UMI ANNUAL SUNDAY SCHOOL LESSON
COMMENTARY

PRECEPTS FOR LIVING®

MISSION STATEMENT

We are called of God to create, produce, and distribute quality Christian education products; to deliver exemplary customer service; and to provide quality Christian educational services which will empower God's people, especially within the Black community, to evangelize, disciple, and equip people for serving Christ, His kingdom, and Church.

UMI

Urban Ministries, Inc.
The African American Christian Publishing & Communications Co.

UMI ANNUAL SUNDAY SCHOOL LESSON COMMENTARY

PRECEPTS FOR LIVING® 2006–2007

INTERNATOINAL SUNDAY SCHOOL LESSONS

VOLUME 9

UMI (URBAN MINISTRIES, INC.)

Melvin Banks Sr., Litt.D., Founder and Chairman
C. Jeffrey Wright, J.D., President and CEO

All art: Copyright© 2006 by UMI.
Bible art: Fred Carter

Unless otherwise indicated, all Scripture references are taken from the authorized King James Version of the Bible.

Copyright© 2006 by UMI.

CONTRIBUTORS

Editorial Staff
Carl Ellis Jr., Editor
Cheryl P. Clemetson,
Ph.D., Director of
Editorial
Kathryn Hall, Managing
Editor
Vincent Bacote, Ph.D.,
Contributing Editor
Cheryl Wilson, Assistant
Editor, Precepts For
Living®
Evangeline Carey, Staff
Writer
Megan Bell, Copy Editor

Product Manager
Vicki Frye

**Cover Design &
Layout**
Trinidad D. Zavala

Bible Illustrations
Fred Carter

**Contributing Writers
Essays/In Focus
Stories**
Luvell Anderson
Rodrick Burton
Evangeline Carey

Rukeia Draw
Hurby Franks
Herb Jackson
Jennifer King
Glen McCarthy
Nathan Munn
Frederick Thomas
Terri Thompson
Cheryl Wilson
Charles Woolery

**Bible Study Guide
Writers**
Luvell Anderson
Charisse Beach
Rodrick Burton
Evangeline Carey
Lisa Crayton
Annette Dammer
Clay Daniel
Sylvia Dozier
Rukeia Draw
Bianca Elliott
George Flennoy
Marcia Gillis
Blanche Hudson, D.Min.
Jennifer King
Vanessa Lovelace
LaTonya Mason
Glen McCarthy
Philip Rodman
Amy Rognlie

Rosa Sailes, Ph.D.
Frederick Thomas
Faith Waters
Charlesetta Watson-
Holmes
Jimmie Wilkerson-
Chaplin
Barbara Williams

**More Light
On The Text**
J. Ayodeji Adewuya, Ph.D.
Evangeline Carey
Moussa Coulibaly, Ph.D.
Clay Daniel
Ronald Davis
S.G. Gregg
Kevin Hrebik
Ransome Merith
Francis Morkeh
Nathan P. Munn
Anthony Myles
C. Fyne Nsofor, Ph.D.
Samuel Olarewaju, Ph.D.
James Rawdon
Rosia Sailes, Ph.D.
Robert Smith, Ph.D.
Raedorah Steward-Dodd
Virginia Stith
James Williams
Louis Wilson, Ph.D.

Dear *Precepts* Customer,

We are excited to bring you this year's *Precepts For Living*®. As you read and study God's Word through the lessons presented in *Precepts For Living*®, we know that you will continue to find this a valuable Bible study tool!

We are also glad to offer to the *Precepts For Living*® *Personal Study Guide* (the workbook) and the CD-ROM version of *Precepts*. In addition, we now offer *Precepts* in Large Print. On our Christian journey, *Precepts For Living*® not only serves as a witness through our learning and sharing more of the Bible, but helps us develop new tools and other ways to delve into a deeper understanding of God's Word. As Paul admonishes Timothy to "Study to shew thyself approved" (2 Timothy 2:15), Christians today are charged with the same responsibility. Challenging ourselves to learn and grow more in God's Word prepares us to be stronger Christians, and to witness to others about the saving power of Jesus Christ.

During your course of study for this year, you will be given the opportunity to discover or expand your understanding and knowledge through the following themes: God's Living Covenant; Jesus Christ: A Portrait of God; Our Community Now and in God's Future; and Committed to Doing Right. This year of study will be meaningful and enriching to your Christian walk.

Precepts For Living® will continue to evolve in an effort to meet our customers' needs. We appreciate your comments and feedback. Please e-mail your feedback to precepts@urbanministries.com or mail your comments to UMI (Urban Ministries, Inc.), *Precepts For Living*®, P.O. Box 436987, Chicago, IL 60643-6987.

We hope that your spirit is edified and encouraged by the contents of this book.

Yours in Christ,

Carl F. Ellis Jr.

Carl F. Ellis Jr.,
Editor

TABLE OF CONTENTS

Fall Quarter, 2006

GOD'S LIVING COVENANT

LESSONS
Unit 1: In Covenant with God
SEPTEMBER

Unit 2: God's Covenant with Judges and Kings
OCTOBER

Unit 3: Living As God's Covenanted People
NOVEMBER

Winter Quarter, 2006–2007

JESUS CHRIST: A PORTRAIT OF GOD

LESSONS
Unit 1: Christ, The Image of God
DECEMBER

Unit 2: Christ Sustains and Supports
JANUARY

Unit 3: Christ Guides and Protects
FEBRUARY

CYCLE OF 2004–2007

Arrangement of Quarters According to the
Church School Year, September through August

	FALL	WINTER	SPRING	SUMMER
2004–2005	The God of Continuing Creation (Bible Survey) Theme: Creation (13)	Called To Be God's People (Bible Survey) Theme: Call (13)	God's Project: Effective Christians (Romans; & Galatians) Theme: Covenant (13)	Jesus' Life, Teachings, and Ministry (Matthew; Mark; Luke) Theme: Christ (13)
2005–2006	You Will Be My Witness (Acts) Theme: Community (13)	God's Commitment— Our Response (Isaiah; 1 & 2 Timothy) Theme: Commitment (13)	Living in and as God's Creation (Psalms; Job; Ecclesiastes; Proverbs) Theme: Creation (13)	Called To Be a Christian Community (1 & 2 Corinthians) Theme: Call (13)
2006–2007	God's Living Covenant (Old Testament Survey) Theme: Covenant (13)	Jesus Christ: A Portrait of God (John; Philippians; Colossians; Hebrews; 1 John) Theme: Christ (13)	Our Community Now and in God's Future (1 John; Revelation) Theme: Community (13)	Committed To Doing Right (Various prophets; 2 Kings; 2 Chronicles) Theme: Commitment (13)

JESUS IS KING OF KINGS AND LORD OF LORDS!

by Evangeline Carey

Observe, meditate, and reflect on the Cross draped in purple and the dove on the front cover, and be reminded that Jesus is in charge of His church—the body of Christ. He is also in charge of His salvation plan and His kingdom-building initiative. He is the only One who could die on the Cross and pay the penalty for our sin. He birthed the church and is seeing it through persecution until His Second Coming (see the book of Acts). Therefore, no finite being can ever take God's place because He shares His glory with no one (Isaiah 42:8).

Believers can be servant-leaders, but never the head of God's church. Instead, we are privileged to be apart of His army of committed Christian soldiers—those who have been set apart—called out of sin and eternal damnation to salvation and eternal life. We have been called to witness for Him, to help build His kingdom, to serve Him—our new Master. He is God—the King of kings and Lord of lords!

In this cycle of *Precepts For Living*®, we will be exploring the 4 central themes: God's Living Covenant; Jesus Christ: A Portrait of God; Our Community Now and in God's Future; and Committed to Doing Right. From our study, we will learn how God made His covenant in the Old Testament with His chosen people and their leaders. We will also learn who Jesus really is, and how He sustains, guides, and protects us.

Our study then turns to the Prophets in Lamentations and 2 Kings, and will help us understand how we should live as God's people according to His commands.

Finally in 1 John and the book of Revelation, we will study the Christian community now and in the future according to God's redemptive plan as we prepare for living in God's new world.

The driving message in all four quarters is that

> **Jesus is Immanuel—God with us!**
> **He is Immanuel**
> **God dwelling**
> **with humanity.**
> **He is Immanuel—Jesus,**
> **God's**
> **one and only Son,**
> **Who came to forgive,**
> **Who came to deliver,**
> **Who came to save us from our sins.**
> **Jesus Christ came to bring**
> **us eternal life**
> **And He now sits on His throne.**

God is building His kingdom and those who have accepted Jesus Christ as their Lord and Saviour will be included. It is imperative that all believers understand that Christianity is about God and His righteousness, and it is propelled by God's Spirit to all nations. Only He can save our soul. Recall that we couldn't save ourselves, but we are redeemed by the blood of the Lamb, Jesus Christ. Jesus is King of kings and Lord of lords over God's creation, including His church, and as such should be at the head of every believer's life. "Who is the King of glory? The LORD, strong and mighty, the LORD mighty in battle" (Psalm 24:8).

As we explore a myriad of Scriptures from Genesis to Revelation—from the Old Testament to the New Testament—we also follow God's kingdom-building progression. Watch Him build His church as He goes from a covenant with the Jews in the Old Testament to a covenant of grace with all believers in the New Testament.

We need to remember that even though John 11:25 and 14:1–14 tell us our salvation was accomplished through Jesus' shed blood, still, Jesus is more than our Redeemer—our Liberator, He is Sovereign God—in charge of His world now and the one to come. He is the King of kings and Lord of lords.

As we study the lessons in this year's cycle, remember that God is establishing His living covenants of law and grace. See with your spiritual eyes His community of believers—the universal church—who is committed to doing right because we have been saved and transformed by the awesome power of God, through believing on His Son, Jesus Christ.

SEPTEMBER 2006
QUARTER AT-A-GLANCE
God's Living Covenant

The study of this quarter is a survey of the Old Testament. Its three units follow the history of God's covenant with the Hebrew people from Noah's day until after the return from exile.

UNIT 1 . IN COVENANT WITH GOD

This unit looks at God's covenants with Noah, Abram, and the people of Israel. It also looks at the people's renewal of the covenant.

LESSON 1: September 3, 2006
God's Covenant with Noah
Genesis 9:1–15

God found it necessary to judge the people of Noah's day by sending a flood to destroy the human race—all except Noah and his family. After the Flood, God made a covenant (a solemn, binding agreement) with Noah that He would never again destroy the entire human race with a flood.

LESSON 2: September 10, 2006
God's Covenant with Abram
Genesis 17:1–8, 15–22

Before Abram left his homeland of Ur, God promised to bless all the world through him, implying he would have many children. At age 86 Abram fathered Ishmael, born to Hagar, his wife's Egyptian handmaid. When Abram was 99 years old God appeared to him to say he would have a son through Sarai and that these descendants would occupy the land of Canaan. God kept His promise as He always does.

LESSON 3: September 17, 2006
God's Covenant with Israel
Exodus 19:1–6; 24:3–8

At Mount Sinai God established His covenant with Israel, a covenant consisting of two sides. God's part was to be their God, to regard them as a kingdom of priests and as His special treasure. The people's part was to obey His voice and keep His commands. This mutual agreement between God and the people of Israel was sealed with the blood of an animal.

LESSON 4: September 24, 2006
Covenant Renewed
Joshua 24:1, 14–24

Some of the Children of Israel were having trouble remaining faithful to the covenant their ancestors had made with the Lord. Before dying, Joshua assembled the tribes of Israel together and reminded them of God's faithfulness to His promises as illustrated by the things He had already done for their people. The people had to make a choice whom they would serve. They pledged that day to serve God and renewed the covenant with Him.

UNIT 2 . GOD'S COVENANT WITH JUDGES AND KINGS

This unit covers God's relationship to the people through the judges in general and Deborah specifically, as well as God's covenant relationship with Samuel, David, and Solomon.

LESSON 5: October 1, 2006
God Sends Judges
Judges 2:16–23

The Israelites showed disobedience and unfaithfulness to God by serving and worshiping idol gods. This angered God, so enemy nations were allowed to rise up against them. Mercifully, however, God raised up judges to deliver the Israelites. God was with the judges and kept the people safe from their enemies throughout the judges' lifetime. The faithfulness of the people lasted only as long as the judge lived, and they would return to their disobedient ways. This cycle of disobedience, despair, and deliverance continued until God decided to test the Israelites by not raising up a judge to deliver them.

LESSON 6: October 8, 2006
God Leads through Deborah
Judges 4:4–10, 12–16

Deborah, a prophetess, was a judge chosen by God to lead Israel. Deborah sought out Barak, an Israelite commander, and told him that God commanded him to go into battle against Sisera's army. Though Deborah told Barak that God would be with him, Barak insisted that he would go only if Deborah went to battle with him. She went and, as promised, God gave them the victory.

LESSON 7: October 15, 2006
God Answers Samuel's Prayer
1 Samuel 7:3–13

The Israelites were afraid they would be attacked by the Philistines. Samuel urged them to turn away from their idols and truly return to the Lord by obeying, serving, and worshiping Him. If they did, God promised to deliver them. As the Philistines approached, the Israelites asked Samuel to pray for them. Samuel prayed to God on the Israelites' behalf and God saved them.

LESSON 8: October 22, 2006
God Covenants with David
2 Samuel 7:8–17

King David wanted to build the temple and discussed this with the prophet Nathan. At first Nathan encouraged David to proceed, but after receiving work from the Lord, he told David God did not want him to do so. David was reminded of how God brought him to the throne. Nathan revealed God's promise to establish David and continue his house forever—a promise fulfilled through Jesus Christ.

LESSON 9: October 29, 2006
God Grants Wisdom to Solomon
1 Kings 3:3–14

King Solomon went to Gibeon to offer sacrifices to the Lord. While there, God appeared to Solomon in a dream and asked him what he wanted. After recalling God's faithfulness to his father, David, Solomon asked God to give him the wisdom to carry out his job. God was pleased with Solomon and granted his request. God promised Solomon unparalleled wisdom along with riches, honor, and the potential for long life, if he continued to follow and obey the Lord.

UNIT 3 . LIVING AS GOD'S COVENANTED PEOPLE

This unit explores the challenge of living in covenant. It also covers the exile as a consequence of breaking covenant with God. Finally, it looks at the restored covenant relationship that God offered.

LESSON 10: November 5, 2006
Elijah Triumphs with God
1 Kings 18:20–24, 30–35, 38–39

Elijah wanted the Israelites to take a stand and decide whom they were going to follow—the one true God, or the Baal idols they were worshiping. The prophet issued a challenge to prove to King Ahab and the people who, alone, was God. When it was Elijah's turn, he wet the altar, cried out to God, who responded by fire, proving He is God.

LESSON 11: November 12, 2006
Josiah Brings Reform
2 Kings 22:8–10; 23:1–3, 21–23

During the repair of the temple, the Book of the Covenant was found and brought to King Josiah. Upon reading it and realizing God's Word was not being followed, Josiah called the people together, read the Book of the Covenant to them and led them in a renewal of the covenant, pledging to follow the Lord and keep His command.

LESSON 12: November 19, 2006
The People Go Into Exile
2 Chronicles 36:15–21; Psalm 137:1–6

The nation of Judah continued to reject the message of the prophets and rebelled against God. Though God gave them many opportunities to turn from their evil ways and honor the covenant, they didn't and continued to do evil. God allowed the Babylonian empire to conquer Judah and take the people into exile.

LESSON 13: November 26, 2006
God Offers Return and Restoration
2 Chronicles 36:22–23; Ezra 1:5–7

After years in captivity, God used King Cyrus of Persia (in fulfillment of Jeremiah's prophecy) to return the exiles to Judah. The Lord moved Cyrus' heart to issue a proclamation that the temple was to be rebuilt and those exiles who wanted to return to Judah and participate in the rebuilding could. They were being given a chance to go home and start again and show faith in God's promise to restore them as people. Not all exiles went, however, only "those whose heart God had moved."

THEMATIC ESSAY

"I WILL BE YOUR GOD AND YOU WILL BE MY PEOPLE": A CENTRAL THEME IN SCRIPTURE

by Evangeline Carey

Scholars tell us that, "It took some 40 men a period of approximately 1,600 years to produce the 66 books that compose the Bible" (Thiessen 2000, 67). God inspired these men to record in their original documents, His inerrant Word "for doctrine, for reproof, for correction, for instruction in righteousness" (2 Timothy 3:16). It should be noted that the central theme, or thread, that runs throughout the collage of Scriptures from Genesis to Revelation is God's desire that the people He created to be in relationship with Him.

Five Historical Books Called the "Pentateuch" (Genesis, Exodus, Leviticus, Numbers, and Deuteronomy)—the Books of the Law

In the Pentateuch, God's great love for mankind and His desire for relationship can be readily seen through (1) His creation of man and woman, (2) His hands-on involvement with Adam and Eve in the Garden of Eden, and (3) the binding agreements He made with His people under the Mosaic Law.

God desired to have a people who would love, honor, respect, and worship Him. He wanted a people who would walk with Him in obedience. When we explore the 66 books of the canon, we find God reaching out to humanity in unconditional love, salvation, and fellowship. God's chosen people (the Israelites) were to be the channel through which the world would come to know the true and living God. He became the Israelites' God, but the Israelites were a complaining, hardheaded, rebellious people who disobeyed God at every turn.

The Additional 12 Historical Books (Joshua, Judges, Ruth, 1 and 2 Samuel, 1 and 2 Kings, 1 and

2 Chronicles, Ezra, Nehemiah, and Esther)

From these historical books, we also come to appreciate God's character and know Him more intimately as we look at how He dealt with the Israelites. These books further explain how God tried to help His chosen people understand and obey His commands and remain in relationship with Him. He raised up priests, judges, and kings to help them stay on His path, but they still broke their covenant–relationship with Him. They perpetuated a cycle of sin or disobedience, captivity (God's punishment for their sins), remorse, repentance, and deliverance.

The Five Poetry Books (Job, Psalms, Proverbs, Ecclesiastes, and Song of Solomon)

These books extol God's unconditional love for His people. They also share how He punishes sin. The whole range of human emotion is expressed in these accounts. We learn how to walk with a holy God in confession. We also learn how to focus on Him and lift our hearts in praise and worship to our God, who is more than enough in our times of need.

Job, the central character of the book of Job, is a model of trust in and obedience to God. From his life, we learn that God is completely and eternally good, in spite of our suffering in a fallen world. We also learn that Almighty God is awesome, that the covenant–relationship with Him still exists, and that Satan cannot do anything to God's children that God does not allow. We learn that Satan had to ask God for permission to afflict Job (1:12).

Psalms, Proverbs, Ecclesiastes, and Song of Solomon also help us picture the unconditional love of God for His sheep. John 3:16 tells us that He loved us so much that He sent His only Son to pay our sin penalty. These books show us that if we are going to let God be our God and if we are going to be His people, we should honor our daily commitment to Him by applying godly morals and wisdom.

The 17 Prophetic Books (Isaiah, Jeremiah, Lamentations, Ezekiel, Daniel, Hosea, Joel, Amos, Obadiah, Jonah, Micah, Nahum, Habakkuk, Zephaniah, Haggai, Zechariah, and Malachi)

These books continue to illustrate how God takes His covenant–relationship with His people very seriously. God raised up spokesmen to warn His chosen people (Israel) to turn from their sinful ways and turn back to Him. He wanted them to honor their agreement with Him. The prophets then called the people back to God and proclaimed His future provision of salvation through the coming Messiah, Jesus. They taught that *God is love, God is merciful, but God is also Judge.*

The Four Gospels (Matthew, Mark, Luke, and John)

Whereas the 39 books of the Old Testament foretold the coming of the Messiah Jesus Christ, who is the eternal King, the four Gospels declare that *Jesus has come and He is the Word of God to man.* "And the Word was made flesh, and dwelt among us" (John 1:14). Jesus has revealed Himself to a lost and dying world as the only way back to a holy God. The gap or gulf between sinful man and a holy God has been closed when sinners believe on the Lord Jesus Christ (John 3:16). With true belief and repentance, Jesus becomes our Lord and Saviour.

The Acts of the Apostles

The book of Acts, a sequel to the gospel of Luke, covers the 30 years after Jesus' ascension into heaven. From the book of Acts, again we see that God stresses to believers *"I will be your God and you will be my people"* as He uses His promised Holy Spirit (the Comforter, Counselor, and Guide) to advance and direct His church outward "from Jerusalem to Judea, in Samaria, and to the uttermost part of the earth" (Acts 1:8).

The 21 Epistles or Letters (Romans, 1 and 2 Corinthians, Galatians, Ephesians, Philippians, Colossians, 1 and 2 Thessalonians, 1 and 2 Timothy, Titus, Philemon, Hebrews, James, 1 and 2 Peter, 1, 2, and 3 John, and Jude)

The epistles, or letters, definitely demonstrate a loving, merciful Father's desire for relationship with His people and His concern for their well-being. Under the anointing of the Holy Spirit, Peter, James, John, and Jude wrote some of the letters, but Paul wrote most of them (among scholars, the author of the book of Hebrews is in dispute) to the infant churches that he helped establish on three missionary journeys.

Paul presented his case for the Good News of the Gospel of Jesus Christ. Often, these letters were written from prison, in chains, after beatings with wooden rods, and in the midst of other perils. In them, Paul explained that God *was* and *is* saying to His followers, *"I will be your God and you will be my people."*

Revelation—The Book of Hope

God used the apostle John, while he was exiled on the island of Patmos in the Aegean Sea, to spell out the hope that believers have of a life beyond the grave in God's kingdom. John had a vision or revelation from Jesus Christ, which unveiled the victorious Lord Jesus' Second Coming. Jesus is coming back to rule the earth! He will no longer be a suffering Servant, but a Judge who vindicates the righteous and judges the wicked.

God, who is Creator, Redeemer, Sustainer, and Judge, gave His revelation to the apostle John nearly 2,000 years ago. This unveiling agrees with what the other 65 books of the Bible proclaim to all believers: that God says and means, "I will be your God and you will be my people forever and ever and ever!"

Sources

Boer, Harry R. *Pentecost and Missions.* Grand Rapids, Mich.: Eerdmans, 1961, 161.

Thiessen, Henry C. *Lectures in Systematic Theology.* Grand Rapids, Mich.: Eerdmans, 2000, 67–255.

Evangeline Carey is a staff writer for UMI and has been an adult Sunday School teacher for more than 25 years.

CHILDREN: THE FOCUS IN BIBLICAL COMMEMORATIONS

by Nathan Munn

This quarter, we will look at the Old Testament history of the people of Israel in order to learn more about what it means to live in covenant with Yahweh, the God of the universe.

We will see that incredible responsibility comes with the privileges of covenant membership. The covenant people of God must not consider His commands as optional recommendations. All that He has commanded must be faithfully obeyed. And when we fail, we must confess our sin to Him, casting ourselves upon His favor and committing ourselves to seeking His righteousness once again.

But the stories we will examine this quarter show us that it is not sufficient for God's covenant people merely to live faithful lives. God intends for the children of His covenant people to grow up into faithful adults as well. He repeatedly instructed the people of Israel to make sure that they taught their children about the true and living God and trained them to walk in His ways, so that there would never fail to be a generation of people who understood the privileges and responsibilities of living in covenant with God (cf. Deuteronomy 4:9; 6:1–2). God's plan was for every Israelite child to grow up saying, "I can't remember a day when I did not know the Lord."

For sure, God commanded the Israelites to instruct their children verbally in the history of His work on their behalf and in the law that He had given them. Their covenant privileges and responsibilities were to be a constant topic of conversation and memorization (Deuteronomy 6:6–9). But God knew the weakness of His people. He knew that the challenges and burdens of everyday living make it difficult for us to spend the time we ought studying His commands and promises for ourselves, much less teaching them to our children. Left to themselves, the people of Israel would soon forget all that God had done for them, and they would disregard the laws He had given to them.

So God established a system of commemorations for the people of Israel. He set the first month of the year to correspond with the anniversary of the Exodus, His greatest, most powerful act of deliverance (Exodus 12:2). He established a schedule of annual festivals and weekly Sabbaths to remind people to make time regularly for remembrance and rededication. And from time to time, the people of Israel established commemorations of their own as additional aids to their memory (e.g., the altar of witness erected by the tribes of Reuben and Gad in Joshua 22, and the festival of Purim established in Esther 9:28). These commemorations benefited everyone: men, women, children, rich, poor, etc. who chose to live with the people of Israel and worship the true and living God (cf. Deuteronomy 16:10–14).

But God had the Children of Israel especially in mind when He established covenant commemorations for the nation. He designed many of the commemorations to be unusual, attention-catching rituals that provoked questioning (as we all know children are certain to do!). Celebration of the Passover involved what would ordinarily be considered extraordinary actions: traveling to Jerusalem, slaughtering and roasting a very special 1-year-old male lamb or goat, eating unleavened bread along with the meat, eating the food in haste and dressing for travel, and burning the leftovers (cf. Exodus 12:3–11; Deuteronomy 16:1–7). The Festival of Unleavened Bread, which followed Passover, required the complete removal of yeast from Israelite homes for seven days and the use of no yeast in any bread (Exodus 12:15, 19). The Festival of Booths required that all native Israelites live in special booths for seven days (Leviticus 23:42–43).

Biblical commemorations were designed so that children would wonder at the reason their parents were doing such odd things and ask why, providing the parents with a ready-made "teachable moment." A parent's answer to one of these questions was guaranteed to remain deep in the hearts of the children since the observance of the Lord's commands had prompted genuine curiosity in the hearts of the little ones.

Commemorations taught Israelite children of their **record** as the people of God. In order to grasp their identity clearly, they needed to know their history, especially concerning their ancestors' time of slavery in Egypt and the incredible way that God delivered them from Pharaoh's oppression (Deuteronomy 6:21–23).

The material we will cover this quarter will help us to see the tragic consequences of a people repeatedly failing to understand their history. The generation that followed Joshua failed to remember that the Lord had brought their grandparents out of Egypt in order to give them the land of Canaan as a place where they could worship and serve Him without fear. They saw the other peoples around them and desired to become like them, because they did not recognize the value and honor of their calling to be the people of God. So they became like the Canaanite people, worshiping and serving idols made of stone, metal, and wood, all because they forgot what God had done for them.

Commemorations taught the Israelite children of their **relationships** with each other. Joshua 22:24–26 tells us of how the tribes who settled east of the Jordan River built an altar of commemoration to remind future generations who lived west of the Jordan River that the eastern tribes were also part of the covenant people of God. The eastern tribes recognized that physical separation from the western tribes would inevitably lead to differences—perhaps different accents or styles of dress. But they were not to be excluded from worship of the living and true God for these kinds of shallow, illegitimate reasons. The relationship between the eastern and western tribes was based on their ancestors' mutual experience of the redeeming work of God, which bound them together permanently.

Commemorations taught Israelite children of their **Redeemer**. The acts of God to bring His people out of slavery demonstrated many of His attributes in real and tangible ways. His great power was manifested in the plagues He sent upon Egypt and, ultimately, in His complete defeat of Pharaoh's army without the contribution of a single Israelite soldier. He acted in mercy, hearing the groaning of the people under the whips of their Egyptian slave masters, desiring that they would instead be able to have rest in a land of their own.

The fact that He acted in response to a promise made 400 years earlier to Abraham demonstrated His absolute faithfulness to keep His promises, which He never forgets or breaks. His holiness was manifested in the law that He gave the people at Sinai and His justice in punishing the faithless Exodus generation by condemning them to death in the wilderness. With commemorations established to help them recall all of these historical events, the Children of Israel could easily remember that Yahweh was the true, eternal, living God who had revealed Himself in time and space as their Deliverer.

Commemorations taught Israelite children about their **responsibilities** under the covenant. The commemorations of the old covenant were designed to remind Israel that God's gracious action on their behalf was in fact an act whereby He purchased them for Himself, giving Him the right to rule their lives. We would prefer not to think of God as one who burdens His people with commands and obligations. But the commemorations of the Exodus teach us that the Lawgiver of the old covenant was much different than their Egyptian taskmasters. The Egyptians burdened the Israelites in order to exploit and weaken them. But the Lord gave them rules and laws in order to protect and bless them (Deuteronomy 6:24–25). He knew the corrupting influence of sin, and, like a loving parent instructing a child to stay out of the street, He told His people what they could and could not do.

The commemorations of the old covenant tell us of our need to firmly grasp the reality of our God and the incredible things He has done to enter into relationship with us by making us His people. Although the Hebrew rituals of the old covenant have passed away because of the work of Christ, we must allow the truth they represent to transform our lives into living commemorations that teach our children and grandchildren about the covenant relationship we have with the God of the universe. When we live our lives as a commemoration to our children and grandchildren, this illustrates the reality of God and His incredible covenant they will ask and learn at an early age of their unique and precious standing as children of the covenant, and pass on their godly heritage to the next generation.

Nathan Munn holds a master of divinity degree from Covenant Seminary in St. Louis, Missouri.

HOW THE COVENANT APPLIES TO US

by Jennifer King

A covenant is not simply an agreement between two parties. Covenants are not arbitrary; they are binding. Covenants are special relationships by which the parties enter into a binding commitment to one another.

In the Bible, we see all types of covenants. Some are made between groups and nations, as is the case recorded in the ninth chapter of Joshua where the people of Gibeon covenanted with the Children of Israel (Joshua 9:6, 15). Another type of covenant is demonstrated in the relationship between David and Jonathan, Saul's son. This relationship was not merely friendship. The Scriptures tell us that "the soul of Jonathan was knit with the soul of David, and Jonathan loved him as his own soul" (1 Samuel 18:1). Throughout the Old Testament, by the covenant between God and the Children of Israel, God offers His love and protection, and in return His people pledge to worship and serve Him alone.

Through Jesus Christ, Christians today are in a covenant relationship with God the Father. This new covenant is expressed throughout Scripture. God says quite explicitly in Ezekiel 36:26–27 (NKJV) that "I will give you a new heart and put a new spirit within you; I will take the heart of stone out of your flesh and give you a heart of flesh." Through Jesus Christ, the righteous Davidic Messiah, God has fulfilled the new covenant. Through His Son's suffering on the cross and resurrection and the pouring out of the Holy Spirit, God has blessed His people for all eternity. But what of our covenanted obligation to one another?

How often have Christians found themselves driving along a busy street, frustrated because, although we are anxious to get to our appointed destination, we cannot? Perhaps we find that the slow pace being set by the driver immediately in front of us begins to irritate and anger us. As our frustration builds, we may find ourselves saying things like, "I wish these people would learn how to drive!" Hopefully, we quickly come to our senses and begin to question our thoughts and hearts. "What in the world," we should be asking, "am I saying? Just who are *these* people I am referring to?" Many times, of course, we are talking about a foreigner who is not a native-born American. Perhaps we come to the rapid conclusion that "they" don't come from this country and probably don't speak English. They are the "others"!

Feeling superior to "others" is an issue that many Christians struggle with. While we will all admit that our reluctance to accept others (those unlike ourselves) is problematic, most of us are far too embarrassed to call it what it really is—discrimination. It is even harder for us to acknowledge that this behavior is totally un-Christian.

The United States has long boasted that it is a cultural "melting pot" where the assimilation of various races and cultures is embraced. In truth, most Americans do very little mixing with folks of other races and cultures outside of work and classroom situations, where diversity is legally mandated. Most of us live in areas where people look like us, and, on Sunday mornings, a great majority of Americans worship with people of the same race and cultural background. While diversity may be the popular buzzword, it is not, for many Christians, a practical reality.

The resentment many of us harbor toward foreigners is understandable in light of current political climate; particularly in the post–9/11 atmosphere. Television further encourages our discomfort in the company of other ethnic groups, particularly Middle Easterners. Since 9/11, needless to say, many Americans are openly hostile toward people of Arabic descent. While it is only natural that we feel most comfortable in the company of people we identify with racially, culturally, and religiously, the world is filled with people of different ethnicities, cultures, and religions. Loving others does not necessarily mean we agree with other's teachings, but Christianity demands that we love those who are different. The ultimate expression of our Christianity is our willingness to love others—those who could be considered strangers.

Reverend Brian K. Woodson, an Old Testament and Hebrew scholar, pointed out that the Hebrew word for "stranger" is *ger* (**gare**). In the Bible, the word is most often used to describe the foreigners or aliens who freely resided among the people of God. Reverend Woodson explained that until the time of Abraham, everyone was a "stranger," since there was no national identity among the Jews yet. Throughout the Mosaic Law, the treatment of the *ger*, or stranger, is favorable. "And if a stranger sojourn with [you] in your land, ye shall not [wrong] him. But the stranger that dwelleth with you shall be unto you as one born among you, and thou shalt love him as thyself; for ye were strangers (*gerim*) in the land of Egypt" (Leviticus 19:33–34). In this passage, God points out the historical similarity between the Jew and the *ger*. More importantly, God recognizes that, like His beloved Israelites, the stranger, as an outsider, is vulnerable and in need of His protection.

Many of the Mosaic laws concerning ritual and sacrifice were extended to strangers. They were expected to rest on the Sabbath (Exodus 20:10), observe the Day of Atonement, Passover (Exodus 12:19), and offer sacrifices (Leviticus 17:8).

Just how inclusive did God intend the relationship to be between His chosen people and the foreigners? Buried in the numerous priestly proscriptives found in Leviticus is a telling account of how God viewed the stranger among His people. Beginning in 24:10, we read that a mixed-race man, the son of an Israelite mother and an Egyptian father, blasphemed the name of God during a fight with an Israelite. The man is brought to Moses, and God tells Moses to take the man outside of the camp and have him publicly stoned. God goes on to tell Moses that laws governing murder and injury are to be equally applied: "Ye shall have one manner of law, as well for the stranger, as for one of your own country: for I am the LORD your God" (Leviticus 24:22). God has already made the stranger safe among His people; He now makes the stranger accountable to Him and His people for his actions.

The interaction between God, His people, and the stranger is chronicled throughout the Old Testament. Ruth, the Moabitess, is a stranger, yet she is included in the lineage of David and Jesus. The interaction with the stranger continues in the New Testament as well. Jesus shows compassion and heals the afflicted daughter of the Canaanite woman (Matthew 15:21–28; Mark 7:24–30). He heals the servant of a Roman centurion (Luke 7:2–10; Matthew 8:5–15). We also see Jesus transcending historical racial hatred between Jews and Samaritans as He witnesses to the Samaritan woman at the well (John 4:1–42). The inclusion of Gentiles in the body of Christ removes a dividing wall (Ephesians 2:13–14).

During Old Testament and New Testament times, strangers were often viewed as enemies. Jesus ushers in a new paradigm. He responds to the stranger not with hatred and distrust, but with loving compassion. Present-day Christians hoping to emulate our Saviour are called to do no less. We must strive, not simply to live, but to live in the new covenant. This means that our love for Christ must motivate us to emulate His love for others. Certainly, we cannot do this on our own. Our "flesh" is unable to see the "beloved" in those who are not like us. It is the empowerment of the Holy Spirit that will enable us to love others the way that Christ would have us love them: completely and unselfishly. We can love our neighbor only when we recognize, as Jesus did, that every person is the neighbor we must love. It is through Christianity that our hearts are transformed and our former discomforts, suspicions, and prejudices against the stranger discarded.

Jennifer King is the Superintendent of Sunday School at Bay Area Christian Church in Oakland, California.

BLACK PERSONALITY

KENNETH B. CLARK (1914–2005)
PSYCHOLOGIST, AUTHOR, EDUCATOR

Just as God raised up men and women of promise in the first century to speak for Him, the dark days of American history show that God also had some "called-out ones" during this period as well. In the middle and latter part of the twentieth century, as an educator and psychologist, Dr. Kenneth B. Clark definitely walked in these shoes.

He and his wife, Mamie Phipps Clark, excelled in the field of psychology at a time when America was relying on inferior data to support the segregation of public education. White psychologists posited that due to the mental inferiority of Black Americans, Black and White children should have "separate but equal education." However, the research of Kenneth and Mamie challenged the notion of this inferiority or differences in the mental abilities of Black and White children, and their findings were used to knock down the segregation law brought forth by the *Plessy v. Ferguson* case.

Dr. Kenneth Clark was the first African American to earn a doctorate in psychology at Columbia University and to hold a permanent professorship at City College of New York. Mamie was also a first in her field, being the first African American woman and the second African American (after her husband) in Columbia University's history to receive a doctorate of psychology. They partnered in a study of whether Black children would choose to play with a Black or White doll if given the choice. Kenneth Clark used this study in 1950 to show that school segregation not only marred the development of Black students, but White students as well. The Supreme Court cited these findings in the famous 1954 case of *Brown* v. *The Board of Education* declaring racial segregation in public schools unconstitutional.

At the time, Justice Earl Warren wrote that "separating Black children from White solely because of their race generates a feeling of inferiority as to their status in the community that may affect their hearts and minds in a way unlikely ever to be undone." Many of us still live with the effects of that separation and that discrimination.

As a graduate student at Howard University, Mamie had been studying self-perception in Black children. It was there that she met, married, and started collaborating with Kenneth. Both conducted the study showing that Black children preferred to play with White dolls over Black dolls. They concluded that this was due to the fact that these children had a poor self-image. According to Kenneth, the total American society had birthed, germinated, and enhanced this poor self-image by shutting Black people in ghettos and marginalizing them.

Dr. Clark was quoted as saying, "It took me 10 to 15 years to realize that I seriously underestimated the depth and complexity of Northern racism. . . . In the South, you could use the courts to do away with separate toilets and all that nonsense. We haven't found a way of dealing with discrimination in the North."

Kenneth was born in 1914 in the Panama Canal Zone to middle-class parents. He later moved with his mom to Harlem in New York City, where he attended public schools.

Dr. Clark's published books include: *Prejudice and Your Child* and *Dark Ghetto*. In 1961, he won the prestigious NAACP Spingarn Medal and in 1985, the Four Freedoms award.

Thank God for people of promise, who fulfill God's calling in their lives. Thank God for Dr. Kenneth B. Clark and his wife, Mamie!

Sources
http://en.wikipedia.org/wiki/Kenneth_Clark_(psychologist)

www.aaregistry.com/african_american_history/283/Kenneth_B_Clark_activist_psyc

www.apa.org/monitor/jun04/itpi.html

www.npr.org/templates/story/story.php?storyId=4627511

TEACHING TIPS

September 3
Bible Study Guide 1

1. Words You Should Know

A. Blessed (Genesis 9:1) *barak* (Heb.)—To endue with power for success, prosperity, fruitfulness, longevity, etc.

B. Dread (v. 2) *chath* (Heb.)—The internal emotion of terror and fear.

C. Establish (v. 11) *quwm* (Heb.)—To make stand; to accomplish.

D. Covenant (v. 11) *beriyth* (Heb.)—An agreement accompanied by signs, sacrifices, and a solemn oath that sealed the relationship with promises of blessing for keeping the agreement and curses for breaking it.

2. Teacher Preparation

A. Prayerfully read the Bible Background and Devotional Reading.

B. Prayerfully study the entire Bible Study Guide. Highlight parts to emphasize.

C. Be prepared to discuss the questions and ways to apply biblical truth to our lives today.

D. Consider talking about the need everyone has for a safe and secure existence and about some common sources of anxiety.

E. Complete lesson 1 in the *Precepts For Living®* *Personal Study Guide*.

3. Starting the Lesson

A. Assign a student to lead the class in prayer, focusing on the Lesson Aim.

B. Ask a student to read the In Focus section.

C. Ask the students to provide examples of people with whom they feel totally secure and to give the reasons why they consider the people to be trustworthy.

4. Getting into the Lesson

A. Allow each student to read some portion of The People, Places, and Times; Background; Keep in Mind; and At-A-Glance.

B. Allow each student to read one of the Focal Verses. As each verse is read, discuss and instruct using the portions of In Depth and More Light on the Text that were highlighted during your preparation.

C. Review Words You Should Know to add intensity to the lesson discussion.

D. Ask the students to respond to the Search the Scriptures questions.

5. Relating the Lesson to Life

A. Ask the students to respond to the Discuss the Meaning questions.

B. Have someone read the Lesson in Our Society section.

6. Arousing Action

A. Allow the students to read Make It Happen and to share a "token" that God gave them.

B. Ask the students to take a few minutes and respond to Follow the Spirit and Remember Your Thoughts.

C. Encourage the students to be prepared for next week's lesson.

Worship Guide

For the Superintendent or Teacher
Theme: God's Covenant with Noah
Theme Song: "The Solid Rock"
Scripture: Psalm 36:5–10
Song: "Never Alone"
Meditation: Heavenly Father, Creator of all things, our hope and our trust are in You, who sustains life. Reassure us in times of uncertainty. Calm all our fears. We can depend on You, Lord. We thank You. We praise You. We glorify Your name. Amen.

GOD'S COVENANT WITH NOAH

Bible Background • GENESIS 9:1–17
Printed Text • GENESIS 9:1–15   Devotional Reading • PSALM 36:5–9

Lesson Aim

By the end of the lesson, we will:

EXPLORE the covenant God made with Noah after the Flood;

REFLECT on God's goodness and care as revealed in the Flood account; and

DECIDE to tell someone about the ways God gives us security.

Keep in Mind

"And I will remember my covenant, which is between me and you and every living creature of all flesh; and the waters shall no more become a flood to destroy all flesh" (Genesis 9:15).

Focal Verses

Genesis 9:1 And God blessed Noah and his sons, and said unto them, Be fruitful, and multiply, and replenish the earth.

2 And the fear of you and the dread of you shall be upon every beast of the earth, and upon every fowl of the air, upon all that moveth upon the earth, and upon all the fishes of the sea; into your hand are they delivered.

3 Every moving thing that liveth shall be meat for you; even as the green herb have I given you all things.

4 But flesh with the life thereof, which is the blood thereof, shall ye not eat.

5 And surely your blood of your lives will I require; at the hand of every beast will I require it, and at the hand of man; at the hand of every man's brother will I require the life of man.

6 Whoso sheddeth man's blood, by man shall his blood be shed: for in the image of God made he man.

7 And you, be ye fruitful, and multiply; bring forth abundantly in the earth, and multiply therein.

8 And God spake unto Noah, and to his sons with him, saying,

9 And I, behold, I establish my covenant with you, and with your seed after you;

10 And with every living creature that is with you, of the fowl, of the cattle, and of every beast of the earth with you; from all that go out of the ark, to every beast of the earth.

11 And I will establish my covenant with you; neither shall all flesh be cut off any more by the waters of a flood; neither shall there any more be a flood to destroy the earth.

12 And God said, This is the token of the covenant which I make between me and you and every living creature that is with you, for perpetual generations:

13 I do set my bow in the cloud, and it shall be for a token of a covenant between me and the earth.

14 And it shall come to pass, when I bring a cloud over the earth, that the bow shall be seen in the cloud:

15 And I will remember my covenant, which is between me and you and every living creature of all flesh; and the waters shall no more become a flood to destroy all flesh.

In Focus

Jean was a Christian who studied the oceans and life in the oceans. Glancing out the window of the speeding train, she caught sight of a tremendous rainbow in the misty sky. A rainbow is the result of a continuous spectrum of light appearing in the sky when the sun shines onto the backs of falling raindrops. As the rainbow disappeared from sight, she reflected on what the sign of the rainbow meant to her Christian life. Her first thoughts were of the storm that rolled dark waters over her soul in 2004.

Jean and her husband had been strolling along the peaceful shores of Bangkok, Thailand, studying shell and coral life. Suddenly, a great tsunami swelled into a horrible tidal wave and in a few minutes killed hundreds of thousands of men, women, and children. Jean survived the ordeal by clinging onto the branches of a treetop. Needless to say, her husband could not hold on, and he was swept away in the muddy water. The loss devastated her. She could not understand why God had allowed her spouse to die, leaving her alone and unprotected. For months, she refused the prayers of her church family and refused to read her Bible.

Then one morning while sitting at her desk, drowning in despair, she picked up her Bible and opened it. Suddenly the light shining through the window in the French doors beside her produced the illusion of a rainbow. In that still, quiet moment God reminded her of His grace. Although she had lost her husband, she had survived the flood. She sank to her knees and began to cry grateful for God's eternal grace and mercy. He had not abandoned her. Now whenever a rainbow appears, she feels the safety of God's love.

In today's lesson, we realize that the rainbow that appeared after the Flood in Noah's time reminded Noah then and us now that we can trust God's promise for our security.

The People, Places, and Times

Covenant. A covenant is a binding agreement between two or more persons in which the following four factors or elements are present: participants, terms, results (or expectations), and security. The Noahic covenant is the first time the actual word "covenant" is used in Scripture (Genesis 6:18; 9:8–17). This covenant was unilateral and unconditional in the sense that God initiated it and guaranteed it without any action on the part of humankind, though God did expect humanity to obey His commands as outlined in Genesis 9:1–7. Thus, the Noahic covenant was universal in scope, including all on the earth.

Background

The global Flood of Noah's day was the greatest judgment that God has ever visited on the inhabitants of the earth. Those that lived on the earth were corrupt and full of violence (Genesis 6:5). The situation was so bad that God decided to destroy all the inhabitants of the earth. However, Noah found grace in the eyes of the Lord. He was a man who lived by God's standards; he was blameless compared to others who lived in his day; and, most importantly, he walked with God. God warned people on the earth of the coming judgment through the preaching and example of Noah for 120 years prior to the Flood, but they refused to repent and obey God (Genesis 6:3; 1 Peter 3:20; Hebrews 11:7). Noah, his three sons, and their wives were the only people who were saved. God also instructed Noah to take groups of air-breathing animals and insects of every kind onto the ark. The floodwaters came from above and below the earth for 40 days and nights, and it took a much longer time for the ground to dry. The total time spent in the ark was 371 days.

At-A-Glance

1. God's Ordinances for the Preservation of Life (Genesis 9:1–7)
2. God's Covenant for the Preservation of Life (vv. 8–11)
3. God's Memorial of Security for Life (vv. 12–15)

In Depth

1. God's Ordinances for the Preservation of Life (Genesis 9:1–7)

Today's Scripture passage describes the beginning of a new period in the history of humanity that Bible scholars refer to as the postdiluvian world—the world after the Flood. There are significant differences between the establishment of society in this postdiluvian period and the beginning of society with Adam and Eve. Adam and Eve began life in a perfect world. There was no knowledge of or experience with fear, sin, evil, and murder. God did not have to provide laws governing events that were nonexistent in a perfect world. However, in a fallen society, some rule of law is required. These ordinances ultimately served to keep humankind from self-destruction. They deterred the evildoers and provided protection for the innocent.

Verses 1–7 discuss such issues as procreation,

family, work, productivity, wildlife, murder, death penalty, war, law enforcement, government, sanctity of life, and abortion. Many of the ordinances established by God are being challenged directly or indirectly by those in our current society. The human heart, independent of God's influence, will always conceive of a *better* way to do things. Unfortunately, the consciences of people today no longer ask the question, "What does God say?" None of the regulations given in this text are temporary. They will apply to the inhabitants of the earth until God brings to an end the world as it is now known.

In verse 1, the loving-kindness of the Lord is immediately presented. God blessed Noah and his sons, enabling them to be fruitful and multiply and fill the earth. Whatever a person sets out to do must be blessed by the Lord; otherwise, it will come to naught. "Except the Lord build the house, they labour in vain that build it: except the Lord keep the city, the watchman waketh but in vain" (Psalm 127:1). A blessing spoken by God is a powerful statement. When God speaks, His words are executed. They materialize. God says that the words He speaks do not return unto Him void (empty) but rather, they fulfill their purpose (Isaiah 55:11). Why? Because God speaks His will and His will is done. The first gift bestowed was fruitfulness, or the ability to produce offspring. This is the ability not only to have children, but to have many grandchildren and great-grandchildren, who in turn have children and multiply. Along with this gift is an obligation for humans to propagate their kind.

There was no divine permission given for eating meat prior to the Flood. Originally, humankind was allowed to eat only vegetables and fruit (1:29). The Scriptures do not say why God allowed the eating of animals after the Flood, but it could have been for the preservation of humanity. God did attach one restriction: The blood should be removed from the meat before it was eaten because the blood represented the life of the animal. Life (represented by the blood) was given by God and was therefore sacred, so God required that people observe and respect life.

The life of a human being is more sacred than that

of an animal because both males and females were made *in the image of God*. Some people try to equate animal life with human life, but the fact that humans are made "in the image and likeness" of God is a substantial and unique distinction.

2. God's Covenant for the Preservation of Life (vv. 8–11)

The covenant that was first promised before the Flood (Genesis 6:18) is now established with Noah and his sons as representatives of the human race. Other beneficiaries of this covenant include all living humans, their descendants, and all living creatures. Divine concern for even the least of creatures is included in this solemn and binding promise given by God. It gives reassurance and addresses the doubts and fears of people by providing evidence of God's commitment to His Word. This covenant originated with God. He established the terms and conditions, even those applying to Himself.

The terms of the covenant established by God are stated in verse 11. It applies to all living creatures ("all flesh") and to the earth. Living creatures would never again be "cut off" from life by the waters of a flood, nor would the earth be destroyed by floodwaters. This promise must have been quite a comfort to a family that had witnessed such a catastrophic event and was now being told to leave the ark of safety and be productive.

3. God's Memorial of Security for Life (vv. 12–15)

Noah and his family, under the protection of God, survive quite a fearful experience. God provided a promise of safety. Additionally, God provided a solemn covenant of reassurance that even extended down to the animal world. It is a covenant that applies to all present and future generations. But God provides even more! He gives the world a visible sign to testify to His solemn oath.

The expression "I do set my bow in the cloud" can be rendered more emphatically, "My bow, do I give in the clouds." In the original Hebrew language, the same word is used for "bow" and "rainbow." It symbolizes a peace bond made between God and humanity. It stands as a witness to the love, grace, and promise of God.

The rainbow does not come every time clouds appear. But whenever the rainbow appears, God is reminded of the covenant. It was not a one-time event; it continues to be a perpetual occurrence. Although this memorial was established for the benefit of humanity, God takes responsibility for honoring its significance. In the midst of the floodwaters, God remembered Noah and brought him to dry ground (Genesis 8:1). Now God promises to remember all creation and to never repeat the disastrous effects of the Flood. This does not imply that God could forget His commitment like people often do. By using these terms, God emphasizes the seriousness of His pledge. It is like saying that His commitment to humanity is a high priority with Him.

Search the Scriptures

1. Whom did God bless immediately after the Flood (Genesis 9:1)?

2. What did God's blessing enable the survivors of the Flood to do (v. 1)?

3. Who would be fearful of humanity (v. 2)?

4. For what purpose did God allow animals to be killed (v. 3)?

5. What was the token of God's covenant (v. 13)?

Discuss the Meaning

1. What distinguishes humanity from all other living creatures?

2. What is the significance of the blood in living creatures?

3. How does a covenant made by God differ from those made by people?

Lesson in Our Society

Thousands of years since the days of Noah, the rainbow still appears in all its beauty and splendor. It reminds humanity that God has been true to His word and that He will continue to be true to His word. Noah and his family did indeed reproduce, multiply, and fill the earth. We see the evidence in civilizations all over the globe. The world continues to exist with all its inhabitants because God preserves humanity and other living creatures.

Make It Happen

God used the rainbow as a token of His commit-

ment to the inhabitants of the earth. Perhaps God has provided you with some "token" that reminds you of His faithfulness to you. It may be a special divine act that you know could not have been accomplished by anything or anyone but God. Why not strengthen and encourage others by sharing your own personal experience?

Follow the Spirit

What God wants me to do:

_____

_____

Remember Your Thoughts

Special insights I have learned:

_____

_____

More Light on the Text
Genesis 9:1–15

1 And God blessed Noah and his sons, and said unto them, Be fruitful, and multiply, and replenish the earth.

The exceeding wickedness of the world, in the days of Noah, made it necessary for God to judge the people at that time. He did this by sending a flood to destroy mankind.

After the Flood, we find a situation in which the once-populated Earth has become desolate and only Noah, his family, and two representatives of every beast are available to begin the process of replenishing the earth. This Scripture reminds us of the same act of blessing and the similar command to be fruitful, multiply, and replenish the earth given to Adam and Eve in Genesis 1:28. The Flood created the kind of situation we find in Genesis 1, in which water covered the whole Earth. This makes the time after the Flood look like a new beginning. The Hebrew word for "blessed" used in this Scripture is *barak* (**baw-RAK**). This is an instance in which man is a beneficiary of God's abundance.

Following the Flood, the earth seems to have experienced a rebirth or some sort of renewal. This renewal brought about the retainment of righteousness after the washing away of wickedness by the Flood. "Noah was a just man and perfect in His gen-

14

erations, and Noah walked with God" (Genesis 6:9). He and his family became the only survivors of the Deluge. As the only ones who bore righteousness, they were given the charge to begin a new generation of righteous people in a renewed Earth. God blessed Noah, commanding him to replenish the earth. The Hebrew word translated "replenish" is *male* (**maw-LAY**), which means "to fill." Noah was blessed and given the charge to fill the earth with his kind.

God bestows blessings on us. His blessing always comes with joy; it is devoid of sorrow (Proverbs 10:22). His blessing causes us to bear fruit and multiply. He blesses us spiritually and materially. Material blessings (especially those that improve our finances) naturally give us a sense of security. But we have been created to need *Him*. It is not enough to find security in God's blessings; having Him as our God and provider—the ultimate source of our blessings—should give us the utmost sense of security.

2 And the fear of you and the dread of you shall be upon every beast of the earth, and upon every fowl of the air, upon all that moveth upon the earth, and upon all the fishes of the sea; into your hand are they delivered.

In this verse, God invests Noah with the capacity to evoke fear and dread in the beasts, fowl, and fish. He is making Noah exude this essential element in order to secure his authority and position. With this declaration to Noah, God reestablishes the dominion He gave to Adam over the beasts (Genesis 1:28).

The Hebrew word translated "fear" in this verse is *mora* (**mo-RAW**), and it denotes the feeling of fear, uneasiness, or terror that is felt in the presence of a superior being. This is the way beasts are meant to react in the presence of man. The Hebrew word for "dread," which is *chath* (**KHATH**), also means "to fear" or "to be afraid," but in this case it refers to great fear; it denotes a sense of being crushed or broken by the feelings of fear and a tendency to withdraw from what is causing the fear. According to God's proclamation in this verse, beasts are meant to be terrified to the point of withdrawing from man's presence.

Thus, fear and dread can be seen as creating an invisible boundary that separates man from beasts and emphasizes man's God-given authority. This invisible restrictive boundary also serves as a protective factor that ensures his security.

In the latter part of this verse, God says to Noah: "into your hands are they delivered." The Hebrew word *yad* (**YAWD**), translated as "hand," means "power" or "rule," while *nathan* (**naw-THAN**), translated as "delivered," means "to give" or "to commit." Together, these words mean that God gave Noah dominion and power over all beasts, fowls, and fishes.

3 Every moving thing that liveth shall be meat for you; even as the green herb have I given you all things.

After giving Noah dominion over the beasts, God further offers them to Noah as meat. Here we see God's sustaining capability as *Jehovah Jireh* (God our provider). God sets an order in place that reveals a purpose: the lesser life (consisting of beasts and herbs) is made to be the means of sustenance for the higher life (man), who is made in God's image. The Hebrew word *oklah* (**ok-LAW**) is translated as "meat" or "food."

God cares for mankind by nurturing, supporting, and maintaining life on Earth. Food is the primary sustainer of life. With this proclamation, God provides a new and expanded diet, which now includes meat. In Genesis 1:29 and 2:16, God gave Adam only plants for food. And during that time, the beasts (in accordance with God's arrangement, not man's) merely coexisted with man and kept him company. Although animals were reared (Abel was a keeper of sheep) and must have been used for fulfillment of man's needs, this new command empowers man to fully utilize animals as a means of sustenance.

4 But flesh with the life thereof, which is the blood thereof, shall ye not eat.

God offers Noah bountiful provisions and the liberty to eat every living thing that moves, but He places a restriction on the eating of flesh that still has blood in it. The Hebrew word translated as "life" here is *nephesh* (**NEH-fesh**). It denotes the breath or vitality in a creature and is used to describe the life force of animals.

This life is in the blood. The Hebrew word *dam* (**DAWM**) is translated as "blood." The shedding of *dam* causes death. The blood is the vehicle for the life of a creature (Leviticus 17:11), and so the prohibition is against the eating of blood, the reason being that blood is used to make atonement for souls (v. 11).

There is no mention of the blood that was used for atonement in Genesis 3:1, when God made coats of skin for Adam and Eve. Yet there are some who believe that blood shed from the animals to make the coats may represent atonement for the sin of Adam and Eve's disobedience to God when they ate from the Tree of Knowledge of Good and Evil.

Significantly, the shedding of the blood of beasts typifies the shedding of the blood of the Lamb of God (Jesus Christ), which brings the ultimate atonement for humankind. Thus, the command not to eat the blood of beasts has significance: It (1) stipulates that blood be used exclusively for the purpose of atonement, and (2) blood is invested with such importance that it will be venerated by men. The veneration of blood in the Old Testament was a standard set by God to foreshadow the New Testament veneration and esteem of the blood of the Lamb (Jesus). The prohibition against eating blood is one of the conditions of the Noahic covenant.

5 And surely your blood of your lives will I require; at the hand of every beast will I require it, and at the hand of man; at the hand of every man's brother will I require the life of man.

Since the life of man is very precious in the sight of God, He declares vengeance on any beast that sheds the blood of man. With this declaration, God places the utmost importance on the protection and preservation of human life. He declares justice for anyone whose blood is shed by either beast or man; on the other side, He declares vengeance on any beast or man who sheds the blood of another man.

God says He will require the blood of life from any killer, whether beast or man. The Hebrew word translated "require" is *darash* (**daw-RASH**). The word

here means "to ask, question, or inquire." It conveys the idea of searching out a matter for the purpose of meting out justice; this means that God will avenge the shedding of blood. Divine protection and preservation are elements of God's grace upon our lives and an expression of His love and care.

6 Whoso sheddeth man's blood, by man shall his blodd be shed: for in the image of God made he man.

God decrees capital punishment for any murderer. This decree was made in the time when men were empowered to mete out retribution against a violation of the law that required death. But such is not the case in the era of grace.

In the time of the law, it was "tit for tat" and "eye for eye." The law encouraged speedy retribution by man. God's declaration could have been an aftermath of the great wickedness that was prevalent before the Noahic Flood. Human life could have been so desecrated or prone to indiscriminate termination that God in a bid to offer protection, preservation, and the highest level of esteem for the life of man had to declare a punishment of death for the shedding of man's blood. With this declaration, He invests human life with great sanctity and esteem. This reveals God's intent for the well-being of man in a new order, after the washing away of wickedness by the Flood.

The Hebrew word translated "image" is *selem* (**SEH-lem**), meaning "copy, resemblance, or representative figure." The word communicates the sense of a replica or essential nature. Thus, man in the image of God bears His essential nature. In the original image of God, before the Fall, man possessed a greater resemblance to God. This was God's original design. Man reflected some of God's own perfections in knowledge, righteousness, and holiness and he had dominion over the creatures. A notable fact is that there was no principle of death or sin at work in man. These attributes made him look like a copy or a representative figure of God in physical form though God has no physical body. And because God incorporated His likeness into man and man came to bear His image, He is offended at the destruction of life. The original design of man was a product of God's creation, which He declared good (Genesis 1:31).

Though humanity has fallen, it still retains some of the elements of God's image. In 9:6, God uses the original design, before the Fall, as a reason for not accepting the killing of man. His image in humankind ought to be venerated, despite the fact that humanity had fallen, because God planned to restore it in Jesus Christ, and He eventually did. It is for this reason that God is mindful of man, according to the psalmist (Psalm 8:4–5; Hebrews 2:7–8).

7 And you, be ye fruitful, and multiply; bring forth abundantly in the earth, and multiply therein.

This is a reiteration of verse 1. It could emphasize the importance of the command that Noah be fruitful and multiply.

The word translated "fruitful," *periy* (Heb. **per-EE**), is derived from the Hebrew word for "fruit," *parah* **(pah-RAW)**, and literally means "to bring forth fruit." The command to be fruitful refers to bearing the fruit of the womb (offspring) and the fruit of labor (rewards, products, and earnings). The command, therefore, is an empowerment for reproduction—that is, on empowering of the reproductive organs of Noah and his generations to beget offspring, as barrenness or infertility would have meant an inability to multiply and replenish the earth. This empowerment for reproduction is a very important blessing for Noah, his household, and subsequent generations that allows them to fulfill God's purpose of replenishment. The command is also given to empower Noah to be fruitful in the work of his hands, to enable him to become productive in his labor, and to equip him to possess abundant wealth.

The Hebrew word *rabah* **(raw-BAW)** is translated "multiply" and means "to become numerous, increase, or become great." It connotes the idea of increasing in numbers. This word is coupled with "fruitful" in this verse to qualify the fruitfulness in terms of great numbers.

8 And God spake unto Noah, and to his sons with him, saying, 9 And I, behold, I establish my covenant with you, and with your seed after you; 10 And with every living creature that is with you, of the fowl, of the cattle, and of every beast of the earth with you;

from all that go out of the ark, to every beast of the earth.

Here, God establishes a covenant with Noah. A covenant is an agreement or a pact between two or more persons. The Hebrew word translated "covenant" is *beryith* **(ber-EETH)**, which originally means "to cut" or "cutting," with reference to the custom of cutting animals in two and passing between the parts in ratifying a covenant (Genesis 15:10, 17; Jeremiah 34:18). In this verse, it indicates a league, agreement, or confederacy.

There are basic factors found in a covenant: the parties, as in the conditions, the results, and security. The parties involved in a covenant may be individual men, i.e. a convenant between one man and another, such as between Abraham and Abimelech (Genesis 21:27). A covenant may be between nations, such as between the Israelites and the Gibeonites (Joshua 9:6–16), or it may be between God and man, as in this case. God is the initiator of this covenant, which is between Him and Noah (including his seed and every living creature). The fact that God Himself initiated and established this covenant makes it unilateral, in the sense that God did not require a promise of acceptance and compliance from Noah for the covenant to be established. Instead, His declaration of the covenant set it in place.

The Noahic covenant was of a universal nature in that it involved all creatures on Earth. And a condition of this covenant was that man would be fruitful, multiply, and replenish the earth. Noah, who is acting here as the representative of humankind, the creatures, and all the earth, received this condition as a command in verses 1 and 7. Another condition is that man not eat flesh with the blood of its life still in it (v. 4). Its being a conditional covenant signified that a violation of God's commands would bring about His displeasure or judgment.

The Hebrew translated "establish" is *quw* **(KOOM)**, which means "to raise up, set up, or decree." It is also used to indicate the continuation or enduring of something. After the Flood, we see a situation in which Noah, his sons, and all the creatures with him come out of the ark to behold a world that lacks established societal laws, regulations, and standards. There is no government, no social system, no communal setting with customs and established practices, not even jungle laws. They have all become extinct. It's a brand-new world. And so, as they emerge from the ark, God "raises up" a standard; He sets up a covenant that comprises commands, conditions, and promises, thereby defining a focus and setting up a pattern for living in a new world.

With God's covenant, Noah and his sons had laws to obey. They could fashion customs based on the covenant, they had assurance and hope of God's love and loyalty because the covenant provided security, and they had a standard to live by.

11 And I will establish my covenant with you; neither shall all flesh be cut off any more by the waters of a flood; neither shall there any more be a flood to destroy the earth.

God makes a promise never again to cut off all flesh by the waters of a flood. This is one of the results of the Noahic covenant. The results of a covenant are either promises of blessings when the covenant is adhered to or warnings of punishment when it is broken.

God speaks to Noah here, recognizing him as a doer of the acceptable righteousness that qualified him to survive the Flood and replenish the earth. Noah is identified as one who found grace in God's sight, who was just and perfect in his generations, and who walked with God (Genesis 6:8–9). Now Noah is a man with the distinguished status of being the head of a new human family, a representative of all races.

Apparently, God gave Noah this promise to assure him that there wouldn't be a destruction by flood again. The flood and resulting destruction must have terrified Noah and his sons; consequently, living in apprehension of another flood would put them in constant terror of God. This focus on God's anger would only make them see the judgmental aspect of God and rarely allow them to see Him as a loving and merciful God.

The Flood is the first recorded judgment of God

against the entire world after the Creation in Genesis 1. God gives Noah this promise based on His plan to bring the perfect means of redeeming man from sin and to make available a superlative form of righteousness, which was to be achieved in Jesus Christ. It was sin that led to the destruction by flood in the first place.

According to this promise, there will never again be a flood that destroys the world. God has appointed a Day of Judgment, the day of vengeance of our God (Isaiah 61:1–2), which will come after the redemptive work of Christ at the Cross of Calvary and when the era of grace has expired.

The Hebrew word for "water" is *mayim* **(MAH-yim)**. Basically, water is one of the most essential substances in human life. This essential element was used by God to destroy life in the Noahic Flood. Here, He promises: "neither shall all flesh be cut off any more by the waters of a flood." God makes this promise to indicate His intention of renewing the use of water. Instead of being used to destroy man, water would be instrumental in his rebirth and renewal.

12 And God said, This is the token of the covenant which I make between me and you and every living creature that is with you, for perpetual generations: 13 I do set my bow in the cloud, and it shall be for a token of a covenant between me and the earth.

In this passage, God introduces a token for the covenant He is establishing with Noah. This token stands as a witness or sign. It is the security that God would keep this covenant for perpetual generations. The security of a covenant is usually given to guarantee its fulfillment. Here, the "token" is the rainbow (v. 13), but in other cases, it could be a solemn oath (particularly with a covenant among men). It could also be a gift (Genesis 21:30) or a sign, such as a heap of stones (31:52).

The Hebrew word translated "token" is *owth* **(OTH)** and refers to a sign as a reminder. It was the evidence that God had entered into a covenant with the earth, and it was also a seal to the covenant. Here, God states the extent to which the covenant is binding: "for perpetual generations." The Hebrew word *olam* (**OLAWM**) is translated "perpetual" and means "eternity; everlasting; forever and ever." In other words, this everlasting covenant is binding on all generations for eternity unto all generations that will come, even in the remotest time in the future. For as long as the covenant is binding, the token shall also be a sign for future generations.

The word "bow" used in this verse is translated from the Hebrew word *qesheth* (**KEH-sheth**) and denotes a bow used for shooting arrows. This refers to the spectrum of colors in a rainbow, which has a bent shape and resembles a bow or an arc in the sky.

No doubt the rainbow is a resplendent reminder of God's glory and a symbol of His faithfulness and mercy (Revelation 4:3; Ezekiel 1:28). It is also a symbol of hope for Noah and his generation. While the rainbow assures man of God's faithfulness to keep His promise not to "cut off" (destroy) all flesh by the waters of a flood and is a continuous expression of His mercy upon man, it also brings hope of His enduring love. Each time it appears, it reminds us that God will never break His covenant with man.

14 And it shall come to pass, when I bring a cloud over the earth, that the bow shall be seen in the cloud: 15 And I will remember my covenant, which is between me and you and every living creature of all flesh; and the waters shall no more become a flood to destroy all flesh.

Clouds, in most cases, precede rain. When a cloud appears in the sky, rain is expected to fall. The Hebrew word *'anan* (**aw-NAWN**) is translated "cloud" and refers to the thundercloud that comes before the rain. It also denotes a cloud mass, such as the pillar of cloud that manifested the special presence of God (Exodus 13:21). However, the cloud God speaks of here is the natural agent that comes

with the rain, and since it figuratively has a divine function of manifesting His presence, the Lord promised that it would be a conveyor of the rainbow. The rainbow that surrounds the throne of God, according to Revelation 4:3, emanates from His very presence. God sets the rainbow in the clouds as a reminder of the covenant between Himself and every living creature on the earth. Therefore, we can be confident that God will never again destroy the human race with a flood. Our God is absolutely trustworthy, and He keeps His promises. He will never break this covenant or go back on His word.

Daily Bible Readings

M: God Is Gracious
Psalm 36:5–9
T: Noah Enters the Ark
Genesis 7:1–12
W: The Flood Rages
Genesis 7:13–24
T: The Water Subsides
Genesis 8:1–12
F: God Makes a Promise
Genesis 8:13–22
S: God Instructs Noah
Genesis 9:1–7
S: God Covenants with Noah
Genesis 9:8–17

TEACHING TIPS

September 10
Bible Study Guide 2

1. Words You Should Know

A. Almighty (Genesis 17:1) *Shadday* or *Shaddai* (Heb.)—Almighty; most powerful.

B. Perfect (v. 1) *tamiym* (Heb.)—Entire; complete; having integrity.

C. Abram (v. 1) *Abram* (Heb.)—High or father; original name of Abraham.

D. Abraham (v. 5) *Abraham* (Heb.)—Father of a multitude or father of many nations.

2. Teacher Preparation

A. Prayerfully read the Bible Background and Devotional Reading.

B. Study the entire Bible Study Guide lesson and complete lesson 2 in the *Precepts For Living® Personal Study Guide.* Highlight important sections to emphasize when teaching the lesson.

C. Be prepared to discuss the questions and various ways the students can apply biblical truths in their daily lives.

D. Be prepared to talk about what it means to have faith in God.

3. Starting the Lesson

A. Assign a student to lead the class in prayer, focusing on the Lesson Aim.

B. Ask a student to read the In Focus section.

C. Challenge the students to share actions of faith that they have taken in response to an inner conviction that they felt came from God.

4. Getting into the Lesson

A. Allow each student to read some portion of The People, Places, and Times; Background; Keep in Mind; and At-A-Glance.

B. Allow each student to read one of the Focal Verses. As each verse is read, discuss and instruct, using the portions of In Depth that were highlighted during your preparation.

C. Use Words You Should Know to add intensity to the lesson discussion.

D. Ask the students to respond to the Search the Scriptures questions.

5. Relating the Lesson to Life

A. Ask the students to respond to the Discuss the Meaning questions.

B. Have someone read the Lesson in Our Society section. Ask the class to make a conscious effort to speak a blessing into the life of a loved one.

6. Arousing Action

A. Allow the students to read Make It Happen and to ask themselves if they have made any consistent effort to hear from God.

B. Ask the students to take a few minutes to respond to Follow the Spirit and Remember Your Thoughts.

C. Encourage the students to be prepared for next week's lesson by reading the Daily Bible Readings.

Worship Guide

For the Superintendent or Teacher
Theme: God's Covenant with Abram
Theme Song: "Blessed Assurance"
Scripture: Hebrews 6:13–20; 11:8–16
Song: "Stand by Me"
Meditation: Oh God, our faith looks up to You.
Our hope is in You alone. Give us eyes to see
Your works and ears to hear Your words.
Produce faith in our hearts. Motivate us to
demonstrate the inspiration given by You. We
thank You for all things, in Christ Jesus. Amen.

GOD'S COVENANT WITH ABRAM

Bible Background • GENESIS 17
Printed Text • GENESIS 17:1–8, 15–22   Devotional Reading • HEBREWS 6:13–20

Lesson Aim

By the end of the lesson, we will:

EXPLORE the covenant God made with Abram to give him a son through Sarai and possession of the land of Canaan;

REFLECT on the trustworthiness of all God's promises; and

IDENTIFY at least one promise we will trust God to keep.

Keep in Mind

"Neither shall thy name any more be called Abram, but thy name shall be Abraham; for a father of many nations have I made thee" (Genesis 17:5).

Focal Verses

Genesis 17:1 And when Abram was ninety years old and nine, the LORD appeared to Abram, and said unto him, I am the Almighty God; walk before me, and be thou perfect.

2 And I will make my covenant between me and thee, and will multiply thee exceedingly.

3 And Abram fell on his face: and God talked with him, saying,

4 As for me, behold, my covenant is with thee, and thou shalt be a father of many nations.

5 Neither shall thy name any more be called Abram, but thy name shall be Abraham; for a father of many nations have I made thee.

6 And I will make thee exceeding fruitful, and I will make nations of thee, and kings shall come out of thee.

7 And I will establish my covenant between me and thee and thy seed after thee in their generations for an everlasting covenant, to be a God unto thee, and to thy seed after thee.

8 And I will give unto thee, and to thy seed after thee, the land wherein thou art a stranger, all the land of Canaan, for an everlasting possession; and I will be their God.

17:15 And God said unto Abraham, As for Sarai thy wife, thou shalt not call her name Sarai, but Sarah shall her name be.

16 And I will bless her, and give thee a son also of her: yea, I will bless her, and she shall be a mother of nations; kings of people shall be of her.

17 Then Abraham fell upon his face, and laughed, and said in his heart, Shall a child be born unto him that is an hundred years old? and shall Sarah, that is ninety years old, bear?

18 And Abraham said unto God, O that Ishmael might live before thee!

19 And God said, Sarah thy wife shall bear thee a son indeed; and thou shalt call his name Isaac: and I will establish my covenant with him for an everlasting covenant, and with his seed after him.

20 And as for Ishmael, I have heard thee: Behold, I have blessed him, and will make him fruitful, and will multiply him exceedingly; twelve princes shall he beget, and I will make him a great nation.

21 But my covenant will I establish with Isaac, which Sarah shall bear unto thee at this set time in the next year.

22 And he left off talking with him, and God went up from Abraham.

In Focus

"Carmen, I was adopted at a young age and never knew my birth parents. It's important that we have children." Ken said this many times during their engagement. Those words were music to Carmen's ears. She had prayed to God for a man who loved her and cherished family life.

After five years of marriage, Carmen had been pregnant twice. Each time she suffered a miscarriage. Four weeks into her third pregnancy, Carmen went for an ultrasound and the doctor informed her she was carrying a healthy fetus. Ken and Carmen were overjoyed. It seemed their faithfulness had finally been rewarded.

However, their real test of faith came three months later when her doctor called her in for another ultrasound to check the fetus' progress. This time the news was not so good. The doctor said, "Carmen, I'm afraid we've detected cervical cancer." Then, in a barely audible whisper, he added, "I would recommend that you abort the child because chemotherapy treatments would affect your baby's development." Carmen answered firmly, "I will not abort this baby. I trust God will deliver me a healthy child."

From the first day of the ordeal, Ken and Carmen were in constant prayer. They had already decided that abortion was not an option and that it was God's will they carry the baby to term. Even though it was difficult, they continued to trust God to confront whatever the outcome. Six months later the doctors witnessed a miracle when a perfect little baby was placed in Carmen's arms.

God's covenant with Abram and Sarai created much doubt, but God fulfilled His promise. Our lesson today affirms that God makes and keeps promises, no matter how insurmountable the obstacles appear.

The People, Places, and Times

Ur. Biblical chronology places Abraham's birth about 2161 B.C. in Ur, located in lower Mesopotamia. The land was originally settled by Nimrod, son of Cush, whose name means "black" or "burnt faced" (Genesis 10). Ur was beginning to grow commercially and politically at this time. Ur was the location of the famous ziggurat temple tower. It had a lucrative woolen trade and other industries that centered around the worship of the moon god Sin (Nannar) and his consort Nin-gal. It became a gathering place, or mecca, for worshipers of these gods.

Canaan. The hill country of Canaan was sparsely populated during the Middle Bronze Age (2100–1550 B.C.), so there was plenty of room for Abraham and his descendants to wander over the hills of central Palestine and the dry lands of the southern area.

Some of the sites at that time were Shechem, Bethel, Dothan, Gerar, Salem, and Beersheba. Located at the southern end of the Dead Sea were the five cities of the plain or circle of the Jordan (Genesis 13:10), namely, Sodom, Gomorrah, Admah, Zeboiim, and Zoar.

Background

Abram originally came from Ur of the Chaldees in Mesopotamia. He was a descendant of Noah's son, Shem. After he was married to Sarai (who was 10 years younger than Abram), he moved with his father, Terah, and his nephew, Lot, from Ur toward the land of Canaan. However, they settled in Haran, a city in northwest Mesopotamia. After Abram's father died, God told Abram to leave his country, kindred, and father's house and go to a land that God would show him. God promised to bless him, make his name great, make him a great nation, and make him a blessing to others. At the age of 75, Abram departed and took Lot with him.

Throughout these years, Sarai was barren. Twenty-four more years passed, and Sarai was still barren. The biological clock had long since expired. The faith of Abram and Sarai was thoroughly tested. Yet, God kept saying that He would make them a great nation. As the years passed, Abram sought to bring God's promise to pass using human means. At one point, Abram asked God if his household steward, Eliezer, would be his heir, but God said no.

Around the age of 85, Sarai gave Hagar, her Egyptian handmaid, to Abram to produce a child named Ishmael. But God had better things in mind. He wanted Abram to be an example to us all. It was always God's purpose to fulfill His promise and make it happen by supernatural means in a covenant relationship through their marriage union. Abram believed in the Lord, and God counted it to him for righteousness (Genesis 15:6; Romans 4:3). Additionally, Abram, whom God later renamed Abraham, was called "the friend of God" (James 2:23).

1. God's Covenant with Abram (Abraham)
(Genesis 17:1–6)

2. God's Covenant with Abraham's
Descendants (vv. 7–8)

3. God's Promise Concerning Sarai (Sarah)
(vv. 15–19)

4. God's Promise Concerning Ishmael
(vv. 20–22)

In Depth

1. God's Covenant with Abram (Abraham)
(Genesis 17:1–6)

The events in our text took place when Abram was 99 years old. It has been almost 25 years since God told him to leave Haran (12:4). The Scripture says that the Lord (or Yahweh [Jehovah], the covenant name of God) appeared to Abram; however, it does not specify the form of the appearance. The Lord declares Himself to be the "Almighty God," which is a translation of the Hebrew word *El Shaddai*. In other words, He is the one who has the power to bring about creation and cause it to do whatever He wills. It is a very appropriate name since it was humanly impossible for Abram and his wife, Sarai, to have a child. God often used names to reveal different facets of Himself to those with particular needs. When Hagar was in despair in the desert, she discovered God to be "Thou God [that] seest me" (16:13). Later in life, when Abraham needed a sacrifice to offer to the Lord in place of his son, he found God to be the "Lord [that] will provide" (22:14, NKJV).

Thus, the awesome God tells Abram to walk before Him and be perfect because a great thing is about to happen. The word "perfect" conveys the idea of moral integrity and a mind that strives for perfection (Philippians 3:15). Abram is to be true to a "God-conscious" life and to fulfill his obligations to God. He is to be devout and pious. The Scripture says that Enoch walked with God (Genesis 5:24) and in doing so pleased God (Hebrews 11:5). Noah also walked with God (Genesis 6:9). Scripture says that without faith it is impossible to please God, so walking with God requires faith (Hebrews 11:6). God wanted Abram to look toward Him as he confronted the situations of life.

The covenant (binding agreement) that God established with Abram in Genesis 15:18 is now to be executed. God wanted to literally "put" or "give" His covenant to Abram. Now the promised things will begin to take place. God will now begin to multiply Abram exceedingly. God was going to provide Abram many descendants. Perhaps Abram thought it had already begun through his son by Hagar. However, Abram would begin to see the reality of the promise and how it would be fulfilled.

Abram reacts to an awesome God with humility and reverence by falling on his face. God acknowledges Abram's act of worship by continuing to speak to him. A third name is now—and throughout the chapter—used for God. First, He is revealed as the gracious Lord of the covenant. Then, He is revealed as the all-powerful and all-sufficient bestower of bountiful blessings. Now He is revealed as the Creator (*Elohim*), who is about to do a creative work in the lives of Abram and Sarai.

The first mentioned result of the covenant is that Abram will father many nations. With the emphatic phrase, "As for Me," God says, "I will do this" (Genesis 17:4). Previous promises mentioned that Abram would father a great nation (12:2) and that his offspring would be beyond counting (16:10). In Abram's day, names described the character or the destiny of the person. God amplified His promise to Abram and proclaimed his destiny by changing his name from Abram ("exalted father") to Abraham ("a father of many nations"). The Ishmaelites, the nations of Keturah (25:14), and the Israelites all acknowledge Abraham as their father. Additionally, all true believers from all nationalities through faith become his children (Romans 4:13, 16–18).

Verse 6 elaborates further on Abraham's posterity. He will be a father of many nations, and he will be exceedingly fruitful (or prolific), which is to say that the nations will be great in number. Abraham can also look forward to future offspring who hold positions as kings.

2. God's Covenant with Abraham's Descendants (vv. 7–8)

God gives (or upholds) the covenant not only to Abraham, but to his descendants as well. It is an everlasting covenant, or a covenant into the hidden future. God will fulfill His commitment to Abraham and his descendants.

God gives Abraham descendants, commits Himself to them, and gives them a place to dwell. He reiterates what He had previously stated in Genesis 12:7 and 15:18. The place of their dwelling is Canaan, the land in which Abraham had sojourned since leaving Haran. The land will be an everlasting (i.e., into the hidden future) possession, like the covenant. Again, God says that He will be God to Abraham and his descendants; that is, He will be with them to fulfill His promises.

3. God's Promise Concerning Sarai (Sarah) (vv. 15–19)

For the last 13 years, Abram's hope of an heir had been focused on Ishmael. According to the terms of the covenant, though, the giving of an heir could not be accomplished through any of Abram's servants, nor could it be accomplished through his son by Hagar. Now God reveals that the covenant will be fulfilled through Abram's barren wife, Sarai. God's covenant will not be implemented by human means through Abram and Sarai's Egyptian handmaid, Hagar. It will be fulfilled by supernatural means between Abraham, a 100-year-old man, and his 90-year-old barren wife. Thus, Sarai is given a new name. She is now called Sarah, which is an alternative pronunciation of Sarai. Both names mean "princess," but now she is so named by the Lord. This serves as a divine affirmation of who she really is. She merits this name because she will be the mother of nations and, in particular, kings. Apart from the Israelites, the other "nations" include those who are made righteous by faith in Jesus Christ (Romans 4:16–25).

Again, Abraham falls on his face, astonished and overwhelmed with joy by the promise that descendants will come through his wife, Sarah. He laughs and wonders in his heart if he and Sarah can do this. Some may see doubt in the way that Abraham reacted, but he is not chastised for pondering the possibilities. In worship and adoration, it is as if Abram were saying to himself, "Will God do so great a thing with us?"

Abraham now understands that the covenant will not be fulfilled through Ishmael; however, he expresses his love for his son by petitioning God on his behalf. He may be asking God to use Ishmael in place of the son Sarah will have (though some may come to a different conclusion), and he could be expressing doubt that the promises can be fulfilled through Sarah. For certain, he simply wants God to be with Ishmael as well as the promised son.

God answers both the silent, internalized question of Abraham's heart and his spoken plea to God for Ishmael. Shall an extremely old and barren couple have a son? "Yes, indeed, and you shall call his name Isaac. My covenant will be established with him and with his seed. I will make it happen through the child of your union with Sarah" (Genesis 17:19, paraphrased). The name Isaac means "laughter" ("glad, happy") and commemorates Abraham's joy.

4. God's Promise Concerning Ishmael (vv. 20–22)

God also says that He will grant Abraham's request for Ishmael ("I have heard thee," v. 20). He will cause Ishmael to be fruitful (or prolific) and will multiply his descendants exceedingly. From his descendants will come 12 princes or tribal leaders, and they will be a great nation (cf. 25:12–18).

God reiterates in no uncertain terms that the covenant will be executed through Isaac and designates the time of his birth to be in one year. God then concludes the conversation and departs from Abraham.

Search the Scriptures

1. How old was Abram in today's lesson (Genesis 17:1)?

2. How did God describe Himself to Abram (v. 1)?

3. To what was Sarai's name changed (v. 15)?

4. What was the name of Sarah's son (v. 19)?

5. With whom did God establish His covenant (vv. 7, 19)?

Discuss the Meaning

1. Up to this point, what made Ishmael special to Abram?

2. What was the significance of God changing Abram's name?

3. Explain how you can share in the blessings of Abraham.

Lesson in Our Society

It is very difficult for a person to believe something that he or she cannot comprehend or visualize. Many sociologists say that the environment has a significant influence on the way a person thinks or acts. From their point of view, a person will not aspire beyond their surroundings or condition in life. Similarly, it is said that words can have a dramatic impact on a person. Constant criticism or, worse yet, berating of children makes them feel worthless. God's words of encouragement can be an effective source of inspiration that results in faithful trust in Him. We can observe how God cultivated and strengthened the faith of Abraham and his wife Sarah by speaking words that enabled them to visualize the fulfillment of His promises, even before there was any evidence to support them.

To Abraham He said, "You are now a father of many nations." From that time forward, even though the elderly couple was still barren, whenever someone called Abraham by his new name, reinforced in their spirit was the fact that he was the father of many nations and Sarah was a princess. What effect do you suppose it would have on your daughter to be called "princess" or "precious," or on your son to be called "champ" or "professor?" What promise can you remind your spouse of that will encourage his or her soul? If you don't know what to say, then pray to God for a vision to share. Abraham prayerfully interceded on behalf of his son, Ishmael. God responded to his request, providing a message and a promise for Abraham to share with Ishmael. Now Ishmael, too, had a tangible reason to believe in God.

Make It Happen

Faith or trust in God results from God speaking to your heart. The most common way to hear from God is by reading or hearing His written Word. If you really want to hear from God, you must put forth the effort to study His Word. Draw nigh to God and He will draw nigh to you. Once you are convinced that God

has spoken to you in a way that is confirmed by His Word, trust Him to be faithful to His promise. He is a God who cannot lie!

Follow the Spirit

What God wants me to do:

_____

_____

Remember Your Thoughts

Special insights I have learned:

_____

_____

More Light on the Text

Genesis 17:1–8, 15–22

1 And when Abram was ninety years old and nine, the Lord appeared to Abram, and said unto him, I am the Almighty God; walk before me, and be thou perfect.

In his past interactions with God, Abram had not fully comprehended God's personality. All he knew of God was what he received from Him: promises, commands, revelations, and the God-established covenant. Here, when Abram is 99 years old, God declares His mighty power. This declaration is the first step toward revealing His personality to Abram. The word translated "Almighty" is *shadday* (Heb. **shad-DAH-ee**). It means "sufficient" or "all-powerful." God assures Abram that He is all-powerful and sufficient for him. This is assurance that should allay his fears and give him hope that all the promises made to him will be fulfilled.

The word *halak* (Heb. **haw-LAK**), translated "walk," literally means "to go" or "to walk," with reference to movement made by the feet. In this Scripture, it is used in a figurative sense to refer to personal behavior. Thus, it means to behave oneself—to live righteously or responsibly. God is charging Abram to walk uprightly before Him.

Because Abram is from a pagan background, as one who lived in Ur of the Chaldees, which was a center of moon worship, God gives him this charge. Moreover, the Lord had called him away from his kindred and out of his country, and he becomes a chosen person through whom God intends to reveal His mighty power.

Today, those of us who express faith like Abraham have been called out of the world to live a sanctified life in view of greater hopes of the manifestation of God's glory.

Though the Abrahamic covenant is considered to be unilateral, God's proclamation, "I am the Almighty God; walk before me, and be thou perfect," adds a second element to it. The covenant lays down certain requirements for Abram to comply with. A bilateral covenant requires fulfillment by both parties.

2 And I will make my covenant between me and thee, and will multiply thee exceedingly. 3 And Abram fell on his face: and God talked with him, saying, 4 As for me, behold, my covenant is with thee, and thou shalt be a father of many nations.

God establishes a covenant with Abram. This covenant comprises great personal promises made to him. God had made these promises to him prior to this time. The word translated "make" is *nathan* (Heb. **naw-THAN**) and means "to give, bestow, grant, or entrust," with particular reference to the establishment of a covenant that was originated by God. As mentioned before, this covenant is generally considered to be unilateral since it was first declared by God without any conditions attached. However, verse 1 adds a second element to it, making the covenant bilateral.

Here, we can identify three of the four elements present in a covenant: parties, conditions, and results. Certainly, God and Abram are the parties involved here. The results are the promises to multiply Abram exceedingly and to make him a father of many nations.

Abram fell on his face while God talked with him. By this, he expressed total submission and a willingness to obey Him. Faithful obedience was the condition required by God in this covenant with Abram.

The promise to multiply Abram exceedingly transcends the promise of making him into a great nation (Genesis 12:2). The former promise refers to Abram's seed, through Isaac and Jacob, becoming the Hebrew nation. The latter promise speaks of the nations that were to come out of him, apart from the nation of

Israel—peoples and nations that were to be his descendants through Hagar (16:15) and Keturah (25:1–2).

God expresses a willingness to multiply Abram exceedingly, which provokes in Abram a willingness to obey God. Like begets like. Because God is ever willing to bless us, it should be easy for us to put our trust in Him (Jeremiah 7:7; Psalm 34:8).

5 Neither shall thy name any more be called Abram, but thy name shall be Abraham; for a father of many nations have I made thee.

Abram means "high father" or "my father is exalted." This meaning is also conveyed in other ancient languages such as Old Babylonian, ancient Egyptian, ancient South Arabic, and Ugaritic. Even in these heathen nations, the name had such a significance. That is, the name was translated with the inclusion of the word "divine" to render it as "my divine father is exalted."

Abraham means "father of a multitude." This new name incorporates God's plan and purpose for Abraham; it points to his destiny, and it reflects God's promise for him.

The word translated "father" is *ab* (Heb. **AWB**), which accounts for the first two letters of the names Abram and Abraham. Abram had been accorded the status of a father even while he was a pagan, but the significance of his fatherhood becomes different now that God is his God. God makes him a father of many nations. This implies a change in his personality and destiny; having been appointed, called, or ordained to be a father of many nations, he has been elevated to a higher status than that of a "high father" in a pagan context.

"Father" also means "founder" and "patriarch"; this promise has been fulfilled over the ages. Abraham is patriarch to many peoples, tribes, cultures, and races. He is patriarch to diverse ethnic, religious, and political groups defined by various geographical locations. He is the father of the Hebrew nation through the seed of the promise, Isaac. However, he is also the father of the Ishmaelites, Midianites, Sheba and Dadan tribes of Arabia, Shuhites, and many others. His descendants grew into an exceedingly wide circle of peoples, kings, princes, and nations. His fatherhood continues down through a long line of physical descendant—progenitors, and also through a "family" that shares his spiritual heritage. All believers who have faith in God are called Abraham's children: "Know ye therefore that they which are of faith, the same are the children of Abraham" (Galatians 3:7).

6 And I will make thee exceeding fruitful, and I will make nations of thee, and kings shall come out of thee.

This promise has two referents. First, it refers to Abraham's physical progeny through Ishmael, Zimran, Jokshan, Median, Midian, Ishabak, and Shuah, who formed various peoples and nations, with their kings. Second, and most importantly, it refers to all believers of all nations who are saved in Jesus Christ. The natural ancestry of Jesus is traced to Abraham (Matthew 1), and believers are kings and priests unto God (Revelation 5:10); they are coheirs with Christ (Romans 8:27; Galatians 3:29).

This promise had been explicitly spoken to Abraham in a figurative sense involving two comparisons that relate to or match the two translations of this promise. The Lord said to Abram, "And I will make thy seed as the dust of the earth: so that if a man can number the dust of the earth, then shall thy seed, also be numbered" (Genesis 13:16). The magnitude of Abraham's fruitfulness is being compared here with the innumerable dust of the earth. This comparison refers to his natural progeny descended from Ishmael, Midian, and others. The "dust of the earth" suggests nature and can represent the natural descendants outside the lineage of the Abrahamic promise. The Lord also said, "Look now toward heaven, and tell the stars, if thou be able to number them: and he said unto him, so shall thy seed be" (Genesis 15:5). This comparison refers to Abraham's spiritual progeny—that is, believers in Christ. "Heaven" and "stars" refer to believers who have been given the kingdom of heaven (Luke 22:29) and who are stars shining in the heavens (Philippians 2:15).

7 And I will establish my covenant between me and thee and thy seed after thee in their generations for an everlasting covenant, to be a God unto thee, and to thy seed after thee.

God reveals the extent of his covenant with Abraham. This covenant is established with Abraham, his immediate offspring, and subsequent offspring even unto distant generations. It is to be everlasting. The Hebrew word *olam* (Heb. **o-LAWM**) is translated "everlasting." It means "eternity" or "perpetual time." God's purpose is to have a people descend from Abraham who will perpetuate faith in Him and service to Him. As the patriarch of a religion that acknowledged the true God, Abraham became the first prophet of God (Genesis 20:7).

God's covenant with Abraham also makes him the founder of a religion that proclaims the worship of the true God. Thus, his fatherhood cuts across all political, social, and religious lines among his progeny. The religion of Abraham was supposed to be an expression of faith and obedience to God, characterized by the practice of righteousness, compliance with divinely stipulated laws and ceremonial practices, and recognition of the prophets, priests, etc., as representatives of God. But in the course of time, alien religious beliefs and practices involving other gods arose, claiming to originate from Abraham. The Ishmaelites and Midianites, for instance, formed major elements of the Arab nation. The Arabs are mostly Mohammedans, who claim that the Islamic religion, which was founded by Mohammed, has its origins from the religion of Abraham.

8 And I will give unto thee, and to thy seed after thee, the land wherein thou art a stranger, all the land of Canaan, for an everlasting possession; and I will be their God.

The nomadic life of Abraham was to be terminated by the possession of the land where he dwelt as a stranger. God promises to turn the immigrant Abraham into a possessor of a foreign land. The Hebrew word *erets* (**EH-rets**) is translated "land" and means "country" or "territory."

By covenant right, Abraham possesses the Canaanite country, but actual possession was realized by the 12 tribes of Israel, third-generation descendants of Abraham. The 12 sons of Jacob eventually became the 12 tribes who settled in the country of the Canaanites. It was a land flowing with milk and honey. God actually dispossessed the original inhabitants of the land to give it to Abraham's descendants in fulfillment of His covenant. God said it was to be for an everlasting possession. Therefore, it is meant to be a permanent home for the descendants of Abraham. It was a perpetual possession.

God never does anything without a purpose. Let us identify a divine purpose here. Before this time, it was not recorded in the Bible that God had a people who assumed a national status and were located in a divinely prescribed geographical location. Giving the land of Canaan to the Israelites fulfilled this purpose; it established a nation possessing a part of the earth and having the true God as its God in a world where other peoples and nations worshiped other gods.

17:15 And God said unto Abraham, As for Sarai thy wife, thou shalt not call her name Sarai, but Sarah shall her name be. 16 And I will bless her, and give thee a son also of her: yea, I will bless her, and she shall be a mother of nations; kings of people shall be of her.

The change of name, already effected in the life of Abraham, is also extended to Sarai, his wife. Here, God commands Abraham not to call her Sarai, but Sarah. The word qara (Heb. **kaw-RAW**) is the Hebrew word translated "call." It means "to call, call out to, or name." Abraham is to call Sarai by the name Sarah. The calling out of a person's name basically accomplishes three things: it gets the person's attention, it makes reference to the person while he or she is absent, and it evokes the meaning or significance of the name, specifying the person's characteristics, as with Jacob in Genesis 27:36, or making reference to the person's destiny, as with Noah in Genesis 5:29.

Sarai and Sarah both mean "princess." Both have their roots from sar (Heb. **SAR**), which means "prince." Sarai or Sarah is a female but the intrinsic meaning of the former name is that of a princess who exercises rule and dominates, while the latter connotes a noble princess (possessing fine personal qualities). The nobility of Sarah is alluded to in 1 Peter 3:4–6. Thus, Sarah, who is to beget peoples, nations, and kings, shares the same promise with her husband. By changing her name, God is making her an exemplary model to her progeny, indicating her participation in His promise.

This is the result of God's covenant with Abraham. The blessing of the Lord upon Sarah was to revive her womb to make it fertile. She had been barren from her youth until the time Abraham received the promise. At this time, she was 90 years old. The word of God brings life to her reproductive organs to enable her to give birth to the promised seed, Isaac.

17 Then Abraham fell upon his face, and laughed, and said in his heart, Shall a child be born unto him that is an hundred years old? and shall Sarah, that is ninety years old, bear?

Abraham responds to God's promise by bowing in reverence and laughing. The word tsachaq (Heb. **tsaw-KHAK**) is translated "laughed" in this verse of Scripture. Abraham's laughter could have been an expression of joy, but it seems to have expressed unbelief, as he questions the possibility of having a child at an old age. He also questions the possibility of Sarah bearing a child at 90 years old. The word tsachaq here could mean either to laugh in merriment or to scorn (as in making sport of something).

Although Abraham is a man who believes in God, his response here indicates a partial consideration of the stark natural realities of his situation. He was 100 years old and Sarah was 90 years old, and that he and Sarah would have a child at their age amazed him. The possibility seemed difficult to grasp; he doubted God.

Abraham had already experienced anxiety over the issue of childbirth. He had been worried over the thought of his steward, Eliezer of Damascus, being his heir, according to the traditions of the Mesopotamians among whom he lived. From his response here, this promise from God was much desired by him, since it was going to be a fulfillment of his lifelong dream.

Placing trust in God's promises is an expression of faith in Him. Although these promises often go beyond our present experiences, we must make up our minds that if God made them, then we must believe them and trust Him for their fulfillment.

18 And Abraham said unto God, O that Ishmael might live before thee!

Abraham expresses a deep affection for Ishmael and hope that he would be the beneficiary of the blessings of God, the heir to His promise. Therefore, he entreats the Lord concerning Ishmael.

The word translated "live" is *chayah* (Heb. **khaw-YAW**) and means "to preserve life, give life, or cause to stay alive." Specifically, Abraham's request concerning Ishmael is that God should cause him to live within the realities of His promise. Generally, it is also a prayer that God would keep him alive.

The birth of Ishmael was the main cause of Abraham's inability to trust in the promise of God—the promise to give him a son through Sarah. Upon having been given Ishmael, he placed all his hopes and affections on him and lost the vision of the promised seed that God would give to him.

There will always be something that will tend to debar us from trusting God, some overwhelming occurrence or seemingly cogent or genuine reasons to turn our minds away from trusting God's promises. We have to resist them.

19 And God said, Sarah thy wife shall bear thee a son indeed; and thou shalt call his name Isaac: and I will establish my covenant with him for an everlasting covenant, and with his seed after him.

God wanted Abraham to keep hope alive by expecting the seed of the promise, so He gave Abraham assurance by repeating this promise to him and further telling him what the name of the child should be.

The first time God promised a child to Abraham was in Genesis 15:4, with specific reference to the fact that it would be a child from his "own bowels," a child that Sarah his wife would bear. The word *yalad* (Heb. **yaw-LAD**) is translated "bear." It refers to the action of giving birth or bearing a child. After Abraham had believed God and his faith was credited to him as righteousness (15:6), an event contrary to his faith took place: the birth of Ishmael. This was a result of yielding to Sarai's pressure to obtain a child through Hagar, her Egyptian handmaid.

God promised that He would establish His covenant with the seed borne by Sarah, Abraham's wife. God's covenant was made within his own generation, with his seed after him, and with further generations to come; thus, the covenant was everlasting.

God commanded that the child be named Isaac, which means "laughter." The prevailing condition of childlessness in the life of Abraham and Sarah brought sadness and anxiety to the greater part of their marriage. The birth of Isaac brought joy and fulfillment, and this was a good cause for laughter.

20 And as for Ishmael, I have heard thee: Behold, I have blessed him, and will make him fruitful, and will multiply him exceedingly; twelve princes shall he beget, and I will make him a great nation.

In response to Abraham's request concerning Ishmael, God promised to make him fruitful and multiply him exceedingly.

Ishmael was Abraham's firstborn. He was born in Abraham's house when Abraham dwelt in the plain of Mamre. He was the son of Hagar, Sarai's Egyptian handmaid. When Hagar conceived him, she began to despise her mistress, Sarai. This led Sarai to mistreat her; she then fled from Sarai's presence into the wilderness. There she was found by the angel of the Lord, who urged her to return to her mistress. There, also, the first proclamation of blessing was made concerning Ishmael. The angel of the Lord also told Hagar that she would bear a son, and that he should be named Ishmael, because the Lord had heard her in her affliction.

The name Ishmael means "whom God hears," and, because God heard his mother in her afflictions, he was so named. Thus, Ishmael's name was based on the circumstances surrounding his birth.

With the institution of the covenant of circumcision and Abraham's request regarding Ishmael in verse 18, God renewed His promise concerning Ishmael. In addition to the blessings of fruitfulness and multiplication, the Lord said that Ishmael would beget 12 princes and would become a great nation. Abraham eventually sent Hagar and her son away. Hagar got an Egyptian wife for Ishmael, who begat the 12 princes. The descendants of these princes peopled the northern and western areas of the Arabian Peninsula, and they eventually formed the chief element of the Arab nation, the wandering Bedouin tribe. These people are now mostly Mohammedans, who look to Mohammed as their spiritual father.

21 But my covenant will I establish with Isaac, which Sarah shall bear unto thee at this set time in the next year. 22 And he left off talking with him, and God went up from Abraham.

God repeats His willingness to establish His covenant with Isaac, the son to be borne to Sarah. Though He had blessed Ishmael, as Abraham requested, His promise to Isaac stands unshaken.

With God there is an appointed time for things to be fulfilled. This is what is indicated by the phrase, "at this set time in the next year." God had set a time for Isaac to be born, and He had chosen to establish His covenant with him. Isaac was the promised child, and Ishmael was not. The early arrival of Ishmael wasn't going to change God's plan. And Sarah had been appointed to bear the promised child. Despite Abraham's doubts, God remained faithful, and His promise came to pass in his life. At God's appointed time, Sarah gave birth to Isaac.

No matter the situation, we must always trust in God's promises. He never fails.

Daily Bible Readings

M: Our Pledge to God
Psalm 119:33–40

T: Moses Chooses Judges
Exodus 18:13–27

W: Moses Goes Up to God
Exodus 19:1–9

T: Preparing for God's Covenant
Exodus 19:9–15

F: God Gives the Commands
Exodus 20:1–17

S: The People Vow Loyalty
Exodus 24:3–8

S: Moses Enters God's Presence
Exodus 24:12–18

TEACHING TIPS

September 17
Bible Study Guide 3

1. Words You Should Know

A. Covenant (Exodus 19:5) *beriyth* (Heb.)—A mutual agreement between two or more people, or a divine agreement between God and mankind.

B. Kingdom (v. 6) *mamlakah* (Heb.)—Denotes a defined kingdom or realm. The Israelites would become a spiritual kingdom of priests whose king would be God Himself. He would have ultimate and exclusive dominion and authority over His subjects, the Israelites.

C. Holy nation (v. 6) *qadosh gowy* (Heb.)—A nation that is set apart or sacred. Unlike other nations, the Israelites were to be set apart for God and distinguished by their allegiance to Him only and to no other gods.

2. Teacher Preparation

A. Read Psalm 119:33–40 in at least two different versions.

B. Read the Lesson Aim and the Keep in Mind verses.

C. Complete lesson 3 in the *Precepts For Living® Personal Study Guide.*

D. Research the many covenants that people enter into today; come prepared to discuss some of these (i.e., marriage, credit cards, salvation).

E. Come prepared to discuss the many reasons people break those covenants and the resulting consequences. (Consequences could include such examples as a broken heart, bad credit, etc.)

3. Starting the Lesson

A. Begin the class with prayer. Thank God for His consistency in keeping His covenant with mankind and for helping Christians to remain faithful to their spiritual covenant with Him and their promises to others.

B. Ask volunteers to read the Keep in Mind verse.

C. Ask a volunteer to read Mathew 5:37.

D. Briefly discuss the question: "Why do promises seem easier to make than keep?" Incorporate the Israelites' covenant-breaking history as an example of what *not* to do.

4. Getting into the Lesson

A. Have volunteers read the Focal Verses.

B. Write the terms "covenants," "broken promises," and "consequences" on the board, and ask for brief examples of each. Discuss what it means to live in a society that seems to place little value on keeping promises/covenants while focusing on the examples that were given.

5. Relating the Lesson to Life

A. Have the students write a brief *covenant keeper* statement for one covenant that they either want to enter into or have not upheld to the fullest. Have them begin the statement with "I will" or "I promise."

B. Have a few volunteers read their statements.

C. Remind the students that God wants Christians to keep their covenants with Him and to honor those covenants they enter into with others.

6. Arousing Action

A. Remind the students that a covenant is an agreement between two parties, and that a spiritual covenant with God demands commitment and respect.

B. In many respects, this is a somber lesson that provokes self-reflection. Some students may experience twinges of guilt or remorse as they analyze their commitments to Christ and others. Strive to end the lesson on an upbeat note. Invite the students to repent of past covenant breaches, reminding them that there is no condemnation in Christ Jesus.

C. Conclude the class with prayer.

Worship Guide

For the Superintendent or Teacher
Theme: God's Covenant with Israel
Theme Song: "Standing on the Promises"
Scripture: Joshua 21:45
Song: "God of Our Father"
Meditation: Dear Heavenly Father, help me to honor the commitments and promises I make to You and others. Amen.

31

GOD'S COVENANT WITH ISRAEL

Bible Background • EXODUS 19:1–6; 24:3–8

Printed Text • EXODUS 19:1–6; 24:3–8   Devotional Reading • PSALM 119:33–40

Lesson Aim

By the end of the lesson, we will:

KNOW the nature and basis of this mutual covenant made between God and the people of Israel;

APPRECIATE the need for respect and commitment in covenants we make; and

COMMIT to doing a better job of keeping our promises to God and others.

Keep in Mind

"And Moses came and told the people all the words of the LORD, and all the judgments: and all the people answered with one voice, and said, All the words which the LORD hath said will we do" (Exodus 24:3).

Focal Verses

Exodus 19:1 In the third month, when the children of Israel were gone forth out of the land of Egypt, the same day came they into the wilderness of Sinai.

2 For they were departed from Rephidim, and were come to the desert of Sinai, and had pitched in the wilderness; and there Israel camped before the mount.

3 And Moses went up unto God, and the LORD called unto him out of the mountain, saying, Thus shalt thou say to the house of Jacob, and tell the children of Israel;

4 Ye have seen what I did unto the Egyptians, and how I bare you on eagles' wings, and brought you unto myself.

5 Now therefore, if ye will obey my voice indeed, and keep my covenant, then ye shall be a peculiar treasure unto me above all people: for all the earth is mine:

6 And ye shall be unto me a kingdom of priests, and an holy nation. These are the words which thou shalt speak unto the children of Israel.

24:3 And Moses came and told the people all the words of the

LORD, and all the judgments: and all the people answered with one voice, and said, All the words which the LORD hath said will we do.

4 And Moses wrote all the words of the LORD, and rose up early in the morning, and builded an altar under the hill, and twelve pillars, according to the twelve tribes of Israel.

5 And he sent young men of the children of Israel, which offered burnt offerings, and sacrificed peace offerings of oxen unto the LORD.

6 And Moses took half of the blood, and put it in basons; and half of the blood he sprinkled on the altar.

7 And he took the book of the covenant, and read in the audience of the people: and they said, All that the LORD hath said will we do, and be obedient.

8 And Moses took the blood, and sprinkled it on the people, and said, Behold the blood of the covenant, which the LORD hath made with you concerning all these words.

In Focus

John, a minister, asked his wife, Arlene, a question as he prepared his Sunday sermon: "Do you believe our Christian relationship with God is a contract or a covenant?"

Arlene, an attorney, replied, "It is definitely a contract."

"Not really," John countered. "It may appear that way, but our relationship with God is a covenant."

Arlene peered over her coffee cup. "John, you are the theologian, but I'm the practicing attorney. A contract is a set of promises made by one party to another, for the breach of which the law provides a remedy."

She continued. "So you see, once we become Christians, we have entered into a contractual relationship with God. If we break God's law, He tells us His remedy or punishment."

John responded, "Biblically, a covenant is an agreement between God and His people in which God makes certain promises and requires certain behavior in return."

Arlene relented. "I see what you are saying. God is not out to get you, like a lawyer would be if you broke a contract."

"Exactly," John laughed and said. "I want the congregation to see God as merciful, gracious, and benevolent toward us, rather than as a suspicious and vengeful ruler according to the law."

That Sunday, the last words of John's sermon challenged his congregation: "I hope all of you will reaffirm your covenant agreement with a Sunday School class, mission group, or some other ministry, because part of our covenant responsibility is to demonstrate that we are God's people by helping others grow in Christ."

The mutual agreement between God and the people of Israel reminds us that we should do all we can to live up to our covenant relationship with God by honoring our commitments.

The People, Places, and Times

The Israelites. Of all the nations in the world, Israel was chosen to be God's covenant people. The Israelites would become His "peculiar treasure" if they lived up to their covenant responsibilities to obey His voice and keep His covenant (Exodus 19:5).

Moses. Moses was handpicked by God (Exodus 3:10) for the job of leading the Israelites out of slavery in Egypt and into a land "flowing with milk and honey" (Exodus 3:8). While his job seemed impossible and fraught with danger, God assured Moses of an eventual victory.

Wilderness of Sinai/Mount Sinai. The wilderness of Sinai was one of the first stops the Israelites made after escaping from Egypt. They stayed there for about a year (Numbers 10:11). It would prove to be a place of national trial and triumph. The Israelites experienced defeat (including making the golden calf while Moses was receiving the Ten Commandments; Exodus 32) and victory (including ratifying the Ten Commandments; Exodus 19–24) while encamped there.

Background

The theme of the book of Exodus is redemption. Originally, Jacob moved to Egypt to escape starvation, but his descendants eventually became slaves under a cruel Pharaoh (Exodus 1:8–14). Exodus chronicles the history of the Israelites from slavery to freedom and the many events that occurred during their stay in the wilderness.

God, aware of the Israelites' plight, selects Moses to lead the trek from bondage to freedom. Moses, in this way, serves as a type of Jesus Christ, our Redeemer and Saviour. God tells Moses that He is aware of the Israelites' dilemma and will lead them to a better land. That land is described as one "flowing with milk and honey" (Exodus 3:16–17), referring to a place where the nation's needs (milk) and desires (honey) will be fulfilled.

True to His promise to Moses, God delivers Israel from slavery in Egypt. He does so by signs and miracles that culminate in the Red Sea parting. The Israelites walk safely through the sea on dry ground, and the Egyptians drown as the sea returns to its normal position.

After three months of trials and testing (Exodus 15–19), the Israelites arrive in the wilderness of Sinai and camp before Mount Sinai. Almost immediately, Moses goes to meet with God. He receives specific instructions to remind the Israelites of their recent deliverance and protection. He must remind the Israelites that God expects them to obey His voice and keep His covenant (Exodus 19:5). If they do, they will be His covenant people (vv. 5–6).

A covenant is basically a legally binding agreement. It affords privileges and responsibilities to each party, and each party must agree to all provisions. The covenant must be signed or ratified. There are numerous consequences, usually outlined in the agreement, for breaking a ratified covenant. The covenant that God initiated and later ratified with the Israelites encompassed their physical, spiritual, and material needs. God was responsible for providing for all these needs, while the Israelites were responsible for obeying Him and serving Him only.

Since obedience can be subjective, God provides

the Israelites with a blueprint for covenantal success. The Ten Commandments (Exodus 20:2–17) outline the conditions that must be fulfilled in order for the Israelites to remain faithful to their covenant with God. As with any agreement, God's covenant with Israel needed to be agreed upon and witnessed to by both parties. This is what takes place in Exodus 24:3–8.

Many argue that the Ten Commandments are not relevant today because the foundation of the Christian life is grace, not the law. That is not so. We cannot be saved or justified before God by keeping the law; still, the moral law of God is unchangeable. When asked which commandment was the greatest, Jesus replied, "Thou shalt love the Lord thy God with all thy heart, and with all thy soul, and with all thy mind. This is the first and great commandment. And the second is like unto it, Thou shalt love thy neighbour as thyself. On these two commandments hang all the law and the prophets" (Matthew 22:37–40).

It is important to note that Jesus did not say that *none* of the other commandments was relevant. He simply revealed how all the commandments hinged on these two. For example, if you loved God and your neighbor, you would not kill, steal, or commit adultery. Thus, the Ten Commandments are still relevant and applicable for Christians seeking to be faithful to their spiritual covenant with God, which was ratified by the blood of our Lord Jesus Christ.

A to A - Glance

1. A Promise Keeper (Exodus 19:1–4)
2. Call to Obedience (v. 5)
3. A New Identity (v. 6)
4. A Mutual Agreement (24:3–8)

In Depth

1. A Promise Keeper (Exodus 19:1–4)

When Moses initially encounters God (Exodus 3), he is unaware that God is a promise keeper. But he soon learns that what God promises, He delivers. That's important to know, since every covenant is limited to its provisions and hinges on the parties' ability to perform them. For example, it would be futile to enter a million-dollar contract with a pauper, fully knowing that party would never be able to provide the monies promised. As Creator of heaven and Earth, God has the resources and power necessary to fulfill His part of the agreement. He not only makes promises, but keeps them as well.

By the time the Israelites arrive at Mount Sinai, it is clear that God is committed to His Word. Despite the Israelites' unfaithfulness on many occasions, including storing up more manna than was directed (16:20), God remained faithful.

At Mount Sinai, God makes it clear that: He (1) alone delivered them from slavery (v. 4), (2) He brought them out for the purpose of serving Him (v. 4), (3) He had specific requirements for their continued relationship with Him (v. 5), and (4) He would ensure an even better future (v. 6). God presents these points to the Israelites on the heels of their redemption. After only three months of freedom, they could easily remember their recent bondage and God's miraculous provision. They also could have faith that God would keep these promises just as He had kept the promise to free them from Egypt.

2. Call to Obedience (v. 5)

God's call to obedience was not an arbitrary one. First, as the Creator of all mankind, He knew the sinful nature of fallen humanity. Second, He had witnessed the Israelites' repeated disobedience to the instructions that Moses received from God and gave to the people. Third, God demands that His chosen people follow Him with a whole heart by serving Him alone and obeying His words.

As former slaves, the Israelites understood what it meant to serve a master or overseer and the many restrictions that doing so entailed. That God commanded only that they obey His voice and follow His commandments must have seemed a light burden compared to what they had formerly experienced. It's also possible, however, that the idea of following by one's heart, instead of being forced to obey at the hands of a cruel taskmaster, would likely have been difficult for people seeking to stretch the bounds of their freedom. The Israelites would soon learn that obedience is not a head matter, but a heart matter. To fully follow God, the Israelites had to be committed to serving Him. They had to do it willingly, not because a cruel taskmaster was forcing them to do it. They would have to do it out of love, not fear.

3. A New Identity (v. 6)

As slaves, the Israelites were likely physically and verbally abused. They were dependent on the benevolence of a cruel Pharaoh who feared they would outnumber the Egyptians and overthrow his kingdom (Exodus 1:9–10). They were lightly esteemed and could never hope to earn positions of respect or affluence.

Then God redeemed them and bestowed a new identity on the entire nation. No longer would they be lowly subhumans worthy of little regard, or treated as animals and worked to death. Imagine how they must have felt when God promised to make them a "kingdom of priests, and an holy nation" (19:6)! God now declares that, to Him, the Israelites are special.

Basically, at Mount Sinai, God affirms the covenant, assuring Israel of His care and provision while giving them a new identity. If the nation would collectively perform its responsibilities, it would become a "kingdom of priests, and an holy nation." Cherished and protected, Israel would be God's "peculiar treasure," preferred over all other nations of the earth. In other words, compared to those nations, the Israelites would become highly favored by God and treated as special.

Such language makes it clear that God had exclusive plans for Israel that did not cease with the crossing of the Red Sea. As He proved with that miracle, God has the needed power and provision to assure the Israelites' longevity and prosperity. Again, however, the promise is conditional, hinging on Israel's obedience to the covenant.

As Christians, we are heirs to the promise of a new identity. The apostle Peter points this out (1 Peter 2:9–10). Like the Israelites, we must embrace this new identity, shedding the "old man" of sin that entices us to disobey God's call to obedience.

4. A Mutual Agreement (24:3–8)

A legally binding contract, or covenant, must be agreed upon by all parties. All parties must affirm their acceptance of contracts and provisions, and then sign or ratify the contract as proof of their mutual agreement. Most contracts also have to be witnessed by a third party (such as a notary public), thus further confirming the parties' mutual agreement. Once ratification has taken place, it is difficult for a party to claim that he/she ignorantly signed the contract or was coerced to do so.

Likewise, the Israelites could not claim to have entered into covenant with God ignorantly or by force. That's because six compelling proofs show that they knowingly and willingly entered into a mutuall agreement with God:

1. Moses provided an oral report of the covenant's provisions (v. 3).
2. The people agreed to all the words they heard (v. 3).
3. Moses provided a written report of the provisions (v. 4).
4. Moses followed Israelite protocol for ratifying covenants by blood (vv. 5–7).
5. Moses read the words of the covenant to the people, who again agreed to obey the words they heard (v. 7).
6. Moses witnessed their agreement and affirmed his witness by sprinkling the people with blood (v. 8).

Thus, the Israelites knowingly entered into a covenant with God. Nonetheless, the promise was conditional. With God's help, the nation could fulfill its covenant obligations. However, if the Israelites failed to live up to their responsibilities, they would not receive the promised preferential treatment. The covenant would be nullified, and the Israelites would experience the full effects of breaching the covenant. The blessings for obedience and the curses for disobedience are fully detailed in Deuteronomy 28.

Search the Scriptures

1. How long did it take for the Israelites to reach Mount Sinai (Exodus 19:1)?
2. Of what did God remind the Israelites, and what did He require (vv. 4–5)?
3. What did Moses write (24:4, 7)?

Discuss the Meaning

1. Why do you think obedience is so important to God (Exodus 19:5)?

2. Why do you think God used the term "peculiar treasure" (v. 5)?

3. Why do you think it was important for the covenant to be in written form (24:4, 7)?

4. Moses sprinkled the blood on the people (Exodus 24:8). What impact do you think the sprinkled blood had on their hearts and minds?

Lesson in Our Society

Reality television shows have become extremely popular. Unfortunately, the success of a contestant on many of these shows hinges on how effectively he or she can "rat" on another contestant or ruthlessly compete. No promise is sacred; any promise can be broken in the pursuit of fame, success, and money. What message do you think such shows send concerning making and keeping promises? How can Christians use such shows to start a meaningful dialogue with an unbeliever about the importance of keeping promises or the consequences of breaking promises? Given your previous actions, if you were the star of a reality television show, would other contestants predict that you would be the promise keeper or the promise breaker? How do you plan to continue or change that reputation?

Make It Happen

Are you ready to be a consistent promise keeper? Are you ready to recommit to prayer, Bible study, church attendance, or financial stewardship? Repent for past disobedience, then ask for God's help. Live a promise-keeping life by remembering that it's not by power nor might, but by God's Spirit that we can remain faithful to Him and His covenant (cf. Zechariah 4:6).

Follow the Spirit

What God wants me to do:

_____

_____

Remember Your Thoughts

Special insights I have learned:

_____

_____

More Light on the Text

Exodus 19:1–6; 24:3–8

1 In the third month, when the children of Israel were gone forth out of the land of Egypt, the same day came they into the wilderness of Sinai.

The phrase "In the third month" might be better translated as "On the third new moon," since the Jewish calendar was developed later. *Sivan* (late May or early June) became known as the third month of the Jewish calendar. The Hebrew phrase *ywm* (**yome**) translated here as "the same day," means "on that very day" or "at that time."

The Children of Israel arrived at Mount Sinai at the beginning of the journey's seventh week. The distance between Egypt and Mount Sinai is approximately 175 miles. When considering the short amount of time it took for them to cover this distance on foot, we get the sense that God did not want them to waste any time. He wanted them to understand right away that their deliverance from slavery was based on His covenantal faithfulness (see Genesis 15). Obviously, in light of this great salvation, the Israelites should respond by being faithful themselves and immediately embracing their covenant with God. As Christians who have received the gift of salvation and eternal life, we should also respond by turning to God in faithful obedience.

2 For they were departed from Rephidim, and they were come to the desert of Sinai, and had (pitched) in the wilderness; and there Israel camped before the mount.

The desert of Sinai was and still is rugged terrain. Moses and the people had to put forth a great deal of effort to get to this hot and lonely place. But this was the place God had chosen to show them His glory from the top of a mountain, 7,363 feet high, at the modern site of Gebel Musa. Our commitment to the Lord might take us to some lonely and hard places;

nevertheless, we must be willing to make the journey. As African Americans, we have come up the rough side of the mountain. In many ways, even our current experience is filled with difficulty, but God is still looking for us to commit ourselves to Him without excuses or compromise. We need to recognize that the Lord is using the rough and lonely places of our lives to show us His glory.

3 And Moses went up unto God, and the LORD called unto him out of the mountain, saying, Thus shalt thou say to the house of Jacob, and tell the children of Israel.

We see the sense of urgency Moses has as He ascends the mountain on the very same day the Israelites arrive there. Moses is in hot pursuit! One of the greatest signs of our commitment to the Lord is our "hot pursuit" of Him. Paul writes to the Philippians, "but I press on to take hold of that for which Christ Jesus took hold of (for) me" (Philippians 3:12, NIV). He goes on to say, "I press on toward the goal to win the prize for which God has called me heavenward in Christ Jesus" (v. 14, NIV). This passage of Scripture indicates that, although we do not do so perfectly, we must be found pursuing Him that is evidence of our commitment.

In Exodus 19:3, God refers to His people as "the house of Jacob" and "the children of Israel." The name Jacob literally means "he grabs by the heel" (Genesis 25:26). Figuratively, it means to supplant or deceive. (It's similar to our saying, "You're pulling my leg.") In Genesis 32:28, we read that God changes Jacob's name to Israel after he had wrestled with God all night. Thus, his name was changed from Jacob "struggling with men" to Israel "prevailing with God and man." The phrase translated in Genesis 32:28 as "hast thou power with God" is better rendered "you have struggled with God." An amazing understanding comes when we hear the last part of the verse: "and hast prevailed" or "and have overcome" (NIV). Jacob had been struggling with his brother, his uncle, and a few others, but it was in his struggle with God that he recognized God as his total resource. He stated, "I will not let you go unless you bless me" (v. 26, NIV).

Thus, in Exodus, God reminds the nation of Israel that until they recognized Him as their total resource like their father Jacob, they would not be blessed. If we recognize the Lord God Almighty as our total resource, it should be no problem for us to commit ourselves to Him. The inclusion of the two names is also a reminder to stay humble. Jacob was just a small herdsman in the desert. Israel was now a large nation of nearly two million people who had just seen God defeat the most powerful nation in the world, Egypt.

4 Ye have seen what I did unto the Egyptians, and how I bare you on eagles' wings, and brought you unto myself.

God uses vivid imagery to remind Israel that His commitment to them is based on the covenant He made with Jacob. The covenant is a bond between two parties. In this case, the bond is sovereignly administered. The phrase "eagles' wings" evokes the same image that God used to describe his relationship with Jacob: "like an eagle that stirs up its nest and hovers over its young, that spreads its wings to catch them and carries them on its pinions. The LORD alone led him" (Deuteronomy 32:11–12, NIV). The way God cared for and protected Jacob is the same way He acted on behalf of Israel and acts on behalf of His children today. God's actions toward Jacob and Israel were based on His covenantal promise to Abraham "to be his God and the God of his descendants" (Genesis 17:1–8, NIV).

The phrase "I bare you on eagles' wings" expresses God's deep love and affection. The Hebrew word translated "bare" is nasa' **(naw-SAW)**, which means "to lift up, carry, support, or sustain." "I lifted you above the circumstances. I protected you by scooping you up and soaring to great heights out of the reach of trouble. It could not get near you." Frequently, we forget how often God has delivered us from the difficult circumstances of life. He has shown that He loves us. Some people even forget to such a great degree that their faith begins to dwindle. But God reminds us today just as He reminded Israel, "Remember my love for you." We can remain faithful to God because of His great love and faithfulness toward us (1 John 4:10, 19).

The eagle is a bird of prey. The image Israel was left with is that of God swooping down on the Egyptians like prey. His judgment was powerful and swift. The Israelites saw the plagues; they saw what the Death Angel did; they saw the sea part as God led them through on dry land; and they saw God wash away their enemies in a swift moment, with crashing waves. By His powerful deliverance, God brought them out of slavery and to Himself at the foot of Mount Sinai to see His glory because He desired an intimate relationship with them. God's love is unchanging. He has delivered us from the slavery of our sins through the Cross of Jesus and has brought us to Himself so that we can enjoy a deep, intimate relationship with Him.

5 Now therefore, if ye will obey my voice indeed, and keep my covenant, then ye shall be a peculiar treasure unto me above all people: for all the earth is mine.

Jesus said, "My sheep listen to my voice; I know them, and they follow me"; and "If you love me, you will obey what I command" (John 10:27; 14:15, NIV). God's covenant is conditional: it is with those who hear (Heb.) *shama*, His voice with a desire to do His will, and not with those who ignore His voice. There are covenant breakers and covenant keepers. Covenant keepers are not perfect, but they have a practice of continually taking their shortcomings to God and following after Jesus. Covenant breakers have the mindset that "No one can be perfect anyway, so what's the use?" Jacob's brother, Esau, who sold his birthright for a temporary moment of pleasure, was considered a covenant breaker (Genesis 25). By instructing them to obey His voice and keep His covenant, God was calling them to set their hearts on the things of God, to set their lives apart from the world, and to show themselves to be His "peculiar treasure."

The English word "peculiar" comes from the Latin word *peculium,* which means "private property." The Hebrew word *ceghullah,* translated as "treasure," means "special possession" or "valued." Thus, God is telling us through Israel, "You are my own special pos-

session, valued property, and a treasure unto me, if you listen to and follow after my Word."

In other words, those who have put their faith in Jesus prove themselves to be God's peculiar people (His own possession). By their desire and willingness to obey God's commands, they show that they are committed to Christ. It is impossible to love the world and serve God at the same time (Matthew 6:24).

6 And ye shall be unto me a kingdom of priests, and an holy nation. These are the words which thou shalt speak unto the children of Israel.

What was the role of the priest? Moses was a mediator between God and the people. He brought the Word of God to the people, and he interceded on behalf of the people before God. Moses represented God to the unbelieving world, and was their representative before God. Thus, Moses was a type of Christ.

Today, under the new covenant, Jesus is our mediator, the only way to get to God. He is the Word (John 1:1, 14). He "ever liveth to make intercession" for us and He offered up His life as the sacrifice for our sins (Hebrew 7:25; 9:26; 10:12). Like Israel, we are to represent God to the world, being His "chosen race, a royal priesthood, a holy nation, God's own people." As God's chosen people, we are to be set apart for His use: to intercede for family, friends, and coworkers; to explain the Word to them; and to introduce them to Jesus. We are also able to come before God because of Christ's work on our behalf.

24:3 And Moses came and told the people all the words of the LORD, and all the judgments; and all the people answered with one voice, and said, All the words which the LORD hath said will we do.

God comes to us as He came to Israel: as absolute sovereign Lord, our King. He pledges to be our God, provider, and protector. In return, He expects us to be loyal to Him. Notice that keeping the regulations and principles of the covenant are merely the outward expressions of a deeper and inward commitment to the Lord.

Moses made a formal declaration of the covenant, and the people responded in the affirmative, meaning they accepted all the conditions. When the people said to Moses, "All the words which the Lord hath said will we do," the covenant was ratified. Similarly, we must count the cost (Luke 14:28). We must not look back: "No man, having put his hand to the plough, and looking back, is fit for the kingdom of God" (9:62). Jesus said, in the same way, "any of you who does not give up everything he has cannot be my disciple" (14:33, NIV).

4 And Moses wrote all the words of the LORD, and rose up early in the morning, and builded an altar under the hill, and twelve pillars, according to the twelve tribes of Israel.

The altar represented God's presence, and the pillars represented the people of Israel. In any covenant or contract, there are usually two parties. Again, the construction of the altar and pillars was a way of formalizing the commitment.

5 And he sent young men of the children of Israel, which offered burnt offerings, and sacrificed peace offerings of oxen to the LORD.

The Hebrew word for "burnt offerings" is *ola* (**o-law'**), which means "to go up." The sacrificial animal was to be consumed on the altar as a fragrance to the Lord. The fire was to burn all night, and the entire offering was to be burned (Leviticus 6). The priest was to lay his hand on the head of the animal, signifying a transfer of the sins of the people to the sacrifice. Then he was to kill the animal and sprinkle the blood on the altar. By doing this, the priest atoned for (or covered) the sins of the people through the blood sacrifice (v. 30).

This animal had to be without spot or blemish to be totally acceptable to the Lord. However, this Old Testament sacrifice for sin was only temporary. Jesus was the Lamb of God who was slain once and for all to atone for our sins throughout all eternity (Hebrews 10:10). Our salvation is secure because the sacrifice of the sinless Son of God was enough to satisfy God's wrath against us once and for all.

Our sins were transferred to Jesus on the Cross. His blood was poured on the altar for our atonement. He

was the perfect Lamb. His offer of forgiveness burns bright, both day and night. All He requires is a willingness to commit ourselves to Him based on what He has done. We do not need to work to gain eternal life.

In addition to the burnt offerings, the Old Testament priests sacrificed peace offerings. Not only do we have peace with God once and for all through the forgiveness found in Jesus, but we also serve God out of a heart that is thankful to Him.

6 And Moses took half of the blood, and put it in basins; and half of the blood he sprinkled on the altar.

According to the *International Standard Bible Encyclopedia,* covenants of the ancient Middle East were ratified in blood. Blood is significant in that it represents the life flow or existence (Leviticus 17:11). A covenant was in effect until death, and was always sealed using blood as part of the official ceremony. Here, God is signified as having accepted the covenant by the blood sprinkled on the altar. Moses also took blood in the basin and sprinkled it on the people (v. 8), signifying that they would keep the covenant as long as they lived. When we commit ourselves to the Lord Almighty, it should be "until death do us part." Death will only usher us into His presence (2 Corinthians 5:8).

7 And he took the book of the covenant, and read in the audience of the people: and they said, All that the LORD hath said will we do, and be obedient.

The Book of the Covenant was the expanded and detailed version of the Decalogue, found in Exodus 20:22–23:33. It included the Ten Commandments (20:1–17) as well as the brief statement of the treaty (19:3–6). By reading publicly, Moses now confirms the covenant between God and His people, and the people agree by replying in the affirmative. The Bible states, "Let the redeemed of the LORD say so" (Psalm 107:2). Nothing solidifies your commitment to Christ like your public testimony of what God has done for you. Committed Christians are not afraid to speak up for the Lord or to declare what God has said.

8 And Moses took the blood and sprinkled it on the people, and said, Behold the blood of the covenant,

which the Lord hath made with you concerning all these words.

Jesus was not only the mediator of the New Covenant, but He was also the Lamb that was slain to take away our sin. It is the shed blood of Jesus Christ that cleanses us from sin (1 John 1:7). The Children of Israel could not (nor can we) make a covenant with God because of the sin in our lives. However, Christ offers us a new and living way to draw near to God. It is because we are sinful that we need a relationship with a merciful God who will allow us to commit ourselves to Him and receive mercy without measure. The blood sprinkled on the people signified God's mercy, which allowed them to enter into covenant with Him, even though they did not have the ability within themselves to keep it. Our God is gracious and kind in that He would deign to commit Himself to us at all. He has shown the riches and kindness of His grace toward us by giving us the gift of salvation through Jesus Christ (Ephesians 2:7–9).

Daily Bible Readings

M: Our Pledge to God
Psalm 119:33–40

T: Moses Chooses Judges
Exodus 18:13–27

W: Moses Goes Up to God
Exodus 19:1–9

T: Preparing for God's Covenant
Exodus 19:9–15

F: God Gives the Commands
Exodus 20:1–17

S: The People Vow Loyalty
Exodus 24:3–8

S: Moses Enters God's Presence
Exodus 24:12–18

TEACHING TIPS

September 24
Bible Study Guide 4

1. Words You Should Know

A. Choose (Joshua 24:15) *bachar* (Heb.)—To make a conscious decision; to elect or choose. It also means to be chosen, as God was chosen.

B. Signs (v. 17) *'owth* (Heb.)—Miracles.

C. Serve (v. 19) *'abad* (Heb.)—To serve or labor for someone as a subject.

2. Teacher Preparation

A. Read the Daily Bible Readings leading up to today's lesson.

B. Read the Lesson Aim and the Keep in Mind verse.

C. Complete Bible Study Guide 3 in the *Precepts For Living® Personal Study Guide*.

D. Be prepared to discuss why surrendering to and serving God is the most important decision one can make and why repentance is the first step, followed by a wholehearted commitment to renew one's covenant with God.

E. Be prepared to discuss why courage and boldness are often needed to make right choices, using an example from a current event (magazine, newspaper, or television).

3. Starting the Lesson

A. Begin the class with prayer. Ask God to open the students' minds concerning how to make right choices and renew their commitment to God.

B. Ask a volunteer to read the Keep in Mind verse.

C. Briefly discuss how the decision to serve the Lord relates to current events and whether the choice the Israelites made was a good or bad one.

4. Getting into the Lesson

A. Ask for volunteers to read the Focal Verses based on the At-A-Glance outline.

B. Write the words "choice," "courage," and "boldness" on the board. Then list and discuss different choices that people make and determine whether they require courage, boldness, or both.

C. Ask how these decisions compare with the choice to accept Jesus Christ as Lord and to serve Him (focus on the simplicity of the Gospel and the courage it takes to live a dedicated Christian life today).

5. Relating the Lesson to Life

A. Ask a volunteer to read the In Focus story.

B. Briefly discuss what influences the choices that people make (e.g., advertising, family, friends, ignorance, books, magazines) have on them.

C. Review the Keep in Mind verse and remind the students that it is never too late to start over (renew their covenant).

6. Arousing Action

A. Reinforce the Lesson Aim. Be prepared to share the importance of making the decision to accept Christ.

B. Ask the students the following question: "What one important spiritual choice have you delayed making?" Briefly discuss some of the students' answers.

C. End the class by offering the opportunity for the students to make a choice for salvation or to renew their commitment to Christ.

Worship Guide

For the Superintendent or Teacher
Theme: Covenant Renewed
**Theme Song: "Give of Your Best
to the Master"**
Scripture: 1 John 4:19
Meditation: Lord, thank You for Your Word.
Thank You for leading me in the path of
Your righteousness. Help me to commit to a
dedicated life of service in doing Your will.
Amen.

COVENANT RENEWED

Bible Background • JOSHUA 24
Printed Text • JOSHUA 24:1, 14–24   Devotional Reading • PSALM 51:1–12

Lesson Aim

By the end of the lesson, we will:

UNDERSTAND that the decision to serve God is an individual one;

REFLECT on the faithfulness God has shown to us; and

COMMIT or RECOMMIT to serving God the rest of our lives.

Keep in Mind

"And if it seem evil unto you to serve the LORD, choose you this day whom ye will serve; whether the gods which your fathers served that were on the other side of the flood, or the gods of the Amorites, in whose land ye dwell: but as for me and my house, we will serve the LORD" (Joshua 24:15).

Focal Verses

Joshua 24:1 And Joshua gathered all the tribes of Israel to Shechem, and called for the elders of Israel, and for their heads, and for their judges, and for their officers; and they presented themselves before God.

24:14 Now therefore fear the LORD, and serve him in sincerity and in truth: and put away the gods which your fathers served on the other side of the flood, and in Egypt; and serve ye the LORD.

15 And if it seem evil unto you to serve the LORD, choose you this day whom ye will serve; whether the gods which your fathers served that were on the other side of the flood, or the gods of the Amorites, in whose land ye dwell: but as for me and my house, we will serve the LORD.

16 And the people answered and said, God forbid that we should forsake the LORD, to serve other gods;

17 For the LORD our God, he it is that brought us up and our fathers out of the land of Egypt, from the house of bondage, and which did those great signs in our sight, and preserved us in all the way wherein we went, and among all the people through whom we passed:

18 And the LORD drave out from before us all the people, even the Amorites which dwelt in the land: therefore will we also serve the LORD; for he is our God.

19 And Joshua said unto the people, Ye cannot serve the LORD: for he is an holy God; he is a jealous God; he will not forgive your transgressions nor your sins.

20 If ye forsake the LORD, and serve strange gods, then he will turn and do you hurt, and consume you, after that he hath done you good.

21 And the people said unto Joshua, Nay; but we will serve the LORD.

22 And Joshua said unto the people, Ye are witnesses against yourselves that ye have chosen you the LORD, to serve him. And they said, We are witnesses.

23 Now therefore put away, said he, the strange gods which are among you, and incline your heart unto the LORD God of Israel.

24 And the people said unto Joshua, The LORD our God will we serve, and his voice will we obey.

In Focus

Mark and James had been best friends since they met as young boys in elementary school over 30 years ago. This Sunday, James decided to visit his lifelong buddy after church. As the two friends sat on Mark's deck barbecuing and watching the game, during the commercial break, James asked his friend, "Man, when are you going to come to church with me? I've been asking you for over a year now, and you still haven't agreed to come."

"Huh?" said Mark. "Look, man, no disrespect to you, but I work nights, and Sunday is the only day of the week I can relax and do my thing. Look at you right now; I'd say you're eating pretty good." "Besides, here's my dilemma: I believe in God, but I don't believe I need to go to church. If God already knows I accept Him, it doesn't matter what I do. I can be the worst of all sinners and still be saved in the end. What's the point in declaring your Christian faith or attending some service every Sunday?"

"Mark, the decision to accept Christ is a choice. You make choices every day. However, the most important choice you will ever make in your life is the choice to accept and serve God. God will not force you to serve Him; you must decide on your own to serve God and live out your life honoring that commitment," James explained.

Mark replied, "Yeah man, I get it. . .but why do I have to attend church to commit to God?"

"Well, let me relate it to you this way," said James. "How will you ever get in the game if you never show up at training camp? All committed athletes have to train before they are allowed to play with the big boys. Baseball players attend spring training; football and basketball players attend training camp. How will you ever learn how to live a godly life if you never commit to do what it takes and receive the training?" asked James.

"You know, my brother, that makes sense. You're actually learning something down at that church," said Mark laughingly. "Come by and pick me up next Sunday; I'll go check out your church."

In today's lesson, Joshua assembles the tribes of Israel together to have them choose whom they will serve. Even today, it remains the most important decision in our lives.

The People, Places, and Times

Joshua. Joshua's history as leader of the Israelites began when he was an assistant to Moses (Exodus 17:9) and one of twelve spies sent to investigate the land of Canaan (Numbers 13). Only Joshua and Caleb brought back a favorable report; the other 10 spies bemoaned the giants of the land. Caleb and Joshua's faith in God's promise to bring Israel into the Promised Land was evident when they reminded the other spies, "If the LORD is pleased with us, he will lead us into that land, a land flowing with milk and honey, and will give it to us. Only do not rebel against the LORD" (Numbers 14:8–9, NIV).

Over the ensuing decades, Joshua proved a faith-

ful servant to God and assistant to Moses. Before Moses died, he received instructions from God to appoint Joshua as the next leader. Joshua, like Moses, proved an apt leader who relied on God to shepherd Israel. The book of Joshua details his leadership years and wraps up with chapter 24, in which Joshua takes the opportunity to remind the Israelites to recommit to God. Before he dies, Joshua leads the nation in renewing its covenant with God.

Your Fathers. Many of the Israelites to whom Joshua spoke did not have firsthand knowledge of God's earlier miraculous deliverance of His people. Yet, they were enjoying the fruits of deliverance. These descendants relied on stories passed down over the years of the victory at the Red Sea and other successful military campaigns. Now, decades later, Joshua again reminds the Israelites of God's faithfulness. Even more, he makes a clear case that the faith of one's ancestors alone is not enough. Each Israelite must make a personal decision to serve God. Joshua also proves his stand on the issue by declaring that "as for me and my house, we will serve the LORD" (Joshua 24:15).

Background

Under the leadership of Joshua, the tribes of Israel received their promised inheritance, a land flowing with milk and honey. After several military campaigns, each tribe has received land. At this point, they are enjoying a time of extended peace, free from enemy attacks (Joshua 23:1). But now they face a greater challenge: the impending death of Joshua. The aged leader calls the elders and the rest of the people together to remind them of the need to renew their covenant with God.

Joshua does so at Shechem, an important location in Israel's history. It was at Shechem that God promised to give the land of Canaan to Abram and his descendants (Genesis 12:6–7). Years later, Jacob would renew his obedience to God at that same location. There, under an oak tree, Jacob buried idols and earrings belonging to his household and others before heading to Bethel to worship God (Genesis 35:2–5).

Joshua's current gathering together of the leaders

at Shechem was another call to obedience, to be demonstrated by following God, not idols. Joshua had earlier called for the key leaders of Israel and all the people, and reminded them of God's care and provision (Joshua 23:1–16). It was important for the leaders to appear, since they were the ones who had been specially appointed as tribal representatives and who could take any special message back to the rest of the individuals under them. (Thanks to Jethro's instructions, Moses had years before, appointed leaders to head groups of specific sizes to assist in shepherding the nations, administering the law, etc.). Joshua offered a moving reminder to obey God (23:11) while warning of the consequences of disobedience. He admonished the people that, although the Israelites had previously enjoyed longevity, they would "perish quickly from off the good land" (v. 16) should they disobey the Lord.

At-A-Glance

1. The Call to Covenant (Joshua 24:1)
2. The Call to Serve God (vv. 14–15)
3. The Call to Commit to God (vv. 16–20)
4. The Call to Recommit to God (vv. 21–24)

In Depth

1. The Call to Covenant (Joshua 24:1)

The Israelites were enjoying the fruit of God's faithfulness to His covenant while living in a Promised Land of plenty. No longer slaves, they were free to live, work, and worship God. The nation, however, was about to face a major trial: the death of Joshua. This former assistant to Moses had courageously led his people by relying on God. He was a faithful servant and leader, steadfast in his devotion to God and God's covenant. Now nearing death, Joshua gathers the leaders to encourage renewed commitment and obedience to God's Word.

The call to covenant renewal before Joshua's death was particularly significant for three reasons. First, it reminded the people that Joshua was not their "real" leader, but just a servant of God who

worked to bring God's people into their inheritance. Second, it made it clear that Joshua's death should not be the end of Israel's commitment to God. Third, it reminded the people of their covenant obligation to serve the true and living God.

2. The Call to Serve God (vv. 14–15)

Joshua, in this second gathering, called for action. Thus, he and the nation present themselves before God for a special message regarding their need to renew their spiritual covenant. Their appearance before God is a reminder that "we must all stand before the judgment seat of Christ" (Romans 14:10). Here, Joshua urges the Israelites to make a choice. Former slaves, the Israelites were living well. Yet, all the things they possessed were essentially gifts of grace (Joshua 24:13). As their leader, Joshua challenges them publicly to make a choice. They were not to be hypocritical by pretending to serve God. Instead, they were to choose whom they were going to serve the gods of their forefathers, or Yahweh.

Some Israelites might have considered it evil to serve the Lord because serving Yahweh might mean a change in their lifestyle. They would have to commit themselves to God's will and His ways. But Joshua assured the Israelites that no matter what choice they made, he and his house would continue to serve the LORD (v. 15).

Just as Joshua challenged the Israelites to choose whom they would serve, we, too, are free to choose or reject God. Salvation is a personal matter, and there comes a time when each person must make a commitment to Christ. Often, a decision to renew one's spiritual covenant is necessary if that commitment has been broken.

3. The Call to Commit to God (vv. 16–20)

The people responded to Joshua's argument by saying that they would never forsake the Lord. They were fully aware of the things He had delivered them from. They understood that it was God who had delivered them out of the hands of their captors and had allowed them to reside in the Promised Land a land flowing with milk and honey. They believed that they had remained faithful to God even though some in this new generation of Israelites had no firsthand knowledge of God's miraculous deliverance. It had been easy for their forefathers to remain faithful and steadfast during those years in the wilderness as they followed Moses because God was their only source. However, this next generation of Israelites began to backslide, and it was Joshua who had to remind them of God's covenant and faithfulness toward them.

At first glance, it appears that verse 19 is a contradiction. Why would Joshua bring the people together to invite spiritual renewal, only to tell them "ye cannot serve the Lord"? It would appear that he was in fact asking for an impossible commitment. Not so. Joshua was not attempting to dissuade the people from making a commitment to God. Instead, he was warning the Israelites that such a commitment could not be fulfilled in their own strength, but only with the help of God. In Joshua's eyes, the people had rebelled against God. Their willful participation in worshiping other gods was a sin for which there was no forgiveness under the law (Numbers 15:30).

Most Christians would say that it is easier to remain faithful and steadfast during times of trials and tribulations. Our belief that God can and will deliver us is what gets us through tough times. But how often do we fall victim to the carnality of life when things are going well? All the bills are paid, the career is on track, the children are obedient, the marriage is solid: Life is good and flowing with milk and honey. Oftentimes, we get too busy for God. Church attendance falls off, our prayer life suffers, and time spent in God's Word decreases. But Joshua was letting the Israelites know then, and lets us know now, that God is a jealous God and will not have any other gods before Him. We, too, must choose Yahweh (God) over little gods (i.e., education, money, houses, cars, prestige).

4. The Call to Recommit to God (vv. 21–24)

Like a true leader, Joshua presented to the people a true and fair case based on their current behavior and asked them to make a choice. Thus, by agreeing to the covenant in their own words, despite Joshua's warnings, the Israelites were knowingly and willingly renewing their covenant with God. Consequently,

subsequent generations could not say that they had entered the covenant unknowingly or unwillingly. They could never say that they did not know what God expected of them, or that they had not been warned of the ramifications of breaking their renewed covenant. The covenant was to bind the people to their promise to renounce their old life of sin and idolatry and to enter into covenant relationship with and remain true servants of God.

Sin happens. Of particular importance is Joshua's warning that one's covenant with God cannot be maintained in the flesh. Although the Israelites were in the midst of a prolonged season of peace, they still were prone to sin. To follow God completely, the Israelites needed to recognize this and make provision to eradicate sin, especially hidden sins (Galatians 5:19–21). In order to fully obey God's covenant, we need to deal with sin. We need to recognize daily how easy it is to sin. We need to renew our covenant daily, to confess our sins, and to accept God's abundant forgiveness, grace, and mercy. Then we can experience the fullness of joy that comes from consistently obeying God's Word.

Search the Scriptures

1. Who presented themselves to God (Joshua 24:1)?

2. What was the Israelites' response regarding the gods of the Egyptians and Amorites (v. 16)?

3. What were some practical methods that Joshua used to remind the people of their renewed covenant (vv. 22–23)?

Discuss the Meaning

1. What do you think would have happened if the nation's covenant with God had not been renewed before Joshua's death?

2. What does it mean to serve God in sincerity and truth (Joshua 24:14)?

3. Discuss present-day gods that people serve.

4. What does it mean to enter into a covenant relationship with God?

Lesson in Our Society

With the proliferation of cults and cultic movements, there are perhaps more religions available today than ever before. The problem is, many of these groups can easily sway the unknowing into spiritual darkness. That is why making the right choice regarding one's spiritual life is so important. But choosing to serve God is not enough. We must decide to live out our lives honoring our spiritual covenant with God. It is a day-in, day-out decision that requires courage and boldness. It is a decision that will make a difference today and throughout eternity.

Where do you stand? Have you chosen to follow Christ? Is your commitment rock solid? Or have you allowed the cares of the world and the deceitfulness of riches to drag you into spiritual quicksand? If the latter describes your situation, consider recommitting to Christ today. He is always ready to covenant with people who have a heart to love and serve Him.

Make It Happen

The decision to accept or recommit to Christ is a very important one. The reality is that all other choices in life will be affected by one's decision to serve God. Do you need to commit or recommit to God? There is a very simple exercise that is taught to small children. It's called the ABC's of salvation. **A**—Ask God to forgive your sins. **B**—Believe that Jesus died on the cross for you. **C**—Call on Jesus to save you. It's really that simple. If you are recommitting your life, pledge your allegiance to God again, as you did in the past.

Follow the Spirit

What God wants me to do:

_____

_____

Remember Your Thoughts

Special insights I have learned:

_____

_____

More Light on the Text

Joshua 24:1, 14–24

1 And Joshua gathered all the tribes of Israel to Shechem, and called for the elders of Israel, and for their heads, and for their judges, and for their offi-cers; and they presented themselves before God.

Joshua was up in years (110 according to verse 29) when he gathered the people to make a covenant renewal. This was his last major act before his death, and he called the people together because he realized that he did not have much time left. As the leader and mediator of the people, he wanted to remind them of what God had done for them and to call them to be faithful to the Lord.

24:14 Now therefore, fear the LORD, and serve him in sincerity and in truth: and put away the gods which your fathers served on the other side of the flood, and in Egypt; and serve ye the LORD.

The instruction to "fear the Lord" does not mean to be so afraid of Him that one has no confidence to live one's life. The Hebrew word for "fear"—*yare'* (**yaw-RAY**)—means "to revere, stand in awe of, honor, or respect." The Israelites were to fear missing out on God's goodness. Such "fear" would involve being constantly in awe of God's majesty and fearing His wrath so much so that they would yield to His authority over them and refuse to do things that would displease Him.

The word "sincerity" comes from the Hebrew word *tamiym* (**taw-MEEM**), which is an adjective that means "complete, whole, entire, or healthful" and refers to what is completely or entirely in accord with the truth and facts. Joshua reminds the Children of Israel to give the Lord their whole hearts and to serve in a way that is truthful, both inwardly and outwardly; in other words, don't just shout on Sunday, but live for Jesus every day.

The word "serve" comes from the Hebrew word *'abad* (**aw-BAD**), which means "to deal bountifully with" or "to be of benefit to someone or something." So often, we want the Lord to bless us and be our friend. However, the real question is, "Are we true friends of the Lord and of benefit to Him?" (cf. Revelation 4:11).

Joshua tells the people to prove their sincerity by making the right choice, i.e., by putting away their idols. An idol can be anything that you spend more time with or think about more than your relationship with the Lord. It could be your mate, your children, your job, a favorite sport, television programs, video

Joshua spoke to the people: "And if it seem evil unto you to serve the LORD, choose you this day whom ye will serve; whether the gods which your fathers served that were on the other side of the flood, or the gods of the Amorites, in whose land ye dwell: but as for me and my house, we will serve the LORD" (Joshua 24:15).

games, movies, etc. Joshua's question is posed to all true believers: "Have you put away your idols?"

The Lord has kept His promise; the people now possess the Promised Land. Jesus has brought you out of slavery and bondage to sin. Don't go back!

15 And if it seem evil unto you to serve the LORD, choose you this day whom ye will serve; whether the gods which your fathers served that were on the other side of the flood, or the gods of the Amorites, in whose land ye dwell: but as for me and my house, we will serve the LORD.

The word "evil" comes from the Hebrew verb *ra`a`*

(**raw-AH**), which means "to be displeasing"; it could also mean "to be injurious, wicked, displeasing or undesirable." It's as if Joshua is saying, "If it is going to cause you personal pain to serve the Lord, if there is nothing attractive to you about that, then serve the false gods of your forefathers." Joshua seems to be using a bit of sarcasm here. After God has been so good to Israel, a point which Joshua has just reminded them of, it ought to be an easy decision to follow Him.

However, Joshua reminds the people that they have to make a choice between evil and God. For Joshua, the choice was obvious. As the head of his household, he made the decision to serve the Lord. In other words, Joshua's house would be defined by God's ways. Great leaders set the tone, and others follow. Thus, the decisions you make about how you will live can impact the destiny of your entire household.

16 And the people answered and said, God forbid that we should forsake the LORD, to serve other gods;

By saying "God forbid," the people are almost invoking a curse upon themselves. After they had looked back at all the wonderful ways God had provided for them, kept them, and helped them, it would be the ultimate insult for them to walk away and serve other gods. In effect, the people are emphatically saying, "We don't want to do anything even close to forsaking Him. May God never allow it to happen; in fact, may He forbid it. It must not happen. We shall make the right choice."

We are faced with choices every day. In times of testing, the question becomes, "Whom will we choose?" When we are tempted to doubt, that is the time to remember in detail how the Lord has brought us "a mighty long way."

17 For the LORD our God, he it is that brought us up and our fathers out of the land of Egypt, from the house of bondage, and which did those great signs in our sight, and preserved us in all the way wherein we went, and among all the people through whom we passed:

The faithfulness of God is undeniable. His faithfulness alone is reason enough for us to make the choice to be continuously faithful to Him. In this passage, the Children of Israel display for us an essential foundation for a lifestyle of faithfulness to the Lord, that is, remembering specific instances of God's faithfulness to us. The phrase "he it is that brought us up" can remind us that we were helpless in our sinful condition. As Israel was helpless to deliver themselves from Egypt, so there was nothing we could do to improve our situation, change our lives, or transform our circumstances. We were unable to save ourselves. We *are* unable to save ourselves.

18 And the LORD drave out from before us all the people, even the Amorites which dwelt in the land: therefore will we also serve the LORD; for he is our God.

The Amorites were a people of war, and they had conquered a great deal of territory. The first Amorites worshiped a god named Mantu, or Amurru, the god of the west; thus, the Amorites were originally known as "the westerners." Amurru was the husband of Aastatum, or Ashoreth, who was considered an equal divinity and the goddess of erotic love, as well as war. It was from among these people that God delivered the Children of Israel.

The entire nation of Israel, represented by the elders, was now renewing their covenant with the one true God, who conquers the greatest of peoples. They refused to indulge in the sexual immorality associated with the gods of the people around them. They would not be slaves to the world around them or to an earthly kingdom. Instead, they would be slaves to the Lord. By declaring their choice, the people of God repented, or turned away from their idols, and gave themselves wholeheartedly to the God who had created them.

Our society is overwhelmed with sexual influences and images. It is the idolatry of our day. The choice that we must make is, will we allow ourselves to be enticed and carried away by the world and its multitudes of gods, or will we repent and renew our covenant daily?

19 And Joshua said unto the people, Ye cannot serve the LORD: for he is an holy God; he is a jealous God; he will not forgive your transgressions nor your sins. 20 If ye forsake the LORD, and serve strange gods, then he will turn and do you hurt, and consume you, after that he hath done you good.

Since God is holy, Joshua challenges the people to put no confidence in themselves. When they look at themselves, it is plain to see that they have failed. In our own strength, we are not able to serve the Lord. However, Joshua tells Israel that God is not looking for men and women who appear to be righteous or who merely give lip service, but for men and women who have integrity of the heart. It is so easy to be overconfident, proud, and arrogant. So many people want to be seen as spiritually "together." But the truth is that God is holy and perfect, and we are frail, weak, and prone to sin. We need His grace, His power, and His holiness working in and through our lives. Jesus said, "Without me ye can do nothing" (John 15:5).

What does it mean that God is jealous? Does the word "jealous" imply that God is capable of human emotions and sins because of His uncontrollable rage? The answer is no. The word "jealous" (Heb. *qannow'*, **kan-NO**) as used here means "angry" and communicates to us how important it is to be faithful to the one and only true God and Creator. God is jealous only in the sense that He owns us, and our hearts and minds should not belong to any other. Loyalty to Him is the only response of those who belong to Him.

Today, many like to think of God as only a God of grace. Joshua reminds us that He is a loving and faithful God who pursues us, provides for us, and protects us with His strength. But He is also the God who disciplines the children He loves. God does not tolerate an attitude of continuous disobedience. Joshua says, "You have made your choice, now stick to it." Renewing their covenant vows did not exempt the people from the curse that comes to the covenant breaker.

21 And the people said unto Joshua, Nay; but we will serve the Lord.

The people respond in the affirmative yet again. They want to assure Joshua, and more importantly the Lord, that they mean business and are sincere. They confirm with deep passion, "We are not only saying it, but we, in fact, will serve the Lord alone." Upon looking at the first chapter of Judges, we see that they kept their word, although their descendants would later stray.

There is no joy or any other feeling to compare with the excitement of making a promise to follow the Lord and keeping it. All the pleasures of the earth stacked up together cannot compare with experienc-

ing His love for you and knowing you are showing your love for Him. Jesus expresses His desire for two-way intimacy with us in John 14:15 and reveals how we can show that we love Him in return: "If you love me, you will obey what I command" (NIV).

22 And Joshua said unto the people, Ye are witnesses against yourselves that ye have chosen you the LORD, to serve him. And they said, We are witnesses. 23 Now therefore put away, said he, the strange gods which are among you, and incline your heart unto the LORD God of Israel.

The people had made a choice. They had voluntarily rejected the idol gods and promised to remain faithful to the God of their forefathers. Every covenant has to be sacred and witnessed; otherwise, there is no accountability for the parties involved. To be a "witness" (Heb. *'ed*, **ayd**) means "to give testimony or bear evidence." Not only was Joshua a witness to their choice, but the people were witnesses for each other. By acknowledging their service to the Lord, the Israelites were reconfirming their covenant with Yahweh. By their own words, they were witnesses to the covenant should they ever decide to break it again.

Although we cannot and will not do it perfectly, we must demonstrate daily our faith in the God of the covenant. Most assuredly, if we do not, our own hearts are witnesses against us, in addition to the all-knowing God.

For the Israelites, the demonstration of their faith in the God of the covenant was the single, but difficult, action of putting away their idols. By putting away all idols and having no other gods before Him, we show to the Lord and to world that we belong to the Lord our God. Deep emotional attachments to and lust for the hidden idols of our hearts will destroy our lives. True covenant keepers will ask God for His grace to be faithful to Him and keep themselves from the idols of today's world (cf. Exodus 20:2–6; 1 John 5:21).

24 And the people said unto Joshua, The LORD our God will we serve, and his voice will we obey.

In previous verses, the Israelites chose to accept and serve God (vv. 17–18). Now they have reaffirmed their choice by expressing their commitment to listen to and obey the Lord. It is said that even today sheep recognize the voice of their shepherd; they will not respond to any other voice. When the shepherd says "come," they follow. Jesus said, "My sheep hear my voice, and they follow me" (John 10:27). Like the people of Joshua's day, we must choose whom we will serve and obey.

Jesus is our Good Shepherd. No matter how educated or wealthy we are, in reality, without a shepherd, we are just like sheep that are prone to self-destruction. The Christian today has the voice of God revealed to him in God's Word from Genesis to Revelation. The HBO of Scripture is Hear, Believe, and Obey. Are you listening? Are you hearing His voice? Renew your commitment to serve God and obey His Word. God is still looking for covenant keepers today.

Daily Bible Readings

M: Pray for Renewal
Psalm 51:1–12
T: Be Strong and Bold
Deuteronomy 31:14–23
W: God Commands Joshua
Joshua 1:1–9
T: Recalling God's Mighty Acts
Joshua 24:1–7
F: God Gives a Land
Joshua 24:8–13
S: Choose Whom You Will Serve
Joshua 24:14–18
S: The People Renew Their Vows
Joshua 24:19–4

TEACHING TIPS
October 1
Bible Study Guide 5

1. Words You Should Know
A. Judges (Judges 2:16) *shaphat* (Heb.)—Refers to those deciding controversies and executing legal, civil, religious, political, and social government.

B. Whoring (v. 17) *zanah* (Heb.)—To commit fornication; to be a harlot. Figuratively, it denotes improper relations with foreign nations or with other deities.

C. Deliver (v. 18) *yasha* (Heb.)—To liberate, save (place in freedom) from external evils.

2. Teacher Preparation
A. Pray for the students in your class, asking God to give them open hearts to accept today's lesson.

B. Carefully read Bible Study Guide 5, making notes for clarification.

C. Complete lesson 5 in the *Precepts For Living*® *Personal Study Guide*.

3. Starting the Lesson
A. Lead the class in prayer. Focus your prayer on the unifying principle of deliverance.

B. Have someone read the In Focus section. Then discuss the key themes as a group.

C. Read the Lesson Aim. Emphasize that the lesson will help the students identify patterns of disobedience and deliverance in their lives.

4. Getting into the Lesson
A. Ask the students to identify examples in their personal lives or within society that reflect cycles of disobedience and deliverance.

B. Ask volunteers to read The People, Places, and Times and Background.

C. Ask the students to silently read the In Depth section as outlined in the At-A-Glance section. Then discuss the story.

D. Ask for volunteers to read Search the Scriptures, and lead the class in discussing the answers.

5. Relating the Lesson to Life
A. Help the students apply the lesson to their lives by answering the questions in the Discuss the Meaning section.

B. Use the Lesson in Our Society section to further help the students relate the Scripture lesson to happenings in today's society.

C. Call the students' attention to the Make It Happen section. Ask them to answer the question and to identify at least one thing they can do to break the negative cycle in their lives.

6. Arousing Action
A. Ask the students to commit the cyclical pattern of Israel's faithfulness to memory: apostasy, affliction, repentance, rescue, and restoration. Give out prizes (e.g., candy) to the students who can remember and recite the pattern.

B. Have the students complete the Follow the Spirit, Remember Your Thoughts, and Daily Bible Readings sections.

C. Ask if anyone would like to share their answer to the question.

D. Close with prayer.

Worship Guide

For the Superintendent or Teacher
Theme: God Sends Judges
Theme Song: "I Love the Lord, He Heard My Cry"
Scripture: Psalm 61:1–5
Song: "He Looked Beyond My Fault"
Meditation: Eternal God, thank You for knowing when I was in trouble and rescuing me from difficult situations, even when I was too stubborn or too blind to recognize that I was in need. Amen.

GOD SENDS JUDGES

Bible Background • JUDGES 2:11–23
Printed Text • JUDGES 2:16–23   Devotional Reading • DEUTERONOMY 6:4–9

Lesson Aim

By the end of the lesson, we will:

EXAMINE the cycle of disobedience, despair, and deliverance the Israelites engaged in;

REFLECT on similar patterns that may exist in our own lives; and

DETERMINE to seek God's help in times of trouble.

Keep in Mind

"Nevertheless the LORD raised up judges, which delivered them out of the hand of those that spoiled them" (Judges 2:16).

Focal Verses

Judges 2:16 Nevertheless the LORD raised up judges, which delivered them out of the hand of those that spoiled them.

17 And yet they would not hearken unto their judges, but they went a whoring after other gods, and bowed themselves unto them: they turned quickly out of the way which their fathers walked in, obeying the commandments of the LORD; but they did not so.

18 And when the LORD raised them up judges, then the LORD was with the judge, and delivered them out of the hand of their enemies all the days of the judge: for it repented the LORD because of their groanings by reason of them that oppressed them and vexed them.

19 And it came to pass, when the judge was dead, that they returned, and corrupted themselves more than their fathers, in following other gods to serve them, and to bow down unto them; they ceased not from their own doings, nor from their stubborn way.

20 And the anger of the LORD was hot against Israel; and he said, Because that this people hath transgressed my covenant which I commanded their fathers, and have not hearkened unto my voice;

21 I also will not henceforth drive out any from before them of the nations which Joshua left when he died:

22 That through them I may prove Israel, whether they will keep the way of the LORD to walk therein, as their fathers did keep it, or not.

23 Therefore the LORD left those nations, without driving them out hastily; neither delivered he them into the hand of Joshua.

In Focus

Lena could hear her grandmother's voice as if it were yesterday. One hot summer night 20 years ago, she and her grandmother were sitting on the front porch.

"Baby, that kind will come to no good end, selling her body for sex," said Lena's grandmother.

A young Lena replied, "But Grandma, she's got such fancy clothes; she must make a lot of money."

"Don't be fooled, girl; it's a hard life she has chosen for herself. The Bible tells us that nothing is worth that lifestyle."

Lena's grandmother died before Lena's 18th birthday. Soon afterward, Lena stopped going to church. In order to survive, the beautiful young woman found herself on drugs and living the life her grandmother warned against.

She remembered telling her friend, Crystal, "I can make money, buy nice clothes, take care of myself, and have fun at the same time."

"What are you thinking? What would your grandmother say?" Crystal had protested.

Though they had talked very seldom in recent years, Crystal continued to pray for Lena. Lena was overjoyed when Crystal agreed to come see her after

Lena's frantic late-night phone call the previous night.

"Were you beaten again?" Crystal asked, looking into Lena's swollen face.

"No. Something wonderful happened," she told her story smiling.

"The other night I was sitting in the dark reminiscing about Grandma and you; and I began trembling. For some strange reason, I started praying. I sat by myself for two days and nights, praying. I wondered if God would even hear me, let alone speak to me, after so many years of disobedience. Just as I was about to give up, I felt His presence. I found my grandmother's old Bible, and it fell open to the book of Judges. I began to read how the Israelites were disobedient time and time again, and how God had mercy on them even though they didn't deserve it. I started to cry because I saw myself in that text. God has shown me mercy that I don't deserve. I realized then that only God could satisfy the longing in my heart. Now I'm sure God has delivered me from that life for good. That's when I decided to call you."

Together they prayed a prayer of thanksgiving.

In the book of Judges, the Israelites discovered what every Christian must remember: If we call out to God in times of despair, He will deliver us.

The People, Places, and Times

Judges. The judges were tribal leaders whom God raised up in times of crisis to deliver Israel from the hand of its enemies. They were endowed with the Spirit of the Lord, who enabled them to be victorious over their foes. Judges ruled Israel from the period of the Israelites' entrance into the land of Canaan to the establishment of the Davidic monarchy. The first introduction (Judges 1:1–2:5) explains that God did not drive out all the Canaanites from the land because Israel did not obey God's command to *them* to drive out all the inhabitants of the land. These leaders are first referred to as "judges" in the second introduction to the book of Judges.

For modern readers, the application of the term "judge" can be misleading. It conjures up an image of an official with authority to administer justice by hearing cases in a court of law. However, only one judge comes close to this image (4:4). The other leaders are portrayed as governors (10:2–3; 11:27; 12:7–14; 15:20; 16:31) or military commanders.

Deliverer. Three of the nine occurrences of the term "deliverer" in the Old Testament are found in the book of Judges (3:9, 15; 18:28). The term refers to the men and women whom God raised up to rescue the Israelites from their enemies. The basic concept is from the Hebrew word for "next of kin," which refers to a person who was responsible for redeeming his kinsman from slavery or despair (Ruth 4:3–4).

Canaan and Canaanites. In the Old Testament, Canaan refers to Palestine, which was east of the Mediterranean Sea and west of the Jordan River; it was the Promised Land of the Israelites. The Israelites occupied Canaan under the leadership of Joshua. The death of Joshua marked the end of the period of conquest and the beginning of the settlement of the Israelites in the land where they encountered various nations. "Canaanites" could refer to the whole indigenous population of Palestine or to any of the numerous ethnic groups that dwelled in the land, including the Midianites, Amalekites, Moabites, and Ammonites. They were descendants of Ham (Genesis 10). The Romans changed the name from Canaan to Philistia (land of the Philistines, Israel's enemies) to humiliate the Jews. "Palestine" is an English term that derives from "Philistia." The General Assembly of the United Nations voted in 1947 to partition the land of Palestine into three territories; we know them today as Israel, Jordan, and Palestine.

Sources

Richardson, Alan. "The Deliverer." In *Interpreter's Dictionary of the Bible,* edited by Keith R. Crim and George A. Buttrick. Nashville, Tenn.: Abingdon Press, 1976.

Wolf, C. U. "Judge." In *Interpreter's Dictionary of the Bible,* edited by Keith R. Crim and George A. Buttrick. Nashville, Tenn.: Abingdon Press, 1962.

Background

The recurring pattern of apostasy, hardship, and moaning by the Israelites, and their subsequent rescue and restoration by the Lord, is the framework for

THE JUDGES OF ISRAEL

JUDGE	YEARS OF SERVING	NOTED ACCOMPLISHMENTS	REFERENCES
1. Othniel	40	Captured a Canaanite city	Judges 3:7–11
2. Ehud	80	Defeated the Moabites	Judges 3:12–30
3. Shamgar	Unknown	Killed 600 Philistines	Judges 3:31
4. Deborah	40	Defeated Sisera/Canaanites	Judges 4, 5(w/Barak)
5. Gideon	40	Raised an army of 10,000, and defeated 135,000 Midianites with 300 soldiers	Judges 6–8
6. Tola	23	Judged Israel for 23 years	Judges 10:1, 2
7. Jair	22	Had 30 sons	Judges 10:3–5
8. Jephthah	6	Defeated the Ammonites	Judges 10:6–12:7
9. Ibzan	7	Had 30 sons and 30 daughters	Judges 12:8–10
10. Elon	10	Unknown	Judges 12:11, 12
11. Abdon	8	Had 40 sons and 30 grandsons	Judges 12:13–15
12. Samson	20	Killed 1,000 Philistines with a donkey's jawbone and was betrayed by Delilah	Judges 13–16

Source: *Life Application Study Bible.* Carol Stream, Ill.: Tyndale House Publishers, 1996, 351.

the stories of the "major" judges: Othniel, Ehud, Deborah, Gideon, Jephthah, and Samson. A new generation has come along and abandoned the Lord, who had delivered their ancestors from slavery in Egypt. They began to follow after and worship the gods of the other inhabitants of Canaan, so that the Lord delivered them into the hand of their adversaries. Thus began the progressive moral and religious deterioration that characterized the relationship between the Israelites and the Lord. Yet, through it all, the Lord never left them and continued to hear and respond to their cries for deliverance.

At-A-Glance

1. God Raised Up Judges (Judges 2:16)
2. The Cyclical Pattern of Apostasy (vv. 17–19)
3. God Tests Israel (vv. 20–23)

In Depth

1. God Raised Up Judges (Judges 2:16)

Joshua and his entire generation had died, and the new generation that grew up did not have a personal relationship with the Lord, nor did they remember how the Lord had delivered their ancestors (Judges 2:8–10). The people did what was evil in the Lord's sight, so He gave them over to their "plunderers." The King James Version translates the word as "those that spoiled them" (v. 16). That is an accurate translation, but its meaning can be overlooked by a contemporary reader. A more modern translation would be, "those that robbed them by force," as in the ransacking of a defeated people after a conquest. Imagine that you are being robbed at gunpoint while the robber's accomplices turn your home upside down and take off with all of your valuables. This is the connotation of "spoiling."

The Lord had sympathy for the Israelites and raised up judges to deliver them from the hands of these marauders. The clear implication is that Israel's deliverance is initiated by the Lord. It is because of the Lord's gracious intervention in the affairs of the Israelites that they are rescued—an intervention that will occur repeatedly as the people forget and rebel against the Lord.

2. The Cyclical Pattern of Apostasy (vv. 17–19)

The narrator's report that the new generation that arose did not walk in the way of their ancestors reminds me of a story an acquaintance once shared about her family. Her parents were the patriarch and matriarch of the family. As long as these two were alive, the children followed their parents' teachings. However, once their parents passed away, the children forgot the ways of older adults. They did things they would never have done while their parents were living, such as divorcing and abandoning the church. How eager they were to disregard the faith of their parents and put it behind them—until a crisis arose in their lives. Then they called on the Lord for deliverance. Once the crisis abated, they returned again to their previous behavior.

As long as the Israelites were suffering under the oppressive yoke of the Egyptians, they looked to the Lord for help. However, once the burden was lifted, they failed to remember what the Lord had done and to pass these memories on to their children. This new generation had not experienced the Lord's graciousness toward the Israelites. Gone were their ancestors who recalled the Lord's deeds and could pass this information down. The Lord was the God of the past. They had tasted of the new gods worshiped by the Canaanites, and the new doctrine and theology were more appealing to them. Yet, when they were being oppressed by the Canaanites and cried out, it was God who raised up judges to deliver them.

The Israelites remained faithful to the Lord until the judge died. Then they resorted to serving and worshiping other gods in a way that was worse than before. Moreover, they remained stubborn and refused to cease doing evil in the sight of the Lord. So began the cycle of apostasy: deserting the Lord to worship other gods, crying out to the Lord, and

affliction at the hands of their enemies and deliverance. Interestingly, verse 17 states that the Israelites went "whoring after other gods." In Hebrew, "whoring" means to commit fornication or to engage in improper intercourse with other deities. Such a depiction of Israel's behavior in pursuing other gods is a sobering indictment of Israel's infidelity.

Interestingly, the people cried out to the Lord, not out of repentance, but rather out of discomfort and anguish. Perhaps that is why they were so quick to fall back into their wicked behavior. In Hebrew, to "turn" or "turn aside" can mean either apostasy (turning away from God and to other gods) or repentance (turning from the direction one is going and returning to God). The Israelites continually walked in the wrong direction.

3. God Tests Israel (vv. 20–23)

The Lord became angry with the Israelites. The Hebrew word for "anger" is translated literally as "nose" referring to the flaring nostrils of someone who is hot with fury (Exodus 11:8). The text says that the anger of the Lord was hot against Israel. This should be a warning to us that God has a limit to His tolerance for sin. God may be slow to anger, but He can be provoked to act (Numbers 11:10; 12:9; Deuteronomy 29:27–28). Since the people failed to obey the commandments that the Lord had given to their ancestors in His covenant, the Lord refused to drive out the nations that remained in Canaan to test whether they would walk in His way like their ancestors before them did. Would Israel turn and follow the Lord's commandments, or would the customs and practices of the remaining nations be a snare to Israel, leading them away from the Lord (Judges 2:3)?

Search the Scriptures

1. What was the function of the judges (Judges 2:16)?

2. Why didn't the Israelites listen to the judges (v. 17)?

3. Why did the Lord raise up judges (v. 18)?

4. What would the Israelites do after the judge died (v. 19)?

5. Why did the Lord refuse to drive out the other nations in the land (vv. 22–23)?

Discuss the Meaning

1. Scripture tells us that the new generation that arose after Joshua and his generation did not follow in the way of their ancestors. Why do you think the people abandoned the Lord to follow after other gods?

2. Many of us can relate a story about someone we know who grew up in the church and, after leaving for college or moving out on their own, refused to attend church any longer. We may even recall hearing them say, "As soon as I'm grown, I am never going to church again." What are some of the reasons young people today stop going to church at the first opportunity that arises?

3. The text states that the Lord had pity on the Israelites because of their groaning under the persecution and oppression by their enemies. Can you recall a time when you cried out to God and He answered your prayers?

Lesson in Our Society

The question at the beginning of the book of Judges was who would govern the people of Israel. The Congolese biblical scholar Fidäle Ugira Kwasi raises a similar question thousands of years later concerning the crisis in his native Democratic Republic of the Congo (RDC) specifically and in sub-Sahara Africa in general. He posed this question in a region where the breakdown of political, economic, and social infrastructures has deprived many people of the bare minimum they need to survive and has created a feeling of hopelessness: "Are we not in a situation where the Lord should raise up judges, who will deliver the impoverished people of the RDC from those who plunder them?" Yet, Kwasi believes that the Lord can deliver his people if they turn to Him, remember their shared experience as Africans just as the Israelites remembered their experience as slaves in Egypt, and recognize that they need to help each other to survive.

Source

Patte, Daniel, J. Severino Croatto, Nicole Wilkinson Duran, Teresa Okure, Archie Chi Chung Lee, eds. "Judges." In *Global Bible Commentary*. Nashville, Tenn.: Abingdon Press, 2004.

Make It Happen

The book of Judges does not offer ready-made answers that we can apply to all the problems in our lives. However, it serves as an example of how to avoid falling into the cycle of disobedience, despair, and deliverance repeated by the Israelites. Identify a habit or ongoing occurrence in your life that leaves a negative impact on you (e.g., procrastinating, never finishing what's started, getting involved with the wrong people, overspending), and ask yourself, "What is at least one thing that I can do to break the cycle?"

Follow the Spirit

What God wants me to do:

_____
_____
_____

Remember Your Thoughts

Special insights I have learned:

_____
_____
_____

More Light on the Text

Judges 2:16–23

16 Nevertheless the LORD raised up judges, which delivered them out of the hand of those that spoiled them.

The fact that the Lord raised up judges for the people of Israel was itself an amazing thing, considering that the oppression they suffered was the direct consequence of their conscious choice to choose the gods of their pagan neighbors rather than the Lord (cf. Judges 2:11–15).

The leaders whom God raises up in these stories are called "judges" (Heb. *shaphat*, **shaw-FAT**). The name comes from the Hebrew verb translated "to judge," although the accounts of the judges do not portray their roles as primarily legal. In fact, only once in the book is the title of judge applied to a specific individual and in that case (11:27), it applies to

Jehovah, not a human being. This verse would seem to indicate that the primary function of the judges was in fact that of "delivering" (Heb. *yasha*, **yaw-SHAH**) or saving the people of Israel.

The author elsewhere makes mention of a special empowering work of the Holy Spirit in the lives of the judges, noting that the Spirit of the Lord came upon them and was instrumental in their success (6:34; 11:29; 13:25).

The word "spoiled" (Heb. *shasah*, **shaw-SAW**) in this case literally means "plundered." The author wants us to conceive of a situation in which the Israelites are completely at the mercy of other nations, who feel uninhibited in taking whatever they want from them.

17 And yet they would not hearken unto their judges, but they went a whoring after other gods, and bowed themselves unto them: they turned quickly out of the way which their fathers walked in, obeying the commandments of the LORD; but they did not so.

The Canaanite society was probably far superior to the Israelite society in many ways at this point in time. Before Joshua led them in the conquest of the land of Canaan, the Israelites had been wandering in the wilderness for 40 years. Conversely, the Canaanites had been established in urban centers for generations. Archaeological evidence indicates that their art, literature, agriculture, trade, and political organization were much more advanced than those of the Israelites. Of course, religion was integral to all systems of Canaanite society. It was inevitable, therefore, that the Israelites would experience a significant temptation to join in the Canaanite lifestyle, including their idolatrous worship.

The point of this verse is not that the previous generations had obeyed the Lord perfectly or provided an example of faithfulness for this generation to mirror (see below). Indeed, their mistakes and outright rebellion were substantial enough to cause the Lord to threaten to completely destroy them before they even entered the Promised Land (Exodus 32:10). However, by the time of Joshua's death, the people of Israel had obeyed the Lord to the extent that they

had taken control of large portions of the Promised Land and removed the previous inhabitants. The question this generation had to answer was whether or not they would pick up where their parents had left off. Unfortunately, they wanted to experience the blessing of being the Lord's people (living in the land He had promised their ancestors) without submitting their lives to His lordship.

The word "whoring" (Heb. *zanah*, **zaw-NAW**) literally means "to commit fornication, adultery, or prostitution." This particular word is probably used here because sacred prostitution was a conspicuous feature of Baal worship. A follower of Baal would appease his god by engaging in sexual relations with a priestess, thereby ensuring that his fields would produce their crop. The previous generation of Israelites had failed to respond appropriately to the sexual temptation presented by the Moabites they encountered en route to the Promised Land (cf. Numbers 25), so it is no wonder that these wicked practices once again led Israel astray.

The use of terms that describe sexual unfaithfulness reminds us that God sometimes talks about His covenant relationship with His people in terms of marriage, especially in the words of the prophets who were to come, such as Hosea, Jeremiah, and Ezekiel (cf. Hosea 4:12, 15). God had to repeatedly remind His people that they did not choose Him, but He chose to love them and enter into relationship with them despite their many flaws (cf. Deuteronomy 9:4–8). When the people of Israel chose to worship other gods, they were arousing the Lord's jealousy, much as an unfaithful spouse arouses jealousy in the heart of his or her wife or husband (cf. Exodus 20:5). This passage is also a reminder of the waywardness of the Exodus generation, who worshiped the golden calf immediately after experiencing the deliverance of God and receiving the covenant at Sinai. The account of the golden calf episode seems to indicate that illicit sexual indulgence was part of the behavior that God found intolerable (Exodus 32:6–7). The Exodus generation died in the wilderness, with the exception of Caleb and Joshua, who led the people in the conquest of Canaan. This generation represents the grandchildren, physically and spiritually, of the Exodus generation.

The repentance implied by following the lead of the judges the Lord raised up (v. 16) is revealed as a fraud, since it does not last. Repentance that is genuine and pleasing to the Lord produces lasting real-life change (Matthew 3:8).

18 And when the LORD raised them up judges, then the LORD was with the judge, and delivered them out of the hand of their enemies all the days of the judge: for it repented the LORD because of their groanings by reason of them that oppressed them and vexed them.

The author directly states that it was not the judges' power or ability that saved the people, but the Lord working through the judges. The Lord "delivered" (Heb. *yasha*) His people, meaning He helped them and saved them by coming to their aid. This is the second time in the Old Testament where this verb is used to describe God's action to save the people of Israel. The first was in Exodus 14:30 (the crossing of the Red Sea).

When the Bible speaks of the Lord "repenting" (Heb. *nacham*, **naw-KHAM**), it does not mean that He has committed wrongdoing and decided to change (cf. Deuteronomy 32:4; 2 Samuel 22:31). Nor does it mean that He has changed His mind in the way that humans change their minds (cf. 1 Samuel 15:29). Rather, God has declared that when He brings judgment upon a nation or people for their wickedness, there is still genuine opportunity for them to repent. If they do repent, God will see fit to cut short their suffering (cf. Jeremiah 18:8–10).

The Lord was moved to pity by the misery of the Israelites' condition, just as He was moved by the misery of their grandfathers in Egypt. In fact, the word used here for "groaning" (Heb. *ne'aqah*, **neh-aw-kaw**) is the same word used in Exodus 2:24 and Exodus 6:5 to describe the suffering of the Israelites in Egypt. Ironically, the current generation of Israelites had chosen to return to Egypt (figuratively speaking) by failing to keep the covenant they had made with God at Sinai.

The enemies of Israel are described as oppressing and vexing the Israelites. The word for "oppressed" (Heb. *lachats*, **law-KHATS**) literally means "to squeeze or press." The word *lachats* was used in Exodus 3:9 to describe the plight of the Israelites under their Egyptian slave masters. The word for "vexed" (Heb. *dachaq*, **daw-KHAK**) literally means "to thrust." The author has painted a visual image of the people of Israel pressed into a tight spot, with an enemy repeatedly thrusting himself (or his weapon) upon them.

19 And it came to pass, when the judge was dead, that they returned, and corrupted themselves more than their fathers, in following other gods to serve them, and to bow down unto them; they ceased not from their own doings, nor from their stubborn way.

The people of Israel "corrupted" (Heb. *shachath*, **shaw-KHATH**, "to destroy, ruin, or decay") themselves in a way that went beyond the disobedience of their forefathers. The Hebrew word reminds the reader of the corruption of the world before Noah's Flood in Genesis 6. In that passage, *shachath* is used three times to describe the corruption of the people and a fourth time to describe, ironically, what God would do to them (destroy them).

Even though the previous generation had followed the Lord during the lifetimes of Joshua and the elders who outlived him, the Israelites of this time still had a legacy of spiritual adultery because their ancestors had worshiped the golden calf. They had the opportunity to either put that legacy behind them and serve the Lord wholeheartedly in the land He had given them, or build on it by rebelling even more than their ancestors.

The Israelites rebelled by "serving" (Heb. *abad*, **aw-BAD**) and "bowing down" (Heb. *shachah*, **shaw-KHAW**) to other gods, thereby doing the exact opposite of what God had commanded in the second of the Ten Commandments (Exodus 20:5). The use of the exact same words that appear in the commandment to describe their idolatry is an indictment of the people for their disobedience of God's law.

The rebellion was manifested by their persistence in their own stubborn way. The word used here for "stubborn" (Heb. *qasheh*, **kaw-SHEH**) is the same word used repeatedly elsewhere in the Old Testament to describe the people of Israel as stiff-necked (cf. Exodus 32:9; Deuteronomy 9:6).

20 And the anger of the LORD was hot against Israel; and he said, Because that this people hath transgressed my covenant which I commanded their fathers, and have not hearkened unto my voice;

The Hebrew expression used here could literally be translated, "and the Lord's nose was hot." Although it is a common expression in the Old Testament, we should note that it is used in Exodus 32:10 to describe the Lord's anger over the golden calf episode.

The word used for "people" (Heb. *gowy*, **GO-ee**) is commonly translated "nation" and is used very rarely in the Old Testament to refer to the people of Israel. In fact, this word is normally used to refer to Gentile peoples—the nations the Israelites are to dispossess. By using "people," the Lord is making it clear that He considers the Israelites to have become just like their pagan neighbors.

The covenant to which God refers is the covenant He had made with Israel at Mount Sinai, the essence of which is the Ten Commandments. At the time God made the covenant, the people of Israel were full and willing participants, pledging, "All the words which the Lord hath said will we do" (Exodus 24:3). Moses led the people in a renewal of this covenant in Deuteronomy 29–30, with the express recognition that the covenant was not only for those alive at that point in time, but for all who were yet to be born (Deuteronomy 29:14–15). Thus, the responsibility fell to every Israelite to see that future generations were carefully instructed in the commands of the Lord.

21 I also will not henceforth drive out any from before them of the nations which Joshua left when he died:

God had originally purposed that the conquest of Canaan was to be gradual—stretched out over several generations. For one thing, the people of Israel were not numerous enough to be responsible for that amount of territory at the time of Joshua. The land would grow wild and unproductive if they were to wipe out all the inhabitants at once (Exodus 23:29). More importantly, however, God wanted future generations of Israelites to manifest their faithfulness to His command by taking care to always be skilled in the art of warfare (Judges 3:1–2). Thus, the life of blessing that God intended for His people to experience was not one void of trials, challenges, and temptations. Every generation would have to answer the question for themselves: "Will we be faithful and trust the Lord to drive out the pagan inhabitants of the land before us?"

God's statement should not have surprised the Israelites, since they had been repeatedly warned by Joshua (Joshua 23:12–13) and Moses (Exodus 23, 34; Numbers 33; Deuteronomy 11) that the land of Canaan had been given to them on the condition of their obedience. They were promised that the very people they were to drive out would become a thorn in their side if they were not faithful to continue to drive them out. This principle holds true even for believers today. Nowhere has the Lord promised to bless those who profess to be His people yet choose to live in purposeful, conscious disobedience. Rather, He often allows us to experience the consequences of our rebellious actions in order to humble us and bring us back to obedience.

God is true to His word throughout the book of Judges. None of the judges led the people in dispossessing the nations Joshua left in the land or in claiming new territory. Rather, their efforts are directed to freeing Israel from the oppression of their neighbors, who rose up because Israel was not faithful to take full possession of the land.

22 That through them I may prove Israel, whether they will keep the way of the LORD to walk therein, as their fathers did keep it, or not.

God had tested the people of Israel before, but the tests He used were somewhat different from those our teachers normally use. We expect a test to come after we have had an opportunity to master certain material. But God uses tests as a learning experience in themselves. The pattern God used was this: He promised to take care of the people of Israel and fulfill the promises He had made to their ancestors by bringing them to the Promised Land. He then brought a situation into the life of the nation in which they would need to rely on the promise He had made in order to survive. Initially, the people always seemed to fail the test—crying out, complaining, and rebelling against the leader God had given. But God did not intend for the test to stop there. Instead, He manifested His faithfulness by providing for the need or solving the problem. Thus, the point of the test was not just to reveal whether or not the people really trusted the Lord; it was also to teach them to trust that God would be faithful to keep the promises He had made (cf. Deuteronomy 8:2–9).

Note that tests are not necessary because of uncertainty as to whether or not God will be faithful to His promise. Tests are necessary only because of human frailty. In times of prosperity, we are often quick to claim that we trust the Lord to provide for us and take care of us. But as soon as a crisis looms, we conclude that God has abandoned us. God uses these experiences so that our faith can grow and mature. We see crises as reason to wonder if God is really faithful or not; He sees them as opportunities for us to prepare for the greater challenges that lie ahead.

The word for "way" (Heb. *derek*, **DEH-rek**) literally means "road" or "path." The imagery is not at all foreign to us. We are responsible for the path we take in life, whether it is the path of the Lord (cf. Jesus' teaching on the straight and narrow way in Matthew 7:13–14) or an alternative that we provide for ourselves. Straying from the path that the Lord has ordained for us is a dangerous and foolish thing to do because we are, in essence, declaring that we do not want to be under the Lord's care. The misconception that we can choose our own path in life but still experience the blessing of the Lord is one of Satan's favorite lies, and the one that he used on our first parents (Genesis 3:3–4).

23 Therefore the LORD left those nations, without driving them out hastily; neither delivered he them into the hand of Joshua.

The Hebrew words used here could literally be translated "And the Lord gave those nations rest." Consider this in light of Joshua 21:44, which speaks of the Lord giving Joshua and the people of Israel rest from war. Ironically, the rest God had promised the people of Israel now passed to those they were to have driven out.

The rest the people of Israel sought after is a symbol to us of the rest that remains as a promise to the people of God. Our own disobedience is the only thing that threatens to keep us from that rest (Hebrews 4:1–11).

God originally left the Canaanites as a test for Israel to see if they would be faithful in continuing to drive them out; now He has left them to be a trial because the Israelites have failed the test.

Daily Bible Readings

M: Love the Lord
Deuteronomy 6:4–9
T: God and the Hebrew People
Psalm 78:1–8
W: Prayer for a Nation
Psalm 85:4–13
T: Israel Disobeys God
Judges 2:1–5
F: A New Generation
Judges 2:6–10
S: Israel Abandons God
Judges 2:11–15
S: Call to Repentance
Judges 2:16–23

TEACHING TIPS

October 8
Bible Study Guide 6

1. Words You Should Know
A. Prophetess (Judges 4:4) *nebiyah* (Heb.)—A woman who has been called to speak for God.

B. Captain (v. 7) *sar* (Heb.)—Chief, ruler, official, or leader; general in a military capacity.

2. Teacher Preparation
A. Read Judges 4 and 5, making notes for clarification.

B. As you study the lesson, pay particular attention to The People, Places, and Times and the Background section. This information will help you lead the discussion and answer the questions in the Search the Scriptures and Discuss the Meaning sections as well as in lesson 6 in the *Precepts For Living® Personal Study Guide.*

3. Starting the Lesson
A. Lead the class in a discussion on the qualities necessary for good leadership.

B. Read the In Focus story. Discuss how the story deals with the issue of leadership.

C. Read the Lesson Aim. Emphasize that the lesson will help the students identify leadership qualities in themselves and surrender their gifts to be used by God.

4. Getting into the Lesson
A. Assign each student to read one of the Focal Verses.

B. Have two students read The People, Places, and Times and the Background section.

C. Ask the students to take about five minutes to silently read the In Depth section as outlined in the At-A-Glance section. Ask if the students have any questions.

D. Ask for volunteers to read the Search the Scriptures questions, and lead the class in discussing the answers in relation to the commentary they just read.

5. Relating the Lesson to Life
A. Help the students apply the lesson to their lives by leading them in exploration of the Discuss the Meaning questions.

B. Use the Lesson in Our Society section to further help the students make the connection between the Scripture lesson and events in today's society.

C. Call the students' attention to the Make It Happen section. Ask them to do the assigned exercise to help identify their leadership skills.

6. Arousing Action
A. Ask the students to identify and make a commitment to attend workshops, classes, seminars, etc. in their church, community, or workplace that can help them sharpen their leadership skills.

B. Remind the students to complete the Follow the Spirit and Remember Your Thoughts sections.

C. Ask the class if anyone would like to share their thoughts or answers to any of the questions.

D. Close with prayer.

Worship Guide

For the Superintendent or Teacher
Theme: **God Leads through Deborah**
Theme Song: **"Let God Arise"**
Scripture: **Matthew 28:19–20**
Song: **"If Jesus Goes with Me I'll Go"**
Meditation: **The Lord our God can use any type of person to carry out His purposes in the world. God is not a respecter of superficial factors such as sex, race, or social status. God chooses people who will be obedient when called.**

GOD LEADS THROUGH DEBORAH

Bible Background • JUDGES 4
Printed Text • JUDGES 4:4–10, 12–16   Devotional Reading • PSALM 91

Lesson Aim

By the end of the lesson, we will:

ANALYZE the qualities Deborah possessed that made her a strong leader;

APPRECIATE the need for leaders and REFLECT on specific qualities we look for in leaders; and

IDENTIFY and SURRENDER for God's use any leadership qualities/potential we may possess.

Keep in Mind

"And Barak said unto her, If thou wilt go with me, then I will go: but if thou wilt not go with me, then I will not go. And she said, I will surely go with thee: notwithstanding the journey that thou takest shall not be for thine honour; for the LORD shall sell Sisera into the hand of a woman. And Deborah arose, and went with Barak to Kedesh" (Judges 4:8–9).

Focal Verses

Judges 4:4 And Deborah, a prophetess, the wife of Lapidoth, she judged Israel at that time.

5 And she dwelt under the palm tree of Deborah between Ramah and Bethel in mount Ephraim: and the children of Israel came up to her for judgment.

6 And she sent and called Barak the son of Abinoam out of Kedesh-naphtali, and said unto him, Hath not the LORD God of Israel commanded, saying, Go and draw toward mount Tabor, and take with thee ten thousand men of the children of Naphtali and of the children of Zebulun?

7 And I will draw unto thee to the river Kishon Sisera, the captain of Jabin's army, with his chariots and his multitude; and I will deliver him into thine hand.

8 And Barak said unto her, If thou wilt go with me, then I will go: but if thou wilt not go with me, then I will not go.

9 And she said, I will surely go with thee: notwithstanding the journey that thou takest shall not be for thine honour; for the LORD shall sell Sisera into the hand of a woman. And Deborah arose, and went with Barak to Kedesh.

10 And Barak called Zebulun and Naphtali to Kedesh; and he went up with ten thousand men at his feet: and Deborah went up with him.

4:12 And they showed Sisera that Barak the son of Abinoam was gone up to mount Tabor.

13 And Sisera gathered together all his chariots, even nine hundred chariots of iron, and all the people that were with him, from Harosheth of the Gentiles unto the river of Kishon.

14 And Deborah said unto Barak, Up; for this is the day in which the LORD hath delivered Sisera into thine hand: is not the LORD gone out before thee? So Barak went down from mount Tabor, and ten thousand men after him.

15 And the LORD discomfited Sisera, and all his chariots, and all his host, with the edge of the sword before Barak; so that Sisera lighted down off his chariot, and fled away on his feet.

16 But Barak pursued after the chariots, and after the host, unto Harosheth of the Gentiles: and all the host of Sisera fell upon the edge of the sword; and there was not a man left.

In Focus

My wife and I have a treasured collection of Academy Award-winning films. One of my all-time favorites is the 1962 film *Lawrence of Arabia*. There is a powerful scene in the film portraying a 10-day march that Lawrence's army made through the desert.

His army staggers along, nearly dead from dehydration, when suddenly an oasis appears, and they throw themselves into the water. Lawrence takes a head count and discovers that one of the camel boys is missing. The boy's camel is found, but he himself is missing.

Lawrence says to several of his men, "We must go back and find him." But the men refuse his order to venture back into the merciless burning sand.

"Master," they plead, "it is

God's will that the boy didn't return with us. His fate was written by God."

Much to their surprise, Lawrence mounts his camel and heads back into the murderous Sahara. By the end of the day, the men believe they have lost their revered leader. On the second day, Lawrence appears out of a wavy veil of heat.

"It's Lawrence; he has found the boy!" they cry out.

Lawrence leans over and hands them the unconscious boy. He glares into their faces and whispers in a hoarse voice: "Remember this: Nothing 'is written' unless you write it."

As a leader, Lawrence knew what God had written in his heart and realized that he had to serve as an example.

In today's lesson, Deborah demonstrates this leadership quality. When God chooses a strong leader, he or she must show a willingness to serve.

The People, Places, and Times

Prophetess. The term *nebyiah*, or "prophetess," is the feminine derivative of the masculine noun "prophet." The term occurs only six times in the Old Testament, referring to Miriam (Exodus 15:20), Deborah (Judges 4:4); Huldah (2 Kings 22:14; 2 Chronicles 34:22) Noadiah (Nehemiah 6:14), and Isaiah's wife (Isaiah 8:3). Miriam and Deborah are endowed with the gift of song, Huldah is consulted by the king for a word from God, Noadiah leads a prophetic guild, and the unnamed wife of Isaiah performs a prophetic act with her husband.

Deborah. One of the major judges in the book of Judges, Deborah is the only female described as judging Israel during a time of oppression at the hand of the Canaanites. As a judge, she consulted God on behalf of the people and rendered decisions. As a prophetess, she delivered oracles of assurance to encourage Israel to battle against its enemy. Israel's victory is recounted in two versions: (1) a prose narrative in Judges 4, and (2) a song known as the Song of Deborah, an ancient song likely composed shortly after the events and preserved in Judges 5. She also plays a military role, accompanying the commander of Israel's army into battle.

Barak. The son of Abinoam from Kedesh-naphtali, he was summoned by Deborah to assume military leadership of the Israelites in a campaign against Canaanite forces (Judges 4:6). Barak deployed men from the tribes of Zebulun and Naphtali to engage the Canaanites in battle near Mount Tabor, a prominent mountain. Barak accepted the call on the condition that Deborah accompany him. Barak is mentioned in the New Testament among the cloud of witnesses to faith for his faithful administration of justice, along with a few other judges: Gideon, Samson, and Jephthah (Hebrews 11:32).

Sisera. The commander of the army of King Jabin of Canaan, Sisera lived in Harosheth of the Gentiles. The army was equipped with 900 chariots made of iron. The Israelites' chariots were made of wood and leather. Sisera engaged in battle against Barak and Deborah and fled when his troops fell by the sword.

Background

The Israelites had been following a pattern of disobedience, despair, and deliverance. They would do evil things in the sight of God. He would allow them to be routed by their enemies, and then He would raise up judges to deliver them from the hand of their adversaries. After the judge died, Israel would repeat the cycle, doing worse than before. After one such incident of transgression, God sold them into the hand of King Jabin of Canaan. Jabin oppressed the people of Israel for 20 years (Judges 4:3). The situation appeared hopeless. King Jabin's army was larger and more technologically advanced than Israel's, causing them to greatly fear the Canaanites. The Israelites cried out to the Lord. This time, the Lord did not raise up a judge to deliver Israel. Rather, He chose a prophetess who was already judging Israel to deliver them.

At-A-Glance

1. Deborah Judges Israel (Judges 4:4–5)
2. Deborah Summons Barak (vv. 6–10)
3. The Lord Defeats Jabin's Army (vv. 12–16)

In Depth

1. Deborah Judges Israel (Judges 4:4–5)

Deborah is judge of Israel during a time of hardship as a result of Israel's disobedience. Her office is under the palm of Deborah, a cultic site located between Ramah and Bethel in the hill country of Ephraim, north of Jerusalem. The palm tree is named in Deborah's honor, attesting to the high regard in which the Israelites held her. The Israelites came to Deborah to settle their disputes. As a prophetess, she would consult the Lord on behalf of the people, as well as receive oracles from the Lord to deliver to the people concerning setting wrong matters right. Deborah served as a mediator between the Lord and the people, as an administrator of justice, and as a problem solver. She is only the second person in the Old Testament to whom the Israelites went for judgment. The other was Moses (Exodus 18:13).

2. Deborah Summons Barak (vv. 6–10)

Deborah summons Barak from Kedesh-naphtali, an undetermined holy place in Naphtali, located in southern Galilee. Barak heeds her command and appears before her. She instructs Barak that the Lord, the God of Israel, has commanded him to muster 10,000 men from the tribes of Naphtali and Zebulun from Galilee and go up to Mount Tabor. Mount Tabor is a prominent mountain in the northeast corner of the Jezreel Valley. It would be difficult for the Canaanites to overlook Barak's deployment of troops there.

Deborah delivers an oracle of assurance to Barak concerning the Lord's plan to use her to draw out Sisera, the commander of Jabin's army. He would be engaged in battle with Barak by the Kishon River. The Lord would give Sisera into hand. Her oracle was intended to summon the troops to battle and assure them of victory through the Lord.

Barak responded, "If thou wilt go with me, then I will go: but if thou wilt not go with me, then I will not go." Barak's reluctance has been attributed to cowardice, a lack of trust in Deborah's prophetic abilities, and a desire for companionship or support. His hesitancy is understandable. This message must

have caught Barak unprepared. The Israelites had been under the cruel oppression of the Canaanites for 20 years (Judges 4:3). The Canaanite army was more sophisticated than any army the Israelites could muster. Israel is often viewed as a united nation, with all 12 tribes ready and willing to fight when called. However, God commanded Barak to deploy troops only from the tribes of Naphtali and Zebulun. (The poetic account in Judges 5 identifies six tribes as heeding the call: Ephraim, Benjamin, Machir, Zebulun, Issachar, and Naphtali. The others were chastised for not responding to Deborah's call.)

The odds might have seemed insurmountable to Barak without God's prophet along. However, that was God's intent. He wanted Israel to recognize that their victory was a result of His divine intervention in their situation, not a result of their physical might. Deborah agrees to accompany Barak to Kedesh. However, she informs him that the glory resulting from the victory would go to a woman rather than to him. Then Barak called the troops from the tribes of Zebulun and Naphtali to Kedesh—10,000 warriors in all—and went up with them to Mount Tabor accompanied by Deborah. The Hebrew verb *zaaq*, translated "called," means "to call or cry out in need." It also means "to call out to" or "call together" for military service, as conveyed in verse 10. Barak's cry was a call for the tribes to take up their weapons and prepare for battle.

3. The Lord Defeats Jabin's Army (vv. 12–16)

Some unidentified persons apprise Sisera of Barak's activities. Sisera, in turn, deploys his troops from Harosheth of the Gentiles to the Kishon River. The approaching Canaanite army prompts Deborah to command Barak, "Up! The time for battle has come." Deborah's presence made it possible for Barak to know exactly when it was time to fight. Once again, Deborah delivers an oracle of assurance that the Lord was going out before the Israelites to defeat Sisera that very day. Barak and his warriors ascend Mount Tabor and pursue Sisera. In a move reminiscent of the defeat of the Egyptians at the Red Sea (Exodus 14:24 ff.), the Lord threw Sisera and all his army into a panic. The poetic version of the events in the Song of Deborah tells how the torrential waters of the River Kishon swept up Sisera's chariots and army (Judges 5:21–22; cf. Exodus 14:26). While his troops begin to scatter, Sisera manages to leap from his chariot and flee. Rather than pursue Sisera, Barak pursues the technologically advanced chariots and the army all the way to Harosheth of the Gentiles, where they are all eventually slaughtered.

Search the Scriptures

1. Who was judging Israel at this time (Judges 4:4)?

2. How many troops did Deborah command Barak to gather (v. 6)?

3. Who accompanied Barak into battle (v. 10)?

4. Who threw Sisera and his chariots and army into a panic (v. 15)?

5. What happened to Sisera's troops (v. 16)?

Discuss the Meaning

1. Deborah is the only female in the Old Testament whom the Israelites consulted for judgment. Why do you think the people placed such trust in her?

2. Deborah is portrayed as a strong leader. She judged the people and gave them the confidence to confront the Canaanites. What are some of the qualities that she possessed that made her such an effective leader?

Lesson in Our Society

Whenever crises have arisen in communities in the African diaspora, God has always used women and men to meet the challenge. God used the voice of Ida B. Wells to protest against the lynching of Black men in the South. Fannie Lou Hamer's faith led her to become an advocate for the voting rights of Black people in America. God called Princess Kasune Zulu of South Africa to speak out against the HIV/AIDS pandemic in Africa.

These women and countless, nameless others have responded to God's call to lead His people, not only during threats to our community, but in every-day acts of faith. They are the missionary board

presidents in our churches, principals in our schools, candy stripers in our hospitals, soldiers in our militaries, and legislators in our governments. They are mentors, care providers, and activists meeting the needs of society. However, what they all have in common is their obedience to God's call, their willingness to go wherever God sends them, and their following through on the mission God gave them.

Make It Happen

Consider the question: What are your gifts? What has God endowed you with to lead His people? Partner with someone in class, and take about five minutes to discuss the leadership skills that God has given you. Then determine what you both can do to strengthen the skills you have in order to be ready when God calls.

Follow the Spirit

What God wants me to do:

_____

_____

Remember Your Thoughts

Special insights I have learned:

_____

_____

More Light on the Text
Judges 4:4–10, 12–16

In keeping with the pattern of the entire book of Judges, the Israelites failed to worship and serve the Lord alone after the death of a righteous leader (4:1). The Lord then disciplined them for their idolatry by allowing a Canaanite king to oppress them for 20 years (4:2). In this case, the king was from the city of Hazor, which is significant because Joshua had defeated the king of Hazor in his initial conquest of the land and burned the city to the ground (cf. Joshua 11:1–14). The fact that this particular king was oppressing the people of Israel points out just how unfaithful they were to the Lord. They had been commanded to continue to drive out the inhabitants of the land after the death of Joshua and had failed miserably (cf. Judges 1:27–2:2).

Furthermore, they even failed to keep the cities that Joshua had defeated from being rebuilt!

4 And Deborah, a prophetess, the wife of Lapidoth, she judged Israel at that time. 5 And she dwelt under the palm tree of Deborah between Ramah and Bethel in mount Ephraim: and the children of Israel came up to her for judgment.

Deborah is introduced to us right away as a "prophetess" (Heb. *ishaah nebiy'ah*, **ish-SHAW neb-ee-YAW**), literally referring to a woman who is a prophet. A prophet was someone who spoke on behalf of God to the people (cf. Deuteronomy 18:15–22). Of course, up to this point in the history of Israel, Moses was the most eminent of the prophets. Joshua was never referred to as a prophet, since his work was not to reveal new words from the Lord but to lead Israel in obedience to what the Lord had commanded through Moses. By learning early on in this story that the Lord is speaking again to His people through a human spokesperson, the reader's hopes are raised that perhaps once again the Lord is going to do something great to deliver His people, just as He did when He revealed Himself through Moses.

At the time this story takes place, Deborah was already in a position of leadership. Her work is described as "judging" (Heb. *shaphat,* **shaw-FAT**), which could include acting as a lawgiver, arbiter, or governor. Deborah is unique among the judges in that she is identified, not as the one whom God has chosen to be a deliverer, but as the messenger to that deliverer (Barak).

The reference to Deborah's location under the palm tree could mean a number of different things. Her home may have been located at that certain spot, or she could have held court outdoors there. The Hebrew word translated "dwelt" (*yashab,* **yaw-SHAB**) can mean either "to sit" or "to dwell."

The passage tells us that the Israelites came to Deborah for "judgment" (Heb. *mishpat,* **mish-PAWT**). The Hebrew wording has led many commentators to assume that Deborah was known as a judge in the legal sense. However, the story emphasizes her role as God's spokesperson by calling her a prophetess and telling us of the command for Barak that she received from the Lord.

6 And she sent and called Barak, the son of Abinoam out of Kedesh-naphtali, and said unto him, Hath not the LORD God of Israel commanded, saying, Go and draw toward mount Tabor, and take with thee ten thousand men of the children of Naphtali and of the children of Zebulun? 7 And I will draw unto thee to the river Kishon Sisera, the captain of Jabin's army, with his chariots and his multitude; and I will deliver him into thine hand.

Verse 6 contains all the biographical information we have on Barak. Since Kedesh was a common city name, it is difficult to know with certainty exactly where Barak was from. Nevertheless, we do know that the area was in the north of Israel and most likely would have been under the oppression of Jabin, king of Hazor.

The word rendered "Hath not" (Heb. *halo,* **ha-LOH**) is probably better understood as "behold" or "indeed." Deborah is not assuming that Barak has already heard from God concerning what he is supposed to do. By every indication, this is the first time Barak has received this message. Deborah gives him the message, however, in a way that prophets commonly gave messages from God: with words chosen to catch his attention and letting him know that it is God Himself speaking.

Mount Tabor rises steeply 1,843 feet above sea level at the northeast corner of the Jezreel Valley, and forces stationed on it could easily control one of the most important crossroads in the region. Tabor also offered the advantage of being a prominent landmark, and there would be little confusion among the forces mustering in response to Barak's summons. Essentially, God was telling Barak to use his forces to defiantly take control of the strategic high ground, forcing the enemy to come to him. Note that God provided the leader as well as the strategy.

Naphtali and Zebulun were regions that would have been subject to the oppression of Jabin, king of Hazor. Hazor (Jabin's capital city) and Harosheth Hagoyim (Sisera's home city) straddled these two areas—Hazor to the northeast of Naphtali, and

Harosheth Hagoyim to the southwest of Zebulun.

God tells Barak that He will draw Sisera and his army to the Kishon River. Evidently, Sisera will hear that the Israelites have taken control of Mount Tabor and move to put down their uprising. The key to Sisera's military power is his possession of 900 iron chariots, something the Israelites had encountered before and found to be intimidating (cf. Joshua 17:16; Judges 1:19). The threat posed by these chariots was perceived to be so great that the Israelites chose to live under Jabin's domination for 20 years (4:3). Chariots were state-of-the-art technology at the time, and the thought of opposing a chariot was understandably terrifying to the ordinary infantryman—not that different, perhaps, from an infantryman of our time opposing a tank. A chariot had the advantage in speed, weight, armor, and firepower (bow or spear).

The Kishon River flows through the Jezreel Valley (also known as the Plain of Esdraelon), a wide plain known for its extremely fertile soil. For most of the year, the Kishon is fed only by springs, and its waters are too minimal to be used for irrigation. During the winter rains, however, the Kishon can become a raging torrent, and large sections of the plain turn to mud. The Lord not only called Barak to lead the people of Israel against Jabin, but He promised to accomplish the task for him—literally, "give" or "deliver" (Heb. *nathan,* **naw-THAN**) him (Jabin) into his hands. Of course, the Lord had already promised to fight for His people if they were faithful to drive out the native peoples. Ironically, God had used the same language in His promise to give the enemy over to the Israelites when Joshua had contemplated his assault on Hazor (Joshua 11:10–13). God had been faithful then, and Joshua had completely destroyed Hazor and burned it to the ground.

8 And Barak said unto her, If thou wilt go with me, then I will go: but if thou wilt not go with me, then I will not go.

Barak hesitated at the task given to him. Even with 10,000 men in his army, the Canaanite force was clearly superior. Barak was not the first or last leader God chose for Israel who hesitated to obey:

Recall Moses (Exodus 3:14) and Gideon (Judges 6).

We must not be too quick to judge Barak for his reluctance. Hebrews 11:32–33 includes Barak and Gideon in a list of courageous men and women who acted in great faith, trusting God to do miraculous things to deliver His people. And we must remember that Barak was not asking any ordinary woman to accompany him. As a prophetess, Deborah was a representative of God Himself. Perhaps Barak's request was rooted in his recognition that mere military would not suffice to win the battle that lay ahead. He knew that victory would require God's direct intervention. In other words, he was willing to step out in faith, but he wasn't interested in signing up for a suicide mission.

9 And she said, I will surely go with thee: notwithstanding the journey that thou takest shall not be for thine honour; for the LORD shall sell Sisera into the hand of a woman. And Deborah arose, and went with Barak to Kedesh.

Deborah's promise to go with Barak at this place in the story is astounding. It comes at the point when God normally promises His presence with the leader He is sending (cf. Exodus 3:12; Joshua 1:5; Judges 6:16). It seems best to understand the promise of her presence as the promise of God's presence, given to help Barak in his weakness. God has repeatedly shown that He is willing to accommodate the weakness of His chosen instruments (cf. Deuteronomy 7:7; 9:4–6). Nevertheless, Barak should have known that God had promised to drive out the Canaanites for the Israelites if only they were faithful to continue to fight (cf. Joshua 13:6; 23:5).

Deborah's displeasure with Barak's hesitation is obvious in her prediction that Barak will not gain glory on this mission. In a touch of beautiful irony, since he has refused to go unless a woman accompanies him, an unnamed woman will gain the glory.

10 And Barak called Zebulun and Naphtali to Kedesh; and he went up with ten thousand men at his feet: and Deborah went up with him.

Ten thousand may sound like a large number of

troops to the modern reader. By comparison, however, the Canaanite army had 900 chariots alone, nearly one for every 10 Israelite soldiers. The implication is that the Canaanite infantry was vast—several times the size of Barak's force. Indeed, when Joshua first conquered Hazor, the king of Hazor conscripted troops from the many outlying cities and villages in his realm. He succeeded in assembling an army "as numerous as the sand on the seashore" (Joshua 11:1–5). Note also that Gideon was able to muster 32,000 men—three times more than Barak—when he prepared for his attack on the armies of Midian (Judges 7:3).

4:12 And they shewed Sisera that Barak the son of Abinoam was gone up to mount Tabor. 13 And Sisera gathered together all his chariots, even nine hundred chariots of iron, and all the people that were with him, from Harosheth of the Gentiles unto the river of Kishon.

The messenger who informed Sisera of Barak's army is not identified; however, as we noted before, the Lord had commanded Barak to position his forces on the strategic high ground—an action that was intended to draw Sisera's attention. Right away, then, we see that the plan the Lord commanded Barak to use is working. Of course, it is working because the Lord is orchestrating the events.

14 And Deborah said unto Barak, Up; for this is the day in which the LORD hath delivered Sisera into thine hand: is not the LORD gone out before thee? So Barak went down from mount Tabor, and ten thousand men after him.

It would have been understandable for Barak to have hesitated at this point. Sisera's powerful cavalry was positioned on a wide plain that presented ideal conditions for their operation. Barak's army probably would have felt much more comfortable fighting in the hills, where chariots would lose their advantage in speed and maneuverability. Yet it is not the military capabilities of Barak's force that matters; it is the fact that the Lord is fighting for Israel. Many scholars see Deborah's question, "Is not the Lord gone out before thee?" as an indication

that the Lord had caused an out-of-season rainstorm, which would have quickly turned the wide plain of the Jezreel Valley into mud.

Barak heeded Deborah's call to bold, definitive action by leading the charge down Mount Tabor into the valley. Barak here shows us that the greatest form of courage is not based on a perception of one's own sufficiency, but on the faithfulness of the God who called him. Without the promise that God would deliver Sisera into his hands, Barak's attack would have been suicidal.

15 And the LORD discomfited Sisera, and all his chariots, and all his host, with the edge of the sword before Barak; so that Sisera lighted down off his chariot, and fled away on his feet.

The word "discomfited" (Heb. *hamam*, **haw-MAM**), which means "to bring into movement and confusion," does not reveal exactly what God did to Sisera and his army, which is why we cannot say with absolute certainty that God sent an unexpected rainstorm. However, this is the same terminology used to describe God's action against the enemy in several other major Israelite triumphs. These triumphs are the destruction of Pharaoh and his army at the Red Sea, where the text specifically says that the Lord made the wheels come off the Egyptian chariots; Joshua's victory over the Amorites (Joshua 10:10); and the Israelites' victory over the Philistines during the days of Samuel, where the Lord used loud thunder to throw the Philistines into a panic.

16 But Barak pursued after the chariots, and after the host, unto Harosheth of the Gentiles: and all the host of Sisera fell upon the edge of the sword; and there was not a man left.

As the Canaanite army realized that the battle was not going their way, they determined it would be best to retreat to fight another day. They headed for their headquarters, Harosheth of Hagoyim, but were unable to outpace the Israelite foot soldiers. One of the possible reasons for this is that the Valley of Jezreel narrows as it approaches Harosheth. The chariots would have been forced to slow down and merge in order to pass through, and a traffic jam probably ensued. If, in fact, a rainstorm was a factor, the charioteers would also have had to deal with the raging Kishon River, which may account for the line in Deborah's song that describes the Kishon as having swept the Canaanites away.

Emboldened by the way the Lord was fighting for them, Barak and his army continued to press the fight against the Canaanites until they were wiped out. Based on some of the content of Deborah's song in chapter 5, some experts have surmised there may have been a second stage to the battle in which soldiers from other areas of Israel joined in the pursuit of the Canaanite army.

Sources

Block, Daniel I. *The New American Commentary: Judges, Ruth.* Nashville, Tenn.: Broadman & Holman Publishers, 1999.

Cundall, Arthur E. *Judges: An Introduction and Commentary.* Downers Grove, Ill.: InterVarsity Press, 1968.

Daily Bible Readings

M: The God in Whom I Trust
Psalm 91
T: Wait for God's Guidance
Psalm 27:1–6
W: Othniel Judges Israel
Judges 3:7–11
T: Courageous Leaders
Hebrews 11:1–2, 32–34
F: Deborah Leads the People
Judges 4:1–10
S: Success Assured
Judges 4:12–16
S: Deborah's Song of Praise
Judges 5:1–12

TEACHING TIPS

October 15
Bible Study Guide 7

1. Words You Should Know

A. Pray (1 Samuel 7:5) *palal* (Heb.)—To intervene, to interpose, to beg, or intercede on behalf of another. Samuel gathered all the Israelites at Mizpeh and told them that he would pray for them.

B. Sin (v. 6) *chata'* (Heb.)—To miss the mark; to err. The Israelites had sinned against God by turning to idolatry; they worshiped foreign gods.

2. Teacher Preparation

A. Prepare for the lesson by reading the Bible Background verses. Prayerfully meditate on the Devotional Reading.

B. Next study the More Light on the Text section and answer the questions in lesson 7 in the *Precepts For Living® Personal Study Guide*. Be prepared to answer the students' questions.

3. Starting the Lesson

A. Concentrate on the Lesson Aim as you begin the lesson in prayer.

B. Ask the students to read the Keep in Mind verse aloud together several times.

C. Introduce the students to Samuel and point out his role as Israel's last judge. Explain that Samuel was a judge, God's spokesperson. Tell the class that Samuel was committed to prayer like his mother, Hannah. He was a judge, prophet, and priest.

4. Getting into the Lesson

A. Read the Lesson Aim to the students.

B. Ask for volunteers to read the Focal Verses and the Background section.

C. Read The People, Places, and Times section.

5. Relating the Lesson to Life

A. Discuss the importance of a prayer life and of intercessory prayer for others.

B. Discuss commitment to God today. Explain

that idolatry is anything that we place higher than God in our lives, such as money, success, or pride.

6. Arousing Action

A. Read the In Focus story. Ask the students if they believe that prayer works and if they place anything above their commitment to God. Are they focused and committed to God in all areas of their lives?

B. Ask the students to think of who they pray for when they speak to God. Remind the students that we should help others, which includes praying for people we know and people we do not know. Remind them that God hears our prayers.

C. Instruct the class to consider praying for someone who expresses they are struggling. Give the students the opportunity to discuss their own personal experiences in receiving answers to prayer when they prayed for someone else.

Worship Guide

For the Superintendent or Teacher
Theme: God Answers Samuel's Prayer
Theme Song: "I Need Thee Every Hour"
Scripture: Psalm 42:5
Song: "A Praying Spirit"
Meditation: Dear Father, I thank You for the effectual, fervent prayer of the righteous. I pray that I will continue to strengthen my prayer life and learn to come to You with every issue of life. Amen.

GOD ANSWERS SAMUEL'S PRAYER

Bible Background • 1 SAMUEL 7:3–13
Printed Text • 1 SAMUEL 7:3–13   Devotional Reading • PSALM 31:14–24

Lesson Aim

By the end of the lesson, we will:

KNOW that praying for others can yield miraculous results;

DISCUSS the effects of praying for others and of knowing that others are praying for us; and

COMMIT to praying for the needs of others.

Keep in Mind

"And Samuel took a sucking lamb, and offered it for a burnt offering wholly unto the LORD: and Samuel cried unto the LORD for Israel: and the LORD heard him" (1 Samuel 7:9).

Focal Verses

1 Samuel 7:3 And Samuel spake unto all the house of Israel, saying, If ye do return unto the LORD with all your hearts, then put away the strange gods and Ashtaroth from among you, and prepare your hearts unto the LORD, and serve him only: and he will deliver you out of the hand of the Philistines.

4 Then the children of Israel did put away Baalim and Ashtaroth, and served the LORD only.

5 And Samuel said, Gather all Israel to Mizpeh, and I will pray for you unto the LORD.

6 And they gathered together to Mizpeh, and drew water, and poured it out before the LORD, and fasted on that day, and said there, We have sinned against the LORD. And Samuel judged the children of Israel in Mizpeh.

7 And when the Philistines heard that the children of Israel were gathered together to Mizpeh, the lords of the Philistines went up against Israel. And when the children of Israel heard it, they were afraid of the Philistines.

8 And the children of Israel said to Samuel, Cease not to cry unto the LORD our God for us, that he will save us out of the hand of the Philistines.

9 And Samuel took a sucking lamb, and offered it for a burnt offering wholly unto the LORD: and Samuel cried unto the LORD for Israel; and the LORD heard him.

10 And as Samuel was offering up the burnt offering, the Philistines drew near to battle against Israel: but the LORD thundered with a great thunder on that day upon the Philistines, and discomfited them; and they were smitten before Israel.

11 And the men of Israel went out of Mizpeh, and pursued the Philistines, and smote them, until they came under Bethcar.

12 Then Samuel took a stone, and set it between Mizpeh and Shen, and called the name of it Ebenezer, saying, Hitherto hath the LORD helped us.

13 So the Philistines were subdued, and they came no more into the coast of Israel: and the hand of the LORD was against the Philistines all the days of Samuel.

In Focus

After graduating from college, Tamara planned to enter law school. She was on the dean's list and was a member of Who's Who Among College Students. Tamara believed that she would be an excellent lawyer. Although she had not decided what aspect of law she would pursue, she knew that she wanted to be financially independent.

Tamara was raised in a Christian home. The entire family regularly attended Bible study, Sunday School, and Sunday service. As a result, Tamara had a strong foundation in God's Word, and she had seen the power of prayer. When Tamara went away to college, her family prayed continually for her. They had a family prayer hour every Friday night. Even when everyone was not under the same roof, they went to God in prayer as a family at the same hour.

As she filled out applications for law school, Tamara remembered the day she had received a full scholarship to attend college. She knew that God had heard the petitions of her heart because she would not have been able to attend college if her family had to pay for her college expenses. Once again, God heard the many prayers that Tamara's church and her family prayed. She was accepted into a prominent law school and was offered a part-time position as a paralegal.

We can accomplish God's purpose for us when we have a strong relationship with Him. Pray and be encouraged; you are a representative for God.

In today's lesson, we see that Samuel prayed to God on the Israelites' behalf, and God saved them. Praying for others shows our compassion and can make a difference in the outcome.

The People, Places, and Times

Samuel. Samuel was the son of Elkanah and Hannah. He served as prophet, judge, and priest. Samuel was born in answer to the prayers of his barren mother, Hannah. Hannah gave Samuel to Eli, the high priest at Shiloh, for dedicated service to God. When Samuel was dedicated to God, he listened to God. Samuel was the last judge in Israel. As the last judge in Israel, he encouraged the Israelites to commit themselves to God and serve Him only.

Kirjath-jearim. This is a place whose name means "city of forests." It was a city in Judah about 10 miles (16 kilometers) west of Jerusalem, near the battlefield where the Ark of the Covenant remained for about 100 years. The ark was kept here from around 1104 B.C. until 1003 B.C. The Israelites tried to harness the power of God to give them victory. Earlier, the Israelites were defeated by the Philistines, who kept the ark. However, the ark soon brought plagues upon every Philistine city it entered. Therefore, the Philistines returned the ark by sending it back to Kirjath-jearim.

Mizpeh. The name means "watchtower" or "lookout." Samuel called the Israelites to come to Mizpeh to pray and fast in sorrow for their sins. Mizpeh was the capital of Judah after the fall of Jerusalem. Later, Saul would be chosen at Mizpeh as Israel's first king. Saul had the blessings but not the approval of God and Samuel.

Ashtaroth. The name of the Canaanite goddess of fertility, sexuality, and war, she was the companion of Baal. Ashtaroth worship usually involved sacred prostitution. The ground was believed to be fertile when she was worshiped in sexual rituals.

Background

Samuel was a judge, prophet, and priest who was obedient to God. Samuel was familiar with the power of God and, like his mother, Hannah, was committed to prayer. Samuel knew that the Israelites were worshiping false gods; they were violating their covenant with God.

The Israelites had suffered defeat by the Philistines when they had tried to use the power of the Ark of the Covenant to gain victory in battle. The Lord had given the Children of Israel strict instructions concerning the ark. Instead of keeping the ark in the most holy place, they were disobedient by moving it to the battlefield. Earlier, God had killed the men of Beth-shemesh because they had gazed upon the ark. The Israelites had experienced 20 years of sorrow because they had not repented of their sins. Samuel urged the Israelites to repent and called them to meet him at Mizpeh so that he could pray on their behalf. The Israelites believed that God had left them, but they did not do anything about it. Samuel urged them to make a change—to do something.

At-A-Glance

1. Samuel Leads Israel to Repent
(1 Samuel 7:3–7)
2. Samuel Leads to Victory (vv. 8–13)

In Depth

1. Samuel Leads Israel to Repent (1 Samuel 7:3–7)

Eleazar, whose name means "God is power" or "God is help," had been selected to take care of the Ark of the Covenant. The ark was taken to a city named Kirjath-jearim, which was near the battlefield because the Israelites wanted to be victorious in battle. Unfortunately, their faith was focused on the ark itself, not on God. Therefore, they believed it would bring them victory if it was nearby when they fought the Philistines. In essence, the ark had become an idol for them. God Himself should have been the focus of their faith, not the ark. Because God will not tolerate such misplaced faith, they were defeated. Because of this defeat, the Israelites realized that God was no longer blessing them. They needed to repent and return to God. Samuel, who was judge, called the assembly at Mizpeh. He directed the Israelites to pray and ask God for forgiveness.

The Israelites prayed and fasted in sorrow for their sins. Fasting is a religious practice associated with making a request of God. When a believer comes to God, physical necessities are minor compared to spiritual needs. Fasting is an act of humbling oneself before God prior to purification. The fasting and prayer represented an act of repentance, of turning from idolatry and turning to God. The Israelites desired to remove any obstacles or sins that had led to their defeat and subjection by the Philistines. They needed to reaffirm their covenant loyalty to God in order to receive His blessings.

Samuel directed the Israelites to gather at Mizpeh and pray. He was active in all his roles as prophet, priest, and judge for the Children of Israel. Samuel prayed to God on behalf of the Israelites and urged them to turn from their sins and turn to God in obedience. After Samuel prayed, he poured out water. The act of pouring the water symbolized repentance. The Israelites no longer desired to worship false gods and to sin. They wanted to return to God by obeying, serving, and worshiping Him. As judge, Samuel made decisions and settled disputes. Although God was the true leader of Israel, Samuel was His spokesman. Samuel was obedient to God's direction and judged the Israelites.

As with Samuel, our commitment to God should be continual. If we are distracted and place anything before God, we should seek Him and repent. When we follow God, there will be distractions; but we must focus on Him. We can easily make excuses, but we must follow God. When we seek God daily with a sincere heart, we can endure and keep our focus on Him.

2. Samuel Leads Israel to Victory (vv. 8–13)

The Philistines knew that the Israelites were not gathered at Mizpeh for a religious observance; they suspected that the Israelites were united in an uprising. The Philistines planned to attack the Israelites, who wanted Samuel to continue to pray for them. The Israelites wanted Samuel to pray for their victory. At Aphek, they had depended on the ark for victory. Now the Israelites depended on the power of God for victory.

Samuel offered a 1-year-old lamb, a spring lamb with the most tender meat, to God. According to Levitical law, an animal could not be offered unless it was at least 8 days old. When Samuel offered the sacrifice, he prayed to God, who heard him. God responded with thunder and lightning, which are associated with the presence of a deity. As God thundered from heaven, the Philistines were confused and defeated. Israel had strength under the leadership of Samuel, who redirected the Israelites to renew their covenant with God. God intervened and gave the Israelites the victory. The Israelites chased the Philistines to Bethcar, which was a high place overlooking the Philistine territory.

After the battle, Samuel set up a memorial of stone between Mizpeh and Shen and named the place Ebenezer, which means "stone of help." God had delivered the Israelites from the hand of the Philistines. Like Joshua, Samuel commemorated God's victories for the Children of Israel with a stone marker (Joshua 4). The Philistines had endured a final defeat at the hands of God. There were no other battles between the Israelites and the Philistines during the time when Samuel was judge.

Like the Israelites, we may need to remember the personal victories that God has given us. When we are experiencing difficult moments, the memories will help us to endure the present suffering with confidence. We have faith that God has already given us the victory if we endure.

Search the Scriptures

1. Who was Samuel's mother, who prayed for him (1 Samuel 1:20)?

2. To whom did Hannah give Samuel when he was a young boy (vv. 24–28)?

3. What false god was Ashtaroth associated with (7:4)?

4. What did the pouring of water by the Israelites mean (v. 6)?

Discuss the Meaning

1. Samuel knew that God hears the prayers of His children. Samuel called the Israelites to Mizpeh to pray to God on their behalf. Do you believe that intercessory prayer is effective? Discuss the importance of praying for others in today's society.

2. Society offers many temptations and distractions that cause us to be disobedient to God. What are some false idols in our society today? Discuss how we can stay obedient and focused on God while we live in this world.

Lesson in Our Society

The Israelites believed that God had abandoned them. In reality, the Israelites had turned from God, who is immutable. God does not change; we change. God continually waits for sinners with open arms and calls out to those who turn from Him to return.

As humans, we live in a world of sin. As believers, we serve a loving God, who hears our prayers and knows our need for help. When we are disobedient, we cannot stay in our current state. We must make a change. We must repent, turn from our sin, and return to God. Today there are many believers who have turned from God and have turned to the world. God stands ready with open arms, but we must do something. Repentance is necessary. If you know someone who has stopped seeking God's guidance, pray for that person. Encourage him or her to return to God.

Make It Happen

Unlike the Israelites, we should seek God at all times. The standards of the world are different from God's standards. Remember that God has complete control; therefore, we are victorious in all situations. Success defined by the world's standards cannot compare with success as a child of God. While we live in the world, we can be strengthened to endure difficult situations by associating with others who will encourage and pray for us.

Seek out a Christian group that has community involvement, or support a community group that encourages those who are alone or homeless. We receive strength when we pray for others and encourage others by our actions and lifestyles. Seek to help those in need; by so doing, you are serving God. When you join a group that prays and seeks to help those in need, you will stay encouraged to do God's will.

Follow the Spirit

What God wants me to do:

_____

_____

Remember Your Thoughts

Special insights I have learned:

_____

_____

More Light on the Text

1 Samuel 7:3–13

3 And Samuel spake unto all the house of Israel, saying, If ye do return unto the LORD with all your hearts, then put away the strange gods and Ashtaroth from among you, and prepare your hearts unto the LORD, and serve him only: and he will deliver you out of the hand of the Philistines.

The ark was returned to Israel and brought to Kirjath-jearim, and all the house of Israel lamented after the LORD" (v. 2). Afterward, Samuel, functioning as judge, prophet, and priest (and king), sets forth the condition for deliverance and guides the house of Israel through the prescription of consecrating themselves before God, whereby covenantal fellowship may be restored. As God's chosen people, they must walk in obedience to the stipulations to receive His promise of mercy and favor (Exodus

19:5). First, they must repent and turn from their detestable idols. The word *Ashtaeroth* is the plural in Hebrew for *Ashtoreth,* who was the goddess of fertility and sexual union; consequently, there were sexual rites surrounding her worship at her many shrines in the land of Canaan.

4 Then the children of Israel did put away Baalim and Ashtaroth, and served the LORD only.

God always fashions, through tests and discipline, the hearts and minds of His people as they turn toward Him. After a period of estrangement—because of their rebellion and apostasy—during which the promise of blessing and protection is deferred, the Israelites return to their God as prodigals. They did not just agree to abide by the dictates of God's law, but wholeheartedly committed themselves to having no other god and to serve Him only. They readily comply with Samuel's call to repentance. The word *Baalim* is the plural in Hebrew for *Baal,* the son of Dagon, the god of the sky who brought forth thunder and rain to fertilize the earth. Of the many strange gods, Baal and Ashtoreth were perhaps the most popular and therefore the most prevalent.

5 And Samuel said, Gather all Israel to Mizpeh, and I will pray for you unto the LORD.

Samuel directs the people to gather at Mizpeh so that he might intercede for them before God. Mizpeh, several miles north of Jerusalem, is a familiar setting. It was the place of national assembly where the people of Israel conferred to bring the Benjamites to justice for the atrocity committed against the concubine of a Levite (see Judges 20:1). Mizpeh would also be the place for the national convention of all the tribes of Israel at which Saul would be elected king, and it would become the capital of Judah after the fall of Jerusalem (2 Kings 25:23, 25).

6 And they gathered together to Mizpeh, and drew water, and poured it out before the LORD, and fasted on that day, and said there, we have sinned against the LORD. And Samuel judged the children of Israel in Mizpeh.

There is no precedent in terms of a previous rite or ceremony of cleansing in which the people draw and pour out water. It is only later, in 2 Samuel 14:14–15, where the Scriptures provide us with some understanding of the significance of their actions. In that passage, Joab contrives to bring Absalom back from exile for the murder of his brother Amnon. He employs a wise woman from Tekoa, who tells a story—much like Nathan, after the murder of Uriah, who shepherds the heart of David toward his blood guilt—but this tale is concocted by Joab to elicit from King David a reason to recall his son home. Alluding to Absalom, the woman says, "For we must needs die, and are as water spilt on the ground, which cannot be gathered up again; neither doth God respect any person: yet doth he devise means, that his banished be not expelled from him" (2 Samuel 14:14).

That the people would pour water on the ground is an acknowledgment that they deserved to be cursed for violating the terms of the covenant. But underlying this act is the appeal for mercy and the knowledge that God honors a contrite heart that knows its bankruptcy. He is a merciful God who says that "the soul that sinneth shall die" (Ezekiel 18:4, 20) but also provides a legal refuge whereby He remains true to His word while some transgressors find refuge by the means of grace He provides. Thus, the people fasted and confessed their sin. And Samuel was leader of Israel at Mizpeh.

7 And when the Philistines heard that the children of Israel were gathered together to Mizpeh, the lords of the Philistines went up against Israel. And when the children of Israel heard it, they were afraid of the Philistines.

Perhaps the Philistines sensed an opportunity, now that all the Israelites have gathered at Mizpeh, to decimate the Israelites once and for all; or perhaps they felt threatened and mobilized their army. Certainly, the reality of the attack of the enemy becomes more evident when God's people turn away from and against the evil influence of the world. God's way is never without opposition and challenge. In any case, the people are afraid. (Fear is the potential enemy within because it tempts us with getting momentary expediency of relief without waiting on God.)

8 And the children of Israel said to Samuel, Cease not to cry unto the LORD our God for us, that he will save us out of the hand of the Philistines.

The people look to and beseech Samuel, God's provision and chosen instrument, as mediator on their behalf. Samuel, in this sense, is a type of Christ, and the deliverance sought from the Philistines foreshadows the greater deliverance and salvation effected in the Person of Christ.

9 And Samuel took a sucking lamb, and offered it for a burnt offering wholly unto the LORD: and Samuel cried unto the LORD for Israel; and the LORD heard him.

Acting as priest, Samuel sacrifices a lamb (refer to the earlier mention). The stage is set. The Lord's face and the promise of His mercies are no longer eclipsed by the iniquity of His people. When Samuel cries out, God accepts and answers his prayer.

10 And as Samuel was offering up the burnt offering, the Philistines drew near to battle against Israel: but the LORD thundered with a great thunder on that day upon the Philistines, and discomfited them; and they were smitten before Israel.

The Philistines are poised for attack, but the Lord's hand against the Philistines is sure, swift, and unmistakable; they were confused and smitten before Israel. The Israelites—as they had done so many times before, from the day of their liberation from the hand of Pharaoh—behold the miracle of what the Lord had done.

11 And the men of Israel went out of Mizpeh, and pursued the Philistines, and smote them, until they came under Bethcar.

"Who is this King of glory? The LORD strong and mighty, the LORD mighty in battle" (Psalm 24:8). So it is when the battle is the Lord's, and all that is left for the Israelites to do is to pursue the scattered Philistines and slay them.

12 Then Samuel took a stone, and set it between Mizpeh and Shen, and called the name of it Ebenezer, saying, Hitherto hath the LORD helped us.

They give God all the glory by erecting a monument between Mizpeh and Shen. Ebenezer means "stone of help." It was only by the help of God that they attained victory over their enemies the Philistines.

13 So the Philistines were subdued, and they came no more into the coast of Israel: and the hand of the LORD was against the Philistines all the days of Samuel.

After their decisive defeat at the hands of the Israelites, the Philistines, though they would continue to harass the Israelites, would never again be an occupying threat in the land. Such is the favor of the Lord to His chosen people when they walk in covenantal fellowship with Him.

Daily Bible Readings

M: Call to Prayer
Colossians 4:2–6
T: The Psalmist Prays
Psalm 31:14–24
W: Hannah Pays Her Vows
1 Samuel 1:21–28
T: Hannah Prays
1 Samuel 2:1–11
F: The Lord Calls Samuel
1 Samuel 3:1–10
S: Israel Returns to God
1 Samuel 7:2–6
S: The Lord Helps the Hebrew People
1 Samuel 7:7–13

TEACHING TIPS

October 22
Bible Study Guide 8

1. Words You Should Know
A. Servant (2 Samuel 7:8) *'ebed* (Heb.)—To serve or to work. A servant obeys the will of God.

B. Seed (v. 12) *zera'* (Heb.)—Literally, a reference to a seed grown in the ground; figuratively, it refers to one's descendants or offspring. It can also refer to a single person or nation.

2. Teacher Preparation
A. Prepare for the lesson by reading the Bible Background and the Daily Bible Readings. Prayerfully meditate on the passage for Devotional Reading.

B. Study the Focal Verses, paying particular attention to the Keep in Mind verse.

C. Read More Light on the Text and complete lesson 8 in the *Precepts For Living® Personal Study Guide* to gain greater insight into today's lesson. Write down any questions that you may have as you read the biblical content.

3. Starting the Lesson
A. Concentrate on the Lesson Aim as you begin the lesson in prayer.

B. Ask for three volunteers to read the Focal Verses according to the At-A-Glance outline.

C. Introduce the students to David and his role as a servant of God. Remind the students that David was the shepherd boy who killed Goliath, the 10-foot Philistine. Explain that David had a heart to please God through obedience.

4. Getting into the Lesson
A. Reread the Lesson Aim to the students.

B. Divide the class into three groups and assign each group a Lesson Aim objective. For example: Group 1—What promises did God make to David as revealed through the prophet Nathan? Group 2—Why are the promises that God made to David still important to Christians today? Group 3—Has God given us any eternal commitments? If so, discuss as a group what they are.

C. Reassemble the class and ask for a representative from each group to present their findings.

5. Relating the Lesson to Life
A. Ask for a volunteer to read the In Focus story. Discuss the importance of trusting in God and accepting His answer even when it does not agree with our plans. Ask for personal examples.

B. Read Lesson in Our Society. Give the students time to offer suggestions.

C. Spend 10 or 15 minutes briefly answering the Discuss the Meaning questions.

6. Arousing Action
A. Ask the students to come up with a specific plan for completing Make It Happen.

B. Ask the students if they have ever had to make a sudden change in their personal plans. Give the students an opportunity to discuss the importance of changing to do God's will.

C. Remind the students to read the Daily Bible Readings to prepare for next week's lesson.

D. Close the class with prayer.

Worship Guide

For the Superintendent or Teacher
Theme: God Covenants with David
Theme Song: "'Tis So Sweet to Trust in Jesus"
Scripture: Hebrews 2:13
Song: "Standing on the Promises"
Meditation: Dear Heavenly Father, thank You for Your direction. I pray that with each passing day, I will increase my faith and trust in Your covenant and eternal plans. Amen.

GOD COVENANTS WITH DAVID

Bible Background • 2 SAMUEL 7
Printed Text • 2 SAMUEL 7:8–17   Devotional Reading • PSALM 5

Lesson Aim

By the end of the lesson, we will:

EXPLORE the promises of God made to David as revealed through Nathan;

REFLECT on why God's promise to David is important to Christians; and

DECIDE to trust in God's eternal commitment to us.

Keep in Mind

"And thine house and thy kingdom shall be established for ever before thee: thy throne shall be established for ever" (2 Samuel 7:16).

Focal Verses

2 Samuel 7:8 Now therefore so shalt thou say unto my servant David, Thus saith the LORD of hosts, I took thee from the sheepcote, from following the sheep, to be ruler over my people, over Israel:

9 And I was with thee whithersoever thou wentest, and have cut off all thine enemies out of thy sight, and have made thee a great name, like unto the name of the great men that are in the earth.

10 Moreover I will appoint a place for my people Israel, and will plant them, that they may dwell in a place of their own, and move no more; neither shall the children of wickedness afflict them any more, as beforetime,

11 And as since the time that I commanded judges to be over my people Israel, and have caused thee to rest from all thine enemies. Also the LORD telleth thee that he will make thee an house.

12 And when thy days be fulfilled, and thou shalt sleep with thy fathers, I will set up thy seed after thee, which shall proceed out of thy bowels, and I will establish his kingdom.

13 He shall build an house for my name, and I will stablish the throne of his kingdom for ever.

14 I will be his father, and he shall be my son. If he commit iniquity, I will chasten him with the rod of men, and with the stripes of the children of men:

15 But my mercy shall not depart away from him, as I took it from Saul, whom I put away before thee.

16 And thine house and thy kingdom shall be established for ever before thee: thy throne shall be established for ever.

17 According to all these words, and according to all this vision, so did Nathan speak unto David.

In Focus

While sipping her Sunday morning tea and holding a little blue Bible, Linda sat at the kitchen table reflecting on her life. Linda was the product of drug-addicted parents. Her mother had abandoned her at age 7 to be raised by her elderly grandmother, and as far as she knew, her father was serving a life sentence in the state penitentiary. One day, Linda's grandmother gave her a little blue Bible and told her that whenever she was afraid or scared, she should just open it up and begin to read. By the time Linda was 12, her grandmother passed away.

After her grandmother's death,

Linda was shuffled back and forth among various relatives and lived in five different foster homes. Many nights Linda lay in her bed and read the stories in the Bible. She prayed to God to help her. As the years passed, Linda experienced many hardships. But despite her circumstances, Linda made it. She graduated magna cum laude from medical school and was immediately hired by a prestigious research hospital, where she met and married Greg, the man of her dreams.

The couple now has two lovely children and a comfortable house in the suburbs. When she was a little girl, Linda didn't really understand why her grandmother had instructed her to read her Bible in times of trouble, but now as an adult she understood what her grandmother was trying to do—she was giving her hope. Her grandmother knew that life would be difficult and that people would disappoint her and break their promises to her, but if she learned to trust and depend on God, He would never disappoint her. Now in her late 40s, Linda's little blue Bible is tattered and worn, but the power of God's Word and the promises found therein are stronger than ever.

It is sometimes hard to trust a promise because we know the potential exists for a promise to be broken. God, however, is trustworthy and never breaks His promises. In today's lesson, we will review God's promise to David and celebrate the eternal nature of this promise, which was fulfilled in Jesus Christ.

The People, Places, and Times

David. David was a man after God's own heart; he ruled according to God's principles. He was a shepherd, poet, and musician. He was loyal to King Saul. David was the first king to unite Judah and Israel. God promised him that he would have the royal Messiah, Jesus Christ, in his lineage. David ruled God's people from 1005 B.C. to 965 B.C. He returned the Ark of the Covenant to the tabernacle. Although David had many accomplishments, he was imperfect; therefore, he stumbled and fell into sin. David recognized his sins and repented; he found forgiveness and restoration through God.

Nathan. He was a prophet in the royal court of David as well as for some of Solomon's reign. His name means "gift" or "God has given." Nathan was a personal adviser to David and spoke for God. Nathan was fearless; he was not afraid to speak the truth. Nathan was one divinely appointed means of accountability in David's life. Throughout David's life, Nathan was able to help David see his own sins.

Jerusalem. This was the capital of Judah and the location of one of David's first victories in battle. It was also the location of the Ark of the Covenant during David's reign as king of Israel.

Background

David was the king of Judah, who defeated the Philistines. At 37 years old, David was crowned king of the tribe of Judah, while Ish-bosheth, Saul's son, was leader of the rest of Israel. David did not force the other tribes to follow him; he gave the matter to God. Eventually, Ish-bosheth was assassinated. David became king of all Israel after the rest of the tribes of Israel pledged their loyalty to him. Many years earlier, David had been anointed by Samuel to be king of Israel, but he had to wait on God to fulfill

His promises. David was obedient to God. When he became king, David unified the people. David conquered Jerusalem and made it the capital city, defeated the Philistines, and brought the ark to Jerusalem. God was with David, who realized that his greatness was from God. David was not motivated by personal ambition. God was first in his life. David recognized God as the ruler of his life. He planned to build a temple for the ark.

At-A-Glance

1. God Speaks through Nathan
   (2 Samuel 7:8–10)
2. God's Promise to David (vv. 11–16)
3. God's Promises Are True (v. 17)

In Depth

1. God Speaks through Nathan (2 Samuel 7:8–10)

David conquered the city of Jerusalem, made it his capital, and brought the Ark of the Covenant to Jerusalem to ensure God's blessings upon the nation of Israel. David also wanted to build a temple, a permanent sanctuary, to house the ark.

Nathan was a prophet and personal adviser to David, and he spoke for God. Initially, Nathan encouraged David to build a temple for the ark. However, when God spoke to Nathan, he realized that God did not want David to build a temple for the ark. God told Nathan to give a message to David. In the message, God reminded David that He had brought him from the role of a shepherd boy to become the king of a great nation. God had fought all of David's battles and had never left him alone. God promised to make David's name great; He had made a similar promise to Abram (Genesis 12:2). God also promised that the Israelites would be secure in the land; they would no longer need to fight and endure affliction from their enemies.

God revealed that He did not want David to build Him a temple. Instead, God told David that He would make him a dynasty. God did not honor David's request to build the temple because His plans far exceeded David's plans. God promised David a dynasty that would last eternally. The throne of David would exist forever through his lineage.

2. God's Promise to David (vv. 11–16)

God made a threefold promise to David. First, God told David that his house, throne, and kingdom would always endure. This meant that David's lineage would be a royal lineage; his house would always be the royal line. Second, God promised David that his family line (David's offspring) would always rule. Finally, God promised that David's earthly kingdom would never be removed. The kingdom would not be taken from future generations in David's lineage.

The promise did not mean that there would not be an interruption in the earthly kingdom. In 930 B.C., the kingdom would be interrupted when the northern kingdom of Israel rebelled against David's dynasty (Hosea 3:4–5). In 586 B.C., Judah would be taken into exile by Nebuchadnezzar (2 Kings 25:1–21). Although there were moments when David's lineage did not rule, the Davidic Covenant stated that the privilege of ruling would belong to David's lineage. The promise in the New Testament is reiterated when Gabriel, an angel of the Lord, promises that Mary's son, Jesus Christ, will receive the throne that was promised to David (Luke 1:32–33). Ultimately, Jesus Christ will fulfill the promise in the new covenant when He returns to reign over His children. This promise is important to Christians today because Jesus Christ will reign on the throne of David at the Second Advent (Revelation 20:1–6). Thus, the promises that God made to David are true for us today.

3. God's Promises Are True (v. 17)

God makes promises that may seem incredible, but He is trustworthy. God never breaks His promises. When God said no to David, He had a purpose. If you seek God's direction but He says no in response, remember that His plans for your life are more than you could have asked. God has blessings that exceed our expectations. Faith is necessary to receive what we cannot see. We must trust and believe that God has already set the plan into action. We cannot see the results at this moment. Faith is an action step that we must take every day in our walk with God.

Faith looks toward God's promises; it does not look back to our disappointments. Be encouraged and trust God. His promises are true.

During the reign of each king, God ensured that a person was present to declare His Word. Nathan gave the vision to David and encouraged him to follow God's direction. David did not believe that he was worthy of God's promises, but he received Nathan's vision from God. As believers, we may not feel worthy of the promises of God, but we must pray for His direction in our lives. The will of God will occur with or without us, but we can pray that we will be a part of His will being done on Earth. Then we will receive the promises of God with praise and adoration.

Search the Scriptures

1. What did David want to build (2 Samuel 7:2)?
2. What was Nathan's role during David's kingship (vv. 2–4, 17)?
3. How did God inform David that his plans were not God's plans (vv. 4–5)?
4. What did God promise David (v. 9)?
5. What did God promise for the people of Israel (v. 10)?
6. What is the Davidic Covenant (vv. 11–13)?

Discuss the Meaning

1. We all have a part in God's plan. Society encourages pride and recognition. Can you take a back seat or move out of the spotlight when God has plans for you? Do you recognize the difference between God's priorities and those of society?
2. David received the message that God did not want him to build a temple. God had other plans for David. Are you able to accept that you may need to redirect your personal agenda in deference to God's agenda? Doing so may include a change in your future. Can you adjust to God's will for your life?

Lesson in Our Society

David's plans were not God's plans. Today's society is governed by political officials who make national decisions. Do you believe that they consult God before making a decision that affects the people of this nation? Do you think they take their position/power for granted or that they submit to God's plans for their lives? What would you do if you held a political office? How can you submit to God's plans in the position you hold today?

Today, we must seek to live for God in our professional and personal lives. We must recognize that God has a perfect plan, and seek His will for our lives. We cannot live for God only when it is convenient. If our plans do not coincide with God's will, then we must ask God to lead us. A sincere heart and a commitment to seek God at all times are necessary to persevere in today's society. We live in the world, but we must be obedient to God's direction for our lives. When we seek our personal agenda, we may need to redirect it when God shows us His will. Can you accept your purpose like David did?

Make It Happen

Develop a personal relationship with God that is reflected in your actions and words. Seek God's will for your life. He has a purpose for you. Ask God to encourage you to stand strong for Him and seek His direction. Find quiet time in the midst of hectic schedules, timelines, and appointments to seek God. Or find a prayer partner, and the two of you can support one another by praying for God's direction and guidance. Make a commitment to encourage others to follow God. When you stand for God and encourage others, you will be encouraged to endure. If you feel that you have missed God's plan for your life, know that God has not forgotten you. Seek God's direction with a sincere heart. He will lead you.

Follow the Spirit

What God wants me to do:

_____

_____

Remember Your Thoughts

Special insights I have learned:

_____

_____

More Light on the Text
2 Samuel 7:8–17

As God reveals more of Himself and His plan of redemption for His people, His track record of faithfulness to His people is established. Here we

see what God is about to unfold to the anointed King David through the prophet Nathan.

8 Now therefore so shalt thou say unto my servant David, Thus saith the LORD of hosts, I took thee from the sheepcote, from following the sheep, to be ruler over my people, over Israel: 9 And I was with thee whithersoever thou wentest, and have cut off all thine enemies out of thy sight, and have made thee a great name, like unto the name of the great men that are in the earth.

Up until this time, God's promises of a coming Messiah had been nonspecific. Here we see the prophet Nathan prophesying to David regarding his destiny. David had purposed in his heart to build a temple to God (2 Samuel 7:1–3). However, God had another plan. The Hebrew word here rendered "sheepcote" is *naweh* (**naw-veh**) and means meadow or pasture. God sent His prophet Nathan to remind David that it was He (God) who had delivered David from the sheepcote, and that He had bigger and better plans for David than simply building a temple.

Echoes of what had been spoken to Abraham, its fulfillment, and the expansion of the covenant—with additional promise and revelation—are evident as God cites all that He has done on David's behalf to bring him to this point. As with Abraham, God gave David a great name (see Genesis 12:2). So often in God's purpose and plan, His chosen instrument is of such an unlikely nature or so extreme that His divine hand in the matter is all the more evident. Note the very election of Israel, in which God fashions an improbable people to rise to such prestige among the nations as they would under King David. In David we see the glory of God's historical resume; He has taken a boy from the "sheepcote" to make a man of great name.

10 Moreover I will appoint a place for my people Israel, and will plant them, that they may dwell in a place of their own, and move no more; neither shall the children of wickedness afflict them any more, as beforetime.

The land was integral to the fulfillment of the promise God made to Abraham (cf. Genesis 15:18–21). The promise to provide "a place for my

Nathan delivered God's word to David: "And thine house and thy kingdom shall be established for ever before thee: thy throne shall be established for ever" (2 Samuel 7:16).

people" was the promise of safe haven—a promise both given and realized. The metaphor of planting is used frequently in Scripture (cf. Psalm 44:2; Jeremiah 2:21; 11:17). To "plant" (Heb. *nata*, **naw-tah**) figuratively means "to be established." Under David's reign, God established Israel; they had obtained a secure place. No longer would they be harassed and oppressed by "the children of wickedness" (i.e., the Philistines, Ammonites, etc.) as before.

11 And as since the time that I commanded judges to be over my people Israel, and have caused thee to rest from all thine enemies. Also the LORD telleth thee that he will make thee an house. 12 And when thy days be fulfilled, and thou shalt sleep with thy fathers, I will set up thy seed after thee, which shall proceed out of thy bowels, and I will establish his kingdom.

The covenant is augmented. The Davidic rule would usher in a zenith of peace, stability, and prosperity in the history of Israel. God promised rest and quiet for His people that had eluded them from the time of the judges. Moreover, God promised to build

David a house—not a literal house, but a dynasty established from David's seed after him. Since their time as nomadic tent-dwellers trekking through the desert, the people of Israel had looked forward to this day. However, it would be Solomon, next in David's immediate bloodline, who would build the temple. It was here that God established David's family in the Messianic lineage to follow (cf. 1 Samuel 2:35).

13 He shall build an house for my name, and I will stablish the throne of his kingdom for ever.

The prophecy here can be said to be twofold with both "near" and "far" revelation. Solomon, David's immediate successor in his bloodline, will build the temple. It is clear from the context that David's immediate offspring is in view (v. 12); however, the "seed" of David may also refer here to the coming Messiah, the Christ (cf. Luke 1:32–33).

14 I will be his father, and he shall be my son. If he commit iniquity, I will chasten him with the rod of men, and with the stripes of the children of men:

The cursing/blessing dimension applies to the natural lineage when marked by iniquity before the coming of the perfect seed, born of the Spirit, who will establish in His person and humanity perfect righteousness. "Chastening" (Heb. *yakah*, **yaw-kaah**) is the operative word here and denotes correction as applied to a son, as opposed to "wrath" as directed to the wicked.

15 But my mercy shall not depart away from him, as I took it from Saul, whom I put away before thee.

The Davidic Kingdom is bound to the covenant. It is sustained by the promise of God, who cannot lie. It bears in itself the bloodline of Christ.

16 And thine house and thy kingdom shall be established for ever before thee: thy throne shall be established for ever.

God, by covenant, will ensure, or guarantee, the posterity of David's kingdom and its rule forever unto eternity.

17 According to all these words, and according to all this vision, so did Nathan speak unto David.

Nathan, like Samuel before him, is the prophet chosen by God to guide the king and guard the royal house of God. He is God's spokesman, God's channel through whom He speaks to David and administers the kingdom.

Daily Bible Readings

M: Samuel Anoints Young David
1 Samuel 16:1–13

T: David's Lyre Soothes Saul
1 Samuel 16:14–23

W. David Protects the Sheep
1 Samuel 17:32–37

T: A Cry for Help
Psalm 5

F: Judah Anoints David King
2 Samuel 2:1–7

S: God's Promises to David
2 Samuel 7:8–17

S: David Speaks to God
2 Samuel 7:18–29

TEACHING TIPS

October 29
Bible Study Guide 9

1. Words You Should Know

A. Statutes (1 Kings 3:3) *chuqqah* (Heb.)—Customs, ordinances, and manners.

B. Righteousness (v. 6) *tsedaqah* (Heb.)—That which denotes moral justice and virtue; a covenantal and relational term.

C. Judge (v. 9) *shphat* (Heb.)—To arbitrate, govern, or rule.

2. Teacher Preparation

A. Read all the Scriptures from the Bible Background and the Devotional Reading. Read the Daily Bible Readings and complete lesson 9 in the *Precepts For Living® Personal Study Guide*.

B. Reread the Focal Verses in a modern translation.

3. Starting the Lesson

A. Open the class with prayer. Focus on the blessing that God hears and answers the prayers of believers.

B. Have the students read the Lesson Aim aloud and in unison.

C. Ask for a volunteer to read the In Focus story.

D. Have the students spend about 10 minutes discussing their experiences with prayers being answered in unexpected ways.

4. Getting into the Lesson

A. Ask for volunteers to read the Focal Verses.

B. Ask for a volunteer to read The People, Places, and Times.

C. Read the Background section.

5. Relating the Lesson to Life

A. Review the Search the Scriptures questions together.

B. Review and discuss the Discuss the Meaning questions. Encourage all the students to participate.

C. Ask for a volunteer to read the Lesson in Our Society section. If time permits, allow the students to discuss the article.

6. Arousing Action

A. Give the students an opportunity to complete the Follow the Spirit and Remember Your Thoughts sections.

B. Close the class in prayer, thanking God for the prayers that He has already answered.

Worship Guide

For the Superintendent or Teacher
Theme: God Grants Wisdom to Solomon
Theme Song: "Whisper a Prayer"
Scripture: 1 Kings 3:12
Song: "Pray for Me"
Meditation: Thank You, Lord,
for lovingly listening to each and every one
of my prayers. Lord, help me to always
trust that You care enough to respond to
me. Amen.

GOD GRANTS WISDOM TO SOLOMON

Bible Background • 1 KINGS 3
Printed Text • 1 KINGS 3:3–14   Devotional Reading • PSALM 119:97–104

Lesson Aim

By the end of the lesson, we will:

REALIZE, through Solomon's example, that God hears and answers prayers;

REFLECT on things we have prayed for and how God responded; and

TRUST that God hears our prayers and will answer in the way that is best for us.

Keep in Mind

"Behold, I have done according to thy words: lo, I have given thee a wise and an understanding heart; so that there was none like thee before thee, neither after thee shall any arise like unto thee" (1 Kings 3:12).

Focal Verses

1 Kings 3:3 And Solomon loved the LORD, walking in the statues of David his father: only he sacrificed and burnt incense in high places.

4 And the king went to Gibeon to sacrifice there; for that was the great high place: a thousand burnt offerings did Solomon offer upon that altar.

5 In Gibeon the LORD appeared to Solomon in a dream by night: and God said, Ask what I shall give thee.

6 And Solomon said, Thou hast shewed unto thy servant David my father great mercy, according as he walked before thee in truth, and in righteousness, and in uprightness of heart with thee; and thou hast kept for him this great kindness, that thou hast given him a son to sit on his throne, as it is this day.

7 And now, O LORD my God, thou hast made thy servant king instead of David my father: and I am but a little child: I know not how to go out or come in.

8 And thy servant is in the midst of thy people which thou hast chosen, a great people, that cannot be numbered nor counted for multitude.

9 Give therefore thy servant an understanding heart to judge thy people, that I may discern between good and bad: for who is able to judge this thy so great a people?

10 And the speech pleased the Lord, that Solomon had asked this thing.

11 And God said unto him, Because thou hast asked this thing, and hast not asked for thyself long life; neither hast asked riches for thyself, nor hast asked the life of thine enemies; but hast asked for thyself understanding to discern judgment;

12 Behold, I have done according to thy words: lo, I have given thee a wise and an understanding heart; so that there was none like thee before thee, neither after thee shall any arise like unto thee.

13 And I have also given thee that which thou hast not asked, both riches, and honour: so that

there shall not be any among the kings like unto thee all thy days.

14 And if thou wilt walk in my ways, to keep my statutes and my commandments, as thy father David did walk, then I will lengthen thy days.

In Focus

Michael awoke in his bedroom to find his wife frantically pulling out drawers and throwing clothes in the middle of the room. "What is it, Elizabeth?"

"It's my first day as manager in the corporate office and the outfit I bought is not right—and I can't find anything else appropriate to wear!"

Smiling at his lovely wife, Michael sat up straighter in bed.

"Liz, why are you worried? You have excellent taste and a closet full of clothes. I'm sure whatever you pick will be fine."

Liz was frantic. "You don't understand, baby, I have worked for this position for two years and I finally got it. My first impression has got to be on point. Everything has got to be perfect from head to toe."

Michael remained calm. "Give me your hands," he instructed his wife.

"What?" Liz replied. "I don't have time to play right now."

"Just give me your hands and let's pray," said Michael.

The couple sat down on the side of the bed and Michael prayed, "Dear God, my wife is very nervous today. She is starting in a new position and needs your help. Guide her and calm her spirit. Give her the confidence to walk worthy of the position you have seen fit to bless her with. In Jesus' name. Amen."

Liz opened her eyes and looked lovingly at her husband, kissed him, and said, "Thank you, man of God." She then proceeded to pick out her navy blue suit and a silk blouse. She dressed and left the house with a renewed confidence.

God hears and responds to people's prayers. In today's lesson, we see how Solomon prayed and asked God for discernment and courage to receive the wisdom He has promised to give us through prayer.

The People, Places, and Times

Gibeon. Located about six miles northwest of Jerusalem's Temple Mount, this ancient city is now known as el-Jib. Gibeon is located on a hill that rises 200 feet (62 meters) above the surrounding area. During the Old Testament era, this land was inhabited by the Gibeonites, also known as the Amorites. Gibeon was one of the ancient Canaanite cities marked for destruction during the time of Joshua. After witnessing the destruction of Jericho, the people of Gibeon recognized that God was on the side of the Children of Israel. Rather than enter into battle, the men of Gibeon tricked Joshua into making a peace covenant with them. In spite of this duplicity on the part of the men of Gibeon, God honored the covenant and ordered the Israelites to come to the aid of Gibeon when it was attacked by five Amorite kings. To ensure Israel's success, God caused the sun to remain in the sky and extended daylight for the battle.

Source

Packer, J. I., and M. C. Tenney, eds. *Illustrated Manners and Customs of the Bible.* Nashville, Tenn.: Thomas Nelson Publishers, 1980.

Background

As a young adult, Solomon ascends to the throne of Israel, shortly before his father, David, dies. What a daunting position for Solomon, or for any young man! David's reign has been legendary. His legacy was as diverse as it was impressive: a dutiful shepherd, an accomplished musician, a fierce warrior, a skillful statesman. As impressive as David's accomplishments were, however, his lifetime love of God was equally as impressive. However, David was not perfect. During his lifetime, he did commit sins, including adultery and murder. Yet, in spite of this, David had a deep and abiding trust in the one true God. Even after sinning, David was humble enough to acknowledge and repent of his sins.

God honored David's faithfulness to Him. It is with David that God enters into one of the greatest biblical covenants. The Davidic Covenant promised that the kingship would remain in David's family forever. The crucial significance of this covenant is that it provided the Messiah, Jesus, a legal heir, with both the legal and identifiable right to the throne of David.

David's abiding devotion to God was echoed in his words to Solomon as he blesses his son and appoints him to the throne: "I go the way of all the earth: be thou strong, therefore, and shew thyself a man; and keep the charge of the LORD your God to walk in his ways, to keep his statutes, and his commandments, and his testimonies, as it is written in the law of Moses, that you mayest prosper in all that thou doest and whithersoever thou turnest" (1 Kings 2:2–3). Here, David reiterates his confidence and trust that as long as his son remained faithful to God and kept God's law, God would be faithful to Solomon and bless his reign.

1. Solomon Demonstrates His Love for God
(1 Kings 3:3–4)
2. Solomon Expresses His Humility
(vv. 5–7)
3. Solomon Requests God's Aid (vv. 8–9)
4. Solomon's Unselfishness Is Rewarded
(vv. 10–14)

In Depth

1. Solomon Demonstrates His Love for God (1 Kings 3:3–4)

That Solomon loved the Lord should not be surprising to us. His father, David, had loved the Lord. One of the finest gifts any parent can share with his or her child is a love for and devotion to God. It is hard to imagine that David would not have shared his experiences with his young son. God had selected, protected, nurtured, elevated, chastened, and forgiven David throughout his lifetime. David's relationship with God was characterized by his unfailing belief that God was always with him and He would hear and answer his prayers. It was this confidence in his covenant relationship with the Lord that inspired David to declare, "The Lord is my shepherd; I shall not want" (Psalm 23:1).

This unique intimacy between David and God served to set the standard for all of Israel's subsequent kings. In the book of 1 Kings we see the expression "David his father" repeated again and again. We may often say that we love someone, but the proof is more clearly demonstrated in how we express that love. Do we love others enough to "please" them? In the case of Solomon, the Scriptures are clear that he offered God more than mere lip service. Solomon's love for the Lord included following his father David's customs and manners. This implies that Solomon praised and worshiped God in the way that his father had done.

Interestingly, the Scripture points out that the site of Solomon's worship differed from David's. Solomon "sacrificed and burnt incense in high places," a reference to the hilly region of Gibeon and not the sanctuaries of Jerusalem. Biblical scholars have wrestled with this discrepancy in worship locale. Some take the position that this is a clear indication that Solomon's earlier marriage to the Egyptian Pharaoh's daughter was the beginning of Solomon's seduction into idolatry. Others, however, argue that this marriage simply amounted to shrewd political alliance to strengthen his kingdom. These scholars argue that references to worshiping in high places are simply a declaration of fact. They point to the clear biblical declaration that "the people sacrificed in high places, because there was no house built unto the name of the Lord, until those days" (1 Kings 3:2). Subsequent kings were instructed to remove and tear down the high places because the proper place for worship was in the temple. However, at this time, the temple had not yet been built.

2. Solomon Expresses His Humility (vv. 5–7)

We are told that Solomon's worship at Gibeon included the sacrificing of "a thousand burnt offerings" (v. 4). The magnitude of the offering suggests that this was an occasion of national importance. More importantly, we should note not only that Solomon shows his love for God by following His statutes, but also that he is an active worshiper!

Following the large-scale sacrifice, "the Lord appeared to Solomon in a dream" (v. 5). Like young Samuel, who was beckoned by God at Shiloh during the quiet hours of the evening, Solomon is called for a divine consultation. God asks Solomon what it is that he wants. What a marvelous opportunity this was for Solomon! The same God who had led the Children of Israel out of Egyptian bondage, parted the waters of the Red Sea, and led them with a pillar of cloud by day and a pillar of fire by night was now asking to be allowed to grant Solomon anything he wanted!

The young king's answer is surprising. Solomon does not ask for material wealth or personal notoriety. These qualities would certainly have bolstered his position as king, especially among the peoples living in the surrounding areas. Solomon could have asked God for anything at all, but he does not.

Instead, in a touching demonstration of personal humility, Solomon acknowledges his shortcomings and simply asks for wisdom.

Although it is implicit from the text that Solomon knows that it is the Lord God who is speaking to him, it is interesting to note how Solomon continually refers to himself as a "servant." Solomon humbly acknowledges that, although he is king, he is now addressing the sovereign of the universe. Solomon begins by stating that he is aware God had shown "great mercy" toward David. In spite of his youth and inexperience, Solomon is keenly aware that his father's greatness was entirely the result of God's benevolence toward David. David's accomplishments did not come by his ability; rather, they were the direct results of divine acts of love and mercy.

3. Solomon Requests God's Aid (vv. 8–9)

Solomon goes on to candidly admit that he is following in his father's footsteps, and that he feels childlike. This indicates, perhaps, that Solomon feels ill equipped to assume the responsibilities of kingship. While Israel's first two kings, Saul and David, were charged with conquering the land, it is left to the young Solomon to organize the spiritual, political, and administrative infrastructure of the nation. Solomon alone is now responsible for the spiritual, social, and economic well-being of God's chosen people.

Additionally, the use of the word "govern" indicates that Solomon's role as king involves judicial as well as executive powers. Hence, Solomon is Israel's chief executive officer, chief financial officer, commander-in-chief, senate, and supreme court! Solomon realizes that governing Israel will require a wise and understanding heart (v. 9). The word "heart" is used figuratively here. The desires, intellectual reasoning, passions, and purposes of a man are all described as matters of the heart. It is only right that Solomon address this matter to God. He recognizes, as did David, that God is the examiner of hearts (1 Samuel 16:7; Jeremiah 17:10). Solomon is not satisfied to simply rule God's people; he wants to provide them with godly leadership. Solomon requests discernment—the godly ability to reason and make

wise decisions—so he can govern God's people wisely and lovingly.

4. Solomon's Unselfishness Is Rewarded (vv. 10–13)

Solomon's selfless and heartfelt request for wisdom pleased the Lord. It is not surprising that God would honor such a request. We should remember that Solomon's request is made within the context of willful obedience and active worship, and that his request for wisdom is made of the very source of all wisdom. Solomon, by his request for a wise and understanding heart to lead God's people, puts God first. Not only does God give Solomon what he asks for, but He blesses the young king with the things he does not ask for: riches and honor.

The blessing of wisdom that God grants Solomon will make him renowned throughout the world and throughout the ages, "so that there was none like [Solomon] before thee, neither after thee shalt any arise like unto thee" (v. 12). The biblical books penned by Solomon—Song of Solomon, Proverbs, and Ecclesiastes—as well as his psalms all attest to his divinely inspired wisdom. Solomon's wisdom would make him as well known as King David himself. Verse 9 points out that Solomon is expected to continue his devotion and faithfulness to the one true God. It is interesting to note here that although God blesses him, Solomon retains the right to choose to do good, to turn away from wickedness, and to serve God. His faithfulness, while a condition of God's continued blessing, is not compulsory. Like us, Solomon must choose to honor the God who so richly blesses and honors those who honor Him.

Search the Scriptures

Fill in the blanks.

1. "And _____ loved the Lord, walking in the statutes of _____, his father: only he sacrificed and burnt incense in _____ places" (1 Kings 3:3).

2. "In _____ the Lord appeared to Solomon in a ____ by night: and God said, Ask what I shall give thee" (v. 5).

3. "And I have also given thee that which thou hast

not asked, both _____ , and _____: so that there shall not be any among the kings like unto thee all thy days" (v. 13).

4. "And if thou wilt walk in my _____, to keep my statutes and my _____, as thy father David did walk, then I will lengthen thy days" (v. 14).

Discuss the Meaning

1. The term "servant leader" is very much in vogue right now. It is bandied about in both religious and secular circles. What, in your opinion, is a servant leader? Does Solomon demonstrate any of the characteristics of a servant leader? If so, which qualities do we see in these Scriptures?

2. What does the fact that God grants Solomon more than what Solomon requests tell us about God's response to our heartfelt prayers?

3. What does Solomon's request for wisdom tell us about the human wisdom he already had?

Lesson in Our Society

Solomon's request for wisdom points out that God hears and answers the prayers of His beloved; it also clearly demonstrates that He values a God-centered worshiper. Although Solomon was the king of Israel, we see that he never loses sight of the fact that he is not in control. Instead, Solomon recognizes, as did his father, David, that God reigns supreme and that His authority extends over all, including kings!

Whatever positions of authority we hold, we must remember that they are from a benevolent God. We cannot reign over any areas of our lives unless we have allowed God to reign over all areas of our lives.

What a mistake it is for Christians to believe that true success—whether it be educational, financial, or commercial—can be ours even if we are unwilling to walk in faithful obedience to God's will. It is only when we are willing to be submissive to the authority of God that we can walk in the majesty and fullness of His blessings and promises.

Make It Happen

Write Matthew 7:7 on a small index card. Next, make a list of all the prayer requests that you have

made in the last 10 days. Begin each morning and end each evening reading Matthew 7:7. By the end of the week, you should have this Scripture memorized. Set aside some quiet time this week to prayerfully and carefully review your Prayer Request list. Be honest with yourself as you look at each request. Does the request benefit anyone other than you? Are the requests consistent with biblical principles and beliefs? Are they made within the context of godly living?

Follow the Spirit

What God wants me to do:

_____
_____

Remember Your Thoughts

Special insights I have learned:

_____
_____

More Light on the Text
1 Kings 3:3–14

3 And Solomon loved the LORD, walking in the statutes of David his father: only he sacrificed and burnt incense in high places. 4 And the king went to Gibeon to sacrifice there; for that was the great high place: a thousand burnt offerings did Solomon offer upon that altar.

In the opening verse of our text, King David is dead and his son, Solomon, has assumed the position of king over Israel. This was not an easy transition of power. Solomon's ascent to the throne was marked by the turmoil of David's household. David had sinned against God in forcing himself upon Bathsheba and ordering the death of her husband, Uriah (2 Samuel 11). Even though God had forgiven David, his sin would have historic consequences. His family would be plagued by calamity and instability (2 Samuel 12:9–14). The result was evident in the children David fathered with his several wives.

David's firstborn son, Amnon, raped his half-sister, Tamar, and was killed by her brother, Absalom. The event forced Absalom to flee, causing father and son to be estranged for several years. Absalom's return did not change his attitude toward his father or his family. Eventually, David was devastated by Absalom's cunning attempt to take the crown by civil war. In the end, Joab, David's military captain, went against David's orders and killed Absalom (2 Samuel 13–18).

Years later, believing David to be too old and ill to find out what he was doing, Solomon's half-brother, Adonijah, attempted to usurp the crown. David was told by Nathan, the prophet, and Bathsheba, Solomon's mother, of the rebellion. David acted swiftly and placed Solomon in position to rule with him in his last days. Thus, David, in effect, established his throne through Solomon before his death (1 Kings 1). This was in accordance with God's promise and David's desire (1 Chronicles 22:8–10).

When Solomon finally became king, he followed the example of worship set by his father. David had ruled Israel for 40 years, and his life had run the emotional gamut. The boy who killed Goliath also played a harp. The youngest son of Jesse would be king of Israel, but he also tended sheep while he wrote poetry to God. He hid from King Saul and lived in caves. He fought wars and commanded armies. He married one woman who rejected him (2 Samuel 6:14–23) and another for whom he committed murder (2 Samuel 12:9). He allowed his lust to overtake him and suffered the brutal deaths of several of his sons. Through it all, David's worship was based on his personal relationship with God and his knowledge of God. David loved God. He called out for mercy and purposed to follow God despite life's circumstances and his shortcomings. As a result, God blessed David. The greatest blessing was God's promise to establish David's throne forever (2 Samuel 7:16).

Solomon also loved God. The Hebrew term for "love" (*ahab*, **aw-hab**) means "affection" and has many applications. Solomon had affection for God because he knew that God had kept His promise to David and would keep His promise to him. Solomon's relationship with God was shaped by David's teaching him who Yahweh was. David had no doubt told Solomon the stories of how God had delivered him from the bear and the lion when he was just a shepherd boy (1 Samuel 17:34–36). When Solomon was a child,

his heart probably leaped when his father told him how he had faced Goliath in the name of the Lord God of Israel (1 Samuel 17:45–51). David probably took the child with him as he made sacrifices before the Lord and spoke of how God returned the ark to Israel (2 Samuel 6).

Because of David's teaching, Solomon knew to follow the religious traditions of his father. He recognized what God had done in elevating him to the throne; therefore, he sacrificed unto the Lord in the manner of the Israelites. Since there was no temple, however, these rituals were customarily performed in the highest mountains. For example, when Samuel made the circuit throughout Israel to judge the people, he presented sacrifices in the mountainous high places of the area (1 Samuel 9:12). The tabernacle and the brazen altar that Moses had built remained in Gibeon, a mountain city five or six miles northwest of Jerusalem (1 Chronicles 16:37–40). The people often sacrificed in Gibeon. *The Message Bible*, a paraphrase edition, calls Gibeon "the most prestigious of the local shrines" (1 Kings 3:4).

God also encouraged the Israelites to build personal altars and present sacrifices. "Wherever I cause my name to be honored, I will come to you and bless you" (Exodus 20:24–26, NIV). It is in this tradition that David erected a tent to house the Ark of the Covenant after it had been rescued from the Philistines. Here, David worshiped the Lord.

Solomon has a choice, and he chooses to worship God at Gibeon, the highest elevation in the area. There, Solomon's enormous sacrifice of 1,000 burnt offerings upon the brazen altar would be seen and spoken of by all. Solomon does not sin by sacrificing at Gibeon. He is not inappropriate in his display of gratitude to God. After all, he is the king, and the people should know that he worships Yahweh, as his father had. Second Chronicles 1:2–3 says that a great number of the dignitaries and rulers of Israel make the pilgrimage with Solomon to present the sacrifice. This would require a large offering because each person has to present a sacrifice before God. Solomon did the right thing in presenting himself and the sacrifice before the Lord.

5 In Gibeon the LORD appeared to Solomon in a dream by night: and God said, Ask what I shall give thee. 6 And Solomon said, Thou hast shewed unto thy servant David my father great mercy, according as he walked before thee in truth, and in righteousness, and in uprightness of heart with thee; and thou hast kept for him this great kindness, that thou hast given him a son to sit on his throne, as it is this day.

The Lord indeed meets Solomon at Gibeon, but the beginning of Solomon's true relationship with God does not take place during the sacrifice. In the still of the night, long after Solomon has gone before the Lord, God visits him in a dream. We've all had dreams that were so powerful that they seemed like real experiences; however, Solomon's dream was more than a visual play of the mind. His dream is reminiscent of Jacob's dream of a ladder leading to heaven (Genesis 28:12) and Joseph's dream of dominion over his brothers (Genesis 37:5–10). God speaks to us through the revelation of His written Word, but Solomon did not have access to the complete Scripture as we do today. Solomon's dream was a prophetic visitation from the Lord.

The term "Lord" is rendered from the Hebrew name for Yahweh, the self-existent one. God needs nothing. Solomon comes before God with the royal trappings of his office and obediently offered his sacrifice; Yahweh neither needs nor is impressed with any show of religiosity. Therefore, the Lord chooses to speak to Solomon away from the busyness of the king's day and the royal entourage that accompanies him.

By addressing Solomon when he least expects it, God leaves him without defenses. Solomon does not have time to strategize. There is no opportunity for a flowery speech. God does not want lavish words; He wants a humble heart. This is not the time for Solomon to be petty or coy; he has to be honest with God. Rather than just bestowing blessings upon Solomon, the Lord urges Solomon to beseech him—to ask with earnest candor and passion for what he wants and needs from God.

Solomon begins his prayer by thanking God for the gracious kindnesses and mercy he had shown to his father, David, who had always come to God with

"truth, and in righteousness, and in uprightness of heart." The word "truth" (Heb. *emeth*, **eh'-meth**) means that David was steadfast in his relationship with Yahweh. David was far from perfect, but he was honest with God, who had saved him from death numerous times, and comforted him in his distress over and over again. No matter what the problem or how deep the shame, David was real with the Lord. He was humble, always seeking God's forgiveness when he failed. As a result, David had been encouraged when he was at his lowest point, and was forgiven when his sin was beyond human understanding. In his heart, the very core of his faith and person, David sought to be morally correct (righteous and upright) before God. Solomon was thankful for the mercy and covenant faithfulness shown to his father.

Next, Solomon acknowledges that his position as leader of a mighty nation is not due to his own brilliance or prowess. Solomon was not David's oldest son. He was not the son who had proven himself triumphant in war or exemplary in the political arena. Solomon was the son God selected to establish David's throne. His appointment is by God's grace and because of God's faithfulness in keeping His promise to David. That faithfulness continued as God allows Solomon to request whatever he wants as the new ruler of Israel.

7 And now, O LORD my God, thou hast made thy servant king instead of David my father: and I am but a little child: I know not how to go out or come in. 8 And thy servant is in the midst of thy people which thou hast chosen, a great people, that cannot be numbered nor counted for multitude.

Before making his request known, Solomon humbles himself. By accepting the title of "servant," Solomon acknowledges that his purpose is to bring honor to his master, Almighty God. Solomon personalizes his prayer for his situation and his time in a way that is almost reminiscent of the old gospel song refrain, "It's me. It's me. It's me, oh Lord, standing in the need of prayer." The passion of a broken spirit can be heard in Solomon's tone. We can almost imagine him falling to his knees and bursting into tears. In this new relationship between Solomon and the Lord, Solomon presents himself to God, not as the king, but as the servant of the self-existent One.

Second, Solomon refers to himself as a child—a little child. Of course, he is not speaking in a chronological sense. The first verse of this chapter indicates that Solomon is a grown and married man. He had been raised in the court of his father and had been privy to David's teaching; however, Solomon recognized that in this new position he was expected to lead his people and to stand with kings of many nations. He was uncertain of where to begin ("go out") or how to reach the desired end ("come in"). The task before him was daunting, and Solomon honestly and humbly confesses that to God. Being overwhelmed is a human failing that often does not get confessed, but Solomon was not hesitant to confess his inadequacies and admit his feelings of insecurity. He stands before God in prayer with "childlike" faith. Solomon realizes that only through God's power and might can he accomplish the tasks ahead.

Solomon also declares that the people he was to lead belonged to God. God had chosen them and had multiplied their numbers so that they had become a great nation. God had delivered them from Pharaoh's army (Exodus 14). He had kept them in the wilderness for 40 years, eating the food He provided and wearing the shoes and clothes He preserved (Deuteronomy 29:5–6). He had allowed Israel to possess the land and had protected them from the surrounding nations. Solomon realizes that any authority he had was for the protection and support of the people whom God had created and placed in his charge. The people belonged to God, and Solomon intended to honor them as God's possession.

9 Give therefore thy servant an understanding heart to judge thy people, that I may discern between good and bad: for who is able to judge this thy so great a people?

Now that Solomon had thanked God and humbled himself before the Lord, he made his request known. Solomon asks for an understanding heart. The word "understanding" (Heb. shama, **shaw-mah**) means to

have power to listen to, obey, or perceive by ear. Solomon wants to be able to listen to the people and determine what should be done. The word "judge" (Heb. shaphat, **shaw-fat'**) means "to govern, vindicate, punish, or decide controversy." Solomon recognizes his responsibility in civil cases and in identifying the direction he must take in governing the nation in all matters.

Solomon asks for discernment. He wants an understanding of good and evil. Knowing the facts would not be enough. Solomon realizes that he must render decisions for the betterment of the nation. He also wants to make decisions that are "good" (Heb. towb, **tobe**), which means "morally pleasing and excellent." Essentially, Solomon asks for the wisdom to do that which pleases God first and then man. In seeking wisdom by which he would recognize that which is evil or bad (Heb. ra, **rah**), Solomon is requesting to know when something is essentially of no moral value and below God's expectation. Thus, Solomon is asking for a discerning heart by which he could please God and bless God's people.

The history of Israel had taught Solomon that the task before him was arduous. Many had ruled before him, but not all had succeeded. Perhaps Solomon was remembering the judges who had ruled Israel and had been victorious, like Deborah (Judges 4:5). He may have been thinking about Gideon, who struggled with his own insecurities (Judges 6:11, 15, 36–40), or he may have been reflecting upon Samson, who disgraced himself before his nation and his enemies (Judges 14:2–3; 16:27). Possibly, Solomon was recalling his father's struggle to do what was right in the cases that came before him, or King Saul's failure as a leader (1 Samuel 13:13–14). Perhaps Solomon was again acknowledging that the nation of Israel was God's precious possession (Deuteronomy 14:2). We do not know what prompted Solomon's question, but he recognizes that no human being acting in his own power and intellect could govern such a nation—especially the nation that belonged to God.

10 And the speech pleased the Lord, that Solomon had asked this thing. 11 And God said unto him,

Because thou hast asked this thing, and hast not asked for thyself long life; neither hast asked riches for thyself, nor hast asked the life of thine enemies; but hast asked for thyself understanding to discern judgment;

God is pleased with what Solomon *does not* say. He is satisfied with Solomon's not asking for long life. Solomon's work was to reign until the time when God would remove him. Solomon is not concerned about how long his reign will last: the almighty God, who had been merciful and gracious to David, could be depended on to care for the life of the king.

Had Solomon asked for riches, he would have been seeking to satisfy his own temporal desires rather than seeking God's desire for His people. Solomon's non-request for wealth was a confession that God would supply his need. Solomon was not looking to be known for his wealth, but for his upright judgment of God's people.

A request for the life of one's enemy seems totally unselfish, but God renders judgment and holds the power of life and death in His hand (Deuteronomy 32:35). Solomon's prayer indicates a primary care for the people of God and their needs. Solomon would rely on God to fight the battles with those who sought to harm the king or the nation. The same God who had protected David would provide for the nation and protect it on every side. God was pleased! Solomon had not asked amiss.

12 Behold, I have done according to thy words: lo, I have given thee a wise and an understanding heart; so that there was none like thee before thee, neither after thee shall any arise like unto thee. 13 And I have also given thee that which thou hast not asked, both riches, and honour: so that there shall not be any among the kings like unto thee all thy days.

While Solomon had no way of knowing it, God had already prepared him for the task ahead. In Solomon's mind, leading the nation was an immeasurable responsibility, but God had already seen what Solomon would need and had provided for him. In fact, God vowed to give Solomon both what he had asked and what he had not asked! As Paul would later write, God is "able to do exceeding abundantly above all that we ask or think" (Ephesians 3:20).

God had much more for Solomon than he could ever have requested. God's blessing so far exceeded Solomon's request that God Himself declares that there had never been a person of such wisdom, wealth, and honor before, nor would there be one to rival Solomon in all the years to come. God favors Solomon as He had never favored another human being. Honor and riches would belong to Solomon because of God's unmerited favor. Solomon had not asked for this overwhelming generosity; God was generous because He is worthy of praise and is faithful to keep His promises.

14 And if thou wilt walk in my ways, to keep my statutes and my commandments, as thy father David did walk, then I will lengthen thy days.

Solomon had declared himself a servant and had asked for wisdom only. God saw fit to further bestow upon him fame and fortune. But Solomon would not be given the opportunity to take God for granted. The word "if" placed a condition on the final blessing: to receive long life. Solomon must walk before God as David had.

Why this condition? Why not, "If you will build me a house" or "If you will write words of wisdom for others to follow?" It appears that this conditional blessing takes us back to our opening verse, 1 Kings 3:3. Solomon worshiped in the "high place." God warned Israel about high places because the surrounding Gentile nations worshiped their gods in the mountains. Although Israel was told to tear down the altars to the pagan idols (Deuteronomy 12:2–3), she failed to eradicate idol worship. While Solomon's sacrifice was offered with integrity, his marriage to an Egyptian princess (1 Kings 3:1) foreshadowed his acceptance of the worship of false gods. God knew that Solomon had a tendency to accommodate himself to the customs of the day and to the cultural activities of his time, and to engage in political bargaining with the nations around him, who did not worship the Lord. God wanted only Solomon's undivided worship and praise. He wanted from Solomon what David, with all of his shortcomings, had never failed to give: total commitment to Yahweh, his God.

The walk, or lifestyle, of the king would be important. If the king followed God, the nation would also. If the king turned to follow other gods, the nation would be scattered and confused. Solomon's walk was more than just his personal journey with God. He was responsible for the entire nation, the people whom God had chosen, who were "a great people, that cannot be numbered nor counted for multitude" (v. 8). Solomon was to follow the path that God had placed before him so that the people would not stray from God's words. By putting God first in his life, Solomon would "keep" (Heb. *shamar*, **shaw-mar**), observe, or give heed to God's covenant law. Not only would Solomon know God and know how to honor Him, but the nation would glorify God as well.

If Solomon does not turn away, God will grant him long life. This conditional promise to Solomon echoes the Ten Commandments (Exodus 20:12). If Solomon honors the tradition and example of his father, God will give him longevity. However, Solomon will have to follow God with his whole heart to please and honor Him and to sustain his own life and reign.

God's promises are sure. He promised David that Solomon would sit upon the throne of Israel. We know now that God's promise ultimately meant that Jesus Christ would sit upon the throne forever. Solomon thanks God for the people. We now know that both Jews and Gentiles are included in God's plan of salvation. God promises Solomon that his life will be long upon the earth only if he continued to honor Him. We now know that, through Jesus Christ, God has given us eternal life. God kept His promises to David and Solomon, and He keeps His promises to us. We can confidently go to God in prayer, humbly asking for His wisdom in all things.

Sources

McGee, J. Vernon. "Thru the Bible: Notes on 1 Kings 3." *Precepts For Living*® CD-ROM. Chicago: Urban Ministries, Inc., 2005.

"The Message Bible." *Precepts For Living*® CD-ROM. Chicago: Urban Ministries, Inc., 2005.

Daily Bible Readings

M: The Incomparable Worth of Wisdom
Proverbs 1:1–7
T: Where Is Wisdom Found?
Job 28:12–28
W: Add to Wisdom Understanding
Psalm 119:97–104
T: Solomon Chosen to Be King
1 Kings 1:28–40
F: Solomon Requests Wisdom
1 Kings 3:3–9
S: God Answers Solomon's Request
1 Kings 3:10–15
S: Solomon Was Wise
1 Kings 4:29–34

TEACHING TIPS

November 5
Bible Study Guide 10

1. Words You Should Know

A. Halt (1 Kings 18:21) *pacach* (Heb.)—To skip or limp. In this context, the word implies hesitating to make a decision.

B. Dress (v. 23) *asah* (Heb.)—To prepare.

C. Bullock (v. 23) *par* (Heb.)—A young calf or ox.

2. Teacher Preparation

A. To review and become more conversant with this text, read 1 Kings 17 and 18 in their entirety.

B. Read the Focal Verses in several modern translations. Make sure to take notes.

C. Complete lesson 10 from the *Precepts For Living® Personal Study Guide*.

D. During your personal devotions, meditate on the passage for Devotional Reading and the Daily Bible Readings for this week's lesson.

E. Read the Bible Background Scriptures to gain insight into today's lesson.

3. Starting the Lesson

A. Ask for a volunteer to open the class with prayer.

B. Have the students read the Lesson Aim.

4. Getting into the Lesson

A. Spend a few minutes determining what your students know about the prophet Elijah and King Ahab.

B. Ask for volunteers to read The People, Places, and Times and the Background sections.

5. Relating the Lesson to Life

A. Have the students divide into small groups and answer the Search the Scriptures questions together.

B. Assign each of the small groups one of the Discuss the Meaning questions. After the groups have discussed the question, have a representative from each group report back to the class.

C. Ask for a volunteer to read the In Focus and Lesson in Our Society sections. If time permits, allow the group to discuss the implications of each.

6. Arousing Action

A. Close the lesson by reading the Keep in Mind verse.

B. Give the reading assignment for the week, and encourage the students to use the Daily Bible Readings for their personal devotions.

C. Before closing the class, ask for prayer requests and praise reports. Then ask for a volunteer to close the class with prayer.

Worship Guide

For the Superintendent or Teacher
Theme: Elijah Triumphs with God
Theme Song: "King Jesus Is A-Listenin'"
Scripture: 1 Kings 18:39
Song: "What a Mighty God We Serve"
Meditation: Lord, You alone are a mighty God. Thank You for being the source of my strength and for always being present in my times of need. Amen.

ELIJAH TRIUMPHS WITH GOD

Bible Background • 1 Kings 18:20–39
Printed Text • 1 Kings 18:20–24, 30–35, 38–39   Devotional Reading • PSALM 86:8–13

Lesson Aim

By the end of the lesson, we will:

KNOW that God's power is absolute—He can do anything He wishes to do;

REFLECT on how God demonstrated His power to the Israelites and how it is demonstrated to us today; and

COMMIT to trusting in God's absolute power and depending on it to work in our lives.

Keep in Mind

"And when all the people saw it, they fell on their faces; and they said, The LORD, he is the God; the LORD, he is the God" (1 Kings 18:39).

Focal Verses

1 Kings 18:20 So Ahab sent unto the children of Israel, and gathered the prophets together to mount Carmel.

21 And Elijah came unto all the people, and said, How long halt ye between two opinions? If the LORD be God, follow him: but if Baal, then follow him. And the people answered him not a word.

22 Then said Elijah unto the people, I, even I only, remain a prophet of the LORD; but Baal's prophets are four hundred and fifty men.

23 Let them therefore give us two bullocks; and let them choose one bullock for themselves, and cut it in pieces, and lay it on the wood, and put no fire under: and I will dress the other bullock, and lay it on the wood, and put no fire under:

24 And call ye on the name of your gods, and I will call on the name of the LORD: and the God that answereth by fire, let him be God. And all the people answered and said, It is well spoken.

18:30 And Elijah said unto all the people, Come near unto me. And all the people came near unto him. And he repaired the altar of the LORD that was broken down.

31 And Elijah took twelve stones, according to the number of the tribes of the sons of Jacob, unto whom the word of the LORD came, saying, Israel shall be Thy name:

32 And with the stones he built an altar in the name of the LORD: and he made a trench about the altar, as great as would contain two measures of seed.

33 And he put the wood in order, and cut the bullock in pieces, and laid him on the wood, and said, Fill four barrels with water, and pour it on the burnt sacrifice, and on the wood.

34 And he said, Do it the second time. And they did it the second time. And he said, Do it the third time. And they did it the third time.

35 And the water ran round about the altar; and he filled the trench also with water.

18:38 Then the fire of the LORD fell, and consumed the burnt sacrifice, and the wood, and the stones, and the dust, and licked up the water that was in the trench.

39 And when all the people saw it, they fell on their faces: and they said, The LORD, he is the God; the LORD, he is the God.

In Focus

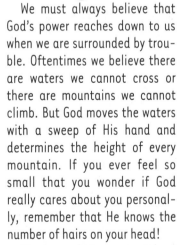

We must always believe that God's power reaches down to us when we are surrounded by trouble. Oftentimes we believe there are waters we cannot cross or there are mountains we cannot climb. But God moves the waters with a sweep of His hand and determines the height of every mountain. If you ever feel so small that you wonder if God really cares about you personally, remember that He knows the number of hairs on your head!

If you need His power, take a step of faith by saying, "I'm going to make a fresh commitment to my marriage." Or the step of faith may take the form of becoming a part of a small group or joining a ministry. When your mind says, "That's what God wants me to do," that's your first step of faith.

You might say, "I don't have the strength to do that on my own. God, give me the strength to do what I can't do on my own." That's how faith grows.

Don't wait until you feel powerful or confident enough to take that step—because you never will. Take the step in spite of the fact that you feel weak, fearful, or even faithless. That's what faith is all about. God does not release His power *before* you take that first step of faith, but it is there the moment *after* you take the step of faith. That's how you learn to depend on God's power in everyday life.

When Elijah cried out, God demonstrated His power to the Israelites. Today's lesson illustrates that we are never as alone as we may feel; God's power is always there with us and for us.

The People, Places, and Times

King Ahab. King of the northern kingdom of Israel, Ahab succeeded his father Omri to the throne and became Israel's seventh king. While none of Israel's northern kings actually served God fully, Ahab is perhaps the most infamous of divided Israel's monarchs. The Bible notes that "Ahab the son of Omri did more evil in the sight of the Lord, above all that were before him" (1 Kings 16:30). Ahab's 22-year reign was marked by his willful disobedience to the laws of God and his sponsorship of the pagan gods, the Baals and the Ashtoreths. This idol worship was probably introduced by his equally infamous wife, Jezebel, a princess of the pagan kingdom of Zidon. Under his direction, a temple for Baal was erected as well as a sacred pole to honor Ashtoreth (vv. 30–33). Rituals of this worship included prostitution and the sacrifice of children. In spite of Ahab's wickedness, God twice defends him and the people of Israel from attacks by Syria's King Ben-hadad.

Ahab's most detestable act was allowing the prophets of God to be slaughtered. It was only through the actions of Obadiah that the remaining 100 prophets were hidden in caves and their lives

spared (18:3–4, 13–14; 19:10). A confrontation between Ahab's prophets and the prophet Elijah at Mount Carmel proved to the people of Israel that the Lord God was the only true God.

Source
Packer, J. I., and M. C. Tenney, eds. *Illustrated Manners and Customs of the Bible.* Nashville, Tenn.: Thomas Nelson Publishers, 1980.

Background

In the opening verses of 1 Kings 18, a severe famine has beset Israel for three years, and Elijah is commanded to come out of exile and confront the wicked King Ahab. We should note the importance of Elijah's steadfast allegiance and obedience to God. Hundreds of other prophets have been "put to the sword" at the king's command. The remaining 150 prophets are alive only because they have been hidden in caves by Obadiah, a man in the king's household who "feared the Lord greatly" (v. 3).

At this point, we know very little about Elijah. He is from Tishbe in Gilead, located east of the Jordan River. In Israel's political circles, Elijah is a newcomer, an unknown. What quickly becomes apparent is that Elijah is on a divine mission. He tells Ahab that he has been sent from the Lord "before whom," he declares, " I stand" (v. 15). Elijah is figuratively throwing down the gauntlet at the king's feet. He has been commissioned by God and has the authority to speak on His behalf.

At-A-Glance

1. Elijah Demands a Decision
(1 Kings 18:20–22)
2. Elijah Challenges Baal Followers
(vv. 23–24)
3. Elijah Rebuilds the Altar to God
(vv. 30–35)
4. Elijah Demonstrates that the Lord God Is God (vv. 38–39)

In Depth

1. Elijah Demands a Decision (1 Kings 18:20–22)

The confrontation between Elijah and Ahab is immediately antagonistic. Ahab accuses Elijah of being the "troubler of Israel" (v. 17, NIV). This insult clearly indicates that he views the drought and subsequent famine as a problem caused by Elijah. Ahab refuses to acknowledge that his sinful apostasy is related to this national calamity. When Elijah instructs the king to "gather all Israel to me at Mount Carmel" (v. 19, NLT), we should take this to mean a representative body of Israel, as the location itself would have prohibited a national assembly of the entire kingdom. Additionally, the king is instructed to bring the prophets of the Baals and the Asherahs, some 850 in total, to Mount Carmel.

When the people gather at Mount Carmel, Elijah again boldly steps forward for God. We must remember that Elijah stands alone confronting the people. The other prophets of the Lord God have either been murdered or are hiding in caves. It is safe to assume that the representatives of Israel gathered at Mount Carmel belong to the majority of the Israelites, who were worshiping Baal. In spite of the isolation and risk involved in this mission, Elijah immediately confronts the people with their guilty indecision and rebukes them for their sins.

On Mount Carmel, Elijah accuses Israel of refusing to commit themselves to the true Lord God. They were, he implies, sitting on the fence and refusing to decide whether they would pledge their allegiance to the God of Jacob or to Baal and the other false gods. While the people of Israel most certainly maintained a belief in the Lord God, their commitment to him had been compromised by idol worship. No doubt many of them feared repercussions from Ahab and Jezebel. We are told, however, that a faithful remnant refused to bow down to Baal (19:18). Jesus taught that "no man can serve two masters; for either he will hate the one and love the other, or else he will be loyal to the one and despise the other" (Matthew 6:24, NLT). In 1 Kings 18, we see Elijah being painfully direct with the people. Israel, he is saying, cannot remain indecisive.

Elijah, sounding like an echo of Joshua's final speech, tells them they must choose whom they will serve.

The people's response to this moving challenge is shocking: "And the people did not answer him a word" (v. 21, RSV). It is reasonable to assume that, in the face of Elijah's truth, there was nothing for them to say. They certainly could not deny that they were worshiping false idols. Nor was there any possible justification they could offer for this grievous sin.

2. Elijah Challenges Baal Followers (vv. 23–24)

Elijah goes on to propose a contest to determine whether God or Baal and the others were the true God. In this contest, Elijah and the prophets of the idol gods would each build an altar and prepare a sacrifice of a bullock, but neither party was to light the customary altar fire. Instead, each would pray and ask their deity to send a fire to ignite the sacrifice. Elijah proposed that whichever deity responded would be recognized as the true God, and the loser would be abandoned by the people.

This contest appears to have taken place in the early morning, and, perhaps, to remove any question about the fairness of the contest, Elijah allows the prophets of Baal to go first. After preparing the altar and killing the bullock, the prophets begin to call on Baal to send down fire. When their calls go unheeded, the prophets resort to shouting and dancing; finally, they began to mutilate themselves. This frenzied behavior continues through the day and into the evening. Elijah begins to ridicule Baal and the false prophets. In keeping with the terms of the contest, Elijah declares their attempts (i.e., their gods) a failure.

3. Elijah Rebuilds the Altar to God (vv. 30–35)

After the failure of the priests of the idol gods to call down fire, Elijah summons the people of Israel to come forward. No doubt Elijah wanted them to see firsthand the power of God that was about to be demonstrated. The first thing Elijah does is to rebuild the altars to the Lord God that had been neglected through the years. Elijah kills his bullock and prepares it for sacrifice. His next moves must have startled the onlookers. Elijah drenches the wood for his fire three separate times. So much water is used that it begins to run over the altar and fills a trench.

The people watching it must have thought the prophet had clearly lost his mind. On the face of things, it certainly is illogical to wet the wood one intends to burn. We must remember, however, that in the three-and-a-half years that God had kept Elijah safely hidden, Elijah had learned of the awesome power of God. The physical laws of nature were, Elijah knew, controlled by the Creator of the universe. In human terms, wetting wood makes it impossible to burn, but in divine terms there is nothing too hard for God! The prophets of Baal had screamed and cried and hurt themselves in an attempt to help Baal be god. Elijah knew that God did not need his help. Elijah had repaired the altar and prepared the sacrifice, but he did not prepare a fire. In fact, he wet the wood for the anticipated fire. Wetting the wood demonstrated to the assembly that God was indeed God and needed the assistance of no one.

4. Elijah Demonstrates that the Lord God Is God (vv. 38–39)

After saturating the altar with water, Elijah prays that God will manifest Himself and prove Himself to be the true God, and that the people gathered in witness would know this without a doubt. Elijah also states that the purpose of this divine demonstration is so that God will turn the "hearts" of the people He loves back to Himself.

As Elijah concludes his prayer, God responds. "The fire of the Lord" strikes the altar with such force that the wood, the sacrifice, and even the very stone altar are all "consumed," or destroyed. What a spectacular display of God's awesomeness this must have been to the onlookers! In their presence, God had demonstrated to Israel that He alone had the power to do what the idol god Baal, whom they had worshiped as the "lord of fire," could not do.

Elijah had previously challenged Israel to serve the one that was God. That the Lord God was God was apparent to everyone present, including the prophets of Baal. This same assembly that had been unable to answer his challenge to choose now "fell on their faces" and cried out, "The LORD, He is God! The LORD, He is God!" (v. 39, NLT).

Search the Scriptures

Fill in the blanks.

1. "So _____ sent unto the children of Israel, and gathered the _____ together to mount Carmel" (1 Kings 18:20).

2. "And _____ came unto all the people and said, How long halt ye between two _____ ? If the LORD be God, follow him: but if _____, then follow him" (v. 21).

3. "And call ye on the name of your _____ , and I will call on the name of the LORD: and the _____ that answereth by fire, let him be God. And all the people answered and said, It is ____ _____" (v. 24).

4. "And _____ said unto all the people, Come near unto me. And all the people came near unto him. And he _____ the altar of the LORD that was _____ _____" (v. 30).

5. "Then the _____ of the LORD fell, and consumed the _____ _____, and the wood, and the stones, and the dust, and licked up the _____ that was in the trench" (v. 38).

6. "And when all the people saw it, they fell on their ____: and they said, The _____, he is the God; the LORD, he is the _____" (v. 39).

Discuss the Meaning

1. After Elijah challenges the Children of Israel to choose to serve God or Baal, we are told that "the people answered him not a word." What does their silence tell you about them? Are today's Christians silent on any significant political or social issues? If so, what are some of these issues and why do you think we are silent?

2. In the face of certain death at the hands of King Ahab, Elijah boldly steps forward for God and

His truth. What do you think it takes for today's Christians to demonstrate this type of godly boldness?

3. Elijah, in his challenge to the people, asks them how long they intend to "halt," or hesitate, in choosing between God and Baal. This implies that their love for God was in conflict with their, perhaps, fear of something else. Is our love for God in conflict with our love for the world? How is our commitment to God affected? In what ways do you think our careers and our desires for personal accomplishments and material attainment conflict with our love for God? What is the result of that "halting" in our churches, our homes, and our society?

Lesson in Our Society

Today's lesson raises many questions for Christians. Perhaps the most significant question is *whom* are we going to serve? Rather than entrust our cares and concerns to Him who, Paul declares, "is able to do exceeding abundantly above all that we ask or think" (Ephesians 3:20), we mistakenly think that our future is in the hands of the modern-day Baals. Too often, it is to these man-made idols of power, prestige, and pleasure that we devote our time, energy, and attention. We think that, like the Children of Israel, we can straddle the fence. This ambivalence only inhibits our developing a total commitment to God. Christians are in a covenant relationship with God, who demands our faithfulness and singular devotion; He demands that we be totally His. He will not play "second fiddle" and share us.

In return for our faithfulness, He brings healing, strength, purpose, and joy into our lives—things that the man-made gods can never provide.

Make It Happen

Think about the areas in your life in which you have been less than confident that God has the solution to your situation. These areas may include your personal finances, employment, or education; your decision about choosing an appropriate life partner; or your relationship with your spouse, your parents, or your children. Select a quiet time to prayerfully consider what steps you have taken in these areas. Just what is it have you done to "fix" things? Now ask yourself, "Have I been trying to handle it on my own?" (Be honest.) If so, pray, surrender, and release the situation to God. Use your Bible to help you. Research those Scriptures that speak about submitting to God. Pay close attention to the biblical narratives that provide us with examples of people who have allowed God to reign in their lives, and note how He never fails to provide. When in doubt, reread today's lesson, and remember that you must choose.

Follow the Spirit

What God wants me to do:

_____

_____

Remember Your Thoughts

Special insights I have learned:

_____

_____

More Light on the Text
1 Kings 18:20–24, 30–35, 38–39

Demonstrating His divine power once again toward His beloved Israel, God stages a showdown between the faithful prophet Elijah and the faithless King Ahab. Elijah, whose name means "my God is Yahweh," lived in Israel during Ahab's reign and Jezebel's influence. Israel means "God prevails" and is the name used for and given to the northern kingdom, which consisted of the 10 tribes under Jeroboam; the southern kingdom was known as Judah.

Ahab, whose name means "father's brother" or "uncle," reigned over Israel from 919 to 896 B.C. and was the first king of Israel to take a heathen wife. Jezebel was a Baal worshiper. Baal means "lord" and was the name of the supreme male divinity of the Phoenicians and Canaanites. Introduced to the community by the king's wife, Jezebel, Baal worship became the national religion of the 10 tribes of Israel.

At this juncture of the journey of Israel's redemption, there is a three-and-a-half-year famine upon the land. There had been the mass murder of God's prophets by order of Ahab's heathen wife, Jezebel. There was a battle for power and provision. The people were distraught, and the leaders were desperate. Dire circumstances forced the king and the prophet into collaboration. At Mount Carmel, a mountain on the Mediterranean coast of northern Israel, the stage was set for God to "show up and to show out"!

20 So Ahab sent unto all the children of Israel, and gathered the prophets together unto mount Carmel.

After three-and-a-half years of famine, Ahab resorted to seeking a showdown with Elijah to relieve Israel's suffering. Calling all the people of Israel and his prophets, this Hebrew noun *nabiy'* (**naw-bee'**) refers to the false or heathen prophets of Baal, which Ahab sets up for the showdown at Mount Carmel.

21 And Elijah came unto all the people, and said, How long halt ye between two opinions? If the LORD be God, follow him: but if Baal, then follow him. And the people answered him not a word.

Elijah enters the scene posing a question so provocative that it leaves the people speechless. In essence he asks, "In light of the manner of oppression upon you since forsaking Yahweh and dabbling in Baal worship, how long will you live trying to serve two masters? What has to happen before you recommit to your covenant with YHWH? When will you get sick and tired of being sick and tired of your faithlessness?" Elijah challenges the people to consider where spiritual compromise had crept in, where deception had effectively divided their loyalty, and where the love of God had been sacrificed to the fear of man.

Elijah's question still echoes down the annals of prophetic history, asking us anew in the twenty-first century, "Why is your heart divided between God and prosperity, between God and hospitality,

between God and peace, between God and anything other than God?"

Conviction was so great that the people have no answer. Their ambivalence expressed by the Hebrew adjective *ca`iph* (**saw-eef'**), consists of worshiping God but serving Baal on the side. It could be compared to Christians who keep another "god" in their lives: substituting New Age language and other spiritual practices for continuing in the doctrines of the apostles and the breaking of bread, or preferring self-help groups to intimate and accountable Christian fellowship. The word "waver" presents a picture of "living with a limp!" Elijah challenges Israel to be healed of the spiritual limp that is stealing their comfort, abundance, and life. He urgently and emphatically pleads with Israel to make up their minds as to which god they would follow.

22 Then said Elijah unto the people, I, even I only, remain a prophet of the LORD; but Baal's prophets are four hundred and fifty men.

Many of God's prophets had been killed on Jezebel's orders, some had fled into remote and desolate caves, and others had been banished from the land. Assessing a situation some might have considered to be a grave disadvantage to Elijah and Yahweh, Elijah confirms that he is indeed the only prophet of the Lord who "remains" (Heb. *yathar*, **yaw-thar'**), meaning "spared" or "preserved alive and present." However, Elijah demonstrates faith in God by standing alone against idolatry. Even in the face of overwhelming odds of 450 to 1, Elijah's knowledge of and belief in God foster his unction to put God to the test.

23 Let them therefore give us two bullocks; and let them choose one bullock for themselves, and cut it in pieces, and lay it on wood, and put no fire under: and I will dress the other bullock, and lay it on wood, and put no fire under: 24 And call ye on the name of your gods, and I will call on the name of the LORD: and the God that answereth by fire, let him be God. And all the people answered and said, It is well spoken.

"And Elijah took twelve stones, according to the number of the tribes of the sons of Jacob...And with the stones he built an altar in the name of the LORD" (from 1 Kings 18:31, 32).

Resorting to efficiency and taking advantage of the stage set for a spectacular demonstration of God's ability to save and restore Israel's covenantal relationship, Elijah issues instructions using immediate, available, and simple props. Knowing that God could stand to be tested and could stand the test, Elijah levels the playing field by building identical altars with common and familiar supplies. Consider how God still does the miraculous through our common lives. All we have to do is be available to God!

Then, in verse 24, Elijah challenges the prophets

to "call" (Heb. *qara'*, **kaw-raw'**, meaning "to summon or invite"), their gods to the stage. Elijah offers to do the same. Both groups of people and prophets were to call "on the name" (Heb. *shem*, **shame,** meaning " reputation and infamy") of their perspective gods. Ever so confident in Yahweh, Elijah concludes that whichever god "answers" (Heb. *`anah*, **aw-naw'**), or responds to, the sacrifices would be worshiped as the one true God. These actions were understood by the people to be sacrifices that would move their deity's hand to end the drought. This divine act in response to the sacrifice would benefit everybody in the land—God's people of Israel and Baal worshipers alike—and would show which deity to glorify as supreme.

The response Elijah provoked was characteristically unusual for the situation. In the face of a famine and drought, Elijah does not pray for rain to water the earth, nourish vegetation, and grow food for the people. Instead, he prays for "fire" (Heb. *'esh*, **aysh**), expecting theophany (the temporal and spatial manifestation of God in some tangible form) accompanied by both natural flames and supernatural fire. Baal was also referred to as "lord of the fire" and was often depicted with a lightning bolt in his hand. The presence of fire, as understood by all the people, would indicate that the sacrifice was acceptable to their god.

Elijah stages this demonstration of faith against seemingly great odds: First, he was outnumbered by prophets; now, he was evoking the agency of power (fire) associated with Baal. The people agreed to his strategic plan for their salvation.

18:30 And Elijah said unto all the people, Come near unto me. And all the people came near unto him. And he repaired the altar of the LORD that was broken down.

Elijah beckons Israel to come close, to gather around him so that they could examine "up close and personal" the destruction done to the altar erected by Saul and the imminent deliverance by Yahweh. Israel watched as Elijah "repaired" (Heb. *rapha'*, **raw-faw'** meaning "healed") the altar that

had been erected by the hands of their ancestors of faith. This same altar had been "broken down" (Heb. *harac*, **haw-ras'**, meaning "ruined"), utterly destroyed, and desecrated during Jezebel's comprehensive strategic plan to institute Baal worship throughout the land.

31 And Elijah took twelve stones, according to the number of the tribes of the sons of Jacob, unto whom the word of the LORD came, saying, Israel shall be thy name: 32 And with the stones he built an altar in the name of the LORD: and he made a trench about the altar, as great as would contain two measures of seed.

Elijah selects 12 stones representing the 12 tribes (Heb. *shebet*, **shay'-bet**) of Israel. The tribes were to be national divisions for civil governance and were never intended to indicate spiritual divisions. This act to restore Yahweh worship is one we can emulate in the church today, both metaphorically and literally. What would it take to make your church and this nation more inclusive and diverse, yet unified as one worshiping body under God?

Elijah chooses to rebuild the altar, assisted by a remnant of the people and using a remnant of the stones to erect it. Proving to be even more peculiar in his method of preparation, Elijah then digs a trench (Heb. *te`alah*, **teh-aw-law'**) around the altar he has erected. This surely piqued the interest of the people—a trench for water around an altar built for fire. Yet it is on this stage, under these peculiar circumstances, that God prevails.

33 And he put the wood in order, and cut the bullock in pieces, and laid him on the wood, and said, Fill four barrels with water, and pour it on the burnt sacrifice, and on the wood. 34 And he said, Do it the second time. And they did it the second time. And he said, Do it the third time. And they did it the third time. 35 And the water ran round about the altar; and he filled the trench also with water.

The altar is built. The bull is dressed (i.e., prepared for sacrifice). The sacrifice is assembled. In addition, Elijah instructs his assistants to pour water on the altar. The Mediterranean Sea made the task of drawing water for this great demonstration rather convenient. Elijah instructs that water be poured on the altar, not just once to merely dampen it, nor twice to simply douse it, but three times, so that the altar and sacrifice are drenched and the trench is filled with the runoff. Lest there be any suspicions of an incendiary device hidden within the altar, Elijah instructs that the altar be saturated with water. It seemed as though Elijah had sabotaged his own sacrifice.

18:38 Then the fire of the LORD fell, and consumed the burnt sacrifice, and the wood, and the stones, and the dust, and licked up the water that was in the trench.

Yahweh responds to Elijah's demonstration of faith immediately and completely. Whereas nothing happened with the altar to Baal, God's fire "consumed" (Heb. *'akal*, **aw-kal'**, meaning "utterly destroyed") the sacrifice, the altar, the dirt, and the water in the ditch! Even though the people were crowded around close to this phenomenal demonstration of God's power, no one was touched by the flames. The fire was completely under God's control, dispelling any doubt that Yahweh is God.

Consider the order in which the altar and sacrifice were consumed: First, the fire came down from heaven, indicating that its source was not the hand of man; then, the fire destroyed the altar in reverse order—the flesh, the wood, the stones, the dust, and even the water in the trench! Of particular note is that, even with Elijah's intentional and meticulous effort to build the altar with stones from the ruins of the previous altar, it was apropos that God ultimately destroy this altar. The altar would never again be needed to make a sacrifice.

39 And when all the people saw it, they fell on their faces: and they said, The LORD, he is the God; the LORD, he is the God.

The Hebrew verb for "saw" is *ra'ah* (Heb. **raw-aw'**), which means "standing close enough for the people to see"; consider God's response to Elijah's sacrifice. Israel "fell" (Heb. *naphal*, **naw-fal'**) prostrate before God in true, unwavering worship and cried out saying, "The LORD [Yahweh] is God! The LORD [Yahweh] is God!" With a made-up mind, Israel responds and vows to worship Yahweh alone as God!

Daily Bible Readings

M: God Is Great
Psalm 145:1–7
T: None Is Like God
Psalm 86:8–13
W: God's Majesty and Might
Psalm 93
T: Who Is the Powerful God?
1 Kings 18:17–24
F: Elijah Taunts the Baal Worshipers
1 Kings 18:25–29
S: Elijah Built an Altar to God
1 Kings 18:30–35
S: Elijah Prays, God Acts
1 Kings 18:36–39

TEACHING TIPS

November 12
Bible Study Guide 11

1. Words You Should Know

A. Covenant (2 Kings 23:3) *beriyth* (Heb.)—An agreement that involves promises on the part of each participant.

B. Stood (v. 3) *'amad* (Heb.)—To stand (by, fast, firm, still, up), take one's stand, or present oneself.

C. Passover (v. 21) *pecach* (Heb.)—To pass, spring over, or spare (Exodus 12:13, 23, 27; cf. Isaiah 31:5). The Passover was an annual Hebrew festival commemorating the last meal eaten in Egypt, in preparation for the Exodus, as Yahweh passed over the protected houses of the Hebrews, slaying only Egypt's firstborn (Exodus 12:12 ff; 13:2, 12).

2. Teacher Preparation

A. Pray for your students, asking God to open their hearts to today's teaching.

B. Review the Lesson Aim.

C. Read 2 Kings 22 and 23 in their entirety. Begin to take notes that specifically address the Lesson Aim objectives.

D. Review the In Depth and More Light on the Text sections.

E. Answer the Search the Scriptures and Discuss the Meaning questions. Also, complete lesson 11 in the *Precepts For Living® Personal Study Guide* so you can be prepared for the class discussion.

3. Starting the Lesson

A. Open the session with prayer, keeping today's Lesson Aim in mind.

B. Read the Keep in Mind verse.

C. Ask the students who completed the study guide pages to tell what they found out about a covenant, Manasseh, Amon, and King Josiah.

D. Read The People, Places, and Times and the Background section.

4. Getting into the Lesson

A. Have the students read aloud the Focal Verses.

B. Present the In Depth insights and commentary.

C. Discuss and meditate on the material present-ed under each point. You will notice that thought-provoking questions are often incorporated into the material.

5. Relating the Lesson to Life

A. Divide the students into small groups and have them discuss the Discuss the Meaning questions.

B. Have the students spend some time meditating on the Lesson Aim.

6. Arousing Action

A. Ask the students what they feel God wants them to do in response to the Follow the Spirit challenge.

B. Challenge the students to think specifically. What attitudes and behavior need to be changed? How will these changes relate to their actions at home, at work, at church, and in the community?

JOSIAH BRINGS REFORM

Bible Background • 2 KINGS 22–23
Printed Text • 2 KINGS 22:8–10; 23:1–3, 21–23   Devotional Reading • PSALM 103:1–18

Lesson Aim

By the end of the lesson, we will:

EXAMINE the events that led Josiah to renew the covenant;

SENSE our need for spiritual renewal; and

SEEK spiritual renewal and ENGAGE in at least one activity that will help us experience spiritual renewal.

Keep in Mind

"And the king stood by a pillar, and made a covenant before the LORD, to walk after the LORD, and to keep his commandments and his testimonies and his statutes with all their heart and all their soul, to perform the words of this covenant that were written in this book. And all the people stood to the covenant" (2 Kings 23:3).

Focal Verses

2 Kings 22:8 And Hilkiah the high priest said unto Shaphan the scribe, I have found the book of the law in the house of the LORD. And Hilkiah gave the book to Shaphan, and he read it.

9 And Shaphan the scribe came to the king, and brought the king word again, and said, Thy servants have gathered the money that was found in the house, and have delivered it into the hand of them that do the work, that have the oversight of the house of the LORD.

10 And Shaphan the scribe shewed the king, saying, Hilkiah the priest hath delivered me a book. And Shaphan read it before the king.

23:1 And the king sent, and they gathered unto him all the elders of Judah and of Jerusalem.

2 And the king went up into the house of the LORD, and all the men of Judah and all the inhabitants of Jerusalem with him, and the priests, and the prophets, and all the people, both small and great: and he read in their ears all the words of the book of the covenant which was found in the house of the LORD.

3 And the king stood by a pillar, and made a covenant before the LORD, to walk after the LORD, and to keep his commandments and his testimonies and his statutes with all their heart and all their soul, to perform the words of this covenant that were written in this book. And all the people stood to the covenant.

23:21 And the king commanded all the people, saying, Keep the passover unto the LORD your God, as it is written in the book of this covenant.

22 Surely there was not holden such a passover from the days of the judges that judged Israel, nor in all the days of the kings of Israel, nor of the kings of Judah;

23 But in the eighteenth year of king Josiah, wherein this passover was holden to the LORD in Jerusalem.

In Focus

Duane and Karen had been happily married for eight years (or so Karen thought) when she discovered that Duane had been see-ing another woman for almost three months. The news of the affair devastated Karen. For months she was on an emotional roller coaster. One moment she was angry, and the next moment she was either bitter or just con-fused. All Karen knew was that she loved her husband and wanted to keep her family together. She couldn't understand why Duane would jeopardize their marriage and all they had worked together to build. For months after Duane ended the affair, the couple strug-gled with Duane's indiscretion. Finally, they decided to seek mar-riage counseling.

After a year of intense counsel-ing, Duane and Karen worked through their problems and were reconciled. Karen was able to for-give her husband's indiscretion and began to trust him once again. God had given them a second chance. As a show of their renewed relationship, the couple decided to renew their marriage covenant. They did so by inviting all their family and friends to witness what God had done in their lives.

God gives us second chances if we accept responsibility and seek

KINGS OF ISRAEL AND JUDAH DURING THE BABYLONIAN CAPTIVITY (735 B.C.–597 B.C.)		
TOOK OFFICE	**KING**	**REFERENCES**
735	Ahaz	2 Kings 15:38–16:20 2 Chronicles 27:9–28:27
715	Hezekiah	2 Kings 18:1–20:21 2 Chronicles 28:27–32:33
697	Manasseh	2 Kings 20:21–21:18 2 Chronicles 32:33–33:20
642	Amon	2 Kings 21:18–26 2 Chronicles 33:20–24
640	Josiah	2 Kings 22:1–23:30 2 Chronicles 33:25–35:27
609	Jehoahaz	2 Kings 23:30–34 2 Chronicles 36:1–4
	Jehoiakim	2 Kings 23:34–24:6 2 Chronicles 36:4–8
598	Jehoiachin	2 Kings 24:6–16; 25:27–30 2 Chronicles 36:8–10
597	Zedekiah	2 Kings 24:17–25:21 2 Chronicles 36:10–20

Source: *Life Application Study Bible.* Carol Stream, Ill.: Tyndale House Publishers, 1996, 609.

to reestablish our relationship with Him. In today's lesson, King Josiah calls the people together and leads them in a renewal of the covenant.

The People, Places, and Times

Josiah. Considered one of the best of all the kings of Judah who followed David, Josiah was the son of the godless Amon and the grandson of the wicked Manasseh (2 Kings 21). Ascending to the throne at age 8, Josiah was apparently blessed with God-fearing advisors who resisted the idolatrous influence of his father and grandfather.

At the age of 16, in the eighth year of his reign, Josiah personally "began to seek the God of David, his father" (2 Chronicles 34:3). It was at this point that he began to purify Judah and Jerusalem from idolatry (2 Kings 22:1–2).

The three decades of Josiah's reign were among the happiest years experienced by Judah. They were characterized by peace, prosperity, and reform. King Josiah dedicated himself to pleasing God and led Israel in their renewed observance of the Mosaic Law.

It is a testimony to the grace of God that a wicked king like Amon could have such a godly son and successor. The spiritual reform brought about by Josiah climaxes with the discovery of the Book of the Law in the eighteenth year of his reign and the celebration of the Passover (2 Kings 22:8–23; 23).

Even though he never knew his great-grandfather Hezekiah, Josiah was like him in many ways. Both had close personal relationships with God. Both were passionate reformers, working diligently to lead their people back to God. Both were bright flashes of obedience to God among a succession of evil kings.

Although Josiah's father and grandfather were exceptionally wicked, his life is an example of God's desire to guide those who set out to be obedient. Even when he was young, Josiah understood that his land was spiritually sick. Idols were everywhere. Josiah began by destroying whatever he recognized as not belonging to the worship of the true God. He continued by renovating the temple, and, in the process, he rediscovered God's Word. Certainly Josiah was someone to emulate. He began well, continued well, and ended well.

Background

The covenant between God and His people is one of the most important overarching theological concepts interwoven throughout the Bible. When God made a covenant with Abram (Genesis 12), He promised to bless Abram's descendants and to make them His special people. In return, Abram was to remain faithful to God and to serve as a channel through which God's blessings could flow to the rest of the world.

In the Mosaic covenant at Sinai, the Israelites promised with an oath to keep the commands of the covenant as found in the Ten Commandments (Exodus 24:3; Deuteronomy 4:13). Their obedience was to be rewarded by God's care and provision, prosperity, victory over their enemies, and the outpouring of God's Spirit (Exodus 23:20–33). Curses would follow disobedience.

Over and over again, the Israelites broke their oath. In contrast, God did not and does not break His promises. His oath to raise up believing children to Abraham (Genesis 22:16–17) is an everlasting covenant that He continues to keep today (Genesis 17:7).

At-A-Glance

1. Josiah Recognized Sin and Repented (2 Kings 22:8–10)
2. Josiah Renewed His Covenant Relationship with God (23:1–3)
3. Josiah Publicly Celebrated His Relationship with God (vv. 21–23)

In Depth

1. Josiah Recognized Sin and Repented (2 Kings 22:8–10)

Josiah began to diligently seek the God of his father David when he was still no more than 16 years old. In the 12th year of his reign, at age 20, he began to purify Judah and Jerusalem from idolatry. It was in the 18th year of his reign (22:8), during his renova-

tion of Solomon's temple, that the Book of the Law was found by the high priest and read before him (vv. 8–28).

When Josiah heard the law (22:11), he was shocked, frightened, and humbled. In grief, he tore his robes and immediately instituted more reforms designed to lead his people back to God. It took just one reading of God's law to compel him to change both the course of his life and that of the nation.

The Word of God should cause us, like Josiah, to immediately take action to reform our lives and bring them into harmony with God's will. The hardest part of repentance is changing the attitudes that produced the sinful behavior in the first place. What needs to be changed in our lives?

2. Josiah Renewed His Covenant Relationship with God (23:1–3)

Josiah did more than repent when the law was read to him—he took action! First, he renewed his personal covenant relationship with God. Then, he led the nation in renewing their covenant before the Lord. To show their consent, all the people stood up, thereby binding themselves to obedience. In general, they were covenanting: (a) to serve only the one true God, (b) to faithfully regulate their conduct by the mandates presented in the law, and (c) to serve God and follow His commands with their whole heart and soul.

It is up to each one of us to personally enter into covenant with God and to walk in obedience to that covenant. No one can do it for us. Blessings follow those who obey, while curses follow those who disobey. Similarly, just as King Josiah led the nation in renewing their covenant, we also have a responsibility to positively affect those who look to us for leadership. Parents, employers, teachers, mentors, and peers are all to take steps to impact those over whom they have influence.

3. Josiah Publicly Celebrated His Relationship with God (vv. 21–23)

God had commanded that the Israelites celebrate the Passover as a yearly holiday in remembrance of their sovereign deliverance from Egyptian slavery (Numbers 9:1–4), but this had not been done for many years. As a result, during the days of the judges who led Israel, and throughout the days of the kings of Israel and the kings of Judah, the Passover had not been observed.

The Passover was an important festival because it was a kind of sacrament uniting the nation to God on the basis of God's grace to them. Every part of the festival and meal had God-ordained symbolic meaning.

When Josiah rediscovered the Passover in the Book of the Covenant, he ordered everyone to observe the ceremonies exactly as prescribed. As is stated in 2 Kings 23:22, "Surely there was not holden such a passover from the days of the judges that judged Israel, nor in all the days of the kings of Israel, nor of the kings of Judah." In other words, this Passover celebration stood out from those in the past in its manner and spirit. It had more enthusiastic participation, was based on purer principles, and was more religiously observed (2 Chronicles 35:1–18).

African American Christians have much to celebrate. Not only have we been delivered from chattel slavery, but we have been liberated from the bondage of sin! In our churches and homes, we need to celebrate with words and songs of praise. In our places of employment, we can have an attitude of joyful celebration as we give testimony of the great things that He has done in our lives! After all, we have been bought with a price . . . have access to God . . . have newness of life . . . are complete in Him! (See John 10:10; Romans 6:4; 1 Corinthians 6:20; Colossians 2:10.)

Sources

Adam Clarke's Commentary on the Bible. Biblesoft, Inc., 1996, 2003.

Keil and Delitzsch Commentary on the Old Testament. Electronic Database. Logos Bible Software, 1996.

Search the Scriptures

1. Why is Josiah described as being one of the best Israelite kings (2 Kings 22:1–2; 23:25)?

2. What happened when the priest read the Book of the Law to King Josiah (vv. 11–13; 23:3–24)?

3. What does it mean to be in covenant with the Lord (v. 3)?

4. What does it mean when Scripture says the people "stood" as Josiah was leading them in renewal of their covenant (v. 3)?

Discuss the Meaning

1. Do you think most Christians have an idea of what it means to be in a covenant relationship with God? Why or why not?

2. What are some of the idols in our society?

3. What are some common attitudes that Christians need to change?

4. What are some Christlike attitudes and behaviors we need to be more careful to express in our homes?

5. What are some ways that we can celebrate what Christ has done in our lives?

Lesson in Our Society

Although Josiah's father and grandfather were extremely wicked, his life is an example of God's willingness to provide ongoing guidance to those who set out to be obedient. Even when he was young, Josiah understood that there was spiritual sickness in his land. Idols were everywhere. Josiah began his search for God by "cleaning up" whatever he recognized as not belonging to the worship of the true God. As he did so, God's Word was rediscovered. The king's intentions and the power of God's written revelation were brought together. Like Josiah, it's time for all Christians to rediscover the power of God's Word!

Make It Happen

How would you describe your relationship with God? Today God's Word is easily accessible. How much change must you make in order to bring your life into alignment with God's teachings? Are you deeply humbled, realizing that you desperately need Him to cleanse and renew you? Good intentions and reforms are not enough. You must allow yourself to be truly humbled and changed by God's Word. What is God saying to you today?

When Josiah realized the terrible state of Judah's religious life, he did something about it. It is not enough to say we believe what is right; we must respond with action, doing what faith requires. This is what James was emphasizing when he wrote, "faith that does not result in good deeds is useless" (James 2:20, NLT). This means that faith requires acting differently at home, school, work, and church. It's not enough to simply talk about obedience. Think about some attitudes and actions that God wants you to change.

Follow the Spirit

What God wants me to do:

_____

_____

Remember Your Thoughts

Special insights I have learned:

_____

_____

More Light on the Text
2 Kings 22:8–10; 23:1–3, 21–23

The kings of Judah had neglected the temple of God, and it fell into ruin. Desecrated with Baal worship, Ashtoreth idols, administrative abandonment, and absence of godly worshipers, the temple merely reflected Israel's spiritual condition. Exposed to and moved by the prophet Jeremiah's preaching, young King Josiah set out to repair the temple buildings and restore the godly worship of Yahweh. Thanks to his leadership, Israel experienced spiritual renewal throughout the nation.

At the helm of this revival was Josiah, whose name means "whom Yahweh heals." The son of King Amon, Josiah ascended to the throne at 8 years old, began rebuilding the temple and restoring the worship of Yahweh at 16 years old, reigned over Judah for 31 years, and was fatally injured in battle and died at 39 years old. King Josiah was assisted in this spiritual revival by many people, but most notably by Hilkiah (**khil-kee-yaw'**, whose name means "my portion is Yahweh"), who served as a high priest in charge of restoring the temple under Josiah's reign; and Shaphan (**shaw-fawn'**), a Levite who served as a secretary, or scribe, to King Josiah.

8 And Hilkiah the high priest said unto Shaphan the scribe, I have found the book of the law in the house of the LORD. And Hilkiah gave the book to Shaphan, and he read it.

As Hilkiah and Shaphan carried out Josiah's instructions in 2 Kings 22:3–7 to restore the temple, they discovered the Book of the Law (cf. Deuteronomy 28:58–61). In Hebrew terminology and understanding, "book of the law" specifically refers to the *Torah* (**to-raw'**), or the first five books of the Bible (also called the book of Moses or the Pentateuch). These "books" were guidelines for moral authority, godly worship, and pious living, as opposed to a list of prohibitions and consequences.

It may be profitable to understand that the word "LORD" displayed in this manner (i.e., with all capital letters) is a translation of the word *Yahweh* (**ya-way**), which means "the existing One" and is the proper name of the one true God. This is significant in this passage, since the Book of the Law was found in God's temple—a book that had been neglected by God's kings in the process of worshiping false gods. Hilkiah's discovery must have certainly resulted in great delight, awe, and distress. In his excitement, Hilkiah handed over the book to be read by his assistant Shaphan, even though it would have been appropriate that Hilkiah read the book himself.

9 And Shaphan the scribe came to the king, and brought the king word again, and said, Thy servants have gathered the money that was found in the house, and have delivered it into the hand of them that do the work, that have the oversight of the house of the LORD.

Following Josiah's instructions (2 Kings 22:3–7), Hilkiah and Shaphan indeed find a great treasury of money available to pay the artisans who labored to restore the temple and the surrounding buildings. The money referred to here amounted to about 10 years' worth of undocumented tithes and offerings given by the people for temple service and upkeep. These funds were duly collected during Amon's reign, yet they had not been used for the priestly portion or

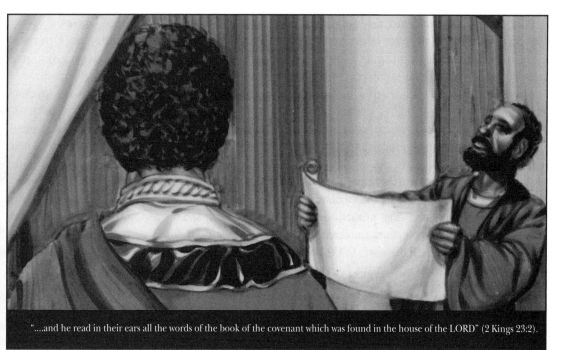

"....and he read in their ears all the words of the book of the covenant which was found in the house of the LORD" (2 Kings 23:2).

the building fund. Josiah so trusted the priests in the temple as men of integrity and honesty, that he instructed that the money simply be gathered and distributed among the workers. As instructed, Hilkiah, the high priest turned project manager, collected all the money and distributed it honestly without account or accountability.

Shaphan was charged with the task of making a progress report to Josiah. He reported that the restorative work was on schedule, that the reserved finances were being managed, and that the Book of the Law had been recovered from the rubble of the temple ruin.

10 And Shaphan the scribe shewed the king, saying, Hilkiah the priest hath delivered me a book. And Shaphan read it before the king.

The word " book" (Heb. *cepher*, **say'-fer**) can refer to a common letter, instructions, written order, commission, request, written decree, or law book. In this instance, it refers to excerpts of the Deuteronomic law recorded in Deuteronomy 28–31, which describe God's fierce judgment upon people who disregard His words. In 2 Chronicles 34:14, this book is referred to as the "book of the Law of the LORD given by Moses,"

which implies that these scrolls might have been transcribed by Moses and could very well have included Moses' signature. Shaphan assumes his usual duty as a scribe, or secretary, and reads the book to Josiah as written.

To flesh out what takes place between this verse and the next verse assigned in this lesson, you are encouraged to read 2 Kings 22:11–20. This interlude records Josiah's repentant response to what he heard, his beckoning his spiritual leaders and prayer partners to seek God's face concerning national repentance and the restoration of the covenant, and the word of a prophetess to interpret Yahweh's denunciation of the people. Like a male prophet, a female prophetess was called by God to speak for Him typically in the midst of a spiritual crisis of national proportions. It is the prophetess Huldah (**hul'da**) who announces the Word of the Lord to Josiah, which in essence was that "God [will] destroy this place and these people." However, God would not do this while Josiah reigned because Josiah had sought the Lord with repentance and weeping.

23:1 And the king sent, and they gathered unto him all the elders of Judah and of Jerusalem.

Upon receiving this comforting and critical word from the prophetess Huldah, Josiah goes into action to revive the land and rid it of idolatry. The first thing he does is to call for a unified gathering of the "elders" (Heb. zaqen, **zaw-kane'**), or those having authority from the nations of Judah and Jerusalem.

2 And the king went up into the house of the LORD, and all the men of Judah and all the inhabitants of Jerusalem with him, and the priests, and the prophets, and all the people, both small and great: and he read in their ears all the words of the book of the covenant which was found in the house of the LORD.

Josiah leads the procession from the courtyard to the temple. Following him into the presence of God are the unified force of godly priests, God's prophets, and all the inhabitants of Israel, regardless of class or caste. With all the people present, Josiah does an unusual thing—he begins to read the book. The magnitude of the task of restoring the temple and Josiah's passion for inciting a revival of godly worship moves him to personally read the book, even though it would have been appropriate, even expected, that the high priest Hilkiah, the scribe Shaphan, or any of the other priests or prophets present perform this task.

By assuming the position of mediator between God and the people, Josiah certainly demonstrates leadership by example. This book of the "covenant" (Heb. beriyth, **ber-eeth'**) is the divine ordinance with signs or pledges between God and Israel. Revival began in the land with the reading of all the words of the Lord, which were heard by all the people of the Lord.

3 And the king stood by a pillar, and made a covenant before the LORD, to walk after the LORD, and to keep his commandments and his testimonies and his statutes with all their heart and all their soul, to perform the words of this covenant that were written in this book. And all the people stood to the covenant.

Josiah "stood" (Heb. `amad, **aw-mad'**, which means "to appoint, ordain, or establish"), as one in a position of authority, on stairs (serving as a "pulpit") to read the Book of the Covenant. While he preaches from this perch, Josiah renews the covenant made with Moses. This renewed covenant called for the people to take three distinct actions to demonstrate renewal: They were charged to "walk" (Heb. yalak, **yaw-lak'**, which connotes a manner of life) after the Lord, to "keep" (Heb. shamar, **shaw-mar'**, which means "to observe or celebrate") God's instructions, and to "perform" (Heb. quwom, **koom**, which means "to fulfill") the words, vows, and acts of the covenant.

Josiah further admonishes the people that they must adhere to this renewed covenant with all their "heart" (Heb. leb, **labe**), which refers to the conscience will, understanding, and emotions, and with all their "soul" (Heb. nephesh, **neh'-fesh**), which refers to the emotions, passions, and character. In essence, the people were to move from habitual to wholehearted worship of the Lord. They were charged to resist rituals and respond in righteousness.

23:21 And the king commanded all the people, saying, Keep the passover unto the LORD your God, as it is written in the book of this covenant.

And Josiah "commanded" (Heb. tsavah, **tsaw-vaw'** meaning "to appoint or ordain as a divine act") the people to keep the Passover. The Passover, or the Feast of Unleavened Bread, was the seven-day feast commemorating Israel's deliverance from the Egyptians and the passing over of the death angel that smote the firstborn of every Egyptian home. It is recorded that Josiah restored and encouraged Israel's priests to lead this "praise party" with much aplomb.

Keeping the Passover was one of the acts of worship on Josiah's restoration and revival agenda. Reading the story in context, one would discover that Josiah's plan was spiritually aggressive and physically thorough. He set out to remove all vestiges and evidences of the worship of Baal, Ashtoreth, and the "gods" of the sun, moon, earth, and sky. This included gathering up all the idols, poles, statues, and buried remains used in false worship and burning them outside the city walls; tearing down the shrines of the priests and prostitutes devoted to these false gods; destroying the rooftop altars and mountainous high places; defrocking the mediums and spiritists; and killing the pagan priests. For revival among God's people, there was first the reading of the Word of the Lord, followed by a purging of the places where the people worshiped.

22 Surely there was not holden such a passover from the days of the judges that judged Israel, nor in all the days of the kings of Israel, nor of the kings of Judah; 23 But in the eighteenth year of king Josiah, wherein this passover was holden to the LORD in Jerusalem.

It is noted that Josiah led this spiritual revival. He is remembered as having "put his money where his mouth is" by providing over 30,000 sheep and goats and 3,000 cattle for anyone in need of an acceptable sacrifice for the temple. Josiah's officials and priests followed his example of generosity and worship. This outpouring of worship was the direct result of the reading of the Word and the cleansing of the temple of foreign gods and their influences.

However, it was not the opulence that made this revival so unforgettable. Yes, it was performed to the letter of the law; yet it was the purity of purpose, the participation of the people, and the pious pageantry that established this record of acclaim. The extraordinary manner and spirit in which this Passover was observed is also recorded in 2 Chronicles 35:1–18. The people kept this renewed covenant as long as Josiah lived.

Daily Bible Readings

M: God Restores Us
Psalm 103:1–12
T: Renewal in the Lord
Psalm 32
W: Return to the Lord
Joel 2:12–17
T: Josiah Made King of Judah
2 Kings 22:1–7
F: A Lost Book Is Found
2 Kings 22:8–13
S: The People Renew Their Covenant
2 Kings 23:1–5
S: Celebrate the Passover
2 Kings 23:21–25

TEACHING TIPS

November 19
Bible Study Guide 12

1. Words You Should Know

A. Wrath (2 Chronicles 36:16) *chemah* (Heb.)—Warmth, heat, anger, rage, indignation; to act violently.

B. Sing (Psalm 137:3) *shiyr* (Heb.)—To celebrate in song, whether that song is triumphant, joyous, or religious in nature; to praise with a loud voice.

2. Teacher Preparation

A. In preparation for today's lesson, examine where you are in light of the Focal Verses.

B. Read the In Depth section and answer the Search the Scriptures and Make It Happen questions so you can be prepared to help the students who may also be struggling with issues in their lives.

C. Also, complete lesson 12 in the *Precepts For Living® Personal Study Guide*.

3. Starting the Lesson

A. As the students arrive today, write the words "rebellion," "obedience," disobedience," "repentance," and "confession" on the chalkboard or newsprint. Then ask several students to define what each word means in light of the Focal Verses. Have them write their answers on a separate piece of paper to review later.

B. Have a student read the Focal Verses following the At-A-Glance outline. Then briefly discuss each point of the outline.

C. Ask a student to lead the class in a prayer that is based on the Lesson Aim.

4. Getting into the Lesson

A. Read the Background section and briefly discuss how each Bible character relates to the lesson.

B. Read the In Depth section and discuss ways that people in the church can demonstrate an attitude or disposition similar to that of the people of Judah.

C. At the end of the In Depth discussion, have the students answer the Search the Scriptures questions and examine the implications of their answers for their personal and corporate lives.

5. Relating the Lesson to Life

A. Give the students several minutes to read and answer the Discuss the Meaning questions.

B. Initiate an open-ended discussion by posing one or more of the following questions: Why are people quick to blame God when things go wrong in society or in their lives? How should God's grace influence the way a person lives? What are some choices you have made that have positively or negatively impacted your relationship with Jesus Christ?

C. The Lesson in Our Society section gives practical application for today's lesson. Be sure to challenge the students to complete this assignment either inside or outside the classroom.

6. Arousing Action

Today's lesson helps remind the students of the importance of making decisions that honor God. Remind the students that even though we serve a gracious God, we face consequences when we make wrong decisions. Adam and Eve, Samson, and Judas are a few biblical figures who help us remember that truth.

Worship Guide

For the Superintendent or Teacher
Theme: The People Go into Exile
Theme Song: "God Has Been Good to Me"
Scripture: Job 2:1–6
Song: "The Lord Will Make a Way Somehow"
Meditation: Lord, as believers we often fail to live as we should. In those moments, forgive us of our sins and help us to walk in newness of life, reminding us of the inheritance we have in You. Thank You for the love and grace You give to us even when we don't deserve it. In Jesus' name. Amen.

THE PEOPLE GO INTO EXILE

Bible Background • 2 CHRONICLES 36:15–21; PSALM 137
Printed Text • 2 CHRONICLES 36:15–21; PSALM 137:1–6   Devotional Reading • PROVERBS 1:20–33

Lesson Aim

By the end of the lesson, we will:

EXPLORE the choices the Israelites made that led to their captivity;

REFLECT on choices we have made and the consequences of those choices;

and IDENTIFY choices we can make that would positively affect our relationship with God.

Keep in Mind

"By the rivers of Babylon, there we sat down, yea, we wept, when we remembered Zion" (Psalm 137:1).

Focal Verses

2 Chronicles 36:15 And the LORD God of their fathers sent to them by his messengers, rising up betimes, and sending; because he had compassion on his people, and on his dwelling place:

16 But they mocked the messengers of God, and despised his words, and misused his prophets, until the wrath of the LORD arose against his people, till there was no remedy.

17 Therefore he brought upon them the king of the Chaldees, who slew their young men with the sword in the house of their sanctuary, and had no compassion upon young man or maiden, old man, or him that stooped for age: he gave them all into his hand.

18 And all the vessels of the house of God, great and small, and the treasures of the house of the LORD, and the treasures of the king, and of his princes; all these he brought to Babylon.

19 And they burnt the house of God, and brake down the wall of Jerusalem, and burnt all the palaces thereof with fire, and destroyed all the goodly vessels thereof.

20 And them that had escaped from the sword carried he away to Babylon; where they were servants to him and his sons until the reign of the kingdom of Persia:

21 To fulfil the word of the LORD by the mouth of Jeremiah, until the land had enjoyed her sabbaths: for as long as she lay desolate she kept sabbath, to fulfil threescore and ten years.

Psalm 137:1 By the rivers of Babylon, there we sat down, yea, we wept, when we remembered Zion.

2 We hanged our harps upon the willows in the midst thereof.

3 For there they that carried us away captive required of us a song; and they that wasted us required of us mirth, saying, Sing us one of the songs of Zion.

4 How shall we sing the LORD's song in a strange land?

5 If I forget thee, O Jerusalem, let my right hand forget her cunning.

6 If I do not remember thee, let my tongue cleave to the roof of my mouth; if I prefer not Jerusalem above my chief joy.

In Focus

Mark was very active in his church. He was a deacon, he taught a teen Sunday School class every Sunday morning, and he was a member of the praise team. However, outside of church, Mark had a very different lifestyle. Unfortunately, he fell into a life of drug addiction, becoming a heroin addict. Eventually, he left the church. Time and time again, his family and friends warned him about the consequences of his addiction. His sister was constantly getting after him to get counseling, but her warnings fell on deaf ears. Mark didn't think he had a problem; "I've got this" was his favorite line. Refusing to seek counseling, he eventually lost his job, home, wife, and family. It was on a trip to the doctor for a routine checkup that Mark discovered he was HIV positive.

Mark's lifestyle had finally caught up with him. Finally, tired of his drug-induced lifestyle, he walked into a Narcotics Anonymous meeting and recommitted his life to Christ. During the NA sessions, he realized that his relationship with God, his marriage, and his family were the most important things in his life.

The people of the nation of Judah continued their evil ways and suffered for their rebellion. In today's lesson, we see how the choices we make can affect our relationship with God and man.

The People, Places, and Times

Dispersion of God's People. The term "dispersion" is used to designate the Jews, who were living outside Palestine and maintaining their religious observances and customs among the Gentiles.

As a result of the Babylonian Exile of Judah after 597 B.C., a sizable Jewish dispersion developed in the eastern regions of Babylonia, Elam, Pathia, Media, and Armenia. In the first century A.D., the Babylonian Jews became numerous and highly favored by the Parthians, who ruled the area in the time of Christ. They were also considered to be of purer stock than Palestinian Jews, which led to some jealousy and pride. They remained true to the tenets of Judaism and became exceptional students of the law and of oral tradition. Their rabbis produced the Babylonian Talmud in the sixth century, one of the most extensive and influential pieces of post-biblical Jewish literature.

Source

Bromiley, Geoffrey W., ed. *The International Standard Bible Encyclopedia.* Grand Rapids, Mich.: William B. Eerdmans Publishing Company, 1979.

Background

In this lesson, both the chronicler and the psalmist share with us the results of a people who have gone astray from the Lord. It is a sobering reminder for believers who make choices abhorrent to the covenant relationship we have with Jesus Christ. For those of us who choose to follow after our own dictates, God's Word reminds us of the ultimate consequences of disobeying the Lord.

1. God's Judgment Is Revealed to His People (2 Chronicles 36:15–21)
2. God's People Acknowledge the Results of His Judgment (Psalm 137:1–6)

In Depth

1. God's Judgment Is Revealed to His People (2 Chronicles 36:15–21)

According to Zodhiates, the primary Hebrew root of the word "rebellion" refers to obstinacy, resistance to truth, disobedience to divine laws, or breach of faith. God had spoken many times to His people about their need to move from rebellion and live submissive and obedient lives, which pleased Him. After all, humility and obedience bring blessings, while disobedience and rebellion cause sorrow and pain. It is with this principle in mind that the prophet Jeremiah had warned Judah that their rebellious and obstinate nature would be the primary factor in their going into exile for 70 years (see Jeremiah 25:1–9).

Many years before the deportation, the people cried out for a human monarch, rather than accepting God as their King. God warned Samuel that their desire to be like other nations would be their downfall (see 1 Samuel 8). Though many of the kings sought to live right, they were human and prone to failure.

Thus, 21-year-old Zedekiah served as Judah's last king before the Exile. He came into power after Nebuchadnezzar deported thousands of Judeans to Babylon. Like his predecessors, Zedekiah rejected God's laws, sought human advice, and caused the people to move further from God. Through the prophets, God declared that even though Nebuchadnezzar would fight against Judah and capture the people, He would use the Babylonian king to do His will. How?

The Scripture makes it clear that Zedekiah would not humble himself before God, choosing a path of disobedience to the Lord. As God's representative to the people and the people's representative before God, the king had a tremendous responsibility to demonstrate his love and loyalty despite being a vassal ruler who had been chosen by Nebuchadnezzar. Unfortunately, Zedekiah chose to obey human authority rather than follow God's divine decrees.

Anytime we choose to live in disobedience to God, there are consequences. Like the Children of Israel, we may mock God's messengers, disobey His Word, and follow our own way of life apart from God. However, before we do, the apostle Paul admonishes us not to be deceived, because God is not mocked, and a person will reap what he sows (see Galatians 6:7).

This lesson brings the dichotomy between God's love and judgment into clear focus. Some would ask, "If God loves His people so much, why would He allow His enemies to vanquish them?" It was vitally important for God's people to learn a difficult, but necessary, lesson. When people harden their hearts and turn from God's law, disaster often comes upon them. It is not God's will for any person to suffer needless persecution, but His desire is that we come into a right relationship with Him. However, because of some of the choices we make, God often allows us to experience heartaches and pain so that we will acknowledge Him and submit to His will. On the other hand, we can choose to go our own way and ultimately forfeit God's blessings on our lives. Certainly, God wants to bless us. But He allows us to decide whether we will receive those blessings by walking in obedience or experience the negative consequences of living disobedient lives.

2. God's People Acknowledge the Results of His Judgment (Psalm 137:1–6)

The author of Psalm 137 is not identified, but he lived in Jerusalem during the reign of Zedekiah and was taken into Babylon when Nebuchadnezzar destroyed the temple and the city. Counting the years of captivity and isolation, the psalmist reminisces of his homeland and its beauty while in the foreign land of Babylon, where the people of Judah would live for 70 years.

It is also possible that the people recalled the freedom and liberty they had once enjoyed in Jerusalem. In Babylon, that freedom was but a painful memory as the people were subjected to humiliation at the hands of their enemies.

The prophet had foretold that God would punish the nation and kingdom that refused to serve Nebuchadnezzar with the sword, famine, and pestilence until God consumed them by His hand (Jeremiah 27:8). Before the Exile, the people chose not to believe Jeremiah. They felt as though his preaching was for others, not for them. But as they faced tremendous persecution and judgment in Babylon at the hands of Nebuchadnezzar, with sadness of heart, they remembered the comfort and ease that had once been theirs in Jerusalem.

Not only did the Babylonians bring tremendous persecution on the people, but they often mocked the Judeans by demanding that they sing "songs of Zion" (v. 3). For the Babylonians, the songs were nothing more than a form of entertainment and a way to further humiliate their enemies. However, for the Jews, the songs of Zion represented being in God's presence and entering into His courts with praise (Psalm 100:4). With the temple destroyed and the people exiled to a heathen land, how was it possible for them to open their mouths and bless the Lord? Their captors' request was an oxymoron that the people could not endure.

How is it that we can sing God's songs in a strange land? We can by recognizing that even in the most difficult circumstances, all things work together for good for those who love God and are called according to His purpose (see Romans 8:28). Though the Jews were suffering due to their own rebellion and disobedience, they could not see the redemptive "light" at the end of the tunnel. Instead, they groaned bitterly because of their circumstance. However, even in the most difficult times, it is important that we (a) see God at work in our lives and (b) maintain the witness of God's purpose before others.

Even when we fail, we must never forget that we still remain in the presence of the Lord. God reminds us to come to Him—even when we fail Him and have to go through difficult and troubling times. Only He can give us rest. The apostle John also affirms that if we confess our sins, God is faithful and just to forgive us and to cleanse us from all unrighteousness (1 John 1:9).

We are never so far from the Lord that we cannot experience His love and grace. If we have strayed from the Lord, made bad choices in our lives, or even rebelled against God's divine decrees, Jesus Christ encourages us to come to God by repenting of and confessing our sins. Like the father in the parable of the prodigal son, our Heavenly Father waits to receive all who will turn to Him today.

Search the Scriptures

1. Why was it necessary for the prophets to warn the people of God's imminent judgment (2 Chronicles 36:15–16)?

2. How did God respond to the people's disobedience (vv. 17–18)?

3. To where were the people deported (vv. 20–21)?

4. What did the Babylonians want the people to do (Psalm 137:3)?

5. What was the people's response to the Babylonians (vv. 4–6)?

Discuss the Meaning

1. Why do we often fail to remember God's benefits and blessings in times of testing?

2. For what purpose does God allow His enemies to hinder the plans and destiny of His people?

3. Does God bless obedient believers with everything they desire from Him? Discuss.

4. Does God test only those believers who are disobedient? Discuss.

5. What is the importance of rejoicing in the Lord despite the problems and challenges we face in life?

Lesson in Our Society

Are the moral, economic, and social problems in the African American community and the larger community due solely to the rebellion of the people, or are there other factors that have a bearing on these problems? In light of today's lesson, write a fact sheet to share with political or community leaders that can shed light on the issues and offer possible solutions that can help alleviate the problems. Be sure to include spiritual issues and suggested solutions. Give a brief report on your findings in next week's class.

Make It Happen

The Africans who arrived in this country in chains came to a strange land, yet many of them survived and flourished despite the hardships they endured. In like manner, today's lesson challenges us to keep our focus on the Lord Jesus Christ despite the hardships we face living in a "strange land." We are often reminded that the world is not our home, that we are "pilgrims" passing through. As the apostle Paul reminds us, "For our light affliction, which is but for a moment, worketh for us a far more exceeding and eternal weight of glory" (2 Corinthians 4:17). Write this Scripture on a piece of paper and put it someplace in your home or workplace to remind yourself of this important truth.

Follow the Spirit

What God wants me to do:

_____

_____

Remember Your Thoughts

Special insights I have learned:

_____

_____

More Light on the Text

2 Chronicles 36:15–21; Psalm 137:1–6

15 And the LORD God of their fathers sent to them by his messengers, rising up betimes, and sending; because he had compassion on his people, and on his dwelling place:

Verses 15 and 16 summarize the root cause of the Exile with language that echoes the words of the prophet Jeremiah (Jeremiah 26:5; 29:19). God, because of his "compassion" (Heb. *chamal*, **khaw-mal'**, meaning "loving concern" or "deep love"), did not leave his people without exhortation, warning, and threatening (cf. Ezekiel 16:3–14; see also Genesis 18:23–32; Ezekiel 18:23; 1 Timothy 2:4). He consistently "sent" them messengers (cf. Jeremiah 7:13). The Hebrew expression *shalach* (**shaw-lakh'**) means "to send a message" (by someone) or "to make a sending." Through the prophets, God called upon the people to repent and return to Him. He wanted to spare them and His "dwelling place" (Heb. *ma`own* or *ma`iyn*, **maw-ohn'** or **maw-een'**, meaning "temple").

The phrase "rising up betimes" is very general—so much so, that it may apply to *all* the times the people gradually turned away from the Lord their God. During the time of King Zedekiah, this turning away from the Lord had reached its highest point (see 2 Chronicles 36:12–16). Thus, the biblical doctrine of retribution is illustrated in this and the following verse. On one hand, we have consequences of sin, which affect later generations (cf. Exodus 34:7). On the other hand, there are also consequences for the sinner himself (Ezekiel 18:4, 20). Our sin will certainly affect others, but in the final analysis it will affect us the most.

16 But they mocked the messengers of God, and despised his words, and misused his prophets, until the wrath of the LORD arose against his people, till there was no remedy.

The people and their leaders refused to listen to the messengers sent by God. The Hebrew verb for "mocked" is *la`ab* (**law-ab'**), which means "to make jokes or jest." The people made fun of God's messengers. They "despised" (Heb. *bazah*, **baw-zaw'**, meaning "to hold in contempt or disdain") His words and scoffed at His prophets.

The phrases "his words" (Heb. *dabar*, **daw-baw'**, meaning "sayings") and "his prophets" are presented as virtually parallel here (cf. 20:20). The distinction drawn between "messengers" (Heb. *mal'ak*, **mal-awk'**, meaning "angel") and "prophets" (Heb. *nabiy'*, **naw-bee'**, meaning "spokesperson") is rhetorical. In this instance, the wording refers primarily to prophets and not to messengers or angels of God. However, the expression is not to be confined to prophets in the narrower sense of the word, for it embraces all the men and women of God who, by word and deed, condemned the godless conduct of the people.

The phrase "no remedy" is translated from the Hebrew word *marpe'* (**mar-pay'**) and is the same word that in 7:14 is translated "to heal the land." No healing was possible because of the people's refusal to repent. They hardened their hearts and forgot the covenant.

17 Therefore he brought upon them the king of the Chaldees, who slew their young men with the sword in the house of their sanctuary, and had no compassion upon young man or maiden, old man, or him that

stooped for age: he gave them all into his hand.

The Hebrew verb `*alah* (**aw-law'**) means "to bring up" or "to bring upon" with the Lord as the subject. The Lord brought judgment upon His unrepentant people when the moral corruption had reached its height (cf. Ezekiel 18:4, 20). This judgment is not represented in its historical details but only rhetorically, in its great general outlines, as a comprehensive destruction and exile.

Prophetic utterances recorded in Jeremiah 15:1–9, 32:3ff, Ezekiel 9:6, and Deuteronomy 32:25 form the basis of this description of the fearful judgment. It was God who brought the Chaldeans and their king against the people of Judah. The subject of the verbs "slew" and "had. . . compassion" is not explicit in Hebrew. From the context, we can infer that the subject of the first and last part of the verse is the Lord; the Chaldeans are described in the middle of the sentence.

The judgment fit the crime. Because they had profaned the sanctuary with their idolatry (2 Chronicles 36:14), they themselves were slain in the sanctuary. The root of the verb "slain" in Hebrew (*harag*, **haw-rag'**) includes the ideas of judicial execution, murder, or violent killing (cf. Genesis 4:8; 9:6; 2 Samuel 4:11–12).

18 And all the vessels of the house of God, great and small, and the treasures of the house of the LORD, and the treasures of the king, and of his princes; all these he brought to Babylon.

This verse depicts a total pillage. The Hebrew expression "great and small" (*gadowl*, **gaw-dole'** and *qatan'*, **kaw-tawn'**) means that nothing valuable was left behind. The king of Babylon took everything back to his country. He carried off everything that was left in the house of the Lord and everything belonging to the king and the princes.

19 And they burnt the house of God, and brake down the wall of Jerusalem, and burnt all the palaces thereof with fire, and destroyed all the goodly vessels thereof.

The Chaldeans totally burnt the city and everything important in it—the temple, the palaces, and the costly vessels. They pulled down the wall of Jerusalem—nothing was left.

The burning of the "house" (Heb. *bayith*, **bah'-yith**), or temple, meant the end of the priesthood. The priests' ministry was to represent the people to God (see Exodus 28:29). However, they were involved in the same sins as the people, thereby making their ministry worthless.

20 And them that had escaped from the sword carried he away to Babylon; where they were servants to him and his sons until the reign of the kingdom of Persia:

All who "had escaped from the sword" (i.e., who had not been slain by the sword) were taken into exile in Babylon. The Hebrew expression *she'eriyth* **sheh-ay-reeth'**), translated "escaped" or "remnant" usually refers to what is left of a people after a disaster such as war (see Genesis 45:7; Isaiah 15:9; Jeremiah 6:9; Amos 5:15; Micah 2:12; cf. Romans 9:27). God is faithful to keep His promises (Genesis 12:1–3). He did not subject the people to total destruction.

Some of the remnant became servants to the king of Babylon and his "sons" (Heb. *ben*, **bane**, meaning "successors") until the rise of the kingdom of Persia, as Jeremiah had prophesied (Jeremiah 27:7).

21 To fulfil the word of the LORD by the mouth of Jeremiah, until the land had enjoyed her sabbaths: for as long as she lay desolate she kept sabbath, to fulfil threescore and ten years.

Nothing that happened was outside the plan of God. The Hebrew verb *male'* (**maw-lay'**), translated "fulfill," denotes completing something in a given period of time. It emphasizes the faithfulness of God in achieving, perfecting, or doing what He said through His messengers that He would do.

It is here that a prophetic word has been linked with, and interpreted by, a clear allusion to a legal passage found in Leviticus 26:34–35. The phrase "to fulfill the word of the LORD by the mouth of Jeremiah" refers to the word of the Lord recorded in

Leviticus 26:34–35 and prophesied by Jeremiah (Jeremiah 25:11–13; 29:10.) Thus, it is not the "word" (Heb. *dabar*, **daw-baw'**) of God spoken by Jeremiah that is referred to, but to the Word of the Lord in general. God is faithful to accomplish His Word.

The period of captivity that came to an end with the rise of the kingdom of Persia is characterized as a time of expiation for the wrong that had been done to the land by the nonobservance of the Sabbath years. By causing the land to remain uncultivated for 70 years, God gave the land a time of rest and refreshment that its inhabitants—for as long as they possessed it—had not given it. The Lord had inflicted the punishment with which the disobedient people had been threatened as early as in the time of Moses (see Leviticus 26:34). Thus, the desolation was a positive blessing given by God. The land would obtain the rest that the sinful people had deprived it by their neglect of the Sabbath observance that they were commanded to keep.

Psalm 137:1 By the rivers of Babylon, there we sat down, yea, we wept, when we remembered Zion.

The rivers of Babylon referred to here are probably the Euphrates with its many canals (cf. Ezekiel 1:1; 3:15; see Acts 16:13). It is possible that the captives were sitting or living by the rivers of Babylon when the remembrance of their native land, Zion, came to them. The term "sat down" is from the Hebrew verb *yashab* (**yaw-shab'**) and denotes dwelling, inhabiting, or settling down. Because the natural scenery around the captives contrasted so strongly with that of their native land, Judah, their remembrance of Zion was forced upon them even more strongly. The pain of being separated from their homeland would have free rein where no hostile eyes were present to suppress it.

2 We hanged our harps upon the willows in the midst thereof.

The captives hung their harps upon the willows (or "by the willows," since the same Hebrew preposition *'al* is used both here and in verse one, "by the rivers" denoting contiguity). They had no further use for them. The time to take delight in music was past. Joyous songs were not suited to their situation.

3 For there they that carried us away captive required of us a song; and they that wasted us required of us mirth, saying, Sing us one of the songs of Zion.

In Babylon, "they that carried us away captive" (Heb. *shabah*, **shaw-baw'**, meaning "captors") and "they that wasted us" (Heb. *towlal*, **to-lawl'**, meaning "tormentors" or "mockers") expected the Jews to sing their native "songs of Zion," or praises to the Lord, referring to sacred liturgical songs (see 1 Chronicles 25:6–7; 2 Chronicles 29:27; cf. Psalm 76; 84; 87; 122). This was intended for humiliation, but the Jews did not feel like doing so because of their captivity.

4 How shall we sing the LORD's song in a strange land?

The phrase "sing the LORD's song" refers to the "songs of Zion" in verse 3. The Jew's captors wanted them to sing songs that they viewed as holy and sacred. The term "strange land" (Heb. *nekar*, **nay-kawr'** and *'adamah*, **ad-aw-maw'**) refers to a foreign land that is considered unclean (cf. Hosea 9:3–9; Amos 7:17; Ezekiel 4:13). The meaning of the interrogatory exclamation is not that the singing of sacred songs in a foreign land is contrary to the law, for psalms continued to be sung even during the Exile and were enriched by new ones.

5 If I forget thee, O Jerusalem, let my right hand forget her cunning.

Jerusalem was viewed as the earthly dwelling place of God. Thus, "to forget" (Heb. *shakach*, **shaw-kakh'**) Jerusalem is to forget the Lord Himself. The people in exile had in fact come to the knowledge of their sins. They now realized that repentance was required in order to get back to that

which they had lost. Repentance and homesickness were inseparable during this time, for all those who gave themselves over to heathenism were disqualified from redemption. Thus, understanding the situation of the exiles and arming himself against the temptation of apostasy and the danger of denying God, the psalmist says, "If I forget thee, O Jerusalem, let my right hand forget her ability or go limp."

6 If I do not remember thee, let my tongue cleave to the roof of my mouth; if I prefer not Jerusalem above my chief joy.

The phrase "if I prefer not Jerusalem above my chief joy" literally means "if I do not raise you above the sum of my joy" or "if I do not place you upon the summit of my joy." The spiritual joy of the psalmist over the city of God is to rise above all earthly joys. His self-cursing, "let my tongue stick to the roof of my mouth," emphasizes his firm devotion to all that Jerusalem represents.

Daily Bible Readings

M: Embrace Wisdom
Proverbs 1:20–33
T: Key to the Good Life
Proverbs 8:32–36
W: Jeremiah Prophesies Judgment
Jeremiah 1:11–19
T: Jeremiah Predicts Jerusalem's Fall
Jeremiah 25:1–11
F: Zedekiah Rebels Against God
2 Chronicles 36:11–14
S: Jerusalem Falls
2 Chronicles 36:15–21
S: Psalm of Remorse
Psalm 137

TEACHING TIPS

November 26
Bible Study Guide 13

1. Words You Should Know
A. Kingdom (2 Chronicles 36:23) *mamliakah* (Heb.)—Dominion, reign, realm, royal rule, and sovereignty of a nation or people.

B. Hands (Ezra 1:6) *yad* (Heb.)—Power, strength, or assistance, both good and evil. It often has connotations of possession or submission.

2. Teacher Preparation
A. Read the In Focus and More Light on the Text sections and reflect on the ways God offers forgiveness and restoration to those who come in faith, repenting of their sins.

B. Read the In Depth section and make mental notes of specific points you want to share with the students to help them truly understand the mercy and grace of the Lord.

C. Complete lesson 13 in the *Precepts For Living® Personal Study Guide.*

D. Spend time in prayer and meditation so you can help the students who may be struggling with certain areas in their lives.

3. Starting the Lesson
A. Write the At-A-Glance outline on the chalkboard and spend a few moments discussing its implications for the lesson today.

B. Let several students read the Focal Verses and ask them to share their feelings on how God used Cyrus and Ezra to restore His people to their proper place in Him.

C. Briefly discuss the Lesson Aim. Give the students a few moments to share their experiences of God's forgiveness while learning the importance of forgiving others.

4. Getting into the Lesson
A. The In Depth section will provide the students with key issues that need to be considered and addressed today. Have the students read this section for better understanding of the lesson.

B. Have the students answer the Search the Scriptures questions.

5. Relating the Lesson to Life
A. Read and answer the Discuss the Meaning questions. In addition, pose the following question for further discussion: How important is it for Christians to recognize when God uses unbelievers to fulfill His purposes?

B. Give the students the opportunity to share and discuss The People, Places, and Times and relate it to where we are in today's society.

C. Challenge the students to discuss what they learned from today's lesson and how they plan to implement them in their relationships with others.

6. Arousing Action
A. Review the Make It Happen section. Have the students share some of their thoughts in class. Encourage them to apply this truth as they interact in their homes and community during the coming week.

B. Encourage the students to read and meditate on the Daily Bible Readings that are provided at the end of the lesson. This will motivate them to further study the lesson during the week.

C. Close the class with prayer.

GOD OFFERS RETURN AND RESTORATION

Bible Background • 2 CHRONICLES 36:22–23; EZRA 1:5–7
Printed Text • 2 CHRONICLES 36:22–23; EZRA 1:5–7   Devotional Reading • JEREMIAH 29:10–14

Lesson Aim

By the end of the lesson, we will:

EXPLORE how the exiles experienced God's forgiveness and the hope of restoration that came with it;

DISCUSS and SENSE the emotions associated with being forgiven and being restored in a relationship; and

DECIDE to tell someone how they can experience God's forgiveness in their life.

Keep in Mind

"Thus saith Cyrus king of Persia, All the kingdoms of the earth hath the LORD God of heaven given me; and he hath charged me to build him a house in Jerusalem, which is in Judah. Who is there among you of all his people? The LORD his God be with him, and let him go up" (2 Chronicles 36:23).

Focal Verses

2 Chronicles 36:22 Now in the first year of Cyrus king of Persia, that the word of the LORD spoken by the mouth of Jeremiah might be accomplished, the LORD stirred up the spirit of Cyrus king of Persia, that he made a proclamation throughout all of his kingdom, and put it also in writing, saying,

23 Thus saith Cyrus king of Persia, All the kingdoms of the earth hath the LORD God of heaven given me; and he hath charged me to build him a house in Jerusalem, which is in Judah. Who is there among you of all his people? The LORD his God be with him, and let him go up.

Ezra 1:5 Then rose up the chief of the fathers of Judah and Benjamin, and the priests, and the Levites, with all them whose spirit God had raised, to go up to build the house of the LORD which is in Jerusalem.

6 And all they that were about them strengthened their hands with vessels of silver, with gold, with goods, and with beasts, and with precious

things, beside all that was willingly offered.

7 Also Cyrus the king brought forth the vessels of the house of the LORD which Nebuchadnezzar had brought forth out of Jerusalem, and had put them in the house of his gods.

In Focus

Sitting in the back of the church, Pearl cried softly as she listened to a teenaged Amanda give her testimony.

Amanda spoke of her first kiss and, nine months later, her first baby. "I was headstrong and squandered the most treasured possession on Earth—my child. I don't deserve life." Amanda fell to the floor convulsing in sorrow as she was surrounded by prayers and loving arms. Amanda's twisted face reminded Pearl of her own situation many years ago.

Pearl thought to herself, I, too, remember crying in my hospital bed, gazing at my infant daughter and feeling like I had to apologize. Somehow, I saw God staring through her newborn eyes, telling

me to go ahead and follow my instincts. Somehow, she seemed to know I was placing her up for adoption. Her face seemed to say, "It's OK, I understand."

My self-hatred lasted two years; then God taught me to forgive myself for winding up in that situation, for signing those adoption papers relinquishing my baby girl.

Today I know I did the right thing. I weighed the alternatives—I did the best thing for her sake. Because God allowed me to release the guilt and shame of an unwanted pregnancy and restored my sense of self and well-being, I now have a relationship with the daughter I gave up many years ago. Her adoptive parents found me and allowed me to become a part of her life. She will be entering college this year. To God be the glory!

In today's lesson, King Cyrus was the instrument of God's forgiveness when His chosen people were given a chance to start again. Our forgiveness can restore relationships also.

The People, Places, and Times

Cyrus. He was the Persian king used as God's tool to bring deliverance, not only to Israel, but also to all the known world. Cyrus allowed the exiles to return to Jerusalem whereby people the world over recognized the Lord's faithfulness to the covenant He made with Israel.

In Isaiah 45:1, God speaks directly to Cyrus, who does not understand the true nature of his role. According to the prophet, Cyrus is the Lord's anointed one (Heb. *mashiyach,* **maw-shee'-akh,** often translated as "Messiah"). It is striking that this term is used of Cyrus and not of the ideal Davidic king. According to Isaiah, a Davidic king does not play a significant role in the expected restoration of God's people. God did not give Cyrus great victories for Cyrus's sake. Rather, the purpose of Cyrus's rise to power is twofold: to liberate Israel and to spread the fame of the one true God of Israel throughout the world.

Cyrus is said to be anointed in the sense that God chose him for a special mission. God, through Isaiah, called Cyrus by name 100 years before his time to prove to the Persian king that He, Yahweh, was the only true God. Josephus says that Cyrus released Israel when he was shown the prophecy of Isaiah 45.

Source
Berlin, Adele, Marc Z. Brettler, and Michael Fishbane, eds. *The Jewish Study Bible.* New York: Oxford University Press, 2004.

Background

God's Word through the prophet Jeremiah was fulfilled (see Jeremiah 29:10–14) and recorded in the book of Ezra. The book of Ezra was written after the exile of the Jews. Ezra is part of the continuous history of God's people, consisting of the books of 1 and 2 Chronicles, Ezra, and Nehemiah. Most scholars would agree that the historical writings presented in these books were primarily the work of one post-exilic author—Ezra.

Ezra was a faithful, godly, and uncompromising leader. His loyalty and passionate love for God's Word was demonstrated as he collected all the Old Testament books together as a unit; originated the form of worship used in the synagogue; and helped build the great synagogue in Jerusalem where the canon of Old Testament Scriptures would be settled. Some of the themes emphasized in the written history of the Chronicles, Ezra, and Nehemiah are hope, revival, reform, and restoration.

At-A-Glance

1. Restoration through the Spirit
(2 Chronicles 36:22–23)
2. Reformation through the Spirit (Ezra 1:5)
3. Contribution through the Spirit (vv. 6–7)

In Depth

1. Restoration through the Spirit (2 Chronicles 36:22–23)

Despite the sin and apostasy that characterized God's people, the Lord was behind the scenes working to accomplish His destiny and purpose in their lives. God demonstrates that He does whatever He will to fulfill His Word and achieve His purposes, even if He has to use the wicked and mighty for His glory. Solomon affirms this principle: "The king's heart is in the hand of the LORD . . . he turneth it whithersoever he will" (Proverbs 21:1). Isn't it wonderful to know that God works behind the scenes orchestrating His plans even through the lives of the unbelieving? (See also Isaiah 45:1–18; Psalm 47:7–8.)

Cyrus was the ruler of Persia, a vast nation stretching from the Indian Ocean to Greece. In his inaugural year as king, Cyrus was strategically positioned by God to fulfill the prophetic word of release and restoration for His people that was spoken by Jeremiah while Judah was still in exile in Babylon. How was this possible? According to Ezra, God "stirred up the spirit of Cyrus" (v. 22). Even though he was not a believer, Cyrus was prompted by the Lord to do what was right and pleasing in His sight. This is why we are commanded by God to pray for those who are in authority, regardless of their political or social views (see Romans 13:1; 1 Timothy 2:1–3). God knows how to turn leaders' hearts toward His people.

Cyrus put his decree in writing so that it would be an official proclamation for all the world to hear. No longer would the Jews be under the ruling hand of the Babylonians. It was time for them to return to their homeland to rebuild Jerusalem and the temple, and God would use Cyrus as His instrument to help the Jews with their work.

Cyrus acknowledged that the power and authority he wielded did not come from himself, but from the one true God who ruled heaven and Earth. God stirred up Cyrus so that he would motivate His people to take the steps necessary to set into motion His plan for future blessings and the restoration of the people.

Also, it is interesting to note that Cyrus spoke a blessing on the people: "The LORD his God be with him" (2 Chronicles 36:23). The principle is that God uses those in authority to encourage us to get involved in community building and family restoration—two important areas of society today. God is looking for yielded vessels whose hearts and spirits are stirred to roll up their sleeves and use their gifts and skills to become "repairer(s) of the breach" and "restorer(s) of paths to dwell in" (Isaiah 58:12–13).

2. Reformation through the Spirit (Ezra 1:5)

The Scripture lesson continues in the book of Ezra as the people return to their homeland. God's Spirit also stirs the hearts of the leaders and common people to commit to rebuilding Jerusalem and the temple. How important it is to be sensitive to the Holy Spirit's leading in our lives! We cannot accomplish any work for the Lord unless we are filled with and directed by His Holy Spirit. Another principle to keep in mind is that we cannot use manipulation, intimidation, or guilt to try to get people to do the Lord's work. If God does not move in people's hearts to get involved in the work of the ministry, all of our efforts are futile.

Almost 50,000 people responded to the Lord's call to get involved, participate in the first pilgrimage to Palestine, and give their all in the rebuilding project. Those who stayed behind in exile gave encouragement and support to the people who returned to the land of Judah. Everyone is gifted to work in ministry, whether that gift is leading, preaching, exhorting, giving, etc., we must help people find their place in ministry and encourage them to share their gifts and skills to further kingdom work.

3. Contribution through the Spirit (vv. 6–7)

God provided the necessary resources to rebuild Jerusalem and the temple. Isn't it wonderful to know that we don't have to depend on ourselves for the provisions needed for kingdom building? Many of the people returned with personal items of silver, gold, and other precious things to make sure there were ample resources for the rebuilding project. The people were so excited that God had forgiven them of their sins and restored them to their former positions that they were willing to do whatever was necessary to support the work of the Lord.

God's Spirit motivates us to be willing givers. When the Lord blesses us with material goods, our first response must be to return a portion of those blessings to Him. When we reflect on all the Lord had done for us, forgiving us of our sins, washing us in His blood, and giving us a new start, we should be willing to bless the Lord with our finances and our lives.

Not only did the people bring their resources to help in rebuilding, but Cyrus also returned the vessels that Nebuchadnezzar had taken from the old temple so they might be restored to their former glory. Once again, God used Cyrus to be His instrument of divine grace and blessing to His people.

The king challenged God's people to rebuild, provisions were made by willing hearts, and precious vessels were restored to the house of the Lord. Just as God restored His people to their proper place in Him, He is still at work restoring lost and broken humanity. We, too, must be willing to help those who are lost and hurting to find their place in the Lord. As we reflect on all God has done for us, we realize that it is not that difficult to be a restorer of humanity. Are you willing to help those who are hurting today?

Search the Scriptures

1. What was the Lord's charge to King Cyrus (2 Chronicles 36:22)?

2. The spirit of King Cyrus was stirred by whom (v. 23)?

3. God's house was built as a result of what (Ezra 1:5)?

4. The chief from what tribes rose up to build the house of the Lord (v. 5)?

5. Who took the vessels from Jerusalem before the Exile (v. 7)?

Discuss the Meaning

1. Is it possible for God to use unbelievers to fulfill His purposes? Discuss.

2. How do we encourage people who have lost hope and who believe that God has forsaken them?

3. What is the importance of getting people involved in the work of the Lord according to their gifts, talents, and abilities?

4. What areas of reformation and restoration are critically needed in the body of Christ? Discuss.

Lesson in Our Society

It is a great source of encouragement to know that the Lord is not only a covenant maker but also a covenant keeper. God delights in forgiving and restoring His people. Therefore, we must be willing to forgive and to restore broken relationships. It is also important that we be sensitive to the work of the Holy Spirit in our lives as well as in the lives of those around us. Together we can help make our communities a shining example of God's wisdom and counsel as we forgive people and work for the common good of our society. This week, be prepared to share that love and forgiveness with people who may have wronged you. See what God does in your life as you take that step of faith.

Make It Happen

There are many people in the world and in the church who need to know or experience God's forgiveness and restoration. Ask the Holy Spirit to help you recognize them, and be willing to give of your time and resources. Remember, God still uses people to play an important role in His redemptive plan.

Follow the Spirit

What God wants me to do:

_____

_____

Remember Your Thoughts

Special insights I have learned:

_____

_____

More Light on the Text

2 Chronicles 36:22–23; Ezra 1:5–7

22 Now in the first year of Cyrus king of Persia, that the word of the LORD spoken by the mouth of Jeremiah might be accomplished, the LORD stirred up the spirit of Cyrus king of Persia, that he made a proclamation throughout all his kingdom, and put it also in writing, saying,

The Hebrew verb *kalah* (**kaw-law'**, which means "might be accomplished"), refers to bringing a process to completion. The Word of God spoken by the mouth of Jeremiah had to be brought to completion to show the faithfulness of God.

To stress even more strongly just how God had fulfilled his Word spoken by Jeremiah, it is briefly mentioned that God stirred up the spirit of Cyrus, king of Persia. The word "spirit" (Heb. `uwr, **oor**, referring to Cyrus's will, mind, etc.) is used as an object with God as the subject. Thus, God incited Cyrus's spirit to act. Cyrus acted in harmony with the prophecy of Jeremiah (25:11ff.; 29:10) for the salvation of God's people.

23 Thus saith Cyrus king of Persia, all the kingdoms of the earth hath the LORD God of heaven given me; and he hath charged me to build him an house in Jerusalem, which is in Judah. Who is there among you of all his people? The LORD his God be with him, and let him go up.

Cyrus said that the Lord had commanded him to build again His temple in Jerusalem, which was in Judah. The Hebrew verb *paqad* (**paw-kad'**), translated "hath charged" here, means "to appoint" or to visit someone for the purpose of charging him or her to do something. Whoever belonged to the people of

"The LORD his God be with him, and let him go up" (from 2 Chronicles 36:23).

God had Cyrus's permission to go up to Jerusalem. Thus, God, in His compassion, made the return and rehabilitation of His people possible.

Ezra 1:5 Then rose up the chief of the fathers of Judah and Benjamin, and the priests, and the Levites, with all them whose spirit God had raised, to go up to build the house of the LORD which is in Jerusalem.

The expression "the chief of the fathers" is a literal translation of the two Hebrew words *ro'sh* (**roshe**) and *'ab* (**awb**) and designates the leaders of Judah and Benjamin. The leaders of Judah and Benjamin, the priests, and the Levites in short, all whose spirit God stirred up, rose to go up to build the house of God as a result of Cyrus's order.

The passage emphasizes that the enterprise was from the Lord (cf. 1:1; 2 Chronicles 36:23; see also Psalm 127:1–2). God incited the people to act. All of God's people were called upon to return, but only those who were willing to go and help build the temple at Jerusalem (or encourage those who did go) were aroused and obeyed God's call. God aroused the spirits of the leaders of Judah and Benjamin and of the priests and Levites (also see 2 Chronicles 36:22; Philippians 2:13; James 1:16–17).

6 And all they that were about them strengthened their hands with vessels of silver, with gold, with goods, and with beasts, and with precious things, beside all that was willingly offered.

The expression "all they that were about them" literally means "all those around them," or their neighbors. It appears to include persons other than the Jews.

The expression "strengthened their hands" means "assisted them with gifts." The people returning to Judah received support not only from other Jews (v. 4) but also from pagans. All their captors assisted them with gifts (see 6:22; Nehemiah 2:18; 6:9; Leviticus 25:34). The return from exile is described as being similar to the Exodus from Egypt, when the Children of Israel left Egypt enriched by gifts from the Egyptians (see Exodus 3:22; 12:35–36).

7 Also Cyrus the king brought forth the vessels of the house of the LORD, which Nebuchadnezzar had brought forth out of Jerusalem, and had put them in the house of his gods;

King Cyrus released the objects taken by Nebuchadnezzar (2 Kings 24:13; 25:13–16; 2 Chronicles 36:10, 18; Jeremiah 52:17–19) to the prince of Judah for use in the house of God that was about to be built. The Hebrew verb *yatsa'* (**yaw-tsaw'**), translated as "to bring forth," refers to going out from a particular location or from the presence of someone. Here, the emphasis is on Cyrus, who gave the order to give the vessels of the temple back to the people going to Jerusalem.

"The vessels of the house of the LORD" are the gold and silver vessels of the temple that Nebuchadnezzar carried off to Babylon and put in the treasure house of his god during the first conquest of Jerusalem while Jehoiakim was king (2 Chronicles

36:7; Daniel 1:1–2). The vessels taken during the second conquest were broken up (2 Kings 24:13). The other gold and silver goods, as well as the large brazen implements that were taken during the third conquest and the destruction of the temple (2 Kings 25:13–17; Jeremiah 52:18), would hardly have been preserved by the Chaldeans, but rather made use of as valuable booty. In the end, it was because of King Cyrus that the Jews were well equipped to rebuild the temple and reestablish Jerusalem.

Daily Bible Readings

M: Prayer for Deliverance
Psalm 57
T: God Promises to Lead and Heal
Isaiah 57:14–19
W: God Forgives
Psalm 130
T: God's Plan Revealed
Jeremiah 29:10–14
F: King Cyrus Plans to Rebuild
2 Chronicles 36:22–23
S: The Exiles Return
Ezra 1
S: Rebuilding the Temple
Ezra 5:7–14

DECEMBER 2006 QUARTER AT-A-GLANCE
Jesus Christ: A Portrait of God

This quarter has three units that introduce Jesus Christ and provide insight into His work. The lessons provide a theological framework for understanding where Jesus came from, as well as practical perspectives on what He came to do.

UNIT 1 . CHRIST, THE IMAGE OF GOD

This unit has five lessons designed to be an appropriate Advent/Christmas study. Lesson 1 asks, "Who is Jesus Christ?" Lesson 2 explores what God has to say in answer to this question. Lesson 3 examines Jesus as the light that conquers the world. Lesson 4, the Christmas lesson, focuses on Jesus Christ as the Word becoming flesh to live among humankind. The final lesson looks at how the issues of humiliation and exaltation converged in Jesus.

LESSON 1: December 3
Who Is Jesus Christ?
Colossians 1:15–23

The issue of Christ's identity is a crucial one. The truths reflected in our text was the apostle Paul's partial answer to the critics of his day, the Gnostics. They denied the humanity of Christ, so Paul found it necessary to declare that Jesus was actually God in the flesh.

LESSON 2: December 10
What God Says about Jesus
Hebrews 1:1–9

Our view of Jesus determines what response we give Him. The readers to whom the book of Hebrews was originally addressed were uncertain of Jesus' identity. They were struggling with whether to remain loyal to their Christian faith or to go back to their old religion of Judaism. To clear up their doubts, the writer asserts Jesus' identity. He states that while God revealed Himself in the past in a variety of ways, He has revealed Himself most profoundly through Jesus, His Son.

LESSON 3: December 17
Light That Conquers
1 John 1:1–2:5

To combat the error of false teachers infiltrating the church of John's day, he writes to assert that Jesus Christ was God in the flesh (incarnate). He presents God as "light," which symbolized perfect holiness and purity. He urged believers to conduct their lives in holiness as Jesus did. In so doing, they will have fellowship with God and with other believers.

LESSON 4: December 24
The Word Became Flesh
John 1:1–18

John presents Jesus as existing from the beginning, Himself the Creator and Source of life. He became human and offered the grace or eternal life and truth for the entire human race.

LESSON 5: December 31
Humiliation and Exaltation
Philippians 2:1–11

The letter to the Philippians was written by Paul during his first imprisonment to counteract false teaching of imprisonment. It was written to counteract false teaching of mysticism and asceticism—teaching that embraced the philosophy of focusing on the spirit world.

UNIT 2 . CHRIST SUSTAINS AND SUPPORTS

The four lessons in this unit focus on various "I am" statements in John's gospel and seek to address people's deepest needs. The first two lessons establish that Jesus has the power to sustain and support us because He came as our authority and judge. The last two lessons explore Jesus as the Bread of Life, Living Water, and the Light of the World.

LESSON 6: January 7
"I Am from Above"
John 8:31–38, 48–56, 58–59

Jesus dialogues with the Jewish leaders seeking to convince them of His heavenly origin. He explains that He can set them free and give them eternal life if they listen to His teaching. He chides them for rejecting His teaching, explaining that if they were the children of Abraham as they claimed to be, they would accept His message.

LESSON 7: January 14
Jesus Is Authority and Judge
John 5:19–29

While on Earth, Jesus conducted His life in complete submission and willing obedience to God the Father. Whatever Jesus saw the Father do, He did. Consequently, the Father has committed all authority and judgment to the Son. The Son of God has the power to raise the dead, give life to whomever He chooses, and to serve as Judge for all people everywhere.

LESSON 8: January 21
Jesus Is the Bread of Life and Living Water
John 6:34–40; 7:37–39

The Feast of Tabernacles was an eight-day celebration immediately following the harvest. Drawing on this time of feast and harvest, which signified bread aplenty and the water ceremony, Jesus declares Himself the Bread of Life and promises Living Water (the Holy Spirit) for those who come to Him.

LESSON 9: January 28
I Am the Light of the World
John 8:12–20; 12:44–46

Throughout the book of John, Jesus has progressively revealed that He did not bring light, but that He IS the light. Since Jesus is the light of the world, through His finished work on the Cross, He has overcome the darkness of sin. The only way a believer in Jesus can daily overcome sin is through constant communication, obedience, and submission to Christ.

UNIT 3 . CHRIST GUIDES AND PROTECTS

This unit explores Jesus' relationship to Christians from a corporate perspective. In lesson 10 we see Jesus as the Good Shepherd. Lesson 11 examines Jesus as the resurrection and the life, while lesson 12 looks at Jesus as the way, the truth, and the life. Finally, in lesson 13, we explore how to remain vitally alive as a community being connected to Jesus, the True Vine.

LESSON 10: February 4
I Am the Good Shepherd
John 10:1–5, 7–18

Jesus as the Good Shepherd has the best interest of the sheep in mind at all times. He is on constant guard to keep His sheep upright and in the fold. He is prepared to meet every need and even to give His life to rescue the sheep from danger. As the Good Shepherd, He protects us from danger and provides for our sustenance.

LESSON 11: February 11
I Am the Resurrection and the Life
John 11:17–27

Jesus is the Giver of physical and spiritual life. In this lesson, we find Jesus coming to the home of Mary and Martha after their brother has been dead and buried four days. Jesus taught that death is not a permanent reality for those who have developed a personal relationship with Him through faith, because He has the power to overcome death.

LESSON 12: February 18
"I Am the Way, the Truth, and the Life"
John 14:1–14

Jesus made it clear that He is the guiding light in the lives of His followers even though He is no longer physically present on the planet. He made it clear that there is no entrance into heaven except through Him, that only because of Him will we be empowered to do greater works than He did.

LESSON 13: February 25
I Am the True Vine
John 15:1–17

In the body of Christ, there is only one secure connection to Jesus Christ. Believers keep the connection secure through faith in the risen Christ, prayer, and the study of God's Word. Knowing that His followers will soon be scattered in a few days, Jesus' words emphasize unity first to Jesus Himself (the True Vine) and then to each other.

JESUS, THE GREAT I AM

by Terri Thompson

Question: How could God be revealed and reconciled to His beloved, mankind?
Answer: Jesus.

Jesus revealed God's character and purposes, and He became the way of salvation for mankind. "And [Jesus] is the radiance of [the Father's] glory and the exact representation of His nature" (Hebrews 1:3, NASB). Jesus "is the image of the invisible God" (Colossians 1:15). The One known to Moses as *I AM*, eternal and self-existent, is now revealed in flesh.

John 1 tells us that Jesus is the Word of God made flesh, dwelling among us and unveiling God's glory for all to see. What is a word except the expression of the person who spoke it? Through words and actions, a person's nature is seen. People are revealed to us by their words. So it is with God through His Word, Jesus.

Jesus demonstrated God's nature perfectly in His words and actions because He always did what He saw the Father doing (John 5:19). He preached the kingdom of God—the rule of God in the hearts of individuals and ultimately over the world—and ushered in a new era in which God could have direct communication with every person. Jesus performed miraculous signs, proving that God's power, authority, and favor dwelled in Him.

Jesus said, "I am the light of the world: he that followeth me shall not walk in the darkness, but shall have the light of life" (John 8:12). He embodied the light of God manifested to mankind. Sin had eclipsed God's light in creation, but Jesus' very presence exposed and dispersed the hidden works of darkness. His acts of light included healing, deliverance, and truth, dispelling the dark works of sin, such as sickness, madness, and lies. His final work on the Cross defeated the darkness of death with luminous rays of eternal life.

The Father gave Jesus all authority to judge. But Jesus turned judgment into grace. "Truly, truly, I say to you, he who hears My word, and believes Him who sent Me, has eternal life, and does not come into judgment, but has passed out of death into life" (John 5:24, NASB). Because of Jesus' death and resurrection, grace overrules judgment for those who believe. Luke gives us a beautiful picture of this when he describes the sinful woman who came and anointed Jesus' feet with perfume and tears. The Pharisees knew what kind of woman she was. They would have condemned her, but Jesus said she loved much because she had been forgiven much. Then He turned to her and spoke the words she could only dream of hearing: "Your sins have been forgiven" (Luke 7:48, NASB).

Using simple metaphors, Jesus gave word pictures describing Himself as God. Men and women watched Jesus and saw the living God in character and color. Jesus portrayed Himself as our very sustenance when He said, "I am the bread of life; he who comes to Me will not hunger, and he who believes in Me will never thirst" (John 6:35, NASB). Without Him, nothing could satisfy the voracious hunger and thirst of a human spirit. During the celebration of living water on the last day of the Feast of Tabernacles, Jesus said, "If anyone is thirsty, let him come to Me and drink" (7:37, NASB).

He proclaimed His ownership of and concern for each of us when He declared, "I am the good shepherd, and I know My own and My own know Me" (John 10:14, NASB). He showed that He was the only way to enter God's fold of sheep when He said, "I am the door; if anyone enters through Me, he will be saved, and will go in and out and find pasture" (John 10:9, NASB).

Jesus asserted that He was the Giver of physical and spiritual life: "I am the resurrection and the life; he who believes in Me will live even if he dies"

(John 11:25, NASB). He boldly claimed to be the only way to reach God the Father: "I am the way, and the truth, and the life; no one comes to the Father but through Me" (14:6, NASB).

Jesus claimed to be the One and only, the Creator, God the great I AM who revealed Himself to Moses: "Truly, truly, I say to you, before Abraham was, I am" (John 8:58, RSV).

But Jesus did more than make lofty claims; He demonstrated God's character through the way He lived. He loved the unlovely, cared for the outcasts, healed the sick, and chased demons out of human homes. He prophesied His own death and resurrection and then fulfilled His prophecies. He showed forth the Father by doing everything He saw His Father doing. He accomplished all that the Father willed, down to the last detail. Then He said, "As the Father has sent Me, I also send you" (John 20:21, NASB).

Jesus is God, and by His actions He revealed God to mankind. Then He sent His disciples and those who would follow in their footsteps to represent Him to a still-dark world. Now we who trace the same path are called to manifest Christ's nature—God's nature—to those around us. But first we must know who we are in Christ.

We are the sheep of His fold if we believe in Him and recognize His voice. Jesus said, "My sheep hear my voice, and I know them, and they follow me" (John 10:27, RSV).

Paul explains in 2 Corinthians 5:18–20 (NASB), "Now all these things are from God, who reconciled us to Himself through Christ and gave us the ministry of reconciliation, namely, that God was in Christ reconciling the world to Himself, not counting their trespasses against them, and He has committed to us the word of reconciliation. Therefore, we are ambassadors for Christ, as though God were making an appeal through us; we beg you on behalf of Christ, be reconciled to God."

So we have the same ministry as our Lord Jesus did. Being full of God's presence, character, and power, we are His light in the darkness, removing obstacles and drawing people to Him. We are to have the same attitude that Christ had. Philippians 2 says that Jesus recognized He was God but did not hold on to that privilege. Instead, He humbled Himself, took the form of a servant, and became obedient to the Father, even to the point of death.

If we abide in Jesus as a branch abides in its vine, we are filled with Christ. He dwells in us, but this is not a cause to boast or to lord it over others. This is our call to follow Christ's example, humble ourselves, and become obedient servants in order to reconcile men to God. We are to be the branches that, drawing nourishment from the vine, produce much fruit. "If you abide in me, and my words abide in you, ask whatever you will, and it shall be done for you. By this my Father is glorified, that you bear much fruit, and so prove to be my disciples" (John 15:8, RSV).

Jesus is the great I AM, the Alpha and the Omega, the Eternal. He came in a physical body to demonstrate God's character and will to men and to reconcile them to God. As we learn to obey His voice and draw our lives from His life, we, too, are called to shine the light of God, revealing Him in the midst of darkness. We, too, reconcile men to God by our lives and words, just as the Word Himself did.

Question: How will God be revealed and reconciled to His beloved, mankind?

Answer: Jesus, in and through us.

_____

Terri Thompson is a short story writer, pastor's wife, women's ministry advisor, and Sunday School teacher.

CHRIST-CENTEREDNESS: THE KEY TO WISDOM

by Luvell Anderson Jr.

If you take a look around, you will undoubtedly see some disturbing things brewing all over the world. Gratuitous wars, legalization of abominable practices, and other such maladies are occurring more and more. Injustice and human atrocities are being committed at the command of those in positions of power and influence. Many are being educated with philosophies that emphasize a concentration on self; it is the Protagorean doctrine "Homo mensura" (man is the measure of all things). This doctrine not only pervades the lives of those in the world, but also crept into the church in large measure. From televangelists to many of our pulpits, we are told how to easily eliminate our problems. Self-help has supplanted the ministry of the Word of God on Sunday mornings. In a study conducted by The Barna Group, 51 percent of Protestants identified having a satisfying family life as their top priority, with understanding and living out the principles of the Christian faith coming in second place.

At the heart of it all, the problem seems to be in the overall philosophy of life that has been adopted. The church has adopted a human-centered philosophy as the way to wisdom. Our actions are motivated more by utilitarianism (i.e., whatever produces the greatest amount of pleasure is the right course of action) than by the Gospel. If we as the church are to recover genuine biblical wisdom, we must reorganize our priorities, placing Jesus Christ at the top of the list, because our relationship with Him determines how things will go with the rest of the items on the list. In short, we must recover Christ-centered preaching and teaching, Christ-centered thinking, and Christ-centered living.

The obvious place to begin our pursuit of wisdom is the Word of God. In 2 Timothy, the apostle Paul charges Timothy to "preach the word" (2 Timothy 4:2). His charge comes after he himself had spent several years faithfully preaching and teaching God's Word. In a letter addressed to the Corinthians, Paul states, "When I came to you, brethren, I did not come proclaiming to you the testimony of God with lofty speech or wisdom. For I decided to know nothing among you except Jesus Christ and him crucified" (1 Corinthians 2:1–2, RSV). Paul emphasized the importance of Christ-centered preaching so as not to deliver to the Corinthians a man-centered wisdom that does not have the power to save human beings from their sins. He knew that only a message that was entirely focused on Christ could save them; it alone provides godly wisdom, since Christ is "the wisdom of God" (1 Corinthians 1:24).

Furthermore, Paul knew that in order for him to preach from the Scriptures faithfully, his sermons must testify of Jesus. When condemning the Pharisees for their unbelief, Jesus said, "You search the scriptures, because you think that in them you have eternal life; and it is they that bear witness to me" (John 5:39, RSV). However, Jesus makes it clear that biblical texts are not moralistic stories meant to show us some principle or rule to follow; instead, they testify about Him.

After we have recovered Christ-centered preaching and teaching in our pulpits and churches, we must internalize the message so that it dominates our thinking. There is no greater impediment to attaining wisdom than self-absorption. When we are overconfident in our own abilities, we, in essence, reject God's Word and open ourselves up to perversion and shame. Scripture gives several examples of the consequences of self-absorption. In the book of Genesis, we find Adam and Eve believing that they were wiser than God, defying His command not to eat of the Tree of Knowledge of Good and Evil. As a result, life on Earth was altered for the worse, catapulting humanity into a state of sin and death.

In Daniel, we read about Nebuchadnezzar, king of Babylon, which was the superpower nation in its day. Nebuchadnezzar ponders: "Is not this great Babylon, which I have built by my mighty power as a royal residence and for the glory of my majesty?" (Daniel 4:30, RSV). Nebuchadnezzar's arrogance brought God's judgment upon him, driving him into the wilderness and reducing him to the level of a wild animal. We also read in Romans how men proclaimed themselves to be wise and instead became fools (Romans 1:22). Paul says that God "gave them up in the lusts of their hearts to impurity" (v. 24, ESV), which led to self-destructive practices. In all of these instances, the thought process of each individual followed the pattern of the world. Each person acted according to the philosophy of the spirit of the age. But God calls us to be transformed by the renewal of our minds (Romans 12:2), by putting off the old nature and putting on the new nature, which is made in the likeness of God (Ephesians 4:22–24; Colossians 3:9–10, RSV). It is the Holy Spirit who transforms us, but we must be willing to yield to Him by shedding any self-centered tendencies and submitting to Jesus Christ.

Finally, after absorbing Christ-centered preaching into our minds, we must begin to act upon it by living it out. It is not enough to be able to recall information, but, in order to claim that we have wisdom, we must evidence wisdom in our everyday lives. Early twentieth century Welsh preacher Martyn Lloyd-Jones explains: "The wise man or woman does not merely have knowledge—you can put that into computers; they have the power of appropriating and assimilating that knowledge until it becomes judgment. It becomes part of them, controlling their point of view, and determining their actions and practice. So our wisdom is judged not merely by the number of books we have read or can quote and recite, but by the way we live, the way we use that knowledge. Christ put that in a famous question—'What shall it profit a man, if he shall gain the whole world [of knowledge and of wealth], and lose his own soul?'" (Mark 8:36). Wisdom is demonstrated by our conduct, not by our erudition or articulation.

We must make Christ the focus of our lives because He is "the wisdom of God." There can be no other focus if we hope to obtain God's wisdom. Christ is also the focus of God's sanctifying work in our lives: "For those whom he foreknew he also predestined to be conformed to the image of his Son" (Romans 8:29, RSV). God is fashioning us to look like Jesus, and it is our calling as Christians to preach, think, and live in a way that reflects our commitment to being conformed to the image of Christ.

Sources

The Barna Group. "What Is a Purpose-Driven Life to Americans?" *The Barna Group*, May 17, 2005. http://www.barna.org/FlexPage.aspx?Page=BarnaUpdate&BarnaUpdate ID=188 (accessed February 16, 2006).

Lloyd-Jones, Martyn. "Humanism—The Fifth Woe." *Sermon Index*. http://www.sermonindex.net/modules/articles/inde .php?view=article&aid=533 (accessed February 16, 2006).

Luvell Anderson Jr. is currently a student at the University of Missouri pursuing a bachelor's degree in philosophy.

TRUE COMMUNITY: THE BASIS OF REAL FELLOWSHIP

by Charles Woolery

The African proverb, "It takes an entire village to raise a child," applies not only to providing for and nurturing our children, but also to taking care of everyone who makes up the village. The village is a community that needs saving. The word "community" is derived from the concept of *common unity*. Community is made up of many components that transcend the idea of just a bunch of people living in the same neighborhood. Rather, a community is made up of citizens, residential homes, businesses, schools, arts and recreation, community centers, and churches. A community also has dark, seedy places, such as drug houses, bars, and nightclubs, which cater to a specific clientele. A community is multifaceted and not monolithic; it has something for everyone. The church is called to give the community a sense of direction and inspire the community to direct its energy to the service of God and humanity. True community can be achieved only when there is an intentional effort made to achieve true unity of purpose.

In the early church, as described in the Acts of the Apostles, there was a village mentality. The second and fourth chapters of Acts state that "all who believed were together and had all things in common; they would sell their possessions and goods and distribute the proceeds to all, as any had need. Now the whole group of those who believed were of one heart and soul" (Acts 2:44–45; 4:32, NRSV). If the church is going to offer salvation to the masses through worship, the Word, and hard work, then it has to work toward bringing about true community. But how can we embrace the concept of true community or a village mentality when many of us have fallen victim to individualism and are stressing individual needs at the expense of community needs? America's defini-

tion of success is based upon individualism, materialism, and how much one can accumulate, as opposed to how much one can give. The prominence of financial accumulation as the criterion for success has negatively affected society, the community, and the church. Many people expect the Lord to bless them with money, cars, clothes, and houses when and if they tithe. With a materialistic mind-set and a me-first mentality, how can we become a true community where the needs of "the least of these" are met? Who is going to care about the hungry, the naked, the illiterate, the poor, and the mentally infirm, if the saints of God are too blessed to be stressed over the urban poor? I'm glad you asked.

True community in the Black community will become a reality when the Black church remembers its origin, purpose, and mission. The American Black church was birthed during a time of systemic oppression and genocide—slavery. The Black church was birthed because there was a need for displaced African Christians to worship God using their own idioms, customs, culture, and spirituality, and singing, dancing, praying, and preaching styles. The Black church gave slaves the freedom, away from the eyes of the slaveholders, to worship in a way that met their spiritual, emotional, and social needs.

Throughout our painful sojourn in America, the Black church has been our weapon to fight against all forms of oppression. Without the Black church fighting for civil and human rights, there would probably be no Black middle or upper class as we now have. The Black church has always fought on the side of the oppressed, whether they were Black, White, Brown, or Yellow. Just as Black America is not monolithic, neither is the Black church. There is diversity within the Black church.

All Black people do not worship exactly alike. Nonetheless, true community can become a reality when church members, that is, disciples of Jesus Christ, remember why the church exists. The church exists to witness to the Gospel: important goals include the aim to save, support, socialize, and strengthen the poor, powerless, defenseless, downtrodden, and voiceless people. The church exists to teach us the value of redistributing our wealth so that everyone can eat, so that everyone can receive an excellent education, so that everyone can have adequate housing, and so that everyone can grow up in a healthy environment. How do we do this? Well, each church should assess the needs of its community. There is strength in numbers. If all churches within a particular community joined forces to combat and defeat the various pathologies that afflict us as diverse people, we could usher in true community.

Finally, true community is not monolithic. True community is not just Christians working together to usher in the rule of God, but it should involve all God-fearing people. A serious discussion of true community must involve bringing together all religious bodies within the Judeo-Christian family. Establishing true community must be intentional within our communities in order to rid them of drugs, violence, crime, poverty, and economic and political apathy. A true community invites all peoples to the salvation table and sets an agenda based not on our differences, but on our similarities and common goals. True community will not happen overnight. It can become a reality in whatever context of ministry we are involved in if we decide to put God's will and the needs of the people ahead of our own.

Let God's will be done on Earth as it is in heaven!

PAMELA ELAINE ROSS

CHRISTIAN EDUCATOR

Words have always been important to Pamela Elaine Ross, and getting people to understand her has also been very important. When she was a child, no one seemed to understand a word she said, except her mother. In second grade, she was sent to a speech therapist. Things began to change. In the meantime, her mother taught her priceless lessons, such as patience, kindness, consideration, and how to love and serve others. These lessons shaped Pamela Elaine Ross into the woman that she is today.

Pamela Elaine Ross has worked diligently in several capacities: Sunday School teacher, School of Ministry instructor, event commentator, radio announcer, and telephone counselor.

Although Pamela is single, she has five godchildren and a multitude of nieces and nephews whom she mothers. Her profession in education has allowed her to teach children with special needs to use today's technology. Headed toward a master's degree in education and in business administration, Pamela has earned certifications in teaching the Trainable Mentally Handicapped, Educable Mentally Handicapped, Learning Disabled, and Behavior Disabled. She also holds CompuPlay Instructor Certification (Computers and Children with Disabilities) and Lekotek Leader Certification (Learning Through Play and Children with Disabilities).

Pamela is a consultant and trainer for using technology as an educational tool. She has served as director of training for United Cerebral Palsy of Greater Chicago, enabling babies 9 months and up and children with disabilities to learn through play, and their parents and service providers to participate in technology training.

In the body of Christ, Pamela trains others to teach the Word of God effectively. She is passionate about the Word of God and helping others to be proficient in their calling to teach the Word. In her training class, she asks her students, "Why do you teach?" Ms. Ross believes that teaching God's Word should be taken even more seriously than teaching in the school system. Her approach to the Word of God makes it practical for everyday life.

Her teaching method involves research, planning, and prayer. Her friends include her Bible, Bible dictionary, Bible commentary, concordances, and downloaded Internet information and software as teaching tools to ensure that she's giving her class her best—her passion. Even after retirement, Pamela sees herself as an itinerant teacher of the Word of God.

TEACHING TIPS

December 3
Bible Study Guide 1

1. Words You Should Know

A. Gnosticism—The thought and practice, especially of various cults of late pre-Christian and early Christian centuries distinguished by the conviction that matter is evil and that emancipation comes through gnosis.

B. Reconcile (Colossians 1:20) *apokatallasso* (Gk.)—An exchange or adjustment; restoration to (divine) favor.

2. Teacher Preparation

A. Pray for clarity in your teaching. Also pray for the students in your class. Ask God to give them ears to hear and a heart to receive the teaching.

B. Study the Focal Verses and memorize the Keep in Mind verse.

C. Review and highlight areas throughout the lesson that specifically deal with the Lesson Aim.

D. Study More Light on the Text for deeper knowledge.

E. Complete lesson 1 in the *Precepts For Living®* *Personal Study Guide.*

3. Starting the Lesson

A. Before your students arrive, write the At-A-Glance outline on the board. Add these questions: Who is God? Who is Christ? Who are today's Gnostics?

B. After your students arrive, have them divide up into small groups, and ask for a volunteer from each group to read the Focal Verses, using the At-A-Glance outline as a guide. Then read Keep in Mind for emphasis.

C. While the small groups work, ask a student to pray the Lesson Aim.

4. Getting into the Lesson

A. Have a student read the In Focus story. Explain that in today's story, God reconciled the two brothers, just as He reconciles us to Himself.

B. Ask a student to read The People, Places, and Times. How does Paul's struggle relate to the students' own ministries? How can we convince others that Christ was God in human form?

C. Ask each group to read In Depth, and have the small groups answer the Search the Scriptures and Discuss the Meaning questions.

D. Have the students reconvene as a large group to discuss their answers.

5. Relating the Lesson to Life

A. Reread Keep in Mind.

B. Ask the students to write a note to a loved one as if the person receiving the note were a 10-year-old child. Ask them to share who Christ is and why they want their loved one to know Him.

C. Ask your students if their understanding of Christ's identity has changed through this study. Does Christ truly feel *real*? How can we get to know Him better?

6. Arousing Action

A. Discuss Lesson in Our Society.

B. Ask your students for a specific plan to implement Make It Happen. Ask for commitments on which to report next week.

C. Remind your students to read next week's Daily Bible Readings to further explore Christ's identity.

D. Close the class with prayer.

Worship Guide

For the Superintendent or Teacher
Theme: Who Is Jesus Christ?
Theme Song: "Stand Up, Stand Up for Jesus"
Scripture: Matthew 18:1–4, 10
Song: "Jesus Loves Me"
Meditation: Sweet Jesus, help me to know You. Help me to know and to share that You are the Creator, Sustainer, Redeemer, and Ruler of our universe. I want to celebrate, trust, honor, and obey You every day. Give me the words to share You, my Jesus, with others. In Christ's name I pray. Amen.

WHO IS JESUS CHRIST?

Bible Background • COLOSSIANS 1
Printed Text • COLOSSIANS 1:15–23   Devotional Reading • ISAIAH 9:2–7

Lesson Aim

By the end of the lesson, we will:

EXPLORE the apostle Paul's view of Jesus Christ as Creator, Sustainer, Redeemer, and Ruler of the universe as presented in our text;

BECOME CONVINCED that because of His identity, Jesus Christ is worthy of our trust, honor, and obedience; and

CELEBRATE Jesus as Creator, Redeemer, and King of our lives.

Keep in Mind

"Who is the image of the invisible God, the firstborn of every creature: For by him were all things created, that are in heaven, and that are in earth, visible and invisible, whether they be thrones, or dominions, or principalities, or powers: all things were created by him, and for him" (Colossians 1:15–16).

Focal Verses

Colossians 1:15 Who is the image of the invisible God, the firstborn of every creature:

16 For by him were all things created, that are in heaven, and that are in earth, visible and invisible, whether they be thrones, or dominions, or principalities, or powers: all things were created by him, and for him:

17 And he is before all things, and by him all things consist.

18 And he is the head of the body, the church: who is the beginning, the firstborn from the dead; that in all things he might have the preeminence.

19 For it pleased the Father that in him should all fulness dwell;

20 And, having made peace through the blood of his cross, by him to reconcile all things unto himself; by him, I say, whether they be things in earth, or things in heaven.

21 And you, that were sometime alienated and enemies in your mind by wicked works, yet now hath he reconciled.

22 In the body of his flesh through death, to present you holy and unblameable and unreproveable in his sight:

23 If ye continue in the faith grounded and settled, and be not moved away from the hope of the gospel, which ye have heard, and which was preached to every creature which is under heaven; whereof I Paul am made a minister;

In Focus

During his 10-year prison stay, Craig wrote to his family members on many occasions, declaring his repentance and asking their forgiveness—but no one answered. Because he was a minister and leader in his community, his highly publicized trial had left a bitter taste in the mouth of his family. Upon his release, he continued to write, but no one in his family would communicate with him, even though he had been out of prison for more than two years.

Just after his release from prison, Craig returned to his community and formed a ministry that provided homes for the community's homeless. Now, Craig was in the news again. Two years had gone by, and Craig had served faithfully without receiving any pay.

One night, as Albert watched the evening news, he saw a newscaster at a ceremony where, to his amazement, his brother Craig was being awarded the key to the city for the good work his ministry was doing in the community. Suddenly, Albert felt convicted, and he saw his brother's life in a different light. He decided that he would pay his brother a visit.

Craig looked thinner than Albert remembered. He looked tired and withdrawn—no doubt the effects of a 10-year prison term. Albert stood in the busy storefront office and embraced his brother awkwardly. Then he said, "Craig, I apologize for not seeking you out sooner. I'm sorry I let your past mistakes keep me away. I wanted to be the first one in the family to welcome you back.

We all got together, and we want to bless your ministry with a $1,000 contribution."

Both men let their tears run freely. After Albert made that first move, love was victorious. A wave of reconciliation swept through their family.

God reconciles people and all things to Himself through the sacrificial blood of Jesus. God's plan to reconcile us to Himself reminds us that reconciliation requires that someone make the first move.

The People, Places, and Times

Colossae. The Colossians lived in *Colossae* (**co-LOS-see**), a city in Phrygia, which was a Roman province in Asia Minor. Close to Hierapolis and Laodicea, Colossae fell in importance as these cities rose. Colossae was close to the great road that led from Ephesus to the Euphrates, the "good and abounding river," often just called "the river" in the Bible (cf. Genesis 15:18; 41:1–3, 17). The largest, the longest, and by far the most important of western Asia's rivers, the Euphrates flows into the Persian Gulf.

Paul. Paul was born Saul of Tarsus and was of the tribe of Benjamin. As a citizen of Tarsus, he enjoyed Roman citizenship. His parents were religious Jews and gave Saul a top-notch education in Jerusalem. Saul became a learned and prominent Pharisee who helped persecute, torture, and scatter Christian disciples. However, this persecution proved critical in spreading the cause of Christ, since the disciples scattered far and wide to survive. After being "blinded by the light" on the road to Damascus, Saul was converted, became known as Paul, and became a great preacher. With his 13 epistles (letters), he wrote more books of the Bible than any other New Testament author, and much of his missionary work is detailed in the last eight chapters of the Acts of the Apostles, written by the apostle Luke. Paul was beheaded by Nero at or near Rome in A.D. 66.

Timothy. A native of Lystra, Timothy had a Greek father, but his grandmother and mother were pious Jews who trained him up in the knowledge of the Scriptures (Acts 16:1). Paul decided to take Timothy along on his journey with Silas, not long after he and Barnabas had argued and parted company.

Tychicus. He was a messenger sent by Paul with the epistles to the Colossians and Ephesians.

Background

Paul wrote this epistle in about A.D. 62 during his first captivity in Rome (Acts 28:16), at about the same time he wrote his epistles to the Ephesians and the Philippians. Although he describes the "ideal church" to the Ephesians, he writes to the Colossians to warn about false teachings. He has been alerted to the problems of the Colossians by Colossae residents Epaphras (Colossians 1:7; 4:12; Philemon 23) and Onesimus (an escaped slave of Philemon who fled from his master but was led to Christ by Paul, who sent him back to Philemon in order to reconcile them as equal brothers in Christ; Colossians 4:9, 18; Philemon 10, 25). Paul wanted the Colossians to be aware that the Gnostics' philosophy was corrupting the simplicity of their belief. Worse, it was obscuring the eternal glory and dignity of Christ. Paul sent Tychicus to deliver the epistles, with directions to check on the state of the believers at Colossae and to exhort and comfort them.

At-A-Glance

1. Christ Is Supreme (Colossians 1:15–18)
2. Christ Reconciles Us through His Death (vv. 19–21)
3. Christ Calls Us To Stay Grounded in Faith (vv. 22–23)

In Depth

1. Christ Is Supreme (Colossians 1:15–18)

This letter to the Colossians is the third of Paul's prison epistles. Even in prison, Paul had heard of the mystic practices that had begun to infiltrate the Colossians' worship of Christ. He wanted the Colossians to know that they were complete in Christ

Jesus is creator of all things that are in heaven and Earth, visible and invisible (see Colossians 1:15–16).

and that Christ is the exact image of the "invisible God" and supreme over all. For if Christ is not above all—if He is not supreme—He is a complete fallacy. Christ must meet each of these criteria for God's fullness to dwell in Him. Paul tells the Colossians that Christ created all things, seen and unseen, in heaven and on Earth—even the powers and dominions. He created them and is the reason for their existence. Nothing can be added to Christ. He is supreme over all.

Christ walked the earth as a visible image of the invisible God. We have testimony and mental images of this fact that are well documented, not only in the Bible but also in a variety of other historically credible texts and teachings. Even those who doubted Christ as Lord and Saviour never doubted that a man named Jesus walked the earth.

Throughout the New Testament, men and women learned from this man named Jesus as He walked their streets, rejoiced with them at a wedding, calmed a stormy sea, or washed their dirty, stinky feet. This flesh and blood image of the invisible God was one of us. He walked, wept, even tossed over the moneychangers' tables in the temple. Finally, the "invisible God" could be physically felt, seen, and heard. Jesus even argued for His Father and taught and healed in His name.

To have this strong, visible "image of the invisible God" assists and comforts us in many ways. We have an image, a completely infallible image, to help us easily understand the "invisible God." This Christ, once we know Him, is a pure and simple way to share our "invisible God" with the unbeliever. In a world with more rulers, factions, and threats than we can number, much less know and control, it is comforting to know that everything was created through Christ. Far beyond and above the complexities of His creation, Christ is before all and holds everything together. More importantly, He's in charge of it all, so we don't have to worry about the myriad powers and principalities that we can or cannot see with our own eyes.

For the Colossians, and for us today, the simple truth could be turned into something twisted by mystic ideas, ritual, popular rumor, or pop culture. As we interact and share with nonbelievers, Christ's identity as God in the flesh is critical. Paul uses many words to share Christ's roles as Creator, Sustainer, and Redeemer of all things. Christ is, in fact, Ruler of the universe, before all things, and only through Him do all things exist. Paul also makes it clear in verse 18 that Christ is the head of the body, the church. As firstborn from the dead, Christ is supreme over all things. This supreme position makes any mystic additions not only irreverent, but also silly. This declaration allows us to be confident that our belief in Christ is perfect and whole—complete.

2. Christ Reconciles Us through His Death (vv. 19–21)

The Father is pleased that in Christ does "all fulness dwell." The *New Living Translation* reads, "For God in all his fullness was pleased to live in Christ." God is pleased with Christ—and pleased to live in Him.

This "fullness" of Christ is critical to God's plan. For it is by Christ that God reconciled everything to Himself. God makes peace with everything in heaven and on Earth by Christ shedding His blood on the Cross—a human being in which God's fullness dwells. Paul's declaration clearly refuted the agnostic teaching that Jesus could not be God.

As we seek reconciliation for ourselves and others, this is a critical point in terms of logic and faith. How could God become human without giving up His divinity? John the Baptist understood the answer to this, and we must search until we, too, understand that Christ was God in the flesh. This image of the invisible God, the tangible Christ-in-the-flesh, allows us to know God in ways that we never could, apart from His becoming human.

If we pass this hurdle through prayer, sharing with others, reading our Bibles, slowly absorbing what is true, and spending time with God and His Son and the Holy Spirit, we will know this is true. And we will fully understand that Christ can be trusted. He deserves our honor and obedience. Once we reach this level, telling others about Christ can be as simple and clear as sharing something funny from our weekend or an intimate moment with our children. As we celebrate Christ and His love in our lives, we'll share with joy the reality of a God who can be touched and felt. Christ as Creator, Redeemer, and King of our lives is a simple truth—and others are bound to want what we have. Maybe they will even ask where we found it.

3. Christ Calls Us To Stay Grounded in Faith (vv. 22–23)

Before we truly knew God—or for some, when we walked away from Him—we were alone, enemies of God in our sinful thoughts and wicked works; but Christ wanted us back. He was willing to die for us, even while knowing how rebellious and angry we might be. He knew what had to be done: He had to endure a horrible death by torture to pay the debt for our sin and for the sins of a multitude of others who would be lost without Him.

So He came, taught, nurtured, and loved. He was tortured, crucified, and buried. Yet He came right back, not weaker but stronger, to reconcile us to Himself and to our Father. He knew that we would struggle to believe and wander off in "wicked ways," but He wanted us just as we are. He loved us first, before we even believed in Him or were moved to look for a way other than our own. And He still loves us—more than most of us will ever understand.

Saul was much like many of us. He hurt and destroyed others, while being positive that he was on the right track. He focused on friends, social standing, and education. He was a Pharisee who was dedicated to smashing this cultlike Christianity. But on the road to Damascus, he was converted, and the apostle Paul emerged. He and many of his epistles changed the world for Christ, spreading the same truth that he had so faithfully set out to destroy.

Paul says he was made a minister by the gifts "dispensed" to him from God to fulfill His Word (vv. 23–25). Paul wrote that the mystery had been hidden from past ages and generations, but that God had manifested it to His saints, showing them the "riches of the glory of this mystery," which is "Christ in you, the hope of glory" (vv. 26–27).

Christ in us, this hope of glory, was a mystery for so long. Paul admonishes the saints to warn and teach every man "in all wisdom," so that we may present "every man perfect in Christ Jesus" (v. 28). Paul claims this as his own labor, something he strives for and something that "worketh in [him] mightily"— even in a Roman prison.

Many of us feel this pull, this urgency that works mightily in us. Yet to share Christ at each opportunity and to declare Him as Ruler of the universe frightens us on many levels. Paul had been whipped and jailed and had suffered many of the tortures he himself had inflicted upon Christians. He was probably afraid, just like every other breathing soul, but he did what he felt he was called to do. He reached out from his prison by writing letters. He worked hard to maintain his faith and surround himself with believers and workers for Christ, even while imprisoned. Paul's letters still teach us today.

Is there something we can do to express our concern for others? Who can you write to today? How can you encourage them in Christ's love, even if they don't know Him yet? Are you willing to step out of your own "prison" and offer Christ's reconciliation to others? Are you willing to face the "torture" of their disapproval or the possibility of cynical stares, ridicule, and rejection?

Search the Scriptures

1. How can we show others an invisible God? What image do we have to show them (Colossians 1:15)?

2. What does it mean to make "peace through the blood of His Cross" (v. 20)?

3. How did we get "reconciled"? What does this mean in God's sight (vv. 20–21)?

4. To stay "grounded and settled," from what do we need to "refuse to be moved" (v. 23)?

5. Make a list of simple daily tasks that can keep us "grounded and settled."

Discuss the Meaning

1. Are you currently prepared to face today's doubters and mystics with a clear, thoughtful description of Christ's identity? Practice a Q&A ses-

sion on "Who is Christ?"

2. Do we need steel-trap memories and long, memorized quotations to tell others about Christ? Why or why not? How can our personal gifts help us explain Jesus to others?

3. What are three things we should celebrate and honor Christ for, according to Paul? Name a few simple ways we can do this daily, in public or in private.

Lesson in Our Society

Mystic practices, such as Wicca (run by modern-day witches), humanistic values, and Hollywood's promotion of immorality and pop culture lurk around every corner. It's difficult to block out the pervasive and constant battering of these external influences. Yet Paul says that by Christ "were all things created, that are in heaven, and that are in earth, visible and invisible, whether they be thrones, or dominions, or principalities, or powers: all things were created by him, and for him" (Colossians 1:15–16). Christ is greater than any other influences or forces. How can we help others see Christ, crucified 2,000 years ago, as the "image of the invisible God" and a powerful force necessary in their lives today?

Make It Happen

This week, ask the Lord to help you find the words to explain "Who is Christ?" Perhaps spend time writing about it in your journal or talking to a child about who Christ is. Take Paul's ideas and add what you know from your own life and your experience with Christ and His love and redemption. Try to find at least one person in need of hope or kindness and introduce him/her to Christ. Next week, report what you said and who you shared with.

Follow the Spirit

What God wants me to do:

_____

_____

Remember Your Thoughts

Special insights I gained today:

_____

_____

More Light on the Text
Colossians 1:15–23

This passage, generally agreed by scholars to be an existing hymn that was used by Paul, carries the reader to the very heights of Paul's Christology. It is as profound in its view of Christ as John 1:1–18. Here, Paul seeks to give expression to the intimate bond between Christ and God, not only in the redemption of fallen humanity, but also in the very creation of the world.

15 Who is the image of the invisible God, the firstborn of every creature:

Here, Paul affirms Christ as the image of the invisible God. An "image" (Gk. *eikon*, **i-KONE**) is something that reflects or manifests the presence of a being or thing that cannot be seen. In Greek thought, an image shares in the reality of what it represents. The word contains the idea of manifestation and representation. The verse echoes the Christian belief that human beings are made in the image of God (Genesis 1:26; 1 Corinthians 11:7; Colossians 3:10). Paul then applies this belief to Christ, who forms the living bridge between the transcendent Creator and the visible world. If people were to ask what God is like, Paul would simply answer that they must look at Jesus, for He perfectly represents God in a form that can be seen, known, and understood by humans (cf. John 14:6–11). Jesus is the perfect manifestation of God, the portrait of God in whom can be seen the personal characteristics and the distinguishing marks of God.

Paul goes on to proclaim Christ as the firstborn of all creation, a phrase that must be understood in its context. The word "firstborn" (Gk. *prototokos*, **pro-tot-OK-os**) is highly significant. Although the English definition is simple, the words "firstborn child" should not be understood in this way here. In a sense, Christ does not belong to God's creation; rather, He stands over against God's creation as the agent through whom all spiritual powers came into existence (vv. 16–17). The word "firstborn" could refer either to first in an order, such as a firstborn child, or to someone prominent in rank and function and,

thus, a title of honor (Exodus 4:22; Psalm 89:27). By using both of these meanings simultaneously, Paul is affirming that Christ is not only begotten before all other creatures, but is also the most favored. To Him belongs the highest honor, which is "higher than the kings of the earth" (Psalm 89:27). The point here is the preeminence of Christ.

16 For by him were all things created, that are in heaven, and that are in earth, visible and invisible, whether they be thrones, or dominions, or principalities, or powers: all things were created by him, and for him:

The passive grammatical form of the phrase "were all things created" (Gk. *ktizo*, **KTID-zo**) indicates that God is the Creator, a point that is reiterated later in the verse with the statement, "all things were created by him, and for him." While the first clause draws attention to the historical act, the second focuses on creation's continuing existence. Jesus is both the Creator and the Sustainer.

Here, the author uses antitheses and synonyms in order to emphasize the scope of Christ's role in creation. The two antitheses appear one after the other—"heaven" (Gk. *ouranos*, **oo-ran-OS**) and "earth" (Gk. *ge*, **ghay**), followed by "visible" (Gk. *horatos*, **hor-at-OS**) and "invisible" (Gk. *aoratos*, **ah-OR-at-os**). These antitheses are followed by synonyms for power and authority regarding divine beings—"thrones" (Gk. *thronos*, **THRON-os**), "dominions" (Gk. *kuriotes*, **koo-ree-OT-ace**), and "principalities" (Gk. *arche*, **ar-KHAY**)—which give a sense of Christ's preeminence and supremacy over everything and the full scope of creation, which was created through Him and for Him.

Contrary to some people's opinions, then and even now, Paul is affirming that Christ is not some kind of a secondary God, but is divine Himself. The author places Christ above all superhuman forces. Everything was created not only by Him and through Him, but also for Him. The formula "by him, and for him" is used to emphasize the supremacy of Christ over creation, thus clarifying the significance of His being firstborn. Therefore, everything is subject to

Him and under His control, and His cosmic role includes a victor's place over all the elements of the world (i.e., thrones, dominions, principalities, and powers). It is only through His ongoing creative power that creation itself continues on.

17 And he is before all things, and by him all things consist.

This verse elaborates on what has already been affirmed in previous verses in terms of the supremacy and preeminence of Christ. The phrase "before all things" is a way of presenting Christ as preexistent and Lord of all created order. What should be understood here is that it was for Him, the Son, that all things were created. Christ is not only the agent of creation, but is also the goal and summit of creation. In other words, creation was created for Him and continues to belong to Him.

The phrase "by him all things consist" shows that it is Christ who holds the world together. All laws that put order into creation—the laws of gravity and rest and the other laws that make the universe hang together—are not only natural and scientific but also divine; they are an expression of the mind of Christ, the Son. Christ is, therefore, all in one. He was before the creation, the beginning of creation, and the end of creation. He is the power that holds creation together, the Creator, the Sustainer, and the final goal of the world.

18 And he is the head of the body, the church: who is the beginning, the firstborn from the dead; that in all things he might have the preeminence.

The first phrase of this verse, "and he is the head of the body," forms a fitting climax to the first part of the poem. Christ's headship is seen primarily over the entire world. By adding the phrase "the church," Paul sets out what Christ is to the church. He begins by using the image of a "body" (Gk. soma, **SO-mah**) and identifies Christ as the head of His body, which is the church. Thus, Christ is not only the head of the celestial "body" (i.e., creation), but also the head of the church, which includes all believers. This is an important theme in Colossians (1:24; 2:17, 19; 3:15).

In Ephesians 1:23, we find a similar expression regarding Christ being the head of the body. God made Christ the supreme head of the church. Paul goes on to say that Christ is the "beginning" (Gk. arche, **ar-KHAY,** meaning origin or first) of the church. Paul is categorically stating that Christ is the source, the starting point, and the origin of the church's life and being. He is the energy, spirit, and motivating factor behind the continued action.

Paul now returns to the event that was at the center of all the thinking, belief, and experience of the early church: the Resurrection. Christ is the "firstborn from the dead." The word "firstborn" (Gk. prototokos, **pro-tot-OK-os**) is again repeated. This time, the word means that Christ is not only the firstborn of all creatures, but also the firstborn of the dead as well. Christ is the first to experience resurrection. Through His resurrection, He conquered death. Thus, He is present in the church forever.

In referring to the church, Paul fused together the "body" theme and the "head" theme in order to affirm that Christ is now the head of the universal church, which is His body; He is "preeminent" (Gk. proteuo, **prote-YOO-o**), or holds first place in all creation. Because He is preeminent, the source of all things, and the firstborn of all creatures and of the dead, supremacy is His. By His resurrection, He has shown that He conquered every opposing power. In life or in death, nothing can bind Him because He is above all things.

19 For it pleased the Father that in him should all fulness dwell; 20 And, having made peace through the blood of his cross, by him to reconcile all things unto himself; by him, I say, whether they be things in earth, or things in heaven.

Christ, as God's Son and image, reflects the divine glory in a unique way, for in Him all the fullness of God was pleased to dwell. God's fullness is in Christ. Hence, no other intermediary between God and man is necessary. Paul then sets down certain great truths about the work of Christ for the whole universe.

The objective of Christ's coming is clear: "to reconcile all things unto himself." Reconciliation is another concept that Paul uses to describe an effect of the Christ event. The Greek terms *katallassein* and *diallassein* are found abundantly in Hellenistic Greek. In a secular sense, they denote a change in relations between individuals, groups, or nations and pertain to relations in the social or political sphere (e.g., a change from anger, hostility, or alienation to love, friendship, or intimacy). When Paul applies this concept to the Christ event, he speaks always of God or Christ reconciling human beings, enemies, or sinners to Himself.

Christ came to unite a fallen humanity with God. The initiative in reconciliation comes from God because it was He who began the whole process of salvation. God so loved the world that He sent His Son to reconcile all things to Himself. The idea of salvation here speaks of a universe in which all of creation is redeemed. Paul is intent on rebutting any idea that part of the universe is outside the scope of Christ's reconciling work.

Through the use of the phrase "whether they be things in earth, or things in heaven" stresses that there is no foreign power or hostile spirit force that can wreak havoc against the church. The means of reconciliation is none other than the blood of the Cross. Through Jesus' death on the Cross, reconciliation was achieved. Therefore, the Cross of Christ is proof of the unfathomable depth of God's love for humankind in restoring and reconciling everything to Himself.

These verses speak of the application of the "truth"—the practical living out of one's faith. The prayer in Colossians 1:9–14 and the hymn in Colossians 1:15–20 show the relevance of Christ's death to the community. Paul stresses the goal of reconciliation and calls the community to put its faith into action. Immediately after the hymn, which focuses on Christ, Paul now focuses on the reader. An important feature that is underscored in these verses and in several parts of this letter is the contrast between now (the present) and then (the past). This is Paul's way of emphasizing for the Gentile converts the great change that faith in Christ has brought into

their lives. He does this by amplifying the significance of the Christ hymn as he reminds the community of their own pagan past.

21 And you, that were sometime alienated and enemies in your mind by wicked works, yet now hath he reconciled

Emphatically, Paul addresses the reader: "And you." He wants his readers to understand that Christ's universal reconciliation also has a personal application, and that without it their faith will be rendered useless. Reconciliation has meaning only in terms of human relationships, rather than in terms of physical or metaphysical events that guarantee salvation in an impersonal way. Reconciliation assumes that there has been an estrangement. To be estranged is to be continuously and persistently out of harmony with God, as expressed in Ephesians 4:18 (RSV): "They are darkened in their understanding, alienated from the life of God because of the ignorance that is in them, due to their hardness of heart."

The word "alienated" (Gk. *apallotrioo*, **ap-al-lot-ree-o-o**) signifies being estranged or shut off from fellowship. The concept is used of the Israelites in Ezekiel 14:5 and of the wicked in general in Psalm 58:3. Paul further demonstrates to his readers that the fruit of estrangement is hostility, as he describes the Colossians to be "enemies in mind." The "mind" spoken of here is the center of a person's' intellectual life. If people harbor hostility in their mind and continue to center their thoughts on it, they will only be led into greater evil, darkness, and disharmony. This is precisely the meaning of the third phrase here. As a practical consequence of their hostility in mind and estrangement from God, the Colossians have been doing evil deeds.

What are the "wicked works" Paul speaks of here? (Given the undisputed instances of the use of this expression in the Pauline epistles, these words may well suggest a combination of idolatry and immorality, as identified in Romans 1:21–32.) In that passage, Paul details the sins of idolatry and immorality, such as covetousness, malice, envy, deceit, and hatred of God. Thus, he paints a dark picture of the "Colossians," a previous pagan existence, when they were separated from God. For every wicked word or deed that came from their hostile minds, the Colossians stood in desperate need of God's grace of reconciliation.

22 In the body of his flesh through death, to present you holy and unblameable and unreproveable in his sight.

In contrast to the Colossians' previous life of alienation, Paul emphasizes that they are now established in peace, harmony, and friendship with God. This is the action that Christ has taken on their behalf: He has reconciled them in the body of His flesh through death. Here, Christ's act of reconciliation is presented in sacrificial terminology. The phrase "in the body of his flesh" is peculiar to the book of Colossians; the expression is not found elsewhere in Pauline literature. The importance and dignity of Jesus' human body in its saving function contrast with the depreciation of the body that seems to have been part of the false teaching of Colossae, thus recalling again the important theme of the body of Christ. The author, in using this Judaic expression, wants to emphasize the cost of redemption in personal terms. In effect, it speaks with greater effect of Jesus' incarnation, of His identity with humankind, and of His submission to death in a human body. This phrase reminds us again of the cost of our redemption—the sacrificial act of Jesus, giving up His body by dying on the Cross to reconcile the whole of creation to God.

The second part of the verse gives us the aim and effect of Christ's reconciliation: "to present you holy and unblameable and unreproveable in his sight." The infinitive verb "to present" represents both the reason for and the result of Christ's reconciliation of humankind to God. It is Christ's sacrifice that results in humankind's being holy and acceptable to God. He carried out His sacrificial work of reconciliation so that He may present us to God holy and beyond reproach. The love that God lavishes on human beings challenges us and calls us to give an adequate

response, which is to live a holy, blameless, and irreproachable life.

23 If ye continue in the faith grounded and settled, and be not moved away from the hope of the gospel, which ye have heard, and which was preached to every creature which is under heaven; whereof I Paul am made a minister;

As Paul often does, he admonished the community to continue in the faith. Reconciliation calls for another kind of obligation: that of standing fast in the faith and never abandoning the hope of the Gospel. "Faith," as used in Colossians, is almost synonymous with the Gospel itself. Thus, the new status a Christian enjoys does not allow him or her to excuse careless living or to enjoy a false sense of security. It is a necessary warning, just in case the Colossian Christians might begin to think that sin does not matter anymore if God loves them and wishes nothing but reconciliation. Christianity is not a once-and-for-all transaction with God; it is an ongoing commitment to transformation, the grace and initiative of which comes from God. It is keeping faith with God through living out the Gospel message in daily life, not just holding on to faith as an intellectual belief.

The author calls for stability and steadfastness, being grounded and settled in the "faith," which he uses synonymously with the Gospel. These metaphors for strength and security are drawn from the picture of a house found in Matthew 7:24–27, described as being built on rock so that it could withstand any adversity (see also Luke 6:49). The New Testament writers often pick up this metaphor (1 Corinthians 3:10, 17; 1 Timothy 3:15; 1 Peter 2:4–10; Matthew 16:17–19). The Colossians' letter calls for steadfastness in times of discouragement and stress (1 Corinthians 15:58).

Paul continues his admonition in the phrase, "and be not moved away from the hope of the gospel, which ye have heard." It is easy to assume that the Colossians had either shifted or been tempted to shift their hope to other promises. Therefore, they needed to be reminded that reconciliation carries with it an obligation, not only to stand fast in the faith but also to not abandon the hope of the Gospel. The admonition to continue in the faith is a timely caution where the danger of drifting from "the faith" is real. The "hope of the gospel," or the hope promised by the Gospel, is none other than faith expressed or put into practice.

Paul brings this section to a high point by stating that the fullness of God's power in Christ has now been brought to fruition in the entire world through the preaching of the Gospel. This Gospel, which "was preached to every creature which is under heaven," is attested to by its universal appeal.

As a seal of authenticity, Paul shifts to the first person, in effect announcing his own stake in the Gospel as he proclaims himself as its minister: "whereof I Paul am made a minister." The term "minister" (Gk. *diakonos,* **dee-AK-on-os**) is worth examining in light of this proclamation. The title is found in 1 Corinthians 3:5, where it is used to designate individuals who helped the Corinthians to faith.

Daily Bible Readings

M: An Angel Promises
Luke 1:5–20
T: Elizabeth Is with Child
Luke 1:21–25
W: A Father Sings His Praise
Luke 1:67–80
T: John Prepares the Way
Matthew 3:1–6
F: A Son Is Promised
Isaiah 9:2–7
S: Into the Kingdom of His Son
Colossians 1:9–14
S: Who Jesus Is
Colossians 1:15–23

TEACHING TIPS

December 10
Bible Study Guide 2

1. Words You Should Know

A. Character—Express image.

B. Canon—The 66 books of the Bible that are the norm for belief and practice.

C. Septuagint—The Greek translation of the Old Testament.

D. Gnosticism—A sect that views the soul as good and the body as evil.

2. Teacher Preparation

A. Read the Focal Verses in various versions.

B. Read The People, Places, and Times and Background, as well as the In Depth section, to get an understanding of the topic.

C. Complete lesson 2 in the *Precepts For Living®Personal Study Guide.*

3. Starting the Lesson

A. Challenge the students with this question: "Who is Jesus?" Encourage all answers, and post them so all may see. You will refer to this listing later.

B. Discuss briefly whom we should listen to when it comes to this question and how it relates to today's Lesson Aim.

C. Explain that this lesson will help them answer the question, "Who is Jesus?" according to the Word of God.

D. Ask for volunteer to read today's poem from the In Focus section aloud.

4. Getting into the Lesson

A. Ask for volunteer to read the Focal Verses and the In Depth section aloud based on the At-A-Glance outline.

B. Discuss briefly the issues of authorship and canonicity. Explain that we believe the Bible is inspired (2 Timothy 3:16–17). Demonstrate how the first verses of Hebrews clearly state that God spoke.

Briefly discuss how the beginning of this book and Genesis are similar (they both begin with the concept of God speaking with humans). Also, the Bible does not waste time arguing God's existence. In both books, God's existence is assumed as a fact. Be prepared to stress this in your class.

C. Ask the class to compare and contrast what the world thinks about the role of angels with what the Bible teaches about angels. You may want to consider using the Search the Scriptures questions at this time.

5. Relating the Lesson to Life

Challenge the students to prepare and memorize a three-minute explanation for their belief in Christ as God's Son. How would they do it?

6. Arousing Action

Close in prayer, thanking God for speaking to His people in Old Testament times and in our present day. Pray that God, through the power of the Holy Spirit, will drive home what was learned today.

Worship Guide

For the Superintendent or Teacher
Theme: What God Says about Jesus
Theme Song: "Bless That Wonderful Name of Jesus"
Scripture: Philippians 2:9
Song: "All Hail the Power of Jesus' Name"
Meditation: Lord, thank You that You did and still do speak. Thank You for sending Jesus, Your Son, at the right time to speak more clearly to us. We give our lives to You in the hope of sharing Christ with others. In Jesus' name. Amen.

WHAT GOD SAYS ABOUT JESUS

Bible Background • HEBREWS 1
Printed Text • HEBREWS 1:1–9   Devotional Reading • LUKE 1:46–55

Lesson Aim

By the end of the lesson, we will:

EXPLORE the truth that Jesus Christ is the exact representation of God, that He came from God, and that He is superior to angels and all created beings;

BECOME CONVINCED that based on who Christ is, we should give Him our highest devotion; and

CELEBRATE Jesus Christ for who He is, and DECIDE to commit or recommit our lives to Him.

Keep in Mind

"God, who at sundry times and in divers manners spake in time past unto the fathers by the prophets, Hath in these last days spoken unto us by his Son, whom he hath appointed heir of all things, by whom also he made the worlds" (Hebrews 1:1–2).

Focal Verses

Hebrews 1:1 God, who at sundry times and in divers manners spake in time past unto the fathers by the prophets,

2 Hath in these last days spoken unto us by his Son, whom he hath appointed heir of all things, by whom also he made the worlds;

3 Who being the brightness of his glory, and the express image of his person, and upholding all things by the word of his power, when he had by himself purged our sins, sat down on the right hand of the Majesty on high;

4 Being made so much better than the angels, as he hath by inheritance obtained a more excellent name than they.

5 For unto which of the angels said he at any time, Thou art my Son, this day have I begotten thee? And again, I will be to him a Father, and he shall be to me a Son?

6 And again, when he bringeth in the firstbegotten into the world, he saith, And let all the angels of God worship him.

7 And of the angels he saith,

Who maketh his angels spirits, and his ministers a flame of fire.

8 But unto the Son he saith, Thy throne, O God, is for ever and ever: a sceptre of righteousness is the sceptre of thy kingdom.

9 Thou hast loved righteousness, and hated iniquity; therefore God, even thy God, hath anointed thee with the oil of gladness above thy fellows.

In Focus

JESUS, I REJOICE IN WHO YOU ARE!

Even though I look around me
And see a world gone mad,
When I behold who You are, Jesus,
My heart is still made glad.

When I see the violence
And the injustice that flourish es so,
Then I glimpse at You, Lord,
My spirit seems to soar!

For I know that my life is in Your hands,
And You are my strength and hope.

I know that in the end You will triumph,
And this helps me to cope.

You are at work in my life,
And your awesome power caus es me to rejoice.
In spite of the desolation far and near,
I can still hear Your voice.

Like the prophet Habakkuk, Jesus,
I will rejoice in You.
For You are the God of my sal vation
And You will bring me through!

Because of who Christ is, indeed we should give Him our highest devotion, honor, and praise. In today's lesson, we cele brate Jesus Christ as the Creator and Ruler over all that exists.

The People, Places, and Times

Authorship. The identity of the author of the book of Hebrews is not clear. Some scholars think it was Paul. Other scholars view the Greek used in the book as being too eloquent to have been used by Paul. There is strong evidence to suggest that Apollos may have written the book. Whoever wrote it, it is clear that he or she had knowledge of the Jewish faith and was seeking to demonstrate or remind readers of the supremacy of Christ over all Old Testament standards.

Location. The place of the writing of this book is equally difficult to ascertain. Without knowing who the author was, it is difficult to determine the location where the book was written for the Jewish readers.

Times. It is generally accepted that this book was written to Jewish Christians before the fall of Jerusalem (A.D. 70), since there is no reference to this significant event in the text. The Jewish people had not experienced the difficulties they would soon suffer under the different Roman Caesars. While all was not calm, there was little persecution.

Background

God wants us to know about Him, His Son, and His Holy Spirit. To do this, He has left us His Word, the Bible. The book of Hebrews is one of many books in the Bible that help us to understand more about our Lord. In fact, there are many Christians who consider the book of Hebrews the fifth gospel because it discusses so much of what it means to be a Christian, especially since many of the early believers came from the Judaic system. This study will develop our faith in the One we serve as Lord of lords and King of kings.

It is obvious that the book of Hebrews was written for those who came from a Jewish background. The repeated references throughout the book to Jewish ceremonies, such as the sacrifices and laws (circumcision, approaching the temple, etc.), were significant to those who had been raised in that atmosphere. For example, later in Hebrews we will read about the sacrifice of Jesus and how it aligns with the book of Leviticus. Also, we will learn how Christ is ordained after the order of Melchizedek and not

according to the Aaronic priesthood. This indicated that Christ's priesthood was in fact superior to Aaron's priesthood. The focus of this particular study, however, is how Jesus is God's Son and is uniquely qualified to meet the needs of humankind.

> **At - A - Glance**
>
> 1. God Has Spoken to Us in Times Past (Hebrews 1:1)
> 2. God Has Spoken to Us through Christ, His Son (vv. 2–3)
> 3. Christ Is Superior to the Angels (vv. 4–9)

In Depth

1. God Has Spoken to Us in Times Past (Hebrews 1:1)

The nature of Christ is all-important to the discussion of salvation. If it could be demonstrated that Christ was not God's Son, the rest of His life would be meaningless to the person seeking to understand Him, His sacrificial death, His resurrection, and His imminent return. The central message and purpose of the book of Hebrews is to demonstrate that Jesus is the superior priest, the ultimate sacrifice, and everything one needs to meet God under the new covenant.

The first verse in Hebrews states how in many places and in many ways God spoke to our fathers. This is important. God did not speak just one time to a few people. Rather, He spoke to many people (Abraham, Isaac, Jacob, etc.) over many years. (Some have determined that the Bible was written over a 1,400-year period.) God spoke to His people through dreams, prophecies, rituals, and other means. Most of the world's major religions cannot say this. They have one man who taught over a set number of years and then left this world. So, from the very beginning, God has communicated with humanity. The author of Hebrews wants the readers to see that it is only in Christ that all the messages, dreams, laws, etc. that God gave were made complete. The fulfillment of the old covenant is in Christ alone.

Jesus is Lord.

2. God Has Spoken to Us through Christ, His Son (vv. 2–3)

Verse 2 declares that in the fullness of time, Christ was born on Earth, and that He is God's Son—the same God who spoke the world into existence (Genesis 1) in the Old Testament. Then, when the time was right for Christ to enter the world, God sent His Son to be the culmination of His plan.

Not only is Jesus the completion of the Old Testament, but He is also heir of all things and Creator of all (Hebrews 1:2). Jesus was with God from the beginning (Ephesians 2:9; Colossians 1:17) and was declared the heir of all things through His obedience to the Father. There are many verses in the New Testament that speak of Jesus as Inheritor and Creator. Colossians 1:16 also supports Hebrews 1:2 when it states that Jesus created everything. Additionally, Colossians 1:15 states that Jesus is the firstborn; as an heir, He receives the inheritance.

There were many heretical teachings during the time when the book of Hebrews was written. One of the most damaging was Gnosticism. Its followers believed that there was a secret way to set the soul free from the body, which they believed was evil. This belief made it difficult to accept that a spiritual being like God would be able to take on human form. Hence, Gnostics did not accept that Jesus had come in the flesh. To them, He was just a spirit or some such thing. However, Colossians 1:19 states, "For it pleased the Father that in him should all fullness dwell." All the fullness of God is found in Jesus Christ.

Like the Gnostics of old, there are still some who say that they know secrets about Christianity. They believe that they have the secret knowledge and that there are only a few who can accept the truth. There are others who do not want to accept that Jesus was truly God and truly human. They do not want to see Jesus for who He really was and is: the Son of God. Gnosticism still exists today. We must lovingly demonstrate from the Scriptures that God wants all of His creation to know and worship Him. God wants the world to know that salvation is found only in His Son's name. We must share the Good News.

3. Christ Is Superior to the Angels (vv. 4–9)

Verses 3–4 state what Jesus did for us. First Corinthians 15:3–8 also includes a miniature Gospel message that encapsulates and restates what Hebrews 1:3–4 states. Some scholars have indicated that these verses in 1 Corinthians may have been taught and used to differentiate Christianity from other religions in the early years. Modern-day evangelists often use these verses as they witness to others.

The book of Hebrews was written for a learned Jewish audience. Many Jews understood multiple languages in those days. For example, many Jews could read Hebrew, Aramaic, and Greek. Some read Latin as well. Jews who lived outside of Jerusalem wanted a copy of the Tanakh (the Old Testament) and they wanted it in the Greek language. As a result, the Septuagint (the Greek translation of the Old Testament) was produced. There are many variations of the story of its development. A simplified version is presented below.

Seventy Jewish scholars were selected to translate a section of the Jewish Old Testament from Hebrew and Aramaic into Greek. They sat down in different rooms and began to work on their respective sections. When completed, each of the scholar's work was compared to the Hebrew and Aramaic to ensure there were no mistakes in the translation. For centuries, the Septuagint was used to translate other later editions of the Old Testament into other languages. The Septuagint was where the verses in Hebrews were taken from.

Hebrews 1:5 quotes Psalm 2:7 and 2 Samuel 7:14. This verse in Hebrews condenses the truth about Christ for all of us, seekers and keepers. Here, Yahweh declares that there has never been anyone like Jesus. Only Jesus is declared to be God's Son. Only Jesus is the begotten of God. We can confidently point to these verses to demonstrate the uniqueness of Jesus for those who would mistakenly say that Jesus is only one of many sons of God.

Jesus is different from anything or anyone else. For example, verse 6 contains another reference to the Septuagint (Deuteronomy 32:43), demonstrating the relationship between Jesus and the angels. Again, the purpose is to eliminate any confusion regarding the uniqueness of Christ. In the Jewish tradition, there were some who made angels much more than the messengers they were. The author of Hebrews does not want the reader to become confused about Jesus' identity. Nor does the author want the reader to think that Jesus was an angel. Therefore, the author states conclusively that, in fact, Jesus is superior to the angels. Verse 7 is a quote from Psalm 104:4, and solidifies this point, reemphasizing that Jesus is superior to the angels.

There were many in the early days of the church who were misinformed regarding angels. In 1 Peter 3:22, Peter states that Jesus is better than the angels. The emphasis, therefore, is not on the fact that the angels are merely servants (their being is such that they are only what God makes them according to the needs of their service), and are, therefore, changeable in contrast with the Son, who is the Ruler and unchangeable. Thus, Jesus is not only superior to the prophets, but He is superior to the angels.

Verse 8 quotes Psalm 45:6–7. Here, the emphasis is on the equality of Jesus with God. Pause and think about this for a moment. Jesus and God are equals. Read Philippians 2:5–11. This is the great section (some say a hymn) of the early church's belief structure. Here, Paul describes exactly what happened when Jesus came to Earth, and why. Notice in verse 6 where it says, "Who, being in the form of God, thought it not robbery to be equal with God." Jesus was in the form, the very image, of God. We read in John 14:9 that Jesus plainly stated that anyone who has seen Him has seen the Father. Also, there were many times that the Jews had wanted to kill Jesus for making Himself out to be God (cf. John 8:58; 10:33). Finally, Hebrews 1:9 refers to Isaiah 61:1.

Search the Scriptures

1. Circle or highlight the word "better" as it appears here and throughout the book of Hebrews. What is Jesus "better" than?

2. What does this mean in your life today?

3. Read Philippians 2:5 11, and put it into your own words.

Discuss the Meaning

1. Because Christianity claims that Jesus is the only way to God, Christians are often accused of being narrow-minded and haughty. How would you answer this accusation?

2. What is the significance of Christ's superiority for your life? How does it apply to any personal situation you may be facing today?

Lesson in Our Society

There are many in the world who will challenge your belief in Jesus Christ. They will say He was a great teacher, a good moral example, or just a man. But as Christians, we believe He is more than that; we believe He is God. Jesus Christ is supreme over the prophets and angels because He is, in His very

essence, God Himself. People are tempted to idolize angels or various human teachers, but only Jesus Christ is the Son of God. We know that Jesus is the second person of the Trinity because the Father has given witness, the disciples gave witness, and His deity is demonstrated by God through the Holy Spirit.

Make It Happen

A coworker has been asking you questions about Christ and Christianity for several weeks. Today, he asks you why you think there is only one way to heaven, through Jesus Christ. You discover that he wants to know what makes Jesus the one he should turn to for salvation. Using today's discussion, generate a short, two- to three-minute response that explains who Christ is without sounding preachy.

Follow the Spirit

What God wants me to do:

_____

_____

Remember Your Thoughts

Special insights I have learned:

_____

_____

More Light on the Text
Hebrews 1:1–9

The letter to the Hebrews begins with a splendid introduction that brings out something of the greatness of Jesus and His saving work. It goes on to point out that Jesus is superior to the angels and thus leads into the first main section of the epistle.

1 God, who at sundry times and in divers manners spake in time past unto the fathers by the prophets, 2 Hath in these last days spoken unto us by his Son, whom he hath appointed heir of all things, by whom also he made the worlds;

In a very deliberate manner, the letter begins with God as the subject. The writer's perspective is noticeably God-centered. God permeates Hebrews. A careful reading of the book shows that the word "God" is mentioned 68 times, thus making Hebrews one of the few books in the New Testament that speaks so frequently about God. Arguably then, from the onset, the reader is confronted with the reality of God and the fact that He has been and continues to be active in history and the world. He is not an absentee God; He is the omnipresent God who intervened in human history with His sovereign Word addressed to humankind. However, His ultimate Word was spoken through One who is distinguished from all others by reason of His unique relationship with God.

The first divine activity mentioned in the book is that God has spoken in "sundry times" (Gk. *polumeros*, **pol-oo-MER-oce**). The word *polumeros* means "sundry parts, parcels, or degrees." As opposed to a full revelation, the word "sundry" refers to the gradual uncovering of the mind and will of God by various methods of communication, one after another. The phrase "divers manners" (Gk. *polutropos*, **pol-oot-ROP-oce**) means "a variety of methods" and may refer to the different ways in which the prophets communicated the different revelations given to them. God spoke in ancient times a great while ago, or "in the past" (Gk. *palai*, **PAL-ahee,** which means "of old," "former," or "long ago"). In the time of the forefathers, or, literally, "fathers" (Gk. *pater*, **pat-AYR**), God spoke to Moses in the burning bush (Exodus 3:2 ff.); to Elijah in a still, small voice (1 Kings 19:12 ff.); to Isaiah in a vision in the temple (Isaiah 6:1 ff.); to Hosea in his family circumstances (Hosea 1:2); and to Amos in a basket of summer fruit (Amos 8:1). Not only did God speak in old days, but He has also spoken in "these last days" (Hebrews 1:2). In the Septuagint, the phrase "in these last days" (Gk. *ep' eschatos hemerais*, **ES-khat-os hay-MER-ah-is**) is often used to refer to the "days of the Messiah." Here in the book of Hebrews, it means that in Jesus, the Messianic Age has appeared: "He hath in these last days spoken unto us by his Son."

Jesus is more than a prophet. It was of Him that the prophets spoke. Jesus Christ alone brings to humanity the full revelation of God, and He alone enables them to enter into God's very presence. Jesus inaugurated a new age. The writer goes on to describe Christ's relationship, to both the Father and creation, to underscore both the significance of Christ's ministry and its superiority to that of the prophets.

First, he has been "appointed heir of all things." The word "heir" (Gk. *kleronomos*, **klay-ron-OM-os**) denotes one who obtains a lot or portion (*kleros*, meaning "lot," and *nemomai*, meaning to "possess"), especially of an inheritance. It referred to a situation in which lots were drawn to divide property or select a winner; the one who drew the lot was the heir. The word came to be used for dividing the property that a father left to his children when he died. If the father had only one son, there was only one heir. Christ, being God's only Son, is the heir of all things. Being an "heir of all things," then, is a title of dignity and shows that Christ has the supreme place in the entire mighty universe. His exaltation to the highest place in heaven after His work on Earth was completed, marked His restoration to His rightful place (cf. Philippians 2:6–11).

Second, it is by or through the Son that God made the worlds. Along with other places in the New Testament, the book of Hebrews shows that Christ is God's agent of creation—God performed the work of creation through the Son (cf. John 1:3; 1 Corinthians 8:6; Colossians 1:16).

3 Who being the brightness of his glory, and the express image of his person, and upholding all things by the word of his power, when he had by himself purged our sins, sat down on the right hand of the Majesty on high;

Verse 3 continues the description of the Son. He is the "brightness" (Gk. *apaugasma*, **ap-OW-gas-mah**) of God's glory. The meaning of the word *apagausma* is not entirely clear. It could mean "effulgence," "outbeaming," "radiance," or "splendor." If the word is understood this way, Jesus is the outshining of the brightness of God's glory. The word could also mean "reflection," in which case Jesus is the reflection of God's glory. What is important to note is that in either case, God's glory is manifested in Jesus, and we see His glory as it really is. The word "glory" (Gk. *doxa*,

DOX-ah) can be used of literal brightness (cf. Acts 22:11). However, it is more commonly used in the New Testament to describe the radiance associated with God and with heavenly beings in general. Glory sometimes indicates the presence of God (cf. Ezekiel 1:28; 11:23) and, to the extent that humans are able to comprehend it, the revelation of God's majesty.

Next, the Son is described as the "express image" (Gk. *charakter*, **khar-ak-TARE**) of God's person or being. The word *charakter* denotes the exact expression, marked likeness, or precise representation in every respect. In Greek, it means two things: (1) a seal, and (2) the stamp or imprint left by a seal on the sealing wax. The imprint has the exact form of the seal. Thus, when the book of Hebrews says that Jesus is the *charakter* of the being of God, it means that Jesus is the exact image or representation of God. So, the writer is saying that when you look at Jesus the Son, you see an exact representation of God. Furthermore, the Son is the One "upholding all things by the word of his power." The word translated "uphold" (Gk. *pheron*, **FER-on**) means "to carry along," "bear with one's self," "bear up," "spare," "abstain from punishing," or "destroy."

Creation is not left on its own. Jesus is the Sustainer of creation—He carries it along. Nothing is excluded from the scope of the Son's sustaining activity; it includes "all things" (Gk. *pas*, meaning "total"). The Son not only was active in creation, but also maintains an interest in it by continuing to move it toward the accomplishment of God's plan. He does all this by the "word of his power." The "word" (Gk. *rhema*, **HRAY-mah**) refers here to a command. The significant thing to note here is that the "word" is both active and powerful (cf. Hebrew 4:12). It is not empty.

The word translated as "purged" is the Greek word *katharismos* (**kath-ar-is-MOS**), which means "cleansing" or "purification." It is most often used in the New Testament of ritual cleansing (Mark 1:44). However, it also has ethical implications (1 Corinthians 5:6–7; 2 Corinthians 7:1; Titus 2:14). Here, it refers to the removal of sin. It implicitly shows the sinfulness of sin—the defiling aspect of sin. The Good News is that Christ has effected a complete cleansing at Calvary. Jesus is the Redeemer. He paid the price of sin by His sacrifice (Hebrews 9:26). He has taken His place on the right hand of glory as the One who makes intercession for us.

Verse 3 ends with the exaltation of Christ. Christ's "sitting down" presupposes both His resurrection and His being vested with the highest authority in heaven, next to the Father. It is generally recognized that sitting is the posture of rest and that the right-hand position is the place of honor. "Sitting at God's right hand," then, is a way of saying that Christ's saving work is done and that He is now in the place of highest honor.

4 Being made so much better than the angels, as he hath by inheritance obtained a more excellent name than they.

As seen in the three previous verses, the author of Hebrews has affirmed the superiority of Christ over the Old Testament prophets. Beginning with verse 4, the writer now affirms the superiority of Christ over the angels. In the first century, angels were of great interest in both Jewish and Greek religious thinking. One of the most commonly held beliefs about angels was that they served as intermediaries between God and humans. It was believed that God spoke to people through the angels and the angels carried people's prayers into the presence of God. Fortunately, because of who Jesus is and His sacrifice on the Cross, we have direct access to God. There is no need for anyone to intercede between humans and God. This being the case, the writer of Hebrews does not mince words concerning the superiority of Christ. Christ is superior to the prophets, angels, priests, and the entire Jewish sacrificial system.

The word "better" is the translation of the Greek word *kreitton* (**KRITE-tohn**) and is rendered "superior" 13 of the 19 times it occurs in the New Testament (cf. Hebrews 6:9; 7:7, 19, 22; 8:6; 9:23; 10:34; 11:16, 35, 40; 12:24). Without a doubt, such a strong emphasis on what is "better" stems from the author's conviction that Jesus Christ is indeed better and has accomplished things that no one else could do.

The author gives various reasons why Jesus is better than the angels. First, he has "obtained a more excellent name than they." In ancient times, a name meant much more than it does today. Names were more than differentiating marks or labels. Instead, a person's name was an indication of his or her character. Jesus is truly God's Son. He is the only begotten Son of God—not a son by adoption, regeneration, or title like the patriarchs, prophets, or other saints might be considered sons of God.

5 For unto which of the angels said he at any time, Thou art my Son, this day have I begotten thee? And again, I will be to him a Father, and he shall be to me a Son?

Here the writer cites several Old Testament passages to make his point regarding Christ's superiority to the angels. The opening question implies that Christ is to be seen in all the Scriptures since there is no explicit reference to Him in the passage cited. In the Old Testament, angels are sometimes designated as "sons of God" (cf. Job 1:6; 2:1). The term was also applied to Israel (Exodus 4:22; Hosea 11:1) and Solomon (2 Samuel 7:14; 1 Chronicles 28:6). But none of the angels, nor anyone else, was ever singled out and given the kind of status this passage gives to Christ. The first quotation comes from Psalm 2:7. The writer clearly views Psalm 2 as messianic and as bestowing great dignity on Jesus. The second quotation comes from 2 Samuel. Although the words were originally used of Solomon, the writer of Hebrews is applying them to the Messiah. The quotation points to the Father Son relationship as the fundamental relationship between God and Christ. No angel can claim such a relationship. Verse 5 and 12:9 are the only passages in Hebrews in which the term "Father" is applied to God. By joining Psalm 2:7 and 2 Samuel 7:14, the writer provides strong biblical support for the claim that the position of the angels is subordinate to the status of the Son. Christ alone enjoys a unique relationship with the Father and God's designation of "my Son."

6 And again, when he bringeth in the firstbegotten into the world, he saith, And let all the angels of God worship him.

The superiority of the Son to the angels finds fresh support in a contrasting quotation concerning the angels. Christ is God's "firstbegotten," or "firstborn" (Gk. *prototokos,* **pro-tot-OK-os**). In this context, the word is a title of honor expressing priority in rank. It speaks of Christ's relationship to others and gives it a social significance. He is to be worshiped. Undoubtedly, the one the angels worship is and must be clearly superior to them.

7 And of the angels he saith, Who maketh his angels spirits, and his ministers a flame of fire.

Here, the writer is quoting Psalm 104:4. This passage can have two meanings. One meaning is that God makes the winds His messengers and the flames His servants. The other meaning is that God makes His messengers (angels) into winds and His servants into flames. This does not downgrade the angels. The point is that, if the angels are superior to humans, the Son is boundlessly superior to the angels. Whereas He has Sonship, they are analogous to nothing more than the elemental forces of wind and fire. Furthermore, the implication is that the angels are temporary in contrast to the Son, who is eternal.

8 But unto the Son he saith, Thy throne, O God, is for ever and ever: a sceptre of righteousness is the sceptre of thy kingdom. 9 Thou hast loved righteousness, and hated iniquity; therefore God, even thy God, hath anointed thee with the oil of gladness above thy fellows.

The contrast implied in verse 7 is borne out by two quotations from Psalm 45, which establish that the Son does not belong to the created order as do the angels. Verses 8 and 9 are extended quotations that express the fundamental contrast between the divine Son of God and the angels. The use of the word "but" (Gk. *de,* **deh**) in the introduction indicates that the writer intends to contrast the Son, whose throne endures forever with the angels, whose existence is ephemeral. The Son's royal estate is brought out by the references to the throne, scepter, and kingdom and by His moral concern for righteousness, which is supreme where He reigns. The writer does not hesitate to refer to Psalm 45:6–7, a passage in which the Son is addressed as God, and alludes to Jesus as the legitimate object of worship. The writer's primary interest in the quotation is not the predication of deity but the eternal nature of the dominion exercised by the Son. The preposition "above" is from the Greek word *para* (**PAR-ah**), which translated means "more than" or "beyond." Therefore, taken in a comparative sense, it reinforces the contrast being drawn between Christ and the angels. Although angels participate in the implementation of God's will (cf. vv. 7, 14) and in this sense are "fellows" (Gk, *metochoi*, **MET-okh-oy**) of the Son, God has assigned His Son to a superior office. Thus, the angels' function is to serve and the Son's is to rule. Angels are subject to change. The Son does not change, and His rule reflects a commitment to righteousness, which explains why God has crowned Him with joy (Hebrews 12:2).

Daily Bible Readings

M: Jesus, the Promised One
Matthew 12:15–21
T: You Will Name Him Jesus
Luke 1:26–33
W: Jesus, Son of God
Luke 1:34–38
T: Mary Sings Her Joy
Luke 1:46–55
F: Listen to Him!
Matthew 17:1–5
S: God's Anointed Son
Hebrews 1:1–9
S: More than the Angels
Hebrews 1:10–14

TEACHING TIPS

December 17
Bible Study Guide 3

1. Words You Should Know

A. Life (1 John 1:1–2) *zoe* (Gk.)—Used in the New Testament to refer to life as a principle, in the absolute sense or as God would have it (John 5:26)—that which the Son manifested in the world (1 John 1:2). The word also has moral associations, as in holiness and righteousness.

B. Light (v. 5) *phos* (Gk.)—Light as seen by the eye; metaphorically, enlightening the mind; phosphorous (literally, "light-bearing"). Primarily, light is a luminous emanation that enables the eye to discern form and color.

C. Darkness (v. 5) *skotia* (Gk.)—Refers to physical darkness (cf. John 6:17); secrecy in general (cf. Matthew 10:27; Luke 12:3); or spiritual or moral darkness, emblematic of sin as a condition of moral or spiritual depravity (cf. Matthew 4:16; John 1:5; 8:12). Except when used to refer to secrecy, darkness always connotes something bad.

D. Propitiation (2:2) *hilasmos* (Gk.)—Signifies a means whereby sin is covered and remitted. The proper meaning of the word is that of reconciling, appeasing, turning away anger, or rendering propitious or favorable.

2. Teacher Preparation

A. Read and study the Focal Verses.

B. Make a list of all the words you think of when you think of light.

C. Complete lesson 3 in the *Precepts For Living*® *Personal Study Guide* to gain additional insight into the lesson.

D. Write the At-A-Glance outline on the board.

3. Starting the Lesson

A. Begin the class with prayer.

B. Read the In Focus story. Ask the students to share some ways they have been a light in the lives of family and friends.

4. Getting into the Lesson

A. Allow the students to take turns reading the Focal Verses based on the At-A-Glance outline.

B. Present the Background section and The People, Places, and Times.

C. At the appropriate time, lead the students in a discussion of what the following terms mean: "life," "light," and "darkness." After the discussion, share the Greek meanings you have been given.

5. Relating the Lesson to Life

A. Instruct the students to answer the Discuss the Meaning questions and relate them to their lives.

B. Ask the students if they have any other insights they would like to share about today's lesson.

6. Arousing Action

A. Read the Make It Happen section.

B. Ask the students to list areas in which they need to change.

C. Have the students pray with a partner in regard to these areas.

D. Instruct the students to read the Daily Bible Readings in preparation for the lesson next week.

Worship Guide

For the Teacher or Superintendent
Theme: Light That Conquers
Theme Song: "Jesus, the Light of the World"
Scripture: John 12:46
Song: "Fix Me, Jesus"
Meditation: Dear Lord, search my heart and see if there is any evil there. Use Your light to reveal any dark places in my life. Forgive me, O Lord. Cleanse me, O Lord. Help me to walk in Your light. Amen.

LIGHT THAT CONQUERS

Bible Background • 1 JOHN 1:1–2:6
Printed Text • 1 JOHN 1:1–2:5   Devotional Reading • EPHESIANS 5:8–14

Lesson Aim

By the end of the lesson, we will:

KNOW the characteristics of Jesus Christ as described in our text;

ASPIRE to "walk in the light" of God's presence; and

DECIDE to pray that God will enable us to live each day in the presence of God.

Keep in Mind

"This then is the message which we have heard of him, and declare unto you, that God is light, and in him is no darkness at all" (1 John 1:5).

Focal Verses

1 John 1:1 That which was from the beginning, which we have heard, which we have seen with our eyes, which we have looked upon, and our hands have handled, of the Word of life;

2 (For the life was manifested, and we have seen it, and bear witness, and shew unto you that eternal life, which was with the Father, and was manifested unto us;)

3 That which we have seen and heard declare we unto you, that ye also may have fellowship with us: and truly our fellowship is with the Father, and with his Son Jesus Christ.

4 And these things write we unto you, that your joy may be full.

5 This then is the message which we have heard of him, and declare unto you, that God is light, and in him is no darkness at all.

6 If we say that we have fellowship with him, and walk in darkness, we lie, and do not the truth:

7 But if we walk in the light, as he is in the light, we have fellow-ship one with another, and the blood of Jesus Christ his Son cleanseth us from all sin.

8 If we say that we have no sin, we deceive ourselves, and the truth is not in us.

9 If we confess our sins, he is faithful and just to forgive us our sins, and to cleanse us from all unrighteousness.

10 If we say that we have not sinned, we make him a liar, and his word is not in us.

2:1 My little children, these things write I unto you, that ye sin not. And if any man sin, we have an advocate with the Father, Jesus Christ the righteous:

2 And he is the propitiation for our sins: and not for ours only, but also for the sins of the whole world.

3 And hereby we do know that we know him, if we keep his com-mandments.

4 He that saith, I know him, and keepeth not his commandments, is a liar, and the truth is not in him.

5 But whoso keepeth his word, in him verily is the love of God per-fected: hereby know we that we are in him.

In Focus

Looking for a way to dispel the darkness in her marriage, Rose visited a nearby shelter for abused women. After crying all night, Rose called her mother. "It's hor-rible living with him," Rose said.

Her mother's understanding was as distant as the California phone call. "Did he lose his job, or hit you?"

"No," she said.

"Is he unfaithful?"

"No, Mother." But Rose thought of her nights in bed listening to Don's snoring and crying herself to sleep, wondering why she stayed with him.

"He never listens, and he yells all the time." Tears fell from her eyes.

"Settle down, baby," her moth-er said. "Stay in that shelter a couple of days, but go back to Don. He is a good man. Try to find out why you are so depressed."

As she talked with her thera-pist, Rose's own words surprised her. "Mama's right. I shouldn't be so depressed. I just need to figure out how to do better, like my husband says."

Ann, her therapist, said, "Look, Rose, your self-esteem is undernourished. You've got to think about what the Bible says: You are a child of God."

"But look at the mess I've made of my marriage. I've gained weight, and I don't decorate the house the way he likes and. . . ."

"Stop it," Ann warned. "It boils down to this question: Are you able to thank God for the way He made you? If not, the first relationship you have to fix is your relationship with God."

Suddenly Rose saw the light that was needed to lift her depression.

In our lesson, John presents God as light that opens doors for believers.

The People, Places, and Times

John. From the beginning, the apostle John has been recognized as the author of this epistle (a circular letter to the churches around Ephesus), although the epistle itself gives no author or recipient name.

John was Jesus' most intimate earthly friend. John accompanied Jesus in His journeys throughout Palestine for over three years, ministering to Him day and night. We are told that John leaned back on Jesus as He talked about His upcoming crucifixion.

Background

Christianity was 60 or more years old and had become a powerful influence in many parts of the Roman Empire by the time this epistle was written. It was natural that there would be attempts to integrate the Gospel with other philosophies that were prevalent at that time. Gnosticism was one such philosophy that was disrupting churches.

Gnosticism taught that human nature was dualistic, that spirit and body were two separate entities. It taught that sin resided in the flesh only, that the body could do as it pleased without affecting the spirit's raptures, and that mental, mystical piety was totally consistent with a full, sensual life. Gnostics denied the Incarnation that Christ was God in the flesh; they held that Christ was a phantom, a man in appearance only.

This epistle appears to be a response to the heretical Gnostic teaching. Throughout the epistle, John goes to great lengths to emphasize that Jesus is the actual, material, authentic manifestation of God in the flesh and that moral transformation results from genuine knowledge of God.

Source

Halley, Henry H. *Halley's Bible Handbook.* Grand Rapids, Mich.: Zondervan Publishing 1965, 671, 672.

At-A-Glance

1. God Is Light, and in Him Is No Darkness (1 John 1:1–6)
2. God's Light Brings Us into Fellowship with One Another (v. 7)
3. God Forgives Confessed Sin (v. 8–2:2)
4. God Calls Us to Walk in His Light (vv. 3–5)

In Depth

1. God Is Light, and in Him Is No Darkness (1 John 1:1–6)

As an eyewitness to Jesus' ministry of teaching and miracles, John was qualified to teach the truth about Christ as being the eternal Word of Life. People had become alienated from this life as a result of the Fall (Ephesians 4:18). John explains how we now can partake in this life through faith in the Lord Jesus Christ (John 3:15).

As one who had actually touched Christ, John was eligible to testify concerning Jesus' humanity, both before and after His resurrection. John could enthusiastically proclaim, "He is God's message of life. This one who is life from God has been shown to us I am speaking of Christ, who is eternal Life. He was with the Father and then was shown to us" (1 John 1:1–2, *The Living Bible*).

In verses 1–4, John writes of the union between Christ and His people. He wanted all Christians to experience the depth of joy available to them because of this life-altering union. Essentially he was saying, "You have already tasted that the Lord is good, but I am now going to show you that your hap-

"This then is the message which we have heard of him, and declare unto you, that God is light, and in him is no darkness at all" (1 John 1:5).

piness may be complete because you are cleansed from sin and filled with the fullness of God." As Christians, we are complete—whole in Him!

In response to the false teachers of his day, John stressed that there was one thing that makes fellowship with God impossible: "walking in darkness." Those false teachers taught that we can have fellowship with God and still walk in darkness. Certainly today there are those who think they can be Christians and still live in evil and immoral ways, but this is inconsistent with biblical teaching. According to the Bible, we can't love God and court sin at the same time.

"God is light." In the biblical sense, and for us today, light represents what is good, pure, true, holy, and reliable. On the other hand, darkness represents what is sinful and evil. The phrase "God is light" means that God is perfectly holy and true and that He

is the only One who can guide us out of the darkness of sin.

Light also relates to truth in the sense that light exposes the true situation—good or bad. In the dark, good and evil look alike; in the light, they can be distinguished clearly. Also, darkness cannot survive in the presence of light. In the same way, sin cannot live in the presence of a holy God. If we are to have a relationship with God, we must put aside our sinful lifestyle. We are hypocrites if we claim that we are His and then live for ourselves. This type of deceit will be exposed.

"In him is no darkness at all" (v. 5). God is absolutely perfect. There is nothing in Him to mar the pure splendor of His character. John lays down this doctrine that God is pure light, as the foundation of all that he had to teach. Spiritual light is to the human soul what physical light is to the world.

Without light, everything would be dismal and full of terror. In the same way, religion would be an empty science without an indwelling God. Aren't we glad that God is light?

People who walk in darkness have nothing on which to base a relationship with God. They know nothing of the real peace and joy that a relationship with God imparts, although by religious practices they may entertain the belief that they are friends of God and are going to heaven. They trust in a name, in forms, and in conformity to external rites. On the other hand, we who have fellowship, or communion, with God are partakers of the divine nature (2 Peter 1:4)!

2. God's Light Brings Us into Fellowship with One Another (v. 7)

A living relationship with Christ opens the door for meaningful relationships with other believers because believers are striving to walk in the light of God's presence. Christian fellowship is grounded in the testimony of God's Word and is renewed daily through the Holy Spirit. It combines Christ-centered social and spiritual interaction.

Unfortunately, Christians all too often neglect to "walk in the light." When this happens, their fellowship with God and with one another becomes vulnerable. Walking in the light produces the fruit of the Spirit: love, joy, peace, long-suffering, gentleness, goodness, and faith. Walking in the light creates a climate that is conducive to positive Christian interaction. On the other hand, when people "walk in the flesh," relationships sour. Let's all do our part to give a testimony of Christian unity to the world so that we will not be judged negatively.

3. God Forgives Confessed Sin (v. 8–2:2)

"If we say we have no sin, we deceive ourselves, and the truth is not in us" (1:8). Pretty harsh words, aren't they? Often it is hard to admit that we have done wrong, even to God. After all, we're Christians! We commit only little sins. God does not care about "little sins," does He? Yes, God cares about all sins, big or small. Remember that God is perfect, and it takes just one little sin to reveal that a person is a

sinner. Furthermore, Scripture tells us, "Sin not" (1 John 2:1), and only confessed sins can be forgiven.

The Bible says, "All have sinned, and come short of the glory of God" (Romans 3:23); therefore, every one of us needs a Saviour. Everyone has had a wrong thought, spoken an angry word, or has committed an angry deed at some time. Most of us would rather pretend that we are strong than humbly and honestly admit our weaknesses. But we do not need to be afraid of revealing our sins to God—He knows them already. He will not push us away, no matter what we've done. Instead, He will draw us to Himself. It's wonderful to know that there is no sin stain so deep that the blood of Christ cannot take it entirely away from the soul! Jesus pleads for us before the Father. Jesus walked on this earth without sin, and He pleases God completely. He has taken our punishment, has brought us into fellowship with God, and is the forgiveness for our sins. Of course, true repentance and faith in the Saviour must come before Christ's blood cleanses us from all sin. How can we be sure that we belong to Him? We can do this by looking within ourselves and asking, "Am I really trying to do what Jesus wants me to?"

Confession is not offered to gain God's acceptance, but to remove the fellowship barrier that our sin has put between Him and us. When we come to Christ, He forgives all the sins we have committed or will ever commit. We don't need to confess the sins of the past over and over again, and we don't need to fear that God will reject us if our slate is not perfectly clean. When we confess, we (1) admit that our sin really was sin and show our willingness to turn from it, and (2) recognize the necessity of relying on His strength to overcome our inclination to sin. Of course, true confession also involves a commitment not to continue in sin. We wouldn't be genuinely confessing our sins to God if we planned to commit them again and just wanted temporary forgiveness. It is also important to pray for strength to defeat temptation.

To people who are feeling guilty and condemned, John offers reassurance. We know we have sinned, and Satan (called "the accuser" in Revelation 12:10) is demanding the death penalty. When you feel this way, don't give up hope; the best defense attorney in the universe is pleading your case. Jesus Christ, your advocate, your defender, is the Judge's Son. He has already suffered your penalty in your place. You can't be tried for a case that is no longer on the docket. United with Christ, you are as safe as He is. Don't be afraid to ask Christ to plead your case—He has already won it (see Romans 8:33 34; Hebrews 7:24 25). As your advocate, Jesus Christ, the righteous One:

1. Admits the guilt of those for whom he becomes the advocate, to the full extent that they are charged by the law of God and by their own consciences.

2. Pleads that His sufferings and death satisfied God's wrath and paid the death penalty for our sin (propitiation).

3. Becomes collateral for our good behavior (Hebrews 7:22). In Him we are both forgiven and purified.

In propitiation, all obstacles to reconciliation to God are taken away, but it is still necessary for man to lay aside his opposition and embrace the terms of mercy before he can receive the benefits.

4. God Calls Us to Walk in His Light (vv. 3–5)

You have probably heard the familiar sayings, "Actions speak louder than words" and "Talk the talk, and walk the walk." Our love for God should result in obedience to His commands. Basically, John is saying, "You may say you are a Christian on your way to heaven, but if you don't do what Christ tells you to do, you are a liar."

If true love exists in the heart, it will be carried out in the life. To put it another way, true love does not exist if it is not combined with obedience. So keep His commandments walk in the light.

Search the Scriptures

1. What qualified John to write this letter to the churches (1 John 1:1–3)?

2. What did he indicate his purposes were in writing it (v. 4; 2:1)?

3. Why did John relate God to light (1:5–10)?

4. What was John referring to when he spoke of darkness (vv. 5, 8, 10; 2:3–5)?

5. What was John referring to when he used the word "propitiation" (2:2)?

6. What did John say confirmed that a person was really a child of the light (1:6; 2:3–5)?

Discuss the Meaning

1. In Matthew 22:37–39, Jesus summarized what it means to keep God's commandments. How should this affect the way we live our lives from day to day?

2. How can we show that we love the Lord with our whole heart?

3. How can we show that we love our neighbor as ourselves?

Lesson in Our Society

Before people can have meaningful relationships with others, they must love themselves. This does not refer to a worldly, self-centered, narcissistic love, but to a proper sense of self-worth. Certainly God values human beings. He made them in His image and showed people that they have infinite value to Him by His willingness to die for them. To achieve a healthy sense of self-esteem and self-worth, people need to have a relationship with God through faith in Jesus Christ and see themselves through God's eyes. To maintain a relationship with God, it is necessary to confess one's sins when they occur. God, who is faithful, will forgive our sins.

The person who aspires to have an honest relationship with God opens the door for meaningful relationships with other believers. That's because all believers have the same objective: to walk in the light of God's presence.

Make It Happen

Think about how you have been living your life. In view of today's lesson, what are some of the ways that you may need to change the way you are living to line up with God's Word? On a sheet of paper, list the areas in which you need to change. Put an asterisk by the areas you want to focus on first.

Follow the Spirit

What God wants me to do:

_____

_____

Remember Your Thoughts

Special insights I have learned:

_____

_____

More Light on the Text
1 John 1:1–2:5

In this passage, John addresses the church at Ephesus regarding false teachings that were circulating about Christ's deity. In this, his first epistle, John testifies about who Christ is and what He has done. John presents the necessity for holiness and righteous living in order to fellowship with God and Christ. His readers must know who God is and who they are in relation to Him. God is light, and no one can have fellowship with Him who does not walk in the light. Those who walk in the light are cleansed from all unrighteousness by the blood of Christ (1 John 1:5–7). Thus, just as John cautioned the church at Ephesus, so he cautions us today that in order to have fellowship with the Father and the Son, we must understand what makes this fellowship possible.

1 That which was from the beginning, which we have heard, which we have seen with our eyes, which we have looked upon, and our hands have handled, of the Word of life;

John's witness, unlike that of his opponents, represented neither innovation nor afterthought. He spoke not out of hearsay or conjecture, but from his own personal experience. Here, John uses the Greek verb for "we have seen" (*horao*, **hor-AH-o**), which simply means "to see" with physical sight. The Greek word *theaomai* (**theh-AH-om-ahee**), translated as "which we have looked upon," expresses the calm, intentional, and continuous contemplation of an object; it is more than a casual look. John had not only physically seen Jesus, but also diligently considered Jesus' person, His conduct, His life, His ministry, His teachings, His sufferings, and His miracles. The word "handled" is from the Greek word *pselaphao*

(**psay-laf-AH-o**), which means "to touch." Its usage here suggests all the evidence available for sense perception other than hearing and sight. John is claiming physical contact with Jesus. The emphasis on the physicality of Jesus confirms the truth that Jesus is God in the flesh, in contrast to the Gnostic belief that the body was evil. Through this writing, John shows the firm ground upon which all believers' faith is built. Jesus, John writes, was from the beginning, and His incarnation was real. And by His incarnation came the "Word of life" (Gk. *logos zoe*, **LOG-os dzo-AY**), the only word that can change death into life and mere existence into real living.

2 (For the life was manifested, and we have seen it, and bear witness, and shew unto you that eternal life, which was with the Father, and was manifested unto us;)

In this verse, John further clarifies Jesus as the Word of life. The life to which John bears witness is the life that was with the Father; it is precisely the life manifested in the historical person of Jesus. That is why John can say he has "seen it" (Gk. *horao*, **hor-AH-o**), can "bear witness" to it (Gk. *martureo*, **mar-too-REH-o**), and can "shew" (Gk. *apaggello*, **ap-ang-EL-lo**), or make an apostolic declaration, concerning it.

3 That which we have seen and heard declare we unto you, that ye also may have fellowship with us: and truly our fellowship is with the Father, and with his Son Jesus Christ.

This verse provides one of the reasons John wrote this epistle. According to John, true fellowship is with the Father and with His Son, Jesus Christ. The Greek word *koinonia* (**koy-nohn-EE-ah**), translated "fellowship," refers to communion, participation, sharing a common life, and partnership. In the New Testament, *koinonia* refers to the supernatural life that Christians share. It is life that is manifested and made possible by the incarnate Christ. It is the eternal life that comes from the Father and becomes the life shared individually and corporately by believers.

4 And these things write we unto you, that your joy may be full.

Clearly, the joy that John desires for his audience is inseparable from the salvation that is present in the Son. In other words, the believer's joy is tied directly to the Son.

5 This then is the message which we have heard of him, and declare unto you, that God is light, and in him is no darkness at all.

Here, John summarizes the substance of his message by unfolding the true Christian doctrine of purity from sin. God is absolute purity. The only method of coming into oneness with His purity is by confession of sins and repentance. In contrast to the false teachers he opposes, John shows the authority that lies behind his own witness as he ties his message to the person of God. God, John writes, is light, and in Him is no darkness at all. In the New Testament darkness is a metaphor for life outside of Christ. But Christians have been delivered from the power of darkness and are now children of the day (Colossians 1:13; 1 Thessalonians 5:4–5). Two important lessons emerge from John's statement: (1) living in darkness conflicts with a Christian's identity as a son or daughter of God, and (2) it is a great tragedy that, although God has revealed Himself to the world, people choose to live and walk in darkness.

6 If we say that we have fellowship with him, and walk in darkness, we lie, and do not the truth:

In this verse, John introduces the first of three tests of Christian fellowship by stating, "If we say. " This is probably in reference to the claims and boasts of the false teachers. They claimed to be righteous (i.e., to walk in the light) while in reality they practiced the deeds of darkness. This is what made their actions so detestable. Having fellowship, or *koinonia* (**koy-nohn-EE-ah**), with God implies a sharing of His divine nature. As such, if one professes to have such communion, and yet walks in darkness, and lives an unrighteous and sinful life, he is a liar and does not know the truth.

7 But if we walk in the light, as he is in the light, we have fellowship one with another, and the blood of Jesus Christ his Son cleanseth us from all sin.

There is only one way to achieve communion with God, and that is to "walk in the light." The word

"walk" here is a translation of *peripateo* (**per-ee-pat-EH-o**) and means "to make way" or "to progress." Walking in the light has two consequences. First, it produces "fellowship one with another." The Greek pronoun for "one another" is *allelon* (**al-LAY-lone**) and refers to two parties. John's point is that if Christians "walk in the light" where God is, then their fellowship (communion) with Him is mutual. Life with God does not result in isolation. Therefore, it should have an effect on our relationship with other believers. We have fellowship with God and other Christians.

Another consequence of walking in the light is that the blood of Jesus continually cleanses us from every defilement due to sin. The efficacy of His passion and death has purged our consciences from dead works and continues to "cleanse" (Gk. *katharizo,* **kath-ar-ID-zo**) us. The present tense of the verb stresses Christ's work as an ongoing provision against present and future sins. Without this continual cleansing, lasting fellowship with God would be impossible, since the guilt that results from sin destroys fellowship. The cleansing John speaks of results in forgiveness, restoration, and the reestablishment of love. The sacrifice of Christ not only atones for past sins but also equips believers in holiness day by day. The blood will never lose its power!

8 If we say that we have no sin, we deceive ourselves, and the truth is not in us.

It is very likely that the heretics of John's day denied that they had any sin or needed any Saviour. This would certainly pertain to the Gnostics, who chose to accept no responsibility for their moral acts. By supposing that they had no guilt or sinfulness, they believed that they had no need of the blood of Christ as an atoning sacrifice. This was and is the most dreadful of all deceptions because it leaves the soul under guilt and the pollution of sin exposed to hell and utterly unfit for heaven.

9 If we confess our sins, he is faithful and just to forgive us our sins, and to cleanse us from all unrighteousness. 10 If we say that we have not sinned, we make him a liar, and his word is not in us.

Walking in the light is demonstrated, not by denying sin, but by confessing and abandoning it. This action links us to God's mercy. If we humble ourselves before God, "confess" (Gk. *homologeo*,, **hom-ol-og-EH-o,** meaning "to acknowledge") our sins, and seek God's mercy, He is "faithful" (Gk. *pistos*, **pis-tos**) to forgive us. The Greek word for "forgive" is *aphiemi* (**af-EE-ay-mee**) and has, at its root, the idea of the cancellation of debts or the dismissal of charges. Moreover, not only did Jesus cancel our debt of sin by dying on the cross, but he cleansed us from all unrighteousness.

The forgiveness that comes from God is related to His faithfulness and justice. God is faithful in Himself, that is, to His own nature (cf. 2 Timothy 2:13), and is faithful to keep His promises (cf. Romans 3:25; 1 Corinthians 10:13; Hebrews 10:23; 11:11). There are numerous places in Scripture where God promises forgiveness to His children (cf. Jeremiah 31:34; Micah 7:19–20). And in keeping His promise, God reveals His faithfulness and justice. *Katharizo* refers to purification from the wickedness of sin so that a new life of holiness may begin. The sinner is perceived as cleansed from moral imperfections and from the injustices that separate him or her from God.

The assertions made in verse 10 are a restatement of the same issues found in verse 8. God requires both admission of and repentance from sin (Leviticus 5:5; 16:21; Psalm 32:1–5; Proverbs 28:13). When a Christian is convicted by God's Word regarding sin, he or she should admit the sin rather than deny it. By denying personal sins in the face of God's testimony, we, in effect, make Him out to be a liar, and His Word has no place in our lives.

2:1 My little children, these things write I unto you, that ye sin not. And if any man sin, we have an advocate with the Father, Jesus Christ the righteous:

As John resumes his discourse on sin and forgiveness, a striking change of mood is observed. Now, he specifically speaks about sin and forgiveness as they relate to believers. He uses a term of endearment: "my little children" (Gk. *teknion mou*, **tek-NEE-on moo**), or "my dear children." This is a tender and affectionate designation that denotes paternal

authority, love, and concern. On one hand, it refers to John's authority as his first century readers' spiritual father. On the other hand, it connotes the obligation of his audience to obey him as his spiritual children. The designation in no way minimizes the seriousness of the issue at hand. There is no question in John's mind that sin and obedience to God are irreconcilable and incompatible. Sin is the enemy. Sin removes the believer from the light. It prevents fellowship with God and destroys fellowship with the children of light. Thus, John warns his readers beforehand against abusing the doctrine of reconciliation. All the words, institutions, and judgments of God are leveled against sin, either that it may not be committed or that it may be abolished. The principle of sin as the power of darkness must be excluded from the believer's life, and individual acts of sin must be resisted.

If any of his "children" should fail and commit sin, John is anxious that they neither deceive themselves about it, nor lie about their actions, nor give up walking in the light. The answer to lapsing into sin is not self-deceit, but the forgiveness of God made available through Jesus Christ. He is the believers' "advocate" (Gk. *parakletos*, **par-AK-lay-tos**), the counselor who speaks in our defense. The advocate does not maintain our innocence but confesses our guilt. Then he enters his plea before the Father on our behalf as the One who has made "atoning sacrifice for our sins." His worthiness to perform this function rests on the fact that even as God is righteous (1:9), so Jesus Christ also is the righteous one—He who suffered, the just for the unjust, that He might bring us to God.

2 And he is the propitiation for our sins: and not for ours only, but also for the sins of the whole world.

Christ is not only the advocate, but also the propitiation for sins. The Greek word *hilasmos* (**hil-as-MOS**), here appropriately rendered "propitiation," is found only in this passage and in 1 John 4:10. However, it occurs often in the Septuagint (Greek translation of the Old Testament), where it signifies a sacrifice of atonement (see Leviticus 6:6–7; Numbers 5:8). For those of us who stumble and commit sin, John is anxious that we not deceive ourselves by living in denial or give up walking in the light. Self-deception is not the answer to the problem of sin. The solution is the forgiveness of God made available through Jesus Christ. Not only is Jesus our advocate—our defense attorney—but He is also our atoning sacrifice who takes our punishment and reconciles us to God. He is worthy to represent us because, like God, who is righteous, Jesus holds the title "the Righteous One."

Christ is a Redeemer, a world-class Saviour. John is careful to say that Christ died not only for the sins of the apostles and not exclusively for the sins of the Jewish people, but also for the sins of whole world, for Gentiles as well as Jews. This echoes John 3:16: It is for the world that God gave His only begotten Son (cf. 1 Timothy 2:4 5; Romans 3:29 30).

3 And hereby we do know that we know him, if we keep his commandments.

For John, the test of knowing God is moral conduct by keeping God's commandments (cf. also Titus 1:16). The Gnostics pretended to have much secret knowledge, but their knowledge left them in possession of all their sinful conduct and unholy habits. They gave no proof that they *knew* God or His Son Jesus. To *know* God carries the same idea of walking in the light and having fellowship with God. It is simply another way of speaking of the reality of God. No one who is still under the power of sin is properly acquainted with God. Too often there is a disconnection between the Christian's profession of faith and his or her practice, doctrine, and deeds. The knowledge of God and the experience of righteousness cannot and must not be separated.

4 He that saith, I know him, and keepeth not his commandments, is a liar, and the truth is not in him.

In previous verses, John dealt with the general question of how we may have assurance that we know God. Here, he deals with those who claim to know God but at the same time break His commandments. For John, knowledge of God is clearly not perceived as academic, theoretical, or speculative, but as practical and experiential. To claim to know God and at the same time to be disobedient to His commandments is, John asserts, to lie and to be devoid of all truth.

5 But whoso keepeth his word, in him verily is the love of God perfected: hereby know we that we are in him.

The true knowledge of God does not end with speculative ideas, as with the Gnostics, but with obedience to the moral law and with the presence of God's love in the believer. The term "perfected" (Gk. *teleioo*, **tel-i-O-o**) carries with it the idea of completion. The form of the verb here indicates a state resulting from an action yet to come. In the present context, therefore, true love for God is expressed, not in sentimental language or mystical experience, but in moral obedience. The proof of love is loyalty; such love is perfected. To be in Christ is to be converted to the Christian faith—receiving the forgiveness of sins, being truly united to Him by a lively faith, having communion with Him, and walking in obedience.

Daily Bible Readings

M: An Angel Speaks to Joseph
Matthew 1:18–25
T: Eyewitnesses of God's Majesty
2 Peter 1:16–21
W: We Preach Jesus Christ
2 Corinthians 4:1–6
T: Live as Children of Light
Ephesians 5:8–14
F: Jesus Is the Word of Life
1 John 1:1–4
S: Walk in the Light
1 John 1:5–10
S: Following Jesus
1 John 2:16

TEACHING TIPS
December 24
Bible Study Guide 4

1. Words You Should Know

A. Logos (John 1:1) *logos* (Gk.)—The Word; denotes the expression of thought, not the mere name of an object. Jesus, in John 1:1, is called "the Word."

B. Witness (v. 7) *martus* or *marturia* (Gk.)—Denotes one who can do or does whatever he has seen or heard or knows.

C. Incarnation—The act of grace whereby Christ became man.

2. Teacher Preparation

A. Read the Focal Verses, the Bible Background Scriptures, and the More Light on the Text section in preparation for the lesson.

B. Prayerfully read John 1, asking God to give you insight into His Word.

C. Read through the entire lesson, paying special attention to the Lesson Aim and the questions under Discuss the Meaning.

D. Complete lesson 4 in the *Precepts For Living® Personal Study Guide.* Be prepared with answers to the questions so you will be able to facilitate a class discussion.

3. Starting the Lesson

A. Ask a student to lead the class in prayer using the Lesson Aim as a guide.

B. Ask for volunteers to read the In Focus; Background; and The People, Places, and Times sections to provide insight on today's lesson.

4. Getting into the Lesson

A. Review the Lesson Aim.

B. Ask for volunteers to read the Focal Verses aloud. Then ask the class, "What are some of the main points of these verses?"

C. As you teach the material in the In Depth section, give the students an opportunity to ask questions or give additional information about what was read.

5. Relating the Lesson to Life

A. Ask the students how the In Focus story relates to today's lesson.

B. Direct the students to the Lesson in Our Society section. Engage the students in a discussion about how they can share Christ with others.

6. Arousing Action

A. Read the Make It Happen exercise and challenge the students to commit to completing it in the coming week. Encourage them to seek God for a deeper revelation of who Christ is.

B. Ask for one or two volunteers to summarize the lesson in one or two sentences.

C. Pray together, asking for God's light to shine through as the students begin a new week. Ask if anyone in the class would desire to make Jesus his or her Saviour, and take time to pray with and lead that person to Christ.

Worship Guide

For the Superintendent or Teacher
Theme: The Word Became Flesh
Theme Song: "O Come, O Come, Emmanuel"
Scripture: John 1:14
Song: "Of the Father's Love Begotten"
Meditation: God, thank You for Jesus. Thank You that He humbled Himself to become a human like us. Thank You that Jesus is the Logos, the living Word of God. Thank You for revealing Yourself to us through Jesus. As we worship this Christmas, grant us a deeper knowledge of who You are, that we may draw others to You. In Jesus' name. Amen.

THE WORD BECAME FLESH

Bible Background • JOHN 1:1–34
Printed Text • JOHN 1:1–18   Devotional Reading • ISAIAH 53:1–6

Lesson Aim

By the end of the lesson, we will:

UNDERSTAND that Jesus is the ultimate expression of the nature and character of God presented to humankind;

REJOICE that God has revealed Himself in this way; and

DETERMINE to receive Jesus as Lord and Saviour or to tell someone else how to receive Him so he or she can become a child of God and express Jesus Christ to others.

Keep in Mind

"And the Word was made flesh, and dwelt among us, (and we beheld his glory, the glory as of the only begotten of the Father,) full of grace and truth" (John 1:14).

Focal Verses

John 1:1 In the beginning was the Word, and the Word was with God, and the Word was God.

2 The same was in the beginning with God.

3 All things were made by him; and without him was not any thing made that was made.

4 In him was life; and the life was the light of men.

5 And the light shineth in darkness; and the darkness comprehended it not.

6 There was a man sent from God, whose name was John.

7 The same came for a witness, to bear witness of the Light, that all men through him might believe.

8 He was not that Light, but was sent to bear witness of that Light.

9 That was the true Light, which lighteth every man that cometh into the world.

10 He was in the world, and the world was made by him, and the world knew him not.

11 He came unto his own, and his own received him not.

12 But as many as received him, to them gave he power to become the sons of God, even to them that believe on his name:

13 Which were born, not of blood, nor of the will of the flesh, nor of the will of man, but of God.

14 And the Word was made flesh, and dwelt among us, (and we beheld his glory, the glory as of the only begotten of the Father,) full of grace and truth.

15 John bare witness of him, and cried, saying, This was he of whom I spake, He that cometh after me is preferred before me: for he was before me.

16 And of his fulness have all we received, and grace for grace.

17 For the law was given by Moses, but grace and truth came by Jesus Christ.

18 No man hath seen God at any time; the only begotten Son, which is in the bosom of the Father, he hath declared him.

In Focus

It was Christmas Eve. The house was warm and comfortable against the snowy evening. The aromas of freshly baked bread, honey ham, and greens floated from the kitchen, filling the house. The children were laughing and chasing one another around the house, while the adults were spread throughout the house. The men were watching football in the family room, and the women were setting the table for dinner. Paula looked around for her grandfather and found him in the living room, silently reading his Bible. "Granddad, why are you sitting all alone?"

Her grandfather looked up with a worried expression. "I'm a little upset with you, missy."

Paula sat on the sofa with him. "Why, Granddad? What did I do?"

Her grandfather leveled his eyes at hers. "I'm concerned about my great-grandchildren. I looked around in church this morning, and I didn't see you or the kids there."

"Granddad, the kids had lots of presents to open this morning, and I had to finish preparing dinner. Besides, we attend church fairly regularly, and the kids are in lots of church programs," retorted Paula.

"Paula, I'm surprised at you. You should realize that the Word of God must be reflected in everything we do, especially during this season. Just as your parents set the example with you, it is your responsibility to set an example with your children so that God becomes as real for them as He is for you."

Paula squeezed his hand and whispered, "I apologize, Granddad; you're right." Just then, her two boys ran into living room and jumped into their great-grandfather's lap.

Today, let us be mindful of the true reason for the Christmas celebration. Without the Word, we are abandoning the purpose for which we were made: to reflect Christlikeness in every aspect of our daily lives.

The People, Places, and Times

Pharisees. During the time the gospel of John was written, the Pharisees were exerting more and more control over all areas of Jewish life. They saw the converted Jews as their opponents and rejected anyone who claimed that Jesus was the Messiah. The Jewish Christians were often made to feel unwelcome in the local synagogues. They were treated as if they had forsaken their Jewish heritage because they had accepted Christ. Despite this opposition, many Jews confessed their faith in Christ.

Greeks, or non-Jews, were also drawn to the Gospel. Many of them had been exposed to varying strains of Gnosticism (an early heresy) and did not believe in the humanity of Jesus. As people from diverse backgrounds became part of the church, it became necessary for the apostles to correct errors in doctrine as well as encourage the existing believers. In the gospel of John, the writer seems to be addressing a mixed audience of believers and unbelievers, Jews and Greeks.

Source
Keener, Craig S. *The IVP Bible Background Commentary: New Testament.* Downers Grove, Ill.: InterVarsity Press, 1993, 261.

Background

The author of the book of John identifies himself as "the disciple whom Jesus loved" (John 13:23; 19:26; 21:7, 20). Most scholars agree that the apostle John is the author of this book. John was well known in the early church and was intimately familiar with Jewish life. He would have been an eyewitness to many of the events recorded in the gospel of John.

Dating of the gospel of John is a matter of debate, with dates ranging from A.D. 50 to 95 or later. However, most scholars accept the later date of A.D. 95. Although we may not know the exact date of the writing, we do know that the first century church was thriving. Even amid the threats of persecution and heresy, the church continued to grow.

John wrote to encourage the believers, most of whom were Jewish. He affirms their Jewishness as well as their faith in Jesus Christ, contrasting them with the Pharisees, who claimed to be the true or real Jews.

Evangelism is one of the main purposes of the book of John. In 20:31, John states: "But these are written, that ye might believe that Jesus is the Christ, the Son of God; and that believing ye might have life through his name." Even today, the gospel of John is known for its evangelistic overtones. The language of John is simple; the message of salvation is clear. However, the book of John is much more than an evangelistic tool; it is a treasure trove of insights for every Christian. In the book of John, Jesus is revealed as the living Word of God.

At-A-Glance

1. Jesus Is the Word (John 1:1–3)
2. Jesus Is the Light (vv. 4–9)
3. Jesus Reveals God's Character (vv. 10–18)

In Depth

1. Jesus Is the Word (John 1:1–3)

The first 18 verses of the book of John summarize the whole Gospel. In these verses, we are introduced to Jesus—who He is, what He does, and the role He plays in the eternal plan of God for the world.

John began his book with the words "In the beginning." He then introduced Jesus as the "Word." The word used here is *logos*. The Greeks understood *logos* to mean not only the written or spoken word, but also the thought or reasoning in the mind. John's Greek readers would have understood the nuances of *logos*, realizing that John was presenting Jesus as the power that controlled all things.

The Jewish believers used the word *logos* to refer to God and would have connected this concept to the wisdom personified in the Old Testament (see Proverbs 8). In tandem with wisdom was ability; in this case, God's wisdom was used to create the universe. Jesus is that wisdom personified. All of these concepts are bound up in the word *logos*.

As believers today, when we read John 1:1–3, we may not realize all the nuances that the author intended. But what we must learn from this verse is clear: Jesus was, is, and always will be. He is God. He is the Creator and the Source of all life. The entirety of our Christian faith rests upon accepting these truths. Without believing in Jesus personally as the *logos*, we will never be able to find any purpose or meaning in life.

Through Jesus, all things were created. The Bible says that "without him, nothing was made that has been made" (John 1:3, NIV). To understand the creation, we must know the Creator.

"John bare witness of him, and cried, saying, 'This was he of whom I spake, He that cometh after me is preferred before me: for he was before me'" (John 1:15).

2. Jesus Is the Light (vv. 4–9)

In this passage, John spoke of Jesus as "the Light." Jesus is life itself, and that life is our light (v. 4). When we receive this life that Jesus offers, our spiritual darkness is replaced by light. As we walk in the light, we learn to comprehend the things of God. We become more like our Creator.

However, many people live in deep darkness. In the Bible, darkness usually connotes sin, guilt, or misery. Even though Jesus is the Light and came to dispel darkness, many people refuse to accept the light of salvation. While here on Earth, Jesus preached to a mostly Jewish audience. They were not only blinded by their sin, but they were hindered by their religion and preconceived ideas.

It's the same today. People are so thoroughly entrenched in their sin and ignorance that they are blind to the light. Their pride is more important to them than anything else, and they are loathe to admit that they could be wrong. It is our joy as believers to shine the light of Jesus to those around us.

God can use anyone and anything to pierce through the darkness. In Jesus' time, God sent John the Baptist to testify, or witness, to the truth of Jesus' words (vv. 6–7). John the Baptist did not seek for people to believe in him, but he pointed the way to Jesus. In this day and age, God uses His written Word and the power of the Holy Spirit to testify to the Light. He also uses believers who are willing and available. Every believer should view himself or herself as a testimony to the truth of salvation through Jesus Christ.

3. Jesus Reveals God's Character (vv. 10–18)

Although Jesus created the world, the world did not recognize Him as Saviour (v. 10). Verse 11 says, "He came unto his own, and his own received him not." Jesus came to the Jews first, but they rejected Him as their Messiah.

His gift of salvation is offered freely to all, but unless one accepts that salvation, the darkness will continue to obscure the light. When we do receive Jesus, God gives us the right to become His children (v. 12). What an amazing statement! We have the

right to become God's children. It's not because of anything we have done to deserve it, but because God's grace makes it possible for us to choose to believe and receive Jesus. We are not children in the physical sense; we are spiritual children of our Father, God. When we receive Christ, we are adopted into the family of God (see 1 John 3:1). We are considered heirs of God (Galatians 3:29), eligible to receive all of His promised blessings.

We cannot become God's children by any other means than through salvation in Jesus Christ. Verse 13 makes this clear: God's children are not born in the natural way of conception and birth. We are born of God spiritually. He chose us. God chose to send His Son, Jesus, to the earth to take on the form of human flesh. John first introduced us to Jesus as the eternally existing Word of God. Now he reveals another facet of *logos*—Jesus. The One who has always existed, the One who is God, has become a human being (v. 14).

Although He had always been omnipresent, He had now come to be one of us. He came to live with us, to feel our pain, to experience our joy, and to know our sorrow. He experienced human life fully. John and the other disciples knew Him intimately as Teacher and Friend. They ate with Him, talked with Him, laughed with Him, and cried with Him.

Verse 14 says, "He dwelt among us." John's Jewish readers would have understood the word "dwelling" to be connected to the word for "tabernacle." In Old Testament times, the tabernacle was where God's glory dwelled. The disciples watched Him perform miracles, and they knew Him as the Messiah.

As modern-day believers, we can't physically touch Jesus. He is no longer here in the flesh. Yet we can see His glory. We can testify to the miracles He has worked in our lives and the lives of others. We can witness to the power of salvation. And, amazingly enough, we can become like Him. In fact, we should strive to become like Him. We are frail humans, but when we receive the *logos*, we will begin to reflect the likeness of Him who is the Living Word.

How can this be accomplished? As we learn to abide, or live, in the Word, our human nature will begin to be transformed. We will begin to think as

Jesus would think. We will begin to act as Jesus would act. We will be light in a dark world.

Because of God's grace, we have the potential to change our world. Because of God's grace, we have received blessing after blessing (v. 16). We have received the ability to comprehend and accept the gift of salvation. We have received the fullness of all that God has to offer us through Jesus.

In verse 17, John reminds his readers that they received the Law through Moses, but that through Christ they received grace and truth. The ideas of grace and truth are sometimes translated as "love" and "faithfulness." In other words, the Law was important, but insufficient for salvation; however, now that Christ has come, we have all that we need for salvation. What an amazing concept. We don't live by following a list of rules; we live according to the grace of a loving Saviour who gently guides us. As we grow in our relationship with Jesus, we receive a greater revelation of who God is.

No one has ever seen God with physical eyes, but Jesus, who is God, has revealed Him to us (v. 18). God has chosen to reveal Himself to us. He has made a way for us to know Him intimately. He longs for us to know Him. But the only way we can know God is through His Son, Jesus. We learn what God is like by learning what Jesus is like. As we draw close to Jesus, He will begin to change us into His image. And when that happens, others will be drawn to Him through us.

Search the Scriptures

1. In the beginning was the _____, and the _____ was with God, and the _____ was God (John 1:1).

2. In him was _____; and the _____ was the _____ of men (v. 4).

3. Yet to all who _____ him, to those who _____ in his name, he gave the _____ to become children of God (v. 12, NIV).

4. The Word became _____ and made his _____ among us. We have seen his glory, the glory of the _____ and _____, who came from the Father, full of _____ and _____ (v. 14, NIV).

5. No one has ever _____ _____, but God the One and only, who is at the Father's side, has made him _____ (v. 18, NIV).

Discuss the Meaning

1. Who is the "Word" (John 1:1)?
2. What is the "light of men" (v. 4)?
3. Why is it important for Christians to recognize the eternal, divine existence of Jesus Christ (v. 12)?
4. How can we receive grace and truth (v. 17)?

Lesson in Our Society

Jesus came into this world in the form of human flesh, yet those around Him did not acknowledge Him for who He is: God. They chose to continue living in darkness rather than receiving the Light.

Things aren't so different in our world today. In our modern society, especially in America, many people have become accustomed to a fast-paced, hectic lifestyle. They are easily distracted, often bored, or generally dissatisfied with life.

Jesus came to give meaningful, real life to all who will receive Him. He is the living revelation of God, who expressed God's truth in a way we can understand. It is our task to share this light with others.

Make It Happen

This week, ask God to reveal Himself to you in a new way. Spend time praying, reading the Word, and meditating on what you have read. Let God's Word permeate your spirit so that you might know God more deeply. Rejoice in the fact that God has revealed Himself to you through Jesus, the Word made flesh, and that He will continue to do so.

Follow the Spirit

What God wants me to do:

_____

_____

Remember Your Thoughts

Special insights I have learned:

_____

_____

More Light on the Text
John 1:1–18

The gospel of John is the fourth book of the New Testament and was written between A.D. 70 and A.D. 90 by the apostle John, the brother of James the "greater" (Matthew 4:21; 10:2; Mark 1:19; 3:17; 10:35). He was one of the sons of Zebedee (Matthew 4:21) and Salome (Matthew 27:56; cp. Mark 15:40) and was born in Bethsaida. "This Gospel was probably written at a time when the church was composed of second- and third-generation Christians who needed more detailed instruction about Jesus and new defenses for the apologetic problems raised by apostasy within the church and by growing opposition from without."

One of the main heresies affecting the church of that day was gnosticism (**NAS-te-si-zem**). Gnosticism was an early-century dualistic heresy that stressed the importance of secret philosophical knowledge for salvation, and that matter was evil. Gnosticism taught that Jesus was one of many emanations of deity that come forth from God, thereby denying the deity and preexistence of Jesus. In order to correct this heresy, John may have written his gospel.

1 In the beginning was the Word, and the Word was with God, and the Word was God.

John begins his gospel with a clear reference to Genesis 1:1. The book of Genesis opens with an affirmation of the nature and character of God, the Creator and Sustainer of the universe. The purpose of the statement in Genesis is threefold: (1) to identify the Creator, (2) to explain the origin of the world, and (3) to tie the work of God in the past to the work of God in the future. Likewise, John is clearly identifying Jesus, the living Word made flesh, as God the Creator (John 1:3) and affirming Him as the only source of life and redemption. This gospel from its very start is heralding the deity of Jesus Christ. John is not referring here to a particular time in the past; rather, he is affirming the preexistence of Jesus.

"Word" here is expressed using the Greek word *logos,* which has several meanings. Ordinarily, *logos*

refers to a spoken word, with an emphasis on the meaning conveyed, not just the sounds produced. But here, *logos* is used as an expression of communication with God. It is more than everyday speech; it is the creative power of God (see Psalm 33:6). John is clearly asserting that the divine Word is the source of creation and of all that is visible and invisible in the world.

John leaves no question as to the nature, character, and glory of the Word—the "Word was God." John is saying that the Word is deity—one with God in nature, character, and glory.

2 The same was in the beginning with God. 3 All things were made by him; and without him was not any thing made that was made.

John begins the second verse by reiterating the divine, preexistent nature of the Word. He proceeds to explain the role of the Word in the beginning. The word "made" (Gk. *ginomai,* **GHIN-om-ahee**) means "to come into being, happen, or become." John is communicating the idea that this creative work happened out of nothing, that the Word not rely on preexisting material to create the universe (Colossians 1:16; Hebrews 1:2).

John also begins to give us a hint as to the name of the Word by referring to the Word as "Him." The Word is more than just an expression of the personality of God; it is the person of Jesus Christ. So John is saying that the Word, which was preexistent with God, was in complete fellowship with God, possessed all the divine nature and characteristics of deity, and created everything.

4 In him was life; and the life was the light of men.

"Life" in Greek is *zoe* (**dzo-AY**) and is used throughout the Bible to refer to both physical and spiritual life. It is frequently qualified with the word "eternal." Jesus was the embodiment of the fullness and quality of life that God offers to those who believe (John 14:6; cp. 10:10). The life that Jesus was to offer would be the light of all humanity.

5 And the light shineth in darkness; and the darkness comprehended it not.

Here, John uses the metaphors of "light" (Gk. *phos*, **foce,** meaning "to manifest," and "darkness" (Gk. *skotia*, **skot-EE-ah,** meaning "dimness" or "obscurity") to illustrate the differences between a life of grace, mercy, and forgiveness and a life of sin and death. The word "comprehend" (Gk. *katalam-bano*, **kat-al-am-BAN-o**) has two possible meanings. One meaning is "to understand, perceive, or learn" and communicates the fact that those who live in the darkness do not receive the light because of a lack of understanding—they don't get it. Another meaning is the idea "to lay hold of or seize" and communicates the fact that the darkness of sinful humanity will never have the ultimate victory over the light of Jesus.

John is saying that some who see the light will be unable to understand and receive it because Satan has blinded them (2 Corinthians 4:4). But John says that no matter how dark the darkness of evil seems in the world, no matter how the global circumstances seem to indicate that the darkness of evil is winning, the darkness cannot overcome the light that comes from the life of Christ.

6 There was a man sent from God, whose name was John. 7 The same came for a witness, to bear witness of the Light, that all men through him might believe.

The apostle John goes on to talk about John the Baptist. The ministry of John the Baptist is prominent in the gospel of John. Here, the apostle John is affirming the prophetic ministry of John the Baptist. Jesus echoed this assertion when He said that John the Baptist was the last of the great Old Testament prophets, who came in the spirit of Elijah (Matthew 11:9–10; Mark 9:13). John the Baptist had a unique call and ministry: to be a witness of Jesus, the Light (cp. Matthew 4:4; John 1:4).

The word "witness" (Gk. *marturia*, **mar-too-REE-ah**) means to affirm by testimony what one has seen, heard, experienced, or knows because of a supernatural encounter with God. Therefore, John the Baptist had the prophetic duty of preparing the way for Jesus by preaching the testimonies of God.

The goal of John the Baptist was the same as the goal of John the apostle: to bring humanity to a place of faith in Jesus as Lord and Saviour. The author is careful to specify that John the Baptist was not the genuine light, but that he came to "bear witness" (Gk. *martureo*, **mar-too-REH-o**), to testify of, or report on the One to come. John the Baptist testified to the world of the nature and character of Jesus so that "all men through him might believe."

8 He was not that Light, but was sent to bear witness of that Light. 9 That was the true Light, which lighteth every man that cometh into the world.

The apostle John makes it clear that John the Baptist was not the Light. He was only to bear witness of the Light. Like the moon that does not shine its own light, but only reflects the light of the sun, so John the Baptist reflects the Light of Jesus Christ, the Son of God. Jesus would be the true Light that would light every man. The word "true" (Gk.*alethinos*, **al-ay-thee-NOS**) refers to that which is sincere, true, or genuine. The apostle John is saying that John the Baptist pointed others to the light to come, and that Jesus Christ was the authentic Light.

10 He was in the world, and the world was made by him, and the world knew him not. 11 He came unto his own, and his own received him not.

Here, the Greek word for "world" is *kosmos* (**KOS-mos**) and refers to the universe (both things and people), the inhabitants of the Earth (i.e., humanity), and the evil world system alienated from God. Gnostics believed that the flesh and the material world were evil. The apostle John may have been refuting this heresy by making the statement that Jesus "was in the world." In other words, Jesus was not alienated from the material world and its inhabitants; this was the world that He had created (cp. John 1:3).

Even though Jesus was in the world that He had made, the world "knew Him not." The Greek word for "knew" is *ginosko* (**ghin-OCE-ko**) and refers to more than just head knowledge. It means "to recognize or perceive" and carries the idea of knowing something intimately. John is conveying the real problem with humanity: The world should recognize its Creator. This recognition should motivate humanity to have a relationship with Jesus, but the world does not recognize Him nor desire to have an intimate relationship with Him.

The rejection of Jesus by the world comes to a head in verse 11. There are two different meanings for the word "own" in this passage. First, He came to His "own" (Gk. *idios*, **ID-ee-os**), meaning "property" or "possessions" (i.e., homeland). Second, His "own" received Him not; the word is masculine in the Greek and refers to His own people, the Jews. For hundreds of years, the Jews had waited for the Messiah; now, when He came, they refused to receive Him as such.

The world belonged to Christ by virtue of His having created it, but the world did not know Him, would not enter into a relationship with Him, and refused to receive Him because they did not recognize Him for who He was. What a scathing commentary on the sinful condition of humanity!

12 But as many as received him, to them gave he power to become the sons of God, even to them that believe on his name:

But there is still hope for sinful humanity. Regardless of how bleak the situation may seem for humanity, God provides hope in the person of Jesus. There will be many who receive Jesus as Saviour and Lord and recognize Him for who He is: the Creator of the universe. The word "receive" (Gk. *paralambano*, **par-al-am-BAN-o**) means "to take what is one's own, take to one's self, or make one's own." As used here, "received" is more than psychologically accepting or making some emotional assent to Jesus. Therefore, to receive Jesus means to take hold of everything that Jesus is (Lord, Saviour, Creator, Redeemer, etc.) and make Him one's own so that His presence affects a person's goals, aims, plans, and desires.

Those who receive Jesus and allow Him to affect their goals, aims, and plans are given the "power to become the sons of God." The Greek word for "power" is *exousia* (**ex-oo-SEE-ah**) and is best translated as "power of authority (influence)" or "power to act."

What John is saying is that whoever receives Jesus is given the power and authority to act in a way consistent with being a child of God, and that this power gives us access to all of the privileges that come through God's grace. It is this power that is used when we become children of God. God's power must be at work in our lives in order for us to live and act in a way consistent with being a child of God (cp. John 1:13).

John goes on to say that the privileges of being a son of God are bestowed on those who "believe" on (Gk. *pisteuo*, **pist-YOO-o**) or have faith in, His name. "Belief" here is more than simply something that happens in the mind. To believe on Jesus Christ means to place complete confidence in the nature, person, and character of Jesus Christ so that He influences the total being (goals, aims, plans, and desires). When you "receive [Jesus]" and "believe in Him," John says, you must entrust Him with your life. Then this trust should lead to some sort of action, whereby you take hold of Jesus for yourself in order to be part of the family of God.

13 Which were born, not of blood, nor of the will of the flesh, nor of the will of man, but of God.

In this verse, Johns tells us that this new birth was not of "blood" (Gk. *haima*, **HAH-ee-mah**), referring to the blood of man or animals. Nor was it a result of the will of the "flesh" (Gk. *sarx*), meaning "carnal nature" or "passions." Rather, the new birth was a result of something supernatural (cf. John 3:5–6).

14 And the Word was made flesh, and dwelt among us, (and we beheld his glory, the glory as of the only begotten of the Father,) full of grace and truth.

John 1:14 is one of the key verses in the New Testament that explains the Incarnation. "Incarnation" is defined as that act of grace whereby Christ took our human nature into union with His divine Person, becoming man. The Word was made flesh. Here, John refers to verse 1 and brings our attention back to the divine Word, or *logos*. The Word, who is God, who created the universe and provided light to all humanity, became flesh. The word "made" here (Gk. *ginomai*, **GHIN-om-ahee**) is the same word used in John 1:3 and means "to come into being." John is not saying that Jesus was some created, lesser god; he is affirming that Jesus existed in eternity past and took on a physical body through the Incarnation.

The divine Word not only took on a physical body, but also dwelt among us. The word "dwelt" (Gk. *skenoo*, **skay-NO-o**) refers to abiding or living in a tabernacle (or tent). One cannot escape John's allusion to the Old Testament tabernacle, which was built as a temporary and mobile dwelling for God (see Exodus 36–40). The original tabernacle was a temporary meeting place. It had provisional status, anticipating the construction of the temple in Jerusalem. In the Incarnation, when the Word was made flesh, humanity did receive a temporary tabernacle; rather, God Himself in Jesus came to live among us.

The idea John is trying to communicate here is that the "glory" (Gk. *doxa*, **DOX-ah,** meaning "perfection, honor, and praise") that we see in the incarnate Word is the glory of the Father in heaven. This is the strongest assertion of the deity of Christ that could be made. "Begotten" is the Greek word *monogenes* (**mon-og-en-ACE**) and means "unique, or one of a kind." While we can claim to be sons (children) of God in a general sense by receiving and believing in Christ, Jesus is the one and only unique Son of God.

And what is it that we see when we behold His glory? A revelation of God's preeminence and dignity, through Jesus, will reveal that He is "full of grace and truth." God's grace is a demonstration of His love. The word "grace" (Gk. *charis*, **KHAR-ece**) is defined as "favor" or "that which affords pleasure." This is the perfect picture of the balance in the nature and character of God. "Truth" (Gk. *aletheia*, **al-AY-thi-a**) can be defined as "that which conforms to reality." So Jesus is the one and only Son of God, and He conforms to the full reality of God in nature, character, and purpose (cp. Colossians 2:9). The truth as it relates to the nature and character of Jesus Christ dispels any heresies that may rise concerning His divine character.

15 John bare witness of him, and cried, saying, This was he of whom I spake, He that cometh after me is preferred before me: for he was before me. 16 And of his fulness have all we received, and grace for grace.

John the apostle then returns to the witness of John the Baptist. Remember that most of the 12 apostles were first followers of John the Baptist, and they held him in the highest regard. John the Baptist continued to remind these early disciples that he was not the Messiah, that he came as "the voice of one crying in the wilderness, Make straight the way of the Lord" (John 1:23).

John the Baptist was born six months before Jesus, but Jesus existed before him in eternity past. Not only was Jesus superior to John the Baptist because of His preexistence, but He is also "preferred" (Gk. *emprosthen*, **EM-pros-then**), meaning to be in front of in rank. Though John the Baptist was born before Jesus and had a significant ministry, Jesus was in front of him in power, prominence, and authority.

The apostle John goes on to explain the magnitude of the effects of the grace that we have received in Jesus Christ as "grace for grace," which can be translated as "grace in exchange for grace" and carries the meaning of "ever-increasing favor." The Bible chronicles the grace of God from cover to cover, from Adam to Abraham to the Children of Israel to the prophets; but until the incarnation of Jesus, this grace was always experienced through an intermediary. Now, in Jesus Christ, we can access the fullness of grace in proportions never experienced by humanity before.

17 For the law was given by Moses, but grace and truth came by Jesus Christ. 18 No man hath seen God at any time; the only begotten Son, which is in the bosom of the Father, he hath declared him.

Here, John contrasts law and grace. The law that was given to Moses cannot compare to the grace given to us in Jesus Christ. The law was not given to Israel to save them. Rather, the law reveals God's standards and certifies our guilt before God. In essence, the law was a temporary fix until the grace of God was revealed through faith in Jesus Christ (cf. Galatians 3:23–24).

In verse 18, John again affirms the divine nature and character of Jesus Christ. The noun for "God" used here is the Greek word *theos* (**THEH-os**) and represents God in His divine nature or deity, rather than as a human being. God is Spirit (John 4:24); no human has ever seen the essence of His deity—not because He is not real, but because human eyes are incapable of looking on Him (Exodus 33:23). Although we cannot see God, His one and only Son, Jesus, "declared" (Gk. *exegeomai*, **ex-ayg-EH-om-ahee,** meaning "go before" or "unfold") the full deity of God to us.

Sources

Tenney, Merrill C. *Expositor's Bible Commentary (John and Acts)* (electronic edition). Edited by Frank E. Gaebelein. Grand Rapids, Mich.: Zondervan Publishing, 1992.

Vincent, Marvin R. *Vincent's Word Studies Vol. 2: The Writings of John* (electronic edition). Hiawatha, Iowa: Parsons Technology, Inc., 1998.

Daily Bible Readings

M: Jesus Is Born
Luke 2:1–7
T: Angels and Shepherds Celebrate
Luke 2:8–20
W: Called to Belong to Jesus Christ
Romans 1:1–5
T: God's Plan for Us
Ephesians 1:3–10
F: The Word Sent by God
John 1:1–9
S: The Word Became Flesh
John 1:10–18
S: New Things I Now Declare
Isaiah 42:5–9

TEACHING TIPS

December 31
Bible Study Guide 5

1. Words You Should Know

A. Mind (Philippians 2:5) *phroneo* (Gk.)—To think, to be minded in a certain way; implies moral interest or reflection, not mere unreasoning opinion.

B. Humbled (v. 8) *tapeinoo* (Gk.)—To make low.

2. Teacher Preparation

A. Read the entire book of Philippians, paying particular attention to the Focal Verses.

B. Review the Lesson Aim to gain insight into the lesson objectives.

C. Read the Background, In Depth, Search the Scriptures, and Discuss the Meaning sections.

D. Complete lesson 5 in the *Precepts For Living® Personal Study Guide.*

3. Starting the Lesson

A. Ask a volunteer to lead the class in prayer, focusing on today's Lesson Aim.

B. Have class members share what they learned this past week based on last week's Make It Happen assignment.

C. Ask a student volunteer to read today's In Focus story.

D. Lead the students in reading this week's Lesson Aim in unison.

4. Getting into the Lesson

A. Read Background and The People, Places, and Times.

B. Ask for a volunteer to read the Focal Verses in a modern Bible translation, such as *The New International Version, The Living Bible,* or *The Message.*

C. Form small groups, and assign each group an In Depth section to review based on the At-A-Glance outline.

5. Relating the Lesson to Life

A. Reassemble the class, and review the Search the Scriptures and Discuss the Meaning questions, allowing five or ten minutes for each group to discuss their answers with the rest of the class.

B. Allow time for the students to share their challenges, frustrations, or successes in living the balanced life.

6. Arousing Action

A. Challenge the students to complete the Make It Happen activity at home this week.

B. Encourage the students to think of creative ways to implement the questions raised in the Lesson in Our Society section.

C. Instruct the class to read the Daily Bible Readings in preparation for next week's class.

D. Close the class in prayer.

Worship Guide

For the Superintendent or Teacher
Theme: Humiliation and Exaltation
Theme Song: "Jesus, Use Me"
Scripture: Philippians 2:3–5
Song: "I Surrender All"
Meditation: Father God, You sent Jesus to be our example. Help us today to follow in His footsteps of servanthood to You and to others. May we please You daily by serving others and submitting to Your will. In Jesus' name. Amen.

HUMILIATION AND EXALTATION

Bible Background • PHILIPPIANS 2:1–11
Printed Text • PHILIPPIANS 2:1–11   Devotional Reading • 1 PETER 3:8–12

Lesson Aim

By the end of the lesson, we will:

UNDERSTAND what it means to walk humbly in the knowledge of who we are in Christ;

SENSE that walking humbly is vital to pleasing Christ our Lord; and

DEDICATE ourselves daily to putting God and others first without feeling put upon or bitter.

Keep in Mind

"Let nothing be done through strife or vainglory; but in lowliness of mind let each esteem other better than themselves" (Philippians 2:3).

Focal Verses

Philippians 2:1 If there be therefore any consolation in Christ, if any comfort of love, if any fellowship of the Spirit, if any bowels and mercies,

2 Fulfil ye my joy, that ye be likeminded, having the same love, being of one accord, of one mind.

3 Let nothing be done through strife or vainglory; but in lowliness of mind let each esteem other better than themselves.

4 Look not every man on his own things, but every man also on the things of others.

5 Let this mind be in you, which was also in Christ Jesus:

6 Who, being in the form of God, thought it not robbery to be equal with God:

7 But made himself of no reputation, and took upon him the form of a servant, and was made in the likeness of men:

8 And being found in fashion as a man, he humbled himself, and became obedient unto death, even the death of the cross.

9 Wherefore God also hath highly exalted him, and given him

a name which is above every name:

10 That at the name of Jesus every knee should bow, of things in heaven, and things in earth, and things under the earth;

11 And that every tongue should confess that Jesus Christ is Lord, to the glory of God the Father.

In Focus

Ben sat in his pastor's office nervous and full of anxiety.

"Margie says God has called her to run for state representative," Ben told Pastor Jones.

"That's wonderful news, Ben," replied Pastor Jones.

"It's really causing a lot of turmoil in our marriage. I don't think it's right for our family. The kids are in high school. It will take her away from our home, our children, and the church."

"Ben, I've known Margie since she was a child. She has strong Christian values. She has faithfully served in the church and this community for years. She has always put the needs of others

before her own. Besides, I think it's important that Christians get off the pew and become active in the political arena."

Ben rubbed his aching head. "I'm not so sure, Pastor. Politics is something that the world has produced, not God."

Pastor Jones gave him a good-natured smile. "Ben, even Christ humbled Himself to serve mankind. A politician's job is to serve his or her constituency. I strongly believe Margie's involvement in politics is an opportunity for our opinions to be heard. If Christians don't act, others who have opposing viewpoints will overtake the dominion God has given us."

"I suppose you're right," said Ben. "I never thought about it that way. I suppose I should practice some humility myself. I know Margie will make a great politician. She's already a terrific wife and mother!" said Ben.

In today's lesson, Paul teaches that we should consider others' interests just as important as our own.

The People, Places, and Times

Philippi. It was a Roman colony in Macedonia. The people of Philippi were proud of their status as Roman citizens, promoting Latin as their official language and taking advantage of their tax-free status. Many of the social and governmental institutions of Philippi were modeled after those in Rome.

The apostle Paul preached the Gospel to the city of Philippi on his second missionary journey. One of Paul's first converts in the area was a prominent Philippian businesswoman named Lydia. She welcomed Paul and his entourage into her home, which apparently was the beginning of the first house church in Philippi.

Background

Primarily a Gentile city, Philippi had no Jewish synagogue in Paul's day. The Philippian church probably comprised several house churches. It was to this body of believers that the apostle Paul wrote his letter to the Philippians, thanking them for their generous and loving support.

Written from prison, probably in Rome, this letter reveals a great mutual affection between Paul and the Philippians. Paul expresses his deep gratitude for their gift but also displays a loving concern for their welfare. The overarching theme of the book of Philippians is joy—so much so that this book is sometimes known as the epistle of joy.

Other significant themes found in the book of Philippians are the character of God, conflict and suffering, and servanthood. In this week's lesson, we will look closely at the idea of servanthood—Christ's and ours.

At-A-Glance

1. Called to Humility (Philippians 2:1–4)
2. Jesus Models Humility (vv. 5–8)
3. Rewards of Humility (vv. 9–11)

In Depth

1. Called to Humility (Philippians 2:1–4)

In Philippians 1, Paul discusses his imprisonment and how it has been used by God to advance the Gospel. This situation, he points out, could also teach the Philippians how to respond to persecution and suffering.

In Philippians 2, Paul instructs the Philippians on the finer points of church life and Christian living. He starts out by reminding them of several aspects of the Christian life that they should already be experiencing: (1) they should be encouraged because of their standing in Christ; (2) they should take comfort in Christ's love; (3) they should be experiencing deep fellowship with other believers, enabled by the Holy Spirit; and (4) they should display great tenderness and compassion toward one another. All of these areas should already have been displayed in their lives as Christians.

Since this is how it should be, Paul goes on to say that they should take the next step and live in unity (v. 2). If the Philippian Christians would do this, Paul says, then his joy will be complete. In other words, Paul would gain great satisfaction in seeing the Philippian church living out the Gospel he had preached to them.

He encourages the Philippian Christians to be "like-minded" and "one in spirit and purpose" (NIV). This doesn't mean that they all had to think alike, but that they would have a mind-set of unity—willingness to work with and serve one another. In this atmosphere of cooperation and fellowship, true unity could flourish.

Paul doesn't merely tell the Philippians to live in unity, but gives practical instruction for doing so. His first instruction is to beware selfishness and pride. Strife or self-ambition (v. 3) is the opposite of unity. In fact, in Galatians 5:20, strife is listed among the acts of the sinful nature. Strife is a natural bent of every human being, but when we choose to walk in God's ways, we begin to learn how to put others' needs ahead of our own. We learn how to choose humility rather than pride.

As Christians, we realize that we have a great priv-

Paul wrote: "Let nothing be done through strife or vainglory; but in lowliness of mind let each esteem other better than themselves" (Philippians 2:3).

ilege—we are children of God (see John 1:12). Along with this position come many blessings and responsibilities. God has given us authority in His name (Luke 10:19). He has "seated us in heavenly places with Christ Jesus" (Ephesians 2:6, paraphrased). He has a rich storehouse of treasure for every one of His children. Yet we must not get so wrapped up in what we have or who we are that we forget the other side of the coin.

In these verses in Philippians, God is calling Christians to lives of voluntary humility. We are called to servanthood. For believers, servanthood includes not only service to God, but also service to our fellow human beings.

2. Jesus Models Humility (vv. 5–8)

In order to learn how to be a servant, we need only to look to Jesus. He is the supreme example of how we should live every area of our lives. He left behind indescribable glory to become a humble servant, and He did it for our benefit. Can we as His followers do any less?

As we look at Jesus' example, we see that humility is a mind-set. In verse 5, Paul urges his readers to have the "mind" of Christ. The Greek word used for "mind" in this verse is *phroneo* (**fron-EH-o**), meaning "to think or feel." Additionally, *phroneo* connotes an attitude that leads to a certain kind of behavior. Obviously, we don't magically become humble when we receive salvation. We must consciously choose to live in an attitude of humility. When our minds are set in an attitude of humility, our behavior will follow suit.

The concept is clearly modeled in parenthood. A mother and father will care for the needs of their infant, even though at times it may be inconvenient or tiresome to do so. God calls us to do the same for those around us. Will serving others be easy? Not always. Will it be worth it? Yes.

Of course, we must strike a balance. We need to care for ourselves, making sure we are taken care of spiritually, emotionally, and physically. However, a great many of us spend way too much time and energy on ourselves. When we consider the sacrificial life of Jesus, the importance of our own interests and desires will pale in comparison.

While here on Earth, Jesus did not flaunt His identity. If anyone had a right to do so, it would certainly have been the Son of God. But the Bible says that although He is God, He didn't let that stop Him from living a life of humble servitude. Verse 6 (NIV) says that Jesus was "in very nature God," but that He "did not consider equality with God something to be grasped." In other words, although He was God, He laid aside His rights in order to become a sacrifice for us. He took on a great handicap—He became human (v. 7). Think about that. Jesus, the eternally existent God, chose to limit Himself by flesh. What a sacrifice! Yet He did it willingly and followed the plan through to the very end—physical death on a cross.

Death by crucifixion was considered the ultimate debasement, the most degrading kind of execution. In Jewish thought, anyone who died by crucifixion was under the curse of God (see Galatians 3:13). But Jesus was willing to do it, knowing that, ultimately, He would bring glory to God by His sacrifice. Jesus' humility was therefore expressed through obedience to God (v. 8).

The concept of obedience is not always a popular one. In this day and age, especially in America, people have a tendency to think they should have the right to do whatever they want to do. When we come to Christ, however, we learn that true freedom comes only through obedience to God. At first glance, this seems to be a paradox. How can we be free if we are obligated to obey?

The key rests in the identity of the One we obey. If God were a raging tyrant, then obedience would not equal freedom. But our God is just and righteous and full of love. When we choose to walk in God's ways,

we begin to desire to submit to Him. We learn to love His commands. As we continue to obey Him, He gives us the power to do what is right, which results in true freedom. We are no longer in bondage to our sin or our own selfishness, but we are servants of the Most High God. As such, we are also servants to one another.

3. Rewards of Humility (vv. 9–11)

The whole point of Philippians 2:5–11 is to stress to the Philippian Christians the importance of maintaining the "mind of Christ" in their relationships with one another. Whereas verses 5–8 focus on Jesus and His sacrifice, verses 9–11 focus on God the Father.

Although death on a cross was seen as a curse, God looked upon Jesus' crucifixion as a glorious, victorious accomplishment. God responded by exalting Jesus to the "highest place" (v. 9). Paul's language here emphasizes and contrasts the depth of Christ's debasement with the glorious height of His exaltation. He who humbled Himself here on Earth has now been raised to the highest position. Along with this, God confers upon Jesus "the name that is above every name" (v. 9, NIV).

In biblical times, a name was not just a name. A name was chosen to reveal something about the person's character or physical being. Jewish tradition also dictated that no one could actually speak God's name (Yahweh). Because of this, the Jews referred to God with other descriptive terms (e.g., the Most High, the Holy One, the Name). When God gave Jesus the "name above every name," He was alluding to this practice. The name that God gave to Jesus is "Lord" (v. 11). In this verse, the word "Lord" is *kurios* (**KOO-ree-os**), the Greek word used for "Yahweh." Jesus is Yahweh God.

Because of God's exaltation of Jesus, all creation will worship Him. Verse 10 says that "every knee" will bow. Bending the knee shows reverence and submission. In acquiescence to Jesus' lordship, every single person—past, present, and future—will one day bow before Him. Every tongue will confess, or declare out loud, that Jesus is God (v. 11). The redemption of man, God's ultimate plan, was accomplished once and for all through the humiliation and exaltation of Jesus.

Source

Arrington, French L., and Roger Stronstad, eds. *Life in the Spirit New Testament Commentary.* Grand Rapids, Mich.: Zondervan Publishing, 1999: 1095, 1104.

Search the Scriptures

1. What was Paul asking the Philippians to do that would make his joy complete (Philippians 2:2)?

2. What is one specific way we can serve others (vv. 3–4)?

3. What role did Jesus model for us (v. 7)?

4. How did Jesus humble Himself (v. 8)?

5. What was the "name above every name" that was given to Jesus (v. 11)?

6. What is the proper response to the name of Jesus (vv. 10–11)?

Discuss the Meaning

1. In verse 1, Paul describes four characteristics of healthy Christian relationships. What are these four characteristics? Do you believe that Christians today display these characteristics?

2. A main theme of our passage today is unity through humility. How is this unity accomplished in the church? In the family?

3. In verse 5, we are told to have the servant mindset that Jesus has. What are some ways listed in this passage that we could follow Jesus' example of humility?

4. What are some things we can do that are *not* listed in this passage?

5. Jesus' obedience and submission to God were part of His humility. Do you think Christians today place importance on obeying God?

6. How would our world be different today if every Christian lived a life of humble servanthood?

Lesson in Our Society

We live in a self-centered world. Everywhere we turn, we are encouraged to spend time, money, and energy on ourselves. Self-improvement books and products are perennial best sellers. Humility is often a foreign concept.

It's easy for Christians to get sucked into the prevailing attitude of the world we live in. After all, humans have a natural tendency toward selfishness. But when we come to Christ and decide to follow Him, we put aside our natural tendencies and begin to take on His characteristics. When we choose to follow Christ in an attitude of humility, we are choosing to glorify God. We are choosing to put others ahead of ourselves, not so we can win favor with God, but because His love in us is urging us onward to Christlikeness.

How can the church be instrumental in modeling servanthood? Should Christians show humility to all people, or only to fellow believers? How would practicing humility in our relationships with unbelievers help draw them to Christ?

Make It Happen

Dedicate some time this week to examining your life in the light of Jesus' example. Reread Philippians 2:1–11. Have you been choosing to walk in the attitude of humility? If not, what are some specific changes you can make in your thought life? What are some tangible changes you can make in your actions? Write these things down, and then ask God to give you the strength and desire to follow through as you seek to become more like Jesus.

Follow the Spirit

What God wants me to do:

_____

_____

Remember Your Thoughts

Special insights I have learned:

_____

_____

More Light on the Text

Philippians 2:1–11

The book of Philippians was written by Paul during the two years when he was in bonds in Rome (Philippians 1:7–13), probably early in the year A.D. 62 or 61.

1 If there be therefore any consolation in Christ, if any comfort of love, if any fellowship of the Spirit, if any bowels and mercies, 2 Fulfil ye my joy, that ye be likeminded, having the same love, being of one accord, of one mind.

The apostle Paul begins the second chapter of Philippians with four statements of encouragement that provide the foundation for the unity that the church has in Christ Jesus. Paul starts off this section with the statement "If there be therefore." The word "if" here is anticipating an affirmative answer rather than a negative one, and it could be correctly translated "since we have consolation in Christ." Paul is saying that we can be sure of possessing these things that we have in Christ (consolation, comfort, fellowship, bowels, and mercy).

The first word of encouragement is "consolation" (Gk. *paraklesis,* **par-AK-lay-sis**) and carries the meaning of comfort, solace, or that which affords comfort or refreshment. This was a common form of solemn appeal used among the Jews of that day. A relationship with Jesus, through salvation, results in a peace that the unsaved person does not experience, a peace that transcends our human understanding (John 14:27; Philippians 4:7). This comfort comes as a result of being in Christ. Paul wrote in 2 Corinthians 5:17, "Therefore if any man be in Christ, he is a new creature: old things are passed away; behold, all things are become new." Comfort that is obtained in Christ is one of the key foundations of unity (cp. Romans 15:5). The same word is used in Luke 2:25, where we read, "there was a man in Jerusalem, whose name was Simeon; and the same man was just and devout, waiting for the consolation of Israel." The consolation of Israel is the Messianic blessing of the nation promised to Abraham but now realized in Jesus the Messiah.

Next, Paul offers the second word of encouragement by saying that our unity is also based on the "comfort of love" that we receive through our relationship with Christ. The Greek word for "comfort," *paramuthion* (**par-am-OO-thee-on**), refers to a persuasive speech or address. It carries the idea that the love we have from Christ ought to persuade us to

maintain our unity. Jesus Christ demonstrated the magnitude of His love for us by leaving the comforts of heaven and willingly going to the cross for our sins (Romans 5:8). Because of this love, we ought to love each other enough to maintain our Christian unity (1 John 3:16).

Paul continues to promote Christian unity by encouraging fellowship. "Fellowship" here is the Greek word *koinonia* (**koy-nohn-EE-ah**), which carries various meanings in the New Testament. It is translated "communion," "communicate," "contribution," "distribution," and "fellowship." Generally speaking, the fellowship described by *koinonia* means more than simply fellowship between church members. The fellowship described by *koinonia* is an intimate association between two individuals and shows the depth of the relationship we have within Jesus Christ (e.g. 1 John 1:7). Our fellowship with Jesus Christ results in fellowship with each other and should motivate us to pursue unity within the body of Christ.

Because of these four "if" statements of encouragement in verse 1 (consolation, comfort, fellowship, any bowels and mercy), in verse 2 Paul exhorts believers to fulfill his joy by promoting unity or "likemindedness" within the church.

But what does true Christian unity look like? True Christian unity finds its fullness in the incarnation of Jesus. Paul describes the four characteristics of Christian unity as being "likeminded, having the same love, being of one accord, of one mind." To be "likeminded" is to fix our thoughts on the same things. The idea here is that Christian unity starts with a unity of focus or agenda. "A double minded man is unstable in all his ways" (James 1:8); likewise, a double-minded church cannot fulfill its true purpose in Christ.

The second characteristic of Christian unity is "having the same love." You cannot have a strong church if the members do not possess the same love for each other. Jesus gave His disciples a new commandment. He said, "A new commandment I give unto you, that ye love one another; as I have loved you, that ye also love one another" (John 13:34). This love then becomes the primary tool for reaching the lost world with the message of the Gospel (see v. 35).

The third characteristic of Christian unity is "being of one accord." "Accord" here is the Greek word *sumpsuchos* (**soom-psoo-khos**), which is in turn derived from two Greek words: *sun* (**soon**), which means "with," and *psuche* (**psoo-KHAY**), which refers to the seat of the feelings, desires, affections, and aversions (our heart/soul). Paul is communicating the idea that if we are to maintain unity in the church, the members need to have a unified soul or passion as it relates to the mission of the church.

Finally, the church should be "of one mind." Whereas being "in one accord" is a call to having a unified mission, being "of one mind" encourages church members to have the same views, especially theological views. Many people do not like to talk about theology or doctrine because they feel that it divides rather than unifies; in reality, however, theology and doctrine divide truth from error. One of the benefits of having an inspired Bible is that it is useful in helping the church distinguish truth from error and keeping the church from doctrinal heresy (cp. 2 Timothy 3:16; Ephesians 4:14).

3 Let nothing be done through strife or vainglory; but in lowliness of mind let each esteem other better than themselves. 4 Look not every man on his own things, but every man also on the things of others.

In these verses, Paul moves on to how this unity affects one's thinking. He starts off by focusing on the two attitudes that could quickly undermine unity in the body of Christ: strife and vainglory. The word "strife" here is the Greek word *eritheia* (**er-ith-I-ah**); it carries the idea of electioneering, or of a church member who causes contentiousness and selfishness by using his or her power, prestige, or status to promote a personal agenda.

Paul further connects "strife" with "vainglory" (Gk. *kenodoxia*, **ken-od-ox-EE-ah**), which means "groundless conceit" or "empty pride." Arrogance and strife go hand in hand. Those who look only after selfish interests cannot promote the unity of the group.

Paul completes his antithesis to vainglory by mov-

ing to the Christian virtue of humility. Instead of vainglory, Christians should develop a "lowliness of mind" (Gk. *tapeinophrosune*, **tap-i-nof-ros-OO-nay**), meaning to have a humble opinion of oneself. This type of humility should not be confused with weakness or a self-debasing attitude; rather, Christian humility recognizes individual abilities but "esteem[s] other[s] better than themselves."

5 Let this mind be in you, which was also in Christ Jesus: 6 Who, being in the form of God, thought it not robbery to be equal with God:

Here, Paul is admonishing the Philippians to change their way of thinking, to push it in another direction that will result in new conclusions and opinions about themselves and others. The word "mind" here again is the Greek word *phroneo* (**fron-EH-o**). Paul is speaking of exercising the mind—that is, entertaining or having a sentiment or opinion. If we are to have unity in the church, we will need first to change the way we think about both ourselves and others.

Paul makes a strong affirmation about the pre-Incarnation deity of Jesus when he says, "in the form of God." The word "form" (Gk. *morphe*, **mor-FAY**) refers to the form in which a person or thing strikes the vision and denotes outward manifestation. Paul is saying that to see Jesus Christ is to see God in the fullness of His deity (see Colossians 2:9).

Even though Jesus possessed the fullness of deity in a bodily form, Paul writes that He "thought it not robbery to be equal with God." The Greek word *harpagmos* (**har-pag-MOS**), translated "robbery," carries dual meanings here: (1) the act of seizing, or (2) a thing seized or to be seized. The word for "equal" here is *isos* (**ee'-sos**), which carries the idea of being equal in quantity or quality. Therefore, being "equal with God" could be interpreted as being equivalent to God Himself. Although Jesus possessed all the characteristics, nature, power, privileges, and glory of being God, He did not use those rights to undermine His redemptive purpose for humanity.

7 But made Himself of no reputation, and took upon Him the form of a servant, and was made in the likeness of men: 8 And being found in fashion as a man, he humbled himself, and became obedient unto death, even the death of the cross.

Verse 7 tells us that Jesus "took upon Him the form of a servant." The word "took" here (Gk. *lambano*, **lam-BAN-o**) conveys the idea that Jesus willfully decided to become a servant—it was not forced on Him—in order to affect our redemption. What Jesus actually took upon Himself was the "form" of a servant. The Greek word *morphe* is the same word used in verse 6 and signifies that Jesus was not just the image of a servant but is the very essence of servanthood.

Jesus was "made in the likeness of men." This aspect of the Incarnation is contrasted to the divine characteristics of Christ's deity. The word used for "made" here is *ginomai* (**GHIN-om-ahee**), which means "to become, come into existence, begin to be, or receive being. The idea is that the preexistent Christ, who possessed all the characteristics and qualities of deity, came into existence as a man to bring us grace and truth (John 1:14).

When Jesus was here on Earth, and as people interacted with Him, they found Him to be a man; He did not have a halo over His head like we see in some artists' renditions. The preexistent Christ became a man through the Incarnation. Paul was making a strong assertion of the humanity of Christ. Jesus was "found in fashion as a man" because He humbled Himself. The word "humbled" (Gk. *tapeinoo*, **tap-i-NO-o**) means "to behave in an unassuming manner" or "to be devoid of all haughtiness." Jesus knew He was God, but He chose to live His life in an unassuming manner to accomplish our redemption. In fact, Jesus' life and sacrifice on the Cross are often referred to as "the humiliation of Christ," an expression that is used to compare His preexistent life to His life experience on Earth. The Cross was the crowning demonstration of the redemptive work of Christ for humanity and the greatest demonstration of God's love for humanity.

9 Wherefore God also hath highly exalted him, and given him a name which is above every name:

Because of His humiliation and suffering, Jesus receives from the Father "a name that is above every name." The Greek word used for "name" is *onoma* (**ON-om-ah**), and it means more than a simple designation given to a person. In Scripture, a person's name signifies everything that the name covers (i.e., one's rank, authority, interests, excellences, and deeds). This definition is consistent with our understanding of the names of the Lord. In Proverbs 18:10 we read, "The name of the LORD is a strong tower." In Isaiah 9:6 we read, "His name shall be called Wonderful, Counsellor, The mighty God, The everlasting Father, The Prince of Peace." This was not the official name of the Messiah, but these names describe the nature and character of the individual with those attributes.

10 That at the name of Jesus every knee should bow, of things in heaven, and things in earth, and things under the earth; 11 And that every tongue should confess that Jesus Christ is Lord, to the glory of God the Father.

Here, the apostle Paul defines the two things that every human being will affirm, whether they presently accept Jesus' name or not: (1) every knee shall bow and (2) every tongue shall confess that Jesus is Lord! This response to the name of Jesus is clear and affirms the deity of Jesus Christ. Paul wants to make it clear that all creation, all things visible and invisible, will acknowledge the reality that Jesus is Lord.

In the Bible, to "confess" something means more than just giving lip service. It means to make a verbal acknowledgment of reality. The Greek word for "confess" is *exomologeo* (**ex-om-ol-og-EH-o**), and it means "to profess that one will do something, promise, agree, engage, and/or acknowledge openly." This type of confession is essential for a person to be saved and thereby experience the new birth. A person must confess Jesus as Lord if he or she is to be saved, and it is through the name of Jesus "whereby we must be saved" (Acts 4:12).

Jesus was not motivated by selfish gain, for this

would be inconsistent with His humiliation; rather, the ultimate glory goes to God the Father. Jesus did not do anything totally for Himself; everything He did was to glorify God. This in no way minimizes the deity of Jesus Christ; rather, it is a clear and striking example of how we are to live our lives. Jesus is God and possesses all the qualities, characteristics, and glory of God. He fashioned Himself as a man and became a servant to redeem us. Jesus' sacrifice is an example of how we are to live with each other.

Sources

Barnes, Albert. *Barnes' Notes on the New Testament* 2nd Edition (electronic edition). Cedar Rapids, Iowa: Parsons Technology, Inc., 1992.

Elwell, Walter A. *Evangelical Commentary on the Bible* (electronic edition). Grand Rapids, Mich.: Baker Book House, 1996.

Kent Jr., Homer A. *Expositor's Bible Commentary (Ephesians Through Philemon)* (electronic edition). Edited by Frank E. Gaebelein. Grand Rapids, Mich.: Zondervan Publishing, 1992.

Vincent, Marvin R. *Vincent's Word Studies, Vol. 3: The Epistles of Paul* (electronic edition). Hiawatha, Iowa: Parsons Technology, Inc., 1998.

Daily Bible Readings

M: The Magi Give Honor
Matthew 2:1–11
T: Jesus Is Presented
Luke 2:22–38
W: Jesus, Our Brother
Hebrews 2:5–3
T: Christ, Our Great High Priest
Hebrews 2:14–18
F: Unity of Spirit
1 Peter 3:8–12
S: Be Like Christ
Philippians 2:1–5
S: Jesus Emptied Himself
Philippians 2:6–11

TEACHING TIPS

January 7
Bible Study Guide 6

1. Words You Should Know

A. Samaritan (John 8:48) *Samareites* (Gk.)—Samaritans were colonists whom the king of Assyria sent to dwell in the land of Israel. After the captivity, they were despised by the Jews (Acts 8:25; John 4:9).

B. Devil (v. 48) *daimonion* (Gk.)—Demons, or devils, are spoken of as spiritual beings who are at enmity with God and have a certain power over man (Matthew 8:16; 10:1; 12:43–45).

2. Teacher Preparation

A. Read and study John 8:31–59.

B. Study references to demons in Matthew's gospel (Matthew 8:16; 10:1; 12:43–45).

C. Read The People, Places, and Times and the Background sections for the lesson.

D. Complete lesson 6 in the *Precepts For Living®* *Personal Study Guide*.

E. Create a skit using the characters and dialogue in the Scripture passage for this lesson. At the close of the skit, include an instruction for the Jews to pick up fake stones and throw them at Jesus as He exits and hides Himself outside the room.

F. Make copies for each of the speaking parts (Jesus, narrator, and Jews). Several people can be in the group of Jews, but have one spokesperson for each speaking part (vv. 48, 52–53, 57).

G. Materials needed: four or five pairs of rolled-up socks to use for stones, robes and blankets to dress participants in the skit.

3. Starting the Lesson

A. As the students arrive, ask for volunteers to sign up for the skit.

B. Have the scene set with a few fake stones lying around; pass out robes or lightweight blankets as outfits for the participants.

C. After the students are settled, begin with prayer.

D. Have a volunteer read the In Focus story, and review the Lesson Aim.

4. Getting into the Lesson

A. Ask a volunteer to read The People, Places, and Times and the Background section.

B. Have the students who signed up for the skit act it out in front of the class.

5. Relating the Lesson to Life

A. Ask the skit participants and other class members to share their thoughts and reactions after hearing the story and participating in the drama.

B. Spend some time answering the questions in the Discuss the Meaning section.

6. Arousing Action

A. Read the Lesson in Our Society section aloud to the class.

B. Ask individual members to share their personal stories.

C. Instruct class members to read the Daily Bible Readings in preparation for next week's class.

D. Close the class with prayer.

Worship Guide

For the Superintendent or Teacher
Theme: "I Am from Above"
Theme Song: "I Will Trust in the Lord"
Scripture: John 8:31–32
Song: "Wonderful Words of Life"
Meditation: Dear God, help me to learn how to respond to my accusers in love. Allow my personal testimony to encourage others in such a way that they will accept You into their lives as Lord and Saviour. Amen.

"I AM FROM ABOVE"

Bible Background • JOHN 8:31–59
Printed Text • JOHN 8:31–38, 48–56, 58–59   Devotional Reading • JOHN 14:23–31

Lesson Aim

By the end of the lesson, we will:

BE REMINDED that freedom from sin comes from a relationship with Christ;

RELATE our love of God through personal testimony; and

SHARE the wonderful story of salvation with others.

Keep in Mind

"Then said Jesus to those Jews which believed on him, If ye continue in my word, then are ye my disciples indeed; And ye shall know the truth, and the truth shall make you free" (John 8:31–32).

Focal Verses

John 8:31 Then said Jesus to those Jews which believed on him, If ye continue in my word, then are ye my disciples indeed;

32 And ye shall know the truth, and the truth shall make you free.

33 They answered him, We be Abraham's seed, and were never in bondage to any man: how sayest thou, Ye shall be made free?

34 Jesus answered them, Verily, verily, I say unto you, Whosoever committeth sin is the servant of sin.

35 And the servant abideth not in the house for ever: but the Son abideth ever.

36 If the Son therefore shall make you free, ye shall be free indeed.

37 I know that ye are Abraham's seed; but ye seek to kill me, because my word hath no place in you.

38 I speak that which I have seen with my Father: and ye do that which ye have seen with your father.

8:48 Then answered the Jews, and said unto him, Say we not well

that thou art a Samaritan, and hast a devil?

49 Jesus answered, I have not a devil; but I honour my Father, and ye do dishonour me.

50 And I seek not mine own glory: there is one that seeketh and judgeth.

51 Verily, verily, I say unto you, If a man keep my saying, he shall never see death.

52 Then said the Jews unto him, Now we know that thou hast a devil. Abraham is dead, and the prophets; and thou sayest, If a man keep my saying, he shall never taste of death.

53 Art thou greater than our father Abraham, which is dead? and the prophets are dead: whom makest thou thyself?

54 Jesus answered, If I honour myself, my honour is nothing: it is my Father that honoureth me; of whom ye say, that he is your God:

55 Yet ye have not known him; but I know him: and if I should say, I know him not, I shall be a liar like unto you: but I know him, and keep his saying.

56 Your father Abraham rejoiced to see my day: and he saw it, and was glad.

8:58 Jesus said unto them, Verily, verily, I say unto you, Before Abraham was, I am.

59 Then took they up stones to cast at him: but Jesus hid himself, and went out of the temple, going through the midst of them, and so passed by.

In Focus

An old story about Harry Houdini, one of the most famous escape artists in history, is a good illustration of how God's having freed us from sin often works in our lives. Houdini had a well-documented challenge for law enforcement agencies in every country he visited. He said he could be handcuffed and locked in any cell, and set himself free in short order. When the heavy doors clanged shut behind Houdini, he used a piece of metal hidden in his belt to set himself free.

It seemed no jail could hold him, but one time something went wrong. He discovered that the lock was unusual. Hours passed, and still he had not opened the door because he could not pick the lock. Bathed in sweat and panting in exasperation after laboring for two hours, Harry Houdini collapsed in frustration and failure against the prison door. But when he fell against the door, it swung open! It had never been locked! Nevertheless, in his mind it was locked, and that mind-set was all it took to keep him from opening the door and walking out of the prison cell.

In a similar way, we must understand what Christ has done for us. The prison doors of our minds keep us locked away and trapped by anxiety, sin, and powerlessness. Christ died to give us freedom, and He has already set us free.

In today's lesson, Jesus dialogued with the Jewish leaders. He told them He could set them free. Do you truly believe you have freedom in Christ?

The People, Places, and Times

Jewish People. There are three names used in the New Testament to designate Jewish people: (1) Jews—to indicate their nationality and to distinguish them from Gentiles; (2) Hebrews—to indicate their language and education and to distinguish them from Hellenists; and (3) Israelites—to acknowledge their sacred privileges as the chosen people of God. The bitter enmity between the Jews and Samaritans continued in the time of our Lord; for example, the Jews had "no dealings with the Samaritans" (John 4:9), and our Lord was contemptuously called "a Samaritan." However, many of the Samaritans quickly embraced the Gospel (John 4:5–42; Acts 8:25; 9:31; 15:3).

Background

The meeting between Jesus and the Jews occurred in the holy temple of Jerusalem around the time of the Festival of Ingathering (Feast of Tabernacles), called *Sukkot,* a Jewish holiday that lasted for seven days. During this time of year, hundreds of Jews from outside Palestine made their pilgrimage to Jerusalem to celebrate the harvest festival. Historically, it was a cultural, political, and religious reunion. It was also a time to keep ancient Jewish traditions alive, to reinforce the faith and reaffirm the covenant of God, and to strengthen ties between Jerusalem and Jewish communities living outside Palestine. During this time, Herod (who initiated the rebuilding of the temple) was king of Judea, and his kingdom was a mixed population of Jewish, Idumean, Samaritan, and non-Jewish people.

The cultural and historical setting is significant because it reminds us that present-day Gentile communities (churches) have people from many different ethnic groups, including people from different denominations, traditions, and cultural backgrounds. Some are viewed negatively in terms of their religious beliefs and practices, while others present an opportunity for outreach and inclusion rather than exclusion from the church.

At-A-Glance

1. Jesus Identifies the True Children of God (John 8:31–38)
2. Jews Charge Jesus with Being Samaritan (8:48–51)
3. Jews Question Jesus (vv. 52–53)
4. Jesus Teaches about Eternal Life (vv. 54–56)
5. Jesus Proclaims His Preexistence (8:58–59)

In Depth

1. Jesus Identifies the True Children of God (John 8:31–38)

After the Pharisees brought a woman to the temple when they had caught her in the act of adultery, Jesus talked to the crowd. He did not condemn nor ignore the sin of the woman, but instead told her to go and sin no more (John 8:11). With this event as the backdrop, Jesus spoke to the crowd about His true children—those who are authentic, genuine believers. Jesus declared that those who believe in Him and obey His teachings are truly His disciples.

Jesus is not only the truth that sets us free from sin, but He is also the source of truth (v. 32). His death on the Cross frees us from the consequences of

"Then said Jesus to those Jews which believed on him, If ye continue in my word, then are ye my disciples indeed; And ye shall know the truth, and the truth shall make you free" (John 8:31–32).

our sins, which include death and eternal separation from God. Because all of us have sinned and fallen short of the glory of God, each one of us needs a Saviour. Each of us needs the gift of salvation that Jesus brings. He is the only One who can redeem us. Jesus restores our relationship with God. The result of sin is death, but instead, by accepting Jesus Christ as our Lord and Saviour, we receive the gift of eternal or everlasting life (Romans 6:23).

Unfortunately, the Jews misunderstood what Jesus was saying to them. They thought that Jesus was saying that they were slaves to man when He told them that "the truth will set you free" (John 8:32). Instead, Jesus explains that everyone who sins is a slave of sin.

Sin, then, becomes our master; it enslaves us. It dominates and controls us. Sin can even prevent us from walking in our calling. But because Jesus is the Son of God, He sets the captives free from sin through His shed blood on the cross. Sin is no longer our master; God is. He breaks the power of sin over our lives. He has set us free!

In verses 37–38, Jesus rebukes the Pharisees by pointing out the difference between how they behave and what they believe regarding their claim as true descendants of Abraham. True children of Abraham would embrace and obey God's Word. Even though the Jews were descendants of Abraham, they were not behaving as such because they sought to kill Jesus. Jesus reminded them that true descendants of Abraham would embrace their inheritance and recognize the God of Abraham. God, then, would also be their Father, and they would imitate His character and follow His guidance.

2. Jews Charge Jesus with Being Samaritan (8:48–51)

By using the term "Samaritan," the Jews were

slandering and showing contempt for Jesus. This was the same as saying Jesus was a heretic. Jesus charged them with being opposed to God; He said they were not friends of God. Thus, they regarded Him as taking sides with the Samaritans and took His statement as evidence that He was possessed with a devil.

Jesus ignored the Jews' charge of being a Samaritan by refusing to recognize national distinctions. He refused to be drawn into a debate about nationality and rightly offered a rebuttal to their charge of being possessed by a demon. Jesus was not in league with the Devil as charged; rather, He honored His Father even though the Jews dishonored Him. In His rebuttal, Jesus explained that whoever belongs to God hears and obeys the Word of God. When the Jews could offer no other claim to counter Jesus' words of truth, they sought to link Jesus with the Samaritans and charged Him with having a demon.

3. Jews Question Jesus (vv. 52–53)

The Jews showed a lack of understanding regarding Jesus' statement about eternal life. When Jesus spoke of never tasting death, the Jews did not understand what He meant. When Jesus said whoever keeps His word will never see death, the Jews considered this statement blasphemy and demanded to know whether Jesus claimed to be greater than Abraham and the prophets. When Jesus offered them eternal life, it outraged them even more. They asked Jesus, "Who do you pretend to be? Even the greatest of the prophets have died, yet how can you—a Nazarene, a Samaritan, and a devil—pretend to keep your followers from dying?"

4. Jesus Teaches about Eternal Life (vv. 54–56)

It should be noted that this debate occurred before the Crucifixion and Resurrection. At that time, the Jews thought that no one could be greater than Abraham. They had no reference point to understand what Jesus was trying to tell them because they did not understand that He was the Messiah. While Jesus was speaking of future time, the Jews only knew of Abraham's time and up to the present time.

Jesus proclaimed His divinity by announcing that "Abraham rejoiced to see my day" (v. 56). He spoke of His knowledge of time before Abraham, including past and future times. Jesus also taught that Abraham rejoiced "to see" his day, thus speaking of Abraham's faith to believe that Jesus is the fulfillment of the promises of God.

5. Jesus Proclaims His Preexistence (8:58–59)

By using the expression "I am" (v. 58), Jesus clearly declared His preexistence. Jesus was telling the Jews that before Abraham was born, "I am." Jesus was once again making Himself equal to God, which the Jews considered blasphemous. Jesus' affirmation of His deity caused the Jews to want to kill Him. But He was able to pass through the crowd unharmed.

Search the Scriptures

1. Explain what Jesus meant by "the truth shall make you free" (John 8:32).

2. What did Jesus mean by the statement, "If the Son therefore shall make you free, ye shall be free indeed" (v. 36)?

3. Even though the Jews were Abraham's biological seed, how did they demonstrate that God's Word had not taken root in their hearts (v. 37)?

4. What kind of death is Jesus speaking of when He says, "If a man keep my saying, he shall never see death" (v. 51)?

Discuss the Meaning

1. How can believers who are incarcerated still be free in Jesus?

2. Does freedom in Jesus allow us to engage in behaviors that might offend weaker brothers or sisters in the faith? Why or why not?

3. In the body of Christ, why and how are we our brother's keeper?

Lesson in Our Society

Some believers feel that it is OK to gamble, drink, and engage in other questionable behaviors that may cause a weaker brother or sister in the faith to stumble. They argue that the Word of God tells them that because they are in Jesus, they are free indeed.

Therefore, if their conscience doesn't persuade them that their actions are wrong, they feel that God is pleased with their walk. How can you personally be a blessing to your weaker brother or sister in Christ? Do you feel that you are truly responsible to God to help a weaker brother or sister in his or her walk with the Lord? When you were growing in your own faith, did someone reach out to help you?

Make It Happen

There are many people today who doubt that Jesus is the Son of God, the One sent to redeem humankind. But as born-again believers, we are given the responsibility to share our personal testimonies to bring the Good News of salvation to the unsaved. Do you know how to witness about the love of Christ? Can you tell someone the Good News that Jesus came to Earth to die for their sins? In the upcoming week, pray and ask God to show you someone who would benefit from your personal testimony and commit to telling your story about the love of Christ in your life.

Follow the Spirit

What God wants me to do:

_____

_____

Remember Your Thoughts

Special insights I have learned:

_____

_____

More Light on the Text
John 8:31–38; 48–56; 58–59

These verses show that what would normally have been a festive, joyful time for Jesus was anything but that. Instead, John records in chapters 7 and 8 that a time of hot conflict and rejection took place. This passage tells about the last in a series of confrontations Jesus had with Jewish leaders, who were beginning to accept His teaching. These included priests who were Sadducees and devout Jewish leaders who were Pharisees.

31 Then said Jesus to those Jews which believed on him, If ye continue in my word, then are ye my disciples indeed;

After hearing about and then seeing Jesus' miraculous powers of healing, feeding over 5,000 people, and bringing dead people back to life, the Jewish leaders were convinced that Jesus was equipped to be what they wanted in a messiah. The miraculous power revealed in His deeds proved Him worthy of their faith. Even when later they were conniving to kill Him, they admitted to one another, "This man doeth many miracles" (John 11:47).

The Jewish leaders endorsed what Jesus did (performing miracles). What He spoke was a different matter. In verse 31, John says, "Then said Jesus...." "Said" is the Greek word *lego* (**leg-o**) and indicates that Jesus repeatedly tried to get them to see that their belief was in a military messiah, which He was not going to be. Over and over He attempted to persuade them to accept Him as the spiritual Messiah that God had sent Him into the world to be. John 12:16 tells us that even Jesus' closest followers didn't fully grasp His true nature and purpose until after His resurrection.

When Jesus said that His real followers "continue in" (Gk. *meno*, **MEN-O**), He meant for his people to decide once and for all that He was who He said He was. In Jesus' day, a disciple was an apprentice who learned a skill by following his master around and imitating what the master did. When Jesus told men to "come, follow me" (Matthew 4:19, NIV), He was calling them to a lifetime of faithfulness. A profession of faith in Christ should be followed by the practice of faith in Him.

George Beasley-Murray says, "The primary duty of a believer [is] to remain in my word." In the prologue to his gospel, John refers to Jesus as the "Word" (Gk. *logos*, **LOG-os**), a word that denotes the essence of God. When Jesus spoke of His Word, He was referring to everything His words and actions revealed about God.

32 And ye shall know the truth, and the truth shall make you free.

Believing in Jesus means more than simply believing that He lived, died, and was resurrected. Belief in Jesus involves more than accepting as truth that He was miraculously born of a virgin or that He performed miraculous acts. This verse shows that Jesus agreed that coming to God through a clear faith in Himself demanded that a person fight through conflicts between a life of faithfulness to God and a life aimed at satisfying natural human desires.

Many Jews assumed that being physically descended from Abraham guaranteed God's pleasure with them. They failed to realize they were spiritual slaves in need of being set free. As a result, they were living a lie. They were blinded to who they were and to who Jesus was and is.

33 They answered him, We be Abraham's seed, and were never in bondage to any man: how sayest thou, Ye shall be made free?

According to some scholars, the rabbis taught the Jews that as descendants of Abraham, Isaac, and Jacob, all Israelites were sons of kings. Here, the use of the word "bondage" (Gk. *douleuo*, **dool-YOO-o**) signifies that these men boldly claimed that Israelites had never been enslaved. In effect, they were saying, "We are not now, nor have we ever been, slaves." This statement shows how desperately these men hated Roman control and wanted a messiah who could free them from it.

Their claim, however, was untrue—a wishful denial at best, an angry lie at worst. The Israelites were enslaved four times. Aside from their deliverance from slavery in Egypt, in 586 B.C. the kingdom of Judah had been conquered and deported, exiled to Babylon for 70 years. Hanukkah, which is still observed today, marked their defeat of and release from oppression under the Syrian King Antiochus Epiphanes about 200 years earlier. Even the men arguing with Jesus could hardly claim to be free. Although they might never have been officially owned as slaves, any Roman legionnaire could order any Israelite soldier to carry his pack for a mile.

34 Jesus answered them, Verily, verily I say unto you, Whosoever committeth sin is the servant of sin.

Twenty-five times John quotes Jesus, saying, "Verily, verily." In the Aramaic language that Jesus spoke, this would have been equivalent to saying, "Amen," "Surely," or "Truly." Repeating the word was a way of adding emphasis to what was being expressed.

Jesus made it plain that everyone who sins becomes a "servant" (Gk. *doulos*, **DOO-los**), or is in bondage. It is apparent here that His concern was for the spiritual, inner man, rather than mere political freedom. The sinfulness with which we are all infected can hound a person into selfish, greedy, or perverted actions. Like Paul, we may grieve at our slavery to sin's power over us. In Romans 7:18 (NLT), Paul wrote, "I know I am rotten through and through so far as my old sinful nature is concerned. No matter which way I turn, I can't make myself do right. I want to, but I can't." That kind of slavery was what Jesus was promising to free his people from.

35 And the servant abideth not in the house for ever: but the son abideth ever.

Jesus' illustration compared a son's place in a family to a slave's. A slave could be sold and sent away at any time. A slave needed a liberator, someone to free him or her from slavery. Without being set free from sin's penalty and power, we live and die in our sin (John 8:21–24; Romans 3:23).

On the other hand, a son always has a place; he is part of the family forever. Likewise, when a person trusts Jesus as Saviour and Lord, that person becomes God's son (Galatians 3:26) and a member of His family forever (Isaiah 56:5).

36 If the Son therefore shall make you free, ye shall be free indeed.

As God's only Son, Jesus has the right to free anyone who is willing to trust Him from the power and penalty of sin. Rather than an unthinking, unemotional act by Jesus, giving freedom from sin is an act of love. Freedom from sin makes it possible for a believer to become part of God's family. Jesus magnanimously turns believers from slaves into sons (cf. Galatians 4:25).

37 I know that ye are Abraham's seed; but ye seek to kill me, because my word hath no place in you.

Jesus agreed with the Jews that they were Abraham's descendants, but they were still trying to kill Him. Their murderous plot proves that they saw Jesus as an ordinary man who could be defeated. Jesus explained that their main reason for wanting to kill Him was that God's "word" (i.e., *logos*), His revealed truth, was not in them. Although the Jews were impressed by what Jesus did, the things He said about Himself angered them. Jesus told them that their thinking made it impossible for them to understand the kind of Messiah God sent Him to be.

38 I speak that which I have seen with my Father: and ye do that which ye have seen with your father.

Here, Jesus compares how children mimic what their fathers say and do. He declares that the Jews' actions are like those of their father Satan (cf. v. 44), and nothing like the actions of the descendants of Abraham.

When John tells us that Jesus spoke of what He had "seen," he uses the word *horao* (Gk. **hor-AH-o**), which means not only to see but also to experience. The word's form indicates a past action with continued results. Jesus was saying that His words revealed what He had seen in His Father's presence. The Jews' repeated objections to what Jesus told them demonstrated what they had seen with their father. Although descended from Abraham, they were not his *children* (v. 39). They were the descendants of Abraham, who, Jeremiah wrote, were circumcised physically, but were uncircumcised in the heart (Jeremiah 9:25–26).

8:48 Then answered the Jews, and said unto him, Say we not well that thou art a Samaritan and hast a devil?

Here, the Jews respond with insults, calling Jesus a Samaritan and saying He is demon possessed. Jews considered Samaritans heretics because they didn't worship at the temple in Jerusalem. They also thought that Samaritans were mixed up with magic power by demons. The Jews may have believed that Jesus' miracles—healing the sick, blind, and crippled; feeding the 5,000; and resuscitating the dead—were acts of magic used to deceive people into believing He was the Messiah (see Matthew 9:34; Mark 3:22; Luke 11:15).

49 Jesus answered, I have not a devil; but I honour my Father, and ye do dishonour me.

In this verse, Jesus uses the negative word "but" (Gk. *alla*, **al-lah**) meaning "to the contrary" or "just the opposite." Jesus insists, "To the contrary, I honour my Father." Then He follows up with "ye dishonour me." To dishonor a messenger was considered an act of disrespect toward the one who sent the message. Jesus was saying that their disbelief in Him and His message dishonored God.

50 And I seek not mine own glory: there is one that seeketh and judgeth.

The Jews viewed Galilee, Jesus' home region, as an ignorant backwoods area. They judged Him to be uneducated in Jewish law (John 7:15); therefore, they considered His message to be unreliable. Jesus had defended the origin of His message at length in John 7:16–18. The disturbing ideas in His message weren't His own, but His Father's, whom they insisted was their God.

The second half of verse 50 can be interpreted in two ways. One is that the Father was looking for acceptance for Jesus, and condemnation would result from refusal to trust Him. Second, Jesus was saying that God the Father was seeking honor for Jesus and judged Him worthy of it, even though these men rejected Him. Whichever interpretation was Jesus' primary meaning, the Father condemns unbelief in Jesus and judges Jesus worthy of praise, honor, and glory. This truth was affirmed at Jesus' resurrection and will be the decisive issue for every person at the final judgment (Romans 14:10; 2 Timothy 4:1).

51 Verily, verily, I say unto you, If a man keep my saying, he shall never see death.

Again, Jesus repeats the word "verily" to emphasize the importance and truthfulness of what He is saying. Jesus follows that declaration with the word "if" (Gk. *ean*, **eh-AN**), which describes a condition that is possible but not certain. "Keep" (Gk. *tereo*, **tay-REH-o**) means "to protect or guard something." Jesus wants his hearers to understand that believing in Him required that they hold fast to and protect what He told them.

Four times the Jews objected to the truth of what Jesus said. Each time Jesus responded with answers that showed He was talking about inner spiritual truths, such as sin (v. 34), the truth of God (v. 40), and glory (v. 50).

When Jesus speaks of seeing "death" (Gk. *thanatos*, **THAN-at-os**), He is implying the idea of experiencing something. To "never see death" didn't mean a believer's body wouldn't die, but that the soul, the essential person, would not. In John 5:24, Jesus makes the same point when He says, "He that heareth my word, and believeth on him that sent me, hath everlasting life, and…is passed from death unto life."

52 Then said the Jews unto him, Now we know that thou hast a devil. Abraham is dead, and the prophets; and thou sayest, If a man keep my saying, he shall never taste death. 53 Art thou greater than our father Abraham, which is dead? and the prophets are dead: whom makest thou thyself?

In response, the Jews repeat the charge they had made (see verse 48) that Jesus was possessed. They are saying, "Now we're absolutely convinced that a demon has control of you." Once again they reject what Jesus is saying to them in literal rather than spiritual terms. They're saying, "Abraham's dead. The prophets are dead. Are You claiming that You're somehow greater than Abraham and all the prophets?"

Rather than speak of keeping Jesus' sayings, which implied experiencing something spiritually, the Jews use the word "taste" (Gk. *geuomai*, **GHYOO-om-ahee**), implying the physical sensation of eating something.

They then ask the key question, which translated literally is, "Who are You making Yourself?" Whom did He claim He was, and, why should they trust Him? This same question faces us today. "Am I willing to trust what Jesus says? Is He who He says He is?"

54 Jesus answered, If I honour myself, my honour is nothing: it is my Father that honoureth me; of whom ye say, that he is your God:

Here, the word "honour" is translated from the Greek word *doxazo* (**dox-AD-zo**), meaning "to glorify, praise, or magnify." When Jesus talked about honoring Himself, He was saying, "If I praise Myself, or if I applaud Myself, the result will be meaningless. I'm not here to honor [praise] Myself. My Father, whom your group says is your God, will honor Me." God would honor Him for faithfully making known the message God sent Him into the world to announce.

55 Yet ye have not known him; but I know him: and if I should say, I know him not, I shall be a liar like unto you: but I know him, and keep his saying.

When Jesus said these men had not "known" (Gk. *ginosko*, **ghin-OCE-ko**) God, He was saying that even though they were actively religious, they had not understood, perceived, or felt His message. Jesus undoubtedly angered them by saying, "If I said I don't really understand God, I'd be lying like all of you are." Jesus, calling them liars, indicated that He took their unwillingness to trust what He said as deliberate, rather than just a lack of insight.

John uses two different Greek words here for the word "know." The first is *ginosko* ("known"). The second, *I-do* (**i-do**), means "to see" or "to perceive with the eyes." This indicates that Jesus is making a comparison. He is saying, "I know God intimately; I don't have to see Him with my eyes to trust His Word."

56 Your father Abraham rejoiced to see my day: and he saw it, and was glad.

Here, John writes in simple past tense: Abraham "saw it, and was glad." This verse does not say *when* Abraham sees God's ministry he will rejoice, or that he rejoiced at the hope or possibility of seeing the Messiah in the future. Most Jews assumed Abraham was alive in God's presence.

8:58 Jesus said unto them, Verily, verily, I say unto you, Before Abraham was, I am. 59 Then took they up stones to cast at him: but Jesus hid himself, and went

out of the temple, going through the midst of them, and so passed by.

Jesus was proclaiming His divine Sonship by once again making Himself equal with God (John 5:18). By stating that before Abraham came into being, "I am," Jesus wasn't saying "I was," or "I came to be." Rather, He said "I am," indicating His eternal preexistence. The Jews considered this the ultimate in blasphemy (Leviticus 24:16) and consequently attempted to stone Jesus for His claims.

Sources

Beasley-Murray, George R. *Word Biblical Commentary: John, Volume 36.* Edited by Bruce M. Metzger, Ralph P. Martin, and Lynn Allan Losie. Nashville, Tenn.: Nelson Reference, 1987, 133.

Hobbs, Herschel H. *An Exposition of the Four Gospels.* Grand Rapids, Mich.: Baker Publishing Group, 1996, 158.

Daily Bible Readings

M: A Voice in the Wilderness
John 1:19–28
T: Jesus Is the Lamb of God
John 1:29–34
W: Promises Fulfilled
Matthew 13:11–17
T: Jesus Gives Peace
John 14:23–31
F: Jesus Is the Christ
Matthew 11:1–6
S: Jesus Promises Freedom
John 8:31–38
S: Jesus Speaks of Eternal Life
John 8:48–59

TEACHING TIPS

January 14
Bible Study Guide 7

1. Words You Should Know

A. Quickeneth (John 5:21) *zoopoieo* (Gk.)—To produce, cause to live, make alive, give life, or to quicken into life; germinating, springing up, growing.

B. Honoureth (v. 23) *timao* (Gk.)—To estimate or fix the value; to revere, venerate, or honor.

C. Life (v. 26) *zoe* (Gk.)—The absolute fullness of life, both essential and ethical, which belongs to God.

2. Teacher Preparation

A. Study the entire fifth chapter of John, including the Bible Background Scripture.

B. Read the Lesson Aim and the Keep in Mind verse.

C. Read and study the Focal Verses; The People, Places, and Times; Background; In Depth; and More Light on the Text to gain insight into the lesson.

D. As you read and prepare to teach the lesson, make notes for yourself that help convey the objectives of the Lesson Aim.

E. Complete lesson 7 in the *Precepts For Living®* *Personal Study Guide.*

3. Starting the Lesson

A. Write the words "authority" and "judge" on the board, and ask for volunteers to define each term.

B. Engage the students in a discussion on who has authority in their lives.

C. Ask a volunteer to read the In Focus story and relate the story to today's Lesson Aim.

4. Getting into the Lesson

A. Ask a volunteer to read the Focal Verses.

B. Read the Keep in Mind verse collectively.

C. Using the In Depth outline, initiate a discussion on the meaning of today's Focal Verses.

D. Review the Search the Scriptures and Discuss the Meaning questions, and discuss the answers.

5. Relating the Lesson to Life

A. Direct the students' attention to the Lesson in Our Society section. Read and discuss the contents.

B. Ask your students for suggestions on how to help spread the Good News of the Gospel to others.

C. Ask the class to share any new insights they may have learned from today's lesson.

6. Arousing Action

A. Read the Make It Happen exercise aloud, and encourage the students to follow through during the upcoming week.

B. Instruct the students to read the Daily Bible Readings in preparation for next week's class.

C. Close the class in prayer.

JESUS IS AUTHORITY AND JUDGE

Bible Background • JOHN 5:19–29
Printed Text • JOHN 5:19–29   Devotional Reading • 2 TIMOTHY 4:1–5

Lesson Aim

By the end of the lesson, we will:

UNDERSTAND that, ultimately, we will face Christ—either as our Saviour or as our Judge;

REALIZE that our eternal judgment is based on whether we accept or reject Jesus during our lifetime; and

DETERMINE to live in such a way that we will hear "well done" from Jesus on the day He serves as our Judge.

Keep in Mind

"Verily, verily, I say unto you, He that heareth my word, and believeth on him that sent me, hath everlasting life, and shall not come into condemnation; but is passed from death unto life" (John 5:24).

Focal Verses

John 5:19 Then answered Jesus and said unto them, Verily, verily, I say unto you, The Son can do nothing of himself, but what he seeth the Father do: for what things soever he doeth, these also doeth the Son likewise.

20 For the Father loveth the Son, and sheweth him all things that himself doeth: and he will shew him greater works than these, that ye may marvel.

21 For as the Father raiseth up the dead, and quickeneth them; even so the Son quickeneth whom he will.

22 For the Father judgeth no man, but hath committed all judgment unto the Son:

23 That all men should honour the Son, even as they honour the Father. He that honoureth not the Son honoureth not the Father which hath sent him.

24 Verily, verily, I say unto you, He that heareth my word, and believeth on him that sent me, hath everlasting life, and shall not come into condemnation; but is passed from death unto life.

25 Verily, verily, I say unto you, The hour is coming, and now is, when the dead shall hear the voice of the Son of God: and they that hear shall live.

26 For as the Father hath life in himself; so hath he given to the Son to have life in himself;

27 And hath given him authority to execute judgment also, because he is the Son of man.

28 Marvel not at this: for the hour is coming, in the which all that are in the graves shall hear his voice,

29 And shall come forth; they that have done good, unto the resurrection of life; and they that have done evil, unto the resurrection of damnation.

In Focus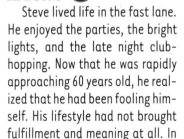

Steve lived life in the fast lane. He enjoyed the parties, the bright lights, and the late night club-hopping. Now that he was rapidly approaching 60 years old, he realized that he had been fooling himself. His lifestyle had not brought fulfillment and meaning at all. In fact, after two divorces, countless women, and estrangement from his only daughter, he was still searching in all the wrong places for peace and happiness. Now he felt all alone, hopeless, and help-less, and the alcohol was no longer dulling the pain.

Even though he sometimes went to church, Steve realized that he still did not know God—the God who would one day be his Judge and ask, "Steve, what did you do with Jesus?"

In today's lesson, we learn that Jesus is indeed the Higher Authority over us all. When we come to the end of our life, we have Him and His judgment to face.

The People, Places, and Times

Jesus. Jesus is God in the flesh. He is fully God and fully man. He is a member of the triune God con-sisting of God the Father, God the Son, and God the Holy Spirit. God the Son took on human flesh and entered this world as a suffering

"Verily, verily, I say unto you, He that heareth my word, and believeth on him that sent me, hath everlasting life, and shall not come into condemnation; but is passed from death unto life" (John 5:24).

servant in order to die on the Cross for the sins of humankind. During His ministry, Jesus not only performed great miracles of healing and deliverance, but also preached to great crowds, trained His 12 disciples, and debated with religious leaders, who later had Him killed. Fortunately, Jesus did not remain in the grave. After three days and nights, He arose from the grave, conquering sin, death, and Satan. Jesus is coming back a second time, but not as a suffering servant. Rather, He is coming with great authority as Judge.

John. One of the "sons of thunder," John was a fisherman and one of Jesus' 12 disciples. With Peter and James, he made up Jesus' inner circle. Scholars believe that John and his brother James were given the title "sons of thunder" because of an incident that happened when he and James went to a Samaritan village to prepare the way for Jesus' arrival. When the Samaritans refused to welcome them, James and John asked Jesus' permission to call fire down from heaven to destroy them (Luke 9:51–56).

Before following Jesus, the apostle John was one of John the Baptist's disciples. He was also the writer of five New Testament books: the gospel of John; 1, 2, and 3 John; and the book of Revelation. He wrote to new Christians and searching non-Christians to prove conclusively that Jesus is indeed who He said He was: the Messiah, the Son of the living God. John made it clear that Jesus was more than just a mere man; He is the eternal Son of God, the Light of the World.

Background

All Jews were required to come to Jerusalem to attend three festivals, or holy days. These included (1) the Feast of the Passover and Unleavened Bread; (2) Pentecost (also called the Festival of Harvest or the Festival of Weeks); and (3) the Festival of Shelters, which commemorated how God kept the Jews during their 40 years of wandering in the wilderness. It was during one of these celebrations that we find Jesus inside the city, near the Sheep Gate and the pool of Bethesda (John 5:1–2).

Crowded onto five porches were hordes of sick people, including the blind, the lame, and the paralyzed (v. 3). Jesus went about doing His Father's business, bringing hope to the hopeless and healing many. Unfortunately, His efforts earned the chastisement of the Pharisees, who were looking for a reason to condemn and kill Him. Even though the Pharisees were supposed to be spiritual men, they were not concerned about the miracles that Jesus performed. Instead, they were more concerned with their religious traditions and finding ways to get rid of Jesus.

At-A-Glance

1. Jesus Answers the Charge (John 5:19–23)
2. Jesus Explains How to Obtain Eternal Life (v. 24)
3. Jesus Gives End-Time Prophecy (vv. 25–29)

In Depth

1. Jesus Answers the Charge (John 5:19–23)

In today's Scripture passage, Jesus is becoming more of a threat to the Jewish religious leaders. He had chosen His first disciples (John 1:35–50), turned water into wine at a wedding (2:1–12), cleared the temple in Jerusalem (vv. 13–16), brought salvation to the Samaritan woman at the well (4:1–25), and healed a lame man at the pool of Bethesda on the Sabbath (5:7–10). The more Jesus grew in popularity, the more His followers increased, and the more the religious leaders viewed Him as a troublemaker.

It is after Jesus has healed the lame man at Bethesda that we pick up today's lesson. Under the Mosaic Law, no one was supposed to do any kind of work on the Sabbath (Exodus 16:26; Leviticus 23:3). The Jewish leaders were looking for a way to condemn Jesus. They were outraged and began to harass Jesus because not only had He broken the Sabbath rules when He healed the lame man, but He also had made Himself equal to God (John 5:16 18). But Jesus meets His accusers head-on. He lets them know that God the Father knew everything that He, the Son, was

doing, and that He (Jesus) would do far greater things than heal the sick (v. 20). He would even raise from the dead anyone He wanted to, just as His Father did (v. 21). In other words, Jesus was equating Himself with God the Father.

Further showing the unity of the Father and the Son, Jesus tells the religious leaders that God the Father leaves all judgment to His Son (v. 22). Jesus was exercising His power of judgment. Moreover, God does this so that everyone, including the Pharisees, will not only glorify the Father, but will also honor and glorify the Son, who is Christ Jesus. Because God the Father sent Jesus the Son, Jesus wanted His hearers to know that if they did not honor Him, they would be dishonoring the Father who sent Him (v. 23).

2. Jesus Explains How to Obtain Eternal Life (v. 24)

The Good News of salvation is that God sent His one and only Son Jesus to die on the cross for our sins. God is also building His kingdom, which will last forever and where He will reign eternally. To be part of that kingdom, we must be saved. To be saved, we must believe that Jesus is the Christ, the Son of the living God (Matthew 16:16). Jesus says here in verse 24 that only those who believe in God, who sent Him, will have eternal life. Those who commit to Jesus will never be condemned for their sins, but have already "passed from death unto life."

Death and life are used metaphorically in verse 24 to refer to spiritual life and death. We will all face physical death. However, when Jesus returns, those who have made Him their Lord and Saviour will be resurrected to live with Him forever.

3. Jesus Gives End-Time Prophecy (vv. 25–29)

Next, Jesus gives an end-time prophecy. He tells His accusers that a time is coming when even the dead will hear His voice (v. 25). Jesus is talking about both the spiritually dead and the physically dead. During His ministry, Jesus showed that He had all power over life and death by raising Lazarus (John 11:43). At His second coming, all Christians who have died will rise to meet Him—the Son of man, who is the Son of God (1 Thessalonians 4:16).

The focus of John 5:26 is life. Jesus tells the leaders that those who have obeyed His commands and followed His directive by walking in godly wisdom will have eternal life. However, He warns in verse 27 that those who continue to disobey God's voice and refuse to accept Him (Jesus) as their Lord and Saviour will face judgment.

Jesus contrasts the events of the end times with the present-day life of a believer (vv. 23, 29). Once again, we see that Jesus has the power to transform death into life. Even in the last days, those who are dead in their graves will hear His voice and respond. He has the final say over who will enter heaven or hell. Jesus is the final Authority and Judge to whom we all must answer. He is at the center of the believer's present and will be at the center of the believer's future.

Search the Scriptures

1. Jesus only does what He sees the _____ do (John 5:19).

2. When we fail to honor the Son, we fail to honor the _____ (v. 23).

3. To receive everlasting life, we need to hear God's Word and _____ on Him (v. 24).

4. God gave Jesus authority to execute _____ because Jesus is the Son of _____ (v. 27).

Discuss the Meaning

1. What does it mean to have everlasting life?

2. How does one get saved?

3. Can one be saved by believing in God, but not in Jesus? Why or why not?

4. Why is Jesus considered the final Authority and Judge?

Lesson in Our Society

Recent studies have shown that traditional evangelical churches are losing membership because many congregants feel that the local church is not meeting their spiritual needs. In fact, on a recent Christian radio program, it was revealed that a startling number of 20- and 30-year-olds have given up on the traditional, denominational church altogether and instead are flocking to larger, nondenominational mega churches.

These trends indicate that we need to get back to the basics. We need to return to the fundamentals of the faith: believing on the Lord Jesus Christ for our salvation and spreading this Good News to the poor in spirit. Only He can bring the dead back to life and meet our needs in the here and now.

Make It Happen

Use this week to assess your relationship with the Lord. Have you lost your spiritual fervor? Are you just going through the motions of worshiping the true and living God? If you feel that you are slipping or have lost your spiritual footing, pray that God will restore the joy of your salvation. Afterward, share the Good News with a loved one, friend, or coworker.

Follow the Spirit

What God wants me to do:

_____

_____

Remember Your Thoughts

Special insights I have learned:

_____

_____

More Light on the Text
John 5:19–29

19 Then answered Jesus and said unto them, Verily, verily, I say unto you, The Son can do nothing of himself, but what he seeth the Father do: for what things soever he doeth, these also doeth the Son likewise.

From the start, Jesus wanted it known that His relationship to the Father was on the Father's authority and in conjunction with His will. Jesus did what any good Son would do, by imitating His Father's example and rejecting the temptation to behave contrary to the Father's desires.

20 For the Father loveth the Son, and sheweth him all things that himself doeth: and he will shew him greater works than these, that ye may marvel.

A clash between Jesus and the Jews arose after Jesus healed a paralyzed man on the Sabbath. Giving medical treatment was judged as work under the rules the priests set forth for observing the Sabbath. Immediately before coming to Jerusalem for the Feast, Jesus had healed a government official's son who was at the point of death. When Jesus stated that the Father would show the Son "greater works than these," He was referring to these recent miracles, but also to those He would perform as His ministry continued.

The important truth this verse reveals is why the Father did this. Jesus declares that the Father showed the Son everything He did. The word "sheweth" (Gk. *deiknymi*, **dike-noo-o**) was used to mean both "to show" and "to explain." The Father showed the Son what He did, how He did it, and He explained how to do it.

The question is, Why did He do that? Jesus says it was because "the Father loveth the Son." What's unusual about this statement is that this is the only time in the gospels that the Greek word *phileo* (**fil-EH-o**) is used to describe the Father loving the Son. "Love," or *phileo*, means to have a strong affection for or to like a person. In all other places, John uses the Greek work *agapao* (**ag-ap-PAH-O**), which refers to a perfect love in which the beloved object is cherished.

A good example of the difference in these two words can be seen at the end of John's gospel. Along the Sea of Galilee, Jesus encountered Peter, who repeatedly denied knowing Jesus as the Sanhedrin, the Jewish court, was trying Him. Three times Jesus asked Peter, "Do you love me?" In our English translations of the Bible (the King James Version and the *New Living Translation,* for example), the word "love" is used all three times. But when John was writing his gospel, the first two times he used the word *agapao*: "Do you love Me perfectly, cherish Me more than anything?" Both times, Peter responded that he did. But the third time, John used the word *phileo*: "Peter, are you sure you really have affection for Me and value our relationship?"

When John used *phileo* to refer to God the Father's love for His Son, it may have been his way of emphasizing that God wasn't just an exalted, holy Being who was beyond the grasp of human understanding and detached from or indifferent to all affection. The Father didn't just cherish His eternal, only begotten Son; He genuinely cared for Him. John uses the same word in 16:27, where Jesus says, "The Father himself loveth you, because ye have loved me." Jesus revealed in the Father's love for Him the kind of love God has for us, a love that cherishes us and accepts us in our human frailty.

21 For as the Father raiseth up the dead, and quickeneth them; even so the Son quickeneth whom he will.

Jesus next mentions resurrection of the dead, and the priests in the group probably became uptight. Most priests were Sadducees, a party that rejected resurrection as impossible. Jesus referred not only to resurrection, but also to giving life. The Father raised the dead, such as the widow's son in 1 Kings 17:17–22. Just as important, the Father was the Source of all life. He gave life to everyone and everything.

Likewise, Jesus, as the Father's Son, has made alive and will make alive "anyone he wants to" (NLT). John uses the word *thelei* (**THEE-lee**), which means "to wish or to will for something." This statement foreshadows bringing his friend Lazarus back to life. For the Jewish leaders, that event would bring to a head their plans to execute Jesus (John 11:27–40). Just as His healing miracles suggested His power to heal the soul of sin's deadly effect (Romans 6:23), so His power to raise the dead physically (Matthew 9:23–25; Luke 7:11–15) symbolized the new spiritual life He would give to those who trusted Him. Later, John records Jesus saying, "The miracles I do in my Father's name speak for me. I give [those who believe in me] eternal life, and they shall never perish" (John 10:25, 28, NIV).

22 For the Father judgeth no man, but hath committed all judgment unto the Son: 23 that all men should honour the Son, even as they honour the

Father. He that honoureth not the Son honoureth not the Father which hath sent him.

Often, as we read the Bible, we think of a verse as a statement that can be understood separately from what the verse before or after it says. Verses 22 and 23 are a good example of when that is not true. These two verses make up one statement by Jesus.

The Father chose Jesus, in His unique position as both the Son of God (v. 25) and the Son of man (v. 27), as His holy agent of judgment. As the Son of man, He understood men perfectly. As the Son of God, He possessed full understanding of the mind and will of God.

The Father did this in order to make it plain that the Son had His full trust and that He accepted the Son on equal terms. Later, Jesus says that to reject Him or the revelation that the Father had sent Him to announce was the same as rejecting the Father (John 15:23; see also 1 John 3:23).

No contradiction exists between what John wrote here and what he wrote later in John 8:15, where Jesus says, "I judge no man." In the first half of that verse, Jesus notes that the Jews judge "after the flesh"—in other words, using superficial standards, such as wealth, education, and social standing. Jesus' point was that He would not judge anyone on that basis. The Jews' judgment was based on human status or standards, but Jesus judged with perfect justice on behalf of the Father for salvation or condemnation.

24 Verily, verily, I say unto you, He that heareth my word, and believeth on him that sent me, hath everlasting life, and shall not come into condemnation; but is passed from death unto life.

The double use of *verily* (Gk. *amen*, **ah-MEEN**) was used to emphasize the importance of a statement as well as to establish the truthfulness of it.

Verse 24, the Keep in Mind verse for this lesson, contains several wonderful promises for the believer. In the Greek language in which John wrote his gospel, the present tense expresses action that is going on continually or habitually. So "he that heareth" refers to a person who keeps listening, pays attention, and lives according to what he has heard. The person who "believeth on him that sent me" is one who trusts

Jesus as Lord because he or she has accepted that He is God's messenger.

The person who trusts that Jesus is God's revelation of truth about Himself, and is, therefore, willing to pay attention to His teaching, *has* life that's worth living forever. John doesn't say the believer will have it (future tense), but that he or she has it (present tense).

Jesus then says that such a person "shall not" come into condemnation. John uses the present tense (Gk. *erchomai*, **er-khom-ahee**). For the person who has decided to trust Jesus, condemnation is behind, not ahead (Romans 8:1).

The greatest promise is found in the final phrase of verse 24. Jesus declares that when a person chooses to trust Him with his or her life, that person passes from the domain of death to the land of life (see Colossians 1:12–14). When John wrote that the believer "passes" (i.e., "is passed," Gk. *metabaino*, **met-ab-AH-ee-no**), the word he used means "to move" or "to change locations or addresses." John describes a completed action that has continuing effects in the present. A believer doesn't have to wait to experience the eternal life of God. Although the fullness of salvation lies ahead, we become God's children now through faith in Christ (John 1:12).

25 Verily, verily, I say unto you, The hour is coming, and now is, when the dead shall hear the voice of the Son of God: and they that hear shall live. 26 For as the Father hath life in himself; so hath he given to the Son to have life in himself.

Little that Jesus said concerned the physical reality of our lives or this world. That is especially true of what Jesus said as recorded in the gospel of John. Verse 25 is a good example. At first glance, many people would think Jesus is speaking of physical resurrection. However, Jesus says, "The hour is coming when the dead shall live." But in the same declaration, He adds, that time "now is." A person can't put off responding to Christ's call to faith, but must pay attention and respond when His call comes (Genesis 6:3; John 6:44).

Jesus isn't referring to the bodily resurrection at His second coming (John 5:28–29; 14:3; 1 Corinthians

15:51–54). He is dealing with those who are spiritually dead in their sin, promising that they have a renewed hope of being brought alive spiritually through faith in Him. That was possible because, as the Father always was, always is, and always will be (Revelation 1:4, 8; 4:8), the Son shares that same life. The Father's purpose for the Son when He sent Him into the world was to share His eternal life with all who will trust Him to do so. As Paul writes in Ephesians 2:4–5 (NIV), "Because of his great love for us, God, who is rich in mercy, made us alive with Christ, even when we were dead in transgressions— it is by grace you have been saved."

27 And hath given him authority to execute judgement also, because he is the Son of man.

The Father trusted the Son, not only with giving life, but also with executing judgment. As the Son of man foretold in Daniel, Jesus was Lord of "an everlasting dominion, which shall not pass away, and a kingdom which shall not be destroyed" (Daniel 7:14). Because Jesus shared the divine nature with the Father, His truth and purposes were open and simple to Him. His dual nature and His death on the cross enabled Him to be the perfect mediator between God and men (1 Timothy 2:5–6)—or in Paul's words, to be both "just, and the justifier of him which believeth in Jesus" (Romans 3:26).

28 Marvel not at this: for the hour is coming, in the which all that are in the graves shall hear his voice, 29 And shall come forth; they that have done good, unto the resurrection of life; and they that have done evil, unto the resurrection of damnation.

At the start of this quarrel, Jesus told the Jews He intended for them to be surprised by His miracles. Through those miracles, He tried to get their attention and to demonstrate the power of God's presence in Him. Now He tells them they shouldn't be surprised—that the Father has given Him the power to give new life to those dead in their sin. Nor should they be surprised that God has authorized Him to

judge those worthy of eternal life. He says, "All that are in the graves shall come forth." Jesus had not forgotten those "in the graves." There will be a bodily resurrection and "one final judgment, but with different results."

The question that Jesus put to the Jews over and over was whether they would accept Him for who He said He was—one whose miracles supported His claim. The difference between doing good and doing evil was between believing Jesus or rejecting Him. The same decision faces each of us today.

Sources

Bamberger, B. J. "Moneychangers." In *The Interpreter's Dictionary of the Bible: An Illustrated Encyclopedia (Volume 3)*, edited by George A. Butterick and Keith R. Crim, 435. Nashville, Tenn.: Abingdon Press, 1962.

Beasley-Murray, George R. *Word Biblical Commentary: John, Volume 36.* Edited by Bruce M. Metzger, Ralph P. Martin, and Lynn Allan Losie. Nashville, Tenn.: Nelson Reference, 1987, 77.

Brown, Raymond E. *The Anchor Bible Series Volume 29: The Gospel According to John I–XII Volume 1.* Garden City, N.Y.: Doubleday & Co., Inc., 1966, 214.

Hobbs, Herschel H. *An Exposition of the Four Gospels.* Grand Rapids, Mich.: Baker Publishing Group, 1968, 115.

Keener, Craig S. *The IVP Bible Background Commentary: New Testament. Downers Grove, Ill.: InterVarsity Press, 1993, 276.*

Daily Bible Readings

M: Jesus Heals a Lame Man
John 5:1–9

T: Whom God Has Sent
John 3:31–36

W: I Am the Christ
John 4:19–26

T: Jesus Taught with Authority
Matthew 7:24–29

F: Christ Will Judge
2 Timothy 4:1–5

S: Honor the Son
John 5:19–23

S: Jesus Speaks of Judgment
John 5:24–30

TEACHING TIPS

January 21
Bible Study Guide 8

1. Words You Should Know

A. Life (John 6:35) *zoe* (Gk.)—Every living soul.

B. Hunger (v. 35) *peinao* (Gk.)—To suffer want or to be needy.

2. Teacher Preparation

A. Begin your preparation to teach the lesson with prayer, asking God to give you wisdom and insight.

B. Read the lesson in its entirety. Read the Bible Background Scriptures and Focal Verses in another translation (e.g., NIV or NKJV).

C. Jot down notes that specifically address the Lesson Aim objectives.

D. Complete lesson 8 in the *Precepts For Living® Personal Study Guide* to gain further insight into the lesson.

3. Starting the Lesson

A. Ask for a volunteer to lead the class in prayer.

B. Read the Lesson Aim aloud. Then ask for a volunteer to read today's In Focus story.

C. Write the phrase "Bread of Life" on the chalkboard. Ask the students what they think this phrase means, and record their answers.

4. Getting into the Lesson

A. Ask for volunteers to read the Focal Verses, The People, Places, and Times and the Background sections.

B. Read the Keep in Mind verse collectively, and use the Lesson Aim to help you explain it.

C. Using the In Depth outline, facilitate a discussion of the meaning of today's Focal Verses.

D. Review the Search the Scriptures and Discuss the Meaning questions, and facilitate a discussion on the answers.

5. Relating the Lesson to Life

A. Read and discuss the contents of Lesson in Our Society.

B. Ask volunteers to explain how Jesus is "bread and living water" to them.

C. Now ask volunteers to share any new insights they may have learned from today's lesson.

6. Arousing Action

A. After having a volunteer read the Make It Happen exercise aloud, encourage the students to follow through during the upcoming week.

B. Instruct the class to read the Daily Bible Readings for the upcoming week in preparation for class.

C. Close the class in prayer.

Worship Guide

For the Superintendent or Teacher
Theme: Jesus Is the Bread of Life and Living Water
Theme Song: "Lead Me, Guide Me"
Scripture: John 6:35
Song: "Let Us Break Bread Together"
Meditation: Dear Lord, help us to always remember that You are our source of salvation and more than sufficient to meet all our needs; without You, we are forever lost. Amen.

JESUS IS THE BREAD OF LIFE AND LIVING WATER

Bible Background • JOHN 6:25–59; 7:37–39
Printed Text • JOHN 6:34–40; 7:37–39   Devotional Reading • EPHESIANS 3:14–21

Lesson Aim

By the end of the lesson, we will:

UNDERSTAND that Jesus is more than sufficient for every human need;

REJOICE in Christ's sufficiency for every need; and

IDENTIFY what Christ has done for us.

Keep in Mind

"And Jesus said unto them, I am the bread of life: he that cometh to me shall never hunger; and he that believeth on me shall never thirst" (John 6:35).

Focal Verses

John 6:34 Then said they unto him, Lord, evermore give us this bread.

35 And Jesus said unto them, I am the bread of life: he that cometh to me shall never hunger; and he that believeth on me shall never thirst.

36 But I said unto you, That ye also have seen me, and believe not.

37 All that the Father giveth me shall come to me; and him that cometh to me I will in no wise cast out.

38 For I came down from heaven, not to do mine own will, but the will of him that sent me.

39 And this is the Father's will which hath sent me, that of all which he hath given me I should lose nothing, but should raise it up again at the last day.

40 And this is the will of him that sent me, that every one which seeth the Son, and believeth on him, may have everlasting life: and I will raise him up at the last day.

7:37 In the last day, that great day of the feast, Jesus stood and cried, saying, If any man thirst, let him come unto me, and drink.

38 He that believeth on me, as the scripture hath said, out of his belly shall flow rivers of living water.

39 (But this spake he of the Spirit, which they that believe on him should receive: for the Holy Ghost was not yet *given;* because that Jesus was not yet glorified.)

In Focus

For the past year and a half, Diane and her husband Mike had struggled to make ends meet in the aftermath of Hurricane Katrina. As residents of a small town in the Mississippi Gulf region, the couple had lost everything: their home, their personal possessions, and their jobs.

One Sunday, Diane told her husband, "I'm not going to church with you today. God doesn't hear our prayers. I've been volunteering at the soup kitchen, helping with the youth, and passing out clothes ever since Katrina hit, and we have been struggling for over a year. And for what? I keep seeing others being blessed, and still we struggle."

Mike looked at his wife in amazement. She had always been the one to keep him together. Now he was hearing something he had never heard before.

"Baby, I'm not sure why God has not blessed us like some others, but I do know that it's because of our faith in God and not our works that we are alive today," Mike replied.

"I suppose you're right," Diane reluctantly agreed. "I know it's not right to think this way, but I'm angry. I don't think God or anyone else is ever going to deliver us out of this situation."

Mike understood why his wife was angry, but he also knew he could not let her give up on God. "Diane, not only has God provided physical food, but He has also given us spiritual nourishment to keep going. Our marriage has never been stronger than it is right now, and we have not been hungry, thirsty, or without shelter since Katrina hit. God has not forgotten about us. We just have to keep our faith."

"You're right," replied Diane. "I'm sorry. Don't leave me; I'll be dressed in 10 minutes and ready to go."

People eat to satisfy their

physical hunger. In today's lesson, we learn that Jesus is our spiritual food, and it is our relationship with Him that sustains spiritual life.

The People, Places, and Times

Bread of Life. Jesus called Himself the "Bread of Life" in contrast to the manna God provided for the Israelites during their wilderness experience. As they traveled through the wilderness, they had to depend on God to supernaturally provide their food. Every day God gave enough food for that day. By God's command, no one could gather more than a day's supply. There had to be a continuous, constant dependence on God; He was their only source of sustenance.

Passover Feast. The Passover Feast was established to commemorate the historical deliverance of the Children of Israel from Egypt. It was one of three annual festivals and was observed during the month of April.

Feast of Tabernacles. This feast was celebrated approximately six months after the Passover feast and lasted eight days. It was a time when the Israelites would remember how God had sustained them in the wilderness.

Background

The Israelites had gathered together in Jerusalem just before the Passover Feast. The people had watched Jesus perform many miracles. Now they followed Jesus across the sea and found Him in the synagogue at Capernaum. The Jews were looking for a prophet like Moses to lead them. Jesus told them they were not following Him because of the miracles they witnessed, but because they wanted more of the loaves and fish to fill their bellies (John 6:26).

Jesus quickly made them aware of their spiritual need by revealing that He is the Bread of Life. He declared that eating bread made from grain sustains only temporarily. Jesus declared that He is the Bread of Life and that God had sent Him from heaven to give eternal life. Just as bread sustains life physical-

ly, Jesus, the Bread of Life, is the very essence of life itself.

At-A-Glance

1. Jesus Responds to the Crowd (John 6:34–35)
2. Jesus Confronts the Crowd's Unbelief (v. 36)
3. Jesus Declares that He Came to Do His Father's Will (vv. 37–40)
4. Jesus Is the Messiah (7:37–39)

In Depth

1. Jesus Responds to the Crowd (John 6:34–35)

Days earlier, a crowd had gathered and had seen Jesus perform many miracles. He had fed 5,000 people with only five small barley loaves and two small fish (John 6:5–13). But the crowd wanted an earthly leader like Moses, and they thought Jesus was the one whom Moses prophesied about (see Deuteronomy 18:15).

Jesus reminded the crowd that God, not Moses, provided the bread in the desert. He identifies Himself as the Bread of Life by stating that it was *He* who came down from heaven and gave life to the world (John 6:33). The crowd misunderstood Jesus' message because they still thought of bread in physical terms (v. 34). However, Jesus identified Himself as the Bread of Life that satisfies forever (v. 35). He is the only one who can satisfy both our physical and spiritual needs and give abundant life that lasts forever.

2. Jesus Confronts the Crowd's Unbelief (v. 36)

The crowd that followed Jesus had seen a number of His miracles. Many had seen Him heal the royal official's son (John 4:46–53) and the invalid man at the pool of Bethesda (5:5–9). But still there was unbelief. Jesus told the crowd that even though they saw Him perform many miracles, they still did not believe in Him. In other words, seeing was not believing.

As Christians, sometimes we ask God for a sign—

"And Jesus said unto them, I am the bread of life: he that cometh to me shall never hunger; and he that believeth on me shall never thirst" (John 6:35).

something that lets us know that God is with us or is listening to us. However, we must learn to have faith and trust in God, knowing that we can always rely on His Word. When we trust God, especially when there are no signs or miracles present, He honors our faith.

3. Jesus Declares that He Came to Do His Father's Will (vv. 37–40)

Throughout the book of John, one of the recurring themes is that Jesus came to do the will of His Father. In these four verses, Jesus consistently talks about the will of God the Father, who sent Him from heaven. Jesus promised to give eternal life to those who remained faithful to Him. For those who claimed to love and obey God, believing and following Jesus

should have been their first priority. Instead, they did not believe nor accept Him as the true Messiah because they wanted to be fed manna from heaven like their forefathers in the desert. They did not realize that Jesus *is* our daily bread.

4. Jesus Is the Messiah (7:37–39)

The Feast of Tabernacles was celebrated to remind the Israelites of God's provision when they were in the desert. On the last day of the celebration, Jesus stood in the midst of the crowd and continued to offer them eternal life. Jesus told them if they were thirsty they needed only to "come to me and drink." He offered them the gift of salvation and promised to give them the water necessary for sustaining life in a desolate place. Jesus shared that whoever believed in Him would have streams of living water and would never be thirsty again. He was comparing the need for water in the desert to the need for the living water—that is, the Holy Spirit.

It is very popular to pursue goals or dreams that satisfy only temporarily. But faith in Jesus is the only source of true satisfaction. He alone is the Bread of Life that satisfies the soul of every human being.

Search the Scriptures

1. Jesus said that He is the _____ of _____ (John 6:35).

2. Jesus came down from heaven not do His own will but the will of _____ the _____ (v. 40).

3. Everyone who believes on the Son will have _____ _____ (v. 40).

Discuss the Meaning

1. The Feast of Tabernacles was held in remembrance of what event?

2. What was the connection between the celebration of the Feast of Tabernacles and Jesus' statement that He is the Bread of Life?

3. Why did Jesus use the words "hunger" and "thirst" as ways of communicating during the celebration of the feast?

4. Does Jesus mean that He came to fulfill our deepest desires and reveal the true meaning of life when He says that those who come to Him will never hunger or thirst?

Lesson in Our Society

The everyday hustle and bustle of work and family life can be overwhelming. Maybe you're tired of trying to keep up with the latest fads and trends. Jesus is the only one who can fulfill our deepest longings and needs. Jesus refreshes, renews, and restores the dry, depleted areas. He gives meaning and purpose, replacing the boredom that comes from seeking after temporary pleasures. This is the abundant life, the eternal life promised to those who give their life to Jesus Christ.

Make It Happen

This week, make a decision to commit your life, schedule, and time to Jesus. Make an attempt to lighten your schedule and make more time for studying God's Word. Let Him be involved in everything you do. Take the time to come into His presence to seek His will, and watch how He will sustain you and meet your every need.

Follow the Spirit

What God wants me to do:

_____

_____

Remember Your Thoughts

Special insights I have learned:

_____

_____

More Light on the Text
John 6:34–40; 7:37–39

34 Then said they unto him, Lord, evermore give us this bread.

The crowd had seen the miracle of the bread and the fish (John 6:1–14). When Jesus talked to them about the bread from God (v. 33), they asked Him to give them that bread. The verb "give" (Gk. *didomi*, **DID-o-mee**) implies a once and for all gift that would be with them "evermore" (Gk. *pantote*, **PAN-tot-eh**), or at all times.

But did the crowd really understand what Jesus meant? No. They understood Jesus' words in a material sense. Just as the Samaritan woman wanted water to be relieved of the task of drawing from the well (4:15), these people had the same materialistic reason for their request. Earlier, Jesus had multiplied five loves of bread and a few fish and fed the entire multitude. Now they followed Jesus in expectation—wanting to be fed again. Therefore, in the next verse, Jesus uses a new form of words to further clarify what He meant.

35 And Jesus said unto them, I am the bread of life: he that cometh to me shall never hunger; and he that believeth on me shall never thirst.

Bread was the primary source of nourishment for the crowd that Jesus addressed. But the bread Jesus spoke of was not like ordinary bread. Jesus identified Himself as the bread that gives life. He is not only the giver of bread (cf. 6:1–15, 27), but He is also the bread that gives life. He came to give Himself so that everyone who believes may live in Him.

In verse 35, Jesus pronounces the first of the notable "I am" (Gk. *ego eimi*, **eg-o' i-mee'**) sayings in the gospel of John (see also vv. 41, 48, 51; 8:12, 58; 10:7, 9, 11, 14; 11:25; 14:6; 15:1, 5; cf. the divine self-definition in Exodus 3:14). However, the "I am" saying bears the essence of His message: He is the answer to the needs of the human heart. It implies the fundamental role Jesus claims to fulfill in relation to the longing of the human spirit. He satisfies the yearning of the soul. Thus, everyone who believes in Him will never hunger or thirst.

36 But I said unto you, That ye also have seen me, and believe not.

The Greek word *alla* (**al-lah'**, meaning "but") introduces a strong contrast. Jesus reminds the crowd that although they had seen Him giving food to the 5,000, they still did not understand the true meaning of this miracle. They were far from understanding the significance of what they had seen. They did not believe; thus, they had not been able to partake of the Bread of Life.

37 All that the Father giveth me shall come to me; and him that cometh to me I will in no wise cast out.

All who come to Jesus will receive the life-giving bread (cf. 1 Timothy 2:4). God is at work in the world by His grace despite people's unbelief. Christ takes the entire responsibility for our full and final salvation. He does not turn away those who come to Him (cf. John 17:6–12). He will keep them and protect them.

38 For I came down from heaven, not to do mine own will, but the will of him that sent me.

The purpose for Jesus' coming into the world and the very sustenance of His life on Earth was to do the "will" (Gk. *thelema*, **THEL-ay-mah,** meaning "desire") of the Father. Jesus was in perfect harmony with the Father in His ministry. This verse reaffirms the unity of Jesus and God and Jesus' divine origin. Jesus is the messenger par excellence.

39 And this is the Father's will which hath sent me, that of all which he hath given me I should lose nothing, but should raise it up again at the last day.

The Greek pronoun *pas* (**pas,** meaning "of all") refers to the entirety of the people given to Jesus by the Father (all believers are seen as one entity, see v. 37a). He will not lose them (cf. 17:6–12), but will "raise" them up (Gk. *anistemi*, **an-IS-tay-mee,** meaning "make to stand up") at the last day, when God will judge all people. The keeping ministry of Jesus will secure those who believe in Him at the time of judgment.

40 And this is the will of him that sent me, that every one which seeth the Son, and believeth on him, may have everlasting life: and I will raise him up at the last day.

The Greek word for "every one" (*pas*, **pas**) is masculine singular; thus, Jesus is referring to each individual believer (each individual member of the whole; see v. 37b). The individual member does not need to fear being ignored among the crowd of believers. The Son and the Father are engaged in the salvation of believers in perfect unity of will and purpose.

The verb "seeth" (Gk. *theoreo*, **theh-o-REH-o,** meaning "to discern") in this context refers to more than physical sight, for which no faith is needed (cf. 2:23; 6:36). It refers to having discernment and recognizing the glory of God in Jesus.

The believer now has both possession of eternal life and the hope of resurrection (cf. Romans 8:23–25).

7:37 In the last day, that great day of the feast, Jesus stood and cried, saying, If any man thirst, let him come unto me, and drink.

The eighth and last day of the Feast of Tabernacles

was a day on which all the people gathered together for a sacred assembly (Leviticus 23:36; Numbers 29:35–39; Nehemiah 8:18). A prayer for rain was recited. Jesus waited until that day to make His proclamation. He offered water to people praying for water (cf. Isaiah 55:1).

The verb "stood" (Gk. *histemi,* **HIS-tay-mee**) implies that Jesus was standing while watching the service. In His standing position, it was possible for a lot of people to see and hear Him declare, "If any one is thirsty, let him come to me and drink" (cf. John 4:10).

38 He that believeth on me, as the scripture hath said, out of his belly shall flow rivers of living water.

The word "belly" (Gk. *koilia,* **koy-LEE-ah**) is often used to refer to the innermost part of a human being, the soul or the heart (cf. Proverbs 20:27; 22:18; Job 15:35). The water Jesus offers not only refreshes one's own soul; but also flows out to refresh the lives of others (cf. John 4:13–14; Isaiah 12:3; Zechariah 13:1; 14:8; Ezekiel 47:9; Joel 3:18).

39 (But this spake he of the Spirit, which they that believe on him should receive: for the Holy Ghost was not yet *given*; because that Jesus was not yet glorified.)

In order to avoid any failure to grasp what Jesus meant, an explicit note is added for the reader. Thus,

the water Jesus offers is not from Earth. It is the Holy Spirit going forth from the dwelling place of God into and through the believer (cf. 1 Corinthians 3:16; 6:19). He is like a living, springing river within the heart of the believer.

The Spirit was present and active, but He was not yet present in the way that Jesus had promised. His full outpouring must wait for the glorifying of Jesus. The word "glorify" (Gk. *doxazo,* **dox-AD-zo**) is central to and characteristic of the gospel of John.

Daily Bible Readings

M: May Christ Dwell Within
Ephesians 3:14–21
T: Do Not Be Afraid
John 6:16–24
W: Jesus, the Heavenly Bread
John 6:25–34
T: I Am the Bread of Life
John 6:33–40
F: Sustained by Living Bread
John 6:41–51
S: Sing for Joy
Isaiah 49:7–13
S: Living Water
John 7:37–41

TEACHING TIPS

January 28
Bible Study Guide 9

1. Words You Should Know

A. Pharisees (John 8:13) *Pharsaios* (Gk.)—A sect that started after the Jewish exile. The Pharisees sought distinction and praise by outward observance of extreme rites and by outward forms of piety, such as ceremonial washing, fasting, prayers, and alms-giving.

B. Light (v. 12) *phos* (Gk.)—Anything emitting light, such as a star, fire, lamp, or torch.

C. Darkness (v. 12) *skotia* (Gk.)—The lack of light; a metaphor used for the ignorance of divine things and the associated wickedness and resulting misery in hell.

2. Teacher Preparation

A. Read and familiarize yourself with the chapters in John preceding the lesson text.

B. Read The People, Places, and Times for information regarding the Feast of Tabernacles and the ceremony of light. Relate this ceremony to the setting and atmosphere in the lesson text.

C. Examine a recent newspaper for headlines that illustrate activities representative of light and darkness.

D. Complete lesson 9 in the *Precepts For Living® Personal Study Guide* to enhance your knowledge of today's lesson.

3. Starting the Lesson

A. Ask the students to define what spiritual darkness means to them.

B. Share recent newspaper headlines with the class that illustrate activities representative of light and darkness.

C. Ask the students to draw on their own experiences and identify a time when they found themselves in a moral dilemma. How did they respond?

4. Getting into the Lesson

A. Ask a volunteer to read the FOCAL VERSES.

B. Explain that today's lesson takes place at the end of the Feast of Tabernacles. Explain the significance of the ceremony of light.

C. Ask the class how an understanding of this ceremony helps reveal how Jesus brought light that overcomes the works of darkness.

5. Relating the Lesson to Life

A. Give the students time to answer the Discuss the Meaning questions.

B. Engage the students in a discussion of what it means to exhibit Christlike behavior.

C. Read the In Focus story aloud, and relate its relevance to the Lesson Aim

D. Ask the class how the image of Jesus being the Light of the World shapes our faith.

6. Arousing Action

A. Challenge the students to follow through on the Make It Happen assignment.

B. Sum up the lesson by having the class read the Keep in Mind verse in unison. Ask each student to spend time in the upcoming week, being a light for Christ.

C. In preparation for next week's lesson, instruct the class to read the Daily Bible Readings found at the end of today's lesson.

D. Close the class with prayer, using the Worship Guide Meditation.

I AM THE LIGHT OF THE WORLD

Bible Background • JOHN 8:12–20; 12:44–46
Printed Text • JOHN 8:12–20; 12:44–46   Devotional Reading • ISAIAH 35:3–10

Lesson Aim

By the end of the lesson, we will:

UNDERSTAND Jesus' statement that He is the Light of the World;

BE CONVINCED of the need to reflect Christlike behavior in all we do; and

ENCOURAGE ourselves and others to overcome darkness by following the light of Jesus to salvation.

Keep in Mind

"Then spake Jesus again unto them, saying, I am the light of the world: he that followeth me shall not walk in darkness, but shall have the light of life" (John 8:12).

Focal Verses

John 8:12 Then spake Jesus again unto them, saying, I am the light of the world: he that followeth me shall not walk in darkness, but shall have the light of life.

13 The Pharisees therefore said unto him, Thou bearest record of thyself; thy record is not true.

14 Jesus answered and said unto them, Though I bear record of myself, yet my record is true: for I know whence I came, and whither I go; but ye cannot tell whence I come, and whither I go.

15 Ye judge after the flesh; I judge no man.

16 And yet if I judge, my judgment is true: for I am not alone, but I and the Father that sent me.

17 It is also written in your law, that the testimony of two men is true.

18 I am one that bear witness of myself, and the Father that sent me beareth witness of me.

19 Then said they unto him, Where is thy Father? Jesus answered, Ye neither know me, nor my Father: if ye had known me, ye should have known my Father also.

20 These words spake Jesus in the treasury, as he taught in the temple: and no man laid hands on him; for his hour was not yet come.

12:44 Jesus cried and said, He that believeth on me, believeth not on me, but on him that sent me.

45 And he that seeth me seeth him that sent me.

46 I am come a light into the world, that whosoever believeth on me should not abide in darkness.

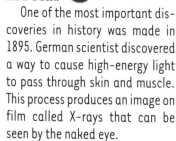

In Focus

One of the most important discoveries in history was made in 1895. German scientist discovered a way to cause high-energy light to pass through skin and muscle. This process produces an image on film called X-rays that can be seen by the naked eye.

The laser beam, which was labeled as "a solution waiting for a problem," was available for 30 years before anyone found a tangible use for the powerful light beam. Today, lasers are used in many areas, such as research, communication, industry, medicine, and environmental care.

However, the most important light ever discovered appeared over 2,000 years ago, when a spectacular star in the heavens prompted many wise men to make a grueling journey through mountains and desert to find its source. At the end of their trek, they found Jesus—the Light of the World.

Jesus' light cannot only penetrate skin and muscle, but it can also overcome the darkness of sin. The light of Christ can heal better than any surgical laser beam. The light of Christ is available for believers as a solution to overcome any of life's troubles.

In today's lesson, we will explore Jesus' statement that He is the Light of the World.

The People, Places, and Times

The Feast of Tabernacles. This was a celebration that is held during the autumn harvest. Each year, Jews would travel to Jerusalem to give thanks for the ingathering or harvest (Exodus 23:16; 34:22; Leviticus 23:34; Deuteronomy 16:13). Fruit was gathered in and people dwelt in booths made of branches and boughs of trees.

The Ceremony of Lights. This was a celebration held during the last days of the Feast of Tabernacles. It involved lighting torches throughout Jerusalem to signify that God provided a way out of darkness by offering His protection to Israel during the wilderness wanderings.

Background

Throughout the gospel of John, Jesus' deity is constantly reaffirmed. John writes that Jesus is the "Word" (John 1:1), the "lamb of God" (1:29, 36), the "bread of life" (6:35), and the "light of the world" (8:12, 9:5). In the Bible, "light" is a symbol of God and His holiness (Acts 9:3; 1 John 1:5), and walking in darkness is a metaphor for stumbling (Isaiah 59:10; Jeremiah 13:16) or being destroyed (Psalm 27:2; Jermiah 20:11). Jesus reaffirms His deity by announcing that He *is* the Light and that anyone who believes in Him will not stay in the darkness of sin.

The setting of this passage is in the temple courtyard at Jerusalem. Jesus is teaching the crowds who had come to celebrate the Feast of Tabernacles. Earlier, Jesus had performed miracles throughout the countryside. The Pharisees had begun to question whether the miracles were done because Jesus' power was demonic or because it was actually from God (John 7–8). Jesus had just spoken to the Jewish leaders about a woman caught in adultery. He told the woman that He didn't condemn her, but instructed her to go and sin no more (John 8:11). It is after this event that Jesus announces that He is the Light of the World (v. 12).

Jesus taught at the Feast of Tabernacles.

1. Jesus Declares He Is the Light of the World
(John 8:12)
2. Jesus Answers the Pharisees (vv. 13–20)
3. Jesus' Final Challenge (12:44–46)

In Depth

1. Jesus Declares He Is the Light of the World (John 8:12)

The light of Jesus illuminates all sin and lights the way to freedom from the darkness of sin. Jesus is the only true light from heaven who dispels the darkness of sin and destroys the works of the Devil. As those who believe in Jesus follow Him, they will be able to shine the light that Jesus gives because they are obedient to God's Word and follow Christ's example.

2. Jesus Answers the Pharisees (vv. 13–20)

The Pharisees didn't want the people to believe in or follow Jesus. Instead, they wanted to make the crowd turn against Him, so they tried to challenge everything He said. When Jesus stated that He is the Light of the World, the Pharisees claimed that He couldn't speak on His own behalf (v. 13). Jesus rebuked them by stating that He was qualified to speak on His own behalf because of who He is and where He comes from (cf. John 7:29).

As the Pharisees continued in their attempt to challenge Jesus, they asked Him, "Where is thy Father?" (John 8:19). By asking this question, the Pharisees were attempting to discredit Jesus yet again. It was obvious that they didn't even know the God they claimed to love and follow. This is why Jesus replied that if they knew Him, they would know His Father. If they knew who Jesus was, they would have fallen on their knees and worshiped Him. They would have recognized Him as the Light of the World.

3. Jesus' Final Challenge (12:44–46)

Jesus has seen the works of darkness firsthand. Throughout the book of John, we read that He continually did miracles among the people. He healed a blind man (John 9:1–12) and brought Lazarus back to life (John 11:38–44). He also reminded the people that by believing in Him they would no longer stay in darkness (12:46). Jesus is the Light that brightens the darkness by setting us free from sin (Romans 6:18). Anyone who believes in Jesus will no longer be a slave to sin. Instead, he or she will become a servant of righteousness and receive eternal life.

Search the Scriptures

1. "He that followeth me shall not walk in _____, but shall have the_____ of _____" (John 8:12).

2. "I am one that bear _____ of _____, and the _____ _____ _____ me beareth witness of me" (v. 18).

3. "If ye had known _____, ye should have known_____ _____ also" (v. 19).

4. "I am come a _____ into the _____ , that whosoever _____ on me should not _____ in _____" (John 12:46).

Discuss the Meaning

1. As believers, how can we be conduits of Jesus' light?

2. In view of the fact that Jesus is the Light of the World, why is it important that we display Christlike behavior toward everyone we meet?

Lesson in Our Society

Abortion, greed, drug abuse, and homosexuality are just a few of the evils that plague our society. In today's lesson, we see that Jesus came to bring light to a dark world plagued with evils. Every day, we are surrounded by sickness, disease, hunger, and depression. It is our duty, as believers in Christ, to illuminate the world by showing God's light and love to those living in darkness by sharing the Good News.

Make It Happen

The coming of light is a metaphor for the coming of salvation. Look around you this week and identify individuals who are walking in spiritual darkness.

Think of various ways that you can demonstrate the light of Christ to help those individuals believe the Gospel and receive salvation.

Follow the Spirit

What God wants me to do:

_____

_____

Remember Your Thoughts

Special insights I have learned:

_____

_____

More Light on the Text

John 8:12–20; 12:44–46

12 Then spake Jesus again unto them, saying, I am the light of the world: he that followeth me shall not walk in darkness, but shall have the light of life.

John 1 declares that Jesus is the "light." Here, Jesus affirms that declaration by proclaiming Himself to be the true "light" (Gk. *phos*, **foce**) of the world. In the Old Testament, light was the first thing God created (Genesis 1:3–4). The use of the word "light" is also symbolic of the law (Psalm 119:105; Proverbs 6:23), wisdom (Proverbs 8:22), and God (Exodus 13:21). But it is here in verse 12 that Jesus gives light new meaning by declaring He *is* the light, thus affirming His deity.

It is interesting to note that Jesus used the term "followeth" (Gk. *akoloutheo*, **ak-ol-oo-THEH-o**, meaning "to join or accompany"), not "receive" or "walk." In the Old Testament, the Children of Israel followed the pillar of fire (and its light) through the wilderness to the Promised Land (Exodus 13:21). Thus, Jesus' promise of "the light of life" for those who follow Him can be perceived as assurance of a life free from the darkness of sin.

13 The Pharisees therefore said unto him, Thou bearest record of thyself; thy record is not true.

In response to Jesus' invitation of salvation, the Pharisees question Jesus' right to bear witness of Himself. "Bearest" (Gk. *martureo*, **mar-too-REH-o**) means "witness." According to Jewish law, no man

could give testimony on his own behalf (Deuteronomy 19:15). Therefore, according to the Pharisees, Jesus is not entitled to speak in His own behalf, and if He does, His evidence is not "true" (Gk. *alethes*, **al-ay-THACE**).

14 Jesus answered and said unto them, Though I bear record of myself, yet my record is true: for I know whence I came, and whither I go; but ye cannot tell whence I come, and whither I go. 15 Ye judge after the flesh; I judge no man.

Jesus answers them by first proclaiming His authority. He validates His right to speak because of His intimate relationship with the Father. Rabbinic law rejected self-testimony and required two or more witnesses to authenticate a case. In contrast, Jesus knew where He had come from and where He was going.

The Greek word for "I go" is *hupago* (**hoop-AG-o**, meaning "to depart"), and is often used to refer to Jesus' death, resurrection, and ascension (cf. John 7:33; 8:21). As a result, Jesus is the only one who could provide a true self-witness because He is the only one who has seen God (John 1:18; 7:29). Therefore, His testimony is true.

In verse 15, Jesus tells the Pharisees that they judge by outward appearances. The verb "judge" (Gk. *krino*, **KREE-no**) means "to separate, pick out, or choose." Jesus renders the Pharisees' judgment superficial as being according to the "flesh" (Gk. *sarx*, **sarx**), meaning they judge by human standards based on what is visible. Those who opposed Jesus had no idea about His origin or His destiny.

16 And yet if I judge, my judgment is true: for I am not alone, but I and the Father that sent me. 17 It is also written in your law, that the testimony of two men is true. 18 I am one that bear witness of myself, and the Father that sent me beareth witness of me.

Once again, Jesus speaks of His divine authority. While the judgment of the Pharisees is based on outward appearances, Jesus does not judge—that is not the purpose of His earthly ministry (cf. John 3:3–7, 16). However, Jesus says that if He were to judge, His judgment would be true, being based on the authority given to Him by His Father.

He is not alone in proclaiming His authority. His testimony is confirmed by the Father who sent Him. In verses 17 and 18, Jesus refers to the Rabbinic law that demands two witnesses (Deuteronomy 17:6; 19:15). Here, Jesus offers Himself as the second witness. It is true that He gives testimony about Himself, but He also has the witness of the Father who sent Him. The phrase "beareth witness" (Gk. *martureo*, **mar-too-REH-o**) means to affirm that one has seen, heard, or experienced something, and implies that Jesus and the Father are continually witnessing.

19 Then said they unto him, Where is thy Father? Jesus answered, Ye neither know me, nor my Father: if ye had known me, ye should have known my Father also.

Because the Pharisees are thinking on an earthly level, they are incapable of understanding who Jesus' Father is (cf. 7:27). They assume that Jesus means a human father. In fact, in biblical times, it bordered on slander to question a man's paternity. Jesus explains to them that if they had truly known who He was, they would have known that He and the Father are one (cf. 14:9). But the Pharisees refused to acknowledge the possibility that Jesus had such an intimate relationship with God.

20 These words spake Jesus in the treasury, as he taught in the temple: and no man laid hands on him; for his hour was not yet come.

The mention here of the "treasury" (Gk. *gazophulakion*, **gad-zof-oo-LAK-ee-on**) provides another connection to the Feast of Tabernacles and the celebration of lights. Josephus speaks of treasuries in the women's court of Herod's temple. It is in this court that containers were lit representing the pillar of fire (i.e., light) and God's protection and guidance in the desert.

No one arrested Jesus because He was under the Father's protection until His work was completed. The hour for His departure from this world had not yet come (cf. John 7:30).

12:44 Jesus cried and said, He that believeth on me, believeth not on me, but on him that sent me. 45 And he that seeth me seeth him that sent me. 46 I am come a light into the world, that whosoever believeth on me should not abide in darkness.

Ultimately, the central theme of this passage is salvation. Here Jesus reiterates His message and His mission: He is the Light of the World and faith in Him is ultimately faith in God. Throughout His ministry, Jesus insisted that He had come to do the work appointed for Him by the Father.

The verb "seeth" (v. 45) is from the Greek word *theoreo* (**theh-o-REH-o**). It implies a continuous contemplation of Jesus, which will result in a better knowledge of the Father. To see Jesus is to see the Father who sent Him (cf. John 1:18; 13:20; 14:9).

The phrase "am come" (Gk. *erchomai*, **ER-khom-ahee**) denotes an action already accomplished and points to the permanent result of believing that Jesus came into the world (cf. 18:37) to deliver humankind from the darkness of sin into the light of salvation.

Daily Bible Readings

M: Promises for God's People
Isaiah 35:3–10
T: Jesus Brings Light
Matthew 4:12–17
W: Jesus Heals a Blind Man
John 9:1–11
T: Who Is the Son of Man?
John 9:35–41
F: Knowing God's Will
Ephesians 5:15–21
S: Jesus Is the World's Light
John 8:12–20
S: I Have Come as Light
John 12:44–50

TEACHING TIPS

February 4
Bible Study Guide 10

1. Words You Should Know

A. Door (John 10:7) *thura* (Gk.)—A portal or entrance.

B. Shepherd (v. 11) *poimen* (Gk.)—A shepherd or pastor; used in this instance to illustrate Jesus' ownership of and commitment to those who follow Him.

2. Teacher Preparation

A. Pray that God will be with you as you prepare to teach today's lesson.

B. Pray for the students in your class, asking God to open their hearts and minds.

C. Study the Focal Verses, using the Lesson Aim as a guide.

D. To help activate the lesson, answer the questions in lesson 10 in the *Precepts For Living®* *Personal Study Guide.*

3. Starting the Lesson

A. Ask the students to share their Make It Happen assignment from last week. Briefly discuss their responses.

B. Concentrate on the Lesson Aim as you begin the lesson with prayer.

C. Instruct the students to read the Keep in Mind verse aloud in unison.

4. Getting into the Lesson

A. Read today's In Focus story, and ask the students to discuss a time when they were unaware of God's protection in their lives.

B. Ask volunteers to read The People, Place, and Times and the Background sections.

C. Write the At-A-Glance outline on the board and instruct the students take turns reading the Focal Verses.

D. Divide the students into four groups. Reflecting on the At-A-Glance outline, assign each group an In Depth section to read silently and discuss within the groups.

E. Ask for one volunteer from each group to share the group's insights about their In Depth topic with the class.

5. Relating the Lesson to Life

A. Spend time answering the questions in the Discuss the Meaning section.

B. Ask the students to (1) explain the difference between the shepherd and the hired hand, and (2) tell which one they would prefer to be and why.

C. Discuss the significance of the terms "thieves" and "robbers."

6. Arousing Action

A. Read the Lesson in Our Society section to the class. Ask each student how he or she can follow the good shepherd.

B. Direct the students to the Make It Happen section, and discuss their responses.

C. Remind the students to read the Daily Bible Readings to prepare for next week's lesson.

D. Ask if there are any prayer requests; then end the class with prayer.

Worship Guide

For the Superintendent or Teacher
Theme: I Am the Good Shepherd
Theme Song: "I Gave My Life For Thee"
Scripture: 1 Peter 2:24
Song: "God Is A Wonder To My Soul"
Meditation: Dear Heavenly Father, Thank You for caring for me. Thank You for sending Your Son to die on the Cross for my sins. Thank You for Your hedge of protection that constantly surrounds me. Amen.

I AM THE GOOD SHEPHERD

Bible Background • JOHN 10:1–18
Printed Text • JOHN 10:1–5, 7–18   Devotional Reading • ISAIAH 40:10–14

Lesson Aim

By the end of the lesson, we will:
UNDERSTAND that Jesus is not only our Life-Giver, but also our Life-Sustainer, inasmuch as He is the Good Shepherd for His sheep;
BE CONVINCED that Jesus cares deeply about us as individuals; and
DECIDE to rely on Jesus as our Good Shepherd by casting all our cares on Him and knowing He cares for us.

Keep in Mind

"I am the good shepherd: the good shepherd giveth his life for the sheep" (John 10:11).

Focal Verses

John 10:1 Verily, verily, I say unto you, He that entereth not by the door into the sheepfold, but climbeth up some other way, the same is a thief and a robber.

2 But he that entereth in by the door is the shepherd of the sheep.

3 To him the porter openeth; and the sheep hear his voice: and he calleth his own sheep by name, and leadeth them out.

4 And when he putteth forth his own sheep, he goeth before them, and the sheep follow him: for they know his voice.

5 And a stranger will they not follow, but will flee from him: for they know not the voice of strangers.

10:7 Then said Jesus unto them again, Verily, verily, I say unto you, I am the door of the sheep.

8 All that ever came before me are thieves and robbers: but the sheep did not hear them.

9 I am the door: by me if any man enter in, he shall be saved, and shall go in and out, and find pasture.

10 The thief cometh not, but for to steal, and to kill, and to destroy: I am come that they might have life, and that they might have it more abundantly.

11 I am the good shepherd: the good shepherd giveth his life for the sheep.

12 But he that is an hireling, and not the shepherd, whose own the sheep are not, seeth the wolf coming, and leaveth the sheep, and fleeth: and the wolf catcheth them, and scattereth the sheep.

13 The hireling fleeth, because he is an hireling, and careth not for the sheep.

14 I am the good shepherd, and know my sheep, and am known of mine.

15 As the Father knoweth me, even so I know the Father: and I lay down my life for the sheep.

16 And other sheep I have, which are not of this fold: them also I must bring, and they shall hear my voice; and there shall be one fold, and one shepherd.

17 Therefore doth my Father love me, because I lay down my life, that I might take it again.

18 No man taketh it from me, but I lay it down of myself. I have power to lay it down, and I have power to take it again. This commandment have I received of my Father.

In Focus

All eyes were on Kevin as he stood behind the microphone trembling. Kevin was the choir director for a world-renowned, gospel choir. At choir practice this evening, Kevin was very nervous. It seemed the whole world was looking at him. Kevin's worst nightmare had actually come true. He had finally gotten up the nerve to tell his fellow choir members about the demons that had been devouring him over the last several years.

"I've been deceiving all of you for quite some time now," Kevin began. He told them how he had almost died one night about a year ago when he overdosed on cocaine before a big gospel concert. Kevin began to cry as he recounted the fornication and debauchery that he had fallen into because of his drug abuse. He admitted that for the past several years, most of the time when the choir was performing, he was high on drugs. He ended his testimony

"I am the good shepherd: the good shepherd giveth his life for the sheep" (John 10:11).

saying, "I was under God's protection through all those dangers, seen and unseen. I truly repented of my sins, and I admitted myself into a substance abuse program. I have been drug free for over nine months now, and I am thankful to God for His hedge of protection."

That night, Kevin's testimony had a greater effect on his fellow choir members than any of the millions of records they had sold.

Today's lesson reveals Christ as the Good Shepherd who invests great amounts of time to redeem His sheep and provide sustenance for all our needs.

The People, Places, and Times

The Shepherd. Jesus pointed out that the most important trait of the good shepherd is that he lays down his life for the sheep. A shepherd's life could at times be dangerous. Wild animals were common in the countryside of Judea, and oftentimes the shepherd had to risk life and limb to save his sheep.

The Sheepfold. In biblical times, a communal sheepfold held everyone's sheep at night. The sheepfold was protected by a strong door, and only the guardian of the door had a key.

Background

Today's lesson follows on the heels of Jesus healing a man born blind (John 9:13–41). Some Jews did not believe Jesus was a healer, while others saw the healings He performed as miracles. Jesus described Himself as both the "good shepherd" and the "door."

As a good shepherd, He owned His sheep and was not a hired hand. As owner, the shepherd was on intimate terms with his sheep; that is, he knew their names and personalities. He invested great amounts of time in the sheep. Unlike the hired hand, the owner will give his life, if necessary, to save his sheep from wolves or other predators.

Jesus also described Himself as the "door" through which one must come to become one of His sheep. There was normally only one entrance into the sheep pen, which reduced the likelihood of uninvited guests entering and harming the sheep.

At-A-Glance

1. My Sheep Know My Name
(John 10:1–5)
2. Jesus Is the Devoted and Dedicated
Shepherd (10:7–14)
3. Jesus Knows His Sheep (vv. 15–16)
4. Jesus Is the Good Shepherd (vv. 17–18)

In Depth

1. My Sheep Know My Name (John 10:1–5)

The door is the main entrance. Jesus explained that anyone who tried to get in any other way besides going through the gate (door) would be a thief—that person would be up to no good. In this passage, Jesus compares Himself to a shepherd who enters the gate; Jesus went on to say that only the shepherd enters through the gate. Only the shepherd has the right to enter the sheepfold and call his own sheep out to follow him.

When the shepherd arrived, he would call his own sheep by name. Because sheep recognize the voice of their shepherd, they follow him out to pasture. Just as a sheep would respond to the voice of the shepherd calling its name, when the Good Shepherd (Jesus) came, all believers recognized His voice and followed Him.

2. Jesus Is the Devoted and Dedicated Shepherd (10:7–14)

These verses consist of a series of four "I am" statements. These statements reveal who Jesus is in relationship to those that follow Him. There are four characteristics that set this good shepherd apart from the thief or robber: (1) He approaches directly—He enters at the gate; (2) He has God's authority—the gatekeeper allows Him to enter; (3) He meets real needs—the sheep recognize His voice and follow Him; and (4) He has sacrificial love—He is willing to lay down His life for the sheep.

At the same time, there is also a vast difference between the good shepherd, the thief, and the hired hand. The thief comes to steal, kill, and destroy the sheep. The hired hand protects the sheep, but does the job only for money and quickly flees when danger comes. In contrast, the good shepherd is committed to the sheep. Jesus is not merely doing a job, He is committed to loving us and even laying down His life for us.

3. Jesus Knows His Sheep (vv. 15–16)

Jesus' followers know Him to be their Messiah—they love and trust Him. Such knowledge and trust between Jesus and His followers is compared to the relationship between Jesus and the Father. Thus, Jesus is the Good Shepherd, not only because of His relationship with the sheep, but also because of His relationship with God the Father.

In verse 16, Jesus tells the Pharisees that He has other sheep. By using this metaphor, Jesus is letting the Pharisees know that He came to save Gentiles as well as Jews. This is an insight into Jesus' worldwide mission: to die for sinful people all over the world. The new Gentile believers and the Jewish believers would form one flock and have one Shepherd.

4. Jesus Is the Good Shepherd (vv. 17–18)

Here, Jesus abandons the sheep metaphor and speaks directly about His relationship with God. Jesus laid down His life of His own accord, and of His own accord He would also take it up again in resurrection. Jesus was living out God's commandment (John 3:16). When Jesus said He laid down His life voluntarily and that He had the power to take it again, He was claiming His authority to control His own death and resurrection.

Jesus, the Good Shepherd, has the best interests of His sheep in mind at all times. He is on constant guard to keep His sheep upright and in the fold. He is prepared to meet every need and even to give His life to rescue the sheep from danger. As the Good Shepherd, He protects us from danger and provides for our sustenance. Like the Pharisees of Jesus' day, we need to be reminded that it was Jesus' choice to give up His life; it was not taken from Him. It is because of His sacrifice that we can have eternal life. The Son's authority to lay down His life and take it up again did not originate with Himself; it came from the Father.

Search the Scriptures

1. What were the people called who did not enter the sheep pen by the door (John 10:1)?

2. Why did the sheep follow the shepherd (v. 3)?

3. Why didn't the sheep follow strangers (v. 5)?

4. What was Jesus' promise to those who enter through the door (v. 9)?

5. Why did the hired hand leave sheep in the face of trouble (v. 13)?

6. How did Jesus plan to save the other sheep (v. 16)?

Discuss the Meaning

1. It is awesome to know that our Creator knows our names and personalities! Discuss the significance that the sheep only follow the Good Shepherd and not strangers (John 10:3–5). Reflect on the importance of deciding to live life according to God's Word. Compare the difference between a believer's life choices and a nonbeliever's life choices.

2. Why did Jesus refer to himself as the "door" (v. 9)?

3. Who were Jesus' other sheep (v. 16)?

4. How can we identify God's protective voice amidst all the perilous voices?

Lesson in Our Society

We live in a society where people make daily decisions to live by pleasure principles rather than God's principles. Such pleasure principles lead to acts of adultery, stealing, debauchery, deceitfulness, and

so on. Jesus died to rescue us from these pitfalls. God commands us to live for Him and in Him.

As the Good Shepherd, Jesus cares for us and protects us from evil. Yet many of us are living outside of the door of His will. What changes are you willing to make in order to know the voice of the Good Shepherd?

Make It Happen

People seek protection from those things that pose a threat to their well-being. Think about your own life. Into what category do you fall? Have you followed the voice of the Good Shepherd, Jesus Christ, our Lord and Saviour, for protection? If you have, thank God for opening your ears, your heart, and your eyes so that you recognize the voice of the Good Shepherd. Or are you a hired hand, a thief, or a robber? If so, ask God to strengthen you so that you might know the voice of the Shepherd and follow Him when He calls.

Follow the Spirit

What God wants me to do:

_____

_____

Remember Your Thoughts

Special insights I have learned:

_____

_____

More Light on the Text

John 10:1–5, 7–18

1 Verily, verily, I say unto you, He that entereth not by the door into the sheepfold, but climbeth up some other way, the same is a thief and a robber.

In this discourse, Jesus employs the familiar analogy of a shepherd and his flock to teach an important lesson about Himself and His relationship with believers. Applying the imagery of the shepherd to kings and priests was a common practice in Middle Eastern culture. In the Old Testament, the shepherd was often used to symbolize a royal caretaker of God's people (cf. 2 Samuel 5:2; Isaiah 44:28). God Himself was referred to as the "Shepherd of Israel" (see Genesis 49:24; Psalm 23:1; 80:1). The "sheepfold" (Gk. *probaton,* **PROB-at-on,** meaning "fold of the sheep") was a walled enclosure open to the sky with one entrance where the sheep were kept. Usually, a sheepfold would hold several flocks. The "shepherd" (Gk. *poimen,* **poy-MANE**), or gatekeeper, set up sleeping posts near the entrance to ward off wild beasts, thieves, and other intruders.

The parable depicts the shepherd as the only one who has authorized access to the flock. The shepherd's position is in stark contrast to a "thief" (Gk. *kleptes,* **KLEP-tace**) or a "robber" (Gk. *lestes,* **lace-TACE**), who must sneak into the fold in some clandestine way. Unlike the stranger, from whom the sheep run away, the shepherd has established a relationship with the sheep. The welfare of his sheep is uppermost in his mind.

2 But he that entereth in by the door is the shepherd of the sheep. 3 To him the porter openeth; and the sheep hear his voice: and he calleth his own sheep by name, and leadeth them out.

The shepherd of the sheep had authorized access to the fold, as evidenced by the "porter" (Gk. *thuroros,* **thoo-ro-ROS,** meaning "gatekeeper") opening the door for him. The shepherd rose in the mornings to call out his own sheep by name. He rightfully entered the fold because the sheep were his, and their best interest was his primary concern; he had no intention of bringing harm to them. Regardless of the number of flocks in the fold, the shepherd called out to his own by name, and they recognized and responded to his familiar "voice" (Gk. *phone,* **fo-NAY,** meaning "sound").

4 And when he putteth forth his own sheep, he goeth before them, and the sheep follow him: for they know his voice.

The shepherd went before the sheep; he did not drive the sheep from behind. The bond between the shepherd and his sheep was so strong and intimate that the sheep willingly followed him out of the sheepfold as he went ahead of them. They knew the sound of his voice, and his voice was reassuring to them. His presence and his rod and staff brought comfort to the sheep (cf. Psalm 23:4).

5 And a stranger will they not follow, but will flee from him: for they know not the voice of strangers.

Jesus used this parable to teach how the shepherd formed his flock. As in verses 3 and 4, the imagery used in verse 5 communicates a sense of intimacy. Note the role the shepherd's "voice" (Gk. *phone,* **fo-NAY**) plays in this discourse. The sheep followed because they knew the voice of the shepherd, but they would never follow a stranger whose voice they did not recognize. From the stranger's voice, the sheep would flee. The sheep that remained safe recognized the voice of the shepherd. The sheep came to the shepherd because he called them, and the proper response of sheep is to come to the shepherd when he calls.

10:7 Then said Jesus unto them again, Verily, verily, I say unto you, I am the door of the sheep.

Up to this point, Jesus has spoken to the Pharisees' situation figuratively. He realized His audience would certainly understand the inferences to be drawn from the illustration of the shepherd/sheep relationship; unfortunately, they missed the spiritual lesson Jesus was trying to teach. So, Jesus shifts metaphors and declares, "I am the door of the sheep." Again, Jesus' hearers would be familiar with the figure of a shepherd as a "door" (Gk. *thura,* **THOO-rah**) of the sheep. Since shepherds habitually lie down across the entrance of the sheepfold with their bodies forming a barrier to thieves and wild beasts, they speak of themselves as the door to let the flock in or out and to protect the flock from intruders. Through the door, the flock goes in and out to graze and to rest. If attacked or frightened, the sheep can retreat into the security of the fold.

Several times in the gospel of John, Jesus describes Himself using the phrase "I am" (Gk. *ego eimi,* **eg-O i-MEE;** cf. 6:35; 8:12; 9:5; 10:7, 9; 10:11, 14; 11:25; 14:6; 15:1, 5). Christ's usage of *ego eimi* in this manner leaves no question about His claim to deity. In fact, to a perceptive Jew who understood the term *ego eimi* as used in Exodus 3:14, Jesus was making Himself equal to God (cf. v. 33).

8 All that ever came before me are thieves and robbers: but the sheep did not hear them.

This verse is not a reference to Old Testament prophets, but to all Messianic pretenders and religious charlatans, like many of the Pharisees and chief priests of the time. Here, Jesus describes them as "thieves" (Gk. *kleptes,* **KLEP-tace**) who divest the unwary of their precious possessions, and "robbers" (Gk. *lestes,* **lace-TACE**) who plunder brazenly by violence. They were the type that did not care about the spiritual good of the people, but only about themselves. As a result, the sheep (i.e., those who are faithful) would not heed their voice.

9 I am the door: by me if any man enter in, he shall be saved, and shall go in and out, and find pasture.

Christ claims to be *the* door, not just *a* door. Here Jesus is explicitly identifying Himself as the means to salvation (cf. Psalm 118:19–21). As the Shepherd, Jesus provides safety and sustenance for His flock. He is the only way of salvation. Through Him, believers find "pasture" (Gk. *nome,* **nom-AY**), or provision for all of their daily needs.

10 The thief cometh not, but for to steal, and to kill, and to destroy: I am come that they might have life, and that they might have it more abundantly.

The thief's motive is diametrically opposed to that of the shepherd. His interest is selfish. He steals the sheep in order to kill them and feed himself, thus destroying part of the flock. In this description, we see a veiled glimpse into the character of the Pharisees and religious authorities who opposed Jesus. In contrast, Christ is the Life-Giver and Life-Sustainer. His interest is the welfare of the sheep. He enables the sheep to have full and secure lives. Conversely, the thief takes life; but Christ gives life to overflowing.

11 I am the good shepherd: the good shepherd giveth his life for the sheep.

The adjective "good" (Gk. *kalos,* **kal-OS**) carries the meaning of being a true or a model shepherd. Here, Jesus is referring to the model of a shepherd found in Ezekiel 34:11–16. According to Ezekiel, the good shepherd gathers, feeds, and protects the sheep. A strong bond exists between sheep and shepherd. It was not unusual for Palestinian shepherds to

risk their lives for their flocks. Wild beasts, lions, jackals, wolves, and bears were on the prowl. In his experience as a shepherd, David's fights with a lion and a bear over the life of his flock convinced him that God was also able to give Goliath into his hands (1 Samuel 17:34–37). When Jesus says, "I am (Gk. *ego eimi*) the good shepherd" (i.e., the true Shepherd), He is expressing the manner in which He carries out His mission of salvation.

12 But he that is an hireling, and not the shepherd, whose own the sheep are not, seeth the wolf coming, and leaveth the sheep, and fleeth: and the wolf catcheth them, and scattereth the sheep.

A "hireling" (Gk. *misthotos,* **mis-tho-TOS**), or hired servant, denotes someone who both has no real interest in his duty and is unfaithful in the discharge of it. As a wage earner, his interest is in the money he makes and in self-preservation. He has no real commitment to the sheep. Therefore, if a wolf shows up, he runs to save his own life, leaving the sheep to fend for themselves. The result is devastating for the sheep. His carelessness exposes the flock to fatal danger. As is the case today, Israel (the Old Testament church) had many false religious leaders, selfish kings, and imitation messiahs; as a result, the flock of God suffered constantly from their abuse.

13 The hireling fleeth, because he is an hireling, and careth not for the sheep. 14 I am the good shepherd, and know my sheep, and am known of mine.

The "hireling" (Gk. *misthotos*) is just that—a hired hand. The image of the hired hand is reflective of Israel's selfish kings and false prophets found in the Old Testament (Ezekiel 34:5–6; Jeremiah 23:1–3; Zechariah 11:15, 17). Both here and in the Old Testament passages, the hired hand's main concern is himself. The sheep are only a means to an end.

By contrast, the "good" (Gk. *kalos,* **kal-OS**, meaning "noble" or "true") shepherd cares for the sheep—so much so that he is willing to lay down his life for them. It is important to note that there is a bond of intimacy between the shepherd and his sheep, as indicated by the phrase "I know" (Gk. *ginosko,* **ghin-OCE-ko**). The use of the Greek word *ginosko* implies Christ's ownership and watchful oversight of the sheep. The reciprocal point that the sheep know their shepherd identifies the sheep's response to Christ's love and intimate care. Moreover, the use of *ginosko* indicates that this knowledge is of high value to the shepherd.

15 As the Father knoweth me, even so know I the Father: and I lay down my life for the sheep.

The deep mutual knowledge between Christ (the Shepherd) and His sheep is likened to the relationship between the Father and the Son. The "knowing" between God the Father and Jesus, His Son, is a uniquely intimate relationship. The connection between the sheep and the shepherd who *knows* his sheep and lays down his life for them shows unity of purpose between the Father and the Son. Jesus is more than the Good Shepherd; He is the fulfillment of God's promises to God's people. Christ voluntarily laid down His life for us. His death was not an unfortunate accident, but part of the planned purpose of God.

16 And other sheep I have, which are not of this fold: them also I must bring, and they shall hear my voice; and there shall be one fold, and one shepherd.

Jesus was addressing His immediate audience—those already in the fold, the Israelites who believed. But the phrase "other sheep" (Gk. *allos probaton,* **AL-los PROB-at-on**) is a direct reference to the Jews and Gentiles who had not yet come to believe. Therefore, they were still outside of Jesus' protection. The fold, then, is a metaphor for the church, and none other than the Shepherd Jesus will gather His sheep together into one fold. As they hear His voice, His people from among Jews and Gentiles will come and be formed into one body of Christ as one flock with one Shepherd. There is one people of God, comprised of believers inside and outside of ethnic Israel.

17 Therefore doth my Father love me, because I lay down my life, that I might take it again.

Jesus reaffirms the love the Father has for Him and picks up again on the theme of His death and resurrection. He will voluntarily lay down His life for the salvation of the world. The Father's "love" (Gk. *aga-*

pao, **ag-ap-AH-o**) is linked with the Son's willingness to lay down His life for the world. The mutual love of the Father and Son come together in one divine purpose of salvation for humankind. The Father in love arranged for the salvation of His people, and the Son in love freely gave His all to accomplish salvation for His people. Naturally, the Father's everlasting love always endures for the Son. However, His death is the supreme manifestation of His sacrificial obedience to the will of God the Father.

18 No man taketh it from me, but I lay it down of myself. I have power to lay it down, and I have power to take it again. This commandment have I received of my Father.

In choosing to die for the sins of the world, Jesus once again proved His sovereign authority over His own destiny. If Christ had not chosen to die, no one would have had the power to kill Him. The work of redemption is done by the Father through the Son. Jesus laid down His life in order to take it up again. In Jesus' death, the penalty for sin is paid in full, and the resurrection is the vindication of the Son as the atonement for sin. In death, the Son becomes the sacrifice for our sins and reconciles us to God. In resurrection, the Son is glorified.

Daily Bible Readings

M: God Tends His Flock
Isaiah 40:10–14
T: A Warning to False Shepherds
Ezekiel 34:1–6
W: I Will Shepherd My Sheep
Ezekiel 34:11–16
T: You Are My Sheep
Ezekiel 34:25–31
F: The Sheep Know Their Shepherd
John 10:1–5
S: I Am the Good Shepherd
John 10:7–11
S: The Shepherd Suffers for the Sheep
John 10:12–18

TEACHING TIPS

February 11
Bible Study Guide 11

1. Words You Should Know

A. Resurrection (John 11:25) *anastasis* (Gk.)—A rising from the dead.

B. Life (v. 25) *zoe* (Gk.)—Denotes life in the fullest sense; life as God has it.

C. Believeth (v. 25) *pisteuo* (Gk.)—To put confidence in; to trust or be persuaded.

2. Teacher Preparation

A. Prepare for this lesson by reading the Bible Background verses, concentrating especially on the Lesson Aim objectives.

B. Meditate on the Keep in Mind verse, and ask the Lord to give you a clear understanding of His Word.

C. Answer the questions from lesson 11 in the *Precept For Living® Personal Study Guide*.

3. Starting the Lesson

A. Write the At-A-Glance outline on the board.

B. Read the poem from the In Focus section.

C. Pray that the Lord would use the class time to speak through His Word to the hearts of His people.

4. Getting into the Lesson

A. Ask for volunteers to read the Focal Verses; The People, Places, and Times; Background; and In Depth sections aloud.

B. Answer the Search the Scriptures and Discuss the Meaning questions in class.

5. Relating the Lesson to Life

Have the students read the Lesson in Our Society section. Then ask them to give examples of times when the Lord demonstrated His power in their lives.

6. Arousing Action

A. Read the Make It Happen section, and challenge the students to take any hopeless situation that they may currently face to the Lord.

B. Instruct the class to read the Daily Bible Readings in preparation for next week's lesson.

B. Close the class in prayer.

Worship Guide

For the Superintendent or Teacher
Theme: I Am the Resurrection and the Life
Theme Song: "The Strife Is O'er"
Scripture: John 11:25
Song: "I Know that My Redeemer Lives"
Meditation: Dear Father, help me to always appreciate what You did for me at Calvary, and the fact that Your resurrection paid my sin debt. Because of You, sin no longer has power over my life. Thank You! Amen.

I AM THE RESURRECTION AND THE LIFE

Bible Background • JOHN 11:1–44
Printed Text • JOHN 11:17–27   Devotional Reading • JUDE 17–23

Lesson Aim

By the end of the lesson, we will:

UNDERSTAND that the power of life and death ultimately rests with Jesus Christ, who is the Resurrection and the Life;

REJOICE in the truth that Jesus can raise us to life from the death sentence of sin, as well as give us eternal life; and

DECIDE to share this life-giving truth with someone during the coming week.

Keep in Mind

"Jesus said unto her, I am the resurrection, and the life: he that believeth in me, though he were dead, yet shall he live" (John 11:25).

Focal Verses

John 11:17 Then when Jesus came, he found that he had lain in the grave four days already.

18 Now Bethany was nigh unto Jerusalem, about fifteen furlongs off:

19 And many of the Jews came to Martha and Mary, to comfort them concerning their brother.

20 Then Martha, as soon as she heard that Jesus was coming, went and met him: but Mary sat still in the house.

21 Then said Martha unto Jesus, Lord, if thou hadst been here, my brother had not died.

22 But I know, that even now, whatsoever thou wilt ask of God, God will give it thee.

23 Jesus saith unto her, Thy brother shall rise again.

24 Martha saith unto him, I know that he shall rise again in the resurrection at the last day.

25 Jesus said unto her, I am the resurrection, and the life: he that believeth in me, though he were dead, yet shall he live:

26 And whosoever liveth and believeth in me shall never die.

Believest thou this?

27 She saith unto him, Yea, Lord: I believe that thou art the Christ, the Son of God, which should come into the world.

In Focus

THE POWER OF GOD

Dear Lord,

Your Resurrection Power makes possible

The impossible.

You and only You

Have just what we need:

Power to live a holy life,

Power to walk with You

And succeed.

You can re-create us,

Make us new creations

Inside out;

Make us all brand new.

You can deliver the inner man

So that we are blessed

In all that we do.

Thank You

For making Your power

Available to us!

Thank You for the Cross.

Without Your love

And tender mercy,

We would be forever lost.

Amen.

Jesus is the Resurrection and the Life. In the book of John, we are reminded that He is the Giver of physical as well as spiritual life.

The People, Places, and Times

Martha. It is thought by some scholars that Martha was the elder sister of Mary and Lazarus. This is because she is referred to as the owner of the house (Luke 10:38). In an earlier meeting with Jesus, it was Martha who became distraught when her sister Mary sat at Jesus' feet instead of helping her serve (Luke 10:38–42).

Bethany. This is a village on the eastern slope of the Mount of Olives, two miles east of Jerusalem. It appears that Jesus preferred to lodge there instead of in Jerusalem. Today, it is known as *el-Azariyeh* (i.e., "place of Lazarus").

"Jesus said unto her, I am the resurrection, and the life: he that believeth in me, though he were dead, yet shall he live" (John 11:25).

Background

Only in the book of John do we find the recounting of Jesus raising Lazarus from the dead. At the start of John 11, Martha and Mary notify Jesus that their brother Lazarus is very sick (v. 3). But instead of rushing to Bethany, Jesus stays where He is for two more days. In biblical times, it was common to bury the dead either on the same day or very close to the time of death. It was also believed that a person's soul hovered around the body for three days after physical death. But by the time Jesus finally arrives in Bethany, Lazarus has been dead four days.

Obviously, Jesus was not in a rush to get to Bethany. He informs His disciples that Lazarus is in fact dead and that He is glad that He was not there to keep Lazarus from dying, so that they may believe (John 11:15). It is this statement that shapes the theological heart of today's lesson.

At-A-Glance

1. Jesus Is in Control (John 11:17–20)
2. Jesus Is Always Right on Time (vv. 21–24)
3. Jesus Is the Resurrection and the Life (vv. 25–27)

In Depth

1. Jesus Is in Control (John 11:17–20)

When Jesus arrives in Bethany, Lazarus had already been dead four days. The professional mourners had arrived, and the situation looked hopeless to the human eye. Everything around Martha and Mary was telling them that it was time to give up hope—that there was nothing more to be done. Mary and Martha must have begun to wonder whether Jesus had forgotten about them or, worse yet, had decided not to do anything about their brother's condition. But in John 11:14, Jesus provides confirmation that He is well aware of Lazarus' condition. He knows exactly what is taking place in the lives of Mary and Martha. But why does He linger and not rush to the scene? Could it be that He waited to demonstrate His power until all hope in human effort was exhausted? Ultimately, Jesus is in complete control of the situation. His delay is for the benefit of His disciples and Lazarus' sisters, Martha and Mary, so they may come to trust in the Lord with all their hearts, instead of leaning on their own understanding (cf. Proverbs 3:5).

Jesus wants us to put our complete confidence in Him because He is in control of all the affairs of life. When things look bad and we cannot see any way out, Jesus wants us to run to Him, like Martha, and place all of our trust in Him alone.

2. Jesus Is Always Right on Time (vv. 21–24)

Martha expects Jesus to do something; she says, "Lord, if You had been here, my brother would not have died" (v. 21, NKJV). Some scholars suggest that Martha's remarks to Jesus were ones of reproach. Some consider Martha a woman of practical duty, eager to put everybody in their rightful place. After all, it was Martha who questioned Jesus regarding her sister Mary's lack of service when Jesus visited their home (see Luke 10:38–41). But here in verse 22, we realize that Martha's faith in Jesus' ability to heal her brother is undiminished. She tells Jesus, "I know" that God will do whatever you ask, which implies that intuitively Martha's assessment of Jesus is that of a righteous man to whom God listens and for whom nothing is impossible.

In response to Martha's statement, Jesus tells her, "Thy brother shall rise again" (v. 23). Judging from Martha's response to Jesus, it appears that she is disappointed. She says, "I know that he will rise again in the resurrection on the last day" (v. 24). Martha's response to the Master implies that she does not yet grasp the full implication of what Jesus was saying. She understood that in the "last day" all would rise, but Martha yearned for a more immediate solution—she wanted her brother back!

Initially, the way Martha addressed Jesus is similar to how we often address Him when things do not go the way we think they should. Oftentimes we ask, "Lord, where were You? If You would have showed up when I called You, this might not have happened." The Lord may not show up when we think He ought to, but we can be sure that He is always right on time.

3. Jesus Is the Resurrection and the Life (vv. 25–27)

When Jesus heard Martha's reply, He responded to her by stating emphatically, "I am the resurrection and the life" (v. 25). In essence, Jesus was telling Martha, "You keep looking forward to some event in the future, but what you are looking for is standing right in front of you." Jesus challenged Martha to place her trust in Him as the One who holds the power of life and death in His hands.

The word Jesus used for "life" is the Greek word *zoe* (**dzo-AY**), which speaks of life in the fullest sense. Jesus has the power to give life because He is Life itself. The power that Jesus has extends beyond merely the physical; He also holds the power to give life to the spiritually dead. Ephesians 2:1 says that we "were dead in trespasses and sins," and it took God to "make us alive," or raise us from our spiritual death. On another occasion, Jesus, addressing a mob of angry Jews, said, "For as the Father raises the dead and gives them life, so also the Son gives life to whom he will" (John 5:21, ESV). The Lord wants us to know that all power in heaven and on Earth is in Jesus' hand (Matthew 28:18), and for this reason we should place all of our trust in Him.

Placing faith in Jesus has implications for the present and is not relegated to some "pie in the sky, we'll do better in the sweet by and by" mind-set. Jesus wants to effect change in our lives right now. As Christians, we must reach the point where our trust in

Christ transcends our understanding of the world around us. When things look impossible from a human perspective, we cannot let this diminish our faith in the One who "upholds the universe by the word of his power" (Hebrews 1:3, ESV). Jesus cares about the troubles of our lives. More importantly, He has the power and desire to do something about it.

Search the Scriptures

1. What is the first thing Martha says to Jesus when she meets Him (John 11:21)?

2. How does Martha understand Jesus' words about her brother rising again (v. 24)?

3. What does Jesus say are the results of believing in Him (vv. 25–26)?

4. What is Martha's response to Jesus' statement in verses 25 and 26 (v. 27)?

Discuss the Meaning

1. Jesus tells Martha, "Your brother will rise again" and raises him from death that same day. Do you think that Jesus wants to demonstrate His resurrecting power in our lives even today? Give some examples of His power at work in your life.

2. What did Jesus mean when He said, "Everyone who lives and believes in me shall never die"? How does this affect our lives right now?

3. Why is it important not to panic or jump to conclusions when faced with a difficult situation? How might those kinds of reactions affect your walk?

Lesson in Our Society

When my wife gave birth to our son, she had complications that threatened her life. Her uterus ruptured, and she was losing a tremendous amount of blood. The doctors were doing everything they could, but the situation was looking worse by the minute. I had a choice to make: either put my hope solely in the impersonal practices of medical science or primarily trust in our personal Lord and Saviour Jesus Christ. When faced with tough circumstances, let us look to Jesus, the One who is able not only to raise us from the dead, but also to powerfully intervene in the dead circumstances of our lives.

Make It Happen

We have all been in situations that looked hopeless. Undoubtedly, we have been tempted to give up hope and count our losses. Think about some of the times that you have given up hope and the Lord came in and "resurrected" the situation. Think about the effect this had on you and what effect it should have on your faith.

Follow the Spirit

What God wants me to do:

_____

_____

Remember Your Thoughts

Special insights I have learned:

_____

_____

More Light on the Text

John 11:17–27

17 Then when Jesus came, he found that he had lain in the grave four days already.

Lazarus had been dead and buried for four days. In biblical times, the Jews believed that the spirit of the dead hovered over the body for three days and could still enter the deceased. Beyond the third day, there was no hope of the spirit reentering the body. Therefore, if Lazarus were brought back from death after four days, it would have been clear to everyone that a real miracle had taken place. Jesus told His disciples that Lazarus' illness was for the sake of the glory of God, that the Son of God may be glorified through it (John 11:4). Bringing Lazarus back from the dead after four days would bear powerful testimony to Jesus as a Life-Giver and demonstrate His power over death.

18 Now Bethany was nigh unto Jerusalem, about fifteen furlongs off: 19 And many of the Jews came to Martha and Mary, to comfort them concerning their brother.

Bethany (now called *El-azariyeh,* or "place of Lazarus") is approximately two miles east of

Jerusalem. This fact is significant because it shows how close Jesus was to Jerusalem. The nearness of Bethany to Jerusalem accounts for the large presence of Jews at the scene of this miracle. Jewish custom provided for a 30-day period of mourning. To console the bereaved during this period of mourning was considered a pious act among the Jews. Here, John draws attention to two things. First, Jesus' proximity to Jerusalem would have allowed Him to get to Lazarus' house within the first three days of his death. Second, because Bethany was so close to Jerusalem, there were many Jews present to witness the great miracle that was about to take place.

20 Then Martha, as soon as she heard that Jesus was coming, went and met him: but Mary sat still in the house.

Upon hearing of Jesus' arrival, Martha hastened to meet Him, while Mary sat in the house. The different responses of Martha and Mary may indicate their personality types: Martha was the outgoing activist and Mary was the contemplative type. It can also be said that because Martha was the older of the two sisters, it was her duty to go out to meet Jesus, while Mary stayed home to continue the mourning rituals with the other mourners.

21 Then said Martha unto Jesus, Lord, if thou hadst been here, my brother had not died. 22 But I know, that even now, whatsoever thou wilt ask of God, God will give it thee.

Martha's words were a confession of her faith in the Lord; they were not intended as a reproach of Jesus, but were the response of a person in great grief. It is probable that the sisters expressed the same ideas to one another as they awaited the coming of Jesus (11:32).

Martha believed that through Christ nothing was impossible with God. She firmly believed that Jesus would have saved Lazarus from death had He been present. But even now that Lazarus was dead, she believed that Jesus could still bring him back to life. The use of the phrase "thou wilt ask" (Gk. *aiteo*, **ahee-TEH-o**), which means "desire, call for, or

crave" implies that she hoped that Jesus would and that He should pray for an immediate resurrection in spite of Lazarus' decomposing body.

23 Jesus saith unto her, Thy brother shall rise again. 24 Martha saith unto him, I know that he shall rise again in the resurrection at the last day.

The phrase "shall rise" (Gk. *anistemi*, **an-IS-tay-mee**) means to "stand up." This statement has a double meaning. It relates to the recall of Lazarus from death to life that was about to take place, as well as to his final resurrection at the close of time. Martha seems to understand Jesus' words to mean that her brother will rise again during the last days. If she understood Jesus' words only in this sense, the assumption is that she had no thought of Lazarus' immediate resurrection (v. 22).

25 Jesus said unto her, I am the resurrection, and the life: he that believeth in me, though he were dead, yet shall he live: 26 And whosoever liveth and believeth in me shall never die. Believest thou this?

Like most Jews, Martha believed in the final resurrection of the dead and the coming rule of God. Therefore, when Jesus stated, "I am the resurrection and the life," He was saying that the promise of resurrection and life is not only some future event, but also was immediately available in the person. To Martha, this would have been a startlingly new revelation. Christ embodies that kingdom with all of its blessings for humankind for which Martha and her people hoped. The power to initiate eternal life and resurrection through which humankind may gain entry into life resides in Jesus. This revelation was both an assurance of resurrection to the eschatological kingdom of God and of life in the present through Him who is Life.

It was crucial that Martha grasp the full importance of what Christ was about to do for Lazarus. In Christ, death will never triumph over the believer. Moreover, Jesus was saying that the person who believes in Him, though he dies, yet will he live; and the person who lives and believes in Him will never die.

In verse 26, Jesus asks Martha a question that is

the basis for determining her faith and the faith of all believers. Jesus asked, "Believest thou this?" Jesus was asking Martha if she had the faith to believe what He said. Did she believe that He (Jesus) is the resurrection and that He has the power of life over death? That is, does she believe in His sovereignty? Unless a person believes in Jesus and His Word, the eternal life He offers cannot be found.

27 She saith unto him, Yea, Lord: I believe that thou art the Christ, the Son of God, which should come into the world.

Here, Martha's reply is a full-fledged confession of her faith in Jesus. In her confession, Martha states, "I believe" (Gk. *pisteuo,* **pist-YOO-o**), which means "to think to be true, be persuaded of, credit, or place confidence in." Martha was agreeing with Jesus' exposition about eternal life for those who believe in Him. Martha's magnificent confession contains some principal elements of the Person of Christ: He is the Christ (God's anointed One) and the Son of God.

Daily Bible Readings

M: Christ Offers Eternal Life
Jude 17–24
T: The Way of Righteousness
Proverbs 8:22–32
W: Jesus Delays
John 11:1–7
T: Jesus Goes to Bethany
John 11:8–16
F: I Am the Resurrection
John 11:17–27
S: Jesus Comforts Mary
John 11:28–37
S: Jesus Raises Lazarus
John 11:38–44

TEACHING TIPS

February 18
Bible Study Guide 12

1. Words You Should Know
A. Troubled (John 14:1) *tarasso* (Gk.)—To agitate, trouble, or cause commotion.

B. Mansions (v. 2) *mone* (Gk.)—Abodes or dwellings.

C. Works (v. 12) *ergon* (Gk.)—Denotes a deed or act.

2. Teacher Preparation
A. Pray and ask the Lord for insight while preparing to teach the lesson.

B. Read the Focal Verses in at least two or three different Bible translations.

C. Complete lesson 12 from the *Precepts For Living® Personal Study Guide* to enhance your knowledge of today's lesson.

3. Starting the Lesson
A. Begin the class with prayer, using the Lesson Aim as a guide.

B. Read the In Focus story aloud and ask the class to list ways God is leading them in their lives.

C. Write the At-A-Glance outline on the chalkboard.

D. Allow time for the class to silently read the Background section and The People, Places, and Times.

4. Getting into the Lesson
A. Divide the class into three groups, and assign each group an In Depth section and a Search the Scriptures question based on the At-A-Glance outline.

B. Reassemble the class, and ask a representative from each group to identify ways Jesus plays a central role in the life of the believer.

5. Relating the Lesson to Life
Initiate a class discussion based on the questions found in the Discuss the Meaning section.

6. Arousing Action
A. Encourage the class to follow through on the Make It Happen section in the upcoming week.

B. Instruct the class to read the Daily Bible Readings for class next week.

C. Close the class with prayer.

Worship Guide

For the Superintendent or Teacher
Theme: "I Am the Way, the Truth, and the Life"
Theme Song: "When We All Get to Heaven"
Scripture: John 14:2
Song: "Order My Steps"
Meditation: Heavenly Father, thank You that when I am troubled I can turn to You for guidance. Give me wisdom and boldness to share Your Word with others so that they, too, might come to know You. Amen.

"I AM THE WAY, THE TRUTH, AND THE LIFE"

Bible Background • JOHN 14:1–14
Printed Text • JOHN 14:1–14   Devotional Reading • EPHESIANS 4:17–24

Lesson Aim

By the end of the lesson, we will:

UNDERSTAND that Jesus is the only way we have access to heaven;

DEVELOP a sense of the importance of trusting Jesus completely; and

SEEK ways to trust the Lord in our everyday lives.

Keep in Mind

"Jesus saith unto him, I am the way, and the truth, and the life: No man cometh unto the Father, but by me" (John 14:6).

Focal Verses

John 14:1 Let not your heart be troubled: ye believe in God, believe also in me.

2 In my Father's house are many mansions: if it were not so, I would have told you. I go to prepare a place for you.

3 And if I go and prepare a place for you, I will come again, and receive you unto myself; that where I am, there ye may be also.

4 And whither I go ye know, and the way ye know.

5 Thomas saith unto him, Lord, we know not whither thou goest; and how can we know the way?

6 Jesus saith unto him, I am the way, the truth, and the life: no man cometh unto the Father, but by me.

7 If ye had known me, ye should have known my Father also: and from henceforth ye know him, and have seen him.

8 Philip saith unto him, Lord, shew us the Father, and it sufficeth us.

9 Jesus saith unto him, Have I been so long time with you, and yet hast thou not known me, Philip? he that hath seen me hath seen the Father; and how sayest

thou then, Shew us the Father?

10 Believest thou not that I am in the Father, and the Father in me? the words that I speak unto you I speak not of myself: but the Father that dwelleth in me, he doeth the works.

11 Believe me that I am in the Father, and the Father in me: or else believe me for the very works' sake.

12 Verily, verily, I say unto you, He that believeth on me, the works that I do shall he do also; and greater works than these shall he do; because I go unto my Father.

13 And whatsoever ye shall ask in my name, that will I do, that the Father may be glorified in the Son.

14 If ye shall ask any thing in my name, I will do it.

In Focus

"Mom, I have given up on Derek. I don't even talk to him about church anymore. I go to church, and he goes to the golf course."

Sharon was putting the finishing touches on her Sunday dinner while she listened to her daughter

Stacey complain about her husband's lack of church attendance.

"Stacey, do you remember when you first got married and you tried to cook Derek's favorite meal by yourself?"

"Boy, do I!" said Stacey as she laughed. "I must have called you over 10 times while you coached me through baked short ribs, fried corn, greens, and cornbread. I made a complete mess of the kitchen. In the end it still didn't taste like yours, but Derek never once complained. He ate the entire meal with a smile and even helped me clean up the kitchen afterward."

"Let me ask you this: How do you think that meal would have turned out if I had not guided you through it, or if I had given up on you and stopped answering your phone calls?" Sharon asked.

"OK, Mom, I get it. But Derek is hopeless. Whenever I say something about church, it ends in an argument."

"Stacey, you can't give up on Derek. Continue to voice your concerns, but do it in a loving way. Try inviting him to Bible class or some other church-sponsored function. Just like I guided you through preparing that meal, you must continue to pray and believe God will guide Derek onto the path of righteousness."

At some point in life, we all have been lost or needed direction and guidance. In today's lesson, Jesus makes it clear that He is the guiding light in the lives of His followers.

The People, Places, and Times

Philip. He was one of the 12 disciples whom Jesus called directly. Philip, along with Peter and Andrew, was from Bethsaida of Galilee (John 1:44).

Thomas. Also called Didymus, or "the twin," Thomas was one of Jesus' 12 disciples. He is the one who said that he would not believe that Jesus was resurrected from the dead unless he could touch the nail prints in Jesus' hands and the wound from the spear in His side.

Background

During His ministry, Jesus repeatedly prepared the disciples for His approaching suffering and death. In John 13, Jesus tells the disciples that one of them would betray Him (v. 21). At the same time, He also informs the disciples that He will soon be leaving them and that they could not follow Him (v. 33). Undoubtedly, these things disturbed the disciples. When Peter asks Jesus where He was going, Jesus responds, "Where I am going you cannot follow me now, but you will follow afterward" (v. 36, ESV). It is not difficult to see why the disciples would have been troubled. They were coming to grips with the fact that the One they had given up everything to follow was now telling them that He was about to leave them to go to a place where they could not follow. It must have seemed as if they were losing the very reason for which they had existed for the past three years.

At-A-Glance

1. Jesus, the Way to Comfort (John 14:1–4)
2. Jesus, the Way to the Father (vv. 5–11)
3. Jesus, the Way to Powerful Living (vv. 12–14)

In Depth

1. Jesus, the Way to Comfort (John 14:1–4)

We've already seen in John 13 that Jesus told His disciples of His approaching suffering and departure. Now, He aims to calm the turmoil raging in their hearts. Jesus encourages them by telling them, "Let not your hearts be troubled" (14:1). Jesus' news apparently throws the disciples' minds into disarray and sends them into a spiritual tailspin, but Jesus provides the key that will lead them out of their mental anguish. He points to Himself as the basis for sustaining peace in the midst of the storm of difficult circumstances by telling them, if "you believe in God, believe also in Me" (v. 1, NKJV). Even though He will no longer be present with the disciples physically, He assures them that where He is going, He is preparing a place for them. This provides great comfort, not only for the apostles, but also for us. Even though Jesus no longer walks the earth in bodily form, we have His promise that He is with us "even to the end of the age" (Matthew 28:20, NKJV) and that He still has the power to calm the storms that rage in our lives. In our times of anxiety and uncertainty, we are directed to place our faith not in our own ingenuity, wit, or financial savvy, but in Jesus Christ the sovereign Lord, who is in control of all the circumstances of our lives.

2. Jesus, the Way to the Father (vv. 5–11)

We live in a religiously pluralistic society. The overarching theme preached from the pulpits of the politically correct clergy is tolerance. To some, it is considered nothing short of arrogance to claim that a religion has the exclusive right to the truth. The mainstream view—that all religions worship the same God—is best expressed in a statement made by nineteenth-century Indian saint, Sri Ramakrishna: "God has made different religions to suit different aspirations, times, and countries. All doctrines are only so many paths, but a path is by no means God Himself. Indeed, one can reach God if one follows any of the paths with wholehearted devotion."

However, what Ramakrishna expresses is in direct opposition to what Jesus Himself says: "I am the way, the truth, and the life: no man cometh unto the Father but by me" (v. 6). Jesus declares that there are not many ways to God, but only one way. Therefore, no matter how sincere one is in following a particular path, if it is not the one true path, it will ultimately lead to a dead end.

Jesus, unlike Ramakrishna, does not point His followers to a path but to a person, namely, Himself: "I am the way." Jesus is not claiming to have uncovered some hidden truth. He is not telling His disciples, "I have experienced enlightenment and now I am able to point you in the direction you must travel." He is claiming something much stronger than that. Jesus declares, "Anyone who has seen me has seen the Father" (v. 9, NIV). Jesus reveals the character and personality of God to us, just as John writes earlier in chapter 1, "No one has seen God at any time. The only begotten Son, who is in the bosom of the Father, He has declared Him" (John 1:18, NKJV). We are to place faith in Christ as the way to the Father because it is only through Him that we can know the Father.

3. Jesus, the Way to Powerful Living (vv. 12–14)

In verses 12–14, Christ notifies His disciples that placing their faith in Him will cause them to lead lives that exhibit the power of God. He says, "He who believes in Me, the works that I do he will do also; and greater works than these he will do, because I go to My Father" (v. 12, NKJV). It is important to note that Jesus says that the works testified of His relationship with the Father: "Believe Me that I am in the Father and the Father in Me, or else believe Me for the sake of the works themselves" (v. 11, NKJV). These were not gratuitous or pointless displays of power, but a demonstration of His authenticity as the Son of God. Furthermore, Jesus lets us know that it is the Father

who is at work through Him: "The words that I speak to you I do not speak on My own authority; but the Father who dwells in Me does the works" (v. 10, NKJV).

Placing all our trust in Jesus produces two results. First, faith in Christ yields fruitful lives that both demonstrate our relationship with Him and glorify the Father. "This is to my Father's glory, that you bear much fruit, showing yourselves to be my disciples" (John 15:8, NIV). Christ comes to give us "abundant life," promising to do anything we ask in His name, to the glory of the Father. Of course, this is not a blank check given to us with which we can expect to receive all of our wildest desires. What it means to "ask in Christ's name" is made clearer in John 15: "If you abide in me, and my words abide in you, ask whatever you wish, and it will be done for you" (v. 7, ESV). When we ask for things in Jesus' name, we are to ask for things that are consistent with His character and purpose. Putting all our trust in Christ guarantees that we will experience power-filled lives because He aims to glorify His Father's name.

Second, placing faith in Christ gives us the power we need to live out the Christian life. Before ascending into heaven, Jesus delivers a parting promise to His disciples: "But you will receive power when the Holy Spirit comes on you; and you will be my witnesses in Jerusalem, and in all Judea and Samaria, and to the ends of the earth" (Acts 1:8, NIV). The only way we can live powerful lives that reflect Christ's presence is by being indwelt with the Holy Spirit. It is the Holy Spirit who gives us power to live the Christian life, and it is only accessible through faith in Christ.

Sources

Smith, Huston. *The World's Religions.* San Francisco: Harper, 1991.

Tenney, Merrill C. *The Expositor's Bible Commentary.* Edited by Frank E. Gaebelein. Grand Rapids, Mich.: Zondervan Publishing, 1981.

Search the Scriptures

1. How did Jesus tell the disciples to deal with anxiety in their hearts (John 14:1)?

2. What do you think Jesus' point was in saying there are many rooms in the Father's house (v. 2)?

3. According to Jesus, how can we know the Father (vv. 6–7)?

4. What does it mean to "ask in Jesus' name" (vv. 13–14; 15:7)?

Discuss the Meaning

1. Suppose you are having a conversation with someone and he or she tells you, "I believe all religions worship the same God. It's just that each one does it in its own way." How would you respond?

2. If Jesus shows the Father to us, what do we know about God's character in Old Testament days? How does this affect our understanding of God when we read Old Testament passages?

3. What kind of "greater works" do you think Jesus meant in verse 12? And how do you know when you are asking for something in Jesus' name?

Lesson in Our Society

In our society, many believe science is the only way by which we can access the truth about the world around us. Many of our scientists believe that faith is a superstitious concept embraced by those who are weak. In what ways does Jesus' declaration, "I am the way, the truth, and the life" challenge that notion? What are some ways that we can share with our family, neighbors, and coworkers the importance of this declaration?

Make It Happen

This week, share with someone that Jesus is the only way to a relationship with God and that He wants to reconcile him or her to God. Also, pray that God will give you the faith to trust Him and allow Him to guide you throughout your everyday life.

Follow the Spirit

What God wants me to do:

_____

_____

Remember Your Thoughts

Special insights I have learned:

_____

_____

More Light on the Text
John 14:1–14

1 Let not your heart be troubled: ye believe in God, believe also in me.

In his letter to the Romans, the apostle Paul says, "Whatsoever is not of faith is sin." Many have included worry in this list to counter those who treat worry as if it falls somehow harmlessly between sin and virtue. Jesus emphasizes this truth by pointing to faith as the relief or antidote for worry or anxiety though He does not treat worry as sin. Here, Jesus tells the disciples not to let their hearts become troubled. In Greek, the word "troubled" is *tarasso* (**tar-AS-so**), and it means "to agitate, disquiet, or stir up."

In the context of this passage, Jesus ushers in faith as a comfort to relieve the anxious disciples, much like a welcome medicine for a nagging illness or parental reassurance for a child's nightmare. In this scenario, the disciples' concern was well founded, since they had just learned that one would betray Jesus, that one would deny Him, and that they couldn't go with Him wherever it was He was going (John 13). Jesus' own heart was "troubled" when He announced that one would betray Him (13:34). It is remarkable that Jesus ministered to them with compassion in spite of the fact that His much more serious anguish was now only hours away.

Peter must have been the most visibly shocked to learn he would deny Jesus, since Jesus immediately responded to his concern with His declaration that Peter would be disloyal (13:38). Jesus immediately follows this with His words of comfort. When our hearts are troubled, when things look their worst, our best response is faith or belief in our Lord; nothing less will open the door to His peace and comfort (Psalm 42:5). Nothing is more important than guarding our hearts (Proverbs 4:23; 1 Corinthians 16:13–14; 2 Peter 3:17), but at the same time, we as believers have good reason to take courage, unlike those without the hope that is ours.

2 In my Father's house are many mansions: if it were not so, I would have told you. I go to prepare a place for you.

The hope of a home in heaven was given as a source of comfort, not only for the disciples, but also for countless believers through the ages, confronting all the multiplied anxieties they as individuals and the church as a whole would face. Jesus' intent was to minister comfort in the face of potentially overwhelming distress; His response (begun in verse 1) was thorough and multifaceted. Added to faith in God and Himself was the reminder of the disciples' (and our) final reward. Here, Jesus reassures them that He would not deceive them by promising them something that was so grand but wasn't the truth. Along with having our name written in the book of life (Isaiah 62:2; Revelation 2:17; 3:12; 21:27), everything becomes new in Christ (2 Corinthians 5:17), including our coming new home in God's kingdom.

3 And if I go and prepare a place for you, I will come again, and receive you unto myself; that where I am, there ye may be also.

This isn't an impersonal second coming to which Jesus refers; He won't be sending a butler, an angel, or anyone else to escort us to our heavenly home, but will come Himself and receive us personally (1 Thessalonians 4:17). The phrase "I will come" is a common, single word in Greek (*erchomai*, **ER-khom-ahee**) and refers to individuals arriving or returning, appearing or making an appearance. The emphasis is on "again," just as being born is common but being born "again" is noteworthy (John 3:3).

As many have said, "Heaven is where Jesus is, and it wouldn't be heaven without Him" (cf. John 17:24). Indeed, heaven would be sufficient if for no other reason than to be with Him. Wherever He is should be where we want to be; wherever He is not should be the place to avoid at all costs. We should all desire to go to heaven, the home of the King of kings and Lord of lords, the Creator of the universe—being ushered by Christ at His Second Coming to God's eternal home will be glorious beyond words (Luke 22:30; Revelation 21).

4 And whither I go ye know, and the way ye know.

Matthew Henry said, "As the resurrection of Christ is the assurance of our resurrection, so his ascension, victory, and glory, are an assurance of ours." Jesus is trying to remind His disciples that they already know in their hearts where He is going and how to get there. Surely this would be one of the things the Comforter would continue to teach them after Jesus' departure (cf. John 14:26).

5 Thomas saith unto him, Lord, we know not whither thou goest; and how can we know the way?

With childlike innocence, Thomas asks a question to which he already knew the answer. Perhaps Thomas's response is an illustration of our own level of spiritual awareness, in reality knowing more than we think we do and being less in the dark than we believe we are at times. The disciples had received a full load of bad news, and, perhaps, had they had more time to digest Jesus' discourse, they might have been less reactive. In any case, Jesus doesn't entrust the matter to their faulty memories and previous knowledge, but continues to explain, just to be certain they do in fact know what they need to know.

6 Jesus saith unto him, I am the way, the truth, and the life: no man cometh unto the Father, but by me.

The most common reading of this verse puts the emphasis on the key words "way" (Gk. *hodos*, **hod-OS**) "truth" (Gk. *aletheia*, **al-AY-thia**), and "life" (Gk. *zoe*, **dzo-AY**). This statement was in response to Thomas's question—a question the disciples should have been able to answer. Surely the emphasis was on the word "I" at the beginning of the sentence. *I* am the way; *I* am the truth; *I* am the life: no man cometh unto the Father, but by *ME*. One can imagine Jesus stopping just short of exasperation; one can see Him explicitly trying to hammer home His point to those closest to Him, those who soon would be without Him, those who would need to teach others about Him, and those who still did not fully understand.

Scripture states that there are two gates and two ways, and also that Jesus is the gate for the sheep and the door (John 10:7, 9). There is a straight gate and a narrow way that leads to life, and a wide gate and a broad way that leads to destruction (Matthew 7:13).

Acts talks about the way of salvation, the way of God, and the Way as the early church had been called (16:17; 18:26; 24:14). By His blood, Jesus opened up for us the "new and living way" (Hebrews 10:20). Even the Old Testament speaks of there being only one way: "ask for the old paths, where is the good way, and walk therein, and ye shall find rest for your souls" (Jeremiah 6:16). In Greek, the word "way" is *hodos* (**ho-DOS**) and refers to a traveler's way or a way of thinking, feeling, and deciding; it is used over 100 times in the New Testament and normally has the aforementioned common interpretation—until Jesus says He is *THE* way.

John clearly establishes that the Word is God (1:1), the Word became flesh (1:14), and the Word is truth (17:17). "Thy word is true from the beginning" (Psalm 119:160). Jesus completes the circle by stating that He is the truth and is one with God (John 10:30); other writers are more explicit regarding His deity (Colossians 2:9; Philippians 2:6; 1 John 5:20). It is truth that sets us free (John 8:32) and that leads us to salvation (Ephesians 1:13). Even His critics know that, as truth, Jesus would never deceive anyone (Luke 20:21). However, people are able to deceive themselves (1 John 1:8). As the embodiment of truth, Jesus stands in perfect contrast to the Devil, in whom there is no truth (John 8:44). In Greek, the word "truth" is *aletheia* (**al-AY-thi-a**) and is used in a variety of contexts, including references to personal excellence and to truth pertaining to God. Again, it is a common word that is used in these ways over 100 times in the New Testament—until Jesus says He is THE truth.

Only because of Christ, we are "dead indeed unto sin, but alive unto God" (Romans 6:11); likewise, He is the only cure for sin (Romans 6:23). No one can ever accuse Jesus of having made mediocre claims. Just in John's gospel alone, preceding His ultimate statement in 14:6, Jesus similarly stated that He was the Bread of Life (6:35); that He came to give life, and life more abundantly (10:10); that He gives life to His sheep (10:28); and that He is the Resurrection and the Life (11:25). In the Greek, the word "life" is *zoe,* the meaning of which includes the absolute full-ness of life. Like the words "way" and "truth," "life" is a common word used well over a 100 times in the New Testament—until Jesus says He is THE life.

The latter part of verse 6 is what is known as an "exceptive statement," meaning "all and only." All may come to the Father through Jesus, and only those coming through Jesus may come to the Father. No matter how politically incorrect His statements may seem, Jesus was, is, and always will be the only way to God the Father and life everlasting.

7 If ye had known me, ye should have known my Father also: and from henceforth ye know him, and have seen him.

Jesus' words are a not-so-subtle rebuke of the disciples for their lack of awareness of just who had been with them for so long. Regardless of the disciples' shortsightedness, Jesus patiently continues to explain that in seeing and knowing Him, they have already seen and known the Father. Jesus immediately extends comfort in His reassurance that they no longer need to be unaware of the Father. As Jesus stated in John 10:30, He and the Father are one. Jesus reveals God to us. The disciples' common awakening experience, which came soon enough and was similar in essence for all of them, is captured by the apostle Paul's pen: "God hath shined in our hearts, to give the light of the knowledge of the glory of God in the face of Jesus Christ" (2 Corinthians 4:6; cf. 4:4; Colossians 1:15). God does this by sending the Holy Spirit after Jesus ascended to heaven.

8 Philip saith unto him, Lord, shew us the Father, and it sufficeth us. 9 Jesus saith unto him, Have I been so long time with you, and yet hast thou not known me, Philip? he that hath seen me hath seen the Father; and how sayest thou then, Shew us the Father? 10 Believest thou not that I am in the Father, and the Father in me? the words that I speak unto you I speak not of myself: but the Father that dwelleth in me, he doeth the works.

Philip wanted a sign. One cannot help but empathize with Philip, since he sounds like so many today who, no matter how much they know or are told, insist on saying, "If I could just see God once, that would settle it for me. If I could witness a real miracle, then I'd become a believer. Why can't God show His face for one split second?" Just like Philip, modern skeptics ignore what is before them. In Philip's case, it was the living Jesus, God in the flesh, worker of miracles, standing before him and talking to him. Yet he didn't understand what he was hearing. In this light, Jesus' response in verse 9 is both understandable and appropriate.

Upon closer examination, it seems evident that more of Jesus' exasperation is showing. Jesus is, in effect, asking Philip, "How could you not know after all this time? Haven't you been paying attention at all? Don't you get it? If you've seen Me, you've seen the Father. How can you look right at Me and ask to see the Father?"

In verse 10, Jesus' response continues: "Philip, do you really not comprehend that I am in the Father, and the Father is in Me. The Father lives in Me. It is He who does the works I do" (paraphrased). When we read these passages consecutively, we see the patient Teacher gently guiding His future apostles, who soon will faithfully carry out His Great Commission in the four corners of the world.

11 Believe me that I am in the Father, and the Father in me: or else believe me for the very works' sake.

Although Jesus' conversation is in response to questions from Thomas and Philip, all the disciples are present and Jesus is addressing all of them in His typical teaching fashion. In this passage, Jesus continues in the same "read-my-lips" tone: "Philip—all of you—it is imperative that you listen very closely and hear me well. Again, I repeat, I am in the Father and the Father in Me." It is no wonder that the early church continued to struggle with the essence of Jesus' words. One can hardly imagine how He could have communicated His deity any more clearly than He did. There were many struggles about Jesus' divinity and humanity through the fifth century, when the Council of Chalcedon finally set the boundaries for orthodox doctrine about the union of divine and human natures in Christ. Today, there are still people who have no problem with Jesus' humanity but struggle greatly with His deity, and sects like the Jehovah's Witnesses, who deny Christ's divinity.

12 Verily, verily, I say unto you, He that believeth on me, the works that I do shall he do also; and greater works than these shall he do; because I go unto my Father.

At this point, Jesus moves on to a different subject, one of many He would address on that auspicious night. One has to wonder if the disciples grasped the fact that the "greater works" to which Jesus referred would not be possible if He had stayed with them when the Holy Spirit came. He also offered them a multilayered message of comfort and courage regarding His impending death and subsequent departure. His message was entirely about comfort and assurances and taking heart for the great things that awaited them. These 11 men—the original pillars of the faith and the architects of the New Testament church—needed at that moment to hear some words of encouragement, reassurance, and hope from their departing Master.

13 And whatsoever ye shall ask in my name, that will I do, that the Father may be glorified in the Son.

Jesus would deny these particular men nothing; He left in their charge the greatest task ever given any human, and He knew what they would need in order to accomplish the work He had given them. Most have heard some preacher at some time try to interpret this as some kind of mysterious combination or formula by implying or claiming that all you have to do is say all the right words and include all the potential caveats and specific disclaimers, and God is almost obliged to accommodate you. Unfortunately, many in the church have a gross misconception of what it means to abide in Christ, which impairs their understanding of how things work in God's kingdom.

When we abide in Christ, His power flows through us to accomplish His purposes in the world. The Holy Spirit is the agent, sent by the resurrected Christ, and we are the vehicles through which He flows. It is not our confession or religious invocation that garners the forces of heaven to do our bidding. It is only when our hearts are surrendered, when we are living in and for God, when our will is attuned to His, and when our prayers are for His purposes, in His name, and for His glory that He will answer, even beyond all we ask or think (Ephesians 3:20).

14 If ye shall ask any thing in my name, I will do it.
Here we find some of the most poignant parting words known to mankind. Jesus, the Saviour, is preparing for His death, burial, and resurrection. He is equipping His disciples with the most important things they will need to know as they carry out His work without His physical presence. The reiteration of verse 13 must be heard in the context of the whole passage. This kind of repetitive reassurance is the type one gives a loved one who needs comfort. We tend to say things more than once when we want someone to genuinely believe us, especially if there is an impending separation.

Yes, when our hearts become one heart like that of the disciples (v. 1), when our faith is sure and steady, when our will is surrendered to Christ, and when our purpose is completely for God's glory, most certainly we, too, can believe like the disciples that our prayers will be answered.

Sources
Henry, Matthew. *Commentary on the Whole Bible.* http://www.ccel.org/h/henry/mhc 2MHC43014.HTM

Daily Bible Readings

M: A New and Living Way
Hebrews 10:19–23
T: Jesus Testifies to the Truth
John 18:33–40
W: Jesus Has Brought Life
2 Timothy 1:8–14
T: Turn from Darkness
Ephesians 4:17–24
F: Walking in the Truth
3 John 2–8
S: Jesus Is the Way
John 14:1–7
S: The Son Reveals the Father
John 14:8–14

TEACHING TIPS

February 25
Bible Study Guide 13

1. Words You Should Know

A. Vine (John 15:1) *ampelos* (Gk.)—A coil or support, which here refers to Jesus as the support of those who follow Him.

B. Husbandman (v. 1) *georgos* (Gk.)—A farmer or gardener; refers to God, who cares for the branches (i.e., the followers of His Son, Jesus).

C. Branch (v. 2) *klema* (Gk.)—A twig or bough; refers to a follower of Jesus Christ.

2. Teacher Preparation

A. Ask God to be with you as you prepare to teach the lesson.

B. Study the Focal Verses in several different Bible translations, paying attention to the Lesson Aim objectives.

C. Pray for the students in your class, asking God to open their hearts to the teaching.

D. To gain further insight, answer and study the questions taken from lesson 13 in the *Precepts For Living® Personal Study Guide* for the lesson.

3. Starting the Lesson

A. Ask the students to share their Make It Happen assignment from last week. Briefly discuss their responses.

B. Concentrate on the Lesson Aim as you begin the lesson with prayer.

C. Instruct the students to read the Keep in Mind verse in unison.

D. Read the In Focus story aloud to the class and ask the students to explain the difference between a vine and a branch.

4. Getting into the Lesson

A. Ask volunteers to read The People, Places, and Times and the Background section.

B. Write the At-A-Glance outline on the board.

C. Divide the students into four groups according to the At-A-Glance outline. Then assign each group an In Depth topic to read and discuss within their group.

D. Reassemble the class and have one volunteer from each group to share the In Depth topic with the rest of the class.

5. Relating the Lesson to Life

A. Spend time answering the questions in the Search the Scriptures and Discuss the Meaning sections.

B. After the discussion, ask each student to elaborate on what fruit they are bearing in their lives as a result of being connected to the vine of Christ?

C. Have the students discuss the distinction between the two kinds of pruning: (1) separating, and (2) cutting back branches.

6. Arousing Action

A. Read the Lesson in Our Society section to the class. Ask each student how he or she may be fruitful.

B. Direct the students to the Make It Happen section, and discuss their responses.

C. Remind the students to read the Daily Bible Readings in preparation for the lesson next week.

D. Ask if there are any prayer requests, then end the lesson with prayer.

Worship Guide

For the Superintendent or Teacher
Theme: I Am the True Vine
Theme Song: "What a Friend We Have in Jesus"
Scripture: Isaiah 5:1–7
Song: "Where He Leads Me"
Meditation: Lord, teach me to obey Your will, forgive others as You have forgiven me, and love others with a sacrificial spirit. Amen.

I AM THE TRUE VINE

Bible Background • JOHN 15:1–17
Printed Text • JOHN 15:1–17   Devotional Reading • PSALM 1

Lesson Aim

By the end of the lesson, we will:

UNDERSTAND that the sole source of fruitfulness is Jesus Christ;

DESIRE to be intimately connected to Jesus and other believers in order to produce the fruit God expects; and

DECIDE to pursue an intimate relationship with Jesus through study of His Word, prayer, and obedience to His directives.

Keep in Mind

"I am the vine, ye are the branches: He that abideth in me, and I in him, the same bringeth forth much fruit: for without me ye can do nothing" (John 15:5).

Focal Verses

John 15:1 I am the true vine, and my Father is the husbandman.

2 Every branch in me that beareth not fruit he taketh away: and every branch that beareth fruit, he purgeth it, that it may bring forth more fruit.

3 Now ye are clean through the word which I have spoken unto you.

4 Abide in me, and I in you. As the branch cannot bear fruit of itself, except it abide in the vine; no more can ye, except ye abide in me.

5 I am the vine, ye are the branches: He that abideth in me, and I in him, the same bringeth forth much fruit: for without me ye can do nothing.

6 If a man abide not in me, he is cast forth as a branch, and is withered; and men gather them, and cast them into the fire, and they are burned.

7 If ye abide in me, and my words abide in you, ye shall ask what ye will, and it shall be done unto you.

8 Herein is my Father glorified, that ye bear much fruit; so shall ye be my disciples.

9 As the Father hath loved me, so have I loved you: continue ye in my love.

10 If ye keep my commandments, ye shall abide in my love; even as I have kept my Father's commandments, and abide in his love.

11 These things have I spoken unto you, that my joy might remain in you, and that your joy might be full.

12 This is my commandment, That ye love one another, as I have loved you.

13 Greater love hath no man than this, that a man lay down his life for his friends.

14 Ye are my friends, if ye do whatsoever I command you.

15 Henceforth I call you not servants; for the servant knoweth not what his lord doeth: but I have called you friends; for all things that I have heard of my Father I have made known unto you.

16 Ye have not chosen me, but I have chosen you, and ordained you, that ye should go and bring forth fruit, and that your fruit should remain: that whatsoever ye shall ask of the Father in my name, he may give it you.

17 These things I command you, that ye love one another.

In Focus

When Kim had accepted Jesus Christ as her personal Saviour three years earlier, she grew in her newfound faith. She attended church services regularly, Bible study on Wednesday nights, and even Sunday School—all of which was helping her in understanding God's Word. Plus, she had a very viable prayer life, seeking God the first thing each morning and closing her day in His presence. Then, life hit her right in the face one day. Her mom went home to be with the Lord.

Over the months, Kim just felt frayed, forsaken, lonely, and so lost without her mom. She often tried to get back into Bible study, but her heart just wasn't in it. Even her prayers seemed to go no further than the ceiling. If the truth be known, Kim even felt forsaken by God. She felt a sorrowful disconnect from the Saviour whom she had grown to love and respect.

What can Kim do to reconnect to the "true vine"—the One who can supply her every need? Today's lesson will help you to understand and answer that question.

The People, Places, and Times

Fruitfulness. Jesus knew that His physical presence with the disciples would soon end. He also knew that these men would need a clear understanding of their position with God and of what was expected of them. So Jesus consciously filled their minds with pictures and ideas to help them survive the days to come. These same lessons Jesus so patiently taught His disciples also provided vital resources for preparing future generations of disciples to grow in their faith.

Background

Jesus is just a few hours away from the Cross, and He and His disciples are walking through a vineyard. He shares a profound message with them in parallelism: the Father is the vinedresser (the owner of the vineyard); He [Jesus] is the vine (the trunk of the grapevine); and believers are the branches (the part that produces fruit). The branches cannot live or produce unless connected to the vine. The vinedresser sees that the branches are taken care of and produce fruit. Similarly, the vinedresser prunes the branches that bear fruit so that they will produce even more. Successful gardeners know that pruning a vine's branches increases its fruit-bearing capabilities. Each spring, vinedressers cut back each vine to its root to enhance its fruitfulness. Likewise, sincere believers (the fruitful branches) must be "pruned," meaning that God must sometimes discipline us to strengthen our character and faith. But branches that don't bear fruit are "cut off" at the trunk and are completely discarded because they are worthless and often infect the rest of the plant.

In the body of Christ, there is only one secure connection to God—Jesus Christ. Anything outside of Him is false and of no benefit. Believers keep the connection secure through faith in the risen Christ, the study and application of His Word, communication in prayer, and obedience to His directives. As a result, the nourishment of His Word that develops in the lives of believers produces fruit that brings God glory. Likewise, believers' connections to one another are solely dependent on each individual's connection to Jesus, the True Vine.

At-A-Glance

1. Jesus, the Vine (John 15:1–3)
2. Conditions for Fruit-bearing (vv. 4–8)
3. Abiding in Love (vv. 9–11)
4. I Am a Friend of God (vv. 12–17)

In Depth

1. Jesus, the Vine (John 15:1–3)

The grapevine is an amazing plant; a single vine bears many grapes. In the Old Testament, the vine was symbolic of Israel, and the grapes (i.e., fruit) symbolized Israel's fruitfulness in doing God's work on Earth. The prophets wrote of Israel as God's vineyard, carefully planted and cared for (Isaiah 5:1–5). In this discourse, John uses the metaphor of the vine and its branches to show the interconnection between the disciples and Jesus, as well as their connection with one another. As the "husbandman," the Father exercises just as much care for the branches as He does the vine. The fruitful branches are synonymous with true believers who, by their living union with Christ, are tenderly and lovingly cared for to produce more fruit. But sometimes the vine yields only rotten fruit. As a result, the Father cuts off every branch that is unproductive.

If believers are "fruit-bearing branches," what would cause a believer to be unproductive (i.e., no longer bear fruit) or an ineffective witness? In nature, there are several things that render the branches of a vine incapable of bearing fruit, includ-

"Every branch in me that beareth not fruit he taketh away: and every branch that beareth fruit, he purgeth it , that it may bring forth more fruit" (John 15:2).

ing disease or old age—both of which cause disconnection from the vine. Likewise, one's spiritual life can become barren and unfruitful, causing disconnection from the vine (Jesus), by not studying God's Word, not witnessing, or an undeveloped prayer life (2 Peter 1:8). When this happens, the husbandman (God) will remove the unproductive branch, who is an ineffective witness. But those branches (believers) that have been pruned and have allowed the Word of God to purge (or cleanse) them, become more productive (fruitful) Christians, and Jesus promises to abide with them.

2. Conditions for Fruit-bearing (vv. 4–8)

The word "abide" refers to fellowship and occurs no less than 15 times in the first 10 verses of John 15. Clearly, then, the Master considered fellowship a matter of great importance. Here Jesus exhorts His

disciples to abide in Him. Because Jesus knew of His impending departure, He continues to use the "branch and vine" metaphor to teach the importance of faithfulness to His disciples.

A branch can survive and produce green foliage after it has been severed from the vine. However, it cannot produce fruit unless it is connected to the root. Jesus was saying that just as He depends on His Father, believers need to abide or remain in Him (Jesus) to stay connected to the root. Abiding, for the disciples and for all believers today, means to make a constant, moment-by-moment decision to depend on Christ. And we must not be passive— believers can't just sit and "remain" until they die. Instead, we must be active.

A vine that produces much fruit glorifies God. True disciples, then, do more than just believe what Jesus says, they let Jesus' words abide in them. When a believer abides in Christ and Christ's Word abides in him, that person's prayers will be answered (v. 7). This does not mean that all prayers are granted. In order to pray and get results, a person must remain in Christ. When we remain in Him, our thoughts and desires conform to His, and we can pray "in Jesus' name," knowing that our requests please God. We can be assured, then, that whatever we ask will be done when we come into a right relationship with God and begin to "bear much fruit" in our lives.

3. Abiding in Love (vv. 9–11)

Here we learn that the basis for "abiding" with Jesus is the love that God and Jesus share with each other. Jesus, then, likens His love for the disciples to the type of love He has for His Father. The highest expression of Jesus' love was expressed on the Cross: He loved us enough to give His life for us. Although we have not been called to die for one another, we must learn to love each other sacrificially as Jesus loved us.

In verse 10, Jesus comes to the essence of His message to the disciples: The only way the disciples (or any believer) will continue to abide in God's love is if they, like Him, practice obedience and keep His Father's commandments. Jesus is delighted to do the will of the Father. Jesus tells us that the basis of Christian joy can be found only in Christ: "and truly our fellowship is with the Father, and with His Son Jesus Christ. And these things we write unto you, that your joy may be full" (1 John 1:3–4). We, too, can have joy by expressing our love toward others by serving, encouraging, and giving of our time to others.

4. I Am a Friend of God (vv. 12–17)

Jesus commanded love. He required His disciples to make peace with one another, to place the interests of others above their own, and to solve their differences quickly. To live as a "branch on the vine" meant that one had to wholeheartedly commit to the work of obeying God's commandments, bearing fruit, and spreading the Gospel.

Jesus called the disciples His friends. However, becoming Jesus' friend was not without a condition: they had to obey His commandments. Jesus told the disciples everything He had heard from His Father. He expected them to lay down their lives if necessary (v. 14). If they followed this command, they would no longer be servants, but friends of God. What an awesome thing to be chosen as a friend of God! Once again, we see Jesus referring to God's own unselfish sacrifice in sending His Son to die on the Cross (John 3:16). Jesus' calling the disciples His friends showed that He trusted them, and that He expected them to spread the Gospel and produce fruit for God's kingdom.

Jesus chose and ordained the disciples. He chose them for a mission, and His Father would answer their requests in order to accomplish that mission. Still today, the Lord chooses every believer to be a branch on the vine—a branch that bears fruit that will last.

Finally, Jesus once again reiterates the central theme of this discourse: "love one another" (v. 17). The disciples must love each other because they would take Jesus' message to a world that despised them. He knew that setting this high standard was essential to preserving the unity of the church. If He commanded it, believers would accept and live out this standard.

Search the Scriptures

1. How does Jesus distinguish between productive and nonproductive followers (John 15:2)?

2. How may we glorify God (v. 8)?

3. What does Jesus promise us when we live in Him (v. 11)?

4. What does Jesus command (v. 17)?

Discuss the Meaning

1. Discuss the symbolism of the vine and the branches (John 15:1–2).

2. Discuss the meaning of bearing "much fruit" (v. 8). Reflect on the importance of living a fruitful life in Christ.

3. How does knowing God's plan for His people change your life?

Lesson in Our Society

In today's society, many Christians believe that obeying God begins and ends with going to church. While God commands us to meet with the "body," He expects us to continue to walk in His light daily. A part of that walk should include spreading the Gospel so that nonbelievers may be saved and weak Christians may be strengthened. In order to accomplish this task we must stay connected to Jesus Christ, the True Vine. When we live by the philosophy of "an eye for an eye" rather than "turn the other cheek," we cut off the support and guidance that God so desperately wants to lend. We must develop a spirit of forgiveness and learn to love one another. We must learn to accept each other's differences without prejudice. We must be actively sharing, reaching out, and building godly relationships that glorify our Father and bear fruit for God's kingdom.

Make It Happen

Think about your own fruitfulness. Pray that God would fill you with the Holy Spirit and enable you to do His will. Then go out and share God's command to love one another with at least three people this week. Explain to them that loving one another comes in many forms: helping, listening, encouraging, and giving. Next week, be prepared to share your efforts with the class.

Follow the Spirit

What God wants me to do:

_____

_____

Remember Your Thoughts

Special insights I have learned:

_____

_____

More Light on the Text
John 15:1–17

The setting is the Passover Feast, or Last Supper; the apostles have just received the news about Jesus' impending death (John 13:33, 36). He encourages them not to be discouraged; His solution is for them to trust God and Himself (14:1). He reminds them of the place He is going to prepare for them, and that He will return to take them there (14:2–3). He promises to send the Comforter, the Holy Spirit, and declares that He would leave His peace with them (14:26–27). Jesus presents His last teaching in chapter 15.

1 I am the true vine, and my Father is the husbandman.

This is the eighth of Jesus' self-referenced "I am" statements, the complete list of which is found only in John's gospel. It is interesting to note that Jesus chose the word "true" in tandem with "vine" in speaking to people intimately familiar with farming language and imagery. The odd language clearly implies that "true" is in contrast to all that is false or untrue. Jesus is the only "true vine" in a world of false or untrue vines. Indeed, the Word often warns of false prophets and teachers (Matthew 7:15; Mark 13:22; 1 John 4:1).

Various versions of Scripture use synonyms for "husbandman," including "vinedresser," "gardener," and "farmer" (2 Timothy 2:6; James 5:7). All are correct interpretations of the Greek word *georgos* (**gheh-ore-GOS**), which can also mean "tiller of the soil." Christ is saying that when God is the Gardener, the garden could not be in better hands or better tended. Also implied is that the Master Gardener will create the ultimate garden with infinite variety and delicacy of fruit, all of which is produced through and because of His only Son, the one true vine.

2 Every branch in me that beareth not fruit he taketh away: and every branch that beareth fruit, he purgeth it, that it may bring forth more fruit.

Some controversy exists in the interpretation of "taketh away" (Gk. *airo*, **AH-ee-ro**), and also of "purgeth" (Gk. *kathairo*, **kath-AH-ee-ro**). The two words are similar enough to constitute a play on words or a rhyme, clearly lost in translation. The latter word, from which we get the word "catharsis," is used only twice in the New Testament (Hebrews 10:2). One of the possible meanings of *airo* is "to raise up, elevate, or lift up," as in raising up a fish when catching it. The "taketh away" interpretation is also legitimate, as in "to take off from something attached, remove, or carry away." In context with the entire vine/branch/fruit metaphor, "lifting up" is acceptable in the sense that an unproductive branch might be lifted and cleaned to enhance its productivity (grapevines are tied up). However, when combined with the syntax of the rest of the verse, the sense of "removing" seems stronger.

The husbandman lifts and cleans the vine (washing with the Word, see v. 3; see also Ephesians 5:26) of all that is unproductive (impure, sinful), removing those parts so the good parts (fruit-bearing branches) that remain will have maximum nourishment and become even more productive. Especially in light of later verses that speak of judgment and unproductive branches being cut off, this seems a more contextually faithful rendering. If anything, a gentle, loving but thorough cleansing rather than a harsh, bloody pruning emerges.

3 Now ye are clean through the word which I have spoken unto you.

Again, the context contributes to a proper rendering; indeed, good hermeneutics must include context and the principle that Scripture interprets Scripture. If "purgeth" doesn't capture the "cleansing sense" of the Greek word *kathairo,* the more explicit phrase "clean through the word" used immediately afterward should steer the interpreter toward it. Following a thorough scrubbing that removes unproductiveness and impurities, "now ye are clean"—a spiritual cleansing that comes only through the Word—the result of which is you'll now be more productive. This is also more in line with reality, rather than straining to make every literal aspect of a metaphor fit human life.

4 Abide in me, and I in you. As the branch cannot bear fruit of itself, except it abide in the vine; no more can ye, except ye abide in me.

To "abide" (Gk. *meno,* **MEN-o,** meaning "to remain" or "to not depart") is the heart of the entire metaphor and the main point of the entire passage. While it seems painfully obvious in nature, Christians seem to struggle with the concept of abiding versus not abiding. Even when Christ drew an explicit parallel with a physical branch and repeats Himself numerous times on the importance of abiding, how many have yet to transfer the weight of the metaphor to their lives? Just as a branch on a fruit vine doesn't exist just to be a branch but to produce fruit, so we exist not for ourselves, but to produce God's fruit; this is possible only with His nourishment, which we receive only when we abide in Him.

5 I am the vine, ye are the branches: He that abideth in me, and I in him, the same bringeth forth much fruit: for without me ye can do nothing.

So much of Christian thought, practice, and doctrine hinges on only a few passages or even one passage (or part of a passage). Yet here, Christ repeats Himself like a logician building an airtight argument. He says the same thing almost every way possible, so that no one can escape the meaning, strength, or importance of His words. With each repetition, He increases the amount of fruit produced: in verse 2, "fruit" and "more fruit," and now "much fruit."

Jesus points over and over to the reality of true nourishment from the True Vine, which alone produces true branches, which again in turn produce true fruit. This type of branch comes from the Greek word *klema* (**KALY-mah**), which specifically refers to a young, tender branch, especially the flexible branch of a vine or a vine sprout, or a young branch that needs a steady supply of nourishment. There is no other source for true fruit and no other chain of supply, though the world tries in vain to imitate Christian fruit.

We do not need to strive to produce fruit, any more than an orange tree strives to produce oranges. All that is necessary is for us to remain attached to the source and to abide and not depart from that nourishment that will inevitably result in the production of fruit. When we plant ourselves in such a position as recipients, God is faithful to meet all our needs in abundance (Philippians 4:19). It is only when we do not abide, when we withdraw from the True Vine and refuse the true nourishment, that we predictably become fruitless and accomplish nothing.

In a real sense, we all grow as close to Christ. We choose to abide in His presence or not, we choose to remain in His Word or not, and we choose whether or not to produce fruit as a result. It is this vital connection to the True Vine to which every believer must attend and that he or she must continually monitor and strengthen. It is also this vital connection that we share with all other believers. No vine produces only one branch, but many; thus, our relationship to other branches is communal or familial.

6 If a man abide not in me, he is cast forth as a branch, and is withered; and men gather them, and cast them into the fire, and they are burned.

Some in the body of Christ question whether this verse is a proof text for being able to lose one's salvation. The context informs us that a branch becomes fruitless only when it is no longer connected to the vine; branches that abide continue to receive nourishment and effortlessly produce fruit because that is their sole purpose and design. Therefore, any fruitless branch is a disconnected branch. If a branch cannot be pruned, cleansed, and its connection restored so it will become fruitful again, it will be cut off and destroyed.

One cannot lose one's salvation, but Scripture is clear that all branches (believers) will have a separate judgment (Revelation 20). This coming judgment reinforces the removal aspect of *kathairo* in verse 2, since the Master Gardener wouldn't allow anything to remain that was worthless or in danger of judgment. At the same time, it seems virtually impossible that any genuinely born-again Christian would receive zero nourishment, produce zero fruit for his or her entire life, and then be cut off at the roots and burned wholesale. What is unmistakable is that abiding in Christ should not be seen as an "option" by Christians.

7 If ye abide in me, and my words abide in you, ye shall ask what ye will, and it shall be done unto you.

It is a genuinely symbiotic relationship that a vine shares with its branches. The vine can't produce its own fruit without branches, and the branches can't provide their own nourishment in order to produce fruit. When we abide in Christ, when we are attached to the Vine, His nourishment flows into us, just as in reality His Spirit indwells us (John 14:7; Romans 8:11; 1 Corinthians 3:16) and we receive His Word into our hearts (Luke 6:45; 8:15; Romans 10:8; 1 John 2:14) and we are predictably fruitful. In Psalm 119:11, David says, "Thy word have I hid in mine heart, that I might not sin against thee." Only in this context—as connected, fruitful believers infused with the Spirit and the Word—will we be able to pray in faith and receive that for which we ask. We receive because our will is conformed to Christ's. We are warned in James 4:2 3 not to "ask amiss," but are also admonished that we have not because we ask not. The qualifications are steep, but the rewards, freedom, and resulting power are immeasurable. "Answered prayer is a privilege of close abiding," says noted scholar Pastor David Guzik. With equal eloquence, Matthew Henry pens, "The promises abiding in us lie ready to be turned into prayers; and the prayers so regulated cannot but speed."

8 Herein is my Father glorified, that ye bear much fruit; so shall ye be my disciples.

While there is contentment and peace for the well-connected branch, fruit and gifts are to be used for the body, for the service of others (1 Peter 4:10). While the primary meaning of "fruit" is that of the vine or tree, the word also refers to good works (Gk. *karpos*, **kar-POS**). Just as a grape does the grapevine no good, and an orange does not benefit the orange tree, our fruit is not for ourselves but for others and for the glory of God (Philippians 1:11). We are not to be shepherds who feed only ourselves (Jude 1:12). Likewise, we enjoy the fruit of others and rejoice whenever we find it (Ezekiel 17:23).

A simple test is to look at the representative list of nine types of fruit in Galatians 5:22–23. Which among them do you want to see in your spouse, your friends, your coworkers, your children? All of them, of course!

In this sense, the body of Christ becomes the ultimate garden, tended by the Master Gardener, who provides through each part an infinite variety and delicacy of fruit (v. 1). As each behavior abides in Christ and becomes fruitful, all are fed and nourished and God is glorified (Colossians 1:10; Hebrews 13:21). As the child resembles the parent, so the true disciple resembles the Master; as He was fruitful, so shall we be fruitful when we abide in Him and His words abide in us. "Ye shall know them by their fruits," Jesus says (Matthew 7:16). While many people will produce similar fruit, each person is unique, and, as in nature, each fruit will look and taste a little different on each branch. All fruit-bearing, in reality, is "growing" Christlikeness.

9 As the Father hath loved me, so have I loved you: continue ye in my love.

Jesus zeroes in on what has been called the ultimate fruit, which is love. Some say all other fruit is secondary to the fruit of love, as its offspring; in fact, some say love is the only true fruit and all others are included within it. Scripture doesn't seem to support this view, since many different types of fruit are specified (Galatians 5:22–23). Also, there is the clear statement in John 21:25 that not everything was included in the gospels and epistles. Each believer may end up producing more of one fruit than another, according to the intent of the Gardener, but all are not only encouraged but also commanded to pursue the fruit of love (see v. 12).

Repeatedly, we are told of God's love for His Son, such as in 2 Peter 1:17, which recalls the pronouncement at Jesus' baptism: "This is my beloved Son, in whom I am well pleased." Jesus loved His disciples with His Father's love, even though, unlike them (and us), He alone was worthy of such great love. It is interesting that no other versions (not even the NKJV) except the KJV interprets *meno* (**MEN-o**) here as "continue," while most use "abide" or "remain," in keeping with the theme of the passage. Christ used the word *meno* over and over in this section of Scripture, and all references are rendered "abide" except this one, which seems strange. The whole

thrust of "abide" has been so well established that when the word is read here (and in the next verse), the syntax is restored and the vine image continued.

10 If ye keep my commandments, ye shall abide in my love; even as I have kept my Father's commandments, and abide in his love.

We are never asked to do what Christ would not do. In the book of John, it is well established that Christ proved His love for His Father by His obedience to Him (John 4:34; 8:29; 12:49; 14:31; 17:4). Following suit, the disciples proved their love by their obedience, and we, in turn, prove our love for Christ by our obedience to Him, and receive His promise of abiding in Him. Roger Hagen says, "Love and obedience are mutually dependent. Love arises out of obedience, obedience out of love."

11 These things have I spoken unto you, that my joy might remain in you, and that your joy might be full.

It is an often-preached sermon that Jesus did not come to give us happiness, but rather joy, and how often, what makes us anything but happy doesn't affect our joy. Joy surrounds the believer from his first introduction to God's love (Matthew 13:20; Luke 15:7) to his final reward (Isaiah 51:11; Matthew 25:21) and throughout his Christian life (Romans 14:17). Jesus Himself was filled with joy on Earth (Luke 10:21) and experienced complete joy (John 3:29). It was only because of the joy that lay ahead of Him that Jesus was able to endure the Cross (Hebrews 12:2). James 1:2 tells us that we are to consider trials as pure joy, and Nehemiah 8:10 says the joy of the Lord is our strength. When we do all that Jesus commands (especially love others), our reward both on Earth and in heaven is His great joy, a gift truly beyond compare and priceless above all precious things.

12 This is my commandment, That ye love one another, as I have loved you.

At first, it must have seemed more an exhortation, until the point when Jesus' discourse changed to a commandment. Commandments were familiar to

Jesus' disciples, and it must have given them pause to hear Him talk about loving one another as a commandment. At the same time, a commandment coming from Jesus couldn't be compared to the commandments they had grown up with under Mosaic Law. While Jesus had taught this previously (Matthew 22:39), considering the many other things the disciples had failed to grasp at first, one wonders if He sensed their lack of understanding and thus felt the need to repeat Himself three times in a single teaching. Only in God's kingdom is such profound simplicity: to obey His command to love one another is to love as He Himself loved us in obedience to His Father. Indeed, it is the greatest commandment.

13 Greater love hath no man than this, that a man lay down his life for his friends.

Teachers and coaches understand the concept that when a bar is set too low, there is no challenge and consequently no improvement. When the bar is set higher, we have to work to reach the goal, and the challenge makes us grow. The higher the bar, the greater the required effort, so Jesus here sets the bar at the highest point possible: that of actually sacrificing one's life in order to attain the highest imitation of His love. Many through the ages have been put to this very test, and it makes us question whether we would have what it takes if that terrible day would ever present itself to us. It is a worthy goal to practice loving unto death as Christ loves, in order to be prepared for the ultimate test of showing the greatest love of all.

14 Ye are my friends, if ye do whatsoever I command you.

In Christ, we are much more than servants; we are sons and daughters (2 Corinthians 6:18), and here we are called friends (for whom He would lay down His life). This speaks volumes to us about all that Christ means as a Friend and Brother, but it also speaks eloquently of His perfect love—He who offers so much to those who once were enemies. In fact, Christ laid down His life while we were still enemies (Romans 5:8, 10; Colossians 1:21). When Jesus told us to love our enemies, He spoke from personal experience (Matthew 5:44). In light of that command, this one in verse 14 should seem painless.

15 Henceforth I call you not servants; for the servant knoweth not what his lord doeth: but I have called you friends; for all things that I have heard of my Father I have made known unto you.

In everything He said and did, Jesus faithfully communicated the Father's love. His very existence was the embodiment of the Father (John 1:1), and the fullness of deity lived in Him (Colossians 2:9). Jesus called the disciples "friends" because of the revelation He disclosed to them. It made them close to Jesus. It wasn't the Father's will that everything that could be known should be made known, but everything that God wanted known was communicated through Christ (Matthew 11:27; 24:36). While servants were common in first century Israel—and still are in some parts of the world—it is easier for most of us to relate to the concept of employees. Bosses don't confide everything to their employees as a rule, but life would certainly be different in corporate America if CEOs suddenly started calling their employees friends and began a policy of total information disclosure.

16 Ye have not chosen me, but I have chosen you, and ordained you, that ye should go and bring forth fruit, and that your fruit should remain: that whatsoever ye shall ask of the Father in my name, he may give it you.

Christ reminds His disciples (his friends) that He chose them and has given them a task. As with them, when we abide in Christ, we receive His nourishment, we are fruitful, we fulfill our purpose as branches, we please the Gardener, we feed and nourish others, we produce seeds for planting, and we become eligible for pruning (cleansing) so we will become even more productive. This is fruit and work that endures (John 6:27), and such a believer has fulfilled the qualifications for prayers being answered. "He answered their prayers because they trusted in him" (1 Chronicles 5:20, NIV).

17 These things I command you, that ye love one another.

According to 2 Peter 1:5, we start with faith and add the various fruit of the Spirit, finally adding love, as if it were the highest attainment of the faith that the Master intended from the beginning. It is almost as though all the other fruit is easier to acquire or produce; indeed, this is possible, since, in the New Testament, so much emphasis is placed on exhorting believers to love, to learn to love, to seek love, to become love. Because it is the highest, it is the hardest; because it most closely resembles Christ, it requires greater surrender and sacrifice. Yet we are virtually surrounded with Scriptures that exhort us to make love our highest priority, to pursue love, and to let love transform us into the very image of Christ, who is love (Romans 12:2; 1 Timothy 6:11; 2 Corinthians 3:18; 2 Timothy 2:22).

Daily Bible Readings

M: How the Word Grows
Matthew 13:18–33
T: Jesus Prays for His Followers
John 17:13–19
W: Abide in Christ
1 John 2:24–29
T: Continue in Christ's Teachings
2 John 7–11
F: The Blessed
Psalm 1
S: I Am the True Vine
John 15:1–8
S: Love One Another
John 15:9–17

Sources

Guzik, David. *Study Guide for John* Chapter 15. http://www.blueletterbible.org/tmp_dir/c/1118938967-8515.html

Henry, Matthew. *Commentary on the Whole Bible,* John 15. http://www.ccel.org/h/henry/mhc2/MHC43015.htm

Hagn, Roger. *John 15:1 17: The Vine and the Branches,* Christian Resource Institute. http://www.cresourcei.org/biblestudy/bbjohn18.html

MARCH 2007
QUARTER AT-A-GLANCE
Our Community Now and in God's Future

This quarter has three units. The first interprets the meaning of God's love using 1 John for insight. Units 2 and 3 draw on passages from Revelation to explore the new community in Christ and how that community will live in God's new world

UNIT 1 . KNOWN BY OUR LOVE

The study has four lessons. Each lesson attempts to interpret the meaning of God's love and how it relates to our relationships with one another. These lessons explore love as a light in our dark world of evil and hate, our hope for experiencing love in its purest form, the source of the love we all need and long for, and ways of loving others as we ourselves would like to be loved.

LESSON 1: March 4, 2007
The Light of Love
1 John 2:7–11, 15–17

John calls believers to exercise love in all their relationships. Loving others is not a new concept; it was enjoined under the Old Covenant (Leviticus 19:18), yet, it is new in the sense that Christ has now given us a new measurement for love. "Love as I have loved you." John asserts we are called to love sacrificially, that is, to look out for the best interest of others without expecting anything in return. What we are *not* to love is "the world" with its evil pleasures and cravings.

LESSON 2: March 11, 2007
The Test of Love
1 John 3:11–24

The person transformed by the Holy Spirit will manifest that transformation in three ways: (1) By the attitude and actions we exhibit in relationship to God, shown by our worship of God and obedience to His will; (2) by the attitude and action we show toward other people, as exemplified by the widow who gave all she had to help others; and (3) by our attitude and actions in relationship to the world.

LESSON 3: March 18, 2007
The Source of Love
1 John 4:7–21

The aged apostle John had come to understand that apart from having a right relationship with God, the believer's greatest challenge is to have the right relationship with other people, especially fellow believers. The basis of our relationship should be that of love. Love, as John explains it, originates with God and is manifested by the coming of Jesus Christ into the world that we might live through Him.

LESSON 4: March 25, 2007
The Way to Love
1 John 5:1–12

John assures believers that eternal life awaits those who believe in the Son. The Gospel of John confirms this: "In Him was life; and the life was the light of men" (John 1:4). Eternity is secure for those who believe and accept Jesus Christ as Saviour and Lord. "He that hath the Son hath life, and he that hath not the Son of God hath not life" (1 John 5:12). Faith in Jesus Christ is validated by loving God and people, and seeking to obey God's Word.

UNIT 2 . A NEW COMMUNITY IN CHRIST

These lessons discuss Jesus' relationship to the community at large. This community forms its identity as Christ evolves in the Gospels. His birth, His life, His death, and His resurrection are key in shaping the community of Christ. These lessons will invite the students to discuss Christ's legacy for the church community, how we worship, and how Christ has committed to both love and protect us.

LESSON 5: April 1, 2007
Christ Is Our King
Revelation 1:8; Luke 19:28–40

The passages in Luke describe the triumphal entry of Christianity. The untying of the colt, and the laying down of the disciples' garments point the reader toward the majesty of the Saviour. In the Revelation text John reminds us that Christ is both Alpha and Omega (the first and the last). These readings are meant to represent Christ as king.

LESSON 6: April 8, 2007 (Easter)
Christ Is Risen
Revelation 1:12, 17–18; John 20:11–16, 30–31

Jesus speaks to John the Revelator, and assures him that He is not dead. He is alive forevermore. Jesus has defeated death and the enemy. He is the beginning and ending of all things.

LESSON 7: April 15, 2007
God Is Worthy of Praise
Revelation 4

John paints a picture of the glorious nature of God—a reminder that all living things should give God praise and honor. John envisions the heavenly throne, and all the day the angels and elders are crying out to God, beholding His glory.

LESSON 8: April 22, 2007
Christ Is Worthy to Redeem
Revelation 5:1–5; 11–14

John describes the "Scroll and the Lamb." It is determined that no one is worthy to open the scroll, except the Lamb of God. The Lamb (Jesus Christ) was born to become a sacrifice or ransom for the sins of mankind.

LESSON 9: April 29, 2007
Christ Is Our Protection
Revelation 7:1–3, 9, 13–17

John has identified the "blood washed" believer. The passage speaks of those who have been washed and made new in the blood of the Lamb. Christ's sacrifice at Calvary had yielded an eternal security for the believer. Those who have been washed by the blood are preserved through persecution; they shall never hunger or thirst again—they are fulfilled in Him.

UNIT 3 . LIVING IN GOD'S NEW WORLD

These four lessons present the promise of life with God after death: the home that God will eventually make for the community of faith, the presence of God in the midst of that new home, and finally Christ's return.

LESSON 10: May 6, 2007
The Final Banquet
Revelation 19:5–10

John admonished us to praise God, reiterating his value as the Messiah. We, His chosen people, must remember to honor Him as a bride would honor her groom.

LESSON 11: May 13, 2007
Our New Home
Revelation 21:1–8

A new heaven and a new earth are coming and will exist in eternity. God is at the center of both—renewing and refreshing His people. He has promised to make all things new, and to wipe away the tears brought by things passed.

LESSON 12: May 20, 2007
God in Our Midst
Revelation 21:9–10; 21:22–22:5

Jesus is our eternal light. He is our guide and our hope for things to come. Nothing impure will enter into His glorious presence, and we should expect to experience His light—the light of life, if we live for Him.

LESSON 13: May 27, 2007
Christ Will Return
Revelation 22:6–10, 12–13, 16–21

The Lord is coming back again, and He will some seeking His bride—the church. All things will be made perfect in heaven. All who wish for better and hope for the fulfillment of Christ can come and find that fulfillment when He returns for us.

COMMITMENT TO TRUTH IS EMPTY WITHOUT COMMITMENT TO PEOPLE

by Evangeline Carey

One church's marquee displayed the mini-sermon, "Know God, Know Peace; No God, No Peace." As the above poem indicates, our desperate and segmented world is in need of God's peace; it is anxious and troubled on every hand. Because for so many people, there is *no* God (the one true God) in their lives, they find themselves with *no* inner peace. God, then, calls every believer to help our lost fellow man to seek, find, and know Him so that God can perform heart-changing surgery. He calls those who embrace His salvation plan to bring the energy of His unconditional love to our world, so that the power of Holy Spirit can save the sin-sick soul; He calls us to take His Spirit-empowered Gospel to those who need Him in the wasteland of their life. In fact in Mark 16:15–16, He says, "Go ye into all the world, and preach the gospel to every creature. He that believeth and is baptized shall be saved." God desires us to lift up Jesus, His one and only Son—the Lamb without blemish—to potential disciples, and He will draw all men unto Himself (John 12:32). He even anoints and empowers us to carry out His will through His Holy Spirit. Thus every believer should not only be committed to the Truth—Jesus—but also to the people for whom He suffered, bled, died, and arose.

God also mandates us in His complete, revealed Word to *love* our fellow man. First John 2:10 says, "He that loveth his brother abideth in the light, and there is none occasion of stumbling in him." God, therefore, calls all believers to take the spiritual blinders off and see both the church and the world through His eyes. He wants believers to see the mental, physical, and spiritual anguish all around us and move out with hands and hearts that bless God and bless others. Therefore, in these perilous times, He calls *all believers* to be godly people. This includes a call to be workers who have a passion for God, who can be a real blessing to God and others, and who can tell the lost that Jesus Himself is the truth that sets us free from the awful bondage of sin. Hence, God does not want us to be lazy Christians, but to have a *two-fold* commitment to His kingdom-building initiative. He wants us to commit to the truth of His living Word and also to the people to whom He sent His Word.

Christian Role Models. God and the world are in need of Christian role model witnesses to illustrate the character of Christianity. Therefore, God needs believers who are in love with Him and will follow Him wholeheartedly. He needs humble people, who are not puffed up with their own importance—who have been delivered by God from any arrogance and pride that might hinder their spiritual mission. He needs believers who will surrender their will to God, be a servant–leader or a follower, and lift up Jesus instead of themselves. He needs workers who will roll up their sleeves and pull their fellowman out of the sludge of physical and spiritual deprivation and suffering. He tells us in 1 John 3:16–17, "Hereby perceive we the love of God, because he laid down his life for us: and we ought to lay down our lives for the brethren. But whoso hath this world's good, and seeth his brother have need, and shutteth up his bowels of compassion from him, how dwelleth the love of God in him?" He further tells us in 1 John 4:7, "Beloved, let us love one another: for love is of God; and every one that loveth is born of God, and knoweth God. He that loveth not knoweth not God; for God is love."

Getting God's Kingdom Perspective. God can and does give us a vision of His kingdom. Phenomenal things are happening with and through Him as we catch the vision and move out to fulfill the call. He tells us in Revelation 7:9 that His kingdom will consist of "a great multitude, which no man could number, of all nations, and kindreds, and people, and tongues." They are the ones whose sins are forgiven because they have believed on the Lord Jesus Christ for their salvation.

God Needs Obedient Believers to Work for Him. God needs believers to be witnesses for Him. He needs those who obey His commands to work in His vineyard. Therefore, He needs workers who will go when He says go; workers who will do when He says do; workers who will speak when He says speak; and workers who will be quiet when He says be quiet—stop, listen, and heed. He needs workers who know what it is to stand in the midst of broken dreams, defeat, ruin, or confusion and doubt, and testify that God is still love and He is still at work in their circumstances. He needs workers who know what it is to sink in the mire of bitterness, despair, and self-pity but, through the prayers of other believers, have come out on the other side and can still inspire others with a quiet and confident faith in God's love and care. He needs workers who know what it is to be in constant pain and suffering and still trust the power of God's deliverance and healing. He needs workers who know what it is to be empty, hurt, lonely, lost, lied to, cheated, and mistreated to live out God's wonderful grace before others so that God can use His unconditional love to draw sincere seekers. He needs ordinary believers to do extraordinary things for Him! God needs us to be committed to Him, obey Him, and press onward to the victory that only He can bring.

Salt, Light, and Grace Moments. I am reminded of two events where believers did not hide their light under a bush but instead illuminated and overshadowed the dark side of human nature. The first one was during 9/11, after the terrorists invaded our shores and wreaked all kinds of havoc and devastation. Some irate American citizens in one large city became vigilantes and decided to storm a Mosque in retaliation. However, a group of devout Christians in the same community decided that this was a "salt and light" moment—a time to show unconditional love and God's grace to the Muslim community. Therefore, these believers surrounded the Mosque so that the hate mongers could not carry out their sinister plans. They became a light not only to the Muslim community, but also to the world. Onlookers saw the love of Jesus Christ up close and personal from those who are called by His name. This was indeed a witness that could be used to draw not only some of these Muslims, but others around the world to the saving knowledge of Jesus Christ.

Finally, an African American nurse recalled another "grace" moment where she and her physician husband (both devout Christians) were able to witness to a declared racist. This nurse shared how they moved their office into a changing racial neighborhood. One day, a desperate, terminally ill White woman reluctantly came in seeking medical help. She announced to the nurse that she did not like Black people and used the "n" word. The nurse determined that she would be "salt and light" to this patient. With God's love and strength, she was able to look past this woman's hatred and see her needs. It happened also that the White woman informed her caregivers that she had no money to pay the doctor for her treatment. Still, the African American nurse and doctor found a way to service her and give her free medications.

As this White cancer patient's health became progressively worse and she was no longer able to make office visits for her treatments, the African American nurse went to her home to assist her. At the same time, the doctor and nurse both prayed for the ailing woman's salvation. There were occasions when the nurse and her 4-year-old granddaughter even read Scriptures to her. Finally, on the last day of her life, with the African American nurse by her side, this proclaimed racist accepted Jesus Christ as her personal Saviour and went on to be with the Lord. At her memorial service, the White woman's son handed the nurse and her husband full payment for his mother's medical bill.

Through grace extended *by believers* in a very difficult situation, God saved a needy soul. Needless to say, in both cases, these believers flavored their world with *agape* (unconditional) love, compassion, and mercy. They became living testimonies; lights in the darkness that overcome evil around them—and showed unbelievers that God is real and His love is alive and well. In fact, God turned the effects of evil into good.

Looking at Our Own Ministries. When we put our ministries on the altar before the living God, He will show us, too, how to love as He does. He will allow us to have His light within us that produces only what is good and true (Ephesians 5:9). We will make the most of every opportunity for doing well in these evil days (v. 16). God will answer people's prayers and meet their requests through us.

God seeks yielded believers who are committed to Christ and His kingdom. The Holy Spirit can stir us to reach out to others with God's love and also give us the spirit of courage to do so. He can give us a passion to pray for others and to help them in their times of need. Just as we need God, our fellowman also needs our help to get to God. Our fellowman needs us to help pray him through his crises.

Serving God through Serving Others. God will be glorified when we truly serve Him through serving people that He loves, even though some may be wearing dirty and tattered clothes, hungry, mentally or physically ill, drugged-out, drunk, stressed out, disenfranchised, or marginalized. Instead of seeking others to serve us or seeking to

bask in the presence of a Holy God all the day long, needy people can be touched by God through us. Our lives may draw them to pray and to seek the Lord. The testimonies of our life can give them hope.

Let Us Hear the Conclusion of this Whole Matter. God can do some awesome things through us when we put our ministries in the hand of the man from Galilee (Jesus) and delight to do His will. He needs some *lovers of God and mankind.* He needs some *consolers.* He needs some *leaders and followers,* who understand brokenness and have the spirit of concern for people. The world is so spiritually poor and needy! Human strength cannot set the captives free; true freedom only comes through the power of an omnipotent God. Can you be counted on to walk *in* and pour *out* God's grace—His compassion, forgiveness, love, mercy—and plant the seeds of His Word so that He can bring in the harvest? God has given us the challenge. He has provided the mission, the resources, and strength to get the job done.

Now go bring joy—Christ—to your suffering world, and remember that commitment to truth is empty without commitment to people.

———————

Evangeline Carey *is a staff writer for UMI and has been an adult Sunday School teacher for more than 25 years.*

WALKING IN THE LIGHT WE SHARE THROUGH FORGIVENESS

by Rukeia Draw

There was a young guy named Javon. He had a reputation around his community for being an admirer of dogs, especially big ones. His neighbor watched as he laid a new driveway one morning. Just as he neared completion of this home improvement project, a large dog went across the cement and left paw prints behind. Javon mumbled something under his breath and smoothed out the paw prints. Afterward, he went indoors and gathered some twine and stakes to mark off the area. He returned only to discover more tracks in the concrete. He cleared the prints again and confidently put up the twine barriers.

Within the next hour, the dog managed to ruin Javon's hard work twice more. The last time he boldly sat in the wet concrete, staring at Javon's door and awaiting the homeowner's eventful return. Sure enough, Jason's appearance came complete with exasperated looks, "shoos," and shaking fists. When Javon returned to the door, he was very upset by what he saw. He retrieved his handgun and shot the persistent dog dead right there!

Stunned, the neighbor rushed over and asked, "Javon, why did you do that? I thought you loved dogs!"

Javon responded, "Yes I do. I like dogs in the abstract, not in the concrete!"

This humorous parable is adapted from a sermon by Rev. Sharon Rhodes-Wickett and is not intended to condone cruelty to animals. It is presented here to make the point that many Christians who like the idea of forgiveness don't often practice it when confronted with the challenges of daily life.

As the Christian story goes, God so loved the people of the world that He sent His only begotten Son as a sacrifice to atone for their sins so that forgiveness could be offered and reconciliation achieved. As the story continues, those who accept this reality are to extend this forgiveness and love to one another and be reconciled (Matthew 6:14; Mark 11:25; 2 Corinthians 2:10; Ephesians 4:32; 5:2; Colossians 3:13). So why is it that the world recognizes believers more by their hypocrisy than by their love for one another?

Alexander Pope is famous for saying, "To err is human, to forgive divine." Elizabeth Large agrees that it is human nature to respond to an offense with anger, grudges, or vengeance; and in spite of religious instruction, many believers respond with all three. Lots of Christians have lives controlled by anger and bitterness. Many are touchy and easily provoked. Others don't know how to let go of grudges. Like the second grader who is full of rage and yells at his teacher, like the molested or abused woman who rehearses acts of molestation and retaliation in her mind a million times over, like the streetwise young man who refuses to let go of payback for the business venture gone sour with his childhood friend, why is it that many of God's children have never adequately learned how to cope with the disappointments and injuries experienced at the hands of others?

The church should dedicate more resources to facilitating forgiveness. Let me give an example that starts with the theologians, the great minds whose task it is to challenge the church to reflect on issues of great importance. There are many systematic theology textbooks, and although they are supposed to cover all the major authoritative teachings of the church, they rarely, if ever, address the topic of love. This trend continues among distinguished Black theologians, with the exception of J. Deotis Roberts and Dwight Hopkins. In contemporary Black theology, forgiveness and reconciliation are overshadowed by freedom and justice. There is, however, ample preaching on forgiveness in local churches. In spite of this, many believers have not moved beyond knowing about forgiveness and believing in its goodness. Christian education in the local church has not typically given congregants the educational experiences they need to practice forgiveness in their daily lives.

Forgiveness helps Christians fulfill God's commandment to love one another (Matthew 22:39; John 13:34; 1 John 3:23). To love another brother or sister in Christ is to walk in the light you both share (1 John 2:10). Love is the bond that holds Christian communities together, and forgiveness is an expression of that love. Mother Teresa said, "If we want to love, we must learn how to forgive." Paul confirms this when he writes that love keeps no record of wrongs (1 Corinthian 13:5). Healthy love relationships are impossible without forgiveness because as Peter Ustinov says, "Love is an act of endless forgiveness." In Matthew 18:22, Jesus communicates this to Peter when He tells him to forgive a person as often as 70 times 7, or 490 times.

Forgiveness is a moral response to injustice. It's a choice to lay down the right to pay an offender back, absorbing the evil and suffering the pain of an injury instead. Based on the merciful character of God and the forgiveness He has already extended to the believer for far greater offenses, such a choice is informed by a conviction that unwillingness to forgive another Christian is hypocritical (Luke 6:36; Ephesians 4:32). The International Forgiveness Institute says forgiveness also reaches out to the offender in moral love by seeking the rehabilitation and betterment of the injurer.

An unforgiving believer walks in darkness because every part of their being is negatively affected—mind, body, and spirit. One guy said, "If you licked my heart, you'd die from poisoning." Like this guy, an unforgiving person drinks poison and expects someone else to die from it. The point is, harboring hostility can be deadly for individuals and those who come too close to them!

Projects looking at the benefits of forgiveness have received millions of dollars in funding lately. These studies have found that people who hold grudges have diminished health compared to those in the general population. They have more frequent doctor visits, more stress-related disorders (anxiety, restlessness, sadness, and depression), lower immune system functioning, and higher rates of cardiovascular disease (high blood pressure, heart disease, and low heart rate).

The most important consequence for those who do not forgive is that it hinders effective communication with the Father. In Matthew 18:23–35, Jesus tells a parable about two indebted men. I'll use my imagination to give a first-person, updated account of the story.

Jesus warns us that God is like the lender who forgave an enormous debt (Matthew 18:35) because He expects a believer's character and treatment of others to reflect His own character and treatment in some small measure. Forgiven people forgive others; there are consequences when they don't.

Believers are an integral part of a loving community, linked by the Spirit of God. Everyone will inevitably, if not regularly, be offended by others in this imperfect community. Love can only prosper where there is forgiveness.

Practicing forgiveness allows believers to be healthy and whole, thereby contributing to the stability, unity, and maturity of the entire Christian community. Remember unforgiveness has serious consequences. Begin using what resources you have to let go of grudges and or help others do so today!

Rukeia Draw is pursuing a Ph.D. in educational studies from Trinity International University in Deerfield, Illinois.

LOVE IS NOT FONDNESS

by Frederick Thomas

Love is one of the most overused and misunderstood words in the English language. Sports fans love their sports teams, and sweets fans love their desserts and candies. We love our pets, and we love our families. Couples fall in love and often fall out of love. Our music resonates with declarations of love, and the movie industry produces several love stories every year.

The question is, what is love? The dictionary has several different definitions of love such as: a deep and tender feeling of affection and thoughtfulness toward a person; a feeling of intense desire and attraction toward a person with whom one is disposed to make a pair; and the emotion of sex and romance. All of these definitions associate love with feelings and emotions. Maybe the problem is that we really do not understand love at all.

We tend to believe that love is an emotion and is based upon how we feel. Since emotions fluctuate, love fluctuates also. Relationships end because people no longer feel like they love each other. Many people do not accept God's love because they cannot feel it. Others feel the immediate rush of passion when they first encounter God and then wonder if God still loves them when the passion is gone.

We tend to associate love with powerful emotions and/or affections. Although many times these emotions and affections are the exciting by-products of love, they do not accurately describe what true love is. I would guess that the tremendously high divorce rate in this country is an indication that people feel that love is based on their own changing feelings and emotions.

The problem with the emotional concept of love is that it is both selfish and self-serving. It is selfish because it concentrates on what one *gets* rather than what one *gives*, and it is self-serving because it is rooted in having one's own needs met by another. Could this possibly be what God meant when He commanded us to love our God with all our being and our neighbor as ourselves?

Does God expect us to live our lives feeling constant passion for Him and affection for our neighbors, whom we may or may not even know? To find out what love really is, we must turn to the source. In John's first letter, the apostle encourages us, "Beloved, let us love one another; for love is of God, and he who loves is born of God and knows God. He who does not love does not know God; for God is love" (1 John 4:7–8). The nature of this love is inherent in the very statement John makes: "love one another."

Love must not be restricted to those who are nice or pleasant to us. Every person is a special creation of God for whom Christ sacrificed His life, and each one is capable of a unique relationship with the Father. That is why we love one another. We are filled with the Spirit of God and God is love. This love is an interest in and a concern for other people; it seeks what is best for the person and asks nothing in return. It makes no difference if the person is rich or poor, Black or White, old or young, male or female.

This love is demonstrated by God because God is love. The Father does not simply love us, He *is* love and the source of love. Love is an essential aspect of His nature. In fact, godly creation of humanity is one way of His self-expression. God is love, and He chose to express that love. He began by creating a physical universe so that the object of His love would be constantly reminded of Him (see Romans 1:20). He created plant and animal life so that His beloved would have something over which to rule even as He ruled over all creation. After God saw that everything else was in place, God created a being in His own image. Because humanity is created in God's marvelous image, people have both the capacity to love and the free will to choose to give or not give love.

Humans are the crowning point of all creation. We are so dear to God that even the way we were formed is unique. God spoke the physical universe and all life into being, but when it came to humanity God got personal. Rather than speaking man into being, our loving Father scooped up a bit of clay and personally formed it in His gentle, loving hands. Then He lovingly took the lifeless form and intimately blew His holy breath into his nostrils and man became a living soul. Here, God expressed His love through doing and giving rather than feeling.

When humanity fell into sin and out of relationship with the loving God, He also made the ultimate sacrifice on our behalf. John says that God loved us so much that He offered His own dear Son to pay the cost of our sin and desertion (3:16). He did not do this after we repented and returned to Him. Scripture teaches that while we were yet sinners, Christ died for us (Romans 5:8). Again, we see God's love in His giving and doing.

That is what love is. It is a decision to give our best on behalf of another. It is an act of the will to sacrifice oneself for the good of another. It is not concerned with what a person is like or what he does or how he dresses or how he looks. It sees one thing only, and that is: "Here is another person created by God to be loved and for whom Christ died." We recognize others as people like ourselves struggling with the aspirations and frustrations of life. Love sees another person beset with the problems of life and asks, "How can I be of help?" That is love.

It is no good claiming that you know God if the love of God is not found in your life. If you cannot treat people objectively and see through the irritating qualities that may offend you—if your reaction to those who offend you is one of opposition, rejection, and instant antagonism—then it is no good saying you belong to Him. If God lives in you, you must be welcoming to all who are in need of love. Rejection is not God's life, and it is not God's love. John's argument is that if the life of God is present in us, then the love of God will be there also. Doing good for others should not be based on how we *feel* about the person. In fact, the best expression of love comes from doing good to those toward whom we harbor feelings of resentment (Luke 6:32–35).

The love of God is seen in both creation and our salvation. In both cases, God gave of Himself while demanding nothing in return. Love should be seen here as an action verb; it is made apparent by what one *does* not by what one *feels*. Beloved, if we are to truly love God and one another, we must give our best both to God and then to each other. "Greater love hath no man than this, that a man lay down His life for his friends" (John 15:13).

Frederick Thomas is the pastor of Family of Faith Community Church in Chicago, Illinois.

THOMAS DORSEY (1899–1993)
PROLIFIC GOSPEL COMPOSER

During the first week of January 2006, billowing flames gutted, ravaged, and razed the Pilgrim Baptist Church, a historical landmark on Chicago's south side. Parishioners and other onlookers were left devastated to see the magnitude of the destruction to the more than 100-year-old edifice. At one time the church had boasted a membership of 10,000 and been the church home of the famous American arranger, pianist, and versatile prolific composer, Thomas A. Dorsey. Not only was Dorsey known as the "Father of Gospel Music," but he was also considered to be one of the most influential figures ever to impact the gospel music genre.

While the fire reduced all but the shell of the Pilgrim Baptist Church to rubble, it did not destroy the community spirit of the congregants. It also could not diminish the legacy of Reverend Dorsey, a versatile musician and composer who had written more than 1,000 songs in his lifetime, half of which were published. From 1932 into the 1970s, Reverend Dorsey organized and directed the choir at Pilgrim Baptist Church. Legendary gospel icons, including Mahalia Jackson, Sallie Martin, and Rosetta Tharpe achieved their first success with Dorsey's soul-stirring, heart-wrenching songs of praise and adoration to the living God.

Considered one of the most revered figures in spiritual music, Rev. Thomas A. Dorsey "was born in Villa Rica, Georgia, to Etta Plant Spencer, a respected church organist, and Thomas Madison Dorsey, an itinerant preacher and sharecropper. A child prodigy, Dorsey taught himself how to play a wide range of instruments. His musical talents were so widely recognized that a gospel tune was called "a Dorsey" until Dorsey himself coined the name "gospel." Then his music was known as "gospel" or "gospel blues."

After moving to Chicago in 1916, Dorsey continued his musical training at the Chicago School of Composition and Arranging. He published his first composition in 1920, and to earn money, he worked as a composer and arranger for the Chicago Music Publishing Company under J. Mayo Williams. He also worked as a music coach for both Paramount and Vocalion Records.

In 1921, after he heard W. M. Nix's inspirational singing at the National Baptist Convention, Dorsey decided to begin composing "sacred" music. He registered his first composition in 1922. After becoming the director of music at New Hope Baptist Church, he combined his sacred music with his blues technique. This collective effort made him one of the progenitors of gospel blues.

In 1932, Dorsey's wife, Nettie Harper, died in childbirth and his newborn son died soon after. One day as he consoled himself, at his piano, he composed a song that has blessed and comforted countless hurting hearts down through the ages: "Take My Hand, Precious Lord."

Elvis Presley's recording of Dorsey's second-most popular God-inspired song, "Peace in the Valley," sold millions of copies. It is considered to be Dorsey's most widely recognized work and was a nationwide hit in both Black and White arenas.

Today, Thomas A. Dorsey is revered in Black church history. Because of his walk with the Lord, Black Americans laud him as a Christian, an accomplished pianist, choir director, and a prolific composer. We praise God that He saved Thomas A. Dorsey. His God-given gift still comforts us through the music that flowed through this wonderful man of God.

Sources

www.answers.com/topic/rev-thomas-a-dorsey

www.ourgeorgiahistory.com/chronpop/1231

TEACHING TIPS

March 4
Bible Study Guide 1

1. Words You Should Know

A. Esoteric—Something that is understood by a limited number of people who constitute an enlightened inner circle.

B. Docetism—An early form of Gnostic heresy that rejected the humanity of Christ based on the sinfulness of flesh. They believed that Jesus only appeared to be human, like a phantom, and did not really die through crucifixion.

C. Heresy—Any teaching that is contrary to clear biblical teaching.

D. Incarnation—A Latin word meaning "having become flesh." The scriptural teaching that the second Person of the Trinity became human through virgin conception and birth (John 1:14; Philippians 2:6–8; 1 Timothy 3:16).

2. Teacher Preparation

A. Pray for wisdom, clarity, and understanding. Ask God to open hearts and spark a genuine discussion during the class session.

B. Familiarize yourself with the content of this lesson, and study the Scripture verses provided in the Bible Background, Daily Bible Readings, and Focal Verses using multiple translations.

C. In addition, complete lesson 1 in the *Precepts For Living® Personal Study Guide.*

3. Starting the Lesson

A. Open the class with prayer.

B. Reiterate today's Lesson Aim.

C. Read the definitions in Words You Should Know aloud.

D. Summarize the context information provided in The People, Places, and Times and Background sections.

4. Getting into the Lesson

A. Ask for two volunteers to read Focal Verses.

B. Summarize the In Depth section. Ask for individual responses to the questions found in Search the Scriptures.

5. Relating the Lesson to Life

A. Select a volunteer to read In Focus and/or Lesson in Our Society. Ask the students to comment on how the content relates to today's lesson.

B. To answer questions in the Discuss the Meaning section, divide the class into groups. Assign one or two questions to each group depending on class size. Tell the students to select a representative to report their responses to the rest of the class.

6. Arousing Action

A. For review, ask half the class to provide a summary of John's teaching on love from the Focal Verses. Ask the other half of the class to share their responses to Remember Your Thoughts.

B. For application, ask the students to complete the Follow the Spirit and Make It Happen sections and Bible Study Guide 1 in the *Precepts For Living® Personal Study Guide* during the week.

THE LIGHT OF LOVE

Bible Background • 1 JOHN 2:7–17
Printed Text • 1 JOHN 2:7–11, 15–17   Devotional Reading • 1 PETER 4:1–11

Lesson Aim

By the end of the lesson, we should be able to:
SUMMARIZE John's teachings on the love of God and love for others;
ASPIRE to treat others with genuine love; and
IDENTIFY at least one act of love we can show, and AGREE to do it during the coming week.

Keep in Mind

"He that loveth his brother abideth in the light, and there is none occasion of stumbling in him" (1 John 2:10).

Focal Verses

1 John 2:7 Brethren, I write no new commandment unto you, but an old commandment which ye had from the beginning. The old commandment is the word which ye have heard from the beginning.

8 Again, a new commandment I write unto you, which thing is true in him and in you: because the darkness is past, and the true light now shineth.

9 He that saith he is in the light, and hateth his brother, is in darkness even until now.

10 He that loveth his brother abideth in the light, and there is none occasion of stumbling in him.

11 But he that hateth his brother is in darkness, and walketh in darkness, and knoweth not whither he goeth, because that darkness hath blinded his eyes.

2:15 Love not the world, neither the things *that are* in the world. If any man love the world, the love of the Father is not in him.

16 For all that is in the world, the lust of the flesh, and the lust of the eyes, and the pride of life, is not of the Father, but is of the world.

17 And the world passeth away, and the lust thereof: but he that doeth the will of God abideth for ever.

In Focus

Dexter and his wife Theresa lounged on the beach surrounded by the crystal waters of Jamaica. Although they had come to Jamaica for a married couples' conference, they were also celebrating their 10-year wedding anniversary.

Surveying the oceanfront, Theresa gasped. "Isn't that Gordon over there under that beach umbrella?"

A cold chill ran through Dexter.

It *was* Gordon, his best friend throughout high school and college; the two had been inseparable—more like brothers. Dexter had not seen or spoken to Gordon in over two years. They had parted with Dexter declaring Gordon his sworn enemy.

"Are you going to speak to him?" she chided.

"No, Theresa, I don't think I can."

"Dexter, just last night you said that you were amazed at how church folk claim to love the Lord, but still treat one another so badly."

Dexter stared through the blinding sunlight and remembered what tore them apart. The two friends had entered into a real estate deal with Ben, one of Gordon's business associates. Dexter felt that Ben cheated him out of his share of the profits on the sale of some income property and that Gordon had betrayed him. What hurt even more was Gordon later admitted that he knew Ben was up to no good soon after they entered the deal, but he never felt comfortable telling Dexter because he was the one who had introduced the two.

Theresa brushed sand from her husband's shoulder and said, "The truth is you lost money on that deal because you didn't listen to your instincts or to me. In the end, Gordon was only trying to protect you."

Dexter knew in his heart that his wife was right. He made his way across the hot sand. When he came face-to-face with Gordon, he was greeted with a smile. "I've prayed for this day," Gordon said. "I've really missed you, my brother."

How we treat people reveals whether or not we truly love them. In today's lesson, John calls for believers to love others as God has loved us. We are empowered to love because God's love is shed abroad in our hearts by the Holy Spirit.

The People, Places, and Times

John. John means "gift of God." John's parents were Zebedee, a fisherman, and possibly Salome, a woman present at the crucifixion (Matthew 4:21; 20:20; 27:56; Mark 1:19–20; 15:40; 16:1). John and his brother James were called to discipleship while working as fisherman on the Sea of Galilee with their father's hired servants (Matthew 4:21; Mark 1:19–20). Early in the ministry Jesus called them by the surname Boanerges, "the sons of thunder," perhaps for their often misguided, natural zeal (Mark 3:17). Jesus had to restrain the zeal of these "sons of thunder" who requested that fire be sent from heaven to destroy a village that rejected them (Luke 9:54), forbade another to perform miracles in Jesus' name (Mark 9:38–41), and jockeyed for special position in glory alongside Jesus (Matthew 20:20–21; Mark 10:35–37). John's legacy, however, would be as the apostle of love.

First, tradition has rendered John as the beloved apostle. Jesus and John shared a close personal relationship. John was with Jesus during the raising of Jairus' daughter (Luke 8:51), on the Mount of Transfiguration (Luke 9:28), in the Garden of Gethsemane (Mark 14:33), and at His trial and crucifixion (John 18:15–16; 19:26–27). Jesus chose John to care for His mother in His absence (John 19:26–27), and John was among those who witnessed the empty tomb (John 20:1–10) and the risen Christ (John 20:19–20; 21:1–2). These experiences may have been the foundation of a relationship wherein

John felt warranted to call himself the disciple whom Jesus loved (John 13:23; 19:26–27; 20:2).

Second, John is credited with writing four New Testament books where a major theme is the love of God. The traditional view is that he authored 1, 2, and 3 John, the gospel of John, and the book of Revelation. He referenced Christian love at least 25 times in his writings.

Asia Minor. After Jesus' ascension, John stayed in Jerusalem at least until Paul and Barnabas's visit (Galatians 2:6–10). He left for Asia Minor sometime after that, perhaps before the fall of Jerusalem with other fleeing Christians. The east meets west in Asia Minor, a central plateau about 3,000 to 5,000 feet in altitude. Asia Minor, also called Anatolia, is bordered by the Mediterranean Sea to the south, the Aegean Sea to the west, and the Black Sea to the north. Being an area of civilization since prehistoric times, it has been home to numerous diverse people (i.e., Saul of Tarsus) and groups (i.e., sons of Shem or Semitic peoples and the Hittites).

The apostle John wrote the first epistle in Asia Minor, the Asian provinces under Roman rule, about A.D. 90. Since the writing lacks a traditional greeting, it probably was intended for general circulation to Christian communities in the areas surrounding Ephesus, the city where the apostle spent his latter years. These churches, located in modern-day Turkey, were likely the same Christian communities addressed by Paul in his letter to the Ephesians and Colossians (Ephesians 1:1; Colossians 1:2), by Peter in his letters (i.e., Pontus, Galatia, Cappadocia, Asia, and Bithynia listed in 1 Peter 1:1), and by John in the book of Revelation (i.e., Pontus, Galatia, Cappadocia, Asia, and Bithynia listed in Revelation 1:11).

Sources

Elwell, Walter A. and Robert W. Yarbrough. *Encountering the New Testament.* Grand Rapids, Mich.: Baker Books, 1998, 366–368.

Packer, J.I., and associates. *Nelson's Illustrated Encyclopedia of Bible Facts.* Nashville: Thomas Nelson Publishers, 1995, 285, 530–533.

Background

The historical context of 1 John includes the infiltration of false teaching throughout the Asia Minor churches. These teachers, whom John identifies as antichrists, have recently departed only after bringing confusion to the believers there. John seeks to strengthen the faith and fellowship of these struggling communities by providing a defense of the apostles' teachings about Christ and by assuring them of their salvation in the midst of this opposition.

Tradition states that John was primarily opposing an early form of Gnosticism, called docetism. This early Gnostic belief denied the incarnation of Christ and attributed His physical appearance to a ghost like phantom; they denounced the atoning and saving work of Jesus's death on the cross, and the victory over sin by the Resurrection. These eastern teachings gradually permeated Asia Minor and Europe, and they presented a serious threat to Christian communities because they challenged New Testament doctrines involving Christ, salvation, and sin.

Sources

Ladd, George E. *A Theology of the New Testament,* rev. ed. Grand Rapids, Mich.: Eerdmans Publishing, 1993, 657–665.

Zodhiates, Spiros, ed. *The Complete Word Study New Testament (KJV).* Chattanooga, Tenn.: AMG Publishers, 1991.

At-A-Glance

1. True Light Is Shown by Love for Other Believers (1 John 2:7–11)
2. True Light Is Shown by Love for the Father (2:15–17)

In Depth

1. True Light Is Shown by Love for Other Believers (1 John 2:7–11)

The commandment instructing believers to love one another would be familiar to John's audience as it is deeply rooted in Christian tradition (Leviticus 19:18). However, it took on new meaning after the coming of Christ (Matthew 22:36–40; John 4:19–21). Since John is opposing the false teachings of the Gnostics, he reorients the faith of his readers toward the work, words, and Person of Jesus Christ. Jesus, who both mediates and embodies the kingdom of God, introduces a love ethic rooted in relationship with the Father. The objective and historical presence of the Messiah inaugurated a new order of divine power to implement the rule of love in inner motivation and external action. The affirmation that the light is already shining references this new reality. Now we can love another as Christ loved us or because we were first loved (John 13:34; 15:9–10; 1 John 4:19–21).

Using Gnostic terminology like "light" and "darkness" to express Christian truth, John calls attention to contradictions between the philosophical and religious ideas of Gnostic and apostolic teachers about the nature of reality, truth, and goodness. Concerning reality, Christians accept the Light that has already shone in the darkness of the world instead of trying to escape to the realm of light (John 1:1–9). Exploring the essence of truth and goodness, John explains light in ethical rather than physical terms. To address the spiritual arrogance and professed moral perfection of the heretics, John insists that the person who believes what is right and does what is right walks in the light. In contrast, a person who does not maintain the truth of apostolic teaching and has broken fellowship with other believers is blinded by darkness. One who abides in the light does so through conduct—not mystical experience—identified as obedience to the law of love (John 2:10).

2. True Light Is Shown by Love for the Father (2:15–17)

John's exhortation not to love the world is not because the material world is evil like the Gnostics propose. Instead, John understands the world to be the totality of human existence under the influence of the evil one. The world is characterized by sensual

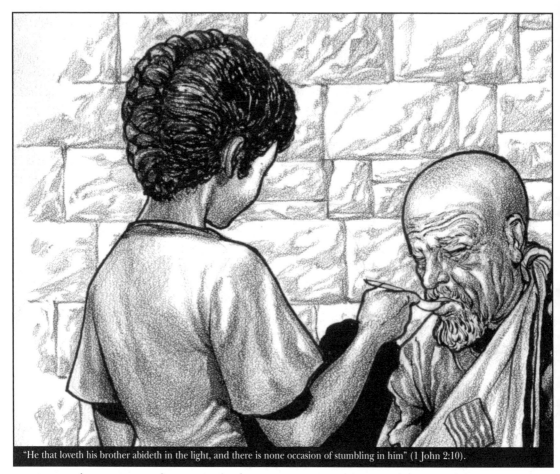

"He that loveth his brother abideth in the light, and there is none occasion of stumbling in him" (1 John 2:10).

indulgences (lust of the flesh), materialism (lust of the eyes), and self-glorification (pride of life). Those who love the world rebel against God's law, have heretical beliefs, and have broken fellowship with God and other believers. All that pertains to the world is passing away, but those who love and obey God live in the light forever.

Sources

Ladd, George E. *A Theology of the New Testament,* rev. ed. Grand Rapids, Mich.: Eerdmans Publishing, 1993, 657–665.

Mansfield, Robert. *Theology of the New Testament Class Supplement Guide.* Tulsa, Okla.: Oral Roberts University, 1999.

McNeile, A. H. *An Introduction to the Study of the New Testament.* Oxford: University Press, 1927.

Search the Scriptures

1. The audience of 1 John is instructed to obey what commandment (vv. 7–8, 10)?

2. Name two characteristics of the believer who loves other Christians (v. 10).

3. Describe John's assessment of the person who hates other believers (v. 11).

4. According to John, is it possible to love God and the world (v. 15)?

5. What ungodly behaviors, values, and attitudes characterize the world (v. 16)?

6. Compare the fate of the world with those that obey God (v. 17).

Discuss the Meaning

1. If John were writing to churches in your area today, what alternative Gospel messages and attitudes would he oppose? Which biblical text or traditional teachings of the church do they contradict?

2. How do you determine authentic Christian spirituality? Why is obedience to the law of love, a valid

requirement for the church today? What other scriptural references are helpful for adopting additional criteria?

3. Evaluate both the beneficial effects of exhortations that assure salvation and the negative effects of spiritual pride on the Christian community. How can confident believers guard against the temptation to become haughty?

4. Why do you believe John places such importance on fellowship and Christian community in the lives of believers?

Lesson in Our Society

There are many competing messages in our society that seek to displace the Gospel message taught, heard, and believed from the beginning: that God first loved us. Because God's love for us, He sent us the Light, which is Jesus Christ. We walk in that light by loving God and others as Christ has shown us. First, we should be sure that we have grasped the truth. Then we must be on guard against philosophies that deny the apostolic teachings of the church, disobey the law of love, and claim a "special knowledge of God" that excludes the entire Christian community. Contrary to John's warning, today many Christians are drinking from the wells of many other religious traditions and new age spiritualities in search of authentic spirituality or "true light." Everyone who drinks from those wells will be thirsty again, but believers who choose not to forsake truth in the face of alternative philosophies or theologies and enticing spirits will receive what will become in them a well of living water leading to eternal life (John 4:14).

Make It Happen

This week, ask the Lord to reveal how you should show love to another believer or what worldly affection you should release. Write this down on a piece of paper or in a journal.

Follow the Spirit

What God wants me to do:

_____

_____

Remember Your Thoughts

Special insights I have learned:

_____

_____

More Light on the Text
1 John 2:7–11, 15–17

7 Brethren, I write no new commandment unto you, but an old commandment which ye had from the beginning. The old commandment is the word which ye have heard from the beginning.

The apostle John makes clear from the onset that the commandment he is about to require the Christians to obey is not new. It is the same old command that they have heard read to them from the Old Testament. *Kainos* (**kahee-NOS**) is the Greek adjective qualifying something that is new relative to quality or form rather than time. For example, Christianity is not a new thing in the African American experience, but today's expression of Christianity can be said to be new, when referring to how it is packaged to express uniquely African American concerns. John, therefore, is not inventing a commandment that has never existed before. Keeping the Ten Commandments given to the Jewish people are not the way to be saved. However, they provide an excellent mandate for how we should act and respond to God, the love of Jesus Christ, and the Holy Spirit. We only need to be creative in applying the old commandments to new situations we face in life.

The Greek word for "commandment" is *entole* (**en-tol-AY**) and is used by Jesus and the apostles with reference to the Law of Moses. In Matthew 22:37–40, Jesus taught that the entire Old Testament is fulfilled in the commandments to love God with all of one's being (Deuteronomy 6:5) and to "love your neighbor as yourself" (Leviticus 19:18, NIV). Thus, John's command to his readers goes back to Moses and is repeated by Jesus. Therefore, John's readers do not have to be afraid or suspicious that he is misleading them with a new commandment. As Christians, we need to be wary of new teachings that are not grounded in Scripture. We must not be too lazy to search the Scriptures and make sure that any new teachings we hear agree with what the Bible says. The Bible, and not any preacher or teacher of it, should be our final authority in matters of faith and practice.

8 Again, a new commandment I write unto you, which thing is true in him and in you: because the darkness is past, and the true light now shineth.

For John, the commandment of love is neither old, nor new, it is both old and new. The old commandment to "love your neighbor as yourself" now has a new dimension to it-the standard is no longer "as yourself" but "As [Christ has] loved you" (John 13:34). Self love is not the Christian standard for loving others; the sacrificial love of Christ is. Christians have been made a new creation in Christ (2 Corinthians 5:17) and thereby enabled to love according to this new love command.

The truth or reality of this new dimension to the love commandment is established in Christ and experienced by Christians. This new commandment is true in Christ, who gave His life to exemplify and establish the new standard of self-sacrifice. It is also true in the saints because they are the beneficiaries of Christ's sacrificial love. As beneficiaries of this new love command, it behooves us to also love others accordingly. Sometimes, loving others as we love ourselves results in a conflict of interest. There is no conflict of interest when we live by the new love command because our own interest will be sacrificed for that of others.

John employs the light and darkness metaphor to explain why he is giving the Christians a new command. For Christians, the darkness that symbolizes their past state of being lost in sin and objects of God's wrath is over. Now, through Christ, the light of salvation is shining on Christians who are the objects and beneficiaries of Christ's sacrificial love. Self-love can easily degenerate into selfishness, self-centeredness, and self-indulgence, which do not reflect the Christians status in Christ. Sacrificial love, however, focuses on the interest of others just as Christ died that we might live. If we are guided by self-love, we would only care for our personal interest, or the interest of our own local church, or our own ethnic group. Sacrificial love reaches out to and

benefits those who are not like us, who cannot repay us, or even who do not like us. It is like an equal opportunity employer that does not discriminate on the basis of race, gender, or creed. Sacrificial love does not discriminate between self and others.

9 He that saith he is in the light, and hateth his brother, is in darkness even until now.

Apparently there were some among John's readers who claimed but had no real experience of being in the light. Being in the light (being saved) is more than mere words. It must be evidenced by an attitude characterized by love for others. Claiming to be in the light does not put one automatically in the light. One must walk the talk by demonstrating the sacrificial love of Christ, especially toward fellow Christians. Anyone who calls herself/himself a Christian but continuously hates another is, in reality, still living in darkness. In this instance, hate is the failure to deny oneself, the unwillingness to lay down one's life for a brother (John 15:13).

Christian love is more than a feeling. It is an attitude fleshed out in action by deeds of love for Christians and others. Salvation is both a private as well as a public matter. Love is the means whereby our private salvation experience is made public for others to see and experience.

10 He that loveth his brother abideth in the light, and there is none occasion of stumbling in him.

John here introduces another metaphor of "abiding" to describe the experience of sacrificial love. In Greek' the word *meno* (**MEN-o**) has a primary meaning of staying in a place, like the house where one resides. Therefore, one who loves his/her fellow Christians is not a stranger to being in the light, but actually resides in the light.

The Greek term *skandalon* (**SKAN-dal-on**) refers to a trap or snare; hence, it is used figuratively for that which causes one to sin or fall morally. If our guiding principle for loving is the sacrificial love of Christ, it exposes and keeps us from tripping over the snares of the devil on our path. Whatever is not motivated by the kind of sacrificial love modeled by Christ is a stumbling block for the Christian. This love should be the driving force behind all interpersonal interactions among Christians. Other motivations for actions such as self-glory, self-interest, and self-indulgence are stumbling blocks and should be avoided.

11 But he that hateth his brother is in darkness, and walketh in darkness, and knoweth not wither he goeth, because that darkness hath blinded his eyes.

This verse is the exact opposite of the previous verse focusing on the implication and consequence of hate. A so-called Christian who habitually hates other Christians is still in a state of moral darkness and has not experienced Christ's deliverance. In the New Testament, the Greek word *miseo* (**mis-EH-o**) can refer to a malicious or unjustifiable feeling against someone. Or it can simply mean to love someone less than another as in John 12:25 (NIV) where Jesus teaches that: "The man who loves his life will lose it, while the man who hates his life in this world will keep it for eternal life." It is clear that to have a malicious feeling against a fellow Christian is not compatible with the sacrificial love modeled by Christ. But neither is it compatible with the exemplary love of Christ to put our own interest ahead of that of other Christians. Instead sacrificial love demands that we consider the interest of others before our own.

To hate another Christian or to be habitually selfish in relating to other Christians is evidence of being in a state of spiritual darkness. Those in this state walk in (engage in acts characterized by) spiritual darkness. Consequently, they do not know where they are going; their existence is like groping in the dark, unaware of the danger ahead. Those who live hating others are unaware of the self-destructive nature of their lifestyle. They think the victims of their hatred are others, without realizing that they themselves are the real victims. They fail to understand the real damage of their hatred to themselves because they've become spiritually blinded by it.

Hatred not only blinds us to its destructive effects on us, it also blinds us to the good qualities in others. When we hate someone, we fail to see the good qual-ities in that person and don't appreciate what God is doing in and through them. In this regard, the one hating is worse off than the one being hated.

In the church today, there are many who falsely claim to be members of God's family. How do we know the true claimants who are in the light as God Himself is in the light from false claimants who are actually in the dark and outside of God's family? We must use the test of obedience to God's word. For example, there is a growing use of paternity tests today to settle the unfortunate dispute of paternity. Hardly anyone contests the result of a paternity test because it is considered highly reliable. In the same fashion, the serious question of spiritual paternity can be resolved definitively by taking a spiritual paternity test. The paternity test for all those who claim to be members of God's family is whether or not they live in obedience to the command to love other Christians in the self-sacrificing way modeled by Christ.

2:15 Love not the world, neither the things that are in the world. If any man love the world, the love of the Father is not in him.

Thus far, the apostle John has encouraged his readers to love others sacrificially as modeled by Christ. The Christian is called to love all humanity. But in these next verses, John is warning his readers against making the world and all its entailments the objects of their love. It is all too easy to love the world and the things in it instead of loving our fellow human beings. The Greek word used for "love" here is *agapao* (**ag-ap-AH-o**) and does not denote the sacrificial love exemplified by Christ mentioned in verse 10; rather, it means to be well-pleased or contented with the things of the world. Barker says it denotes "the love that entices by an evil desire or a forbidden appetite . . . . It is the world's ability to seduce believers, to draw them away from love of the Father." It is a seductive passion for the things of the world that lures its victims away from God.

The "world," (Gk. *kosmos*, **KOS-mos**), which is the object of this evil desire, is a system or order whose values are opposed to God. The "world" in this context is to be differentiated from the physical, material world and its inhabitants. Any culture, value system, institution, or ideology that is opposed to God can be rightly termed "worldly." The Christian is not to love the world or the things in the world. The things in the world can be material, spiritual, ideological, or systemic. They all have one thing in common, that is, their opposition to God.

Love for this world and the things in it cannot coexist with love for God. Therefore, love for this world is evidence of the absence of love for God. When a Christian loves God, he/she shows it by submitting to the commands of God. Love for God entails obedience to His commands. In the same way, to love the world is to submit to its controlling influence knowingly or unknowingly. There is a struggle for mastery between these two loves. Jesus makes clear that "No one can serve two masters. Either he will hate the one and love the other, or he will be devoted to the one and despise the other. You cannot serve both God and money [mammon]" (Matthew 6:24, NIV). Jesus' words remind us that we can truly only serve God, or we choose to serve whatever "mammon" represents in our lives. If indeed we are children of God, then we would obey His command to love other Christians as Christ loves us. Love for other Christians is an indication that we are the children of the heavenly Father who is love Himself.

16 For all that is in the world, the lust of the flesh, and the lust of the eyes, and the pride of life, is not of the Father, but is of the world.

John here gives reason for his conclusion in the previous verse that love for God and for the world cannot coexist in the same person. John reasons that all that constitutes love for the world (i.e., various kinds of lusts and arrogance) are not of the Father. The Greek source of the word translated "lust" here is *epithumia* (**ep-ee-thoo-MEE-ah**) and denotes a strong desire, craving, or longing. The strong desire may be positive or negative, depending on the object and the underlying motive. The context here suggests that it is a strong desire that is opposed to God; hence, it is rightly translated "lust." No doubt this lust defines further what love for the world includes in verse 15. The other aspect of love for the world is

"pride," which translates the Greek word *alazoneia* (**al-ad-zon-I-a**) and means self-confidence, boasting, or arrogance. It is characterized by a careless and empty trust in one's own power and resources that despises and violates divine laws and human rights. Any pride or self-confidence not rooted in God is not of God.

The lust of the flesh, the lust of the eyes, and the pride of life have been summarized as sensuality, superficiality, and showmanship. The lust of the flesh refers to those negative desires that originate from fallen human nature. They are not bad because of their association with our physical bodies but because they are pursued in ways that violate God's commands. The same is true of the lust of the eyes. The eyes, in themselves, are not evil, but they become a gateway for the strong desire to acquire those things that the eyes find very appealing, even if it is at the cost of disobeying God's Word. The pride of life, most likely, refers to conceit that stems from or depends on one's means of livelihood. Compare 1 John 3:17 and Mark 12:44 where in both passages the word *bios* (**BEE-os**) refers to one's goods or means of livelihood respectively. Again, it is not the ownership of goods that is wrong; rather it is the arrogant dependence on one's possession in a manner that fails to recognize God's provision of all good things that is wrong.

Adam and Eve's experience recounted in Genesis 3:6 illustrates the dynamics of these three desires: she "saw that the tree was good for food" (the lust of the flesh), "and that it was pleasant to the eyes" (the lust of the eyes), "and also desirable for gaining wisdom" (the pride of life) then both proceeded to disobey God's prohibition.

Unlike the negative example of Adam and Eve, we see in Jesus' encounter with the Devil a positive example of how love for the Father was tested by means of lust of the flesh, the lust of the eyes, and the pride of life. According to Luke 4:1–13, the devil tried to cause Jesus to disregard God's Word by tempting Him with food, the splendor of material things, and the arrogant display of His power. Each time Jesus refused to yield by submitting Himself to the authority of God's Word, which He quoted time and again to ward off the Devil.

These strong desires and pride are bad because they are not of God. That is, they do not come from God. God is not their author, the world is. As Christians, we must be careful that our desire for things does not have mastery over us that we are willing to disregard God's commands. Our love for God, which translates into obedience to His commands, must override our desires for the things of this world, such as the desire for power, possessions, prestige, and popularity.

17 And the world passeth away, and the lust thereof: but he that doeth the will of God abideth for ever.

John here discusses a second and final reason why his readers should not love the world. As a system opposed to God, the world and its strong desires are only momentary and therefore not worth the cost of losing an eternity with God. Who in their right mind would like to trade in a brand new Cadillac with a 10-year warranty for a 20-year-old Volkswagen Beetle that hardly runs? The irrationality of making a decision like this is incomparably better than forfeiting eternity with God on account of the fleeting and illusory pleasures that the world promises those in love with it. The world and its lusts are both transitory. Therefore, any promise of success, pleasure, power, and prestige held out to those who desire these things is bound to be transitory too. The ungodly system of the world does not have any eternal values, so it can't offer what it does not have.

The lure of the prospect of becoming rich quickly and easily has become a major problem bedeviling the younger generation of African Americans. The get-rich-quick mentality is like some of the popular fast foods, which instantly gratify your hunger as well as your taste buds; but their long-term effects on your body are destructive. The seductive promises of quick success that the ungodly system of the world offers are usually prominently displayed, as it were, in large and bold print; but the destructive aspects of these promises are hardly expressed, and if at all expressed, they are in very small print tucked away in an obscure corner.

The contrast, in verse 17, to the world and its lust is the one who does the will of God. So, by implication, the world here refers to that which is opposed to the will of God. Doing the will of God, unlike loving the world, holds a promise of eternal life. In this context, doing the will of God is another way of describing obedience to God's commands, not least the new command to love others. Doing the will of God is not something one does occasionally or when one feels like it. Rather it is a lifestyle that one is intentionally committed to so that it becomes habitual.

Sources

Barker, Kenneth L., ed. "1 John." *Zondervan NIV Bible Commentary, Volume 2*. Grand Rapids, Mich.: Zondervan, 1994, 1088–89.

Brown, Raymond E. *The Epistles of John, Volume 30*. Garden City, New York: Doubleday & Company, 1982, 286.

Daily Bible Readings

M: Partakers of the Divine Nature
2 Peter 1:5–11
T: Living in Love
Romans 12:9–21
W: Fulfilling the Law in Love
Romans 13:8–14
T: Serve with Love
Galatians 5:13–26
F: Love Deeply
1 Peter 4:1–11
S: Called to Live in Love
1 John 2:7–11
S: Live for God
1 John 2:12–17

TEACHING TIPS

March 11
Bible Study Guide 2

1. Words You Should Know

A. Laid down (1 John 3:16) *tithemi* (Gk.)—Denotes to place aside, put down, set forth, fix, establish, or appoint.

B. Bowels (v. 17) *splagchnon* (Gk.)—Regarded as the seat of both violent passions, such as anger and love, and tender affections, especially kindness, benevolence, and compassion. Refers here to a heart in which inward affection and mercy reside.

C. Condemn (v. 21) *kataginosko* (Gk.)—To accuse, find fault with, or blame; to be in the wrong.

2. Teacher Preparation

A. Pray for your students in your class, asking God to open their hearts to today's lesson.

B. Study the Focal Verses in at least one other translation.

C. Read the Bible Background and The People, Places, and Times section.

D. Complete lesson 2 in the *Precepts For Living® Personal Study Guide*.

E. Answer the Search the Scriptures and Discuss the Meaning questions.

3. Starting the Lesson

A. Before the students arrive for class, write the Lesson Aim on the board.

B. Ask one student to lead the class in prayer.

C. Read the Focal Verses and the Keep in Mind verse aloud in unison. Ask for volunteers to read the In Depth section and explain the verses.

4. Getting into the Lesson

A. To help the students focus on today's lesson ask for a volunteer to read the Background and The People, Places, and Times sections. Discuss these sections briefly.

B. Have volunteers read and then solicit responses to the Search the Scriptures questions.

C. Ask a student to read the Discuss the Meaning questions and generate a thorough discussion around class responses.

5. Relating the Lesson to Life

A. Have the students read the In Focus story and complete the Lesson in Our Society exercise. Briefly discuss with the class various societal ills such as crimes of passion, hate crimes, or murder. Ask students to share honestly how they think the contents of their hearts would measure against "God's love thermostat."

B. Ask the students to share any insights they may have on how to overcome such ills and still be obedient to the commandment to love.

6. Arousing Action

A. Direct the students' attention to the Make It Happen section. Ask the students to seriously consider how they respond in various situations. Help them identify ways of coping with mistreatment by making a list of "natural" responses versus godly responses.

B. Remind the students to read the Daily Bible Readings, Remember Your Thoughts, and Follow the Spirit sections for the week.

C. Ask the class if there are any particular prayer requests and end the lesson with prayer.

Worship Guide

For the Superintendent or Teacher
Theme: The Test of Love
Theme Song: "Spirit of the Living God"
Scripture: 1 John 3:11–24
Song: "Blessed Be the Name of the Lord"
Meditation: Lord, Jesus, we thank You for loving us and showing us how to love one another. Give us the strength and grace to love according to Your precious Word. We love You and will continue to give Your holy name praise. In Jesus' name, we pray. Amen.

THE TEST OF LOVE

Bible Background ● 1 JOHN 3
Printed Text ● 1 JOHN 3:11–24   Devotional Reading ● 1 CORINTHIANS 13

Lesson Aim

By the end of the lesson, we will:

SUMMARIZE John's teachings on how Christians are to relate to one another;

IDENTIFY ways of coping with ill treatment from others; and

AGREE to put these coping techniques into practice during the coming week.

Keep in Mind

"Beloved, now are we the sons of God, and it doth not yet appear what we shall be: but we know that, when he shall appear, we shall be like him; for we shall see him as he is" (1 John 3:2).

Focal Verses

1 John 3:11 For this is the message that ye heard from the beginning, that we should love one another.

12 Not as Cain, who was of that wicked one, and slew his brother. And wherefore slew he him? Because his own works were evil, and his brother's righteous.

13 Marvel not, my brethren, if the world hate you.

14 We know that we have passed from death unto life, because we love the brethren. He that loveth not his brother abideth in death.

15 Whosoever hateth his brother is a murderer: and ye know that no murderer hath eternal life abiding in him.

16 Hereby perceive we the love of God, because he laid down his life for us: and we ought to lay down our lives for the brethren.

17 But whoso hath this world's good, and seeth his brother have need, and shutteth up his bowels of compassion from him, how dwelleth the love of God in him?

18 My little children, let us not love in word, neither in tongue; but in deed and in truth.

19 And hereby we know that we are of the truth, and shall assure our hearts before him.

20 For if our heart condemn us, God is greater than our heart, and knoweth all things.

21 Beloved, if our heart condemn us not, then have we confidence toward God.

22 And whatsoever we ask, we receive of him, because we keep his commandments, and do those things that are pleasing in his sight.

23 And this is his commandment, That we should believe on the name of his Son, Jesus Christ, and love one another, as he gave us commandment.

24 And he that keepeth his commandments dwelleth in him, and he in him. And hereby we know that he abideth in us, by the Spirit which he hath given us.

In Focus

Randy and his sister, Michelle, were driving down the highway on their way to church one Sunday morning when a blue sedan cut in front of Randy and caused him to swerve onto the shoulder, barely missing a barrier wall.

Startled, Randy asked Michelle, "Are you OK, Sis?"

"Yes, but what happened? One minute I was reading my Sunday School lesson for this morning, and the next minute, we barely missed hitting the wall."

"Yea, I know. Some fool just cut in front of me."

The incident so enraged Randy that he took off in hot pursuit of the blue sedan.

"Slow down, Randy. It's not that crucial. I'd like to get to church in one piece," said Michelle.

Once Randy caught up with the blue car, he rolled down his window and began to shout at the man behind the wheel. "What's wrong with you, man?" shouted Randy. "You almost killed us!"

The man responded to his inquiry by forcing Randy's car off the road and causing it to roll over, resulting in Michelle's death.

At the trial, the man in the blue sedan was charged with vehicular manslaughter and sentenced to 25 years in prison.

Several years after the incident, Randy, racked with guilt, still mourned the death of his sister. He decided to seek pastoral counseling. After several counseling sessions, Randy realized that anger, self-hatred, and guilt were eating away at him. And in order for him to begin to rebuild his life, he needed not only to forgive himself, but to forgive the driver of the blue sedan as well. The next week Randy visited the prison and forgave the man who caused the accident that resulted in the death of his sister.

In today's lesson, believers are challenged to resist hatred and mistreatment of one another, which is a worldly response, and submit to love, which comes from God.

The People, Places, and Times

Cain. The eldest son of Adam and Eve and the brother of Abel, Cain was a farmer and Abel was a shepherd. Both brothers brought sacrifices to the Lord. Abel brought fat portions from some of the firstborn of his flock, and Cain brought the fruit of the ground. The Lord was content with Abel's offering and rejected Cain's (Genesis 4:3–5). The Lord was pleased with Abel's offering because it was an expression of his faith in God's promise of salvation. Abel was commended for his righteousness, faith, and attitude toward God (Hebrews 11:4).

God rejected Cain's sacrifice. The Lord pointed out Cain's error and admonished him to repent and present an acceptable sacrifice. But Cain rejected God's admonition and allowed bitterness and envy to creep into his heart. Out of retaliation against divine rejection, Cain killed his brother. The Lord confronted Cain about his sinful attitude and act. Instead of confessing and repenting, like his parents, Cain claimed ignorance about the state of Abel. As a result, God judged Cain, declared a curse over him and drove him out of the land of Nod, east of Eden (Genesis 4:8–16). When Cain appealed to God on the basis that his punishment was greater than he could bear

and someone would find him and kill him, the Lord put a mark of protection on Cain as a warning to everyone that sevenfold retribution would fall on anyone who tried to kill him.

Background

The book of first John was written to dispel arguments over the true identity of Jesus Christ. Speculations ranged from Jesus being a misguided fool, a simple teacher, or someone who suffered from delusions of grandeur. Today these same arguments exist, creating doubt and apprehension in the minds of some Christians, and causing many to ask the question, "Who is Jesus and was He really God?" The purpose of this epistle is to restore confidence in the believer's mind and reiterate that Jesus is God. The author of this letter, the apostle John, enjoyed a personal relationship with Christ. He walked and talked with Jesus, witnessed His miracles, saw Jesus heal, watched Him die, witnessed His resurrection and ascension to heaven. John pens this letter using clear, simple, and practical terms.

In chapter 3, John presents God as "love," and out of this love we are given permission to become the children of God. This love that the Lord so lavishly and graciously bestows upon us should be extended to other people. Our love for others should go beyond mere words. Our actions should be motivated by love and a pure heart. When we walk in God's abundant love, we can serve others with sincerity of heart and selfless motives. Whatever we do, our actions should please the heart of God and not seek the applause or approval of other people. God has given us a blueprint on love. His Word tells us how we should love and reminds us that God is love!

At-A-Glance

1. Loving One Another (1 John 3:11–15)
2. Laying Down Our Lives (vv. 16–20)
3. Living in Obedience to God (vv. 21–24)

In Depth

1. Loving One Another (1 John 3:11–15)

Christianity is a religion of the heart. As Christians, our hearts should mirror the love of God. It is His love that purifies our hearts. However, if we are not careful to spend quality time with God in prayer, worship, and devotion, impurities can invade our hearts. John references this truth in verse 12 as he reminds us of the story of Cain and Abel. Abel's death was a result of Cain's envious rage. Why does the Bible compare Cain's behavior to Abel's? Cain's wicked behavior exposed the "righteous" actions of Abel. In a similar fashion, our lives should represent the righteousness of Christ Jesus. If we live according to the Word of God, our righteous living will shine brightly in a world full of darkness and expose the immoral and sinful acts of the world.

We must be careful not to confuse "righteous-living" with "self-righteousness." Our righteousness is rooted in Christ Jesus. When we respond to situations and people through the eyes of God, people will see the love of God. They will experience compassion not condemnation, and our actions will draw people to Christ. Jesus Christ is our primary focus, and He alone should get the glory through our lives. When we act out of self-righteousness, we are seeking to draw attention to ourselves and glorify our flesh. True Christian love is not distinguished by following church rituals, public prayer, or even Bible reading. We are called to serve! We show God's love by how well we treat others. Living a Christian life will not always make us popular; yet, it is the commandment of God to live according to His precepts. The peace, joy, and contentment we obtain from abiding in God's love far outweigh any desire to exalt our flesh or seek the approval of others.

John tells us that we cannot love God and hate our brother or sister (v. 15), for if we do, the love of God is not in us. John further explains that anyone who hates his brother or sister is a murderer! This is a powerful statement; it tells us that if we are children of God then we ought to love as He loves. We may not be responsible for the actual physical death of another person but we can assassinate someone's character through malicious gossip and slander. When we participate in this kind of behavior how can we say the love of God resides in us? James 3:10–12 says with our tongue we bless the Lord and curse men who are made in God's likeness. How can bitterness and love occupy the same heart? As believers, we must allow the Word of God to change us from the inside out.

In order to love others, we must begin with loving God. God requires that we recognize who He is in our lives. When we show reverence for God, it is an extension of our love for Him. By doing this, the Lord will reveal Himself to us and transform the way we respond to Him and to others. The Word of the Lord will eventually become so embedded in our hearts that we will learn how to love according to Scripture.

2. Laying Down Our Lives (vv. 16–20)

Laying down your life for others is the ultimate expression of self-sacrifice. Jesus' atoning death on the cross is the greatest example of this kind of love. This does not mean that Christians have to become doormats and allow others to walk all over us; however, it does imply we cannot serve the Lord out of our flesh. We must allow the Word of God to change our carnal ways of thinking and behaving. This involves surrendering to God's will. For example, if we see someone in need and have the opportunity to provide for that person, we should give generously. Moreover, if we are aware of another's needs and refuse to help or show no compassion, then how can the truth of God be in us? We should offer more than lip service when it is in our ability to help a brother or sister in need. Serving one another should be motivated by love and not self-gratification. Serving others involves putting others' (Philippians 2:2–3) first.

At times, we may feel guilty for not fulfilling the mandate to love one another. We may feel we are not doing enough to meet the needs of others. God is greater than our hearts and He knows the motives behind our actions. If we know we have made a sincere effort to help others and our conscious accuses us, we should turn our focus on God's love. His love will sustain us and give us peace. Keeping Jesus at the center of our lives will give us victory over feelings of condemnation.

3. Living in Obedience to God (vv. 21–24)

Living in obedience to the Word of God means accepting the name of His Son, Jesus Christ, and loving one another as He has commanded. Loving others is not always easy. But Scripture tells us that we should not marvel or be surprised at the world's response to us, nor should the primary purpose of Christian love be motivated by a desire to gain honor or recognition. However, if we maintain a effective prayer life, we can rest assured that the Lord will give us the strength to cope with every situation. We are not to return evil for evil, but to do good to all people and always be prepared to give a response for the hope we have in Christ Jesus (1 Samuel 17:47; 2 Timothy 2:3–4; Romans 12:17–21).

Search the Scriptures

1. What does it mean to pass "from death unto life" (1 John 3:14)?

2. What does it mean to "not love in word, neither in tongue; but in deed and in truth" (v. 18)?

3. What did the Lord tell us to believe in (v. 23)?

Discuss the Meaning

1. List some reasons why we may feel condemnation and explain how we can prevent condemnation.

2. Why does the Bible tell us that we should not be surprised if the world hates us?

3. Describe what it means to lay down your life for someone else. Give some examples.

Lesson in Our Society

Violence in our society is commonplace. Today's In Focus story gives an example of how a common, everyday practice like driving a car can quickly escalate into a tragic occurrence. We know an impure heart can hinder our prayer life and make obedience to God's Word futile. The root of bitterness and envy, if left unchecked, can grow like cancer, choking the Word of God in our hearts. If God had a "love thermostat" that measured the level of love in your heart

how would you measure up? Would your heart be full of God's Word, or bitterness, resentment, or envy? Would it be hot, warm, cold, or overflowing with love?

Make It Happen

We are responsible for controlling our actions not the reactions of others. How well do you respond to ill treatment? Do you have a "Cain" attitude and display anger? Do you yell, scream, or accuse? Do you turn the other cheek or withdraw? Or do you contemplate revenge? Make a list of incidences where you have responded to situations with anger, hatred, rage, etc. Pray and ask the Lord to align your behavior in accordance with His Word. Ask Him to help you to identify ways to cope with mistreatment from others. Next time you are in a similar situation write down your response. Did you respond the same? Remember practice makes perfect! Share your responses with the class next week.

Follow the Spirit

What God wants me to do:

_____

_____

Remember Your Thoughts

Special insights I have learned:

_____

_____

More Light on the Text
1 John 3:11–24

11 For this is the message that ye heard from the beginning, that we should love one another.

John's message is clear: Love for one another is an integral and original part of the Gospel message. In this verse John states that love should not be an afterthought. Obedience to Jesus' command to love one another as He loves us is expected of anyone who accepts the Gospel message. That love shows us that the Gospel includes both the benefits of salvation and the responsibility of Christians to love one another.

Paul uses the metaphor of debt to describe the mutual nature of this love. He says, "Owe no man any thing, but to love one another . . . ." (Romans 13:8). Loving one another, therefore, can be viewed as a debt that Christians owe to each other.

12 Not as Cain, who was of that wicked one, and slew his brother. And wherefore slew he him? Because his works were evil, and his brother's righteous.

Cain is cited here as an example of one who did not show love for his brother. Cain is characterized as "that wicked one" The word "wicked" (Gk. *poneros*, **pon-ay-ROS**) is also translated as "hurtful" or "evil" and refers to someone who is bad or would cause harm. It is used here to show the source of the evil character that led Cain to slay his brother Abel. If we are characterized by love, it will affect our behavior. Likewise, if we are characterized by hatred, it will certainly be mirrored in our behavior. Hence the saying that we sin because we are, by nature, sinners. We are not sinners because we sin.

The reason Cain slew his brother Abel was because his "works were evil." Notice that same Greek word, *poneros*, translated earlier in the verse as "wicked one," is now also used to describe the quality of Cain's works. Cain's murderous act was most assuredly not motivated by love, unlike his brother Abel, but by hatred.

From the example of Cain, we see that hatred facilitates envy, violence, and murder. While we may not literally murder people, we may assassinate their character and reputation because of hatred. We must avoid hating others, especially Christians, because of the murderous and devilish nature of hatred.

13 Marvel not, my brethren, if the world hate you.

The world here is representative of all those opposed to God. John is saying that we as Christians should not be surprised because the world hates us. It is the expectation for Christians to love one another in obedience to Christ's command. Such acts of love, then, translate into acts of righteousness.

14 We know that we have passed from death unto life, because we love the brethren. He that loveth not his brother abideth in death.

Obeying Christ's command to love one another gives Christians an inner knowledge and assurance of their passage from spiritual death to spiritual life. Love for fellow Christians is a dynamic experience that testifies to the reality of the spiritual journey from death to life in Christ. Metaphorically, John compares brotherly love as a rite of passage representative of a significant change or progress in one's spiritual life. It is crucial to note that John is not saying that one can pass from death to life simply by loving others—that would be salvation by works. Rather, John's point is that having love for others is *evidence* that one has matured and has now passed from death of sin to a life based on faith in Christ. So love is the *evidence of* and not the *means of* salvation.

A nominal Christian who does not love others, in reality, has not embarked upon the spiritual journey from death to life; that person is still in a static state of death. The absence of love for others is a convincing sign that one has yet to come alive spiritually; it is a sign that one has not allowed the Holy Spirit, who enables us to produce the fruit of love, to come into their hearts enabling them to love one another in obedience to Christ's command.

15 Whosoever hated his brother is a murderer: and ye know that no murderer hath eternal life abiding in him.

This is an echo of Cain's experience mentioned in verse 12. John presents to his readers the serious consequence of hatred and establishes the parallel between hatred and murder: anyone who, like Cain, hates his brother is also a murderer. Typically, one could assume that this verse means that a true Christian cannot hate his fellow Christian. But it is a fallacy to believe that Christians are incapable of hatred and murder. The Bible records several instances of murder. Moses killed an Egyptian (Exodus 2:12); David had Uriah killed to conceal his adultery with Bathsheba (2 Samuel 12:9); Nebuchadnezzar killed Zedekiah's sons to punish him for his rebellion (Jeremiah 39:6); and finally our Lord and Saviour, Jesus Christ, was killed (Acts 5:30; 1 Thessalonians 2:15). Having established this link with Cain, John now concludes that hatred of others is the spiritual equivalent of murder and that no murderer is entitled to eternal life.

The word for "abiding" is the Greek participle *menousan* (derived from the root word *men-o*), which means to remain, last, or to endure. Its use here by John is very important. John was saying that although believers possess eternal life, those who hate or murder do not have Christ's Spirit residing within them. Thus, hatred is the equivalent of moral murder.

16 Hereby perceive we the love of God, because he laid down his life for us: and we ought to lay down our lives for the brethren.

The love of God for others is made known not just in words, but in concrete, practical acts of love. The Greek word *ginosko* (**ghin-OCE-ko**), translated here as "perceive" refers to obtaining knowledge. Very practically, God demonstrated His love to us by sending His Son to lay down His life on our behalf. This demonstration of divine love is the heart of the Gospel. Christ gave His own sinless life to pay the penalty incurred by our own sins. And the pardon resulting from this sacrificial act of love He now offers to all who will accept it by faith in Him. Divine love is a giving love. God loves and gave His Son. The Son loves and gave His life. The Greek word *agape* (**ag-AH-pay**), translated here as "love," finds its ultimate definition in this unconditional act of giving by Jesus.

If Christians follow this model of divine love, then they too ought to give something of themselves to express their love for one another. Jesus says, there is no greater love than this self-sacrificing love (John 15:13). That is why Christians are called to a self-sacrificing love rather than to a self-preserving love. And as beneficiaries of this kind of love, it is incumbent on us to love the children of God and others in the same way.

17 But whoso hath this world's good, and seeth his brother have need, and shutteth up his bowels of compassion from him, how dwelleth the love of God in him?

John says when anyone has the material means to help the needy but refuses to respond compassionately by giving, the existence of a Christlike love in such a Christian is open to question. By means of a rhetorical question, John shows that God's love does not exist in anyone who has the ability yet refuses to help those in need. To be sure, at issue is not whether or not God loves the person who fails to show compassion, but whether or not such a person possesses God's kind of love toward others.

Our material possessions are not given to us only for self-indulgence. God's command to love others requires that we use our possessions as a means of obeying that command. Some regard worldly possessions as an end in themselves. But John says they are a means for expressing God's love that is in us. It is God's love in us that should open the door of compassion inside of us, thus enabling us to reach out to others in need.

The Greek word *splagchnon* (**SPLANGKH-non**) literally means "bowels" or "intestines," but figuratively it means "tender mercy or inward affection" and is used to indicate that compassion is essentially a quality of one's inner emotions. As such, it has to be unlocked from the inside by love before it can be expressed outwardly. Anybody can perceive a need, but not everybody has the key to unlock the inner door of their compassion to minister to another's need. What is the state of the door of your compassion?

18 My little children, let us not love in word, neither in tongue; but in deed and in truth.

Addressing his readers as children not only suggests that John was advanced in years, but it also shows the family atmosphere that John was trying to create among his readers. There is no better institution that reflects the kind of sacrificial love John is writing about than the family. Including himself in the admonition, John says, "let us not love in word, neither in tongue." The construction suggests like a father giving advice, John was asking them to stop merely talking about love and begin showing love in deed and truth.

Christian love is more than a feeling: It involves the essential ingredient of giving. Many times when people say they love another, the only real action on their part is that of their mouth (i.e., "in tongue"). An expression of love that is backed up by only the action of the tongue is not true love as exemplified by Christ's self-sacrificing love. True love engages in actions that are centered on others. The world is sick and tired of passive love. Only active love will attract outsiders and cause them to want to become members of God's family.

19 And hereby we know that we are of the truth, and shall assure our hearts before him.

The word "hereby" (Gk. *toutos,* **TOO-oo**) refers to verse 18 and points to an active expression of love shown in a way that corresponds to Christ's exemplary self-sacrifice as opposed to passive love. When Christians demonstrate this kind of active love, they know as a result that they belong to the "truth" (Gk. *aletheia,* **al-AY-thi-a,** meaning what is true in things pertaining to God and the duties of man, morality, and religious truth). In the parable of the sheep and the goats, the sheep on Christ's right were commended for their acts of love toward others and were rewarded accordingly by Christ (Matthew 25:31–46). In the future when Christ returns, we shall all stand before Him to be judged and rewarded according to our deeds.

20 For if our heart condemn us, God is greater than our heart, and knoweth all things.

The Greek word *kardia* (**kar-DEE-ah**) literally refers to the "heart," but here it is used figuratively and denotes the center of all physical and spiritual life. Therefore, if the testimony of our hearts is negative, it stands to reason that we have not been sacrificially reaching out to love others like Christ. Fortunately, God is greater than our hearts and therefore knows better than our hearts the actual motives for our service. The Greek word for "condemn" is *kataginosko* (**kat-ag-in-O-sko**), which means to find fault, blame, accuse, or condemn. The underlying motives for our actions may not be known by others, but deep inside we know our motives. Just as we cannot deceive our hearts regarding our motives for serving or loving others, we cannot deceive God who is greater than our hearts and knows all things.

21 Beloved, if our heart condemn us not, then have we confidence toward God. 22 And whatsoever we ask, we receive of him, because we keep his commandments, and do those things that are pleasing in his sight.

As Christians we must learn to listen to our inner voice so we can have confidence before God. The Greek word for "confidence" is *parrhesia* (**par-rhay-SEE-ah**), which means open or without concealment. It may be easy to deceive others, but God knows our hearts (i.e., motives). Therefore, John says, if our hearts are open and honest, we can go confidently before the throne of grace and petition God.

Verse 22 discusses the resulting benefits of a positive testimony of the heart. If we have a confident heart because we keep God's commandments and do the things that please Him, then we will also have the assurance that we shall receive whatever we pray for. Thus, we can equate the kind of love we have toward others with whether or not our prayer life is fruitful. John's point is that disobeying Christ's command to love can hinder our prayers. But if we obey His command to love, then disobedience will not be a hindrance to our prayers.

23 And this is his commandment, that we should believe on the name of his Son Jesus Christ, and love one another, as he gave us commandment.

In this verse, John provides the crux of his epistle. When Christians act in obedient, self-sacrificing love, we obtain boldness in prayer and confidence toward God. Obedience to this command to have faith in Christ and show love for one another brings us into a new covenant relationship with God whereby we become not just His creatures, but His children. Believing on the name of Jesus Christ includes accepting the fact that Jesus is the Son of God who gave His life to pay the penalty for our sins, thus reconciling us back to God.

The second part of the commandment is to love one another. The sequence is important. The command is that we both have faith in Christ and also love one another. Faith in Jesus Christ is the basis of our new relationship with God, and love for one another is the expression or evidence of that saving faith in us.

24 And he that keepeth his commandments dwelleth in him, and he in him. And hereby we know that he abideth in us, by the Spirit which he hath given us.

To keep God's commands, which includes loving one another, is to abide in God and to have God abide in us. As referenced previously in verse 15, the word "abideth" (Gk. *meno*) means to continually be present. This mutual indwelling characterizes the relationship between God and His Son Jesus and points to their unity (John 17:21). At another level, the believers' mutual indwelling with God is also a reference to the familial union between God and His believing children.

God is present in believers through His Holy Spirit who dwells in (cf. Romans 8:9,11) them. It is through the presence of the Holy Spirit within believers that they have a sense of belonging in God's family. Paul says, "For ye have not received the spirit of bondage again to fear; but ye have received the Spirit of adoption, whereby we cry, Abba, Father" (Romans 8:15). This context shows that by the Spirit of adoption we know that we are children of God (cf. Romans 8:16). Furthermore, keeping God's commands, especially to love one another, is a result of believers' union with God. Since God is love, it is to be expected that His children will also be characterized by love. Just as we love members of our earthly family and enjoy getting together with them, so believers must enjoy helping others if indeed they have the love of Christ toward one another.

Daily Bible Readings

M: Love Is Eternal
1 Corinthians 13
T: Jesus Commands Us to Love
John 13:31–35
W: A Widow's Gift of Love
Mark 12:38–44
T: God Loves Us
1 John 3:1–5
F: Avoid the Wrong
1 John 3:6–10
S: Evidence of New Life
John 3:11–15
S: Love as Christ Loves
John 3:16–24

TEACHING TIPS

March 18
Bible Study Guide 3

1. Words You Should Know

A. Love (1 John 4:7) *agapas* (Gk.)—Christian love based on esteem and spiritual affection toward God and man. It is directed by the will, not by feeling, and can be commended as duty.

B. Perfect (v. 18) *teleios* (Gk.)—To carry through completely; to accomplish, finish, and bring to a close by fulfillment.

2. Teacher Preparation

A. Read the Daily Bible Readings for today's lesson.

B. Study the Focal Verses in several different translations, paying particular attention to the Keep in Mind verse.

C. Read the More Light on the Text section, and take notes you read the biblical content.

D. Complete lesson 3 in the *Precepts For Living® Personal Study Guide.*

3. Starting the Lesson

A. Before the students arrive, write the At-A-Glance outline on the chalkboard, along with the words "identify" and "implement."

B. After the students arrive, assign three students to read the Focal Verses. Be sure each student has paper and pencils to take notes.

C. Assign several students to answer the Search the Scriptures and Discuss the Meaning questions later in the class time.

D. Ask a student to open the class in prayer.

4. Getting into the Lesson

A. Have a student read the In Focus story. Ask the students to comment on how it relates to today's lesson.

B. Ask a volunteer to read the Bible Background. Briefly review last week's lesson to see how it relates to today's lesson.

C. Direct the student's attention to the words "identify" and "implement" on the chalkboard. Ask the students to identify ways to display divine love and what they can do to implement this kind of love on a daily basis. Write their comments under each word on the board.

D. After the students have read the In Depth section, ask them to give the answers to the Search the Scriptures and Discuss the Meaning questions.

5. Relating the Lesson to Life

A. Read Lesson in Our Society.

B. Then give the students an opportunity to participate in a discussion that compares God's view of love and the world's view of love.

6. Arousing Action

A. Have the students read the Make It Happen section. Ask the students to write down particular needs that are present in their family, church, or community. Ask the students to implement a plan on how they could help.

B. Remind the students to read the Daily Bible Readings for next week.

C. Close the class with prayer.

Worship Guide

For the Superintendent or Teacher
Theme: The Source of Love
Theme Song: "You Are a Mighty God"
Scripture: 1 John 4:7–21
Song: "Blessed Assurance"
Meditation: Lord Jesus, we thank You for Your undying love. Give us the power to love according to Your Word. Give us the wisdom to continuously look to You as our everlasting source of unselfish love. In Jesus' name, we pray. Amen.

THE SOURCE OF LOVE

Bible Background • 1 JOHN 4:7–21
Printed Text • 1 JOHN 4:7–21   Devotional Reading • JOHN 21:15–19

Lesson Aim

By the end of the lesson, we will:

KNOW the nature and basis of this mutual covenant made between God and the people of Israel;

APPRECIATE the need for respect and commitment in covenants we make; and

COMMIT to doing a better job of keeping our promises to God and others.

Keep in Mind

"We love him, because he first loved us" (1 John 4:19).

Focal Verses

1 John 4:7 Beloved, let us love one another: for love is of God; and every one that loveth is born of God, and knoweth God.

8 He that loveth not knoweth not God; for God is love.

9 In this was manifested the love of God toward us, because that God sent his only begotten Son into the world, that we might live through him.

10 Herein is love, not that we loved God, but that he loved us, and sent his Son to be the propitiation for our sins.

11 Beloved, if God so loved us, we ought also to love one another.

12 No man hath seen God at any time. If we love one another, God dwelleth in us, and his love in perfected in us.

13 Hereby know we that we dwell in him and he in us, because he hath given us of his Spirit.

14 And we have seen and do testify that the Father sent the Son to be the Saviour of the world.

15 Whosoever shall confess that Jesus is the Son of God, God dwelleth in him, and he in God.

16 And we have known and believed the love that God hath to us. God is love; and he that dwelleth in love dwelleth in God, and God in him.

17 Herein is our love made perfect, that we may have boldness in the day of Judgment: because as he is, so are we in this world.

18 There is no fear in love; but perfect love casteth out fear: because fear hath torment. He that feareth is not made perfect in love.

19 We love him, because he first loved us.

20 If a man says, I love God, and hateth his brother, he is a liar: for he that loveth not his brother whom he hath seen, how can he love God whom he hath not seen?

21 And this commandment have we from him, That he who loveth God love his brother also.

In Focus

A popular song from several years ago included the following lyrics: "I'll do anything for you. Anything you want me to, I'll do. Anywhere you want me to go, I'll go. Anything you want me to be, I'll be." What the songwriter seemed to convey is that love will cause one to do anything, go anywhere, and be anything for the one you love, regardless of the cost. You might ask, "How can I acquire that kind of love so that those characteristics are part of my life?" It is not easy.

Often, we are faced with unbearable situations. However, when we allow the love of Jesus Christ to permeate our lives and become our source, God's love will fill our hearts, thus enabling us to be victorious over any negative feelings we may have.

In this week's lesson, John admonishes his readers to hold to the truth of the Gospel. He gives practical applications on how showing God's divine love toward one another enables us to live a victorious life.

The People, Places, and Times

Commandment. Jesus gave the

"love" commandment to His disciples. This commandment was designed to govern the disciples' behavior and interactions with their enemies and neighbors. The commandment to love one another within the church is intended to produce a compelling testimony to those outside the church. Treating each other with love is one way of demonstrating to people outside the church that we are followers of Jesus. It gives evidence to the world that we possess qualities of Christ (Matthew 5:43–45; Luke 10:25–37; John 13:35; 17:21–23).

Propitiation. The act of propitiation means to atone or take on the sins and punishment of another. Three crucial New Testament passages regarding propitiation are: Romans 3:25, 1 John 2:2 and 4:10. Each of these passages presents the thought that God's opposition to sin is more than a token. Christ is the answer; He was appointed to make propitiation for our sins by offering up His sinless life and shedding in His blood (Romans 3:24–25). Christ's sacrificial death is the supreme example of divine love (1 John 4:10).

Background

The apostle John apparently sent this pastoral letter to several congregations. John is known as the apostle of love. His authoritative inscription gave new generations of believers' assurance and confidence in God. John writes this letter with confidence and boldness. He warns the church not to believe every spirit. Instead, he wants them to try the spirits whether they are of God (1 John 4:1).

Docetism was rampant. Docetism was an early belief that denied Jesus had come in the flesh. Docetists believed that the divine being only appeared to be human, like a phantom, and did not really die through crucifixion. Therefore, John makes it clear: "Every spirit that does not confess that Jesus Christ has come in the flesh is not of God. And this is the spirit of the Antichrist, which you have heard was coming, and is now already in the world" (1 John 4:3, NKJV).

In verse 7, John restates that God is the source of love and declares that the only way we can convey genuine love toward others is by depending on God.

At-A-Glance

1. God Loved Us First (1 John 4:7–12)
2. God's Love Abides in Us (vv. 13–16)
3. God Loves Others Through Us (vv. 17–21)

In Depth

1. God Loved Us First (1 John 4:7–12)

Love must be demonstrated, not just felt or thought; it is the motivation that should precede our actions. Love is the active response we give to God because of who He is and what He has done. Here John starts out by calling the church "beloved." He assumes that those who are part of the community have followed the standard set before them regarding loving one another (see 1 John 3:11). However, John is quick to remind them to love one another because they belong to and know God.

Love is a divine characteristic of God. It was best displayed at the Cross of Calvary. The apostle Paul tells us that "God showed his great love for us by sending Christ to die for us while we were still sinners" (Romans 5:8, The Living Bible). Therefore, believers in Jesus Christ should not only love others, but also strive to display the type of selfless love demonstrated by Christ (cf. Philippians 2:5–8).

John's description of love is in sharp contrast to society's definition. The world places emphasis on self-gratification, which is rooted in self-centeredness. God's love is just the opposite. Everything Jesus did on Earth exemplified the love of God. He was the personification of self-sacrificing love. Jesus demonstrated the power of love in every situation. He expressed compassion in every relationship; He served His disciples and put their needs before His own. He endured humiliation and degradation on the Cross, and He suffered public scrutiny for wrongs He did not commit. Jesus is the perfect example of agape love. Many people wouldn't even consider sacrificing their personal agenda in order to help others.

Yet showing self-sacrificing love is exactly what God admonishes us to do.

John clarifies how God has demonstrated His love toward people by paraphrasing John 3:16. He says, "God sent his only begotten Son into the world, that we might live through him" (v. 9). Only by accepting the death of Jesus Christ as our way of salvation can we experience the love of God. It was this type of self-sacrificing love that emanated from the Cross and that seeks the best for others. The apostle emphatically makes his point by saying that people who do not love in the way God has challenged us to don't know Him.

John affirms a basic truth when he says, "No one has seen God at any time" (v. 12). This is a familiar truth that John has presented before (see John 1:18) and probably something the church already knew. Nevertheless, a reasonable question is: Since the community has not seen God, how can they know who God is? God is manifested through the lives of those who love Him and have allowed His love to mature in them. Since we are instruments of God's divine peace and love, we must also show the world we are born of God through the various acts of love and service we give to others. Some people may never set foot in a church or open a Bible, but they can get to know God and His love for them by how we treat them.

2. God's Love Abides in Us (vv. 13–16)

At times, we fall short of God's "love" standards. This shortcoming is attributed to our fallen human nature. Fortunately, for us, the Lord has given us a Helper—the Holy Spirit. The apostle John affirms that the way to know whether we abide in God and He in us is through the Holy Spirit (v. 13). When the Holy Spirit controls our lives, we are able to give love and be patient with others.

Regrettably, so many of us still live and love according to the standards of this world. In our society, the concept of "love" has been misconstrued and distorted. Society often depicts love as conditional and suggests love is whatever makes a person feel good. Individuals will sacrifice moral principles and the rights of others all in the name of love.

Similarly, people get involved in relationships as long as it fits their needs; then as soon as the relationship is no longer satisfying, it is tossed aside like an old pair of shoes. We should count our blessings because God does not abandon us like an old pair of shoes. He knows our weaknesses and gives grace in our frailties. He loves us even when we feel worn out, tired, and useless. When we rely on Him, God restores and renews our strength. His love is immeasurable and unending. When we abide in Him, He will sustain and guide us in all righteousness.

God creates out of His love and He loves what He creates. We are an expression of God's love! Since we are also the recipients of God's love, we should be an extension of His love. No one has ever seen God, yet Jesus revealed the attributes of God in all that He did on Earth. When we exhibit godly qualities, we are introducing others to God.

3. God Loves Others Through Us (vv. 17–21)

The characteristics of God are absolute. He is completely good and holy, which means He cannot and does not condone sin. Therefore, because He loves us and wants to protect us, He cannot overlook sin in our lives. We must chose then how we want to live. Do we want to live according to our fallen human nature, or do we want to live in accordance with the Spirit? John explains that once we allow God's love to control our lives, it will grow and become complete. As a result, we will be able to come boldly before God's throne of judgment, confident that He will not cast us away. Why? Because the love of God dwells in us, we do not need to worry that God will reject us in the Day of Judgment. This does not mean that we will live a sinless and perfect life like Jesus did. However, God knows each heart and is aware of those whose motives are pure.

It is easier to say we love God, whom we have not seen, than it is to love other people that we see. However, we certainly cannot hate God's children, whom we see and interact with every day, and still say we love Him. That is why the source of our love is tested by what we *do* not just by what we *say*. If God is our source, then what we do will magnify His characteristics. If the world is our source, then what we do will amplify the standards of our society.

Our lives represent God's transforming power when we depend on Him as our source of love. John reminds us that Jesus commanded us to love one another even as He has loved us (John 13:34). His purpose for living in us is to transform us into the image of His Son, Jesus Christ. The love of God is immeasurable and hard to fathom. We cannot earn His love; it is a gift to us. As we submit and surrender to the love of God, we will allow His love to shine brightly through us by showing love to others.

Search the Scriptures

1. How was Jesus made a propitiation for our sins (1 John 4:10)?

2. What is meant by "perfect love casts out all fear" (v. 18)?

3. Why does the Bible say a man is a liar if he says he loves God but hates his brother (v. 20)?

Discuss the Meaning

1. Explain why we might fall into the trap of loving according to the world's standard. Why is God's way of loving so difficult for some of us?

2. Discuss why it is important to depend on God as the source of love.

3. Give examples of what we can do to allow God to love through us.

Lesson in Our Society

According to the world's standards, love is whatever feels good and satisfies the flesh! However, this is not God's definition of love. God's love is not self-gratifying—but self-sacrificing. How do you view love? Is your view in line with the world or with God's Word? Are you depending on God as your source of love for others?

Make It Happen

Based on today's lesson, reflect on ways you can show love toward others. For example, you could volunteer your time in the food pantry, deliver home cooked meals to someone sick or shut-in, donate or buy clothes for needy families, or offer to babysit for a single parent. Pray and ask the Lord to use you to meet a particular need in your church, family, or community. Share the results with the class next week.

Follow the Spirit

What God wants me to do:

_____

_____

Remember Your Thoughts

Special insights I have learned:

_____

_____

More Light on the Text

1 John 4:7–21

7 Beloved, let us love one another: for love is of God; and every one that loveth is born of God, and knoweth God.

After dealing with the matter of discerning the spirits, John returns to the discussion on love that he began in chapter 3. He now calls Christians to demonstrate what he identifies as one of the distinguishing marks of a true believer. He calls for Christians to love one another because God is the source of love. This statement is not meant to stand alone. John is not catering to our appetite for deep philosophical and theological discussion. He tells the early church that God is the source of love because he wants to emphasize what it means to be in a true relationship with God. In other words, John wants to distinguish between those who are in a right relationship with God and those who are not. For those who love "have been born of God" John says. They are God's children and He is their Father. This is why John tells us that God is the source of love; for if we truly love as God loves, we demonstrate that we are God's children by manifesting His love toward others.

Expressing love toward one another is one method of demonstrating that we know God. The Greek word for "knoweth" is *ginosko* (**ghin-OCE-ko**) and denotes intimate knowledge. John uses the present tense of the verb here to emphasize that this knowledge is not temporary but ongoing. Thus the one who loves can say that he truly knows God and will continue to know Him.

8 He that loveth not knoweth not God; for God is love.

Since love is a distinguishing mark of a true Christian, John says that the one who does not love has not been born of God. He puts this statement in the past tense to indicate that regardless of the orthodoxy of their profession of faith, one who does not love has never entered into a relationship with God. John's point is not that love must be perfectly demonstrated at all times, but there should be some sign that the practice of true love is present in the life of a believer who claims to be a child of God.

John reveals God's character by simply stating, "God is love." Just as God is Light (1 John 1:5) or Spirit (4:24), so, too, God is love. Since God is love, it would be inconsistent to claim that we know God if we do not express love.

9 In this was manifested the love of God toward us, because that God sent his only begotten Son into the world, that we might live through him.

Next, John turns to the supreme example of God's love—His Son, Jesus Christ. For God, love is more than simply kind words spoken to another or warm feelings stored up in the heart. True love acts on behalf of another and for the sake of another. Love is expressed action and exercised by a function of will, not by mere feelings or emotions. This is not to say that emotions are exempt, but that they are not the primary motivator. John says that the supreme demonstration of love is God sending His only Son into the world to give His life for humankind. Because He loved us so much, God willingly gave up His Son for us. God sent His Son that we might truly live, and by so doing, He demonstrated the reality of His love toward us.

10 Herein is love, not that we loved God, but that he loved us, and sent his Son to be the propitiation for our sins. 11 Beloved, if God so loved us, we ought also to love one another.

God sent His one and only Son into the world as a demonstration of His love in order that we who were spiritually dead might have life. John makes it clear that it was not our love for God that moved Him to give up His Son, but rather God's love for us. In fact, Scripture tells us that it was while we were still in our sin that God demonstrated His love toward us by sending His Son to die for us (see Romans 5:8).

In verse 10, the word "propitiation" is the Greek word *hilasmos* (**hil-as-MOS**), which relates to the removal of sin through atonement or sacrifice. There can be little doubt, then, that when John used the term *hilamos* he was emphasizing that God sent Jesus Christ to be the atoning sacrifice—to remove the guilt we incurred because of our sins so that we might have eternal life. Herein lies the supreme example of love. While we were in a state of disobedience toward God because of our sins, God gave up His Son to remove our guilt and called us to Himself to receive eternal life. Now that's love!

In light of this supreme example of love, how can we not love one another? Only by accepting the death of Jesus Christ as our way of salvation can we really experience the love of God. I'm sure you have heard the saying "a chip off the old block" when referring to a son who resembles his father. So too, it is with Christians. We must become loving and caring toward others just as God is with us. As consider Christ's sacrifice on the Cross, we are reminded of God's great love for us. We cannot produce this kind of love in our own strength—it comes from God. When the love that God placed in our hearts is ignited, only then are we able to fulfill His command to love one another.

12 No man hath seen God at any time. If we love one another, God dwelleth in us, and his love is perfected in us.

It is a fundamental truth that no one has actually seen God with their natural eyes. Thus the question emerges, "How does one truly *see* God?" Ultimately, we see God in His Son; but in reference to John's point, we see God in everyday life as we demonstrate true love toward one another. God is the source of love. Therefore, when we show love toward one another, we bear witness to the world of the reality of God's divine presence within us.

The word "perfected" is the Greek verb *teleioo*

(**tel-i-O-o**) which means to accomplish, complete, or bring to an end. Therefore, when we love others, we perfect or complete God's command to love as He, through Christ, has loved us.

13 Hereby know we that we dwell in him, and he in us, because he hath given us of his Spirit.

God lives in His people through the Holy Spirit as an assurance of the reality of the relationship we have with Him. The term "dwell" (Gk. *meno*, **MEN-o**) means to abide or remain. Thus, John affirms that the same Spirit of the living God that taught Jesus also abides within every believer.

When couples marry, a ring is placed on the third finger of the left hand as a symbol of the couple's commitment to one another. Every time he or she looks at the ring, it is a reminder of the commitment to abide with one another throughout this life. God's has demonstrated His commitment to us by giving us something that is much greater than a ring. He gives us His assurance of love by giving us the Holy Spirit!

14 And we have seen and do testify that the Father sent the Son to be the Saviour of the world.

Here John notes the reality of eyewitnesses who have seen and have given testimony to the fact that God sent His Son into the world to be our Saviour. It is worth mentioning that John's statement should not be taken out of context. At first glance, it would appear that the term "we" (Gk. *hemeis*, **hay-MICE**) is referring to the disciples who walked and talked with Jesus (see 1 John 1:1–4). However, some scholars indicate that John is referring to the entire church community because of their abiding faith in God, rather than the original eyewitnesses of Jesus' earthly ministry. Whatever the case, John wants his readers to know that "whoever confesses that Jesus is the Son of God" has God in them and they are "in God."

15 Whosoever shall confess that Jesus is the Son of God, God dwelleth in him, and he in God.

Again, here John restates that anyone who "shall confess" (Gk. *homologeo*, **hom-ol-og-EH-o**, meaning to acknowledge, profess, or agree) that Jesus

Christ is the Son of God will dwell with God and He in them. Loving one another, the presence of the Spirit in us, and our confession of faith that Jesus is the Son of God are all equally important assurances that God abides in us and we in Him. It is not enough to say that we believe in Christ, love the Lord, or have the Spirit. All three together signify the reality of our communion with God and together provide assurance to our hearts that we are rooted in God and He in us.

16 And we have known and believed the love that God hath to us. God is love; and he that dwelleth in love dwelleth in God, and God in him.

Here John tells us that God is love. He restates what he has suggested throughout this passage, that those who "dwelleth" (Gk. *meno*) or abide in God have the benefit of a personal relationship with the true and living God. As a result, those whose lives demonstrate true, Christian love are assured that God will continue to live in them and they in God.

17 Herein is our love made perfect, that we may have boldness in the day of judgment: because as he is, so are we in this world.

The reality of God's love among believers is a means of confidence on the Day of Judgment. The Greek word used here for "boldness" is *parrhesia* (**par-rhay-SEE-ah**), which means to be open, frank, or have freedom in speaking. Here John reintroduces the theme of boldness found in 1 John 2:28 and 3:21–22. He reminds readers how God's love is made "perfect" (Gk. *teleioo*) or complete within us. Once we allow God's love to control our lives, it will grow and become complete. As a result, we will be able to come boldly before God's throne of judgment, confident that He will not cast us away.

18 There is no fear in love; but perfect love casteth out fear: because fear hath torment. He that feareth is not made perfect in love.

In this verse, John shows the disparity between fear (Gk. *phobos*, **FOB-os,** meaning dread or terror) and love (Gk. *agape*, **ag-AH-pay,** meaning affection, benevolence, or goodwill)—the two cannot coexist.

The word "torment" is the Greek word *kolasis* (**KOL-as-is**), which means correction, punishment, or penalty. Yet John says that it is not God's will that any of His children be tormented. When we fear, we are not considering the perfect love God has for us, which in turn prohibits us from demonstrating love toward others (cf. 2 Timothy 1:7).

19 We love him, because he first loved us. 20 If a man say, I love God, and hateth his brother, he is a liar: for he that loveth not his brother whom he hath seen, how can he love God whom he hath not seen?
Expressing love for one another is an outward sign that a person loves God. We cannot see God, but we can see our brothers. In this light, John says that anyone who claims to love God and hates his brother is simply a liar. The word "liar" is the Greek term *pseustes* (**psyoos-TACE**), which refers to a faithless man. In short, John is saying it is impossible to have faith in God if one does not show love toward other people. Yes, we may commit loving acts from time to time, but if our motives are false, the deception will not prevail. When we love or fail to love others, we demonstrate whether or not we truly love God.

21 And this commandment have we from him, That he who loveth God love his brother also.
Finally, the apostle returns to a now familiar thought—love one another. It is God's great love for us that ignites our love for Him. The more we understand His great love for us, the more we are motivated to love Him. Jesus Himself said, "A new commandment I give to you, that you love one another: just as I have loved you, you also are to love one another. By this all people will know that you are my disciples, if you have love for one another" (John 13:34–35, ESV). Love is not an option for Christians. Love for God and love for one another go hand in hand.

Daily Bible Readings

M: Be Reconciled to God
Romans 5:1–11
T: Be Reconciled to One Another
Matthew 5:21–26
W: Care for One Another
John 21:15–19
T: Investing in Eternity
1 Timothy 6:11–19
F: Knowing God through Love
1 John 4:7–12
S: God Is Love
1 John 4:13–17
S: Love Brothers and Sisters
1 John 4:18–21

TEACHING TIPS

March 25
Bible Study Guide 4

1. Words You Should Know

A. Begat (1 John 5:1) *genneao* (Gk.)—To procreate, give birth or father; to bear, bring forth, be begotten, or be delivered.

B. Witness (v. 6) *martyreo* (Gk.)—To bear record, testify, or have a good report.

2. Teacher Preparation

A. To prepare for today's lesson, read the Bible Background and The People, Places, and Times section.

B. Study the Focal Verses. Use several biblical translations to help you understand the meaning of the verses.

C. Complete lesson 4 in the *Precepts For Living® Personal Study Guide.*

D. Review and answer the Search the Scriptures and Discuss the Meaning questions.

3. Starting the Lesson

A. Open the class with prayer.

B. Share the information in Words You Should Know with the students.

C. Read the Focal Verses and the Keep in Mind verse aloud in unison.

4. Getting into the Lesson

A. Ask for several volunteers to read the In Focus; The People, Places, and Times; and the Background section.

B. Have the students answer the Search the Scriptures questions.

C. Allow time for an open discussion of the Discuss the Meaning questions to increase understanding of the lesson.

5. Relating the Lesson to Life

A. Read the Lesson in Our Society section.

B. Ask the students to share any insights they may have received from today's lesson.

6. Arousing Action

A. Call the students' attention to the Make It Happen suggestion and encourage them to practice it this week.

B. Challenge the students to faithfully read the Daily Bible Readings.

C. Ask if there are any prayer concerns and end the session with prayer.

Worship Guide

For the Superintendent or Teacher
Theme: The Way to Love
Theme Song: "Great Is the Lord"
Scripture: 1 John 5:1–12
Song: "I Worship You, Almighty God"
Meditation: Lord, Jesus, thank You for being our Life-giver and Sustainer. Teach us to live as those who possess eternal life. Give us strength to walk with confidence and boldness, and make us fruitful witnesses for Your kingdom. In Jesus' name, we pray. Amen.

THE WAY TO LOVE

Bible Background ● 1 JOHN 5:1–12
Printed Text ● 1 JOHN 5:1–12   Devotional Reading ● JOHN 17:1–5

Lesson Aim

By the end of the lesson, we will:

SUMMARIZE John's teaching on the relationship between love, faith, and eternal life in Christ;

ACCEPT the truth of Jesus' identity as God's Son and Life-giver; and

COMMIT to live as one possessing eternal life.

Keep in Mind

"And this is the record, that God hath given to us eternal life, and this life is in his Son" (1 John 5:11).

Focal Verses

1 John 5:1 Whosoever believeth that Jesus is the Christ is born of God: and every one that loveth him that begat loveth him also that is begotten of him.

2 By this we know that we love the children of God, when we love God, and keep his commandments.

3 For this is the love of God, that we keep his commandments: and his commandments are not grievous.

4 For whatsoever is born of God overcometh the world: and this is the victory that overcometh the world, even our faith.

5 Who is he that overcometh the world, but he that believeth that Jesus is the Son of God?

6 This is he that came by water and blood, even Jesus Christ; not by water only, but by water and blood. And it is the Spirit that beareth witness, because the Spirit is truth.

7 For there are three that bear record in heaven, the Father, the Word, and the Holy Ghost: and these three are one.

8 And there are three that bear witness in earth, the Spirit, and the water, and the blood: and these three agree in one.

9 If we receive the witness of men, the witness of God is greater: for this is the witness of God which he hath testified of his Son.

10 He that believeth on the Son of God hath the witness in himself: he that believeth not God hath made him a liar; because he believeth not the record that God gave of his Son.

11 And this is the record, that God hath given to us eternal life, and this life is in his Son.

12 He that hath the Son hath life; and he that hath not the Son of God hath not life.

In Focus

People want to believe that life can go on after physical death. They wonder what the connection is between love, faith, and eternal life and what hope of life after death we can find in Jesus Christ. They desire to have a life full of power, fortune, and fame, but they are unsure how living a better life on Earth relates to eternal life with Christ. Instead of turning to God, they seek fulfillment in material *things* and have no idea that their inward yearning is actually to be in concert with God.

A fulfilling and abundant life must be centered in Jesus Christ. Not only can He fill any void in our lives, but He gives us eternal life. Faith in Jesus Christ will grant us eternal life and empower us to love in the way that God wants. The life we live and the life to come can only be found in Jesus, the Son of God. It is His great love for us that gives us access to His promise of life forevermore.

This week John admonishes us to believe that Christ is the source of present and eternal life. He affirms that those who love and follow Christ will have eternal life.

The People, Places, and Times

Eternal life. This identifies everlasting life at its fullness without end. All believers are promised eternal life with God at the time of their conversion (John 11:25–26). The appearance of Moses and Elijah before Jesus and the three disciples (Matthew 17:2–9) affirmed eternal life; and through His resurrection, Jesus Christ became the "firstfruits" of eternal life for all believers (1 Corinthians 15:19). Eternal life is more than a never ending existence, it is the life of God as revealed in His Son Jesus.

Love. The word "love" is often misused because of its many definitions. The classical Greek word *agape* (**ag-AH-pay**) is translated as "charity" (1 Corinthians 13:2, KJV), and can only be found in religious texts. Charity is defined as benevolent or brotherly love. The Greek word *agape* refers to the God kind of love. John uses this word to show us how God loves us so much that He sent His Son to die for all creation. Love is made evident through giving. God did not give us what we wanted; He knew what we needed. Thus, Jesus Christ is the epitome of God's love.

Faith. Love and faith are similar in that they are both evidenced by action. God demonstrated the greatest act of love when He gave His Son as an eternal sacrifice on our behalf (John 3:16). Faith, on the other hand, is best evidenced through obedient service. Scripture commands us to act in faith (Matthew 6:33; James 2:17–18) and it reveals that faith works by love (Galatians 5:6).

Background

The book of first John was written to help the early church realize the certainty of God's presence in the life of every believer. The first two chapters describe the conditions of fellowship with God made possible through the blood of His Son. Chapter 3 explains that obedience is the key to our fellowship and we should attempt to live sinless lives. Chapter 4 defines how confession leads to forgiveness and allows believers to celebrate our fellowship with God.

Finally, in today's lesson from chapter 5, John concludes his first letter by summarizing the key factors regarding achieving a right relationship with God. These are powerful verses and speak to the essence of the tremendous gift we have in Christ—life everlasting! John admonishes all believers to: (1) have love for one another; (2) be obedient to God; (3) receive the power to overcome the world; and (4) receive eternal life.

At-A-Glance

1. Trusting in Christ (1 John 5:1–3)
2. Overcoming in Christ (vv. 4–5)
3. Testifying in Christ (vv. 6–10)
4. Living in Christ (vv. 11–12)

In Depth

1. Trusting in Christ (1 John 5:1–3)

John begins the final chapter of his letter by demonstrating the relationship between having faith in Christ, loving God, and obeying God's commands. Because John was writing to believers who were influenced by Gnosticism, he had to make his points about the relationship between God, Jesus, and man succinct. He establishes three tests of true faith; every believer must (a) believe in Jesus as the Son of God; (b) show love for God and His children; and (c) obey God's commandments.

In verse 1 John states, "Whosoever believeth that Jesus is the Christ is born of God." Our faith in Christ is the doorway to our relationship with God (John 14:6). True faith expresses itself in love for God and His Son, Jesus Christ. If we love God, we must also love His Son because the Father and Son are one. John acknowledges that Jesus *is* the only begotten Son of God—the head of the church, and the Anointed One sent by God.

How do we *show* that we love God's children? Sometimes the greatest test of how much we love a person is demonstrated in how well we treat them. John says, the proof of our love for God is that we love others and obey God's commandments. John made it clear that no one can say they love God and at the same time hate their brother. To do so would make one a liar (1 John 4:20). Thus, true love flows out of our service to others as well as an obedient heart toward God. When we love God, we love those whom He loves.

John goes on to say that keeping God's commandments should not be grievous (v. 3). The word "grievous" refers to an excessively heavy load or something that is too difficult to endure. Fortunately, for the true believers, God's commands are not too much to bear because He gives us the strength to fulfill their demands. Therefore, if we say we love God, then we should obey His commandments no matter how difficult they may seem.

2. Overcoming in Christ (vv. 4–5)

The idea of God's commandments not being grievous and our overcoming are closely linked. The world's system pressures believers to disobey God's commandments. However, the Bible tells us that through faith in Jesus we have overcome the world. It is only through the power of faith that believers can obey God's commandments in a world set against Him. Only a believer who has submitted his or her life to Jesus Christ, and walks in true love, can be victorious over the demonic forces that manipulate the world. This means that by God's grace, we can enjoy peace, joy, love, and God's sufficient grace when we depend on Him.

Our situations may not change immediately, but the Lord will give us what we need to endure. We can defeat the enemy's' tactics by looking to Jesus as our source and provider. Faith that overcomes the world is a faith that trusts and loves God and His Son. As we grow closer to God, we realize that the world's sinful pleasures are only momentary inconveniences. It is the things we cannot see that are eternal and have the greatest impact in the kingdom of God!

In verse 5 (NIV), John asks a rhetorical question and immediately answers it: "Who is he that overcomes the world? Only he who believes that Jesus is the Son of God." You cannot overcome the world unless you believe that Jesus is the Son of God. John makes it clear: We can only overcome the world if we love God, obey His commands, and love others as He loves us. That kind of love results from faith in Jesus Christ as the Anointed One sent from God.

3. Testifying in Christ (vv. 6–10)

At the time John wrote this letter, certain false teachers called Gnostics were attacking the deity of Christ. The Gnostics believed that it was impossible for deity and humanity to become one because they regarded the material world as evil. John's statement in verse 6 was meant to refute this heresy. Jesus initiated His ministry at His baptism "by water"—He ended His earthly ministry at the cross "by blood." The water bears witness to Christ's identity as God's Son while the blood represents His work of redemption and the full atonement of sin.

To the elements of water and blood, John adds the third witness—the Holy Spirit called the "Spirit of truth" (v. 6). The Holy Spirit reveals the truth about Jesus' redemption and righteousness on a continuous basis. The water, blood, and the Holy Spirit stand in perfect agreement with the testimony about Christ. The Holy Spirit affirms Jesus Christ as the Son of God and leads our hearts in the knowledge of God's Word.

Next, John points out the parallel between Jesus' divinity and His earthly ministry. In order to convict someone under Mosaic law, two or three witnesses were necessary. Therefore, John says, if we readily receive the witness of men testimony, we should certainly accept the testimony of God concerning His Son because His is greater (v. 9). To believe on the Son of God is to have unshakable trust in Christ. In contrast, anyone who refuses to believe what God says about His Son is in effect calling God a liar (v. 10).

4. Living in Christ (vv. 11–12)

John concludes his teaching on love by pointing out that our eternal life comes from God through faith in His Son. Jesus Christ is much more than an anointed prophet or great teacher. He is higher than the highest priest—greater than any philosopher. He is the only Son of God, and therefore is God Himself. It is the believer's faith in Christ's deity that makes us overcomers and guarantees our victory over all situations and circumstances.

Living with the knowledge that we have eternal life gives us supreme tranquility and total satisfaction knowing our present and future is secured with God. In Christ, we are new creations and transformed from "death" to "life." It doesn't matter who we are or what we've done in the past; if we have confessed Christ as Lord, we possess eternal life. We don't have to wait to die. The gift of everlasting life resides in our hearts today! Jesus is our sustainer and giver of life! We rest in the knowledge that our time on Earth is temporary but what we have in Jesus will last forever (2 Corinthians 3:12–18; John 3:36).

Search the Scriptures

1. By what standard do we know that we love the children of God (1 John 5:1–2)?

2. What three bear record in heaven of the testimony of Jesus (v. 7)?

3. What three bear witness in Earth of the testimony of Christ (v. 8)?

Discuss the Meaning

1. If the commandments of God are not burdensome, why do we struggle with obedience?

2. John said believers know for sure that they have eternal life. What is the source of their confidence?

Lesson in Our Society

It seems that every day the world wakes up to some new horror. Violence, diseases, wars, famine, and natural disasters strike the world with deadly regularity. Believers, though subject to the turmoil of the world, are yet overcomers of the world. Think about your world. What specific steps can you take to live in victory over the temptations you face? How can you demonstrate that you are an overcomer through Christ?

Make It Happen

This week think of what it means to be an obedient overcomer and have eternal life in Christ. Think about your personal goals and life choices. What eternal values are you creating in your life, family, church, or community?

Follow the Spirit

What God wants me to do:

_____

_____

Remember Your Thoughts

Special insights I have learned:

_____

_____

More Light on the Text
1 John 5:1–12
1 Whosoever believeth that Jesus is the Christ is born of God: and every one that loveth him that begat loveth him also that is begotten of him.

In chapter 4, John noted love as an indispensable evidence of genuine salvation. If we have really been born again, we will love one another. Here in chapter 5, John begins by adding faith as another distinguishing characteristic of genuine salvation. He has made mention of faith as a distinguishing mark of genuine salvation and returns to it here. The point is that if we have truly been born again it will be demonstrated by the reality of our faith in Jesus as the Messiah.

Our faith in Jesus brings us into the family of God, and into a loving relationship with "the one who begets," namely God. It is only natural that if we love and respect the Father we will love His children as well. In saying this, John reminds us of what he says in chapter 4—genuine love for God will be demonstrated by loving our brothers and sisters in Christ (1 John 4:19–21).

2 By this we know that we love the children of God, when we love God, and keep his commandments.

What is the evidence that we truly love the children of God? Earlier John said that we should demonstrate genuine love for God by loving His children. Now he tells us that we demonstrate true love for God's children by loving God and doing what He says. These two realities are inseparable. We cannot love God and fail to love His children, nor can we love God's children yet fail to love God. The two go hand in hand.

When we keep God's commands, we demonstrate our love for God and for His people for this is the heart of the law according to our Lord (Matthew 22:37–40). However, we cannot keep God's commands in our own strength, nor do we attempt to keep God's law to earn salvation. Rather, we keep His commands out of love and gratitude for the salvation He accomplished for us, and in so doing we demonstrate our love for Him and for His people.

3 For this is the love of God, that we keep his commandments: and his commandments are not grievous.

Here John states emphatically what he implied in the previous verse. Genuine love for God is demonstrated by what we do for one another and not just by what we say or feel about them. Remember our Lord's words to the disciples: "If you love me, you will keep my commandments" (John 14:15, ESV).

Some people may feel it is too difficult to do what God wants. But John tells us that God's commands are not "grievous." The Greek word used here is *barus* (**bar-OOCE**), which means heavy in weight or burdensome. God's commands are not beyond our ability to perform, John says, because of God's power working within us.

We may not keep God's commands perfectly, but we must not allow that fact to be an excuse to avoid doing what God commands. By His power' we are daily equipped to battle and overcome our sinfulness. In so doing, we fulfill the law (cf. Romans 13:8).

4 For whatsoever is born of God overcometh the world: and this is the victory that overcometh the world, even our faith.

In this verse, John tells us why God's commands are not a burden for us. He says that those who have been born of God have overcome the world. If we are truly God's children, then we are victors. Jesus said, "But take heart! I have overcome the world" (John 16:33, ESV). It is by believing in Jesus that we become God's children and thus share in the victory of our Lord over the world. The Greek word for "world" used here is *kosmos* (**KOS-mos**). In this context, the word most likely refers to the world system as it is set against God or, more specifically, to the things in the world that draw us away from loyalty to God. In Jesus Christ, we have overcome the world; His sacrifice has freed us from bondage to the world. As a result, we who are in Christ have overcome our bondage to the world and its influences, enabling us to do what God commands of us.

John goes on to identify the source of our victory. He tells us that we have overcome the world by faith—our faith in Jesus as the Messiah, the Son of the Living God. The Greek word for "faith" is *pistis* (**PIS-tis**), which means conviction of the truth or belief. In the New Testament, the word *pistis* often signifies the belief that Jesus is the Messiah through whom we obtain eternal salvation in the kingdom of God. Notice that John does not say that it is our efforts to keep God's commands that have given us victory; rather it is our faith (or belief) in the finished work of Christ on our behalf that has given us victory.

5 Who is he that overcometh the world, but he that believeth that Jesus is the Son of God?

John begins here by asking a rhetorical question: "Who is it that overcomes the world? Only those who believe that Jesus is the Son of God" (paraphrased). It is not enough to say that we believe. We must recognize that the source of overcoming power is faith in Jesus as the Son of God. "Jesus is the way, the truth, and the life" (John 14:6). Our victory comes form our confidence in the authority of Christ.

6 This is he that came by water and blood, even Jesus Christ; not by water only, but by water and blood. And it is the Spirit that beareth witness, because the Spirit is truth.

In this verse John proceeds to defend Jesus against the false teachers. Members of a Gnostic group known as the Docetists held that Jesus was not truly human. They believed that Jesus *appeared* to be human throughout His life, but that events such as His death were great illusions. In their view, Jesus appeared to be a human, but could not have been so because deity cannot take on flesh, which they perceived as evil.

John refuted this belief as heresy that separated the man Jesus from the spiritual Christ. He wanted his readers to know that Jesus had come in the flesh, and

"And this is the record, that God hath given to us eternal life, and this life is in his Son" (1 John 5:11).

that Jesus and Christ are one. He came by water and blood. If John were indeed refuting the false teaching of the various Gnostic heretics, and it appears that he is, then his point would be that Jesus was always divine and human; He was the Christ both at His baptism and at His death. He never ceased nor did He ever cease to be Jesus Christ—the Anointed One.

John goes on to say that the Holy Spirit is the one who bears witness to this truth because the Holy Spirit Himself is truth. John does not say how the Spirit bears witness, but most likely the Spirit's witness is an inner witness of the heart. He assures us of the truth about who Jesus is. Thus, we are reminded of Jesus' words regarding the work of the Holy Spirit in the life of the believer (cf. John 16:13–15).

7 For there are three that bear record in heaven, the Father, the Word, and the Holy Ghost: and these three are one.

In this verse, the reality of the Triune godhead is affirmed. In Mosaic Law, valid testimony rested on the statements of two or three witnesses. It is worthy to point out that these words are not found in any Greek manuscript before the 16th century. Nevertheless, John's point here is not to emphasize the doctrine of the Trinity as much as to emphasize the Person of Jesus Christ—there are indeed three witnesses to the truth of who Jesus is.

8 And there are three that bear witness in earth, the Spirit, and the water, and the blood: and these three agree in one.

The three things that bear witness of who Jesus is are the Holy Spirit, the water, and the blood. The Holy Spirit convicts us inwardly. Jesus' baptism (water) and redemptive death (blood) are outward forms of witnessing to the truth that Jesus is the Son of God. In the Jewish law, it was not enough just to have more than one witness; the witnesses had to agree as well. They could not give conflicting testimony. John says that the witnesses that attest to who Jesus is are in total agreement.

9 If we receive the witness of men, the witness of God is greater: for this is the witness of God which he hath testified of his Son.

Here, John reasons, if we accept the testimony of men, should we not accept the testimony of God, who is greater than men? In other words, God's testimony is far greater because He is God. John is not seeking to add another witness to the truths about who Jesus is. He is simply communicating that the witness just presented is from God. The spirit, water, and blood are a single form of divine testimony. It is what God has said about His Son through the witnesses whom He ordained that the true testimony about Jesus comes to us, not through the testimony of the false teachers.

10 He that believeth on the Son of God hath the witness in himself: he that believeth not God hath made him a liar; because he believeth not the record that God gave of his Son.

To believe in the Son of God, John says, is to have God's testimony concerning His Son in our hearts. The nuance of the verb "hath" (Gk. *echo*, **EKH-o**) means to wear or possess, meaning metaphorically, the one who believes God's testimony wears or possesses it in his heart—he has received an internalized witness.

The person who believes has accepted God's witness as true. However, John says, that the person who fails to believe God's witness concerning His Son is in effect calling God a liar. Anyone who does not accept God's truths essentially rejects the Spirit of truth. If we reject God's truths, we reject Him and have no part of His family.

11 And this is the record, that God hath given to us eternal life, and this life is in his Son. 12 He that hath the Son hath life; and he that hath not the Son of God hath not life.

God's testimony is clear. He promises eternal life to everyone who believes Jesus is the Son of God. The Greek word for "record" is *marturia* (**mar-too-REE-ah**), which means evidence, testimony, or to summon as witness. Here the divine testimony conveys that the promise of eternal life is found in Jesus Christ who is truly the divine, human Saviour and the giver of eternal life itself.

Because eternal life is found only in Jesus Christ, the one who does not have Christ does not have eternal life. Once again, we see the Greek word *echo*, or "hath," which means possession, (cf. v.12); used here, the idea is relational and implies the union of someone or something. Thus, to have the Son is to be united with Him.

Daily Bible Readings

M: Jesus Calls Disciples
Mark 1:16–20
T: God's Love Saves Creation
John 3:16–21
W: Jesus Seeks the Father
John 17:1–5
T: We Belong to God
Romans 8:9–17
F: We Are God's Heirs
Galatians 4:1–7
S: Love God's Children
1 John 5:1–6
S: God Gives Eternal Life
1 John 5:7–13

TEACHING TIPS
April 1
Bible Study Guide 5

1. Words You Should Know

A. Alpha and Omega (Revelation 1:8)—The first and last letters of the Greek alphabet. This phrase is used to express God's eternity and indicates that He is the beginning and the end.

B. Colt (Luke 19:35) *polos* (Gk)—A young horse or donkey; a foal or filly.

C. Blessed (v. 38) *makarios* (Gk.)—A word that expresses the special joy and satisfaction granted the person who experiences salvation.

D. Sovereign—Superior to all others in position, power, and influence. God is always in control; He rules and reigns and governs all things.

2. Teacher Preparation

A. Start your week by reading the Daily Bible Readings leading up to today. Conceptualize the Lesson Aim, while studying the Focal Verses, Background, and In Depth sections.

B. Add to your learning by reading The People, Places, and Times and More Light on the Text.

C. Complete lesson 5 in the *Precepts For Living® Personal Study Guide*.

3. Starting the Lesson

A. Open the class with prayer, including the Lesson Aim.

B. Tell the students that today's lesson is about Jesus being both Lord and Saviour. Divide the class into two groups and have one of them define the term "Lord" and identify its characteristics. Have the second group define "Saviour" and identify its characteristics. Have a representative from each group write their responses on the chalkboard.

C. To further motivate the students to learn from today's lesson, ask a volunteer to read the In Focus story.

4. Getting into the Lesson

A. Solicit other students to read Focal Verses; Background; The People, Places, and Times; and In Depth. Use this information to help the students understand what was going on when John and Luke were writing. Encourage the students to ask questions.

B. Ask the students to imagine themselves as members of one of the seven churches in Asia. Ask them to think about how they might respond to John's revelation letter while they were being persecuted. Ask them to consider what instruction they can take from the letter to help them endure any trials they may be going through.

5. Relating the Lesson to Life

Have the students reread Luke 19:28–40. Ask them which of the following people they identify with when they are in the midst of a trial: the owners of the colt, the disciples, or the Pharisees?

6. Arousing Action

A. Direct the students' attention to the Lesson in Our Society and Make It Happen sections.

B. Close the class with prayer, thanking God for His fruitful Word and the completion of the work He began in each student through this lesson.

Worship Guide

For the Superintendent or Teacher
Theme: Christ Is Our King
Theme Song: "Ride on King Jesus"
Scripture: Revelation 1:1–8; Luke 19:28–40
Song: "Our God Is an Awesome God"
Meditation: Dear God, we acknowledge You as the greatest power in heaven and Earth. No one can take away Your authority. You are great and greatly to be praised. Amen.

CHRIST IS OUR KING

Bible Background ● REVELATION 1:1–8; LUKE 19:28–40
Printed Text ● REVELATION 1:8; LUKE 19:28–40   Devotional Reading ● PSALM 118:21–28

Lesson Aim

By the end of the lesson, we will:

UNDERSTAND that Christ should be our guide;

BELIEVE deeply that Christ is King; and

IDENTIFY and YIELD to His lordship over our lives.

Keep in Mind

"Saying, Blessed be the King that cometh in the name of the Lord: peace in heaven, and glory in the highest" (Luke 19:38).

Focal Verses

Revelation 1:8 I am Alpha and Omega, the beginning and the ending, saith the Lord, which is, and which was, and which is to come, the Almighty.

Luke 19:28 And when he had thus spoken, he went before, ascending up to Jerusalem.

29 And it came to pass, when he was come nigh to Bethpage and Bethany, at the mount called the mount of Olives, he sent two of his disciples,

30 Saying, Go ye into the village over against you; in the which at your entering ye shall find a colt tied, whereon yet never man sat: loose him, and bring him hither.

31 And if any man ask you, Why do ye loose him? Thus shall ye say unto him, Because the Lord hath need of him.

32 And they that were sent went their way, and found even as he had said unto them.

33 And as they were loosing the colt, the owners thereof said unto them, Why loose ye the colt?

34 And they said, The Lord hath need of him.

35 And they brought him to Jesus: and they cast their garments upon the colt, and they set Jesus thereon.

36 And as he went, they spread their clothes in the way.

37 And when he was come nigh, even now at the descent of the mount of Olives, the whole multitude of the disciples began to rejoice and praise God with a loud voice for the mighty works that they had seen;

38 Saying, Blessed be the King that cometh in the name of the Lord: peace in heaven, and glory in the highest.

39 And some of the Pharisees from among the multitude said unto him, Master, rebuke the disciples.

40 And he answered and said unto them, I tell you that, if these should hold their peace, the stones would immediately cry out.

In Focus

Breathing hard, Monica answered the phone. It was her pastor.

"Hello, Monica, are you all right?" he asked with concern.

"I can't go," she blurted out abruptly.

Aware of her struggle, he responded gently, "The rest of the team is counting on you to go."

"But everyone says with my weight I won't last a day in the African heat," Monica countered.

"But you've lost 50 pounds over the last year," her pastor reminded her.

"Yes, I know, but I still weigh over 200 pounds."

"Your weight loss was motivated by your desire to become a team leader on this missionary trip. Don't you remember your misery before you yielded to God? What's your real fear?"

"I don't know if I'll be looked down upon because of my size," Monica said.

"Don't worry about that. The question is, will you be faithful to your commitment?"

"I understand," she said.

One week later, when Monica stepped out of the airport and into the humid heat of Accra, Ghana, her stomach fluttered with nervousness. After that first night when her group met with the villagers, her discomfort disappeared, and she realized that this was going to be a wonderful mission trip.

In today's lesson, the passage in Revelation affirms that Jesus is

302

the ruler of all things. The Luke passage reminds us that by yielding to God's guidance, we symbolically demonstrate Jesus' kingship in the world.

The People, Places, and Times

Seven Churches of Asia. About 50 miles apart geographically forming a pointed arch, the Seven Churches of Asia are located in the Roman province of Asia (a region lying in modern western Turkey) moving clockwise north from Ephesus and coming around the arch to Laodicea. They were perhaps postal centers serving seven geographical regions. Apparently the entire book of Revelation (including the seven letters) was sent to each church.

Mount of Olives. A ridge of hills a little more than a mile long, overlooking Jerusalem to the east but separated from the city by the Kidron Valley.

Background

When Roman authorities began enforcing emperor worship, Christians—who held that Christ was Lord, and not Caesar—were persecuted. John wrote the book of Revelation to encourage them to remain faithful and to continue to resist the demands of emperor worship. The hostility against Christians was so great that some people within the church were advocating a policy of compromise (Revelation 2:14–15, 20). John himself had been exiled to the island of Patmos for his activities as a Christian missionary (Revelation 1:9).

In spite of the present state of the church, John directs their attention to the victory they will have through Christ in the future. He informs the church that the final showdown between God and Satan is imminent, and that Satan will increase his opposition against them, but that they must keep their eyes on God's promise to vindicate them when their King, whom they upheld, returns. He assures them that God is the Alpha and Omega, the beginning and the ending, the sovereign ruler over all human history.

His majesty is further evidenced by Luke 19:28–40, which describes the triumphal entry of Christ into Jerusalem. The crowd welcomed Him with shouts of "Hosanna!" and the words of Psalm

118:25–26, giving Him a Messianic title as the coming King of Israel.

In Depth

1. The Soon-Coming King (Revelation 1:8)

John identifies this book as "The Revelation of Jesus Christ," which could mean that it discloses information given to him from Jesus Christ or that it unveils information about Jesus Christ, or both.

When the Roman officials saw that Christians were not worshiping their emperors, they persecuted the church. The persecution was so fierce that some Christians advocated a policy of compromise. God was very concerned about the affairs of the church, its connected nations, and the world; therefore, He gave a vision to John revealing "things that must shortly come to pass," signifying the coming of Christ. John reports that this revelation knowledge comes from God through *His* angel. John is not referring to any ordinary angel or ministering spirit (Hebrews 1:14), he is referring to Jesus as Mediator. Though Christ is God Himself (John 10:30), He serves as a mediator between God and all humankind (1 Timothy 2:5), and He receives instructions from the Father (Luke 6:38).

John accepts his assignment to record God's revelation, Jesus' testimony of it, and the things he saw. Then he proclaims a blessing upon the person who reads it, hears it, and takes it to heart because he warns that the time when they shall soon see the fulfillment of his prophecy is at hand. John assures the church that although it looked like the Roman rulers were in control, he encouraged them to look for the soon-coming King who is the sovereign ruler over all.

Lastly John encourages them to look up because they will see this sovereign King "coming with clouds," unless they shrink back. Then they will see Him and wail with those who crucified Him. He dou-

"Blessed be the King that cometh in the name of the Lord: peace in heaven, and glory in the highest" (from Luke 19:38).

bly affirms Christ's sovereignty by including His words, "I am Alpha and Omega, the beginning and the ending" and confirms His majesty by referring to Him as the *Almighty*.

2. The Majesty of the King (Luke 19:28–40)

In the book of Revelation, John admonished his readers that Christ is both Alpha and Omega (the first and the last letters of the Greek alphabet); thus, He is both ruler and Saviour and worthy of all praise.

Luke 19:28–40 records the "Triumphal Entry" wherein Jesus entered Jerusalem mounted on a donkey ("colt") to publicly claim that He was the chosen Son of David to sit on David's throne (1 Kings 1:33, 44). Many in the multitude of the disciples recognized Him as a majestic King, placing their clothes on the donkey's back so Jesus could sit comfortably upon it, and lining the streets with clothes so the donkey could walk upon them as it carried Jesus into the city. They rejoiced and praised God with a loud voice saying, "Blessed be the King that cometh in the name of the Lord." But the Pharisees couldn't imagine a King riding on a donkey. In their minds, there was nothing majestic about that! They asked Jesus to rebuke His disciples for carrying on, but they were rebuked by His words.

We must not be like the Pharisees, who were with Jesus and did not recognize Him. It is imperative to know that we will be persecuted for the name of Jesus Christ (Matthew 10:22). However, we will fare well through these trials knowing that it is only preparation for His soon coming. Our Lord is in control and He is sovereign. He is majestic and deserves our praise in the midst of our trials.

Search the Scriptures

1. What did Jesus send two disciples for when He arrived at the Mount of Olives (Luke 19:30)?

2. What was the multitude of disciples' response to Jesus' public proclamation of His Kingship (vv. 35–38)?

3. How did the Pharisees respond (v. 39)?

Discuss the Meaning

Read the following paragraph and offer solutions based on the lessons from the text.

Cassandra was deep in debt. When she went to borrow money from her cousin Janet for the third time, Janet shared her testimony about God's goodness and provision for her. Though Cassandra listened intently, she wasn't interested in getting saved, until after her financial situation got even worse. Finally, she allowed Janet to lead her to Christ. Now, two years later, Cassandra loves God and her church, she is a faithful tither and a dedicated giver, although she is still struggling financially. Cassandra learned of a financial seminar at church that would help participants work through their financial needs. Cassandra is beginning to see the light at the end of the tunnel.

Lesson in Our Society

In our world, countries are being torn apart by war, terrorism, famine, poverty, social injustices, cultural disparities, and political agendas. On most days, everything looks and feels like it's out of control. In spite of the despair, we are reminded of the power, love, and mercy of God. We are reminded of who God is through the rising and setting of the sun, the miracle of birth, and the beauty of nature. Although humanity can create and destroy, God's unconditional love for us as revealed in Jesus Christ provides us the courage to stand for justice and show love.

Make It Happen

This week, identify the one thing you struggle with most—financial instability, emotional or physical healing, lack of forgiveness, or past abuse. When the area is identified, find at least two Scripture verses that remind you of God's promises of victory. Take the issue to God in prayer, confessing your attempts to handle it on your own. Repent and release it to God. Every time the situation presents itself, defer it to God and confess His scriptural promises.

Follow the Spirit

What God wants me to do:

_____

_____

Remember Your Thoughts

Special insights I have learned:

_____

_____

More Light on the Text
Revelation 1:8; Luke 19:28–40

Under the Roman Emperor Domitian in A.D. 90–95, many believers were suffering economically, politically, and socially. Some were even being killed for their faith in Jesus Christ. God wanted to remind His church of His sufficiency and His unconditional love for them. He wanted to give them hope in their "fiery furnace." God used His faithful, humble servant, the apostle John, to get the job done. Exiled on Patmos, John's earthly life was drawing to a close. It was here that God revealed His vision of present and end-time events by showing John God's ultimate triumph over Satan and evil.

God had John write to seven churches in Asia Minor to disclose His plans—His agenda. These churches included: Ephesus, Smyrna, Pergamum, Thyatira, Sardis, Philadelphia, and Laodicea (Revelation 2 3). God's message, through John, also included all the churches throughout history (i.e., the universal church).

In His revelation, God also warned those who had become lethargic and indifferent in their Christian walk to wake up and rekindle the fires of their love for Him. The triumphant, victorious God wanted them to know that He always expects wholehearted service and nothing less would be acceptable.

Not only in this revelation did God divulge the full identity of Christ, but He also let believers know that at Christ's Second Coming, He would vindicate the righteous and judge the wicked. Troubles were not going to last forever! Evil and injustice would not prevail. Believers could anticipate dramatic future changes and know in the midst of the fierce battle between good and evil that God has already won the war. In fact, God unfolded His blueprint for a new heaven and a new earth—the New Jerusalem (Revelation 21:1).

Yes, God has already triumphed! Victory came when Jesus died on that cruel, rugged cross at Calvary and arose from the dead. He arose conquering pain, suffering, death, sin, evil, and Satan. He arose securing eternal life for all those who believe in the Lord Jesus Christ as Saviour and Lord. God wanted His children the sheep of His pasture to know that He is building His eternal kingdom and that because they are on His side they are on the winning side.

8 I am Alpha and Omega, the beginning and the ending, saith the Lord, which is, and which was, and which is to come, the Almighty.

This revelation is both the Word of Almighty God and the testimony of Jesus Christ. God spoke through His Word what He wanted the churches to know and what He promised will come to past. The Greek word for "Almighty" is *pantokrator* (**pan-tok-RAT-ore**) and means the all-ruling (i.e., God as absolute and universal sovereign), omnipotent One. The Lord God is the everlasting Lord and ruler of our past, present, and future. Thus, it is stated metaphorically in this passage that He is Alpha and Omega (Alpha and Omega are the first and last letters of the Greek alphabet), the beginning and the ending. God also declared that at Jesus' Second Coming, He would not return as the Suffering Servant. He is returning as King of kings and Lord of lords, Ruler, and Judge to reign forever and ever over His eternal kingdom.

This passage reminds us that without Jesus, we are forever lost. There is *nothing* or *no one* who can save us from our sins. Jesus was the perfect sacrifice—the only One who could pay our sin-penalty and restore our broken intimate relationship with God. He is 100 percent God and 100 percent man (fully God and fully human). In essence, there is no other way to have peace with God except through His Son, Jesus. Christ must, then, be the Alpha and Omega (the beginning and end) of our lives. We must yield to His lordship in our lives. He must be our Saviour as well as our King and our Lord.

Luke 19:28 And when he had thus spoken, he went before, ascending up to Jerusalem.

The writer of Luke's gospel (the Gentile physician, Luke) was not an eyewitness of Jesus' ministry. Yet he wrote to give an accurate historical account of the life of Christ and to present Jesus as the perfect human and Saviour. Therefore, in this passage of Scripture, he gave meticulous details gathered through accurately preserved eyewitness accounts of "The triumphal Entry of Christ" into Jerusalem. This was Jesus' last trip before He was tried, executed on a cruel cross, and then arose from the dead.

When Jesus went to Jerusalem, He did so knowing Satan's intent to destroy Him (John 8:44; 12:31, 32). Actually Jesus was in the process of fulfilling His earthly mission to save believers from their sins. He was continuing the process of establishing His eternal kingdom, which will reign forever and ever as John saw in His vision on the island of Patmos.

What a wonderful blessing to know that the kingdom of God is not a distant memory from biblical times. We can celebrate today and reflect on the joy so many experienced in Jesus' times when He lived on Earth. This is Good News! The kingdom of God is not limited to our boundaries. In the kingdom of God, there is a present and future joy in knowing that Jesus' love will reign supreme.

29 And it came to pass, when he was come nigh to Bethphage and Bethany, at the mount called the mount of Olives, he sent two of his disciples, 30 Saying, Go ye into the village over against you; in the which at your entering ye shall find a colt tied, whereon yet never man sat: loose him, and bring him hither.

During Jesus' last week in Jerusalem, as He and His disciples journeyed to Jerusalem from Jericho (Luke 19:1), they came to Bethphage and Bethany. These two villages were just a few miles outside of Jerusalem located on the eastern slope of the Mount of Olives.

The Jews were looking for a king to establish an earthly kingdom and topple the Roman rulers who dominated the nation. However, this text does not describe an impressive military procession. In making His grand entrance into Jerusalem, it is significant that the King of kings and Lord of lords chose a donkey as His mode of transportation. One would think that the Saviour of humanity would select a *choice* steed or white stallion to proclaim to the world who He really was—to declare His royalty, His majesty. However, Jesus made the statement riding on that donkey. His choice of a donkey indicated that He came in peace, fulfilling the prophecy of Zechariah. His kingdom was not of this world.

31 And if any man ask you, Why do ye loose him? thus shall ye say unto him, Because the Lord hath need of him. 32 And they that were sent went their way, and found even as he had said unto them. 33 And as they were loosing the colt, the owners thereof said unto them, Why loose ye the colt? 34 And they said, The Lord hath need of him. 35 And they brought him to Jesus: and they cast their garments upon the colt, and they set Jesus thereon.

Theologians believe that when the disciples took the donkey, it was part of the expected hospitality one extended to a famous visitor (in this case Jesus—a recognized rabbi) attending the Passover Feast. Consequently, once the disciples explained who wanted the colt, the colt's owner did not balk. He probably had heard of Jesus' reputation even if He had not personally witnessed His miracles, and willingly gave the colt to the disciples.

36 And as he went, they spread their clothes in the way. 37 And when he was come nigh, even now at the descent of the mount of Olives, the whole multitude of the disciples began to rejoice and praise God with a loud voice for all the mighty works that they had seen. 38 Saying, Blessed be the King that cometh in the name of the Lord: peace in heaven, and glory in the highest.

This triumphal entry was important *to* and *for* the Jews because it was Jesus' final and official offer of Himself to them as their Messiah-King. The Word of God says, "Rejoice greatly, O daughter of Zion; O daughter of Jerusalem: behold, thy King cometh unto thee: he is just, and having salvation; lowly, and riding upon an ass, and upon a colt the foal of an ass" (Zechariah 9:9). Jewish history, however, shows that in mass, they rejected their Messiah-King. They rejected their Saviour. Yet He was the only one who could restore their intimate relationship with a personal Holy God. He was the only one who could give them eternal life. Because of the Israelites' disobedience and rebellion, they would not make Jesus Saviour, King, and Lord of their lives. Many people today are no different.

Jesus was unlike any king that the world had ever seen or known. His mission was also unlike anything the world had ever seen or known. Jesus, the King of glory, entered Jerusalem on the road to His death and resurrection to finish what He came into the world to accomplish in the first place.

As Jesus entered the city, the multitude began to rejoice and praise God (Luke 19:37). The word "rejoice" in Greek is *chairo* (**KHAH-ee-ro**) and means hail or greet with joy, and rejoice greatly. The word "praise" in Greek is *aineo* (**ahee-NEH-o**) and it means to extol or respond in praise.

Note that the crowd said, "Blessed be the King that cometh in the name of the Lord. Some theologians question how Jesus could have received such an enthusiastic welcome by the inhabitants of Jerusalem just one week before His crucifixion. The answer might be found in the composition of the crowd who greeted Jesus on that Palm Sunday. Josephus, an early Jewish historian, claimed that nearly three million people came to the city of Jerusalem for the Feast of Passover. Many in the diverse crowd were *not* citizens of Jerusalem. Therefore, many were foreign Jews, had *not* seen or witnessed His miracles.

In verse 38, the word "peace" in Greek is *eirene* (**i-RAY-nay**) and refers to a state of tranquility, safety, prosperity, and harmony. The word "glory," in Greek, is *doxa* (**DOX-ah**) and means to render or esteem glorious; to honor or magnify. The people exalted Jesus and proclaimed peace and glory in the highest. Their actions seemed to imply that they were celebrating the coming of their King; however, a week later many yelled, "Crucify him, crucify him" (Luke 23:21). They were disappointed that He was not who they thought He was. His mission was not what they thought it should be.

39 And some of the Pharisees from among the multitude said unto him, Master, rebuke thy disciples. 40 And he answered and said unto them, I tell you that, if these should hold their peace, the stones would immediately cry out.

The Pharisees (the religious leaders of that day) always had problems with Jesus. Time and time again, Jesus challenged their personal authority and power. Not to mention the fact that they had already rejected Him as King of the Jews, the Pharisees also feared a revolt among the people that would raise the attention of the Roman authorities, causing trouble for them. As usual, the Pharisees's main focus was on themselves, their position, their authority, and their power. Therefore, when they addressed Jesus as Master, they were being facetious. The word "master" in Greek is *didaskalos* (**did-AS-kal-os**) and means teacher. However, the Pharisees did not consider Jesus to be their teacher and definitely did not acknowledge His supreme authority as ruler of all. They did not recognize Jesus as their God. They definitely did not recognize Him as their Lord.

The crowd began to praise Jesus. In contrast, the Pharisees had been looking for a reason to kill Him. Since they did not accept Jesus as God's Son, they deemed the people's words both blasphemous and sacrilegious. However, Jesus told the Pharisees that if these people were silent, the stones along the road would cheer in honor and praises to Him—the King of kings and Lord of lords.

Both the passages of Scriptures from Revelation and Luke's gospel remind us that indeed Jesus Christ is the Alpha and Omega (the first and the last—the beginning and the end) of all things. He is who He says He is—the "all-sufficient" God, and the only Saviour *for* and *of* humanity. He is the Son of the living God, who is worthy to be honored and praised. He is the Sovereign Lord who holds supreme and permanent authority over all.

Daily Bible Readings

M: Jesus Is the Cornerstone
1 Peter 2:4–10
T: Jesus, God's Son
Hebrews 3:1–6
W: Children Praise Jesus
Matthew 21:14–17
T: Give Thanks
Psalm 118:21–28
F: The Lord Needs It
Luke 19:28–34
S: Blessed Is the King
Luke 19:35–40
S: Christ Will Return
Revelation 1:1–8

TEACHING TIPS

April 8
Bible Study Guide 6

1. Words You Should Know

A. Hell (Revelation 1:18) *hades* (Gk.)—Literally means the unseen world or the unseen realm.

B. Rabboni (John 20:16) *rhabboni* (Gk.)—The highest degree of honor for a master or teacher.

2. Teacher Preparation

A. To prepare for today's lesson, pray that God will enlighten you with His Word.

B. Start early enough in the week to conceptualize the Lesson Aim, while studying the Focal Verses, Background, and In Depth sections.

C. Add to your study by completing lesson 6 of the *Precepts For Living® Personal Study Guide.* Read The People, Places, and Times and the More Light on the Text section.

3. Starting the Lesson

A. Before your students arrive, write this question on the board: How Do You Find Jesus?

B. Open the class with prayer, including the Lesson Aim.

C. Initiate discussion about the question on the board. Ask the students to share times when they felt that Jesus was nowhere to be found. Remind them that God never leaves us or forsakes us (Joshua 1:5).

4. Getting into the Lesson

A. Inform the students that today's lesson is about discovering Jesus' sovereignty and submitting to His lordship. Tell them that John and Mary will serve as examples on how to find Jesus.

B. Solicit volunteers to read In Focus; The People, Places, and Times; Background; and In Depth. Allow time for a discussion between each section.

5. Relating the Lesson to Life

A. To help the students understand how to apply today's lesson to their everyday lives, direct their attention to Lesson in Our Society and Discuss the Meaning.

B. Have the students share the most significant point they learned from today's lesson and how they plan to use it this week.

6. Arousing Action

A. Have the students read the Keep in Mind verse aloud in unison.

B. Read the Make It Happen section and assign it as homework.

C. Remind the students to read the Daily Bible Readings in preparation for next week's lesson.

D. Close the class in prayer.

CHRIST IS RISEN

Bible Background ● REVELATION 1:9–20; JOHN 20:1–18; 30–31
Printed Text ● REVELATION 1:12, 17–18; JOHN 20:11–16, 30–31
Devotional Reading ● ROMANS 14:7–12

Lesson Aim

By the end of this lesson, we will:
UNDERSTAND that Christ is sovereign and infinite;
BELIEVE in the power of Christ's resurrection;
IDENTIFY and AFFIRM Christ's power for our lives.

Keep in Mind

"And when I saw him, I fell at his feet as dead. And he laid his right hand upon me, saying unto me, Fear not; I am the first and the last: I am He that liveth, and was dead; and behold, I am alive forevermore, Amen; and have the keys of hell and of death" (Revelation 1:17–18).

Focal Verses

Revelation 1:12 And I turned to see the voice that spake with me.

1:17 And when I saw him, I fell at his feet as dead. And he laid his right hand upon me, saying unto me, Fear not; I am the first and the last:

18 I am He that liveth, and was dead; and behold, I am alive forevermore, Amen; and have the keys of hell and death.

John 20:11 But Mary stood without at the sepulcher weeping: and as she wept, she stooped down, and looked into the sepulcher,

12 And seeth two angels in white sitting, the one at the head, and the other at the feet, where the body of Jesus had lain.

13 And they say unto her, Woman, why weepest thou? She saith unto them, Because they have taken away my Lord, and I know not where they have laid Him.

14 And when she had thus said, she turned herself back, and saw Jesus standing, and knew not that it was Jesus.

15 Jesus saith unto her, Woman, why weepest thou? whom seekest thou? She, supposing him to be the gardener, saith unto him, Sir, if you have borne him hence, tell me where thou hast laid him, and I will take him away.

16 Jesus saith unto her, Mary. She turned herself, and saith unto him, Rabboni; which is to say, Master.

20:30 And many other signs truly did Jesus in the presence of His disciples, which are not written in this book:

31 But these are written, that ye might believe that Jesus is the Christ, the Son of God; and that believing ye might have life through his name.

In Focus

It was Resurrection Sunday. Many across the country call it Easter. It is a time when believers throughout the world celebrate the fact that Jesus Christ, God's one and only Son, died on the Cross to pay the penalty for our sin.

Forty-five-year old Iris came to church to celebrate as well. When the pastor asked that members of the congregation stand and give a testimony of what Resurrection Sunday meant to them, Iris did not hesitate to share her story. Iris stated emphatically that she knew, without a doubt, that Jesus Christ is risen. Admittedly she was in the final stages of cancer, and the somewhat demure scarf she tied around her head to shield her baldness from the extensive chemotherapy treatments attested to her plight.

One would have thought that Iris's testimony would be filled with sorrow and disappointments of how God had let her down. Instead, she reaffirmed her commitment to trusting the Lord and Saviour Jesus Christ for her soul's salvation. She reaffirmed the fact that even if God did not heal her body on this side of the grave, that she still believed in Him; she still trusted in Him. Iris ended her testimony with this statement, "If I live, I believe in the Lord Jesus

Christ; and if I die and go on to be with Him, I still believe in what He did for me at Calvary."

Needless to say, her words stirred the hearts of everyone in the sanctuary. Indeed, this was the message of Resurrection Sunday—Jesus is no longer dead. He is alive! And anyone who believes that the Lord Jesus Christ is Saviour will receive everlasting life.

During this season, Christians celebrate the fact that after three days and nights in a borrowed tomb, Jesus rose with all power in heaven and in Earth. Death could not hold Him. Jesus fulfilled His purpose for being born in the first place—to show mercy to humanity, die, and rise again so that believers everywhere could have everlasting life.

In our lesson, John reminds us that Christ is worthy of our appreciation for what He has done for us.

The People, Places, and Times

Mary Magdalene. She was known as Mary Magdalene because she came from the town of Magdala. The first record of her appearance is in Luke 8:2, when she was among a group of women who "ministered unto Him of their substance," after Jesus had healed them of their evil spirits and infirmities. "Seven devils went out" of Mary Magdalene. She was present at Jesus' crucifixion and waited there until His body was to be taken to a sepulchre. Jesus appeared to her first, where He found her at the sepulcher weeping and waiting for His body.

Sepulchre. A tomb; usually a natural cave enlarged and adapted by excavation. When an owner's means permitted, they were prepared beforehand and stood in gardens, by roadsides, or even adjoining houses. Joseph of Arimithea prepared Jesus' sepulchre in his garden.

Background

The apostle John wrote both the gospel of John and the book of Revelation. John and his brother James were apostles, and Jesus called them Boanerges, or "sons of thunder" because of their fiery personalities. They were the sons of Zebedee, a fisherman on the Lake of Galilee; their mother's name was Salome.

Scholars infer that John came from a well-to-do family: Mark 1:20 records that Zebedee had "hired servants," and the apostle John associated with Annas the high priest (see John 18:25). But the family was not above manual labor, as Zebedee was in a boat with his sons mending nets in Mark 1:19–20. According to John 19:25–26, Salome was probably the sister of Jesus' mother Mary. Salome, whose name means "peaceful," asked Jesus to reserve seats of honor in the kingdom of heaven for her sons (Mark 20:20). She was with her sister Mary at Jesus' crucifixion and later at the sepulcher.

Salome and Zebedee apparently trained their boys in the nurture and admonition of the Lord, because when Jesus called them as disciples the text records that "straightway he called them: and they left their father Zebedee in the ship" (Mark 1:20). John was known as the "disciple whom Jesus loved," and his love for Jesus was is recorded in several texts, including John 13:25, where he laid his head on Jesus' breast.

Sources

Smith, William. *Smith's Bible Dictionary.* Peabody, Mass.: Hendrickson Publishers, Inc., 2000, 94, 315–316, 581, 757.

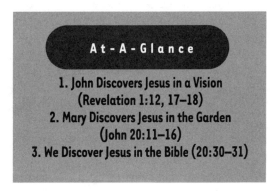

At-A-Glance

1. John Discovers Jesus in a Vision (Revelation 1:12, 17–18)
2. Mary Discovers Jesus in the Garden (John 20:11–16)
3. We Discover Jesus in the Bible (20:30–31)

In Depth

1. John Discovers Jesus in a Vision (Revelation 1:12, 17–18)

In the midst of a seemingly hopeless situation, where Christians are being persecuted on account of their faith and John is imprisoned on the island of Patmos for being a faithful witness of the Gospel, he

"And when I saw him, I fell at his feet as dead. And he laid his right hand upon me, saying unto me, Fear not; I am the first and the last" (Revelation 1:17).

hears a voice—the voice of Jesus. Jesus tells John to write everything he sees in a book and send it to the seven churches in Asia.

It is interesting to note that John turned to see the *voice* that spoke, and not the *person* who spoke. When he turned around, he saw Jesus. John fell at His feet, a sign of great respect and awe, and was so overpowered with the greatness of Jesus' glory that he "fell as dead." First Samuel 6:20 reads, "Who is able to stand before this holy LORD God?"

John records that Jesus laid His right hand on him. Why not His left hand? The phrase "right hand" is often associated with power and depicts God as a sustainer and protector. For example, according to Mark 16:19, Jesus sits at the right hand of God. Sometimes the word "right" means authority. It may be that when Jesus laid His right hand on John, He was strengthening, appointing, and commissioning him for the assignment he'd been given.

Jesus comforted John and told him not to be afraid and reminded John of His sovereignty, letting him

know that if He was dead and now lives, surely He can protect John from harm. He even tells John that He has the keys of hell and death, absolute control over their domain.

2. Mary Discovers Jesus in the Garden (John 20:11–16)

Mary Magdalene had never had a problem finding Jesus. The Bible records several appearances she made including ministering to Jesus (Luke 8:2), watching the crucifixion (John 19:25), waiting long afterward for His body to be taken down (Matthew 27:61), and viewing His body so that she could anoint it with sweet spices on the next morning (Luke 23:55–56). However, this time she got up earlier than the others and found His tomb empty. Even the two angels at the tombs could not comfort her.

In many accounts, the risen Jesus was not recognized. It is not known if He intentionally prevented His recognition or if He looked different. It could have simply been that since Mary Magdalene witnessed Jesus' crucifixion and burial she had no reason to expect to see Him alive. And since she was in a garden, she expected that the person talking to her was a gardener. "Where have you laid Him?" she asked. It wasn't until He called her by name that she recognized Him. She was so ecstatic she called Him, "Rabboni," meaning *my great master,* a strengthened form of "rabbi."

3. We Discover Jesus in the Bible (20:30–31)

John saw Jesus alive and exalted in a vision recorded in Revelation 1. Mary found Him in a garden, and John tells us that we can learn of Jesus in the Bible, especially the Gospel he wrote. He writes that Jesus performed many miraculous signs and that not all of them are recorded in his book, but that he carefully selected and recorded specific ones that would stir up our faith to "believe that Jesus is the Christ, the Son of God," so that we will "have life through His name."

Hebrews 11:6 (NIV) reads, "And without faith it is impossible to please God, because anyone who comes to him must believe that he exists and that he rewards those who earnestly seek him." John and Mary both discovered that He is Lord and that He is great. We are called to discover His greatness. He is the all-powerful One. He has proven that He is both sovereign and infinite. If we are in Christ, we do not have to fear death. He has already conquered it. His resurrection is a testament of hope for His people—if we suffer with our Lord, we shall also reign with Him in eternity.

Search the Scriptures

1. What did John do when he saw Jesus (Revelation 1:17)?

2. How did Jesus encourage John (vv. 17–18)?

3. Who did Jesus show Himself to first (John 20:11)?

4. Who did Mary think Jesus was when she saw Him (v. 15)?

5. When did she recognize Him (v. 16)?

6. What does "Rabboni" mean (v. 16)?

Discuss the Meaning

1. Mary is alone in the garden at the empty tomb of Jesus. Although Mary is in a place that represents life and beauty, she finds herself dealing with the pain, mystery, and uncertainty of what happened to Jesus. Mary does not run away from the empty tomb. Instead, she seeks to find Jesus. How do you respond to Jesus when you are unsure about where Jesus is in our time of need? Do you seek Him with joy, expectancy, or intensity?

2. Why do you think Mary was surprised to see Jesus?

Lesson in Our Society

The good thing about the trials and tribulations of life is that they force us to face our limitedness, inadequacy, and imperfection, and cause us to look for a greater power. Many people, at the point of desperation in their trials, seek the power of drugs and alcohol, illegal practices, lottery and chance, horoscopes, fortunetellers and soothsayers, or government assistance for guidance and relief. Many others, when they are just as desperate and at the end of their ropes, find Jesus and trust Him as their Lord and Saviour. How can you point someone who is having a desperate time or looking for a desperate measure to Jesus?

Make It Happen

Make a place for prayer in your house by choosing an area that is not heavily trafficked. A closet or a corner of a room will do just fine. Give this place a name: "prayer closet," "refuge," or "altar." Pick a time that you will meet with God in that place every day. If it is difficult to find time, purpose to wake up earlier. It is OK to start out with five minutes, then increase the time as you become accustomed to meeting with Him. Use your time in your place to pray, worship, meditate on Scripture, study the Bible, sing, dance, or just to quiet your head and listen.

Follow the Spirit

What God wants me to do:

_____

_____

Remember Your Thoughts

Special insights I have learned:

_____

_____

More Light on the Text
Revelation 1:12, 17–18; John 20:11–16, 30–31
12 And I turned to see the voice that spake with me.

Nearly 2,000 years ago while the beloved apostle and eyewitness of Jesus, John, was exiled on the Isle of Patmos, Jesus gave him a revelation of end-time events. John received a vision from the risen Christ, and he recorded it for the benefit of not only the seven churches in the province of Asia: Ephesus, Smyrna, Pergamum, Thyatira, Sardis, Philadelphia, and Laodicea (Revelation 1:11), but for believers throughout history. God gave this vision so that believers would have hope so that we would know that Jesus is risen from the dead and when He returns to Earth the second time, He is going to be victorious over sin, death, and Satan. Almighty God will have both ultimate and permanent victory. John was to let the churches know that no matter what trials or tribulations they face, Jesus the Son of the living God will protect them with His far-reaching love and reassuring power.

In his vision, after hearing a loud voice behind him—"a great voice, as of a trumpet" (v. 10)—John turned to see who spoke to him. The Greek word for "see" is *blepo* (**BLEP-o**), which means to know by experience; to see with the mind's eye; to discern mentally, observe, perceive, or discover. "I turned to see the voice that spake with me," is of course a figure of speech. Once John turned, in his vision, he then saw the seven golden candlesticks or seven golden lampstands that represented the seven churches.

1:17 And when I saw him, I fell at his feet as dead. And he laid his right hand upon me, saying unto me, Fear not; I am the first and the last.

John saw a revelation of God and His glory. The word "glory" in the Greek is *doxa* (**DOX-ah**) and means dignity, glory, honor, praise, and worship. When used in the New Testament, it is speaking of the heaviness, awesomeness, or intrinsic worth of God's being. John saw the awesomeness and majesty of the glorified Son of God. John had enjoyed periods of intimate fellowship with Jesus in Christ's earthly life. He had lived with Jesus for three years and had already seen Him as the Galilean preacher. Frequently, he had laid his head upon the bosom of the Saviour—the Son of Man. But now, in this text, John (mere human flesh) beholds the pure essence or holiness of God. He was no longer a suffering Servant. When John stood in the presence of the awesomeness of Jesus, the King of kings and Lord of lords, terror consumed John. Therefore, he prostrated himself before the Sovereign God—the One who holds the key to death and hell and is worthy of praise and worship. He fell at Jesus' feet like he was dead. The word "dead" in the Greek is *nekros* (**nek-ROS**). It means destitute of life, force, or power; inactive, inanimate, or inoperative.

In the Bible terror was a common response to divine visions (Genesis 15:12; Luke 1:12–13), and reaction by those who received revelations of God (Ezekiel 1:28; 11:13). In the Old Testament, those receiving the vision often fell on their faces, unless the revealer touched and strengthened them" (cf. Daniel 8:18; 10:10).

John saw that Jesus' power was no longer veiled and Jesus' righteousness was revealed to be a consuming fire. The vision of the glorified Jesus was so breathtaking that it overwhelmed John to the point that He fell at Jesus' feet. This vision of Jesus inspired reverent fear in John.

Jesus let John know that He is the first and the last and He is God. The word "first" in the Greek is *protos* (**PRO-tos**). It means first in time or place in any succession of things or persons; first in rank, influence, or honor; chief. Jesus is letting us know that everything—all creation has its beginning in Him. Nothing would exist without Him.

The word "last" in Greek is *eschatos* (**ES-khat-os**) means uttermost, end, last in time or in place, or the uttermost part. All eternity rests in Jesus' capable hands. Eternal life rests in His hands and none other. Again, He holds the key to death and hell. He will win the victory over death, sin, and Satan in the end.

18 I am he that liveth, and was dead; and, behold, I am alive forevermore, Amen; and have the keys of hell and of death.

Jesus reveals Himself to John in His complete sovereignty. He lets John know that He is alive. Although He died on that old rugged cross and was placed in a borrowed tomb, He now lives! And because He lives, He is alive forever more. Because He lives, He has conquered hell. The Greek word for "hell" is *hades* **hah-dace.** It means the nether world, the realm of the dead, the grave, death, or hell. Because Jesus conquered death, He holds the keys of hell and death; He has control over them both. He is not only sovereign over physical death, but over the life after death. Thus in Jesus' death and resurrection, He took all authority that Satan may have had over death (Hebrews 2:14–15). This means that even though believers may be afflicted by Satan and in trial and trouble, no believer can die apart from God's divine permission.

John 20:11 But Mary stood without at the sepulcher weeping: and as she wept, she stooped down, and looked into the sepulcher.

The apostle John wrote his gospel to prove conclusively that Jesus is indeed who He says He is—the Messiah—the Son of the living God. In his account of Jesus' resurrection, he tells how Mary Magdalene—that same Mary from whom Jesus drove out seven demons (Luke 8:2)—was among the first to see the risen Christ. Not only did He choose a woman from a culture that held little value in a woman's word to be first to see Him, but a woman who had a personal relationship with Him as well. Early that Sunday morning, after Jesus had spent His appointed time in the grave, this Mary was standing outside of the tomb crying. While weeping, she stooped and looked inside the tomb and found it empty.

According to biblical scholars, burying the dead was not just a crucial duty in Judaism, but a pious one as well. It was also an important act of love because not being buried was too horrible to be permitted, even for criminals. But because of the lateness of the hour and the advent of the Sabbath after Jesus was crucified, Joseph of Arimathea had to hurry to take Jesus' body to the tomb. Therefore, even though the nearest of kin would remain home mourning for their dead for seven days; Mary Magdalene came early to complete the work of preparing the body that they had been unable to finish after the crucifixion. Since the first day of the week began at sundown on what we would call Saturday night, the Sabbath had ended hours before she approached the tomb where Jesus lay. Mary approached the tomb before daylight to demonstrate her devotion to Jesus.

12 And seeth two angels in white sitting, the one at the head, and the other at the feet, where the body of Jesus had lain. 13 And they say unto her, Woman, why weepest thou? She saith unto them, Because they have taken away my Lord, and I know not where they have laid him.

Instead of finding Jesus' body, Mary Magdalene saw two white-robed angels sitting at the head and foot of the place where the body of Jesus had been lying. It is clear that Mary thought that someone had just taken Jesus' body and placed it someplace else.

Bible scholars tell us that white linen garments were worn by not only Jewish priests, but by some other ancient priests and by angels in Jewish tradition. White linen also served as wrappings for the "righteous" dead.

14 And when she had thus said, she turned herself back, and saw Jesus standing, and knew not that it was Jesus. 15 Jesus saith unto her, Woman, why weepest thou? whom seekest thou? She, supposing him to be the gardener, saith unto him, Sir, if thou have borne him hence, tell me where thou hast laid him, and I will take him away.

These passages of Scripture make it clear that Jesus had risen from the dead. No one took His body to another grave site. He was no longer dead! Because Jesus was now alive and standing and the last time she had seen Him, He lay dead; Mary did not recognize who He was. She thought that he might be the gardener. Bible scholars tell us that gardeners were at the bottom of the social scale. If it had been the gardener, he would have been tending to the gardening and not to the tomb itself. Therefore, he definitely would not have moved the body. Also since tomb robbers were not likely to come during the period of mourning, it never occurred to Mary that the man she saw was a tomb robber. However, Mary's major concern was finding the body of Jesus so that she could finish ministering to Him. She wanted to find her Lord and Saviour.

16 Jesus saith unto her, Mary. She turned herself, and saith unto him, Rabboni; which is to say, Master.

The Greek words for "Rabboni" is *rhabboni* or *rhabbouni* (**hrab-bon-EE**) which means master, chief, prince, and is a title of honor Mary used to address Jesus. The title is of Chaldee origin and means Lord or Teacher. Now that Mary saw who Jesus really was, she made it very personal and called Him, "my teacher." Because she had a personal relationship with Him, she owned Jesus as Her own personal Master.

20:30 And many other signs truly did Jesus in the presence of his disciples, which are not written in this book: 31 But these are written, that ye might believe that Jesus is the Christ, the Son of God; and that believing ye might have life through his name.

Thomas believed because he had seen Jesus with his own eyes. Jesus recognized that other believers who did not share Thomas' experience would believe as well. They would believe even though they had not personally seen Jesus.

Jesus did many other signs in His disciples' presence so that they, too, would know without a doubt that He was the Son of God. The Greek word for "sign"

is *semeion* (**say-mi-on**). It means an unusual occurrence, miracles, and wonders by which God authenticates the men sent by Him or by which men prove that the cause they are pleading is God's. Therefore, miracles are an indication of God's supernatural power. Many of these signs or miracles are not even recorded in the Bible. However, Jesus said that believers are blessed if they believe without seeing signs and miracles. In fact, we have the proof that He is who He says He is in His inerrant holy Word.

If we believe on the Lord Jesus Christ, we will have life eternally. This is the Good News of salvation. Without Him, we will be eternally separated from God because of our sins. There is no forgiveness of sin there is no eternal salvation outside of Jesus Christ. He is the one and only way back to God. Isn't that Good News?

Daily Bible Readings

M: This Is My Body
Luke 22:7–23
T: Jesus Is Lord of All
Romans 14:7–12
W: Mary Finds an Empty Tomb
John 20:1–9
T: Jesus Appears to Mary
John 20:10–18
F: Jesus Appears to His Disciples
John 20:19–23
S: Jesus Appears to Thomas
John 20:24–31
S: Jesus, the First and Last
Revelation 1:9–12a, 17–18

TEACHING TIPS

April 15
Bible Study Guide 7

1. Words You Should Know

A. Elders (Revelation 4:4) *presbuteros* (Gk.)—In the New Testament church, the term refers to leaders who were responsible for the direction and government of the local and regional bodies.

B. Beasts (v. 6) *zoon* (Gk.)—A living being. The word appears 20 times in Revelation and always refers to those beings that stand before God's throne and render glory, honor, and praise to Him.

2. Teacher Preparation

A. To prepare for today's lesson, study the Focal Verses, Background, and In Depth sections.

B. Complete lesson 7 in the *Precepts For Living® Personal Study Guide.* Read The People, Places, and Times and More Light on the Text.

C. Reflect on how your church is organized—the leadership, and who has governing authority in and outside of the church—and be prepared to discuss.

3. Starting the Lesson

A. Assign a student to lead the class in prayer, focusing on the Lesson Aim.

B. Ask for a volunteer to read the In Focus story for today and relate it to the Lesson Aim.

C. Ask two volunteers to read the Focal Verses. Then ask: What are some of the key points in the verses? How can we relate those points to where we are today?

D. Use the questions in the Search the Scriptures section as a closed Bible quiz. Then have the class review the answers together.

4. Getting into the Lesson

A. Select a student to read the Background sectioin. Then ask for a volunteer to explain what John saw and another volunteer to explain "the things which are."

B. Discuss The People, Places, and Times and ask the students what type of crown they would most want to have and why.

5. Relating the Lesson to Life

A. Share your testimony of salvation with the class. Explain why it is important that you strive to live a life that is pleasing to God.

B. Break the class into four groups and assign each group a question from the Discuss the Meaning section.

C. The Lesson in Our Society section can help the students see how the lesson parallels many present-day situations. Ask the students if it is possible that they have let something in their lives become more important than serving God.

6. Arousing Action

A. Read the In Focus story. Ask the students if they believe that prayer works and if they place anything above their commitment to God.

B. Instruct the class to consider praying for someone who expresses they are struggling. Give the students the opportunity to discuss their own personal experiences in receiving answers to prayer when they prayed for someone else.

Worship Guide

For the Superintendent or Teacher
Theme: God Is Worthy of Praise
Theme Song: "Lord You Are Good"
Scripture: Psalm 111
Song: "Great Is the Lord"
Meditation: Lord, I thank You for being the beginning and the end of my life. I will praise You because You are good and Your mercy endures forever. Amen.

GOD IS WORTHY OF PRAISE

Bible Background ● REVELATION 4
Printed Text ● REVELATION 4   Devotional Reading ● PSALM 111

Lesson Aim

By the end of the lesson, we will:
DESCRIBE John's picture of worship;
BELIEVE that God is the only God worthy of worship; and
IDENTIFY ways and commit to worship Him through holy living.

Keep in Mind

"Thou art worthy, O Lord, to receive glory and honour and power: for thou hast created all things, and for thy pleasure they are and were created" (Revelation 4:11).

Focal Verses

Revelation 4:1 After this I looked, and, behold, a door was opened in heaven: and the first voice which I heard was as it were of a trumpet talking with me; which said, Come up hither, and I will show thee things which must be hereafter.

2 And immediately I was in the spirit: and, behold, a throne was set in heaven, and one sat on the throne.

3 And he that sat was to look upon like a jasper and a sardine stone: and there was a rainbow round about the throne, in sight like unto an emerald.

4 And round about the throne were four and twenty seats: and upon the seats I saw four and twenty elders sitting, clothed in white raiment; and they had on their heads crowns of gold.

5 And out of the throne proceeded lightnings and thunderings and voices: and there were seven lamps of fire burning before the throne, which are the seven Spirits of God.

6 And before the throne there was a sea of glass like unto crystal: and in the midst of the throne,

and round about the throne, were four beasts full of eyes before and behind.

7 And the first beast was like a lion, and the second beast like a calf, and the third beast had a face as a man, and the fourth beast was like a flying eagle.

8 And the four beasts had each of them six wings about him; and they were full of eyes within: and they rest not day and night, saying, Holy, holy, holy, Lord God Almighty, which was, and is, and is to come.

9 And when those beasts give glory and honour and thanks to him that sat on the throne, who liveth forever and ever,

10 The four and twenty elders fall down before him that sat on the throne, and worship him that liveth forever and ever, and cast their crowns before the throne, saying,

11 Thou art worthy, O Lord, to receive glory and honor and power: for thou hast created all things, and for thy pleasure they are and were created.

In Focus

Young Dr. Rice worked the final midnight shift of his emergency room internship. Even though he bandaged cuts, set broken bones, and treated the pain of patients, he felt his silent prayers were his most durable medication. As he stood behind the partition with a teenager named Paul, blood flowed from Paul's nose as if a faucet were open. "What happened?" Dr. Rice asked the nurse.

"He is a regular cocaine user," the nurse explained. After years of sniffing cocaine, the small crystals of powder had weakened Paul's nose membranes.

"I'm so ashamed," Paul said, pressing an ice pack to his face.

After examining Paul carefully Dr. Rice said, "The membranes in your nose have deteriorated, and you will need extensive surgery. The operation will repair your nose, but only God can repair your life. Have you tried praying and asking God to help stop your drug addiction?"

"I'm not addicted to cocaine. I can quit anytime I want," Paul said fighting back tears.

In a gentle voice, Dr. Rice went on. "Did you know that if you put cocaine ahead of God, you are worshiping the drug? Try Jesus, He can perform surgery on your life."

"People keep saying that, but it's really hard," Paul answered.

"It's not hard, Paul. Do you want to pray and ask God for help?"

John reminds us that all living things should give God praise and honor. Then we can find the true joy that surpasses all understanding.

The People, Places, and Times

Crowns. There are two types of crowns mentioned in the New Testament that are translated from the Greek words *diadema* and *stephanos*. *Diadema* suggests authority. In Revelation 12:3, a woman representing God's people is wearing a crown containing 12 stars that represent the 12 tribes of Israel. Later, the Antichrist is pictured as having 10 horns, and each horn has a crown (Revelation 13:1). The final mention of *diadema* refers to Jesus returning to Earth as the conquering King riding a white horse and wearing many crowns.

The other type of crown, the *stephanos*, usually denotes a wreath or victor's crown. These are the crowns of life promised to believers in the church of Smyrna (2:10), and worn by the 24 elders who cast them at God's feet (4:10). The apostle Paul tells us that God intends to honor His faithful saints with various types of *stephanos*. There is the victor's crown (1 Corinthians 9:25), a crown of righteousness (2 Timothy 4:8), and the crown of glory (1 Peter 5:4).

Background

Chapter 4 begins the third and final segment of the book of Revelation as outlined by Jesus to John. "Write the things which thou hast seen, and the things which are, and the things which shall be hereafter" (Revelation 1:19). The vision of the risen Lord in chapter 1 are the things "which thou hast seen" and the messages to the seven churches in chapters 2 and 3 are "the things which are." And now we come to the things "which shall be hereafter."

This third section of Revelation looks ahead to the future, and chapters 4 and 5 form the prologue to the events that are to follow. The focus now shifts from Earth to heaven and provides a glorious vision of heaven that will spread through chapters 6–22.

The key feature of chapter 4 is the throne and the Person occupying the throne. All of heaven bows before the throne and worships Him who lives forever and ever.

At-A-Glance

1. The Throne of God (Revelation 4:1–7)
2. The Worship of God (vv. 8–11)

In Depth

1. The Throne of God (Revelation 4:1–7)

The phrase "After this" (v. 1) brings us to part three of the Lord's outline: "the things which shall be hereafter." After the Lord completed His message to the seven churches, John looks up and sees a door being opened in heaven. The open door is similar to the open door the Lord promised to the church in Philadelphia: "I know your deeds. See, I have placed before you an open door that no one can shut. I know that you have little strength, yet you have kept my word and have not denied my name" (3:8, NIV). This door is on Earth and represents the opportunity to reach Philadelphia and the region with the Gospel. It was a door that no human could close.

The second door is in heaven, and could symbolize the only way into heaven. Jesus declared, "I am the door: by me if any man enter in, he shall be saved" (John 10:9). He is the only way into heaven, and it is He who calls out to John, "Come up hither" (Revelation 4:1b). It is only by the call of the Lord that we come into the kingdom of heaven. The prophet Isaiah pictures God as a vendor in the marketplace calling out to all who would listen to come and drink of the water of life (Isaiah 55:1). Jesus issued the call to all weary souls to "come and I will give you rest" (Matthew 11:28).

The door to heaven can only be opened from

"Thou art worthy, O Lord, to receive glory and honor and power: for thou hast created all things…" (from Revelation 4:11).

above. That's why Christ said, "No one can come to me unless the Father who sent me draws him" (John 6:44, NIV) and "no one can come to me unless the Father has enabled him" (v. 65, NIV). When the Lord opens doors on Earth, no human can close them; likewise, no human can open the door to heaven for himself.

The purpose of the vision of heaven was to show John future events that would taking place. John was immediately transported "in the spirit" into heaven. This is the second time the phrase "in the spirit" is used. In the first instance, it refers to John being in a state of prayer led by the Holy Spirit (Revelation 1:10; cf. John 4:23–24; Romans 8:26–27). Here the

phrase refers to the Holy Spirit giving John a vision of things that could not be perceived through mere human eyesight. A similar expression with the same meaning will be later in the book (17:3; 21:10). All true prophecy comes to us from holy men of God who spoke "as they were carried along by the Holy Spirit" (2 Peter 1:21, NIV).

When he enters heaven, the first thing John sees is a throne and the person sitting on it. Thrones are indications of a ruler's dignity, and the throne that John sees is quite similar to the Ezekiel's vision of the throne (Ezekiel 1:26–28). The only description given of the Person on the throne is "One who sat on the throne." This phrase or a similar phrase is repeated throughout the heavenly description (Revelation 4:9; 5:1, 7). The Person sitting on the throne radiated with the brilliance of precious stones. The jasper was clear as crystal and the sardine (carnelian stone) was blood red. The jasper stone indicated God's pure glory (see Revelation 21:11), and the sardine speaks of redemption and judgment. The rainbow is symbolic of God's covenant with Noah (Genesis 9:11–16), and signifies His covenant relationship with us, Noah's descendants.

Circling the throne were 24 much smaller thrones, and seated on them were 24 elders dressed in white and wearing golden crowns on their heads. The 24 elders are believed by some scholars to represent the church in heaven. Jesus promised several things to the church that overcame. He said they would sit with Him in heaven (3:21), they would be clothed in white (3:5; cf. Revelation 6:11; 7:9, 14), and they would be rewarded with victor's crowns (2:10).

The number 12 is often used in the Bible to express God's elective purposes is the number of divine government (12 tribes of Israel, 12 apostles, 12 foundations in the New Jerusalem, 12 gates, 12 angels at each gate, etc.), subsequently, the number 24 (being a multiple of 12), has a similar significance. Some believe it may symbolize the royal priesthood of the church (1 Peter 2:9), or a heavenly counterpart to the Old Testament priestly divisions (1 Chronicles 24:4). Those who believe the 24 elders represent the redeemed in heaven often link their presence with Christ's promise to His church at Philadelphia: "I also will keep thee from the hour of temptation, which shall come upon all the world, to try them that dwell upon the earth" (Revelation 3:10).

In Scripture, a storm is often the symbol of God's awesome presence and power and generates holy fear in the hearts of people (see Exodus 19:11, 16; 20:18–20). In Revelation, these storms are a recurring theme and are generally associated with God's awesome judgment. The rainbow around the throne is a symbol of God's love and relationship to His people. The thunder and lightning are symbols of His awesome presence and the vindication of the saints (4:5; 6:18; 8:5; 11:19; 16:18). It is beautiful to consider the rainbow, but we must never lose sight of the coming storm for all who reject God's grace.

The number seven appears 57 times in the book of Revelations and is representative of completeness and perfection (see Genesis 2:2; Leviticus 14:7). The seven spirits of verse 5 refer to the Holy Spirit in His perfect fullness as seen in Isaiah 11:2. Around the throne was a sea so calm it looked like beautiful crystal. The stillness indicates calmness in the presence of God. There is absolutely no turbulence in the water. This quiet sea is reminiscent of the shepherd leading his sheep to still waters where they can drink without fear (Psalm 23:20). Referring to a fuller manifestation of God's kingdom, David wrote, "There is a river, the streams whereof shall make glad the city of God, the holy place of the tabernacles of the most High" (Psalm 46:4).

In the center of all this around the throne were four living creatures covered with eyes. The faces of the four creatures are similar to the four cherubim Ezekiel saw in His vision: "As for the likeness of their faces, they four had the face of a man, and the face of a lion, on the right side: and they four had the face of an ox on the left side; they four also had the face of an eagle" (Ezekiel 1:10). The creatures in John's vision are different in that each of the four creatures of Ezekiel's vision had four faces. The place and duties of the creatures are quite similar to the vision Isaiah witnessed at the beginning of his ministry: "Above it stood the seraphims: each one had six wings; with twain he covered his face, and with twain he covered his feet, and with twain he did fly. And one cried unto another, and said, Holy, holy, holy, is the Lord of hosts: the whole earth is full of his glory" (Isaiah 6:2–3). Regardless of the class of angels, their mission is clear. They constantly worship the Lord and proclaim His glory.

2. The Worship of God (vv. 8–11)

Because the four living creatures never rest from worshiping God, they are the worship leaders of the heavenly kingdom. They praise God for His divine attributes. Their worship combines the Trisagion ("holy, holy, holy") of Isaiah with the self-proclamation of Jesus, "which is and which was and which is to come, the Almighty."

In Scripture, the number three is often representative of perfection. God, being **three times** holy, is perfectly holy. John said it best in his first epistle when he related God's holiness to light, "This then is the message which we have heard of him, and declare unto you, that God is light, and in him is no darkness at all" (1 John 1:5).

Following their lead, the 24 elders join in the worship. Their worship is both verbal and physical. The elders prostrate themselves before God and cast their crowns at His feet. Their prostrate position demonstrates absolute submission to His will, and casting their crowns at His feet indicates giving their best and their all to Him. The reward they received for victorious living is offered back to God as an act of reverence.

They worship God because He is worthy, meaning that God is inherently deserving of glory honor and power. They esteem Him as the Creator of all things, and they acknowledge that the only reason anything that exists is for His pleasure.

The point of this chapter is summed up with the phrase, "for thou hast created all things, and for thy pleasure they are and were created." God is worthy of the praise and worship from all His creation because He is the Creator of all things. Just as the elders prostrated themselves and threw their hard won crowns at His feet, we too should completely submit our lives to God. The highest form of earthly worship is to give God our best everyday.

Search the Scriptures

1. After Jesus finished giving John the message to the seven churches, what did John see (Revelation 4:1)?

2. To what instrument did John compare the voice he heard and what was the purpose of John's call (v. 2)?

3. How many smaller thrones surrounded the great throne occupied by God (v. 4) ?

4. How many beasts or living creatures were before the throne and what form did their faces have (vv. 6–7)?

5. What praise did the four living creatures repeat constantly day after day (v. 8)?

Discuss the Meaning

1. How do the 24 elders is in heaven represent the people of God throughout the ages?

2. Explain the significance of the clothing and the crowns worn by the 24 elders.

Lesson in Our Society

In today's society, many people worship things other than the One True God. Some people worship their possessions, others their jobs, and some worship themselves. The easiest way to determine what someone really worships is to look at how they spend their time. You will spend the most time thinking about and attending to the thing that matters most to you, and the thing that matters most is the thing you worship. Believers should periodically examine their lives to see if they have allowed anything to come before God.

Make It Happen

Believers worship God in song and in prayer, but the worship that God truly desires from His people is to be shown in our daily lives. Make a list of ways you can worship God through holy living. You may find the Daily Bible Readings helpful in preparing your list. Over the next week, put your list into practice and be prepared to share your experiences with the class next week.

Follow the Spirit

What God wants me to do:

_____

_____

Remember Your Thoughts

Special insights I have learned:

_____

_____

More Light on the Text
Revelation 4

It seems that in this day and age, everybody has something to say about heaven. People sing and talk about who they will see and what it will be like. Heaven has almost become associated with being a cosmic gathering party for the saints. Surely there will be the joy of seeing loved ones; humanly speaking, there might be even some surprise heavenly residents. However, this will not be our focus. In heaven, the center of attention is not on *who* made it there, but on *the One* who sits on the throne.

The ultimate mind-boggling fact about heaven is that the saints are in God's presence. John gives us a recap of his heavenly visit; although he most definitively is honored to receive a heavenly call to the throne, he avoids any hint of personal privilege. John had received an invitation he was not worthy of and could not refuse.

1 After this I looked, and, behold, a door was opened in heaven: and the first voice which I heard was as it were of a trumpet talking with me; which said, Come up hither, and I will shew thee things which must be hereafter. 2a And immediately I was in the spirit

The opening phrase literally means "after these things, I looked and behold." The word *idou* (**id-OO**) translated "behold" is a Greek word used to emphasize what follows. In this context what follows is a door in heaven and a voice that sounded like a trumpet. It was as if John was saying, "Now that the church knows what God thinks about some of its priorities on earth (cf. Revelation 2–3), God wants to declare what heaven's priority is." One thing is for sure, heaven had John's attention. Most commentators suggest when a heavenly trumpet is sounded, it is time to listen up (Revelation 1:10; Exodus 19:16) for God is about to speak. And, speak He did. God commanded John to come up here, for he would be shown great things that had yet to come.

John himself did not ascend to heaven; rather he was taken in the spirit. When the revelation began (1:10), John says he was in the spirit. Unbridled communion with God is always a working of the Spirit (Galatians 5). There is no earthly invocation adequate to tantalize God to invite us into His presence. No church program is so appealing to Him that He is compelled to show Himself. The church enters into

His presence, He does not enter into ours. The invitation comes from Him alone. We enter His presence boldly, not because of what we do, rather because of what He has done (Hebrews 4:14–16).

2b and, behold, a throne was set in heaven, and one sat on the throne.

As John was sovereignly prepared to be in God's presence, suddenly he saw a throne set in heaven, and the one who sat on the throne. This is the focus of this section. Attempts could be made to elaborate on earthly thrones to provide examples of what it means to sit in the place of absolute authority and power. However, Jesus declared that heaven *is* God's throne (Matthew 5:34).

If heaven is God's throne and John saw a throne set in heaven, then heaven is filled with the presence of God. The word "set" (Gk. *keimai*, **KI-mahee**) implies more than that which occupies time and space; in this passage it means something that has predestined continuity and purpose. A passage in Luke explains the significance of this word in relation to Jesus. Simeon, a man full of the Holy Spirit says to Mary and Joseph, "Behold, this child is set for the fall and rising again of many in Israel; and for a sign which shall be spoken against" (Luke 2:34). The throne is about an eternal plan that sees its fulfillment in an eternal Person, in whom all power, rule, and authority reside.

The second part of verse 2 literally means, "for, on the throne was one sitting." The Greek word for "sitting" originates from the Hebrew word *yashab* (**yaw-SHAB**), which means to inhabit a permanent dwelling place.

The relationship between the throne and the One sitting on the throne are irrevocable, eternal in nature, and affirm the will of God. When God's throne and the One sitting on the throne are the subject, all thoughts must be directed at who He is, what He has done, and why we have been granted the privilege to be in His presence.

Given the description of the New Jerusalem in chapter 22, we can only imagine the inexpressible wonders John must have seen. These things could have gotten John's full attention; however, He was in the presence of God. When God is the focus of praise and adoration, nothing else, however majestic, really matters. All sights and sounds become nothing more than distractions unless they also are focused on Him. John was in God's presence, and God cannot be denied.

3 And he that sat was to look upon like a jasper and a sardine stone: and there was a rainbow round about the throne, in sight like unto an emerald.

The one sitting on the throne is God the Father. Christ Himself is at the right hand of the Father (Mark 16:19; Romans 8:34) and in the midst of throne (Revelation 5:6). The question—or rather dilemma—for John then is describing the incomprehensible and indescribable. John does not even try. John does not say he saw the Father, he says he saw a vision of the *One* seated. The word *horasis* (**HOR-as-is**) is the Greek word for "vision," which is translated "look" in verse 3. This is a different word than the one used in verse 1 where the apostle "perceives" with his own mind. What John is "seeing" now is a divinely granted manifestation of God's character and purposes. Whenever God is envisioned or wherever God is, He is all there.

There is quite a bit of scholarly discussion about which contemporary gem stones might be similar to the stones John describes. Some suggest the jasper is a diamond, the sardine stone was red, and the emerald as today was green. The jasper and sardine were the first and last stones (Exodus 28:17, 20) on the breastplate of the high priest. It just might be that these stones represent God's holiness and wrath. On the other hand, the rainbow is described to evidence God's completed work of grace and salvation. In His presence, there are no imperfections and no tasks left undone.

4 And round about the throne were four and twenty seats: and upon the seats I saw four and twenty elders sitting, clothed in white raiment; and they had on their heads crowns of gold.

There are those that argue that the thrones upon which the elders sit is symbolic of the "fact" that the redeemed share in God's authority. The church is not a group of heavenly stockholders. They have paid no price, while the Father through His Son has paid the ultimate price. "Behold," as John says, what follows.

Some believe the 24 elders represent angels who have significant responsibilities. While others believe the elders represent the redeemed of the Lord. This is understood because they are sitting, clothed in white, and their heads are crowned with gold. The 24 elders have been thought to refer to the 12 tribes in the Old Testament and the 12 apostles of the New Testament. It is most probable, however, that these elders are the redeemed or represent the redeemed, for they clearly pay homage to the Master by offering praise on behalf of the saints (Revelation 5:8–10). What is most important is not who the elders are, but rather what they are doing. They are sitting down in the presence of the Lord God, Yahweh.

Is it imaginable for someone to be sitting in God's presence? What gall! What audacity! How do those who have been redeemed (or represent the redeemed) dare sit in the very presence of God? How do those who have been delivered from unspeakable acts of sin and rebellion sit in His presence? How? Why? The answer is that the redeemed are neither stepchildren nor the riffraff nor the undesirables of heaven. They sit in His presence because not only was it *His* house, it was also *their* house. The word for "sit" used in this context is the same word used in verse 2 to speak of Him who sits on the throne. This is no temporary dwelling place; the redeemed will be in His presence forever.

There is a time to give an audible praise and a shout-out for what God has done, but for now all John records is that the elders are sitting. Maybe they are so emotionally consumed and so in awe of God that their silence is the only form of praise they can give. Could it be that there should be times when in His presence the best thing to do is just to be mesmerized because He just *is*? John does not end his description of the elders with what they were doing; he goes on to mention what they were wearing white garments.

John says the elders were "clothed," which in

Greek is *periballo* (**per-ee-BAL-lo**). Significantly, John uses a verbal construction that is known as a perfect passive. The perfect tense conveys action completed in the past with on going effects. The passive suggests the elders had nothing to do with clothing themselves. They were as little children clothed by the caring hand of a loving parent. The elders' presence in heaven was all God's doing.

If this were an earthly convocation and the question were asked, "How did you get here?" The responses would be many: train, bus, car, walked, and/or flew. In heaven, if a similar question were asked, there will be one answer given by all. Him! Him! Him! And the respondents would be clothed with blood-washed clothes and wearing crowns (*stephanos*) on their heads.

These crowns were not *diadema* (**dee-AD-ay-mah**), the crown of kings. Some suggest the crowns also represent the authority of the saints, but the overwhelming testimony of the Scripture is that the crowns are those "given" to the victorious (2 Timothy 4:8; Revelation 3:11), and they testify of what God has done, not what the redeemed have done. As on earth, a crown's value is derived from the position of the one that bestows the crown. John envisions these elders as having only one responsibility—to point to the immeasurable, incomprehensible grace of God.

5 And out of the throne proceeded lightnings and thunderings and voices: and there were seven lamps of fire burning before the throne, which are the seven Spirits of God. 6 And before the throne there was a sea of glass like unto crystal: and in the midst of the throne, and round about the throne, were four beasts full of eyes before and behind. 7 And the first beast was like a lion, and the second beast like a calf, and the third beast had a face as a man, and the fourth beast was like a flying eagle 8 And the four beasts had each of them six wings about him; and they were full of eyes within: and they rest not day and night, saying, Holy, holy, holy, Lord God Almighty, which was, and is, and is to come.

John has clearly stated that the focus of the heavenly beings is the complete, unadulterated adoration of God. In fact, everything in heaven focuses on God. All of creation has but one purpose: to glorify Him.

Most would agree that the thunder and lightning represent that which conveys the awesome presence of God. The seven Spirits refer to the perfection and fullness of God as evidenced in the work of the Holy Spirit (see Isaiah 11:2). The sea of glass might be a clear representation of the Old Testament *laver* (called a sea), where the high priest had to wash before ministering before the Lord.

The four beasts (called "living creatures" in the NIV and NKJV) possibly represent the cherubim or seraphim (angels). There is also the possibility that the attributes of God are represented by the four beasts. The four beasts each have six wings: two wings to cover their eyes so they do not look upon the face of God, two wings to cover their feet in humility as they minister at the foot of the throne of God, and two wings so to fly and do the bidding of God. In contrast to these creatures who use wings to stay covered, the redeemed approach God's throne boldly and will see Him face to face (1 Corinthians 13:12).

The statement "Holy, holy, holy, Lord God Almighty, which was, and is, and is to come" might also be said this way: "He's the One. Yes, He's the only One. Yes, yes, we know there can be no other. He is the Lord God Almighty!!!" The only other instance where the trilogy "holy, holy, holy" is used is in Isaiah 6:3. The conclusion the angels declare in that passage is that the whole earth is full of His glory, and so it is in heaven.

9 And when those beasts give glory and honour and thanks to him that sat on the throne, who liveth forever and ever, 10 The four and twenty elders fall down before him that sat on the throne, and worship him that liveth forever and ever, and cast their crowns before the throne, saying, 11 Thou art worthy, O Lord, to receive glory and honor and power: for thou hast created all things, and for thy pleasure they are and were created.

As the elders testified to the worship of "the living creatures," they could do nothing but fall down before Him, give back the crowns they had been given, and declare His praises. This was no inadvertent falling; the elders cast themselves down. The Greek word for "fall down" is *pipto* (**PIP-to**). It does not matter where the praise is coming from or who is giving it; when God is praised, the honorable response is for everyone else in the room to fall down and worship. They worship Him because He is "worthy" (Gk. *axios*, **AX-ee-os**). God supremely deserves to receive the glory, and honor, and power that is given to Him.

Through John, the Spirit of the Lord says to the church that the reason the redeemed are to offer continual, unbridled praise to God is because (1) all things were created by Him and (2) all things were created for His pleasure. God has one design for us, which is to glorify Him. Think about it. God is complete in every way. Psalm 50:12 (NIV) says, "If I were hungry I would not tell you, for the world is mine, and all that is in it." Colossians 1:16 says, "For by him were all things created, that are in heaven, and that are in earth, visible and invisible, whether they be thrones, or dominions, or principalities, or powers: all things were created by him, and for him." Yet, God created us anyway; we are the unnecessary necessity, made in God's image to glorify Him.

Too often, God's people hold back their praise. Life is chaotic and problems can be persistent. However, God is on the throne. All things are created by His will and for His pleasure. Praise and thank Him for what He has done, praise and adore Him for who He is, and praise and honor Him because He didn't have to do it. Hallelujah to the Lamb!

Daily Bible Readings

M: Praise to a Gracious God
Psalm 145:8–12
T: Great Is Our God
Psalm 111
W: God's Eternal Purpose
Ephesians 3:7–13
T: None Is Like God
Jeremiah 10:6–10
F: Live a Life of Love
Ephesians 4:25 5:2
S: Endure Hardships
Revelations 2:1–7
S: God Is Worthy of Praise
Revelation 4

TEACHING TIPS

April 22
Bible Study Guide 8

1. Words You Should Know

A. Angels (Revelation 5:11) *aggelos* (Gk.)—Spiritual creatures who act as guardians, watchers, and/or messengers from God to man.

B. Worship (v. 14) *proskuneo* (Gk.)—To bend the knee toward or to render reverence and homage to one who is considered vastly superior.

2. Teacher Preparation

A. Pray for your students.

B. Read the Focal Verses in another translation.

C. Complete lesson 8 in the *Precepts For Living® Personal Study Guide*.

3. Starting the Lesson

A. Assign a student to lead the class in prayer, focusing on the Lesson Aim as well as thanking God for the opportunity to study His Word this week.

B. Review the highlights of last week's lesson. Ask volunteers to share how the lesson affected them.

C. Ask the students to share their experiences from last week's Make It Happen suggestion. Ask them to share any insights from their Daily Bible Readings.

D. Have the students silently read the Focal Verses for today's lesson. After they have read the verses, ask: What are some of the key points in the verses? How can we relate those points to where we are today?

E. Review the Search the Scriptures questions. Ask the students to attempt to answer the questions without opening their Bibles. Then after each question is answered, open the Bible to the verse and review.

4. Getting into the Lesson

A. Divide the class into groups and have them read Background. After reading the section, ask the class to explain the responsibilities of their nearest relative and how this might pertain to Jesus.

B. Discuss The People, Places, and Times.

5. Relating the Lesson to Life

A. Separate the class into four groups and assign each group a question from the Discuss the Meaning section. After the groups talk over the questions, have each group present their conclusions to the rest of the class.

B. Lesson in Our Society can help the students see how the lesson parallels with many present-day situations.

C. Using today's lesson, ask the students what they plan to do to find people who are discouraged with life and encourage them.

6. Arousing Action

A. The Make It Happen section contains a suggestion of what may be done to implement principles learned. Because it is a suggestion, you may want to adjust the implementations to the specific needs of your class.

B. Challenge the students to read the Daily Bible Readings for the week.

C. Encourage the students to study next week's lesson and come to class prepared to share what they have learned in their studies.

D. Close the class with prayer, thanking God for His redemption.

Worship Guide

For the Superintendent or Teacher
Theme: **Christ Is Worthy to Redeem**
Theme Song: **"Redeemed by the Blood"**
Scripture: **Psalm 40:1–5**
Song: **"Praise the Name of Jesus"**
Meditation: **Lord, I thank You for sending Your Son, Jesus, to pay the cost of my rebellion. Worthy is the Lamb to receive power, glory, and honor. Amen.**

CHRIST IS WORTHY TO REDEEM

Bible Background • REVELATION 5
Printed Text • REVELATION 5:1–5, 11–14   Devotional Reading • PSALM 107:1–9

Lesson Aim

By the end of the lesson, we will:

UNDERSTAND that Jesus died for our sins;

BELIEVE that our iniquity was covered by His sacrifice; and

EXPRESS our appreciation to Jesus Christ for what He has done for us.

Keep in Mind

"And every creature which is in heaven, and on the earth, and under the earth, and such as are in the sea, and all that are in them, heard I saying, Blessing, and honor, and glory, and power, be unto him that sitteth upon the throne, and unto the Lamb forever and ever" (Revelation 5:13).

Focal Verses

Revelation 5:1 And I saw in the right hand of him that sat on the throne a book written within and on the backside, sealed with seven seals.

2 And I saw a strong angel proclaiming with a loud voice, Who is worthy to open the book, and to loose the seals thereof?

3 And no man in heaven, nor in earth, neither under the earth, was able to open the book, neither to look thereon.

4 And I wept much, because no man was found worthy to open and to read the book, neither to look thereon.

5 And one of the elders saith unto me, Weep not: behold, the Lion of the tribe of Juda, the Root of David, hath prevailed to open the book, and to loose the seven seals thereof.

5:11 And I beheld, and I heard the voice of many angels round about the throne and the beasts and the elders: and the number of them was ten thousand times ten thousand, and thousands of thousands;

12 Saying with a loud voice, Worthy is the Lamb that was slain to receive power, and riches, and wisdom, and strength, and honor, and glory, and blessing.

13 And every creature which is in heaven, and on the earth, and under the earth, and such as are in the sea, and all that are in them, heard I saying, Blessing, and honour, and glory, and power, be unto him that sitteth upon the throne, and unto the Lamb forever and ever.

14 And the four beasts said, Amen. And the four and twenty elders fell down and worshipped him that liveth forever and ever.

In Focus

Mom Macy had lived a long and productive life in her home and church, raising her eight children to reverence and love Jesus Christ. All but one of them accepted Jesus as their own Lord and Saviour. William, her youngest son, decided that he could control his own destiny better than God. Mom Macy grieved for his soul, but in her prayers, she put him in the hands of God. She believed that

God was faithful and one day her son would accept Jesus Christ as Lord and Saviour. Ultimately, her time of prayer for her son stretched out into years, and although she was sometimes weary, she still did not give up hope that one day William would accept Jesus into his life. On her death bed, as she took her last breath, she reminded God of His promises to her—that He would never leave or forsake her and that He would save her and her household.

It was the Sunday after his mother's funeral when William came forth and acknowledged to the pastor and the congregation that he wanted to accept Jesus Christ as his Lord and Saviour. He admitted that he had been running from God and His mother's prayers for a long time; but now in his 60s, he could run no longer. He recognized that he had made a horrendous mess of his life and needed God to take control. Needless to say, the church rejoiced. They knew how long Mom Macy had prayed and trusted God for her son's salvation. They realized that God had heard her mother's cry for help. Now Mom Macy's son, William, would be in the Lamb's book of life. God had been faithful!

This week we will look at John's heavenly vision in Revelation 5. The question asked by an angel was, "Who is worthy to open the book, and to loose the seals thereof?" (5:2). There was no one worthy, or righteous enough, to get the job done except the Lamb of God (John 1:29, 36). This week's lesson will give us a glimpse of who this Lamb is.

The People, Places, and Times

Praise. Praise is essentially the believer's response to God's revelation of Himself. God reveals Himself to us through His Word, His works, and especially His Son, Jesus Christ. We, in turn, recognize the hand of God in our lives and acknowledge the Person we have come to know.

Praise, however, is much more than acknowledging God working in our lives. It is an expression of the pleasure we find in Him. We revel in God as He reveals Himself to us. We can praise God privately in our homes and corporately within church. Praise commends God for His attributes and His works. It speaks of His blessings toward His people and creation. It offers thanksgiving and confesses the daily need for Him in our lives. Praise glorifies God for who He is and expresses our love to Him. When we praise God, we join the angels and other believers who, from the very beginning of time, have expressed their love and gratitude to Him for His mighty acts.

Worship. The term "worship" has a dual meaning: (1) to show reverence and (2) to submit. Worship is a matter of the heart and soul. It expresses our inner relationship with God and acknowledges His glory, which is the sum total of who He is. Our greatest act of worship is obedience to God's Word in our daily lives and submission to His will.

Background

In the tenth year of King Zedekiah, Jerusalem was under siege from the Babylonians and Jeremiah was in prison for prophesying the fall of Jerusalem. The word of the Lord came to the imprisoned prophet and told him that his cousin, Hanamel, would ask him to redeem his land. God instructed Jeremiah to honor his cousin's request and buy back the land because He was the nearest relative. Under Levitical law (see Leviticus 25:25), it was the nearest relative's right and duty to redeem lost property and possess it.

As God had said, Hanamel came to Jeremiah in prison and asked Him to redeem the land. Jeremiah honored his cousin's request and bought back the land for about seven ounces of silver (Jeremiah 32:1–25). However, paying for the land was only the beginning of the redemption.

When Hanamel lost the land, two scrolls or contracts were drafted containing the terms for redeeming the land. One scroll, left unsealed, became a public record. The other scroll was sealed with seven seals and kept in storage at the temple. After the redeemer presented the temple priest with necessary proof of ownership, the priest would retrieve the scroll from storage, unseal it, and read it. If everything was in order, the redeemer would then receive ownership to the land.

When God created the heavens and the earth, He gave authority over the earth to man. When Adam sinned, evil sinked its way into humanity. In Revelation 5, John still sees the heavenly vision and the central issue is: "Who is qualified to open the scroll?"

At-A-Glance

1. The Scroll of Redemption (Revelation 5:1–5)
2. The Song of Redemption (5:11–14)

In Depth

1. The Scroll of Redemption (Revelation 5:1–5)

The fifth chapter of Revelation is a continuation of the heavenly scene begun in chapter 4. However, now John's attention is focused on a scroll in the right hand of the one sitting on the throne. The scroll contains writing on both sides and is sealed with seven seals.

Some refer to the scroll as the "Book of Redemption." The scroll represents the result of sin that separates people from the eternal life we were created to have. It contains the terms for our redemption, the provision for eternal life, and the full account of what God has in store for the world. The seven seals symbolize that the contract of ownership is in full force until the original owner or his kinsman-redeemer meets the terms. Breaking the seals symbolizes voiding the terms of the contract and freeing the people from its requirements.

Scroll contracts were common and very important during biblical times. A scribe would take a roll of parchment and begin writing the contract and its requirements. At certain points, he would stop writing and seal with wax all that he had written previously. When opened, the scroll would be read a section at a time after each seal was broken. Our heavenly scroll has seven divisions that will be opened successively with each part introducing and explaining the next.

John's attention is diverted from the scroll by the voice of an angel he described as strong or mighty. The angel is not identified, but he has the authority to speak out in the presence of God. There are those who believe the angel here is Gabriel, the archangel because his name means "strength of God." Gabriel also affirmed to Zechariah, the father of John the Baptist, that he stood in the presence of God (see Luke 1:19). Whoever the angel is, he shouts out a challenge to all creation: "Who is worthy to open the book, and to loose the seals thereof?" (Revelation 5:2).

The thundering challenge is met with absolute silence. No one in all creation utters a peep. No angel in heaven, no person on Earth, no demon in hell, not even Satan dares to raise his voice. John is bitterly disappointed and wails in grief. He realizes the importance of the scroll. He knows that unless someone is found to open the seals and read the book, pain, misery, war, hatred, prejudice, and suffering would continue. God's kingdom would never come to Earth and humanity is lost in sin and has no hope.

One of the 24 elders comforts the stricken apostle, "Weep not: behold, the Lion of the tribe of Juda, the Root of David, hath prevailed to open the book, and to loose the seven seals thereof" (v. 5). This Lion of Judah and Root of David is none other than the risen Lord, Jesus Christ. He is worthy because He has prevailed over death and the grave, and has broken the curse of the law. These two titles are two Old Testament references to Jesus. Judah was one of Jacob's (Israel's) 12 sons. Although he was not the eldest, he was the first leader of the 12 tribes. God promised that the Messiah would come from Judah's tribe whose symbol was the lion (see Genesis 48:8–12). Jesus, a descendant of the tribe of Judah, will return to earth like a conquering lion after the great tribulation.

Jesus, the Lion of Judah, proved Himself worthy to break the seals and open the scroll by living a perfect life of obedience, offering Himself up as a sacrifice on the cross, and rising from the dead to demonstrate His power over sin and death.

The Root of David is a reference to the promise God made to David that one of His descendants would occupy the throne forever (see 2 Samuel and Luke 1:31–3). David's dynasty was interrupted when Judah was carried into captivity by Babylon around 584 B.C., and it remains so to this very day. However, the prophet Isaiah foretold that a branch would grow from Jesse's (David's father) roots (Isaiah 53:7). This term for Jesus will be used again by Jesus Himself during His final words to His church (Revelation 22:16).

After hearing the elders' words, John looked up; but instead of seeing a lion, he saw a lamb. The Lion represents Jesus' power and authority, but the Lamb represents His submission to God's will and His sacrifice for the sins of all humankind. Although Christ, the Lion will lead the final battle where Satan is defeated (Revelation 19–21), it is Christ, the Lamb, who won the greatest battle of all. He defeated the forces of evil by dying on the cross and rising from the dead.

The Lamb was before the throne and was surrounded by the four living creatures and the 24 elders. The Lamb looked as though He had been killed but was alive. The wounds inflicted on Jesus' body during His trial and crucifixion are still visible in heaven. The Lamb had seven horns symbolizing its prefect power. Seven is the number of perfection and seven horns symbolize perfect power. The Lamb is omnipotent. Although He looked like a little lamb, He had all the power of God. The seven sets of eyes, described as the seven spirits of God sent out to all the earth, demonstrate that the Lamb is the all-seeing vision of the Holy Spirit; He is omniscient. The eyes also represent the seven virtues of the Holy Spirit in the nature of Jesus: wisdom, understanding, counsel, might, knowledge, reverence, and respect for God's will (see Isaiah 11:2).

John watches intently as the Lamb approaches the throne, only Jesus can stand at God's right hand. The Lamb takes the book from God's hand. As the Son, Jesus takes possession of the book, the four living creatures and the 24 elders fall down before the Lamb in worship.

2. The Song of Redemption (5:11–14)

Each of the elders and living creatures had a harp and golden bowl containing the prayers of the saints. The prayers of the saints are the intercessory prayers of the saints for the coming of God's kingdom when they will reign on earth with Christ. The prayer of the saints is: "Your Kingdom come, your will be done on earth as it is in heaven" (Matthew 6:10, NIV).

The elders and living creatures begin singing a new song to Jesus extolling His worthiness to take the scroll and open the seals. The Lord's worthiness is based on His suffering on the cross to redeem God's people. The elders and living creatures are joined in their praise by millions of angels surrounding the throne and singing in a mighty chorus extolling the Lamb's worthiness to receive a seven-fold acknowledgment of power, riches, wisdom, strength, honor, glory, and blessing. This huge chorale is soon joined by the entirety of creation both living and dead from all races and cultures.

God's message of salvation is unlimited. It is not limited by race, culture, country, or history.

All of creation joins in singing, "Blessing, and honour, and glory, and power, be unto him that sitteth upon the throne, and unto the Lamb forever and ever" (Revelation 5:13). The four living creatures affirm their agreement with the Lamb's exaltation with the word "amen," and the 24 elders prostrate themselves in gratitude before the throne and worship the eternal God.

The heavenly song of the Lamb praises the work of Christ. He was slain, purchased us with His blood, gathered us into a kingdom, made us priests, and appointed us to be rulers on earth. Although the song of the Lamb is a heavenly celebration, as we look toward heaven we can begin singing it now.

Christ's worthiness to open the scroll proves that Jesus, and not Satan, holds the future. Christ is in control, and He alone is worthy to dictate the course of our individual lives and set into motion the last days of history.

Even in the difficulties of the present, we should always remember that our current suffering is nothing compared to the glory we will receive later. Thus, we can confidently worship the Lord for what He has done, what He is doing, and what He will do for us in the future.

Search the Scriptures

1. Where was the scroll located when John first noticed it (Revelation 5:1)?

2. What question did the mighty angel ask of all creation concerning the scroll (v. 2)?

3. Why did John break down and bitterly weep (v. 4)?

4. What sevenfold acknowledgement is the Lamb worthy to receive (v. 12)?

5 How did the 24 elders respond to creation's worship of God and the Lamb (v. 14)?

Discuss the Meaning

1. Why do you believe it was necessary for the Lamb of God, rather than the Lion of Judah, to take the scroll from the right hand of God?

2. How would humanity be affected if no one was found worthy to break the seals and read the scroll?

Lesson in Our Society

Why is it important for us to understand why John's revelation is applicable to us today or in the future? We are reminded that only Jesus Christ has the power to save us from our sin and show us a new way to live a life that is rooted in the kingdom of God on Earth. Discuss how you understand the meaning of John's revelation personally and globally.

Make It Happen

What a great day of praise it's going to be for those who claim Jesus Christ as Lord and Saviour. The events of our world make it appear that this great day of praise is coming soon. Believers must tell people about it while there is still time. This week, share with someone how they, too, can be redeemed from the law of sin and death before Christ returns.

Follow the Spirit

What God wants me to do:

_____

_____

Remember Your Thoughts

Special insights I have learned:

_____

_____

More Light on the Text
Revelation 5:1–5, 11–14

1 And I saw in the right hand of him that sat on the throne a book written within and on the backside, sealed with seven seals

Continuing the account of his trip to heaven, John once again relates what he "saw." As stated in the last lesson, there is a difference between seeing things from a human perspective and seeing things from a divinely-inspired revelation. The Greek word for "saw" is *eido* (**i-DO**) or *oida* (**OY-da**), which can mean to perceive/know by the faculties of the mind

and/or to know by experience. Has John's heavenly journey joined that which is in his head with that which is in his heart? The enlightenment view of Immanuel Kant implies that knowledge is based solely on experience. However, such a view is woefully inadequate. Personal experiences alone, without an irrefutable word, can fool you.

John was about to enter into a revelation that would equally grip his mind and his heart. John saw a book (some translations say "scroll"), which no one could open. Based on the context of this passage, it is evident that the scroll unfolds the consummation of all history—"the mystery of God" seen by the Old Testament prophets. It reveals how God's judgment will come, how His kingdom will be established, and what will be the inheritance of the saints who will reign with Christ. Thus, John wept uncontrollably because no one could open the scroll. In fact, no one could open the book in heaven or Earth, save One. This scroll seemed to have John's attention, at least for the moment. There are three things that John noticed: the scroll was in the right hand of God, the scroll was sealed, and no one was found worthy in heaven or earth to open or even look upon its contents.

The Greek word *grapho* (**GRAF-o**) literally means "to write," referring either to that which was being written or the contents of that which has been written. In the New Testament, *grapho* is only used 10 times outside of the book of Revelation. In each of these instances, *grapho* refers to those things that have been recorded and written in the Old Testament. Is this scroll heaven's version of the Bible? After all, knowingly or unknowingly, John was writing the last "book" of the Bible, and this revelation would be included in that Bible. The text suggests, however, something other than the Bible is in view.

The word *grapho* is used 17 times in Revelation and 8 of those times are in the fifth chapter. Why? The text gives us our clues in answer to this question. The focus has not changed from Revelation 4. He is still at the center of attention and this is His scroll.

The "book" represented in chapter 5 is different

from all others. The Bible says in 2 Peter 1:21 (NIV), "For prophecy never had its origin in the will of man, but men spoke from God as they were carried along by the Holy Spirit." In 2 Timothy 3:16–17 (NIV) it says, "All Scripture is God-breathed and is useful for teaching, rebuking, correcting and training in righteousness, so that the man of God may be thoroughly equipped for every good work." The Bible is God's Word to us so that we might be like Him.

But this "scroll" in Revelation is different. God writes this scroll for Himself, and for the eyes of His Son Jesus Christ. The good news for us is that this is a finished product. It contents have been sealed—decreed and preordained. Most scholars suggest that the writing in the front and the back represent the fact that nothing more can be added and nothing can be taken away. This is not like one of those encyclopedias that, to keep up, you have to get the latest edition every year. The last word has already been confirmed, for with God what was, what is, and what will be is done! Praises to the Lamb!!

Every principality that has or will oppose God has been vanquished. The words "within" and "backside" are adverbs modifying the word "sealed," which is a perfect passive participle. Taken as a whole, the phase "written within and on the backside, sealed" simply means the content of the book contains that which has already happened and has permanent future effects.

From God's perspective, every journey of sorrow has come to its joyful end, every satanic opposition has been overcome, every lie has been exposed, every deceit has been destroyed, and every trial has been triumphed over. The word "sealed," in the Greek is *katasphragizo* (**kat-asfrag-ID-zo**) which means to cover with a seal, to close up or close with a seal. In other words, the deal is done; it has been authenticated, the game has been played, and the victor is wearing the crown. The word used for "seal" in this context is not the same as that used in reference to the sealing of the saints in Ephesians 1:13 or even the seals later mentioned in Revelation. This scroll does not just bear the mark of authenticity. This scroll is authentic in its very essence. How do we know this?

Because there is only One worthy to open the scroll and affirm its contents.

So, what is in the scroll? Before that question is answered, later in the book of Revelation, the first order of business is to open the scroll. How do we know what is on the mind of God? Look at what God does. God has authorized that the only one who is worthy to open the scroll must be completely like Himself. There is only One worthy to open the scroll; there is only One who is worthy to reveal the mind of God and purposes of God, the Lord Jesus Christ.

2 And I saw a strong angel proclaiming with a loud voice, Who is worthy to open the book, and to loose the seals thereof?

A strong angel was proclaiming who is worthy to open the book and release its seals. John is making a point: The book is authentic; it has been authenticated. The contents reflect its authenticity, and nobody has a right to open up God's book.

The mighty angel of verse 2 is contrasted with the One who is worthy. The angel just might be mighty in heaven, but not nearly mighty enough to have a right to open the book. The power to open the book cannot be power that has been granted. The power of attorney can give someone extreme authority to represent someone else. Angels have power, but that power has limits. An eternity of unbridled commitment and service to God does not make an angel worthy of opening the book.

The One who authenticates the book is the One authorized to open the book. This One is the Son of God. Christ's authority derives from His identity and His sacrifice. He alone is worthy to bring justice and offer redemption to the world (Revelation 5:12). First Corinthian 1:23–24 says, "But we preach Christ crucified, unto the Jews a stumbling block, and unto the Greeks foolishness; But unto them which are called, both Jews and Greeks, Christ the power of God, and the wisdom of God." Christ alone has authority and is worthy to save and to judge.

3 And no man in heaven, nor in earth, neither under the earth, was able to open the book, neither to look thereon.

No one except the worthy One has or ever will be worthy of opening the book—not Moses, the most humble man on Earth; not Abraham, a friend of God; not David, a man after God's own heart; and not even the archangels Gabriel or Michael. Opening this book requires bloodstained hands.

4 And I wept much, because no man was found worthy to open and to read the book, neither to look thereon.

God has brought John to heaven and revealed Himself in unspeakable ways. To know more about God, John would have to draw closer to Him. In other words, he must forget about what is in the book and focus on the One who can open up the book.

Have you ever felt like weeping because the future seems totally unclear and unknowable? You know God has been good. You know He has always been on time. You thought you knew what it was to be totally dependent on God until life presented you with unanswered questions. John found himself in such a spot. Who could open up the book? One of the 24 elders supplied a simple, profound answer.

5 And one of the elders saith unto me, Weep not: behold, the Lion of the tribe of Juda, the Root of David, hath prevailed to open the book, and to loose the seven seals thereof.

One of the elders told John not to cry but just behold. The word "behold" (Gk. *idou*, **id-OO**) is a reference to something in between or something associated with something else. John had sat with Jesus, ministered with Jesus, and been chastised by Jesus, but now the charge is just "behold" Him. Look and see what the Lord will do next. The elder was simply saying, "You are crying, but if you turn your focus toward the Lamb, the Lion of Judah and the Root of David, your tears will cease."

Only Jesus is worthy to open up the book and release its seven seals because He has prevailed. Again, from heaven's perspective, there are no prophecies to be fulfilled, no victories to be won, and no sacrifices to make—all has been fulfilled. John must learn, as these elders teach him, that the only

adequate response in the presence of the Lamb is to fall down and praise Him for what He has done.

5:11 And I beheld, and I heard the voice of many angels round about the throne and the beasts and the elders: and the number of them was ten thousand times ten thousand, and thousands of thousands; 12 Saying with a loud voice, Worthy is the Lamb that was slain to receive power, and riches, and wisdom, and strength, and honor, and glory, and blessing.

John says he heard *the voice* of many angels. How do you hear the voice of a choir too large to be counted? Technically, the phrase "ten thousand times ten thousand" literally means "an innumerable number." Symbolically, most linguists understand and interpret the phrase to mean a number that cannot be counted. How does a congregation that is too large to be counted speak in one "voice"? They have but one focus, the Lamb that was slain.

The word used for lamb (*arnion*, **ar-NEE-on**) is one that denotes a young, innocent lamb. The only other instance of this word being used outside of the book of Revelation is in John 21:15. In Revelation, *arnion* is used 29 times, and 28 of these times refer to Christ, the Lamb of God. Our redemption requires a perfect sacrifice, and among humankind there was none until the coming of the Lord.

The use of the word "slain" (Gk. *sphazo*, **SFAD-zo**) literally means "to be put to death by violence." However, the Lord was not slain because He was unable to resist. He has slain because He willingly chose to submit to the will of the Father and to become the sacrifice for our sins (cf. Isaiah 53:10).

That is why heaven can sing and shout loudly with one voice. You want to know how a church can come together and stay together to achieve a divinely inspired vision? Focus on God. When God is in the house and that house is filled with praise, worship, and adoration for Him, all other matters become unimportant.

13 And every creature which is in heaven, and on the earth, and under the earth, and such as are in the sea, and all that are in them, heard I saying, Blessing,

and honour, and glory, and power, be unto him that sitteth upon the throne, and unto the Lamb forever and ever. **14 And the four beasts said, Amen. And the four and twenty elders fell down and worshipped him that liveth forever and ever.**

John says that every creature gives glory and honor to the Lamb. Philippians 2:10–11 says, "that at the name of Jesus every knee should bow, of things in heaven, and things in earth, and things under the earth; And that every tongue should confess that Jesus Christ is Lord." Wouldn't it be a shame to let the animals over which we have authority and dominion give God more praise than we do?

We should "praise" (Gk. *eulogia*, **yoo-log-EE-ah**) Him without ceasing. We should "honor" (Gk. *time*, **tee-MAY**) Him as being more valuable than the sum of all we possess. We should bask in the awesomeness of His "glory" (Gk. *doxa*, **DOX-ah**) and marvel at His matchless "power" (Gk. *kratos*, **KRAT-os**) as demonstrated through His love toward us. As human beings, we are gifted with *dunamis* (**DOO-nam-is**) power—the power to do God's will. Never, however, will we possess *kratos* power. *Kratos* power sustains the purposes of God.

To "worship" means more than singing, praying, and shouting. The same Greek word *proskuneo* (**pros-koo-NEH-o**) is used of those who follow the beast (see Revelation 13:4). Interestingly, *proskuneo* is not commonly used in the epistles. Only in Revelation and in the Gospels does the term *proskuneo* appear with any frequency. Scholars suggest *proskuneo* worship is worship that unites the act of worship with seeing that which is worshiped. Worship that is focused on our sovereign God and our Lord and Saviour Jesus Christ should be a part of our lives every day.

Daily Bible Readings

M: Thanks for Redemption
Psalm 107:1–9
T: Serving the Living God
Hebrews 9:11–15
W: Life in Exile
1 Peter 1:13–21
T: Praise for Redemption
Psalm 40:1–5
F: That Your Love Might Overflow
Philippians 1:3–11
S: The Scroll Is Opened
Revelation 5:1–5
S: Worthy Is the Lamb
Revelation 5:11–14

TEACHING TIPS

April 29
Bible Study Guide 9

1. Words You Should Know

A. Seal (Revelation 7:2) *sphragis* (Gk.)—A mark indicating ownership, authenticity, and protection.

B. Great Tribulation (v. 14)—The persecution of God's people during the final days before the triumphal return of Christ.

2. Teacher Preparation

A. Pray that God will give the students an understanding of how the blood of Christ cleanses believers from sin and provides for their deliverance in all situations.

B. Review the Focal Verses. Review them in the *New Living Translation* (see the PFL CD-ROM) or the *New International Version* as well.

C. Study the Background section.

D. Complete lesson 9 in the *Precepts For Living® Personal Study Guide*.

E Read the In Depth and More Light on the Text sections.

F. Create a three-column chart. Label the first column, "Resurrection: What Jesus Did"; the second, "Redemption: What We Have"; and the third, "Revelation: Therefore We Can."

G. Materials needed: *New Living Translation* of the Bible, display of the three-column chart, and individual copies of the chart (optional).

3. Starting the Lesson

A. After opening with prayer, read and discuss the In Focus story.

B. Briefly explain the chart. Then discuss how the ideas from the story might be included on the chart.

4. Getting into the Lesson

A. Refer to The People, Places, and Times as the terms are encountered in the lesson. Focus the class discussion on defining these future events.

B. Discuss the Focal Verses using the At-A-Glance outline and questions from Search the Scriptures. Have the students fill in the first two columns of the chart as you proceed through the text of the lesson.

C. Refer the students as needed to the concepts that are clarified in the In Depth section.

5. Relating the Lesson to Life

A. Direct the students to review the items listed in the first two columns of the chart.

B. Use the Discuss the Meaning questions to help the class reflect on the freedom believers have to go to God in prayer. Complete the last column of the chart as you discuss this section.

C. Read the Lesson in Our Society section. Discuss how it relates to the third column. Add to the chart during the discussion.

6. Arousing Action

A. Have the students identify ways to implement the Make It Happen activities this week. Ask the students to consider sharing their responses with a prayer partner for this activity.

B. Encourage the students to either journalize their praise report about their increased trust in God's protection or focus on a personal prayer thanking God for His deliverance.

CHRIST IS OUR PROTECTION

Bible Background • REVELATION 7
Printed Text • REVELATION 7:1–3, 9, 13–17   Devotional Reading • PSALM 121

Lesson Aim

By the end of the lesson, we will:

UNDERSTAND that the blood of Christ cleanses and preserves those who place their faith in Him;

BELIEVE that Jesus' sacrifice on Calvary took away the penalty of sin and provided eternal life for believers; and

INCREASE our commitment to rely on God for protection and comfort.

Keep in Mind

"These are they which came out of great tribulation, and have washed their robes, and made them white in the blood of the Lamb" (Revelation 7:14).

Focal Verses

Revelation 7:1 And after these things I saw four angels standing on the four corners of the earth, holding the four winds of the earth, that the wind should not blow on the earth, nor on the sea, nor on any tree.

2 And I saw another angel ascending from the east, having the seal of the living God: and he cried with a loud voice to the four angels, to whom it was given to hurt the earth and the sea,

3 Saying, Hurt not the earth, neither the sea, nor the trees, till we have sealed the servants of our God in their foreheads.

7:9 After this I beheld, and, lo, a great multitude, which no man could number, of all nations, and kindreds, and people, and tongues, stood before the throne, and before the Lamb, clothed with white robes, and palms in their hands;

7:13 And one of the elders answered, saying unto me, What are these which are arrayed in white robes? and whence came they?

14 And I said unto him, Sir, thou knowest. And he said to me, These are they which came out of great tribulation, and have washed their robes, and made them white in the blood of the Lamb.

15 Therefore are they before the throne of God, and serve him day and night in his temple: and he that sitteth on the throne shall dwell among them.

16 They shall hunger no more, neither thirst any more; neither shall the sun light on them, nor any heat.

17 For the Lamb which is in the midst of the throne shall feed them, and shall lead them unto living fountains of waters: and God shall wipe away all tears from their eyes.

In Focus

Pastor Sam called Vera, a seasoned saint and prayer warrior, to assist him with evangelizing the gang-infested community where his church was located. At their first meeting, Vera asked, "Pastor Sam, what are you doing to minister to the members of this community?"

"I'm taking karate lessons." The athletically built pastor smiled.

"Karate lessons?" Vera quickly asked.

Pastor Sam sheepishly responded, "It's very dangerous in this neighborhood. I need to protect myself."

"How can karate protect you or teach the residents of this community about Christ?"

"What do you mean?" the pastor asked.

Vera asked for a pad of paper and pencil and began drawing circles. After the first circle she said, "This circle represents our life." She then drew a bigger circle around the first one. "The bigger circle represents Christ. The Bible says that you are in Christ. Do you believe that?"

"Of course," the pastor answered.

Vera drew an even bigger circle around the first two circles. "This

"These are they which came out of great tribulation, and have washed their robes, and made them white in the blood of the Lamb" (from Revelation 7:14).

circle represents the Father. You are in Christ and Christ is in the Father." Then she drew a small circle inside the first circle. "That circle represents the Holy Spirit who lives inside you. You are in Christ. Christ is in the Father. And the Holy Spirit lives in you."

Pastor Sam agreed and Vera continued, "Before the Devil can harm you, he has to first go through the Father and get permission from Him. If the Father gives him permission to attack you, he then must go through the Son. If the Son gives him permission to attack you, then you have the Holy Spirit living within you. So why karate? The safest place in the world is 'in Christ.'" Do you agree with Vera or Pastor Sam? Can you give a sound reason for Pastor Sam's karate lessons?

In today's lesson, John teaches that the future of the believer is secure through the blood of Christ, the

Lamb. His vision affirms that God's people are protected by the Lamb.

The People, Places, and Times

John. The entire revelation is seen through the eyes of the apostle John who is writing the vision he had on the Isle of Patmos during his exile.

Lamb. The lamb was one of the sacrificial animals mandated as a presentation to God under the Mosaic Law. Jesus Christ is the perfect Lamb of God who was offered as a sacrifice for the sins of humankind.

Servants. In this lesson, the term "servants" refers to people who have been redeemed by Christ. They have bound themselves to Jesus through acceptance of Him as the sacrifice for their sin.

Multitudes. These are people of all nations, languages, and backgrounds who have trusted Christ as their Lord and Saviour.

Angels. Messengers of God. The angels in this lesson have several tasks to perform. Four are holding back the wind of worldwide destruction. One angel has come to proclaim the sealing of the servants of God. All angels are declared to be worshiping God at the throne in the presence of the Lamb.

Elders. The elders were venerable people representing the entire church, both Old and New Testament saints. According to *Matthew Henry's Commentary*, the elders represent "the church triumphant in heaven." Others believe the elders represent angels who have great authority.

Throne. God's throne represents His power and authority. It is here that Jesus will be seen as the Lamb.

Source

Henry, Matthew. *Matthew Henry's Commentary.* Precepts For Living® CD-ROM. Chicago: UMI (Urban Ministries, Inc.), 2005.

Background

The concept of sacrificing and giving offerings to God was established after the Garden of Eden. Both Cain and Abel presented sacrifices to God (Genesis 3). The law delivered to Moses identified a system of offerings and sacrifices and ordained priests to accept and mediate these sacrifices on behalf of the people. The Mosaic Law identified sin and the system of sacrificial offerings in order to cover the stain and pay the penalty of sin. This was done through animal sacrifices brought to the priests at the tabernacle. Bulls, goats, lambs, and other animals were offered to God in a ritual of confession and cleansing before the altar.

The animal's slain body was placed on a fire and the smoke went upward as a symbol of confession before God. Each year the high priest symbolically placed blood in the Holy of Holies to represent the sins of the people; however, Hebrews 10:4 states that "It is not possible that the blood of bulls and of goats

should take away sins." These acts of regularly bringing a sacrifice to the altar and annually going into the holiest place (the Holy of Holies) were only a "shadow" of the real sacrifice that would come (10:1).

Jesus Christ, the son of God, is the ultimate sacrifice. His death on Calvary is the sacrifice that God accepts as atonement for the sins of man. Hebrews 9:12 states, "Neither by the blood of goats and calves, but by his own blood he entered in once into the holy place, having obtained eternal redemption for us." John the Baptist said of Jesus, "Behold! The Lamb of God, who takes away the sin of the world (John 1:29 NKJV). Jesus Christ was the Lamb that was slain so that man could stand before God. Since Christ's death on Calvary, believers have access to God through faith in Jesus Christ. They have the privilege to stand before God despite the sinful nature they were born with and the deeds and thoughts they've experienced.

Jesus' sacrifice dispels the wrath of God. Those who accept the sacrifice of Christ have a personal relationship with Christ, the protection of God in the midst of trials, and the right to dwell with God eternally. God's unmerited favor (grace) is given to those who receive Jesus Christ as Lord and Saviour. In the end, they will stand before His throne offering praise continually for the sacrifice made by the Lamb.

At-A-Glance

1. Sealed Servants (Revelation 7:1–3)
2. Standing Multitude (7:9, 13–14)
3. Secure Followers (vv. 15–17)

In Depth

1. Sealed Servants (Revelation 7:1–3)

This segment of John's vision begins with the four winds in the four corners of the earth set to bring the final destruction to the world. Before those events, however, the people who have trusted Christ will be identified. This is reminiscent of the first Passover when Israel was told that death would come to the land of Egypt. They would be spared if the blood of the sacrifice was placed on their doorposts to identify those who belonged to God (Exodus 12:7, 13).

The servants in Revelation 7:3 are God's people—those who are in Christ. For their protection, angels will be dispatched to place a seal on each person's forehead. A seal is a sign of ownership and authentication. God will identify each person who belongs to Him. By placing His seal upon them, God protects His servants from the dangers and turmoil that would otherwise consume them.

2. Standing Multitude (7:9, 13–14)

This scene in heaven is a celebration of redemption by those for whom Christ has given His life. The Bible says that all humanity has sinned and fallen short of God's standard of righteousness (Romans 3:23)—all our righteousness is as filthy rags (Isaiah 64:6). Without access to God, humanity is condemned to eternal damnation. Jesus Christ came to Earth to satisfy the justice of God by dying for the sins of the world. He is the way to God.

The multitude represents all nations, kindreds (tribes), people, and tongues (languages). The term "nations" can also be translated "Gentiles." The term "kindred" is a reference to every tribe on Earth, both Jews and Gentiles. The words "people" and "tongues" indicate that all language groups and backgrounds are numbered in the multitude who are in Christ—who will come before the throne.

The multitude is also described as wearing white robes and holding branches from palm trees. Their redemption is signified by the garments they wear. Those who trust in His sacrifice shall be cleansed from sin, washed in blood of the Lamb with spotless garments that are as white as snow (cf. Revelation 1:5; 7:14). In ancient civilizations, palm branches were used to pay homage to royalty, conquering heroes, and those who were esteemed to be honorable. The multitude around the throne are those who pay homage to Christ, realizing that He has delivered them from sin and protected them in the midst of their suffering on Earth.

This multitude is giving true worship and honor to the Redeemer who secured their salvation. While the number is great, each individual will have the opportunity to stand before Christ and worship Him. Each believer will meet Jesus—face-to-face! The multitude will stand before Christ as righteous because of His sacrifice.

3. Secure Followers (vv. 15–17)

The multitude in John's vision has come through great tribulation and suffered persecution for their faith. In the midst of the turmoil, the multitude is challenged by life's circumstances: poverty, hunger, fear, loneliness, isolation, and defeat. They face hardships caused by the wrath of natural disasters: hurricanes, earthquakes, storms, drought, and scorching desert heat. Nonetheless, these believers maintained faith in the shed blood of Christ on Calvary and had an assurance that they would one day see Jesus face to face. Through it all, they learned to trust in Jesus; they learned to trust in God.

Now they have been redeemed. Their faith has been vindicated and God's promise has been kept. They came through tribulation knowing that they were secure in Christ. They held on to the promised Word and had faith in Christ's accomplishment of salvation. They have been delivered from the vicissitudes of life and the cruelty of the world system.

This heavenly scene is reminiscent of James Weldon Johnson's masterful poem, "The Creation." Johnson described God's compassion with the words, "This Great God, like a mammy bending over her baby." In Revelation 7, we see that comfort as God wipes the tears away from the eyes of His creation. Before the seat of His power and presence, God will provide for their hunger and their thirst. Now redeemed through the sacrifice of God's only begotten Son, the multitude, the servants of God, will dwell forever before His throne.

Source

Johnson, James Weldon. "The Creation." *God's Trombones: Seven Negro Sermons in Verse*, 1927.

Search the Scriptures

1. Why were the angels stationed in "the four corners of the earth" (Revelation 7:1)?

2. What was the mission of the angel from the east (vv. 2–3)?

3. Who are the people before the throne and how are they described (v. 9)?

4. How did the robes become white (v. 14)?

5. What comfort is provided to those who belong to God (v. 16–17)?

Discuss the Meaning

In the opening verses of Revelation 7, the earth is poised for great danger. Jesus Christ's sacrifice paved the way for the protection of the believers from destruction and made them eligible for the seal to be placed upon them. How does this great sacrifice provide protection for us in our daily trials and tribulations?

Revelation 7:14 uses the terms "washed" and "blood" together. What do the "washed" robes represent? In what way have modern believers also been washed?

Revelation 7:17 speaks of the comfort given to those who have come before the throne of God. What comfort can we take in the knowledge of God's compassion as described in this verse?

Lesson in Our Society

Our daily news is rife with reports of violence against children. Our world seems to see conflict resolution as the art of getting even. Increasingly, we see elderly people lose their jobs as their retirement funds are bartered to keep corporate interests afloat. Healthcare is not available to the poor, and changes in care options and housing are causing others to struggle. In such a world, where can we turn when we are overwhelmed or face difficulty? Believers turn to God.

When you have accepted Christ as Saviour, you can depend on His ability to protect you in the midst of turmoil. On the spiritual level, the blood of Jesus was shed on Calvary to remove sin and secure eternal life for believers. God is equally concerned for the daily

needs and relationships of His people. The sacrifice of Jesus on Calvary provided power through the indwelling of the Holy Spirit to strengthen the Christian's walk each day.

How does the knowledge of this power help you apply God's promises to today's struggles? What confidence can you draw from God's promises of comfort in times of distress and concern? How closely does your faith in God regarding spiritual matters match your trust in God for daily support?

Make It Happen

This week, examine your commitment to Christ by asking yourself the following questions at the end of every day: Am I satisfied that my response to the activities and events of my day reflected my trust that God was in control? Did anything in my personal actions and responses today dishonor the sacrifice I know Jesus paid for me personally? What tears and concerns do I need God to touch in my life today? Which promises of God can strengthen my commitment to honor Christ's sacrifice tomorrow?

Follow the Spirit

What God wants me to do:

_____

_____

Remember Your Thoughts

Special insights I have learned:

_____

_____

More Light on the Text
Revelation 7:1–3, 9, 13–17

1 And after these things I saw four angels standing on the four corners of the earth, holding the four winds of the earth, that the wind should not blow on the earth, nor on the sea, nor on any tree.

John says he saw four angels holding back the judgments of God. Some suggest the four angels have been delegated authority over certain aspects of nature and others have been delegated to do battle with Satan and his cohorts. The "four winds" (Gk. tessares anemos, **TES-sar-es AN-em-os**) of the earth represent the totality of human existence as understood by humankind. Clearly, God is going to judge every sphere of human knowledge and existence. Then John saw another angel carrying the seal of the living God. This seal was God's affirmation that although the end is fast approaching, it is not the end for the people of God. God will not destroy all humankind. He promises that His people will be spared from the ultimate consequence of judgment, which is total separation and alienation from Him.

2 And I saw another angel ascending from the east, having the seal of the living God: and he cried with a loud voice to the four angels, to whom it was given to hurt the earth and the sea, 3 Saying, Hurt not the earth, neither the sea, nor the trees, till we have sealed the servants of our God in their foreheads.

John identifies the angel in this verse as being very distinct from the other four angels holding back the judgments of God. Just as we have been given certain responsibilities, "another" angel is assigned the task of sealing the saints. Angels are assigned varying responsibilities as dictated by God. This particular angel was called by God to command the other four angels to withhold judgment on the earth until God's people were protected from hurt.

While the earth and all its inhabitants will receive the just reward for acts of unrighteousness, God's chosen people will be protected by the righteousness of God because they belong unconditionally to Him. God's people are marked as His possession. Therefore, as God's people, we are secure from any imaginable impending judgment that could separate us from God (cf. Romans 8:34–39).

The world may crumble around us, but we will not crumble with it. God has decreed protection from any and everything that might come our way to thwart spending eternity with Him. This is no ordinary seal; it is the seal of the living God. A seal that is only given to those whose robes have been washed in the blood of the Lamb.

7:9 After this I beheld, and, lo, a great multitude, which no man could number, of all nations, and kin-dreds, and people, and tongues, stood before the throne, and before the Lamb, clothed with white robes, and palms in their hands;

John says after he witnessed what God had done to secure the future destiny of His people, he was given a vision of God gathering His people together. It is as if John were saying, "I knew God was good, but now I see just how expansive the grace of God is." There is no nation, no ethnic group, no subculture, no people group, or language that will not be represented in heaven.

John says this number was beyond the ability of man to number. The phase "no man could number" employs the Greek word *dunamai* (**DOO-nam-ahee**) translated as "could." Here "could" means to be able to do something, or to have power by virtue of one's own ability and resources. The use of *dunamai* signifies an action that has taken place without any specific reference to a location, time, or place. No human being past, present, or future has the ability to dictate who gets in, or who stays out, or how many will ultimately experience the eternal love and grace of God. Ultimately, only God can make that decision. What joins us together is not that we look alike, talk alike, walk alike, eat the same foods, live in the same neighborhoods, or go to the same churches. What joins us together is nothing but the blood of Christ.

The only attire acceptable in heaven are souls that have been washed white in the blood of the Lamb. Those who have been saved from eternal damnation and judgment stand before the Lamb with palms in hands that are freed of sin. Christ's victory over the grave and death gives us our reward (cf. 1 Corinthians 15:55–57).

7:13 And one of the elders answered, saying unto me, What are these which are arrayed in white robes? and whence came they? 14 And I said unto him, Sir, thou knowest. And he said to me, These are they which came out of great tribulation, and have washed their robes, and made them white in the blood of the Lamb. 15 Therefore are they before the throne of God, and serve him day and night in his temple: and he that sitteth on the throne shall dwell among them.

John must have been somewhat surprised by the inclusiveness of God's family because he appears to have asked one of the elders a question. Did John ask a question or in someway convey a sense of amazement? Something prompted one of the elders to ask, "Who were these people standing around and throne in white robes?" They are the survivors of the great tribulation. The word "tribulation" (Gk. *thlipsis,* **THLIP-sis**) can refer to personal afflictions (1 Thessalonians 3:3; 1 Peter 4:3) or a time of affliction (Matthew 24:4–8; Mark 13). It is a time marked by intense oppression and suffering. The Good News is that whatever horror may come, the blood of Jesus covers all believers.

So what does it mean to overcome, to survive, to have the privilege of spending eternity with God? The Greek term for "therefore," *dia houtos* (**dee-AH HOO-tos**) gives the answer. *Dia houtos* means "for this reason." It is because we are washed, because we have survived; it is for *this reason* that we serve and worship the Lord.

There are a number of Greek words used to convey the idea of service. It may be significant that the Greek word translated "serve" in this verse is *latreuo* (**lat-RYOO-o**) and has connotations of service rendered with an expectation of reward. Can we dare expect God to reward us for serving Him when He has already paid the ultimate price—made the ultimate sacrifice? YES, we can. Do not overlook the connecting conjunction between serving Him in His temple *and* dwelling among us. In other words, He is our reward!

The word used to convey "dwell" is the Greek word *skenoo* (**skay-NO-o**). It literally means to pitch a tent and live among us and connotes a spiritual and psychological residing. There will be no more feeble attempts to please God or wonder what His will is for the day; we will know innately because He will be among us leading the way.

16 They shall hunger no more, neither thirst any more; neither shall the sun light on them, nor any heat. 17 For the Lamb which is in the midst of the throne shall feed them, and shall lead them unto living fountains of waters: and God shall wipe away all tears from their eyes.

Here the elder has told John that the blood of the Lamb has secured our past, present, and future. Whatever happened in the past, or whatever you may be going through in the present, does not affect the future of those who have been washed in the blood. The Lord Himself is preparing to meet our needs for eternity. He will feed us. He will give us eternal life, and He will never allow us to experience pain and sorrow again.

Daily Bible Readings

M: Thanks for Faithful Followers
Colossians 1:3–8
T: The Lord Will Keep You
Psalm 121
W: God Is Our Deliverer
Psalm 3
T: God Is Good
Psalm 34:1–10
F: Protection in Trials
Revelation 3:7–13
S: Salvation Belongs to God
Revelation 7:1–3, 9–10
S: The Lamb on the Throne
Revelation 7:11–17

TEACHING TIPS

May 6
Bible Study Guide 10

1. Words You Should Know

A. Omnipotent (Revelation 19:6) *pantokrator* (Gk.)—Almighty or ruler of all. The word is only used to describe God.

B. Righteousness (v. 8) *dikaioma* (Gk.)—The character or quality of being right or just. John uses the word to denote the righteousness of saints, who do good works to bring honor to Christ's name.

C. Prophecy (v. 10) *propheteia* (Gk.)—Signifies the speaking forth of the mind and counsel of God.

2. Teacher Preparation

A. Begin with prayer and then read the Devotional Reading and Focal Verses.

B. Read the Lesson Aim.

C. Consult the *Precepts For Living®* CD-ROM for additional commentary and background history.

D. Complete lesson 10 in the *Precepts For Living® Personal Study Guide*.

3. Starting the Lesson

A. Open with prayer.

B. Ask the students to explain the significance of marriage.

C. Ask two students to volunteer to read the In Focus story and Lesson Aim.

4. Getting into the Lesson

A. Have a student read Background and The People, Places, and Times and discuss it with the class.

B. Review the Words You Should Know section.

C. Have a volunteer read the At-A-Glance outline. Discuss the In Depth section with your class.

D. Review the Search the Scriptures section and have the students complete the answers.

5. Relating the Lesson to Life

A. Review the Discuss the Meaning section with the class.

B. Ask two or three students to share how we, as a community of believers, can honor our Bridegroom, Jesus.

6. Arousing Action

A. Have the students reread the Lesson Aim out loud.

B. Remind the students that we should honor Jesus, who is the Bridegroom, through service to others.

C. Close the class with prayer.

Worship Guide

For the Superintendent or Teacher
Theme: The Final Banquet
Theme Song: "All Hail the Power of Jesus' Name"
Scripture: Psalm 45
Song: "Joyful, Joyful, We Adore Thee"
Meditation: Heavenly Father, I praise Your name. Only You are worthy of all honor and glory. I acknowledge You as the Head of my life. Help me to humbly serve You and others. Amen.

THE FINAL BANQUET

Bible Background • REVELATION 19
Printed Text • REVELATION 19:5–10   Devotional Reading • PSALM 148:1–14

Lesson Aim

By the end of the lesson, we will:

UNDERSTAND that the Christian community is built on the recognition of Jesus as the Head and Bridegroom of the church and that other believers are fellow bride members;

SENSE deeply that Jesus Christ is to be honored as a bride honors her groom; and IDENTIFY ways in which we, in community with one another, can serve our Bridegroom.

Keep in Mind

"And I heard as it were the voice of a great multitude, and as the voice of many waters, and as the voice of mighty thunderings, saying, Allelujah: for the Lord God omnipotent reigneth" (Revelation 19:6).

Focal Verses

Revelation 19:5 And a voice came out of the throne, saying, Praise our God, all ye his servants, and ye that fear him, both small and great.

6 And I heard as it were the voice of a great multitude, and as the voice of many waters, and as the voice of mighty thunderings, saying, Allelujah: for the Lord God omnipotent reigneth.

7 Let us be glad and rejoice, and give honor to him: for the marriage of the Lamb is come, and his wife hath made herself ready.

8 And to her was granted that she should be arrayed in fine linen, clean and white: for the fine linen is the righteousness of saints.

9 And he saith unto me, Write, Blessed are they which are called unto the marriage supper of the Lamb. And he saith unto me, These are the true sayings of God.

10 And I fell at his feet to worship him. And he said unto me, See thou do it not: I am thy fellow servant, and of thy brethren that have the testimony of Jesus: wor-

ship God; for the testimony of Jesus is the spirit of prophecy.

In Focus

Russell's shoulders were slumped as he got off his knees from morning devotion. His face was covered with tears because he realized that he had been disobedient.

He had not been to church for months because he was at odds with the new pastor. He didn't agree with how money was being allocated for the building fund, so he decided to leave the committee. As a result, his church attendance gradually diminished. Now several months had passed since he had attended Sunday services.

When fellow church members and family questioned his lack of attendance, his answer was, "My faith is a personal matter. I can be a Christian without regular church attendance. What's wrong with reading Scripture, listening to religious music, and watching televangelists?" Each time Russell mouthed those words, he felt

himself sinking deeper into the troubled waters of pride.

Can we be Christians, those who follow Christ, and separate ourselves from the community of faith? Maybe, but it is like removing a burning ember from a fireplace. After it is removed from the warmth of the other burning embers, it begins to lose its heat and soon it grows cold. It still holds the heat of an ember, but it doesn't burn with the same intensity and power as it did when gathered with other burning embers. The same is true of our spiritual fires. God's gift of community strengthens us.

In today's lesson, John admonishes us to honor God and work together in community with one another in order to serve our Bridegroom.

The People, Places, and Times

Worship. The concept of worship in Scripture is adoration and love manifested in service. Christ's teachings reveal that worship is a service offered to God not only in public praise and prayers in the temple, but also in service to others (Luke 10:25–37; John 4:21–24).

Multitude. The multitude of voices that came from heaven was composed of the 24 elders, the four living creatures, angels, and believers.

Background

In the book of Revelation, the apostle John reveals the full identity of Jesus Christ. The church was experiencing persecution under Emperor Domitian during A.D. 90–95. While on the isle of Patmos, John is given a vision of future events. These events include judgment and the ultimate triumph of God over evil. He was offering hope for believers and warnings against unrighteous behavior.

There are seven letters written to the churches in the Roman province of Asia. The scene then shifts to visions of God and of the Lamb; afterward, we have the opening of the seven seals. In between the opening of the sixth and seventh seals, John reveals that God's people will be marked as His own and guaranteed His protection over their souls.

John then records a woman bringing forth a man-child. This birth precipitates a great conflict between God and Satan, beasts opposing themselves to God, the Lamb on Mount Zion, and His followers. Seven angels pour out God's judgment upon the earth from seven bowls. One of these angels from the group of seven reveals to John a vision of a "great whore" called Babylon riding a scarlet beast. Among other things, she symbolizes the Roman Empire riding a scarlet beast.

Babylon has become a dwelling place of demons and is full of unclean things. The city was an evil and immoral empire, a world center for idol worship. Nations went into collusion with Babylon thereby earning God's wrath. Merchants in the Roman Empire became rich by exploiting the sinful pleasures of their society. Once God dispenses judgment against Babylon, there is grief, torment, pestilence, and famine instead of the luxury and consumption of the past.

The world mourns Babylon's fall. Merchants weep because no one buys their cargo anymore. Babylon was the hub of trade and merchants depended on her. Those who refused to worship the beast had been excluded from buying and selling. However, these merchants had colluded with Babylon.

The apostles, saints, and prophets are commanded to rejoice because God has judged in their favor and against Babylon. In Babylon, the blood of prophets and saints had been shed. The fall of Babylon serves as justice for believers and avenges the blood of God's servants.

In our lesson, a "great multitude" in heaven is praising God for the victory. There is a harmony of praise from saints, angels, churches, and ministers. It is appropriate to give honor and praise to the Bridegroom.

Source
The New Interpreter's Bible (Volume 12). Nashville, Tenn.: Abingdon Press, 1998, 692–694.

At-A-Glance

1. Honor God with Praise (Revelation 19:5–6)
2. Honor God, the Bridegroom (vv. 7–8)
3. Honor God through Service (vv. 9–10)

In Depth

1. Honor God with Praise (Revelation 19:5–6)

John hears a voice from the throne commanding God's servants and all who fear Him "to praise our God." He had triumphed over Babylon and all evilness. The call for all to praise God is a reminder we should be offering a harmony of praise to God in honor of what He has done and is yet to do. When we are in harmony with one another, recognizing the sovereignty and righteousness of God, it ushers in a sense of community among believers.

"There is one body and one Spirit—just as you

were called to one hope when you were called—one Lord, one faith, one baptism; one God and Father of all, who is over all and through all and in all" (Ephesians 4:4–6, NIV). All believers in Christ belong to one body; all are united under one Head, Christ Himself. As we acknowledge Jesus as the Head and ourselves as the body, our focus is upon Him. When our full attention is on Christ, we will discover His will for our lives.

For example, every day people travel to their places of employment. Imagine if you were told to come to work every day, but you never knew your job title. It would cause you to wonder what was your purpose for being present every day. You would feel disconnected from coworkers and confused. But the solution is to seek clarification of your role and responsibilities from someone in authority. In the same way, Jesus, the Head, knows what our purpose is within the body of believers. All we need to do is humble ourselves and seek Him. We will discover the plans He has for us (Jeremiah 29:11–3).

There is a voice that sounds like a "great multitude" and the "sound of many waters" speaking in a melodious song of praise, asserting God's sovereignty (Revelation 19:6). The proof of His sovereignty is the defeat of Babylon and judgment of the wicked. As we serve Christ, it must be done in complete recognition of His status as "the Almighty." He alone is the ruler of all. In submission, there is unity between the Bridegroom and the bride (the church). That unity precedes a sense of community.

2. Honor God, the Bridegroom (vv. 7–8)

After a song of praise, the multitudes in heaven now rejoice and celebrate the marriage of the Lamb (Revelation 19:7). The Lamb is Jesus Christ, who gave Himself as a sacrifice for our sins. He has defeated the enemy and dispensed judgment. He now reigns with dominion power as the One who is now publicly betrothing the bride to Himself. The bride is the church, composed of all believers from all times.

When a couple has a wedding ceremony, the celebration is conducted among family and friends. The couple is publicly announcing to the community: "We are now one." In the same manner, the Lamb shall publicly take the bride to Himself in the presence of the heavenly multitude. Jesus Christ will take those who have served and honored Him to reign with Him for eternity. The only precise manner to be prepared is to accept Christ and serve Him. In service to others within the community, we honor Jesus. Like a bride who honors her husband, when we serve with love and humility, others recognize that we belong to Jesus.

The bride is clothed in "fine linen, clean and white: for the fine linen is the righteousness of saints" (19:8). The garment is a symbol of righteousness—not of the works of believers, but the provision of God's salvation by grace through faith in Christ. She had washed her robes and made them white in the blood of the Lamb. The "fine linen," referred to as "the righteousness of saints," are works of godliness and goodness produced by the Holy Spirit as the believer yields to God (3:5; 5:8). In doing so, we bring honor to Christ's name both now and in the hereafter.

3. Honor God Through Service (vv. 9–10)

The marriage feast (Matthew 22:1–10; Luke 14:15–24) is a time of celebration and praise to God for His goodness. Those who are called to attend and accept the invitation will indulge in a feast composed of the promises of the Gospel. These promises opened, applied, and sealed by the Spirit of God in holy eucharistic ordinances compose the marriage feast; and the whole collective body of all those who partake of the feast is the bride, the Lamb's wife. The Lamb, the Son of Man, has communion with the churches. The consummation is the demonstration that the dwelling of God is with humanity and in the midst of the throne (Revelation 21:3; 22:3).

Traditionally, during weddings the bride and groom may partake of Holy Communion. It represents the union of the bride and groom to Christ through His body and blood. While at the wedding reception, the bride and groom share a feast with their guests in the spirit of celebration and unity. It is in serving and sharing our provisions with others that we reflect the love and the spirit of unity among believers (Acts 2:44–47).

John falls down at the angel's feet to worship him, just as the elders and the living creatures had done before God (Revelation 19:10). The angel informed John that this is the wrong thing to do. He explains that he is "a fellow servant" of all who hold the testimony of Jesus. John may have seen the angel as a divine figure like the Son of Man since its voice comes from the throne. Angels are messengers and servants of God. They are created slightly above humans, and are "fellow servants." Jesus came to serve. He was even willing to wash the feet of His disciples (John 13:13–16). We must imitate Jesus and become humble servants.

Search the Scriptures

1. How can believers honor God (Revelation 19:5)?

2. Who reigns and gives us total victory (v. 6)?

3. Who will be present during the marriage of the Lamb (v. 7)?

4. How do the saints' garments become clean and white (v. 8)?

5. Who does the angel tell John to worship (v. 10)?

Discuss the Meaning

Deacon Wicks and his wife were thrilled that their daughter's wedding day had finally arrived. Deacon Wicks wanted to give his full attention to his beautiful daughter, so they closed the plumbing business for the weekend.

In the middle of the wedding ceremony, a loud noise was heard coming from the fellowship hall. One of the ushers notified Deacon Wicks that a hot water pipe had burst. Water was flooding the kitchen and threatening to destroy all the caterer's food. They needed a plumber.

How do you think Deacon Wicks responded? How would you respond?

Lesson in Our Society

Many people profess to know God. They even attend church regularly. However, we need to honor God not with lip service, but in service to others. There are children who lack the basic necessities of life like clothes, food, and shelter. Many widows are homebound and alone. Prisons are overflowing with youth from our communities. In some instances, these children, widows, and youth are members of our churches. Believers cannot be concerned about themselves only. Jesus came to serve by fulfilling His Father's will. Where is the focus of your attention? How are you serving God?

Make It Happen

This week, ask God to help you honor Him with your life. Ask for a fresh refilling of the Holy Spirit to empower you for service. Seek ways to serve others in your home, church, and community.

Follow the Spirit

What God wants me to do:

_____

_____

Remember Your Thoughts

Special insights I have learned:

_____

_____

More Light on the Text

Revelation 19:5–10

5 And a voice came out of the throne, saying, Praise our God, all ye his servants, and ye that fear him, both small and great.

This verse is a lead vocal in one of those remarkable hymns sung in heaven after the fall of Babylon. It is a clarion call to perform the utmost service for which we were called from the kingdom of darkness (1 Peter 2:9). It is a charge emanating from the highest place of authority (the throne) to those who are servants of God and who constitute a community of people that fear Him.

The Greek word translated "voice" is *phone* (fo-NAY); it means sound and denotes something that is spoken. The first mention of "voice" in verse 1 of this chapter refers to that of "much people in heaven" (this is the redeemed in heaven). In this verse, we find the second mention of the word "voice", which emanated from the throne. The word *thronos* (THRON-os) is translated "throne" in this verse. It is a stately seat of authority and power occupied by a king, priest, or some sort of ruler.

John mentions three classes of creatures that could have spoken this charge (9:1–5): the people in heaven, the 24, or the four beasts. But none of these made this call. "A voice came out of the throne" (v. 5) implies that the sound was articulate and distinct. This is definitely the throne in heaven where God is seated. John saw these things in his vision of heaven, at the Isle of Patmos, and narrates them as he saw and heard them. His earlier descriptions of the voice he heard while in the Spirit were different. He said he heard a voice which sounded like a trumpet (Revelation 1:10) and another voice was like the sound of many waters (v. 15). He also heard the voice of many angels (5:11), a voice from heaven (14:15), and a voice out of the temple (16:1). But the particular sound emanating from the throne was described in a peculiar way: "And out of the throne proceeded lightnings and thunderings and voices" (4:5). The throne is the seat of authority and power; it produces sounds and voices, and it gave the call to praise God. Because of these abilities, the throne of God is seen as a divine personage.

The throne is the place from which God rules and judges the world in general and His people in particular. It bears such appellations as: "the throne of grace" (Hebrews 4:16), "the throne of the Majesty" (8:1), "throne of his glory" (Matthew 19:28), "the throne of God" (Hebrews 12:2), and the "great white throne" (Revelation 20:11). These appellations reveal to us its status, attributes, and ownership.

John's narrative of a voice coming out of the throne and charging the servants of God to praise Him bears a parallelism with David's declaration: "But thou art holy, O thou that inhabitest the praises of Israel" (Psalm 22:3). The NIV footnotes provide another meaning to the latter part of this Scripture with this expression: "enthroned on the praises of Israel." Where the KJV uses the word "inhabitest," the NIV uses "enthroned." The overall idea we derive from these two words is a place where God dwells, sits, or is positioned. This is no other place than His throne. It then means that the throne of God is an embodi-

ment of praises; a living, divine personage that gives off lightnings, thunderings, and voices with the authority to charge the servants of God to praise Him. In other words, God dwells or sits on praises as His throne.

The Greek word translated "praise" is *ainos* (**AH-ee-nos**), which primarily meant "a story or narration," but came to denote "praise." Praise of God is one of the most characteristic features of biblical piety. We, the chosen people of God, ought to praise Him for His glory (Ephesians 1:12). Our praise unto God can be expressed by being filled with the fruit of righteousness (Philippians 1:11). The fruits of our lips, that is, our utterances are meant to be sacrifices of praise unto God (Hebrews 13:15). The trial of our faith is also meant to bring praise at the appearing of Jesus Christ (1 Peter 1:7). In all of these, we are meant to make our whole lives and conduct a form of praise unto God.

The charge to praise God is given to His servans—they that fear Him—both small and great. The Greek word *phobeo* (**fob-EH-o**) is translated "fear" in this Scripture; it means to revere. We have been called out of the world to live lives that praise God. We are His servants. A very important quality that enables us to achieve this aim is fear (reverence). In an effort to dispel negative fear from the Israelites when God descended on Mount Sinai in full view of the people to give them the Ten Commandments, Moses told them that God wanted His fear (reverence) to be with them to keep them from sinning (Exodus 20:20). The fear of God enables us to respect God's authority, obey His commandments, and abstain from sin.

6 And I heard as it were the voice of a great multitude, and as the voice of many waters, and as the voice of mighty thunderings, saying, Alleluia: for the Lord God omnipotent reigneth.

John speaks of hearing a voice which he describes in a pair of similes: "as the voice of many waters" and "as the voice of mighty thunderings." The Greek word *ochlos* (**okh-los**) is translated "multitude" in this verse. It means a crowd, a great number of people or a great multitude. Apparently, John is still referring to the "great voice of much people" (v. 1), but here he uses a pair of similes to denote a dual meaning. First, the similes describe sound effects—the kind of effects created by many waters and mighty thunderings. Second, the words he uses ("water" and "thundering") are symbolic. Water symbolizes the people used in verse 1 and also the "multitude" used in this verse, with further amplification that denotes nationality and tongue or language (Revelation 17:15). "Thunder" symbolizes divine power (2 Samuel 22:14). Thus, we are made to understand here that multitudes of people from different nations and of various tongues spoke with divine power.

This great multitude is responding to the charge to praise God which came out of the throne (v. 5). The preface to the proclamation made by this multitude is a short doxology: "Alleluia" meaning "praise the Lord." This is followed by an exalting declaration of God's omnipotence and continuous reign. The Greek word *pantokrator* (**pan-tok-RAT-ore**) translated "omnipotent" is the same word that is translated "almighty." It means all-ruling or ruler of all and refers to God's unlimited power.

While verse 5 gives the charge to praise God, verse 6 introduces a chorus by the great multitude singing the divine hymn in a response to that charge. This response focuses on God's absolute and universal sovereignty and infinite reign as main points and ultimate reasons why we ought to praise Him. God's omnipotence and infinite reign provide enough assurance for us that: There is nothing too hard for Him (Jeremiah 32:17), no one can hinder His purpose (Isaiah 43:13), with Him all things are possible (Mark 10:27), and His grace will reign unto eternity (Romans 5:21). When we personalize all these truths about God, then we can access His manifold blessings and benefits.

All human aspirations have favorable achievements (blessings or benefits) as their goals. Since progress toward their life goals is always desired, many people seek direction for their lives. They seek a course of life that will lead to greater fulfillment, a

pathway in various circumstances and situations that will lead to desirable accomplishments, and a means out of prevailing adverse conditions that will bring about relief or ease. The ultimate is divine direction, and only God gives it: "I am the LORD your God....who directs you in the way you should go." (Isaiah 48:17, NIV). Those seeking direction for their lives must begin their search by serving, honoring, and praising God. Divine direction is sure to give your life a meaning because it will lead you to the realization of God's purpose for your life.

7 Let us be glad and rejoice, and give honor to him: for the marriage of the Lamb is come, and his wife hath made herself ready.

The first part of verse 7 is a continuation of the declaration of praise in verse 6. It opens up with an admonishment that is meant to encourage believers to rejoice. The Greek word *agalliao* (**ag-al-lee-AH-o**) is translated "rejoice" in this verse; it conveys an active sense of rejoicing, jubilant exaltation; to jump for joy and be exceedingly glad. While the Greek word *chairo* (**KHAH-ee-ro**) is translated "glad" conveys the idea of being cheerful, being well-off, and maintaining a consistent rejoicing attitude.

We are further admonished to honor the Lord. The Greek word *doxa* (**DOX-ah**) is the Greek word translated honor, and it means glory and praise. This admonishment is followed by the introduction of a great heavenly occasion: the marriage of the Lamb. This event is presented here as the reason for being glad, rejoicing, and honoring the Lord. The marriage of the Lamb is the great celebration of the union of Christ and His bride, the church. Christ is spoken of here as the Lamb because of His atoning sacrifice—the sacrifice of being slain to redeem us unto God by His blood out of every kindred, tongue, people, and nation to be made kings and priests who reign on the earth (Revelation 5:9–10). But the marriage celebration is the ultimate climatic ceremonial union that places the redeemed on the highest status of relationship with Christ. In addition to being kings and priests (Revelation 5:10), branches (John 15:5), sheep (10:14), stones (1 Peter 2:5), a new creature (1 Corinthians 5:17), and the church (Colossians 1:18), we are also called the bride in respect to the marriage of the Lamb. The marriage culminates at our assumption of the ultimate status: "His wife." Thus, the church is called the wife at her marriage to her Bridegroom (Christ), and this spiritual union is based on His atoning sacrifice.

This verse portrays the accomplishment of the marriage and the readiness of His wife. While this sounds prophetic to us now, it reveals a certainty of the fulfillment of the marriage. The atoning sacrifice of Christ that purifies His believers prepares them as His wife. The readiness of the wife is also portrayed in the parable of the 10 virgins (Matthew 25:1–13). The five wise virgins were ready for the groom because they had extra oil for their lamps, and their flames burned until his arrival. The oil symbolizes the Holy Spirit's anointing, which means they remained fervent in Spirit (Romans 12:11). The flame symbolizes faith; they continued in faith (Colossians 1:23) until the arrival of the bridegroom.

Jesus asks, "Nevertheless when the Son of man cometh, shall he find faith on earth" (Luke 18:8). As the bride of Christ, therefore, we are to live in readiness as a virgin betrothed to her future husband (2 Corinthians 11:2); we must always honor Him as a bride would honor her groom. We must always remember that we belong to Christ under the marriage contract—that is, the covenant of redemption—and our engagement to Him will eventually be consummated in the "marriage of the Lamb."

8 And to her was granted that she should be arrayed in fine linen, clean and white: for the fine linen is the righteousness of saints.

The bride is usually in her best attire on her wedding day. The atoning sacrifice of Christ sets in place a wholesome and complete process that enables the church to be prepared for the marriage of the Lamb and be donned as the bride, thus eventually becoming His wife.

The Greek word translated "granted" is a form of the verb *didomi* (**DID-o-mee**), and means "to give, to bestow." This word speaks of the grace given to us by

God (Ephesians 2:8), which makes us beneficiaries of Christ's atonement and redemption. It is the grace by which we are sanctified and justified.

Justification means the act of declaring righteous. Through the redemptive work of Christ, we were justified freely by His grace (Romans 3:24). And so those of us who believe have the righteousness of God, which is by faith in Christ (Romans 3:22). This righteousness (described as imputed righteousness) becomes personal to every believer, and our response is living a life pleasing and acceptable in the sight of God. A sanctified life—a life of purity—is what is described in this verse as "the righteousness of saints" and symbolized by clean white fine linen.

The clean white fine linen is the wedding garment. It qualifies the bride (the church) for the marriage of the Lamb. In the parable of the king and the wedding banquet in Matthew 22 when the guests came for the wedding banquet, one man was found not to be dressed in wedding garments and the king ordered that he be thrown out (vv. 11–12).

The grant given to the "wife" to be arrayed in fine linen spells out the wholesome process of atonement, sanctification and justification to bring her to the status of a bride fit to marry her Groom and become His wife. In preparing the bride and getting her ready for the marriage, we see the inestimable value of the work of Jesus as the Messiah anointed to bring her salvation. For "Christ loved the church and gave himself up for her to make her holy, cleansing her by the washing with water through the word, and to present her to himself as a radiant church, without stain or wrinkle or any other blemish, but holy and blameless" (Ephesians 5:25–27, NIV). The radiance of the prepared bride is seen in the clean white fine linen that clothes her.

9 And he saith unto me, Write, Blessed are they which are called unto the marriage supper of the Lamb. And he saith unto me, These are the true sayings of God.

It is apparent from the narrative that John hears various voices during his vision of heaven, but one thing stands out clearly: he also has an attendant angel who speaks to him about what he is made to behold. This angel testifies to everything he sees (Revelation 1:1–2). And so after the heavenly hymn, the angel asks John to write a commendation extolling those who are privileged to be invited to the marriage supper of the Lamb.

It is usually an experience of great worth to be invited to the grand wedding banquet of a highly placed person. The worth, bliss, and experience becomes incomparable when you are invited to the marriage of the Lamb. For He is the hope of our salvation; the ultimate goal of our faith and service to Christ.

The Greek word translated "blessed" in this verse is *makarios* (**mak-AR-ee-os**). This word denotes someone who is fortunate, supremely blessed, well off, and happy. It is used to describe those who are privileged and fortunate to be invited to the marriage supper of the Lamb. In fact the Scripture says that they are "called."

The church constitutes people who are called out of the world. The word "church" is derived from the Greek word *kuriakos* (**koo-ree-ak-OS**) which means one belonging to the Lord. However, the Greek term *ekklesia* (**ek-klay-SEE-ah**) also came to mean "church." *Ekklesia* originally referred to an assembly called out by legislative authority; it referred to a body of citizens gathered to discuss the affairs of the state, among the Greeks. But the adoption of the term by Greek-speaking Jewish Christians and their Gentile adherents in the New Testament times is what gave force and acceptability to use the word *ekklesia* to refer to the church, which is how the writers of the new Testament applied the term.

The invitation to share in the marriage supper with Jesus is extended to all those who hear and receive the invitation. Not everyone will accept the invitation, but all are welcome to come. In Luke 14:15–24, Jesus extends an invitation to a great feast that many turned down. Nevertheless, the feast took place in spite of the naysayers letting us know that Jesus' marriage supper will happen even if only a few accept His offer.

The marriage supper of the Lamb is an eschato-logical fulfillment of the Last Supper Christ had with His disciples before His crucifixion, which was also a Passover meal. The Last Supper, sometimes called the Lord's Supper, is the taking of bread, which symbolizes His body, and wine, which symbolizes His blood. He speaks of this supper as something that will be fulfilled in the kingdom of God (Luke 22:16).

The Last Supper is observed by the church in accordance with Christ's institution. This, He says, we should do in remembrance of Him. Today it is known as the Holy Communion. The messianic significance of the Last Supper is based on the fact that Christ is the real Passover Lamb sacrificed for our redemption through His broken body and shed blood. The Old Testament Passover lamb is a figure of the real Lamb of God (Christ) who takes away the sins of the world.

10 And I fell at his feet to worship him. And he said unto me, See thou do it not: I am thy fellow servant, and of thy brethren that have the testimony of Jesus: worship God: for the testimony of Jesus is the spirit of prophecy.

The awesomeness of these revelations filled John with so much reverence that he fell at the feet of the angel to worship him. The Greek word translated "worship" here is *proskuneo*. It conveys a sense of prostrating oneself in homage, doing reverence, or showing respect, as an act of worship. It indicates an absoluteness in a physical act of adoration. For a moment John was so overwhelmed with the greatness of the things spoken to him and impelled by the last sentence of this verse: "These are the true sayings of God," that he fell at the angel's feet to pay obeisance to him as if he were doing it to God.

The angel restrained John from worshiping him, and told him he was a fellow servant along with him. *Sundoulos* (**SOON-doo-los**) is the Greek word translated "fellowservant." These are two words joined together to form one; it simply implies servants serving the same master or Lord, or fellow servants who belong to the same community of brethren. The angel also says that the brethren have the "testimony" (Gk. *marturia,* **mar-too-REE-ah**), meaning witness or evidence of Jesus. In other words, the brethren bear the witness of Jesus (1 John 5:9), and those who believe in Jesus have this witness in themselves (v. 10); they are the ones who keep the commandments of God (Revelation 12:17). The word "record" (1 John 5:11) means witness or testimony. The record (witness) is this: "that God hath given to us eternal life, and this life is in his Son."

Jesus said, "for the works which the Father hath given me to finish, the same works that I do, bear witness of me, that the Father hath sent me" (John 5:36). The works of Jesus are express testimonies. A testimony shows that something exists or is true.

After dissuading John from worshiping him, the angel charged him to worship God, and told him, "the testimony of Jesus is the spirit of prophecy." The Greek word *propheteia* (**prof-ay-TI-ah**) is translated "prophecy" here. It means to speak forth the mind and counsel of God. It foretells the will and plans of God.

The church is the bride which forms the Christian community where all are servants of Christ who is the Head of the church and the Bridegroom of the bride. The church's great responsibility is to serve her Head and to honor her Bridegroom.

The Christian community exists temporarily in the world, and it is supposed to distinguish itself by paying obeisance to the King (Jesus Christ), living as the sanctified body, fulfilling righteousness, and living in readiness for the great marriage of the Lamb.

In active fulfillment of this, believers should consistently attend the gathering of the righteous, perform Christian duties, and be light and salt to the various secular communities in which they find themselves.

Daily Bible Readings

M: Parable of the Wedding Banquet
Matthew 22:1–14
T: The Song of the Lamb
Revelation 15:1–5
W: He Will Reign Forever
Revelation 11:15–19
T: The Heavens Praise
Psalm 148:1–6
F: The Earth Praises
Psalm 148:7–14
S: Hallelujah!
Revelation 19:1–5
S: Give God Glory
Revelation 19:6–10

TEACHING TIPS

May 13
Bible Study Guide 11

1. Words You Should Know

A. Tabernacle (Revelation 21:3) *skene* (Gk.)—The tent of meeting in the Old Testament; the future dwelling place of God in the new earth.

B. Death (vv. 4, 8) *thanatos* (Gk.)—Physical death; the separation of man from God.

2. Teacher Preparation

A. Begin with prayer.

B. Read the Devotional Reading and the Lesson Aim.

C. For additional commentary and background history, consult the *Precepts For Living®* CD-ROM and complete lesson 11 in the *Precepts For Living® Personal Study Guide*.

3. Starting the Lesson

A. Open with prayer using the Lesson Aim as a guide.

B. Ask for a volunteer to read the In Focus story. Next, ask the class to think about what they expect to experience in heaven and allow the students a few minutes to share their thoughts with the class.

4. Getting into the Lesson

A. Have a student read Background and The People, Places, and Times. Then discuss the information with the class.

B. Review the Words You Should Know section.

C. Have volunteers read the In Depth section based on the At-A-Glance outline.

D. Review the Search the Scriptures section and have the students search out the answers.

5. Relating the Lesson to Life

A. Review the Discuss the Meaning section with the class.

B. Discuss the first step we must take to ensure that we spend eternity with God.

6. Arousing Action

A. Have the students reread the Lesson Aim in unison aloud.

B. Have the class read Luke 16:19–31 silently and compare it to the Focal Verses.

C. Ask two or three students to share how we can honor God and prepare ourselves for our new home in heaven.

D. Instruct the class to read the Daily Bible Readings in preparation for next week's lesson. Close the class in prayer.

Worship Guide

For the Superintendent or Teacher
Theme: Our New Home
Theme Song: "Come, We that Love the Lord"
Scripture: 2 Corinthians 5:1–10
Song: "When We All Get to Heaven"
Meditation: Lord, thank You for loving me. I know whatever we experience here on Earth is only temporary. Give me the strength to endure the trials and tribulations of this life. I look forward to the new home You have prepared for me in heaven. Amen.

OUR NEW HOME

Bible Background • REVELATION 21:1–8
Printed Text • REVELATION 21:1–8   Devotional Reading • 2 PETER 3:10–18

Lesson Aim

By the end of the lesson, we should:

UNDERSTAND that heaven is a real and desirable place planned for believers;

LONG to experience eternity with Christ; and

EVALUATE our relationship with God to make sure we're ready for heaven.

Keep in Mind

"And I heard a great voice out of heaven saying, Behold, the tabernacle of God is with men, and he will dwell with them, and they shall be his people, and God himself shall be with them and be their God" (Revelation 21:3).

Focal Verses

Revelation 21:1 And I saw a new heaven and a new earth: for the first heaven and the first earth were passed away; and there was no more sea.

2 And I, John, saw the holy city, new Jerusalem, coming down from God out of heaven, prepared as a bride adorned for her husband.

3 And I heard a great voice out of heaven saying, Behold, the tabernacle of God is with men, and he will dwell with them, and they shall be his people, and God himself shall be with them, and be their God.

4 And God shall wipe away all tears from their eyes; and there shall be no more death, neither sorrow, nor crying, neither shall there be any more pain: for the former things are passed away.

5 And he that sat upon the throne said, Behold, I make all things new. And he said unto me, Write; for these words are true and faithful.

6 And he said unto me, It is done. I am Alpha and Omega, the beginning and the end. I will give

unto him that is athirst of the fountain of the water of life freely.

7 He that overcometh shall inherit all things; and I will be his God, and he shall be my son.

8 But the fearful, and unbelieving, and the abominable, and murderers, and whoremongers, and sorcerers, and idolaters, and all liars, shall have their part in the lake which burneth with fire and brimstone: which is the second death.

In Focus

"How do you know for sure you have eternal life?" Roger asked Hal. Roger was only 30 years old, but he was one of the homeless people who slept and lived beneath Chicago's downtown underground streets where delivery trucks accessed the buildings above.

Roger had arrived in Chicago as part of the Hurricane Katrina relief effort in the fall of 2005. Things had not gone well for Roger. He had been institutionalized many times since his arrival in

Chicago. Defeated, hopeless, and abandoned, he roamed the alleys and streets of downtown Chicago barely surviving.

Roger's foul breath and pungent odor was in stark contrast to Hal's business suit and cologne. Three days a week Hal spent his lunch hour distributing Bibles and praying with the homeless who rummaged the alleyways behind his office building.

Hal had ministered to Roger before. Over time Hal discovered that Roger's family, his three small children, wife, mother, and two brothers had all died in the aftermath of the hurricane.

"The Bible says you are offered eternal perfection through His perfection," Hal responded.

"Ain't nobody perfect," Roger said sitting on the curb. "So nobody can expect eternal life. Not my wife who loved God, or any of my family."

Hal sat down beside Roger on the curb and asked, "Were your wife and family baptized?"

"Yes, we all were," retorted

Roger, "but what good has it done? They are all gone now."

"Well, Roger, when your wife and family received Christ as their Saviour, God placed His eternal Spirit within them and gave them eternal life and their souls were saved. If you have accepted Christ, you too have that same promise. And I know times have been hard for you, but because you have accepted Christ as your Saviour, you will see them again. But now is the time for you to begin rebuilding your life and start living as Christ would want you to."

After Hal prayed for Roger, he asked if he could come by on Sunday so the two could attend church together. Roger agreed. Several weeks later, Roger rededicated his life to Christ and his tears about things of the past gave way to anticipation for a brighter future.

In the book of Revelation, we are assured that a new heaven and a new Earth are coming and will exist in eternity renewing and refreshing God's people.

The People, Places, and Times

The New Jerusalem. The New Jerusalem represents the glorified church. It is the future home of believers. God's dwelling with men will now be possible because Adam's curse will be removed, Satan will be judged, the wicked will be punished, and the universe will be sinless, except for the lake of fire.

This city takes the place of and supercedes the historical Jerusalem, which passed away with the first Earth, and becomes part of the new Earth. The inhabitants will include God the Father in full glory, glorified Old Testament saints, New Testament church saints (the bride of Christ), multitudes of unfallen angels, and the Lord Himself (Hebrews 12:22–23). Since God the Almighty and Christ the Lamb dwell in the midst of the Holy City, there will be no need for a physical temple to worship. Everyone will have direct access to God and the Lamb who dwell in their midst.

Background

According to our text, a great multitude of believers have come out of the Great Tribulation. As a result of their faithfulness, they are rewarded by God to enter into heaven. They enter into eternal peace in the presence of the Lamb, who they worship continually.

After much conflict between God and Satan, there is a pouring out of the last plagues. In the bowls of God's wrath is the final and complete judgment upon the earth, including Armageddon. The final victory has been given through the destruction of Babylon, which ushers in a multitude giving praise in triumphant song to the Lamb of God for the victory.

The final banquet occurs during the marriage of the Lamb to His bride, the church. John describes it like a wedding. The bride (all believers) has been adorned in "fine linen, clean and white" (Revelation 19:8). The color white represents the cleansing of believers' sins through the blood of the Lamb. Jesus is the Bridegroom.

According to some Bible scholars, after the millennium (1000 years), Satan is released once more but Christ quickly defeats him. Christ dispenses the final judgment on believers and non-believers. The Antichrist, false prophet, Satan, death, hades (hell), and the wicked are thrown into the lake of fire, which is the second death. In contrast, believers will experience a new heaven and a new earth. We will spend eternal life in the presence of God in the New Jerusalem.

At-A-Glance

1. Our New World (Revelation 21:1)
2. The New Jerusalem (vv. 2–4)
3. Our New Inheritance (vv. 5–8)

In Depth

1. Our New World (Revelation 21:1)

The apostle John has a vision of the new heaven and earth that God will establish. The earth, as we know it today, will no longer exist. As Romans 8:19–24 suggest, the world will be "renewed" when God brings an end to the history of this world. Therefore, we need to remember that this life is only temporary. One day, if we live for Christ, we will experience the new world that was promised. In Isaiah 65:17 and 66:22, the prophet speaks of the new heaven and earth that is to come. The promise is now fulfilled.

Those who are the heirs of it will inhabit the new world—the ones who are "washed in the blood of the Lamb" and have overcome the enemy by faith. They will have glorified bodies that are suited for the new world where only holiness and purity reign. God will dwell in the midst of this world.

2. The New Jerusalem (vv. 2–4)

John sees the Holy City descending out of heaven. The New Jerusalem is where God dwells among His people. He leaves His throne and descends to the New Jerusalem where His people dwell. This new tabernacle is the church of God in its new and perfect state. It is a beautiful, holy place prepared for God and His people. His presence will be continual and for eternity. Similar to the way a bride adores her bridegroom, we shall be one with God and overflow with love, joy, and delight.

Christians can also experience oneness with God now. We can experience His presence through worship, prayer, studying His Word, and in service. "Draw nigh to God, and He will draw nigh to you" (James 4:8). We can be one in the Spirit. Christians do not have to wait until we get to heaven, God's presence dwells with us now.

That same covenant of love that now exists between God and His people will be perfected in the end. God Himself will be our God. Christians will experience perfect happiness that comes from receiving the fullness of God's love through His presence with them. Our love and happiness will be for eternity.

The promise and prospect of living in a new home is exciting, especially since we know pain, sorrow, and death will cease. Today, we experience many life situations that can test our faith. How often have you found yourself crying over family problems, sickness in your body, or the death of a friend or family member? The trials of this world seem endless. Every day some catastrophe is reported on the news. The newspapers are full of stories of murder, robbery,

and rape. How easy is it to wonder what will happen next or whether God notices what's going on. No matter the circumstances, we can be confident that God is sovereign. "God shall wipe away all tears from their eyes." He will end all crying, pain, and death. All of the various trials we now have to suffer will end in praise and honor and glory to Jesus Christ when we see Him (1 Peter 1:6–7). In our new home, His peace and love shall reign continually.

3. Our New Inheritance (vv. 5–8)

The Word and promises of God ratify the truth and certainty of this blessed peace and eternal happiness. God orders His words to be recorded. We can be fully confident in what God says because "the word of the Lord endureth forever" (1 Peter 1:25). He is the Creator of this world (Genesis 1:1), as well as the new heaven and earth. Everything begins and ends with God. Even the waters, which previously were a threat to God's people (Revelation 12:15; 15:2), are now under the control of the One who created them. They have been made new so His people can drink freely of the water of life and be refreshed. Christians will not have to fear the former threats of life (like natural disasters, disease, or crime) because all sin is gone and all creation submits to the authority of God.

The New Jerusalem could be compared to the Garden of Eden before the fall of Adam and Eve. The Garden of Eden was a perfect place where man and God were one. It contained plants, herbs, and fruit-bearing trees of all kinds, including the Tree of Life, and free-flowing rivers. There was no death, disease, sickness, or pain. If Adam and Eve had obeyed God, they could have lived forever. The Tree of Life had the power to give Adam and Eve eternal life with God. Now we can experience eternal life with God in a new paradise (Revelation 22:2). The only requirement for entrance is belief in Jesus Christ as Lord.

Through confession and belief in Jesus Christ (Romans 10:9–10), we are saved. The Holy Spirit empowers us for service. If we remain faithful, God will bestow upon us an "eternal inheritance" (Hebrews 9:15). He gives us all things as well as the enjoyment of eternal blessedness. Whatever we now suffer, it shall pass away and a greater inheritance awaits us.

In contrast, the state of the wicked is different (Revelation 21:8). "The fearful, and unbelieving" are those who fear taking up the Cross of Christ and serving Him, so their unbelief leads to more sin. The sinners mentioned include "the abominable, and murderers, and whoremongers, and sorcerers, and idolaters, and all liars." These sinners have committed acts that separate them from God. It is important to note that any thought, word, or deed that is against God's Word separates us from Him. We cannot live unrighteous lives and inherit eternal life. "Not everyone that saith Lord, Lord, shall enter into the kingdom of heaven" (Matthew 7:21). After their physical death, they must die another death, a spiritual death. Their inheritance is eternal separation from God.

At funerals there is a distinct difference between the deaths of Christians versus unbelievers. Family and friends of Christians can rejoice in the midst of their sorrow because the person is "absent from the body, and present with the Lord" (2 Corinthians 5:8). There is an assurance that the Christian is at peace with God and enjoying His presence. In contrast, the unbeliever's family and friends grieve over their death but have no assurance of eternal life. Thus, a funeral becomes a warning that if we die without Christ, we will spend eternal life in the lake of fire. While we are alive, every individual must make a personal decision: Where do I want to spend eternity? What inheritance do I want?

John's vision of the New Jerusalem is a city with many gates facing different geographical areas of the world (Revelation 21:13). The city has four equal sides, relating to the four quarters of the world, east, west, north and south. On each side are three gates signifying that from all quarters of the earth there will be some who will get safely to heaven and be received there. There is as free an entrance into heaven from one part of the world as from the another part. Men, women, and children from all nations and languages, who believe in Christ, have by Him access to God. It is an individual choice whether to accept or reject Him. Only those who accept Christ will have access to God and experience the fullness of His love in the New Jerusalem.

Search the Scriptures

1. Where does the Holy City originate (Revelation 21:2)?
2. What will God remove from His people in the New Jerusalem (v. 4)?
3. Who will experience the second death (v. 8)?

Discuss the Meaning

Julie and Malika were college roommates and best friends. Julie grew up in a Christian home. She shared her faith with Malika on many occasions. Malika, however, grew up as an atheist, so whenever Julie shared her faith, Malika would listen but never believed in Christ. She thought Julie was just another religious fanatic but never told her. One day while Malika was driving Julie home from the mall, a drunk driver crashed into them. They both died instantly. What happened to Julie and Malika's souls? What can Julie's parents share with Malika's family during this time of bereavement?

Lesson in Our Society

In today's society, most people live in the moment. Their lives revolve around the here and now. People seek to fulfill their every desire by whatever means necessary. This pursuit for material possessions, position, and power often leads to immoral behavior. The result is a corrupt world in which pain and grief is the norm.

Christians live in this world but know we have another home; therefore, the focus of our attention is on God and not this world. We live by faith as humble servants of Jesus Christ. Even though trials and tribulations may come, when we die, the Lord shall allow us to abide with Him for eternity in heaven. Those who have rejected God shall receive their reward as well in the lake of fire for eternity.

Make It Happen

During the upcoming week, evaluate your relationship with God. First, ask yourself, "Am I saved?

Have I confessed, repented, and accepted Jesus as my Lord and Saviour?" If not, read Romans 10:9–10 and pray to accept Christ into your life. Second, once you are certain of your salvation, ask God to reveal any areas in your life that He is not pleased with. As the Holy Spirit reveals these areas, repent and seek God's forgiveness and help to live differently. Talk to your pastor if you need additional spiritual guidance. And third, ask God to help you to have a closer relationship with Him through praise, worship, and service.

Follow the Spirit

What God wants me to do:

_____

_____

Remember Your Thoughts

Special insights I have learned:

_____

_____

More Light on the Text
Revelation 21:1–8

1 And I saw new heaven and a new earth: for the first heaven had passed away; and there was no more sea.

John received a divine revelation from God to look into the final stage of history concerning what God had purposed for His created order as a result of His creating activities (Genesis 1–2; 1 Peter 3:1–15; Colossians 1:15–17). The terms "heaven" and "earth" used in this context of Scripture do not have mythical connotations or meaning, but they designate the resulting *cosmos,* which has an idea of the Greek word for "ornament" or "beautiful arrangement." Since the beginning of time, God has always upheld, guided, and ruled His creation through His sovereign activities. Now God unfolds to His servant, John, His ultimate plan and design for the final consummation of all things.

The word "new" has been used by God to describe His new order of creation to be established in accordance to His purpose. The adjectives "new' and "first" used by God in this portion of Scripture to

qualify the different states of heaven and Earth, seem to describe a previous and latter *cosmos* standing in opposition to each other. The previous had passed away in the sense that God has completely transformed the universe. The latter had come to take its place and God intends that it stay forever without ever reversing into a negative direction again (Isaiah 65:17–18). It is important for the believer to always remember that the Almighty God has the supreme power and authority to do whatever He wills for and through His entire creation. And nothing or nobody has the audacity to thwart God's purpose (Job 42:1–2).

2 And I John saw the holy city, new Jerusalem, coming down from God out of heaven, prepared as a bride adorned for her husband.

Jesus Christ promised the believer who endures faithfully to the end a new home in heaven where there is complete peace, holiness, excellence, and love. It is a place of ultimate fulfillment of God's perfect will for the faithful ones (John 14:1–10). Conventional wisdom teaches us to understand the fact that "charity begins at home." The home represents a place for true nurture and an anchor for emotional and spiritual strength. Also, it denotes the idea of a final destination. It is a place where our day ends after a hard day's work; our souls receive replenishment from our drives and aspirations for a good future. The apostle John saw the New Jerusalem, God's Holy City, descending from God's presence—heaven. It is a representation of God's idea of a place for renewing and refreshing His people after both their turbulence and success. It has no tears, sorrow, and pains; it is a place where we never die and wickedness is totally shut out. It was specially "prepared" by God Himself for His people.

A metaphor of a potentially good and promising marriage was used by John to describe the efficacy and reality of what the new order brings to God's people. The efforts and time spent in preparing a bride for a husband in order for the latter to be accepted gives us the indication of God's intentions for our new home—the New Jerusalem. It should also help us to begin to appreciate the fact that our new home is excellent beyond all our human imaginations or dreams. It has been already prepared for us and it is waiting for us. It is the new and permanent place that Christ went ahead to prepare for us.

3 And I heard a great voice out of heaven saying, Behold, the tabernacle of God is with men, and he will dwell with them, and they shall be his people, and God himself shall be with them, and be their God.

God's everlasting presence will be with His people in our new home. In the Gospel narratives, God has declared many times that He will always be with His people. He will never leave us nor forsake us (Hebrews 13:5). It is important to note that this promise was made to His chosen people who are living in a fallen world system where Satan and evil powers operate to subvert God's purpose for His creation. However, in our new home, the content and context of God's abiding presence is totally different. The word "tabernacle" (Gk. *skene*) used in this text does not literally mean the physical temple or sanctuary as described in most of the texts in the Old Testament (Exodus; Leviticus 1; 2 Kings; 1 and 2 Chronicles). Rather, in figurative sense, it referred to a dwelling place of God. It includes the idea of God's kingdom, glory, and power tangibly filling up this "renewed" world which He created for His people.

The consequences and impact of a fallen human nature and society will be no more. In the Gospel of John, "the Word (Jesus) became flesh and dwelled among us" (John 1:14). God's presence in the new world becomes the light that dispels all forces of evil and destruction; it is also the splendor of the new city. The Almighty God will be our provider and protector from all kinds of evil. The concept of "Emmanuel" (God with us) will become an everlasting reality in this new world.

4 And God shall wipe away all tears from their eyes; and there shall be no more death, neither sorrow, nor crying, neither shall there be any more pain: for the former things are passed away. 5 And he that sat upon the throne said, Behold, I make all things new. And he said unto me, Write: for these words are true and faithful.

The fall in Eden brought with it death, sickness, and poverty. The Bible teaches about three types of death. Spiritual death is the result of the broken relationship between God and man (Ephesians 2:1ff.); physical death occurs when our spirit is separated from the body (James 2:26); and eternal death occurs when we depart forever into condemnation by spending our eternity in the lake of fire (Revelation 20:14–15; 21:8). But in our new home, the Scriptures reveal that all these three kinds of death "shall be no more."

Sickness is often the evidence of disease. Humankind is internally and externally broken spiritually, psychologically, and physically. Poverty has stricken society on many levels. This poverty is expressed spiritually, as a lack of the knowledge of God; physically, as poor health and malfunctioning of the body; materially, as a lack of resources and money; and socially, as political vulnerability and social oppression. God has promised us that "there shall no more be pain" in the new world. Poverty has produced misery and mourning in families and society. However, when we go to our new home, "there shall be no more sorrow, nor crying." The "former things are passed away" because the fallen world system will be transformed into a new created order where God's entire creation is launched into an era of shalom (peace). Our new home is a place where believers will experience the fullness of God in ways that are unimaginable. God not only speaks words that are true and faithful, but His own names are Faithful and True (Revelation 19:11). He keeps His word and acts in accordance with His divine nature at all times. Whatever the Almighty God has promised the believer concerning our new home, He is also more than able to perform.

6 And He said to me, It is done. I am Alpha and Omega, the beginning and the end. I will give unto him that is athirst of the fountain of the water of life freely.

God's Word and activities are fulfilled in accordance to His divine purpose. He is the originator of all good and perfect things (James 1:17). He is also the consummation of all things that bring glory and honor to His name on Earth. In the "beginning of the beginnings" of all that was and is, God IS.

"Water" symbolizes the life that God willingly gives to all who seek Him with all their hearts, minds, and souls/spirits. It is a gift from the Creator God. This means it is not based on an individual's personal work, neither does she/he have to merit it. This can be likened to our salvation which we received by the grace of God through faith and not by our own works, so we have no cause to boast (Ephesians 2:8–9). Let us remember that God is the source of all that we are and have in this life. He is the foundation of life, and has promised us a home in heaven where all our needs will be totally satisfied according to His perfect will.

7 He that overcometh shall inherit all things; and I will be his God and he shall be my son. 8 But the fearful, and unbelieving, and the abominable, and murderers, and whoremongers, and sorcerers, and idolaters, and all liars, shall have their part in the lake which burneth with fire and brimstone: which is the second death.

We can draw on the fact that even though God hates sin, He still loves the sinner (Romans 5:8). God's love for the sinner is expressed in His act of grace to send His only begotten Son, Jesus, to die for all humankind (John 3:16). Whoever believes in God's redemptive plan and lives in obedience to His Word becomes an overcomer (1 John 5:4). He/she also becomes an inheritor of God's prepared place where there is no lack of any good thing, neither is there any evil because of God's perpetual presence. However, those who refuse or rebel against God's offer of redemption are condemned. The new home that our heavenly father is preparing for us is a pure and holy place. God's divine presence of light will expose all forms of darkness or imperfections. According to the Scriptures, sin did not originate from God, neither does He sanction any evil activity. The "second death," which is damnation into the lake of fire where there is complete separation between man and God, will become the final home for the sinful and wicked.

What can disqualify us from going to be with the Lord forever in our new home is rejecting God's offer of grace to receive salvation in Jesus Christ. God has so many rooms and space in His final prepared place for all who trust and obey Him. Therefore, there is no shortage of resources for all who will open up to faithfully accept God's divine provision of the way to escape hell and destruction. For those of us who have already accepted God's grace by faith and have become members of God's beloved family, we must always depend on the Holy Spirit to walk in the ways of His perfect will. Even though God's Spirit is at work in us to preserve and guide us to the end, we must always keep in mind the fact that we still have to make choices in submission to the spirit that will sustain us in God's purpose forever. Our consistent practice should be to reckon ourselves as dead to sin and alive to God on a daily basis by renewing our minds and walking in Christ on earth as transformed people who have a home prepared for us by our Heavenly Father. Let us make the right choices of accepting God's grace of salvation and also walking obediently in His Word so that we may not fall into the category of the cowardly, unbelieving, abominable murderers, sexually immoral, sorcerers, and idolaters, which will only reveal us to be unsaved and lead us into the brimstone of the lake of fire—the second death.

Daily Bible Readings

M: Our Citizenship Is in Heaven
Philippians 3:17–21
T: The Coming of the Kingdom
1 Corinthians 15:20–28
W: Our Heavenly Dwelling
2 Corinthians 5:1–10
T: Longing for a New Home
Hebrews 11:10–16
F: The Day of the Lord
2 Peter 3:10–18
S: New Heavens and a New Earth
Isaiah 65:17–19, 23–25
S: God Will Dwell among Us
Revelation 21:1–8

TEACHING TIPS
May 20
Bible Study Guide 12

1. Words You Should Know

A. Holy (Revelation 21:10) *hagios* (Gk.)—The quality of being set apart from what is common.

B. Glory (vv. 24, 26) *doxa* (Gk.)—A state of radiance, weightiness, and importance or the recognition of that state in someone else.

C. Fruit (22:2) *karpos* (Gk.)—A symbol of abundance and provision or of the natural outcome of a person's inner identity.

2. Teacher Preparation

A. Read the Bible Background and the Focal Verses.

B. Read Genesis 2:4–17 for background on the description of the New Jerusalem; read also Revelation 21:1 8, 11–21 for a more complete picture of John's vision.

C. Complete lesson 12 in the *Precepts For Living® Personal Study Guide*.

3. Starting the Lesson

A. Begin the class with prayer, thanking God for His kindness in storing up a secure and imperishable inheritance for His people, and revealing the wonder of that inheritance through His holy Word.

B. Ask a volunteer to read In Focus story.

C. Share honestly your struggles to "seek those things which are above," and some of the things that keep you from doing so.

4. Getting into the Lesson

A. Ask a volunteer to read the Focal Verses.

B. Ask people what they imagine heaven to be like, and take down their responses for everyone to see.

5. Relating the Lesson to Life

A. Have class members write down specific elements of their lives that keep them from thinking about their wonderful inheritance in Christ (these elements may be fear of death and the unknown, a worldly mind-set, a lack of faith, etc.).

B. Have the class look through the passage and write down specific pictures and promises that help them overcome these obstacles. Tell them to cross out the obstacles and write the promises above them.

6. Arousing Action

A. Allow your students to answer the Discuss the Meaning questions as a group.

B. Have the students brainstorm how they plan to accomplish the Lesson in Our Society exercise.

C. Challenge the students to complete the Make It Happen assignment.

D. Instruct the class to read the Daily Bible Readings in preparation for next week's lesson. Close the class with prayer, using the meditation from the Worship Guide below.

Worship Guide

For the Superintendent or Teacher
Theme: God in Our Midst
Theme Song: "I Want To Be Ready"
Scripture: 1 Thessalonians 4:13–18
Song: "Just to Behold His Face"
Meditation: Lord, give me faith to believe the astonishingly great promises You give me in Your Word. Let my hope be set on things above, and my thoughts be filled with an earnest longing for the day when I will see You face-to-face.

GOD IN OUR MIDST

Bible Background • REVELATION 21:9–22:5
Printed Text • REVELATION 21:9–10, 22–22:5   Devotional Reading • EPHESIANS 1:15–23

Lesson Aim

By the end of the lesson, we will:

UNDERSTAND that Jesus has prepared a wonderful place for us with Him;

REALIZE that we can never find lasting comfort in temporal things; and

DETERMINE to place our hope in Jesus Christ, who loves us and has prepared such a wonderful future for those who trust Him.

Keep in Mind

"And there shall be no night there; and they need no candle, neither light of the sun; for the Lord God giveth them light: and they shall reign forever and ever" (Revelation 22:5).

Focal Verses

Revelation 21:9 And there came unto me one of the seven angels which had the seven vials full of the seven last plagues, and talked with me, saying, Come hither, I will show thee the bride, the Lamb's wife.

10 And he carried me away in the spirit to a great and high mountain, and showed me that great city, the holy Jerusalem, descending out of heaven from God.

21:22 And I saw no temple therein: for the Lord God Almighty and the Lamb are the temple of it.

23 And the city had no need of the sun, neither of the moon, to shine in it: for the glory of God did lighten it, and the Lamb is the light thereof.

24 And the nations of them which are saved shall walk in the light of it: and the kings of the earth do bring their glory and honor into it.

25 And the gates of it shall not be shut at all by day: for there shall be no night there.

26 And they shall bring the glory and honor of the nations into it.

27 And there shall in no wise enter into it any thing that defileth, neither whatsoever worketh abomination, or maketh a lie: but they which are written in the Lamb's book of life.

22:1 And he showed me a pure river of water of life, clear as crystal, proceeding out of the throne of God and of the Lamb.

2 In the midst of the street of it, and on either side of the river, was there the tree of life, which bare twelve manner of fruits, and yielded her fruit every month: and the leaves of the tree were for the healing of the nations.

3 And there shall be no more curse: but the throne of God and of the Lamb shall be in it; and his servants shall serve him:

4 And they shall see his face; and his name shall be in their foreheads.

5 And there shall be no night there; and they need no candle, neither light of the sun; for the Lord God giveth them light: and they shall reign forever and ever.

In Focus

Just recently Darnell's wife, Sherry, had lost her battle with cancer and went home to be with the Lord. Darnell was in deep meditation replanting his wife's butterfly garden and contemplating whether their 7-year-old daughter, Mykalia, understood that Mommy was not coming back, when she came and knelt beside him.

Kneeling in the dirt, Mykalia asked, "Daddy, you're planting flower seeds, so why do you call this a butterfly garden?"

"Because, I'm growing flowers whose nectar attracts butterflies."

"But the caterpillars eat a lot of the flowers," she said.

"Mykalia, caterpillars *are* butterflies." Darnell smiled.

"I thought caterpillars were moths," she said pushing a few seeds in the ground with her thumb.

"They can be," he said.

"Then how come you don't call it a moth garden, Daddy?"

"Because the most beautiful thing a caterpillar can become is a butterfly. Butterflies fly in daylight for everyone to marvel at their bright colors while the moth

363

is drab and only flies at night flying blindly into flames or scorching light bulbs."

"Well, how do you know which caterpillar will be a butterfly, and which will be a moth, Daddy?"

"It depends on *how* they feed. Moths eat all the food they will ever eat as caterpillars, but butterflies continue to live on the nectar of plants. Only God knows for sure which is which."

Mykalia nodded and smiled with understanding. "So Mommy is like the caterpillar who became a butterfly, right Daddy?"

Darnell looked down and kissed his daughter on the forehead and thought of the saying "out of the mouth of babes."

"You're absolutely right, baby, Mommy became a butterfly that soared in the magnificent light of God to live with Him forever."

Our lesson reminds us that our earthly body and homes are not our final dwelling place—we are meant to be God's majestic butterflies to soar forever in His eternal light.

The People, Places, and Times

Bride. The imagery of the bride is used widely in the Bible as a description of the people of God. In the Old Testament, the prophets presented Israel (the Old Testament church) as a bride who had committed repeated adulteries (Jeremiah 3; Ezekiel 16; Hosea 3). The prophets also proclaimed that God was faithful to His unfaithful bride and would restore her (Jeremiah 33:10–11; Isaiah 61:10; 62:5). In the book of Revelation, bride imagery is used often of the church (the New Testament Israel) and her relationship to Christ. The bride belongs to Christ, who is the Bridegroom (John 3:29). In Revelation, the church, as the bride of the Lamb has prepared herself for marriage by performing righteous deeds (19:7–8). In Revelation 21, the great wedding is portrayed with the church prepared for her Bridegroom (vv. 2, 9).

The bride pictured here has not earned her status through righteous deeds. These acts were the church's obedient response to God's saving grace. The garments of righteousness were *given* to her.

New Jerusalem. Since Jerusalem was a significant focus of God's activity in the Old Testament and the place where the church was founded at Pentecost, the New Testament writers fittingly used the city in a figurative sense to speak of the Christian's salvation and future hope. In Galatians 4:26, Paul refers to the "Jerusalem which is above" when pointing out the Christian's spiritual status of freedom from the law's curse. The author of Hebrews speaks of a "heavenly Jerusalem" (Hebrews 12:22) to denote the beauty and security of the New Covenant. The book of Revelation refers to "the holy city, new Jerusalem" (21:2) and "that great city, the holy Jerusalem, descending out of heaven from God" (10). Here the angel identifies the city with the bride, the church; the following description, in which Jerusalem is massive and radiant with jewels and perfect in symmetry shows the wonderful destiny of God's people, when He will dwell among them forever.

Lamb. In the book of Revelation, the unqualified designation "Lamb" (Gk. *arnion*, **ar-NEE-on**) occurs eight times in symbolic reference to Christ and unites the two ideas of redemption and kingship. On one side are statements referring to a Lamb that has been slain (5:6, 12); those "who have washed their robes, and made them white in the blood of the Lamb" (7:14); and "they overcame him by the blood of the Lamb, and by the word of their testimony" (12:11). The stress here falls upon the redeeming work of Christ as the Lamb of God. On the other side, also connected with the title is the idea of sovereignty. It is the Lamb that was slain that has power to take the book and loose its seals (5:6–7); there is reference to the wrath of the Lamb (6:16); and the Lamb is seen in the midst of the throne (7:17). In the general term, "Lamb," two ideas unite: victorious power and vicarious suffering. At the heart of God's sovereignty, there is sacrificial love.

Sources

Ellis, Terence B. "Bride." In *Holman Bible Dictionary*, edited by Trent C. Butler. Nashville, Tenn.: Broadman & Holman, 1991.

McDonald, H.D. "Lamb of God." In *Evangelical Dictionary of Theology*, edited by Walter A. Elwell, 618–619. Grand Rapids, Mich.: Baker Book House, 1984.

"And there shall be no night there; and they need no candle, neither light of the sun; for the Lord God giveth them light: and they shall reign forever and ever" (Revelation 22:5).

Background

After John's vision of the new heaven and the new Earth, the believer's final and eternal habitation, the angel, shows him a more specific picture: the church, here described as "the bride" (Revelation 21:9) and "the holy Jerusalem" (v. 10). The "new Jerusalem prepared as a bride adorned for her husband" (21:2) is now shown to be a realm of perfect life, beauty, bounty, and wholeness. This passage explains in graphic detail the implications of that glorious statement, "the tabernacle of God is with men, and he will dwell with them" (v. 3). The rich imagery used here and elsewhere in the Scriptures seeks to portray in shimmering detail how great is the believer's inheritance: being with God Himself in all His glory! One might imagine the apostle Paul had this passage in mind when he said, "'No eye has seen, no ear has heard, no mind has conceived what God has prepared for those who love him" (1 Corinthians 2:9, NIV).

At-A-Glance

1. The Glorious Identity of God's People (Revelation 21:9–10)
2. The Glorious Inheritance of God's People (21:22–27)
3. The Glorious Abundance of God's People (22:1–5)

In Depth

1. The Glorious Identity of God's People (Revelation 21:9–10)

The apostle John describes the church as the bride. What do we learn about the church's glorious identity from this term? If the church is Jesus' bride (for He indeed is the "husband" of v. 2), then she is bound and betrothed to Him in a holy and unbreakable covenant. This suggests that her duty to is to love and respond to her husband, but more importantly it communicates the overwhelming love and commitment of Jesus Christ to His bride. If human beings consider themselves bound by the vows they take on their wedding day, how much more will Jesus consider Himself bound to His people, since in Him all God's promises are "yes" (2 Corinthians 1:20), and since He has sealed the covenant of marriage between God and His people with His very own blood?

In the Old Testament, God's presence dwelled in Jerusalem and the people were blessed by His holiness and His favor. In the new heavens and the new earth, God will dwell in the midst of His people as never before. Christ, the great Mediator, will usher them into God's presence with robes of righteousness, and they will be thoroughly acceptable in His sight. How great is the love of the Father, and how secure is the identity of the saints!

2. The Glorious Inheritance of God's People (21:22–27)

What is the hope of the Christian? It is that God Himself will become the temple in the midst of His people. For the temple is the place where God dwells, whether a physical location, as in the Old Testament, or in the church, His temple in the New Testament (see 1 Corinthians 3:16, Ephesians 2:20). Until the time described in Revelation 21, God's people experience His presence through the Holy Spirit; but in glory, both Father and Son ("the Lord God Almighty and the Lamb," 21:22) are described as the temple—meaning that in the new heavens and the new earth God dwells directly, intimately, and fully with His people! And just as God's people no longer worship God indirectly, they will no longer be sustained by indirect things, like the light from the sun and moon. God Himself will sustain them!

Who could hope for such a glorious inheritance? John's vision identifies those fortunate ones as the "nations," the same word used elsewhere to refer to "Gentiles." Just as promised in the New Covenant, the gates will never be shut (v. 25) to outsiders; rather they will come forth into the New Jerusalem praising God! We should not think, however, that the open

access to the nations means that all will come into the heavenly city. John gives us two ways to know those who will not come in.

First, those whose *identity* is defined by uncleanness, detestable practices, and falseness will not be found in the heavenly city (v. 27a). In fact, the radiant beauty and symmetry of the city (21:11–21) symbolizes the faithfulness of the bride, even as she by faith is built on the foundation of the Lamb.

Second, we see that the New Jerusalem contains only the elect, those whose names are written in the Lamb's Book of Life. On one hand, only those who are made pure by their faith in Christ will come in; on the other, only those whom God has called before the foundation of the world. Just as so often happens in the Bible, God's sovereign call and man's responsibility come together mysteriously. It has been said that on the outside of the gates of heaven is written: "Whosoever will may come," and on the inside of those gates: "Chosen from all eternity."

3. The Glorious Abundance of God's People (22:1–5)

To paint a picture of the greatest possible abundance and blessing, John's vision returns to the place of God's original purpose: the Garden of Eden. Just as is true in Eden (Genesis 2:10), a life-giving river flows in the New Jerusalem; this "water of life" symbolizes the everlasting life given by God through the Spirit (see John 7:37–39) and the "life abundant" Jesus promises in John 10:10. Just as the tree of life stood in Eden (Genesis 2:9) as a sign of perfect fruitfulness and the provision of every human need, so in the New Jerusalem that tree will stand amidst the river, represented by 12 trees (a number symbolizing divine government and completeness). Humankind was not commanded to leave the earth as an untilled garden, but to work the ground and produce good things, thereby mirroring the creativity and benevolent reign of God over His creation. And though humankind fails miserably at the task God calls us to (this is the story of Genesis 3 to Revelation 20!), God brings about His purpose nonetheless, redeeming not only His chosen remnant but all the earth as well! And so the new heavens and new Earth are a place of perfect abundance—a world fit for God and His people to reign. This is true, redeemed urban living!

What will life be like in this gloriously abundant dwelling place? As we saw in Revelation 21:3–4, God will heal and bind up all wounds—especially the wounds of sin and spiritual brokenness, which are washed away as the nations partake of the tree of life (22:2). Although the divine Judge had frequently cursed the stubborn rebelliousness of mankind and set them apart for destruction (see Joshua 7:12), here no curse is possible, for God now dwells in perfect purity with a purified people. In the mystery of God's trinitarian being, Father and Son are shown to dwell on one "throne" (22:3). Even as God exists in loving fellowship with Himself in three persons, so now all God's people will be enfolded in that perfect triune love and communion. The sublime happiness promised to the saints might be summed up by showing that the great blessing of Numbers 6:24–27 (NIV) is now perfectly fulfilled: "'The LORD bless you and keep you; the LORD make his face shine upon you and be gracious to you; the LORD turn his face toward you and give you peace. So they will put my name on the Israelites, and I will bless them.'"

Search the Scriptures

1. How is John shown to be "carried away" to his vision of the New Jerusalem (Revelation 21:10)?

2. What typical context of worship is noticeably absent in the heavenly city (v. 22)?

3. What are the three characteristics of those who will never enter the City of God (v. 27)?

4. From where does the river of life flow in the New Jerusalem (22:1; cp. Genesis 2:10)?

Discuss the Meaning

1. How can we explain to ourselves and others the elements of judgment that we find among the glorious, hope-filled promises in this passage?

2. Why is it often hard to have a true longing for heaven?

3. How would you use this passage to help someone (yourself or someone else) who struggles with the fear of death?

Lesson in Our Society

The human race continues to encounter injustice, oppression, and misery. In particular, the African American community possesses a living history of oppression—one that continues today through racism and economic injustice. God provides opportunity, to seek to redress wrong and injustice through political or social means. And yet social justice can become an idol, and bitterness may ensue when cruelty and oppression continue. This passage reminds us that hope for a paradise on this earth is a misguided hope. The Christian's hope is set immeasurably higher. In the new heavens and new earth, God's bride, the church, becomes as perfectly radiant as the New Jerusalem; only there will true healing take place. And so the Holy Spirit reminds us, through John's vision, that even as we seek to see the Gospel transform our society in the here and now, we are always to "seek those things which are above" (Colossians 3:1).

Make It Happen

Think about circumstances or relationships in your life that leave you feeling bitter or resentful because of the way you've been treated. How do you respond when you feel slighted? Does a focus on making things right in this world keep you from longing for the next? Take this opportunity to repent of your misplaced hope and turn to Christ for mercy. In light of the incredible promises of God about your identity and your abundant inheritance, take time each day to intentionally rejoice and give thanks for the glory that awaits you in God's presence.

Follow the Spirit

What God wants me to do:

_____

_____

Remember Your Thoughts

Special insights I have learned:

_____

_____

More Light on the Text
Revelation 21:9–10, 22–22:5

9 And there came unto me one of the seven angels which had the seven vials full of the seven last plagues, and talked with me, saying, Come hither, I will show thee the bride, the Lamb's wife.

John's vision of heaven is told from two points of view: from heaven and from Earth. Revelation 21:9 is one of those verses that tells the narrative from the earthly viewpoint. Here John is approached by one of the seven angels who had the seven vials full of the seven last plagues. We are first introduced to these angels in Revelation 15 where one of the four beasts in heaven gave them the seven golden vials full of the seven last plagues which are also called the wrath of God (v. 1). A vial is a bowl; this term is translated from the Greek word *phiale* (**fee-AL-ay**).

The pouring out of the last plagues from these vials signifies the release of the final series of God's judgment in which the exercise of His wrath is concluded. After these, John told us of the fall of Babylon the great (Revelation 17–18), the triumph of the heavenly army led by Christ (Revelation 19), the binding, incarceration, and final judgment of Satan (Revelation 20) and then the passing away (the transformation) of the first heaven and earth which were replaced by a new heaven and earth (Revelation 21:1). After this renewal, John beholds the Holy City, the New Jerusalem (v. 2).

In this verse, the angel invites John to come, proposing to show him the bride, the Lamb's wife. The Greek word *numphe* (**noom-FAY**) is translated "bride." It means a betrothed or newly married young woman. This word is one of the most important figures used to refer to the church. It signifies the relationship between Christ and the church, also called the Lamb's wife. But as we shall find in the next verse, the name "bride" also refers to the holy Jerusalem, the City of God.

10 And he carried me away in the Spirit to a great and high mountain, and showed me that great city, the holy Jerusalem, descending out of heaven from God.

Here John is transported in the spirit by the angel to a great high mountain where he was shown the great city, the holy Jerusalem, descending out of heaven from God. This verse runs parallel with verse 2 where he described this city using a personifying marital analogy: "prepared as a bride adorned for her husband." The Greek word translated "city" is *polis* (**POL-is**) from the root *ple*, which means fullness or from the root *polus*, which means many or plenteous. The meaning conveys the idea of a populated place. This city is called "the bride" and "the Lamb's wife" (21:2, 9) just as the church is also referred to as the "Lamb's wife" in Revelation 19:7. Consequently, both the body of believers and the city are referred to as the bride, the Lamb's wife.

The fact is, in a sense, they are significantly alike. The holy Jerusalem is a city out of heaven; it is not heaven, but it possesses the features of heaven. It is the dwelling place of the resurrected bodies of the church (the redeemed bride), God, and Christ (Revelation 21:3; 22:3).

Jesus said, "In my Father's house are many mansions I go to prepare a place for you. And if I go and prepare a place for you, I will come again, and receive you unto myself; that where I am, there ye may be also" (John 14:2–3). This city is undoubtedly the promised prepared place for the redeemed bride. Our bodies are our temporary habitations for our spirits and souls. The apostle Paul calls them "earthen vessels" (2 Corinthians 4:7). Our earthly homes are also temporary, but we have a final dwelling place. This is the Holy City, a wonderful place Jesus has prepared for us in heaven.

First Peter 2:5 says: "Ye also, as lively stones, are built up a spiritual house." Though this city will be established physically here on earth, it descended from heaven, a spiritual realm, and possibly each member of the church is represented by a stone which was used to "prepare" this city and therefore has a part in it (Revelation 22:19): the gates are named after the 12 tribes of Israel (21:12); the wall and foundations of the city are named after the 12 apostles (v. 14); most likely, it is a place where the names of members of the church have been immortalized.

And this could be the reason why the city bears the same appellation with the church.

The church is a holy nation (1 Peter 2:9); a human prefiguration of the heavenly Jerusalem, and the church makes up the City of God here on Earth (Hebrews 12:22). Therefore, the prepared bride (the Holy City) is a structure laid out as a city to provide a permanent dwelling place for the redeemed bride (the church), another structure in the image of God. One is in the form of a city, while the other is in human form, and both bear the presence of God.

When God called Abraham to leave his country, God promised him he would possess a foreign country; this promise filled Abraham with the vision of a great city a city with foundations, whose architect and builder is God (Hebrews 11:10).

The earthly Jerusalem has been called to be the City of God (Psalm 48:1–2), the Holy City (Isaiah 52:1; Matthew 4:5), and the city where God has chosen to put His name (2 Chronicles 6:6). Today it is the most famous holy city in the world and aptly called the "spiritual capital of the world." The earthly Jerusalem is a prefiguration of the New Jerusalem from heaven.

21:22 And I saw no temple therein: for the Lord God Almighty and the Lamb are the temple of it.

John tells us here that the city lacks a temple. What is translated "temple" here is the Greek word *naos* (**nah-OS**). This refers to the inner sanctuary where only the priest could lawfully enter, and it is contrasted with *hieron* (**hee-er-ON**), which also means temple, but denotes the entire temple complex with all its courts and auxiliary buildings. *Naos*, the inner sanctuary or Holy of Holies, is the location of the Ark of the Covenant in the Mosaic tabernacle and Solomon's temple. This is the place where God manifested His presence.

23 And the city had no need of the sun, neither of the moon, to shine in it: for the glory of God did lighten it, and the Lamb is the light thereof. 24 And the nations of them which are saved shall walk in the light of it: and the kings of the earth do bring their glory and honor into it.

John further tells us that the city has no need of the natural agents of light the sun and moon. While these two agents of light are the main illuminators of planet Earth, they also cause some discomforting conditions to its inhabitants. God's desire to shield His people from the scorching effects of the light of the sun and moon is expressed by David: "the sun shall not smite thee by day, nor the moon by night. The LORD shall preserve thee from all evil: he shall preserve thy soul" (Psalm 121:6–7). This desire is ultimately fulfilled in the New Jerusalem.

Sun and moon are features of the heaven and Earth that have passed away (Revelation 21:1). The light rays and heat of the sun will not be needed in the Holy City. These two heavenly bodies are also objects of worship for various people. In the New Jerusalem, the glory of God and the Lamb is declared here to be greater, more enduring, and blissful than sunlight and moonlight.

The Greek word translated "glory" is *doxa* (**DOX-ah**). It is used here to denote the supernatural brightness or splendor emanating from God; this is the brightness manifested in Christ when He was transfigured. This glory will illuminate the city, and cause it to shine on the entire face of the earth and the saved nations shall "walk in the light of it." The Greek word translated "walk" here is *peripateo* (**per-ee-pat-EH-o**); it figuratively denotes "to live." This means the nations will live by the light of God and the Lamb that shines from the Holy City.

It is very important to note that most of the things, activities, features, or manifestations of the book of Revelation run parallel to other books of the Bible, particularly those of the Old Testament. Some of the features and activities John saw in his vision are eschatological fulfillments of some prophecies of Scripture. For instance, Isaiah and Micah prophesied about the coming glory and the exalted status of the house of God in Isaiah 2:2–3 and Micah 4:1–2. This prophecy pictures a similar situation as is revealed by John: peoples of all nations flowing to the house of God to be taught His ways and to "walk" in His paths in the last days (Revelation 21:24). In addition to the figurative meaning "to live," the word "walk" is also applied to the observance of religious ordinances. One of the main attractions to the City of God is: " for out of Zion shall go forth the law, and the word of the Lord from Jerusalem" (Isaiah 2:3). The saved nations will live by the light of the Word of God, as they shall observe His statutes that come from the Holy City.

Jesus is the light of God—our light now and unto eternity, and our hope of glory. As we walk in His light, He will guide us to the realization of this great and glorious experience in the Holy City.

God promised that the Children of Israel would possess the wealth of kings and of nations (Isaiah 60:11). That promise is ultimately fulfilled in the times of the New Jerusalem. Although the original promise implied that the wealth would come from Gentile kings and nations, here it indicates that the wealth will come from a homage paid by saved nations and kings to the New Jerusalem because of its powerful and overwhelming presence on Earth.

25 And the gates of it shall not be shut at all by day: for there shall be no night there. 26 And they shall bring the glory and honor of the nation into it.

The promise (actually a prophecy) in Isaiah 60:11, continues here. It attains ultimate fulfillment in the New Jerusalem. The Greek word *pulon* (**poo-LONE**) is translated as "gates" and refers to the gateway or gate tower of a walled city. Open gates indicate admittance and readiness. Here it connotes consistent influx that does not necessitate a closure.

The sun and the moon, which regulate signs, seasons, days and years, and divide the day from the night (Genesis 1:14), will no longer impose a set time to shut the gates of the Holy City. Thus, the absence of these heavenly bodies means the absence of day and night.

While verse 24 makes particular reference to the kings of the nations bringing glory and honor to the New Jerusalem, this verse seems to be referring to the nations or the citizens of nations bringing glory and honor to the Holy City. The word "glory" here could be referring, by metonymy, to material gifts, honorarium, or prized possessions; the nations take pride in that they bring them to show honor.

27 And there shall in no wise enter into it any thing that "defileth," neither whatsoever worketh abomination, or maketh a lie: but they which are written in the Lamb's book of life.

By designation, the New Jerusalem is called "the Holy City," and in accordance to this appellation, there is a divine restriction a restriction against anything that defiles or causes abomination and lies.

The Greek word translated "defileth" is *koinoo* (**koy-NO-o**). It means to render unholy, to make common, pollute, or make unclean. This refers to things and practices that would defile the city by rendering it common or ordinary. The Holy City assumes the status of the Holy of Holies; it is a place of great beauty, lavishly built of precious stones, so nothing unclean would enter it. The word translated "abomination" is *bdelugma* (**BDEL-oog-mah**), and it denotes an object of disgust or an idolatrous object. This is speaking of idols. God and the Lord Jesus are the only objects of worship in the Holy City. No idol will be there. In Ezekiel's vision, he was made to see "where the idol that provokes to jealousy stood' at the entrance of the temple's inner court facing the north (Ezekiel 8:3, NIV). The image of the beast is also called "the abomination that causes desolation." There will be no abomination in the Holy City. The word translated "lie" is *pseudos* (**PSYOO-dos**). It simply means falsehood or that which is not true. Jesus is the Truth; anything contrary to Him is a lie and will not enter the Holy City.

Any creature or act that is described this way is forbidden entry into the Holy City. This divine restriction brings about an ultimate realization of a city devoid of evil on earth. It is an eschatological fulfillment of God's prescribed course of conduct for human life, which is described as "the way of God in truth" (Matthew 22:16), "the paths of righteousness" (Psalm 23:3), "the way of holiness" (Isaiah 35:8), and "the path of life" (Psalm 16:11). This prescribed course, prophesied in Isaiah 35:8, is laid down in its entirety, in the faith we profess as Christians and will be perfectly realized in the Holy City.

No impure or unholy creature will enter His glorious presence, which fills the entire city. The only qualified entrants and occupants of this New Jerusalem are those whose names are written in the Lamb's book of life. This book is a register containing the names of those who accepted Jesus as their Lord and Saviour, those who serve Him, those who live the life of God in Him. The Greek word translated "life" is *zoe* (**dzo-AY**). This is the life of God and the life of Christ in the believer; it is eternal life.

22:1 And he showed me a pure river of water of life, clear as crystal, proceeding out of the throne of God and of the Lamb.

John's vision in the Spirit continues. He is being made to have a panoramic view of the Holy City. He is shown a pure river containing the water of life. David spoke prophetically of this river: "There is a river, the streams whereof shall make glad the city of God, the holy place of the tabernacles of the most High" (Psalm 46:4). The Greek word translated "river" is *potamos* (**pot-am-OS**). It denotes running water, like a stream, flood, or river. David reveals to us in that passage that the river makes glad the city of God. It is water of life that brings the life of God.

This river had been foreshadowed by the river in the Garden of Eden (Genesis 2:10). The river from the millennial temple (Ezekiel 47:1 12) also foreshadows this river; it brings life to all creatures wherever it flows. Zechariah also prophesied the issuing out of "living waters" from Jerusalem (Zechariah 14:8).

A figurative reference to this river describes one of the greatest spiritual realities of the Christian faith: the outpouring, deposit, and flow of the Holy Spirit in the life of the believer. Jesus said: "He that believeth on me out of his belly shall flow rivers of living waters But this spake he of the Spirit " (John 7:38).

2 In the midst of the street of it, and on either side of the river, was there the tree of life, which bare twelve manner of fruits, and yielded her fruit every month: and the leaves of the tree were for the healing of the nations.

The New Jerusalem is naturally prefigured by the Garden of Eden, the first place where humans lived during the dispensation of innocence. Both have rivers, and Eden is the first place where the tree of life was mentioned. Everything in the Holy City is of the greatest proportion, being the ultimate and the most perfect reality in comparison to other references or similarities in the Bible which are mere prefigurations. For instance, the Bible talks about one tree of life in the middle of the Garden of Eden, but here there are numerous trees; they abound on both sides of the river.

The Greek word *xulon* (**XOO-lon**) is translated "tree." The tree of life conferred immortality on anyone who ate its fruit, hence its name (Genesis 3:22). In Ezekiel's vision, he revealed that the fruit of the tree of life was meant for food and healing (Ezekiel 47:12). Here John tells us the same thing: the fruits and leaves are for the healing of the nations.

There are four things that the Bible metaphorically calls the tree of life: wisdom (Proverbs 3:18), the fruit of righteousness (Proverbs 11:30), fulfilled desire (Proverbs 13:12), and a wholesome tongue (Proverbs 15:4).

This tree is said to bear 12 kinds of fruit every month. As a tree of life, it bears fruit to confer immortality on its eater and to maintain life in the Holy City. Thus, it ensures that the inhabitants of the city produce fruit: the fruit of the Spirit (Ephesians 5:22–23), the fruit of the lips (praise) (Hebrews 13:15), the fruit of the mouth (positive communication) (Proverbs 13:14), and the fruit of righteousness (Philippians 1:11).

3 And there shall be no more curse: but the throne of God and the Lamb shall be in it: and his servants shall serve him: 4 And they shall see his face; and his name shall be in their foreheads.

The worst thing a person can say to someone else is a curse. The Greek word translated "curse" here is *katanathema* (**kat-an-ATH-em-ah**). It denotes a wish that evil may befall a person. Curses served as protective and punitive measures against a violation of the terms of a treaty; they were intended to consign a person to calamity or destruction. The curse in the Garden of Eden was a divine judgment against man's disobedience. But in the Holy City curses have no place. The occupants of this city are not objects of divine wrath and punishment, so no calamity or destruction can come upon them. They are the redeemed who have qualified as occupants of the New Jerusalem by their faith in Christ and distinguishing themselves with lives that are above sin, curse, and calamity.

The New Jerusalem is certainly a place that will offer ultimate bliss to the believer. It will offer the greatest rewards and privileges that are not available in our present world. The throne of God and Christ will be there, bringing the habitation, presence, and direct government of God to the redeemed. And most of all, the "divine prohibition" will end. God's order which forbids man from seeing His face will no longer exist. This Old Testament order, communicated by God to Moses, stated: " Thou canst not see my face: for there shall no man see me, and live." (Exodus 33:20). Over the ages the physical sight of God had been denied to humans, because the consequence was death. But in the New Jerusalem, there will be a new order: God's servants will serve Him, and they will see His face and behold Him physically. His name (seal of ownership) will be on their foreheads.

5 And there shall be no night there; and they need no candle, neither light of the sun; for the Lord God giveth them light: and they shall reign forever and ever.

In the beginning, God created light. This light came from the two heavenly bodies (sun and moon), and one of their functions was to bring about day and night (Genesis 1:14). Here the passage says there shall be no night. The Greek word translated "night"

is *nux* (**noox**). Figuratively, the night stands for various periods and conditions in human life. It can mean a time of ignorance and helplessness (Micah 3:6), it denotes the depraved condition of mankind (1 Thessolonians 5:5–7), and it also means a time of inactivity or death (John 9:4). In the Holy City, it means there will be no ignorance; the depraved conditions of mankind will not exist and death will be no more.

Nothing in our present world can give us enduring comfort and eternal joy. We must place all our hopes on Jesus Christ, serving Him wholeheartedly. He has prepared a wonderful and glorious future for those who put their trust in Him. Everything we do should be aimed at securing our places in the New Jerusalem. It is a place where God will dwell with His people.

Daily Bible Readings

M: The Hope of Our Calling
Ephesians 1:15–23
T: The Glory of the Lord
Isaiah 60:18–22
W: An Unshakable Kingdom
Hebrews 12:22–28
T: The Hope of Glory
2 Corinthians 3:7–18
F: John Sees the Heavenly City
Revelation 21:9–14
S: God Will Be the Light
Revelation 21:22–27
S: Blessings to Come
Revelation 22:1–5

TEACHING TIPS

May 27
Bible Study Guide 13

1. Words You Should Know

A. Prophecy (Revelation 22:7, 10, 18, 19) *propheteia* (Gk.)—A revelation from God given through the mouth of a prophet; may or may not deal with the future directly.

B. Quickly (vv. 7, 12) *tachu* (Gk.)—An adverb that may refer to imminence ("soon") or suddenness ("quickly").

2. Teacher Preparation

A. Read the Bible Background and the Focal Verses.

B. Read Revelation 21 and 22:1–5 for the content of the prophecy repeatedly referred to in these verses.

C. Think about people in your church and your students, in particular. Consider what makes them struggle with doubt about their futures? Do they seem to lack knowledge or faith? Consider in advance the way this passage speaks to the doubts and anxieties of those in your class.

3. Starting the Lesson

A. Begin the class with prayer, thanking God for His faithfulness in sending Christ to the world for our salvation and in sending His Spirit as a deposit guaranteeing what is to come.

B. Ask someone to share with the class a time in their life when they had a crisis of faith and struggled with deep doubts about what they had been taught.

C. Ask volunteers to read Keep in Mind.

D. Discuss the question: "Why do we fail to believe the things we read in the Bible?"

4. Getting into the Lesson

A. Ask a volunteer to read the In Focus story and relate it to the Lesson Aim.

B. Ask the class what they like best about getting to the end of a story. Write down their responses and revisit these responses when you have covered the "end of the story" here in Revelation.

C. Ask a volunteer to read the Focal Verses.

5. Relating the Lesson to Life

Have class members come up with three or four different groups of people with whom they interact—perhaps coworkers, family members, friends, etc. Ask them to imagine themselves walking into these various groups and saying simply, "Jesus is coming back." What do they think the response would be in each of those situations? What kind of explanations would help each group understand the significance of that statement? How can this passage be used to help them to understand more clearly the meaning of Jesus' return?

6. Arousing Action

A. Allow your students to answer the Discuss the Meaning questions as a group.

B. Have the students brainstorm how they plan to accomplish the Lesson in Our Society exercise.

C. Challenge the students to complete the Make It Happen assignment.

D. Close the class with prayer.

Worship Guide

For the Superintendent or Teacher
Theme: Christ Will Return
Theme Song: "Soon and Very Soon"
Scripture: Revelation 17:14
Song: "When The Roll Is Called Up Yonder"
Meditation: Lord Jesus, thank You that our hope in Your return is as solid as the ground on which we stand. Give us grace that we might hold You in reverence and not be casual about the thought of Your glorious return. Help us to humbly rejoice as we think about the joy of everlasting fellowship with You. Amen.

CHRIST WILL RETURN

Bible Background • REVELATION 22:6–21
Printed Text • REVELATION 22:6–10, 12–13, 16–21   Devotional Reading • JOHN 16:17–24

Lesson Aim

By the end of the lesson, we will:

UNDERSTAND that Jesus will one day return for us;

BELIEVE that we shall see Him face-to-face; and

REST with the peace of an assured glorious ending.

Keep in Mind

"He which testifieth these things saith, Surely I come quickly. Amen. Even so, come, Lord Jesus" (Revelation 22:20).

Focal Verses

Revelation 22:6 And he said unto me, These sayings are faithful and true: and the Lord God of the holy prophets sent his angel to show unto his servants the things which must shortly be done.

7 Behold, I come quickly: blessed is he that keepeth the sayings of the prophecy of this book.

8 And I John saw these things, and heard them. And when I had heard and seen, I fell down to worship before the feet of the angel which showed me these things.

9 Then saith he unto me, See thou do it not: for I am thy fellow servant, and of thy brethren the prophets, and of them which keep the sayings of this book: worship God.

10 And he saith unto me, Seal not the sayings of the prophecy of this book: for the time is at hand.

22:12 And, behold, I come quickly; and my reward is with me, to give every man according as his work shall be.

13 I am Alpha and Omega, the beginning and the end, the first and the last.

22:16 I Jesus have sent mine angel to testify unto you these things in the churches. I am the root and the offspring of David, and the bright and morning star.

17 And the Spirit and the bride say, Come. And let him that heareth say, Come. And let him that is athirst come. And whosoever will, let him take the water of life freely.

18 For I testify unto every man that heareth the words of the prophecy of this book, If any man shall add unto these things, God shall add unto him the plagues that are written in this book:

19 And if any man shall take away from the words of the book of this prophecy, God shall take away his part out of the book of life, and out of the holy city, and from the things which are written in this book.

20 He which testifieth these things saith, Surely I come quickly. Amen. Even so, come, Lord Jesus.

21 The grace of our Lord Jesus Christ be with you all. Amen.

In Focus

Chris laughed along with the television audience as he listened to his friend, Jason, a popular comedian, deliver his punch lines with ease. A phone call interrupted him in mid-laughter. It was Jason.

"Are you watching the show I taped last week?" Jason asked.

"Yeah, I told you I would. Pretty funny stuff. I can never figure out where you're headed."

"That's the secret of a good punch line." He chuckled.

"Now I got a good one for you. I told you I would start reading the Bible; today I have just finished the last chapter," Jason said.

"You started with the last chapter?" Chris asked nervously. It wasn't that unusual. Jason always read the ending before considering any book.

"Jason, why would you do that?" Chris asked, thinking the end-of-the-world horrors might be too much for a new Christian.

"Nobody told me where to start, so I figured I'd find out how everything was going to come out. You know, to see if the ending was worth it," Jason replied.

Chris tried to explain, "But Genesis and the walk of Christ ." Before he could finish, he heard Jason howling in laugher.

"Don't worry, the ending told me what I needed to know. We win in the end! Now I want to know more about how and why."

In the book of Revelation, Christians are assured of the ultimate happy ending—a triumphal procession in Christ!

The People, Places, and Times

David. At the height of the nation's history, David, the king of Israel, united his people and gained victory over their enemies. His devotion to the Lord was such that God said of him, "I have found David son of Jesse a man after my own heart; he will do everything I want him to do" (Acts 13:22, NIV). God gave David an enduring promise: "Your house and your kingdom will endure forever before me; your throne will be established forever" (2 Samuel 7:16, NIV). David's descendants failed to remain on the throne because of unfaithfulness, but the promise remained: "Your throne, O God, will last for ever and ever; a scepter of justice will be the scepter of your kingdom. You love righteousness and hate wickedness; therefore God, your God, has set you above your companions by anointing you with the oil of joy" (Psalm 45:6–7, NIV). The New Testament unfolds the mystery: Jesus is the eternal King who will fulfill the prophecy by sitting forever on the Davidic throne (cf. Acts 2:34–35). This great weight of expectation, this messianic longing, this anticipation of God's faithfulness in fulfilling His promise all are bound up in Jesus' self-affirmation in Revelation 22:16: "I am the root and the offspring of David." Jesus is the King for whom God's people have always longed; His coming is the hope of the elect and the reward of God's remnant.

Background

Revelation 21 and the first part of chapter 22 portray, in visions and images, the wonderful future awaiting God's people in the new heaven and the new Earth. Drawing heavily on the book of Isaiah, John's vision concludes by showing the certainty of the promise. Just as the prophecies of the Old Testament have been fulfilled in Christ's first coming, so the prophecy of Revelation will be fulfilled—ultimately, through Christ's second coming. And just as Christ's first coming was great news for some (the poor in spirit, who believed in Him) and bad news for others (the proud of heart, who rejected Him), so also His unstoppable Second Coming will be wonderful news for those who belong to Christ, and woeful news for those who spurn the message of His Gospel. Revelation, like the Bible as a whole, is both a book of promise and a book of warning. John's remarkable vision calls the church to examine itself, to "give diligence to make [its] calling and election sure" (2 Peter 1:10), and to take comfort in the incomparable power and mercy of Christ, who comes for His own and for their redemption.

At-A-Glance

1. Christ Is Coming Certainly and Quickly (Revelation 22:6–10)
2. Christ Is Coming as King and Lord (22:12–13, 16)
3. Christ Is Coming for the Faithful Who Belong to Him (vv. 17–21)

In Depth

1. Christ Is Coming Certainly and Quickly (Revelation 22:6–10)

The words of the Bible can be hard to hang on to because the promises are so otherworldly and because our sight is so limited. God, in His mercy, frequently gives added testimony to the certainty of what He reveals. To call the Lord the "God of the holy prophets" (v. 6) is to show that these words, just like the prophets' words, are breathed out by God and cannot be false. Just as the prophets were able to say, "Thus says the Lord," so also the angel, with the same authority, promises that these words are "faithful and true," and that these things "must shortly be done" (v. 6). Likewise, when John is com-

"He which testifieth these things saith, Surely I come quickly. Amen. Even so, come, Lord Jesus" (Revelation 22:20).

manded not to seal up the prophecy, but to write it down, God shows us that the vision is true. The record of that vision is also inspired by Him and is utterly reliable.

In light of the vision's glory and the authority with which it is revealed, we should not be surprised that John feels compelled to worship the messenger (v. 8), even though he has already been rebuked for doing so (19:10). The angel's response shows that the angel himself submits to the powerful words of the prophecy. He calls himself a "fellow servant of them which keep the sayings of this book" (v. 9). He shows that, though many may long to see visions and dream dreams, it is the words of God that should command His servants' greatest loyalty and obedience. Through the "ordinary" communication of words and sentences, the God of the universe speaks, and blesses His people! It is no accident then that "blessed is he that keepeth the saying of the prophecy of this book" (v. 7).

2. Christ Is Coming as King and Lord (22:12–13, 16)

Hear the powerful, kingly language of Jesus as He promises His coming! Only a king would speak this way, promising a "reward" (v. 12) and daring to examine and understand the fullness of a person's deeds. In the language of Isaiah (Isaiah 44:6; 48:12), Christ's voice thunders in testimony to His preeminence. In the Old Testament, this kind of language beginning and ending, first and last (v. 13)—could apply to Yahweh alone. Can there be any doubt that Jesus is laying claim to the same divine status? If not the divine King, could He send His angel to do His will (16a)? If not the divine King, could He lay claim to David's lineage and the promises of Isaiah (chapter 11) concerning the eternal King to come? This testimony matters greatly to the Christian not only that Christ might be rightly worshiped, but also that the believer may know the certainly of His coming! If Jesus is the faithful and true King, on par with the perfections of Yahweh, how could He fail to come through on behalf of His beloved ones?

When Christ comes as King and Lord, He will "give every man according as his work shall be" (v. 12). Does this passage teach a form of salvation by works? There seems to be at least three good reasons to say no. First, this verse alludes to two passages (Isaiah 40:10 and 62:11), both of which use the same word ("reward," or "recompense") and both of which refer to God coming to bring salvation (not to reward good behavior).

Second, the New Testament elsewhere makes clear that in the Gospel God brings salvation to His people on the ground of Christ's righteousness alone. They receive that righteousness by faith, not by works.

Third, the book of Revelation (5:1–10) establishes that Jesus, the slain Lamb, is the only One who can open the scroll because no human being can earn the right to open it. So in what sense does Christ reward each one according to His works? Verse 11 reveals the key: each person acts according to his true nature and the state of his heart toward Christ. Even in light of Christ's decisive second coming, only those God called will persevere to the end, through the faith the Spirit has given them.

3. Christ Is Coming for the Faithful Who Belong to Him (vv. 17–21)

The book of Revelation, with all its vivid imagery and difficult symbolism, is simply a letter. It begins like a letter, with a greeting and a blessing to the seven churches (Revelation 2–3); and it ends like a letter, with a benediction (22:21). Fittingly, this letter concludes with an invitation: in light of the sure coming of Christ as King and Lord, will you be found to belong to Him? Verse 17 reminds us of the full, free offer of Christ in the Gospel. The Holy Spirit extends the invitation to accept Christ as Lord, and even the bride, the true church, is pictured urging all to come unto Christ. Echoing John 7:37–39 and Jesus' invitation there, John beseeches those in the seven churches and beyond to recognize and satisfy their thirst by receiving the water of eternal life in the Gospel.

This invitation is strengthened and complemented by the following warning: no one must add or take away from the words of Revelation (vv. 18–19). Echoing the words of Deuteronomy 29:19–20, John urges the people of God to spurn false teaching and idolatry. John's stern words call to mind Luke 12:48 (NIV): "From everyone who has been given much, much will be demanded; and from the one who has been entrusted with much, much more will be asked." The seven churches (indeed, the whole church) receives so much through this prophecy, this peek into God's plan for the ages! The church's faithfulness is demanded in return—a faithfulness springing from true faith. Likewise, this passage pictures a great law court with four faithful witnesses: the angel, John, the Holy Spirit, and finally Jesus Himself (v. 20). And where there is a law court, there is accountability and justice; all who hear are accountable to respond to the message! John demonstrates the beautiful, simple response of faith: "Amen. Even so, come, Lord Jesus."

Source

Beale, Gregory K. *Revelation: A Commentary on the Greek Text.* Grand Rapids, Mich.: Eerdmans, 1998.

Search the Scriptures

1. What evidence do you see that John's prophecy in Revelation will come true (Revelation 22:6–10)?

2. What was John's response to hearing the vision given by the angel (v. 8)? What was the angel's response to John's action (v. 9)?

3. For what purpose does Jesus say He will return quickly (v. 12)?

4. To whom does Jesus give the message of Revelation (v. 16)?

5. Who extends the invitation and who is invited to receive the invitation (v. 17)?

6. How does "the punishment fit the crime" (vv. 18–19)?

Discuss the Meaning

1. Why do you think that Jesus, through the angel and John's vision, goes to such lengths to reinforce the certainty and security of His promise in verses 6–10?

2. Why is it important that Jesus announces His identity in verses 13–16? How does His identity relate to the hope of the Christian?

3. Why do you think the gracious invitation of verse 17 and the stern warning of verses 18–19 are put next to each other?

4. How is this last part of Revelation a happy ending? What do you find surprising or unexpected about this ending?

5. How does this passage help you understand the book of Revelation as a whole?

Lesson in Our Society

Throughout church history, countless individuals and communities have predicted with confidence the exact date on which Jesus will return. Without exception, they have been wrong. As a result, the whole idea of expecting a miraculous return of Christ has been largely discredited in the minds of many. The book of Revelation, when it focuses on the return of Christ, does not list a series of mysterious hints that the church is left to decode. Nor does it merely tell us what we want to hear, flattering us by sparing any sense of accountability and judgment at Christ's return. Before a world that mocks its expectation as "pie in the sky" and a church that often misunderstands its message as a riddle to solve, the book of Revelation focuses on the faithfulness and preeminence of Christ. Because Jesus is the first and the last, the King of kings, and the true descendant of David, the Christian can rest in His promises. Thanks be to God for His indescribable gift!

Make It Happen

If you could have written the last chapter of the Bible, how would you have written it? Often the Spirit uses the parts of the Bible we find most surprising to drive home the Word's significance. Read through these last few verses of Revelation and write down the parts you find unexpected. Think through what each surprising part means for the church and for you individually, and resolve to make that meaning part of your regular prayers and conversation with others in the church.

Follow the Spirit

What God wants me to do:

_____

_____

Remember Your Thoughts

Special insights I have learned:

_____

_____

More Light on the Text
Revelation 22:6–10, 12–13, 16–21

The context of the last chapter of the last book of Scripture brings to a close human history. Like ultimate bookends of man's inimitable story, our beginning and our end are contrasted and captured by authors Moses and John. In Genesis, the serpent tempts the first Adam, he falls, and Paradise is lost. In Revelation, the serpent is destroyed, the second Adam is victorious, and Paradise is restored. The significant elements of the garden Paradise were two people, the tree of life, and a river that watered the garden (Genesis 2:9–10). In the New Jerusalem the fountain of life flows from the throne of God (Revelation 22:1–2; 4:6), and lining both sides of the river are many trees of life (22:14) that are not only

freely accessible, but ever fruitful for the enjoyment and healing of many nations (Psalm 46:4). In Eden, one tree was forbidden; in Paradise, nothing is forbidden.

This succinct picture of our final Paradise supersedes the original, in particular, because of the absence of temptation, death, and evil.

6 And he said unto me, These sayings are faithful and true: and the Lord God of the holy prophets sent his angel to show unto his servants the things which must shortly be done.

This is the third time the angel used the words "faithful and true," which also are applied directly to Christ (Revelation 3:14; 19:11). As Christ is faithful and true, so His words sent via prophets or angels are faithful and true. Implied perhaps is an indictment on future man's predictable slowness to grasp each newly revealed facet of God's glory. For the most part, we are wise to detect the "con" in the many schemes men concoct to swindle their fellowmen. Sooner or later, however, one would think we would learn "it's too good to be true" doesn't apply to the revelations or character of God.

The same "truth assurances" could be said for both the book of Revelation and the entirety of God's Word. The apparent redundancy here must indicate the special importance to the church of these particular words—even while underscoring that God always has, in the same trustworthy manner, revealed the future through His prophets. The phrase translated as "who tells his prophets what the future holds" is only found in the NLT, explaining why the prophets of the past are linked to the current vision given to John.

The hinge phrase "must shortly be done" (v. 6) is rendered among translators with the most variety, yet all clearly concur that the Greek word *tachos* (**TAKH-os**) means quickness or speed. Still, Pastor David Guzik had an interesting alternate translation of "suddenly," and quotes expositor G. Campbell Morgan (early twentieth century pastor of Westminster Chapel, London) as saying that the original Greek did not intend "quickly" as per common usage. Few would say 2,000 years equates with "quickly," but "suddenly" could happen at any time, even the far distant future. This rendering also agrees with other verses that describe His coming as a thief in the night, taking a self-indulgent, self-absorbed world by surprise (Matthew 24:38–41; 1 Thessalonians 5:4).

Ever since John penned his vision, these words of imminent hope have been available for all to see and react to as they choose. When Christ finally does return, no one will be able to claim total surprise, and they also will have no one to blame if His coming isn't welcome.

7 Behold, I come quickly: blessed is he that keepeth the sayings of the prophecy of this book.

After reinforcing this element of surprise, the angel encourages believers, but subtly implies that those who *don't* "keep the true sayings in this book" *won't* be "blessed" at Jesus' sudden appearance. In this Revelation beatitude believers will be blessed, more likely ecstatic, as our time of vindication and the completion of our redemption will have come at long last. In stark contrast, one can imagine an almost deafening, collective, "Oh, no!" coming from the entire unsaved world, as it simultaneously realizes both its folly not to have believed, and its imminent, certain judgment.

Here rendered "sayings" but generally rendered "words," John uses the Greek word *logos* (**LOG-os**), a word he used multiple times in 36 verses of his gospel and which has come to represent the entire Word of God.

It is important that each succeeding generation anticipate, prepare, watch, and be ready for Jesus' return. For those unfamiliar with the term, the Greek word *parousia* (**par-oo-SEE-ah**) is Christ's Second Coming (Matthew 24:3; 1 Thessalonians 2:19; 2 Timothy 2:8). Rather than just looking for a distant event, each generation in a sense has been running along the edge of the cliff, from the time of the apostles until now. Our sense of time must surrender to God's.

8 And I John saw these things, and heard them. And when I had heard and seen, I fell down to worship before the feet of the angel which showed me these things. 9 Then saith he unto me, See thou do it not: for I am thy fellow servant, and of thy brethren the prophets, and of them which keep the sayings of this book: worship God.

For the second time, John tries to worship the angel, and again is immediately rebuked. It is a natural human tendency to want to express gratitude and love to the bearer of good news. But to supersede gratitude and begin to worship any created being is sinning against God who alone is to be worshiped (Exodus 20:3; Deuteronomy 5:6; 6:13). Satan attempted the supreme insult to God by trying to get Jesus to worship him and was rebuked with a reminder of the first commandment (Matthew 4:9–10). The fact that Jesus openly received worship on several occasions from people is one of the strongest arguments for His deity (Matthew 8:2; 14:33; John 9:38) moreover, He was worthy to receive worship from angels (Hebrews 1:6).

10 And he saith unto me, Seal not the sayings of the prophecy of this book: for the time is at hand.

In Daniel 8:26, the command was given, to "shut up the vision" and not yet reveal what the Lord says. But now the message or "saying" or *logos* is given for publication. "At hand" is the Greek term *eggus* (**eng-GOOS**), which means near, nigh, or ready. This is breaking news the church needs to hear, so it can begin to watch and pray for Christ's second coming. This is an evangelistic word for the church, the Gospel of Christ is to be revealed, proclaimed, and told to all who will hear, for all too soon there will be no more opportunity to repent and receive the grace of God. While urgent, the message is still positive because it implies that right up until the end of life, there is still time to choose (Hebrews 9:27).

22:12 And, behold, I come quickly; and my reward is with me, to give every man according as his work shall be.

This writer does not see enough consistency with the standard interpretation of "quickly" over the possibly more literal rendering of "suddenly." Both, as a result, intend for the church, the bride of Christ, to prepare herself and be ready at any time for the return of her beloved Bridegroom. Whether He returns "quickly" or "suddenly," both achieve the intended result of urging believers to be prepared for Christ's return because no one really knows when it will happen. The main point, repeated over and over in Scripture, is to be ready for Christ's return whenever it happens.

It is misguided thinking to take this verse out of context and try to say we are justified by works; too many other Scriptures clarify this issue (James 2:20; Titus 3:8). This verse was not intended to make a doctrinal statement, but rather was an exhortation to preparedness, which includes an ever ready, healthy, fruitful (works producing) faith. A positive take on the verse is that Jesus will come with "rewards" (Gk. *misthos*, **mis-THOS**), like wages or payment for services, for those who have been faithful. While no one is saved by works, those who are saved will be rewarded according to their "works" (Gk. *ergon*, **ER-gon,** meaning employment or labor).

13 I am Alpha and Omega, the beginning and the end, the first and the last.

Alpha is the first letter of the 22-letter Greek alphabet and Omega is the last; thus the connection to the beginning and the end, and the first and the last. Psalm 90:2 says Jesus is from "everlasting to everlasting," and He is the same "yesterday, and today, and forever" (Hebrews 13:8). If Genesis and Revelation are the bookends of human history, Jesus is the holder of the bookends both preexisting and post-existing our temporal time frame. This is true not only in the sense of existence, but in character and holiness, without beginning or end, and without change (Malachi 3:6). Alpha and Omega, moreover, is one of many self-proclaimed images of Christ found in Scripture. The same names are applied to God (cf. Isaiah 41:4; 44:6) and here are specifically applied to Christ (cf. Revelation 1:17; 2:8), giving another insurmountable argument for His deity.

22:16 I Jesus have sent mine angel to testify unto you these things in the churches. I am the root and the offspring of David, and the bright and morning star.

Jesus places His stamp of approval on the testimony of the message of Revelation to the church (the word "you" in the Greek is plural), which includes our present age. No mortal could be both root (the Creator) and offspring (Isaiah 11:1); Jesus is both the Lord of David and the son of David (Matthew 22:42–45).

The fallen angel, Lucifer, once called a morning star (Isaiah 14:12; also day star in some versions), has from the beginning lied to mankind and falsely presented himself as an angel of light (2 Corinthians 11:14). Jesus affirms that He alone is the true Morning Star. Here two ordinary Greek words are combined to form a unique metaphor: *orthrinos* (**or-thrin-OS**) for "morning" and *aster* (**as-TARE**) for "star." The Greek word *phosphoros* (**foce-FOR-os**) means light bearing, and is translated both "daystar" and "morning star." It is used only once in the New Testament (2 Peter 1:19) and is applied to Christ both there and in Revelation. The Morning Star will continue to shine, as He always has shone for eternity.

17 And the Spirit and the bride say, Come. And let him that heareth say, Come. And let him that is athirst come. And whosoever will, let him take the water of life freely.

Both the Spirit of God, who indwells God's church, and the bride of Christ (the church, believers) are invited. Those who have yet to decide for Christ are also invited to come to the water of life! We, along with the Spirit, wait expectantly but we also serve as a testimony that the human heart is satisfied by coming to Jesus, and any who comes to Him may freely drink of the water of life (John 7:37–39; Revelation 22:1), both now and forever.

18 For I testify unto every man that heareth the words of the prophecy of this book, If any man shall add unto these things, God shall add unto him the plagues that are written in this book: 19 And if any

man shall take away from the words of the book of this prophecy, God shall take away his part out of the book of life, and out of the holy city, and from the things which are written in this book.

Matthew Henry makes the interesting observation that the words of warning resemble previous words of protection found in Scripture: "This sanction is like a flaming sword, to guard the canon of the Scripture from profane hands." Henry's words are reminiscent of the angel guarding the tree of life with a flaming sword (Genesis 3:24). God installed similar sanctions for the protection of the law (see Deuteronomy 4:2; 12:32; Proverbs 30:5–6). God will judge appropriately offenders for their violation of His *logos* The clearly promised curse balances the previous promised blessing offered to the faithful (v. 12) and together retain a familiar blessing/curse theme from the Old Testament as the New Testament closes.

20 He which testifieth these things saith, Surely I come quickly. Amen. Even so, come, Lord Jesus.

Christ's parting words are filled with mercy and hope. When Jesus ascended after His resurrection, He promised to be with them by His Spirit; now He promises He will soon return. The Greek word for "testify" is *martureo* (**mar-too-REH-o**) and means to give or bear witness, just as the apostles were eyewitnesses who became witnesses throughout the New Testament. His coming will be fulfilled as completely as the fulfillment of sending the Holy Spirit, the Comforter and Teacher of the church. Once Christ does return, it will be the end for all who rejected Him. Perhaps believers can then comfort themselves with the keenness of Jesus' genuine sorrow for the unbelievers' coming judgment. The primary message for the church is to be and remain ready.

The book of Revelation started with the Spirit (1:10), the church lives and exists because of the Spirit, and individual believers are raised to newness of life only through being born of the Spirit (John 3:5, 8; Galatians 4:29). The heartbeat of every Christian (the body and bride of Christ) is the Spirit. The Spirit has been our teacher of truth, always leading us

toward Christ. The Spirit within you will confirm these words, "that when I come, whatever the day and year, it will seem to happen suddenly, and will take many by surprise." All born again believers, will be ready because of the Spirit and will wait expectantly, no matter how long it takes.

21 The grace of our Lord Jesus Christ be with you all. Amen.

It is no coincidence that both the book and the Word end with a word of grace. Christ came to bring us grace. When Christ's work on earth was finished, He left to prepare a place for us, and as surely as He came according to His promise, He will return as promised for His bride. Love is grace, and grace is love. Until we are perfected in Him, we can find no better comfort, stronger peace, or more enduring hope, than the presence of His grace to sustain us until His return.

Source
Henry, Matthew. "Commentary on Revelation 22." In *Matthew Henry's Commentary on the Whole Bible*. Peabody, Mass.: Henderson Publishers, 1991.

Daily Bible Readings

M: Pain Becomes Joy
John 16:17–24

T: Jesus Overcomes
John 16:25–33

W: One Body, One Spirit
Ephesians 4:1–6

T: May Christ Rule Your Hearts
Colossians 3:12–17

F: Worship God
Revelation 22:6–11

S: The Reward for Faithfulness
Revelation 22:12–16

S: The Invitation
Revelation 22:17–21

JUNE 2007
QUARTER AT-A-GLANCE
Committed to Doing Right

The three units in this quarter look at a number of Old Testament prophets in near chronological order. Although the prophets' careers spanned several hundred years, their messages were consistent: Being related through faith places certain requirements on God's people—one such requirement is to do right.

UNIT 1 . LIFE AS GOD'S PEOPLE

These lessons examine the need for justice, the peoples' accountability for wrongdoing, the nature of true worship, and the abundant life that God offers.

LESSON 1: June 3
Amos Challenges Injustice
Amos 5:10–15, 21–24

Justice is an attribute of God. We have been created in the likeness of God and are expected to be just and fair in all our dealings with others. Amos chided the people of Israel for their failure to show justice to the poor by oppressing them and devising schemes to rip them off. Amos reminds the people that God holds them accountable. God refused to accept the oppressors' worship, and promised to send judgment on both people and land. God would take away their wealth and send them into captivity.

LESSON 2: June 10
Hosea Preaches God's Accusation against Israel
Hosea 4:1–4; 7:1–2; 12: 8–9

Hosea identifies many sins the people of Israel had committed in rejecting the covenant commands of God. King Jeroboam started the people down this treacherous path when he established an alternative place and mode of worship at Bethel. Since God had not judged the nation so far, the people boasted that judgment would never come. The prophet pleaded with them to repent and return to God in order to avoid His judgment.

LESSON 3: June 17
Isaiah Calls for True Worship
Isaiah 1:10–11, 14–20

Isaiah was sent by God to call his people away from sin and back to a restored relationship with Him. The people thought they could bring their offerings at the appropriate times and then do whatever they pleased the rest of the time. Isaiah warned the people of judgment if they refused to turn back. At the same time he promised them God's blessings if they repented and remained faithful to their covenant promises.

LESSON 4: June 24
Isaiah Invites Us to God's Feast
Isaiah 55:1–3, 6–11

Jesus, the Son of David, will someday come and draw many nations and people to Himself. Using the image of the great feast to which we are invited, Isaiah says that God is the one who generously provides all good things for us.

UNIT 2 . WHAT DOES GOD REQUIRE?

The first lesson provides us with a panoramic view of God's requirement for righteous living. The next four lessons then relate this to God's justice, God's judgment, the people's disobedience, and the need for trust in God. The texts come from Micah, Zephaniah, Habakkuk, Jeremiah, 2 Kings, and 2 Chronicles.

LESSON 5: July 1
Micah Announces God's Requirements
Micah 3:1–4; 6:6–8

Those who plot evil against others will be judged by God. Micah was filled with the Spirit to reveal the people's sin to them. He preached concerning God's judgment on them. He tells the people that religious rituals will not cover their sins. God requires three things of us: to act justly, to love mercifully, and to walk humbly with God.

LESSON 6: July 8
Zephaniah Announces God's Justice
Zephaniah 3:1–5, 8–9

Israel's leaders have turned away from God. The officials, the rulers, the prophets, and the priests have been arrogant and treacherous. They have profaned God's sanctuary and done violence to His Law. But the day will come when God will judge all the nations. Israel's God will be acknowledged by the nations, and God's people will be held in honor by them.

LESSON 7: July 15
Habakkuk Announces the Doom of the Unrighteous
Habakkuk 2:6–14

Habakkuk questioned God as to why evil in Israel was not punished. God told him that He would use the Babylonians to punish Israel. Habakkuk could not understand why God would use a people even more wicked to punish them. God's answer was that Babylon would be punished and those who trusted in the Lord would be rewarded.

LESSON 8: July 22
Jeremiah Announces the Consequences of Disobedience
Jeremiah 7:11–15; 2 Kings 23:36–37

Jehoiakim did evil in the eyes of the Lord and was one of the very last rulers before the fall of Jerusalem. The people thought they would be safe because they had the temple in Jerusalem, but Jeremiah warned them of the danger of this fallacy. The people trusted in a religious institution rather than being obedient to God, and now they were going to have to bear the consequences.

LESSON 9: July 29
Jeremiah Invites Jews in Babylon to Trust God
Jeremiah 29:1–14

The Babylonians had encircled Jerusalem and taken many of the people captive. False prophets were encouraging the captives to rebel against their captors. However, because their captivity was sent by God, Jeremiah told the people not to listen to them. Jeremiah instructed the Jews to trust in God even in captivity, because He had good plans for their future.

UNIT 3 . HOW SHALL WE RESPOND?

This unit emphasizes hope, personal responsibility, and repentance as appropriate responses for those who are committed to doing right. And it also reminds us that God's judgment is just.

LESSON 10: August 5
Lamentations Urges Hope in God
Lamentations 3:25–33, 55–58

Here the prophet expresses the horror of being torn from the Jewish homeland and taken away to Babylon. But in the midst of this third lament, the prophet says that God is good to those who hope in Him, to those who wait for His salvation. He acknowledges that this suffering is good, because it has come from the Lord.

LESSON 11: August 12
Ezekiel Preaches about Individual Responsibility
Ezekiel 18:4, 20–23, 30–32

Some people do not take responsibility for their actions, but seek to blame others instead. Ezekiel says that each of us bears responsibility for our own sins.

LESSON 12: August 19
Zechariah Calls for a Return to God
Zechariah 1:1–6; 7:8–14

Zechariah invites the people to return to God with the sure promise that God will return to them. Zechariah says that when we return to the Lord, wholeness and happiness becomes available to us as well.

LESSON 13: August 26
Malachi Describes God's Just Judgment
Malachi 2:17–3:5; 4:1

The people expected God to return to the temple, and that a glorious future would arrive. When these things did not happen, they became cynical toward God and slipshod in their obedience to Him. Malachi told the people that God would indeed be coming back, but that it would be a day of judgment.

GOD IS FAITHFUL, IN SPITE OF OUR FAILURES

by Glen A. McCarthy

God, who is the great I AM, is indeed who He is, and will be who He will be regardless of people's disposition toward Him. Faithfulness is one of God's most noted attributes and one of the great biblical motifs. This facet of God's character is ascribed to Him throughout the history of His relationship with His chosen people, Israel.

The Jewish understanding of God's relationship with and commitment to them as a people is rooted in the indelible mark of an irrevocable divine choice: God's choice to enter history as the God of Israel. God's covenant with Israel is the substratum of Israel's faith in Him. God's sovereign choice was motivated by His free, yet irrevocable, love for the people of Israel and, through Israel, for the world as a whole. Israel believed that God's election of them was based solely on His unalterable love and hence could not be abrogated from the human side.

This election by God was not because Israel was superior in any way to other people groups; indeed, in some respects Israel was thought to have as many negative characteristics than other groups. Nor was God's election conditional upon Israel's obedience to the commands that He imposed on them as the expression of His will for their conduct. God's election brought with it His commands and the threat of severe punishment should Israel fail to live up to their election. Although Israel struggled endlessly against their election, causing the most disastrous consequences for themselves and for the rest of the nations, the divine election remained unaffected because it was unconditional, based solely on God's love. In Jewish theology, God's anger is a passing phase that can only temporarily obscure His overwhelming love for Israel. Israel was confi-

dent of her election and of God's special love for her amid all the families of the earth.

Throughout the Old Testament, Israel failed God by not carrying out His divine mandate or upholding His standards of holiness and righteousness. Moreover, Israel's sin caused much cynicism among the nations of the world.

Israel and the Gentile nations all fell victim to the distortion of their respective identities. Israel was God's chosen people, chosen to bring salvation to the world and reconciliation between God and all people. Unfortunately, Israel succumbed to vain pride in their own election, causing God to become angry with and seemingly indifferent toward them. The nations responded to Israel with resentment and rage due to envy. By their actions, they placed obstacles in the path of God's plan to consummate creation through Israel's election. In the end, however, there is a limit to what human freedom can do. In this case, the nations were unable to nullify God's purposes: the election and redemption of Israel, and, through Israel, the redemption of humanity.

In the New Testament, the apostle Paul, the first and probably the most significant Christian theologian, discloses two great mysteries: first, that all of Israel (all believers) will be saved (Romans 11:25–26), and second, that Gentile believers are heirs together with Israel through the Gospel (Ephesians 3:3–6). Paul believed that Gentile believers had been adopted into the family of God through faith in Jesus Christ and received the same love from God that Israel received (Galatians 3:7, 4:5; Ephesians 1:5). This idea should be very encouraging to Christians. God's covenant with Israel through Abraham is everlasting from God's standpoint (Genesis 17:13, 19) but capable of being broken from a human standpoint (Genesis

17:14; cf. Isaiah 24:5; Jeremiah 31:32). The heart of God's often repeated promise in the Old Testament was that He would be Israel's God (Genesis 17:8; Jeremiah 24:7; 31:33; Ezekiel 34:30–31; Hosea 2:23; Zechariah 8:8). This promise was God's pledge to be the Protector of His people and the One who provided for their well-being and guaranteed their future blessing (Genesis 15:1). God's covenant with Israel, through Abraham, also included everlasting possession of the land (Genesis 12:7; 15:18; Acts 7:5); however, the land could be temporarily lost because of disobedience (see Deuteronomy 28:62–63; 30:1–10).

In Galatians 3:6–29, the apostle Paul gives a theological premise for asserting that Gentile Christians are indeed the seed of Abraham through faith (see Genesis 3:7). Throughout the chapter, he elucidates the covenant that God made with Abraham and his seed in Genesis 17:7–8. Paul speaks of the promise of an everlasting covenant and of the possession of the land of Canaan by Abraham and his seed, bringing out the singularity of the word "seed." He goes on to assert that Jesus Christ was that "seed" to whom, along with Abraham, the promise was made, and that anyone who is in Christ is Abraham's seed as well (Galatians 3:15–16, 29). From Paul's perspective, a true Jew was one who had experienced circumcision of the heart, not merely outward circumcision of the flesh. He wanted his audience to know that this circumcision of the heart was according to the spirit and not the letter of the law (Romans 2:28–29).

What is important to know is that just as God's love for Israel was unmerited, so is His love for Christians. God elected Israel through his covenant with Abraham 430 years before the law was instituted; therefore, the inheritance of Israel was by promise and not by the works of the law. The law was instituted because of transgression, to make Israel aware of God's high standards of righteousness and holiness. This perfect law humbles us while simultaneously convincing us that we are in need of a Saviour and can be saved from sin only through forgiveness. God wants people to know that He is faithful, that His love is unconditional and consistent.

God is love (1 John 4:8, 16), and His love for us is based on who He is and not on what we do. He is our God, and we are His people. His nature, which contains both paternal and maternal elements, obligates Him to provide for, protect, console, and nurture us. God's love for us is based on the integrity of *His* character, not ours. When we come to understand how much God loves us, we should strive to love Him and others in the same way (1 John 4:19; John 13:35). This kind of love is made manifest in the life and earthly ministry of Jesus Christ.

Israel forgot that her election was for service, to be a sign of the infinite and unwarranted gift of God rather than an indication of any inherent superiority to other people. But God was faithful to Israel throughout the Old Testament and still is, through His promises of restoration. Sometimes we, as the church, forget that we, too, were called out through salvation for service. As children of God, we are to be imitators of Christ, who came to serve instead of to be served. He taught us that greatness in the kingdom of God is achieved through serving other people. This service consists not only of feeding the poor, clothing the naked, and visiting the motherless and the fatherless, and the widows/widowers in their affliction, but also of allowing God to use us as instruments of justice. We are called to defend the poor and to change unjust systems and structures within our society that exploit, dehumanize, and oppress the marginalized. Our obedience to God's command should be based on our love for God. Many times we feel unworthy due to our failures in conduct, but we can rest assured that God's mercy and grace will be extended toward us. It is our faith that connects us to the covenant promises of Abraham. God is faithful in His love. Christians are a part of God's family and receive salvation, along with all the covenant promises to Abraham—as long as we stay in the faith, regardless of our failures (1 Corinthians 1:9; 1 Thessalonians 5:24).

Glenn McCarthy *holds a bachelor of arts in biblical theological studies and is currently in seminary pursuing a masters of divinity.*

IMPARTING MORE THAN INFORMATION

by Hurby Franks

We are in the midst of a postmodern generation. Though very difficult to define, essentially, postmodernism is the questioning or outright rejection of accepted "modern" thought in the areas of culture, architecture, philosophy, and religion. In other words, postmodernists redefine or regard as more complex truth in these areas. Beginning in the mid to late 1970s, people began to define truth as a personal concept instead of a universal one. It becomes harder for us as Christians to present the Gospel as truth when some postmodernists feel that everyone has his or her own truth. In order to combat this problem, we need to impart the *application* as well as the *information* of the Gospel.

I have seen examples of this need in my own Christian walk. For four years, I was a college campus minister. Over that four-year period, I noticed that, in the Bible Belt (an area of the United States typically associated with the southern states), almost everyone claimed to be a Christian. However, the truth of the Gospel did not always have an effect on how college students lived their lives. Students tended to apply the parts of Scripture they felt were "true" for them, while discarding the parts that did not agree with their lifestyles, labeling those verses as "untrue" for them. As I talked with my colleagues in other parts of the country, they informed me that the prevailing theory for students in their areas was that the Gospel, as well as all of Christianity, is just another "truth" in a long list of possible "truths." In order for this perspective to change, Christianity needs to be shown as not only true, but relevant for everyone.

Amos and Hosea speak to these issues in the first four lessons of the fourth quarter. Amos calls for God's people not only to care about but also to deal with issues of injustice. He points out how the people of God have taken advantage of the poor and have committed other sins that afflict the just.

Amos says that as a result of the mistreatment of the poor and the just, the Lord God of hosts will not accept the sacrificial offerings of His people. The greater concern of the Lord God of hosts is that "judgment run down as waters, and righteousness as a mighty stream" (Amos 5:24, KJV). Hosea also rebukes God's people, pointing out how the sin of Israel has affected the land. Because of the lying, stealing, adultery, etc. of God's people, the land literally suffers. In Hosea 7, God says that when He would have healed the land, more iniquity was discovered. However, the Lord offers restoration. Isaiah continues with the theme of the Lord not accepting Israel's offerings in Isaiah 1; however, he also says that if God's people put away evil, seek justice, and plead for the poor, the land will be restored. In other words, if they (and we) commit to doing right, restoration will take place.

In today's society, non-Christians need to see how much Christians are committed to justice and righteousness. One complaint from non-Christians that I heard quite often on the college campus was that Christians care only about themselves and about adding to their numbers, instead of being concerned with issues that everyone should care about. However, as we can see from the first four lessons of the fourth quarter, the Lord mandates that we not only care about injustices, but that we also repent and rid ourselves of any injustices that we as Christians are committing. The Lord challenges us to start with ourselves when it comes to righting injustices; when we do, He will bring change to the environment and to the people around us.

The next four lessons of this quarter continue with the theme of God's requirement of justice. In these lessons, the Lord speaks of the justice that He will bring. The prophet Micah continues to highlight the need for the people of Israel to act justly. Micah challenges us "to do justly, and to love mercy, and to walk humbly with [our] God"

(Micah 6:8, KJV). Zephaniah declares that God's justice will ultimately triumph over evil. Habakkuk announces that the unrighteous who have built their cities with the blood and labor of others will be doomed by the Lord of hosts. Finally, Jeremiah announces that the disobedient and the unjust will answer to the Lord of hosts.

The Lord requires His people to care about justice in every area. However, there are some areas in which we do not have the ability to make immediate changes. In such areas, we are required to pursue justice and trust God to bring it to pass in His time. Repeatedly in these passages, the Lord declares that He will bring justice. For example, in Zephaniah 3:8–9, the Lord requires us to wait on Him, and He will allow His people to call on His name and to serve Him in the end. All those who are opposed to God will be dealt with by Him in the end. In the meantime, we as Christians are called to live justly, be merciful to others, and keep walking with God.

The last four lessons of the fourth quarter continue to emphasize the need to do the right thing. Added into the equation is the need to keep our hope in God, be responsible for ourselves, and repent. In Lamentations, we are encouraged to wait on the Lord and seek Him. We are encouraged to place our hope in God, even in hard times. Ezekiel informs us that we are not to blame our sins on our fathers or our predecessors, but to take full responsibility for our own actions. The Lord says that He will judge each individual according to his or her own ways. Zechariah calls for all of us to return to God, a turning that once again includes taking care of the poor and overcoming evil. Zechariah says, "oppress not the widow, nor the fatherless, the stranger, nor the poor; and let none of you imagine evil against his brother in your heart" (Zechariah 7:10, KJV). Finally, Malachi reiterates how just God is in His judgment. The prophet uses vivid imagery to describe what will happen to those who have been unjust. He even foreshadows the end of time with his statements in Malachi 4:1.

In all 13 lessons of this quarter, the prophets are imparting more than just information to us, the people of God; they are imparting challenges. According to all these verses, what are we as Christians being called to do? The prophet Micah says it best: "He hath shewed thee, O man, what is good; and what doth the Lord require of thee, but to do justly, and to love mercy, and to walk humbly with thy God?" (Micah 6:8, KJV). First, we are called to seek justice. Injustices are happening all around us. Our call is to be just to others, to pursue and pray for justice, and to place our hope and trust in God that He will bring about ultimate justice. God also calls Christians to love mercy. As much as we are to pursue justice, we are also to be merciful to those who need to be shown mercy. Finally, Christians are to walk continuously with God, and He will show us when and how to pursue justice and mercy. Also, because God is our guide, He will convict us when we do wrong and show us when we need to ask for forgiveness and mercy from others.

As previously mentioned, we are in the midst of a postmodern generation. There are many theories in the Christian world as to the best way to minister in a postmodern society. In *Christian Apologetics in the Postmodern World*, three possible responses to postmodernity are given. One possible response is to continue to provide evidence of the truth of the Gospel. Although some postmodernists tend to pursue other "truths," Christians can provide evidence that the Gospel is the ultimate truth. Another possible response is to attack the critiques of Christianity and Western culture. Finally, the book argues that the key aspects of postmodernity can be used to support and defend orthodox Christianity. Postmodernists believe that "the truth" should have a positive impact on society. If we Christians pursue justice and mercy the way we should, postmodernists will come to understand that justice and mercy are parts of the main purpose of the Gospel. Also, seeing our mercy toward others will introduce non-Christians to the mercy and restorative power of Jesus Christ. It will help them see the kingdom of God as more than a club looking for new recruits. They will see it as a society of people who have been changed by God and want to see others changed as well. In other words, imparting the application of the Gospel to our lives as Christians will allow non-Christian postmodernists to hear the information of the Gospel.

Source

Phillips, Timothy, and Dennis Okholm, eds. *Christian Apologetics in the Postmodern World*. Westmont, Ill.: InterVarsity Press, 1995.

GODLINESS AND JUSTICE: TWO SIDES OF THE SAME COIN

by Rodrick Burton

Justice means many things to many people. For African Americans, justice often brings thoughts of historic *injustice* inflicted on us. To the patron in the barbershop or beauty shop, justice may mean "just us." To others, justice means punishing the guilty. But what does justice mean as defined by the Bible? Shouldn't Christians speak with absolute clarity concerning justice? In short, how is justice connected to godliness.

For the average person, justice is usually associated with the court system. Popular courtroom television shows capitalize on this association, and media coverage of popular court cases reinforce this view. Similarly, the average person associates the term "godliness" with the church and religion. Further exploration of the term might mean a treacherous walk on the plank of political correctness. In contemporary society, to acknowledge the "God" in "godliness" may mean offending a Hindu, an atheist, or a Wiccan. With that said, what should godliness mean to Christians?

God's love is manifested in these three things: godliness, mercy, and justice. To the Christian, godliness should mean a lifelong effort to conform to God's laws and wishes as they are manifested in Jesus Christ and His teachings. This conformity must not be the hollow piety that the prophets warned about, but a devoutness flowing from fellowship with God through Christ. God did not create us as robots with a "default setting" for love; He made us mentally free to accept or reject Him. Yet, as we study the Scriptures and meditate on the love shown to us through the sacrifice of Jesus, our desire to respond to this unmerited love should manifest itself in a lifestyle that is characterized by godliness.

What does godliness entail? Worship, of course, and praise, absolutely. These dispositions are aimed at God vertically, but what of our fellow man, with whom we coexist on a horizontal plane? How does justice come into play? Jesus called us to love all humanity as He did, including our enemies.

God's mercy was manifested as Jesus allowed Himself to be put to death for crimes He did not commit. In so doing, He abated the eternal death penalty we deserved as convicted sinners. It cannot be emphasized enough that, although we all deserved death, Christ secured our full pardon in the divine *supreme court*. This transaction leads to fidelity. The promise of eternal life is good because God's faithfulness (fidelity) is exhibited in His covenant with Abraham, which extends to all believers through Christ. This is fidelity and faithfulness indeed! God fills us with this fidelity through the indwelling Holy Spirit.

Lastly, God's love is manifested in justice. Outlaws and evildoers must pay. Wrongs committed are not forgotten but dealt with. Why is this? God knows His creation. He set boundaries out of love, and crossing these boundaries has consequences. God's rules and laws are typically viewed negatively because they are limiting; in reality, however, they protect us because sin has inclined us as humans to abuse our freedom. This is especially relevant in our society, where the cult of individuality trumps everything, even common sense. The new American mantra is that anything should be permitted as long as it breaks no laws. God knows us better than we know ourselves, and the contortion of justice into "just us" is an injustice to God, the Owner and Dispenser of justice.

So what does justice look like for those proponents of godliness? For some it means reaching out to members of our communities who are trapped in cycles of oppression. Just as the prophets Amos and Micah warned Israel that God was disgusted with the exploitation of the poor, He must also be disgusted as our most precious commidity—impressionable youth—are seduced into lifestyles of sexual exploitation and oppression. As proponents of godliness, Christians must strive to liberate our culture from the toxic embrace of an oppressive iconography. As proponents of godliness we must challenge the sexual exploitation of our culture and expose the vile wickedness that it is. To leave this ideology unchallenged is to deny justice to the weak and vulnerable in our society.

Godliness includes a relentless drive to extend fairness, truth, and mercy to all who enter our sphere of influence in order to ensure that *justice* is not for *just us,* but for everyone, believer and nonbeliever alike. It means looking at the crime in our communities and working with the police to see that offenders are punished for their crimes. We must work harder to rehabilitate offenders, mentoring them as they return to our communities so that they can be transformed from purveyors of injustice into champions of justice.

Justice is not about *just us.* It is about God's world, redeemed by the sacrifice of His Son. Because of His love for a fallen humanity, God sees that justice exists to repel the walls of inhumanity, which, without Him, would collapse on top of us. To exhibit godliness is to show God's love to all people. Therefore, when we act justly, we are exhibiting godliness—the love God wants all His children to exhibit.

BLACK PERSONALITY

REV. HENRY SOLES, COMMITTED TO DOING RIGHT

PROLIFIC GOSPEL COMPOSER

Rev. Henry Soles is the chaplain of the Chicago Bulls. One hour before each game, players, media members, and even members of the opposing team are invited to the chaplain's office for 20 minutes of prayer, Bible study, discussion, and maybe a song or two. Reverend Soles' prayers are never for one team or the other to win; he prays that each team will do its best and that there will be no injuries.

The players appreciate someone who cares about them, not just about their fat paychecks or their fame. Reverend Soles does just this. He provides a place where they can safely share what is on their hearts, knowing that what is said in the chapel remains there. Reverend Soles says, "Athletes are ordinary people with extraordinary gifts."

When Michael Jordan's father was brutally murdered, Michael came to Reverend Soles for spiritual counsel and consolation. Then, when Reverend Soles' mother died, Michael wore a black armband to the game to show his solidarity with him. This is the kind of relationship that Reverend Soles has with the players.

Being chaplain of the Bulls has opened up some exciting opportunities for ministry. Once, Reverend Soles and his wife, Rev. Effie Soles, led a team of NBA players to Nairobi, Kenya, where they shared basketball skills and the Word of God. As a result of their ministry, a number of African athletes made commitments to Christ.

Another time, Reverend Soles accompanied the Bulls to Osaka, the second largest city in Japan. Mayor Richard J. Daley of Chicago sent a letter of introduction to the mayor of Osaka, and Reverend Soles was able to use his connection to introduce some of the Japanese church leaders to their own mayor. Reverend Soles found that many Japanese were far more open to hearing the Gospel from an African American Christian than from a White American Christian.

Reverend Soles began his sports ministry when he was asked to do a chapel service for the Chicago Bears. Then he began focusing his attention on the Chicago White Sox, even accompanying them to spring training in Florida. It was hard for the players to be separated from their families, and they didn't even know if they might be cut from the team. During these times of stress, the players really needed lots of prayer.

But Reverend Soles does not just minister to the "up-and-in"; he also ministers to the "down-and-out." One of his passions is volunteering at Serenity House, a ministry for those recovering from addictions to drugs and alcohol. His work there earned him their Man of the Year award for 1996.

In addition, Reverend Soles is a board member of CHAD (Community Housing Association of DuPage). This organization was instrumental in building 100 housing units for low-income residents when there was a need for affordable housing in the western suburbs of Chicago. Reverend Soles is also vice president of Gospel Outreach, a youth ministry in the Robert Taylor Homes housing projects in Chicago. He also serves on the board of the DuPage Prevention Partnership and Koinonia House, a residence for ex-offenders returning to society. Besides being involved in all of these community activities, Reverend Soles and his wife are associate ministers at the DuPage A.M.E. Church in Lisle, Illinois.

We could go on about Reverend Soles' many accomplishments and ministries, but we are especially proud of him because he was the first editor at UMI (Urban Ministries, Inc.), the publisher of the book that you are reading at this very moment!

TEACHING TIPS

June 3
Bible Study Guide 1

1. Words You Should Know

A. Houses (Amos 5:11) *bayith* (Heb.)—Buildings that are used to dwell in. The rich in Amos's day had luxurious houses built out of hewn stone, which only the wealthiest could afford.

B. Seek (v. 14) *darash* (Heb.)—To inquire, ask, or search for. Amos encouraged his hearers to search for life in the living God, not in dead idols.

2. Teacher Preparation

A. Pray for wisdom, clarity, and understanding. Ask God to open hearts and spark genuine discussion during the class session.

B. Familiarize yourself with the content of this lesson, and study the Scripture verses provided in the Bible Background, Daily Bible Readings, and Focal Verses using multiple translations.

C. In addition, complete lesson 1 in the *Precepts For Living® Personal Study Guide.*

3. Starting the Lesson

A. Begin the lesson in prayer, concentrating on the Lesson Aim.

B. Ask the students to read the Keep in Mind verse aloud from the NIV or some other translation.

C. Introduce the students to Amos and to the instructions that he received from God. Tell the class that Amos was a humble, obedient man of God.

4. Getting into the Lesson

A. Ask for volunteers to read the Focal Verses.

B. Ask for another volunteer to read the Background section and The People, Places, and Times.

5. Relating the Lesson to Life

A. Discuss the exploitation that existed in Amos's time and the complacency of the rich and powerful.

B. Discuss the attitude of self-sufficiency described in the text and as it presently exists. Is there a great and ever-growing divide between the wealthy and the impoverished in today's society?

6. Arousing Action

A. Read In Focus. Ask the students to make an honest assessment of themselves. Are they living their lives for God, or are they living to obtain prestige and material possessions? Are they making the division between the rich and the poor more obvious? Ask each student to consider what he or she strives for daily, whether it is a life lived for God or a life lived for the world.

B. Ask each student to think of his or her immediate response upon seeing a homeless person. Give the students an opportunity to discuss their own personal encounters if possible.

C. Give the students an opportunity to complete the Follow the Spirit and Remember Your Thoughts sections.

Worship Guide

For the Superintendent or Teacher
Theme: Amos Challenges Injustice
Theme Song: "God Never Fails"
Scripture: Isaiah 30:18
Song: "What A Mighty God We Serve"
Meditation: Dear Lord, today's society is filled with many injustices and hardships. But I am glad that Your authority is not limited to the confines of people's thoughts and deeds. As we call upon You, O Lord, strengthen us to take action against injustice in our homes and in our community at large. Amen.

AMOS CHALLENGES INJUSTICE

Bible Background • AMOS 5:10–15, 21–24; 8:4–12; 2 KINGS 13:23–25
Printed Text • AMOS 5:10–15, 21–24   Devotional Reading • PSALM 82

Lesson Aim

By the end of the lesson, we will:

EXPLORE the themes of justice and judgment as presented in the book of Amos;

FEEL that injustice betrays the character of God and should be avoided; and

PRAY for courage to act against injustice, both in our personal lives and in our society.

Keep in Mind

"But let judgment run down as waters, and righteousness as a mighty stream" (Amos 5:24).

Focal Verses

Amos 5:10 They hate him that rebuketh in the gate, and they abhor him that speaketh upright-ly.

11 Forasmuch therefore as your treading is upon the poor, and ye take from him burdens of wheat: ye have built houses of hewn stone, but ye shall not dwell in them; ye have planted pleasant vineyards, but ye shall not drink wine of them.

12 For I know your manifold transgressions and your mighty sins: they afflict the just, they take a bribe, and they turn aside the poor in the gate from their right.

13 Therefore the prudent shall keep silence in that time; for it is an evil time.

14 Seek good, and not evil, that ye may live: and so the LORD, the God of hosts, shall be with you, as ye have spoken.

15 Hate the evil, and love the good, and establish judgment in the gate: it may be that the LORD God of hosts will be gracious unto the remnant of Joseph.

5:21 I hate, I despise your feast days, and I will not smell in your solemn assemblies.

22 Though ye offer me burnt offerings and your meat offerings, I will not accept them: neither will I regard the peace offerings of your fat beasts.

23 Take thou away from me the noise of thy songs; for I will not hear the melody of thy viols.

24 But let judgment run down as waters, and righteousness as a mighty stream.

In Focus

Shanice and Tamara had been friends since college. After gradu-ation, the two decided to share an apartment as roommates. Shanice wanted to live in the ren-ovated town houses where an old housing project had once stood. Many people who had lived their entire lives in the housing project had been forced to move as the area gentrified. Slowly, the old buildings in the neighborhood were replaced with upscale, luxu-ry town houses.

When Shanice and Tamara toured the neighborhood with a leasing agent, Shanice was impressed. After the tour, she said, "This area definitely fits my image. It looks very upscale." Tamara was quiet while Shanice talked to the leasing agent. Tamara walked out of the office while Shanice continued to talk. Shanice told the leasing agent that she would call her tomorrow. "I know we'll be residents of this community," Shanice reassured the agent as they said their good-byes.

When Shanice came outside, she saw Tamara talking to a homeless person. Shanice called out to her. "Come on, Tamara. We're going to be late for our appointment."

Tamara finished talking to the person and approached Shanice. "What are you talking about? We don't have any appointments this afternoon," said Tamara, looking confused.

"I know we don't have any appointments. I just wanted to

give you an opportunity to get away from that home-less man. I know you are drawn to anyone who needs help."

Tamara shook her head. "That *homeless* man's name is Albert. He used to live here before they ren-ovated this building. He told me that several former residents of this building are now either homeless or living in a shelter.

"Why is that my concern?" asked Shanice.

Tamara knew that Shanice was materialistic. She prayed that her friend would learn to lead a more selfless life. Concerned, Tamara asked, "Do you think that my conversation with Albert was just a coinci-dence?"

"No, I think he wants to discourage people from living in this neighborhood because he can no longer afford this luxury. He's poor, but I'm not and I don't plan to be. I plan to work so I can have nice things that tell others who I am," replied Shanice.

"You've given your life to God, right?" asked Tamara.

"Yes. I go to church and I give my tithes. That should be enough," retorted Shanice.

"Well, it's not. When we see something that is unfair, God wants us to take action. God does not stand for injustice or complacency. Your heart should be focused on sharing God's love with everyone regardless of their appearance—not just on materi-al possessions. When you give your life to God, He expects your life to reflect Jesus Christ. It's not about you, Shanice; it's about God and living for Him."

In today's lesson, we will explore the themes of justice and judgment in the book of Amos.

The People, Places, and Times

Amos. The name Amos means "burdened" or "one who is supported (by God)." Amos had not received training in the religious schools of his day and even denied having any connection with the formal reli-gious community. He was a Judean sheep breeder, a shepherd, a fig grower, and a layperson. Yet God commanded this humble, reluctant servant to speak for Him (Amos 7:15).

When God called Amos to prophesy, Israel had

already split into the northern and southern king-doms, which occurred after King Solomon died (see 1 Kings 12:1–22:53). Amos was from the southern kingdom of Judah. However, God called him to be a spokesman to the northern kingdom around 750 B.C., when Israel was at the height of its prosperity and power. God used Amos to carry His message to a stiff-necked, disobedient people. Amos gave a prophetic message about the future of various cities—from Damascus, a Syrian city, to Gaza, a Philistine city.

Amos is called a "minor" prophet because his prophetic book is not as long as those of other prophets; however, his message is in no way minor.

Tekoa. Tekoa was Amos's hometown, located in the rugged sheep country of Judah approximately 10 miles south of Jerusalem and 12 miles west of the Dead Sea. Amos made his living from the wilderness of the dry pastureland near Tekoa.

Background

Amos prophesied during a time of peace under Jeroboam II, who became king of Israel in 793 B.C., and Uzziah (Azariah), who began to reign in Judah in 792 B.C. When God gave Amos the vision of His future judgment, Israel and Judah were economically sta-ble. Amos's prophecy was to all the surrounding nations as well as to Judah and Israel because each nation refused to follow God's commands. Selfishness, materialism, and sin were rampant, and God wanted His people to know that He would neither forget nor tolerate such behavior.

Unfortunately, the rich sought to gain greater riches at the expense of the poor. The ruling powers reserved the rich soil in the valley for growing cash crops such as wheat. This resulted in the peasant class having smaller land holdings and therefore being barely able to produce enough crops to sustain their lifestyle. At the same time, trade with the Phoenicians increased the material possessions of the nobility and merchant class, leaving the peasant class exploited, in servitude, and in debt. Illegal and immoral slavery resulted from overtaxation of the poor and land grabbing by the rich. These things bred cruelty and indifference toward the poor. Amos warned the corrupt businessmen that God was angry and would show no mercy when He judged them.

Sources

Life Application Study Bible. Wheaton, Ill.: Tyndale House Publishers, Inc., 1996, 1657–1671.

Pfeiffer, Charles F., Howard F. Vos, and John Rea, eds. *Wycliffe Bible Dictionary.* Peabody, Mass.: Hendrickson Publishers, 1998, 61.

At-A-Glance

1. Justice for All: A Plea to Repent
(Amos 5:10–13)
2. Turn to God: A Plea for Restoration
(vv. 14–15)
3. True Praise and Worship
(5:21–24)

"But let judgment run down as waters, and righteousness as a mighty stream" (Amos 5:24).

In Depth

1. Justice for All: A Plea to Repent (Amos 5:10–13)

In biblical times, it was considered commendable for the rich to defend the poor (Isaiah 5:7; 28:17). Unfortunately, the relationship between Israel's poor and rich had deteriorated. The poor were being mistreated and abused by the rich, and God was not pleased. God's prophet, Amos, mourned for Israel as he reiterated God's passionate plea for justice.

Amos refers to "the gate," which was the location of the town courts. The poor depended on the court system to be fair and just. Justice should have been rendered and upheld at the gate. Instead, contrary to covenant law, the rich landowners began to abuse the court system by bribing judges, who in turn ignored the laws (Deuteronomy 16:18–20). Ultimately, this led to the poor losing their land to the rich landowners. When the poor did not have enough money to pay their taxes, they used grain as payment. In the end, the rich landowners lived in magnificent houses, while the poor were relegated to working the land as slaves of the rich.

God was not pleased that the rich were taking the possessions of the poor. The rich boldly sinned when they prospered through unfair taxation and land grabbing. They had become pious and worshiped idols. In view of their behavior, God, through His prophet Amos, told them that they would never enjoy the houses they had built on the land that had once belonged to the poor, nor would they drink the wine from the vineyards they had planted.

God created all of humanity. God expects us as Christians to be fair and just with everyone. He expects us to stand up and take action when we encounter injustice. We can pray to God for strength to act against injustice in all areas of our lives. Amos was not intimidated by the religious leaders whom he encountered. He had a prophetic message from God that he spoke boldly. Today, God can give us courage to stand for justice and against injustice.

2. Turn to God: A Plea for Restoration (vv. 14–15)

Amos encouraged Israel to turn to God. The message is the same today. We must return to God if we have turned to the world and injustice. Every day we must cling to God and speak to Him in prayer.

Amos hoped the Israelites would worship God, who otherwise would send judgment. Amos hoped they would live as God had intended. The message is the same for the world today. We must seek God and live according to His Word. The Bible tells us to live for God. When we talk to God, He will instruct us. Our lives are meaningless and without justice unless we seek life in the living God. There is no real life in material possessions. We must seek God at all times. He desires justice for all, and when we follow Him, we uphold justice.

3. True Praise and Worship (5:21–24)

The life of Israel was filled with apostasy, which is the act of rebelling against or falling away from what one has believed. Amos warned the Israelites to turn from idolatry. He announced the "day of the Lord," or God's impending judgment. God's promises to His people are still true today. God promised that He would hear the Israelites and accept their sacrifices as long as they truly worshiped Him. When the Israelites turned from God, He refused to hear them or accept their sacrifices, deeming their worship to be false. Likewise, God is not pleased when our worship is a charade. He hates it when we try to look good through our worship while our lives are sinful and our hearts are not sincere. God cannot hear our prayers or accept our worship when we are hypocrites. Our image in public does not matter as much as our attitude toward God. Are you sincere in your worship? Are you focused on pleasing God and not the world?

When our worship is not sincere, God does not accept it. It is empty worship. God considered Israel's worship to be empty. Their worship was for show; it was not from a sincere heart. Worship without heartfelt obedience and sincere commitment to God is empty. The result was God's judgment. We are all accountable to God. We all must answer to Him and give an account for our lives and for our sins. God's judgment is inevitable and unavoidable. He sees and evaluates the motives of everyone. When God's judgment does come, it will be fair and just.

Search the Scriptures

1. When Amos prophesied, what were the rich doing to the poor (Amos 5:11)?

2. How did God characterize the times that Amos live and prophesied (v. 13)?

3. What did God want His chosen people to do to redeem the times (v. 14)?

4. What had the Children of Israel been worshiping (v. 26)?

Discuss the Meaning

1. Since we are vessels of God, we should stand for justice. Amos had a prophetic message for the people of Israel concerning prosperity. How is this message relevant to today's society?

2. Believing in God is a personal and communal experience, and God expects us to take a stand against injustice. Amos spoke boldly against the rich who oppressed the poor. Amos was humble and obedient to the will of God. Discuss ways that we can address the injustices in today's society with compassion.

Lesson in Our Society

In today's lesson, Amos was obedient to God's instructions. He pronounced God's judgment upon Israel. Just as in biblical times, God requires justice and truth from those who follow Him. As believers, we must remember that nothing has meaning without God. We are vessels that God can use to end injustice. We can make many excuses to be complacent, but God requires that we treat all of humanity with love, including the poor, the downtrodden, and all who have been treated unfairly.

Make It Happen

Complacency ends when action begins. Seek God with a sincere heart. Make an effort to end social injustice. You can volunteer at shelters or help with a community organization that helps the impoverished. One person can make a difference. Talk to your family and friends, and encourage them to open their eyes to see the injustice in your community. Encourage them to ask God for direction and for the courage to do His will.

Follow the Spirit

What God wants me to do:

_____

_____

Remember Your Thoughts

Special insights I have learned:

_____

_____

More Light on the Text
Amos 5:10–15, 21–24

The book of Amos discusses God's impending punishment of Israel at the hands of an enemy nation. The Israelites' sins included wallowing in sin and perverting justice. King Jeroboam (786–746 B.C.), the son of Joash, was the ungodly leader of the northern kingdom of Israel. It is true that he had managed to secure the nation from external threats by the surrounding nations and had succeeded in extending its borders on all fronts; however, he had led the nation into idolatry and the abuse of justice. The southern kingdom of Judah, ruled by Azariah son of Amaziah (783–742 B.C.), was in a subservient relationship with and paid tribute to the northern kingdom. As a result, there was no immediate sign of an enemy power ready to pounce on Israel and secure an easy victory over her. However, the prophet Amos received a vision from the Lord and foresaw the eventual judgment of Israel. He called for the destruction of the royal temple at Bethel in the northern kingdom, which had become the center for collecting revenues, offerings, and tributes. The temple became the leading symbol for abominable activities that were set over against godly systems of justice in the region.

10 They hate him that rebuketh in the gate, and they abhor him that speaketh uprightly.

In ancient Israel, the "gate," as described here, represented the place where justice was sought. It was the source of legal authority and a platform for truth and integrity. Issues of fairness, justice, and equity concerning the poor, oppressed, and needy were legally dealt with at the gates of the city. The phrase, "him that rebuketh" (Heb. *yakach*, **yaw-KAHH**) was often used in a legal context. It referred to a person who was actively involved in legal issues in courts to foster truth and justice (Genesis 31:37; Job 9:33). The legal, moral, and spiritual standards of Israel were abused and perverted to the point that anyone who stood up to confront the unjust system was labeled as an enemy of society. This seems to illustrate the fact that whenever the conscience of a society becomes seared to the point that it consistently pursues what is immoral and ungodly, those who dare to stand up for the truth are hated and are portrayed as infidels. Yet such situations should not discourage an upright person or prevent him or her from standing boldly for the sake of moral integrity, even though doing so may displease the "powers that be," for it always pays to obey God rather than humans. As believers we have been called to stand our ground against all forms of injustice in society, which are contrary to the will of God (Isaiah 58:1–14; James 2:1–5).

Jesus taught His disciples to pray that the kingdom of God might come. The implication is that we should not only pray, but also work in a purposeful manner on a daily basis with the aim of transforming the fallen world system in which we live. We do this by employing sound and healthy principles from God's Word to impact the minds and hearts of society.

The Lord Jesus, our great example, declared His "manifesto" prior to beginning His earthly ministry. He was anointed to preach the Gospel to the poor, to heal the brokenhearted, to preach deliverance to the captives, to recover sight to the blind, to set free those who are oppressed, and to preach God's acceptable Year of Jubilee, which is freedom, justice, and liberty (Luke 4:18–19). The prophets of the Old Testament and the disciples of the New Testament spoke forthrightly against all forms of evil social structures and systems that were perpetrating injustice and inequity. God has called us as believers to do the same wherever we find ourselves.

11 Forasmuch therefore as your treading is upon the poor, and ye take from him burdens of wheat: ye have built houses of hewn stone, but ye shall not dwell in them; ye have planted pleasant vineyards, but ye shall not drink wine of them.

The Scriptures clearly teach that justice is an attribute of God, and we should emulate His characteristics and qualities (Acts 10:34–35; Romans 1, 2; 3:23). The Bible describes God as one who is morally perfect and always takes action against sin and injustice. Accordingly, He deals justly with ALL people, rich and poor, meting out punishment (Genesis 2:17; Romans 1:32) and rewarding (Deuteronomy 7:9–13; Psalm 58:11; Hebrews 11:26) as necessary. Because God is righteous and just, He defends and vindicates the oppressed whenever they are unjustly treated. He vowed, through Amos's prophecy, to punish the wicked leadership—indeed, all evildoers—by preventing them from enjoying their ill-gotten treasure and wealth.

God is just and holy. We are created in the likeness of God and are therefore expected to reflect these qualities when dealing with others. Israel displeased God when both the leadership and the people failed to deal fairly with the prevailing situation, in which the oppressed were manipulated, taken advantage of, and marginalized. We should learn from their experience. When we use our position, status, and power to wrongly acquire wealth by taking advantage of the marginalized and powerless in society, it can have consequences similar to those that befell Israel. We should be ready to stand with and defend the poor and needy in their fight against social injustice and be committed to always treating the weak and downtrodden with fairness and dignity. Failure to do so will bring God's displeasure on us.

12 For I know your manifold transgressions and your mighty sin: they afflict the just, they take a bribe, and they turn aside the poor in the gate from their right.

God knew about the nature and scope of Israel's "sin culture." The weak were being deprived of their rights and denied the opportunity to fight for their rights in the legal system. God is willing to forgive the sins of those who transgress His laws and principles when they repent. However, He abhors deliberate and consistent sin among His people (Hebrews 10:26–29). The term "just" (Heb. *tsaddiyq*, **tsad-DEEK**), refers to a person's innocence as declared by due process of the law (Exodus 23:7–8). The great Judge and King who sits on His throne with all authority and power fights against all kinds of injustice and wrongdoing stemming from lack of due process. But He gives rewards for deeds that are justly done. The biblical view of justice reveals God as the source and dispenser of true freedom and liberty for all humankind (John 8:31–35). The fallen world system in which we live, with all its imperfections and depravities, does not often reflect the kind of justice that is achieved through due process of the law. Ethnic, religious, racial, and social identities are exploited and twisted to undermine due process based on justice and fairness. However, as believers who are called to bear witness of God's truth, we should allow ourselves to be influenced by the Holy Spirit to refrain from such ungodly tendencies. We have been set aside by God to NOT "turn aside the poor in the gate from their rights."

13 Therefore the prudent shall keep silence in that time: for it is an evil time.

When the day of God's judgment comes, neither persons of integrity and sound moral judgment nor the wicked will be able to dismiss it! God has a way of proclaiming His righteousness and justice. Even in our work for justice, God demonstrates His sovereign justice among the nations. It will be impossible for anyone to deny or challenge the moral and legal basis of God's actions. The discerning heart need only rely on God's infinite wisdom as He does what is right in His own sight.

14 Seek good, and not evil, that ye may live: and so the LORD, the God of hosts, shall be with you, as ye have spoken.

The word "seek" (Heb. *darash*, **daw-RASH**) refers to one who diligently inquires after God or makes a total commitment to His worship or service (Genesis 25:22; Deuteronomy 18:11). When the whole commu-

nity and the entire fabric of society in which we live begin to say and do things that run counter to God's purposes and biblical truth, the committed person who desires to please God at all times must devote him or herself to seeking and understanding God's will so that they can walk in it. The Scripture teaches that we should ask, seek, and knock at the door of God's righteousness and before His throne of justice, and He will make a way for us (Luke 11:9–13). As we walk through His open door, we will be showered with blessings, not only in this life, but in the life to come. We live because He lives! By His very nature, God is the defender of people of integrity and low estate who lay themselves on the altar of sacrifice for the sake of His kingdom. God gives wisdom, grace, and strength to enable us to overcome any inhibiting and misleading situations that may come our way.

15 Hate the evil, and love the good, and establish judgment in the gate: it may be that the LORD God of hosts will be gracious unto the remnant of Joseph.

God admonished His people not only to refrain from sin, but to hate it with all their souls, spirits, and bodies, and to walk in a godly manner, loving Him and their neighbors. As people who are created in the image of God (*imago Dei*), we must "be like Him" (Genesis 1:16–28; 1 John 17:18). God is love. We are created to reflect His love by loving Him (vertical relationship) and all people (horizontal relationships) in all that we say and do (Colossians 3:16–17). Our decision to live as God's people, who are committed to engage unjust and evil structures or ideas with the principles of God's Word, helps to transform human life and society according to God's purpose. Establishing good judgment "in the gates" can be done through actively engaging social, economic, spiritual, and cultural evils, which are contrary to a biblical worldview. We must help to shape the world in which we live according to God's purpose. When God's people set their hearts and minds to faithfully serve and worship Him in spirit and truth and turn away from what is evil, the favor of God rests upon them. This kind of favor flows graciously to the generations of the righteous who please Him. On the other hand, when God declares His judgment on an evil generation, He also graciously makes a way of escape for those who heed His warning and repent. "The remnant of Joseph" (v. 15) to whom God promised to be gracious are those in society who decide to do what is right when they heed God's warning against sin. The implication is that, in any society where evil and injustice are rampant, God's Spirit still has the power to work in the hearts and minds of those who decide to turn their lives over to God. Let us remember that when God decides to judge His people for wrongdoing, He still shows mercy to those who walk in His way with integrity.

5:21 I hate, I despise your feast days, and I will not smell in your assemblies. 22 Though ye offer me burnt offerings and your meat offerings, I will not accept them: neither will I regard the peace offerings of your fat beasts.

God rejected the feast days of His people because they were observed in sin and perversion. He minced no words in telling them that He would not accept such ungodly feasts, nor would He look upon such offerings with favor. What God was looking for was upright and diligent hearts behind all the religious services. He also required that all the ceremonial activities and rituals be in accordance with the divine guidelines He had given His people. Obedience is always better than sacrifice. The lesson here is that, according to "God's logic," the means justifies the end. He is not interested in our rituals, ceremonies, and religious events if they are outwardly (or mechanically) nice, but lack truth and integrity based on His perfect will. God requires the believer to have a broken and contrite heart that seeks to totally please Him. Religious services that are devoid of His holy presence and have nothing to do with justice, fairness, and mercy are abominations to Him.

Outwardly impressive public or religious acts of goodwill that are selfishly done do not move the heart of God. The phrase "your feast days" (Heb. *chag*, **khag**) refers to the three main festivals that God established in Israel: Passover, Pentecost, and the Feast of Tabernacles (Exodus 23:14–19;

Deuteronomy 16:13–17). All of these festivals were being abused by Israel at this time in their history. God rejected what Israel did in these feasts, which had a form of godliness but lacked the power thereof. The implication is that events, activities, or procedures may be established by God Himself, but His people can pervert, abuse, and misuse them to achieve their own selfish ends. This usually occurs when God's people begin to consistently live in sin, turning their hearts toward the world, the flesh, and Satan without repentance. Our "solemn assemblies" today may be likened to some of the church traditions and activities that some Christians grew up performing in their local churches, but that have lost their spiritual significance. The keeping of ordinances like the Lord's Supper and water baptism could be hated by God when, as with the feasts of Passover, Pentecost, and Tabernacles, their real spiritual value or significance is lost.

23 Take thou away from me the noise of thy songs; for I will not hear the melody of thy viols.

Celebrations and rejoicing in God's presence played an important part in Israel's temple worship established by God. The Israelites used many kinds of musical instruments to praise and worship God for His goodness and faithfulness (2 Chronicles 7ff; Psalm 149). Making a joyful noise in praise to our Maker as an act of our spiritual worship is a good thing. However, when the noise of our songs becomes mere outward ritual, centered on ourselves and not on God and His glory, it becomes empty and unacceptable to Him. What God required as an act of true worship—something that was missing in Israel's approach to singing and making melody to the Lord—was a total commitment to doing what was right before Him regarding justice and righteousness toward the poor and powerless.

24 But let judgment run down as waters, and righteousness as a mighty stream.

God illustrates the nature of judgment (justice) and righteousness by using the phrases "run down as water" and " as a mighty stream," respectively, which speak of the ongoing and unobstructed movement of an ever-flowing body of water. These phrases also describe how justice and righteousness are to be viewed among God's people: We are to stay within the boundaries of His divine covenant, which should be carried out in a consistent manner as long as we serve Him. The issue is to understand how the consistency of God's dealings with His people is based on His nature and character. God never changes. He is not haphazard in His dealings with humankind. His ability to keep His word in accordance with His purpose should be a great lesson for all God's people as we walk with Him and relate to others in our families, communities, and societies. God's judgment and righteousness, expressed as they are through His love and holiness, should always be foundational pillars of reference in our walk with the Lord.

Daily Bible Readings

M: A Plea for Justice
Psalm 82:1–8
T: Where Is Justice and Truth?
Isaiah 59:9–15
W: Do What Is Just
Jeremiah 22:1–5
T: God Admonishes Israel
Amos 3:1–10
F: Protect the Poor
Amos 8:4–8
S: Seek Good, Not Evil
Amos 5:10–15
S: Let Justice Roll Down
Amos 5:20–25

TEACHING TIPS

June 10
Bible Study Guide 2

1. Words You Should Know

A. Truth (Hosea 4:1) *'emeth* (Heb.)—Faithfulness, sureness, stability. The prophet Hosea used the term to show that there was no stability in the land because God's statutes, God's edicts, were not being obeyed.

B. Mourn (v. 3) *'abal* (Heb.)—To lament (agonize, grieve, groan). Because the sin and disobedience of God's chosen people are so rampant, there are individual and environmental agonizing, grieving, and groaning throughout the land—widespread suffering.

2. Teacher Preparation

A. Prepare for the lesson by reading the Bible Background verses. Prayerfully meditate on the Devotional Reading.

B. Study the Focal Verses, paying special attention to the Keep in Mind verse.

C. Read More Light on the Text and complete lesson 2 in the *Precepts For Living® Personal Study Guide*.

D. Review the Teaching Tips and plan how you want to present the lesson.

3. Starting the Lesson

A. Concentrate on the Lesson Aim as you begin the lesson in prayer.

B. Ask for volunteers to read the Focal Verses.

C. Introduce the students to Hosea. Tell the students that Hosea was obedient to God's command to find a wife. Inform the students that Hosea's love for his unfaithful wife, Gomer, mirrors God's unconditional love for the Children of Israel and for all humanity.

4. Getting into the Lesson

A. Ask for a volunteer to read the In Focus story. Ask the students to comment on how the story relates to today's lesson.

B. Ask for a volunteer to read the Bible Background.

C. Ask the students to comment on the fact that Hosea knew Gomer would be unfaithful before he married her.

5. Relating the Lesson to Life

A. Read The People, Places, and Times.

B. Have the students comment briefly on the love of Hosea for Gomer and the love that God has for humanity today. Ask the students to comment on spiritual and physical adultery.

C. Read Lesson in Our Society. Give the students time to make suggestions.

6. Arousing Action

A. Ask the students to derive a specific plan to complete the Make It Happen assignment.

B. Give the students an opportunity to complete the Follow the Spirit and Remember Your Thoughts sections.

C. Remind the students to read the Daily Bible Readings for the week, which will help them grow in their walk with God.

D. Close the class with prayer.

HOSEA PREACHES GOD'S ACCUSATION AGAINST ISRAEL

Bible Background • HOSEA 4:1–4; 7:1–2; 12:7–9; 14:1–3; 2 KINGS 15:8–10
Printed Text • HOSEA 4:1–4; 7:1–2; 12:8–9   Devotional Reading • HOSEA 14

Lesson Aim

By the end of the lesson, we will:

KNOW that although God is displeased when we sin, He forgives and restores us when we truly repent;

FEEL the need to confess and be restored when we sin; and

ASK God to forgive us for any known sin of acting callously or selfishly.

Keep in Mind

"Hear the word of the LORD, ye children of Israel: for the LORD hath a controversy with the inhabitants of the land, because there is no truth, nor mercy, nor knowledge of God in the land" (Hosea 4:1).

Focal Verses

Hosea 4:1 Hear the word of the LORD, ye children of Israel: for the LORD hath a controversy with the inhabitants of the land, because there is no truth, nor mercy, nor knowledge of God in the land.

2 By swearing, and lying, and killing, and stealing, and committing adultery, they break out, and blood toucheth blood.

3 Therefore shall the land mourn, and every one that dwelleth therein shall languish, with the beasts of the field, and with the fowls of heaven; yea, the fishes of the sea also shall be taken away.

4 Yet let no man strive, nor reprove another: for thy people are as they that strive with the priest.

7:1 When I would have healed Israel, then the iniquity of Ephraim was discovered, and the wickedness of Samaria: for they commit falsehood; and the thief cometh in, and the troop of robbers spoileth without.

2 And they consider not in their hearts that I remember all their wickedness: now their own doings have beset them about; they are before my face.

12:8 And Ephraim said, Yet I am become rich, I have found me out substance: in all my labours they shall find none iniquity in me that were sin.

9 And I that am the LORD thy God from the land of Egypt will yet make thee to dwell in tabernacles, as in the days of the solemn feast.

In Focus

William and Debra were high school sweethearts who attended the same church. They had made a commitment to God and to each other at an early age. When they went to different colleges, they committed to be faithful to their relationship. William was the first man whom Debra had loved. While at college, Debra maintained her faithfulness to William by not dating anyone. She called William every week and wrote to him when she had time. She was committed to her love for him.

William was at college on a basketball scholarship. He did not have much time between studying and practicing to write to Debra. He loved Debra, but he struggled to remain faithful to her. He knew that he planned to marry Debra, so he didn't think the "college days" really mattered. William always told himself, "Debra is my heart. I would never hurt her." Nevertheless, William had many female admirers and did not remain faithful to Debra.

Finally, one Christmas, the year before they were to graduate, William proposed to Debra, who quickly accepted his proposal. Before they were married, the couple counseled with William's pastor on God's expectations for their marriage. The pastor encouraged the couple to pray together and to be honest with one another. He reminded them that marriage is a gift from God that He Himself designed. After the first session, Debra said, "We have always treated our commitment to one another seriously," but William looked away and did not comment.

Soon after their marriage, the

couple decided they wanted to start a family. When they did not become pregnant immediately, Debra became concerned. She made an appointment with her physician for a thorough physical. One week later the doctor called her back for a follow-up appointment and requested that William come to the appointment with her. Once seated in the doctor's office, the doctor said, "I have determined the reason why you have not conceived. Debra, you have a sexually transmitted disease that has caused some scaring and we need to treat immediately. William, I will need to check you as well." Debra was speechless and almost fainted. William was shocked and at a loss for words. He realized that it was his past behavior that had caused this dilemma—how could he tell Debra the truth about his unfaithfulness?

In today's lesson, unfaithfulness had become a problem between God and His chosen people, Israel. Because they worshiped other gods and broke their covenant with the one true God, they were going to be judged.

The People, Places, and Times

Hosea. The name Hosea means "salvation." Hosea served from 753 to 715 B.C. as a prophet to the northern kingdom of Israel. He came to be called a "minor" prophet due to the relatively short length of his prophetic book. Hosea was obedient to God's directive to marry a whore, Gomer, who was unfaithful to him and would cause him many headaches and heartaches. Hosea's marriage to Gomer is a picture of the relationship between a faithful God and unfaithful Israel. It illustrates the love of a merciful but jealous God for His sinful people.

Gomer. Gomer was Hosea's unfaithful wife, the daughter of Diblaim. According to the *Wycliffe Bible Dictionary*, the name Gomer comes from a Hebrew term signifying "lump or double cakes of figs and raisins." Some theologians believe that the name is figurative, i.e., "Gomer, the daughter of raisin cakes," meaning that she was wholly given up to her harlotry, since raisin cakes were used in certain fertility cult rites (457). She was also the mother of

Jezreel, Lo-ruhamah, and Lo-ammi (the second and third children may not have been Hosea's). As Gomer violated her sacred vows of marriage to Hosea, so did Israel act toward God.

Source
Pfeiffer, Charles F., Howard F. Vos, and John Rea, eds. *Wycliffe Bible Dictionary.* Peabody, Mass.: Hendrickson Publishers, 1998.

Background

The prophet Hosea wrote the book of Hosea around 715 B.C. and recorded events that took place between 753 and 715 B.C. Hosea's prophetic years spanned the reigns of Uzziah through Hezekiah as kings of Judah. Jeroboam II was the first of seven kings of Israel during this time, all of whom were wicked and promoted oppression of the poor, increased taxation, and idolatry with no regard for God. Because of political turmoil, the kings turned to foreign alliances. They had illicit relationships with Assyria and Egypt in an effort to bolster their military might. Israel became subject to Assyria and was required to pay tribute, and the Assyrians robbed Israel of her resources. After Samaria fell in 722 B.C., Israel went into captivity.

When Hosea prophesied, the people were greedy. The Children of Israel had accepted and were practicing the idolatry and immoral behavior of the Canaanites who surrounded them. They were unfaithful to God. God sustained Israel through agriculture, but there was an economic crisis due to Israel's sinfulness. Thanks to God's covenant agreement, Israel had provisions of grain, oil, clothing, and wool. Although God provided, Israel stepped outside the covenant relationship and worshiped other gods, including Baal, giving these other gods credit for providing them with gold and silver. The Israelites ignored the fact that these other gods were false. Instead, they attempted to combine God and Baal to receive all the benefits of a good harvest. God, through Hosea, let His people know that they needed to turn from their wicked ways and turn back to Him.

In Depth

1. God's Disobedient People: God Charges Israel (Hosea 4:1–4)

Hosea charged Israel with disobedience. The nation of Israel was suffering from moral and spiritual decay. God was not pleased that the religious leaders of Israel had not turned the people from idolatry. The people did not have faith in God. Instead, they turned to Baal, a false god.

God does not accept behavior that does not recognize His lordship. Murder had occurred in Israel without much concern over its existence. The behavior of the Israelites resulted in ecological crisis and violence.

Leaders are held accountable because they provide instruction. God held the religious leaders accountable for the events that had occurred in Israel. The religious leaders led the Israelites into idolatry and immorality. The priests exhibited faithlessness. The leaders lacked good judgment due to sexual indulgence and insobriety. God blamed the religious leaders and held them accountable for their failure to lead.

Israel had broken her covenant with God, just as Gomer was unfaithful to Hosea. Israel did not have "truth, nor mercy, nor knowledge of God" (Hosea 4:1). There was no loyalty, devotion, or intellectual understanding of God's authority and covenant relationship with Israel. When Hosea charged Israel with sin, he listed five of the Ten Commandments. The punishment for their sins was a drought that would have a direct impact upon the people. The religious

leaders, including the priests, did not teach God's law. As a result, God would end the line of priests. The priests did not teach the people the knowledge of God, and He held the priests accountable. Although God loved Israel faithfully, she did not respond to His love. Like Gomer, Israel was unfaithful to God and was spiritually adulterous toward Him. Later, God warned Israel, through Hosea, of a final judgment.

Even as believers, we make mistakes. We must turn to God and ask to be forgiven in order to restore our fellowship with Him. Although we can blame others for our sinfulness, we must take responsibility for our actions and seek God. When we blame others, we do not feel a need to seek forgiveness. We do not think that we have committed sin. We can easily see the sins of someone else, but God's focus is on us. We must look within ourselves and see our lack of faith and our own sinfulness. We must seek the forgiveness of God, who is merciful. He will restore us if we repent and turn to Him.

2. God's Disobedient People: God Knows (7:1–2)

God desired the love of Israel, just as Hosea desired the love of Gomer. God allowed Hosea to feel what He felt many times with Israel. Israel's faith wavered. Although other prophets had warned the people, they continued to sin. Israel's relationship with God deteriorated through spiritual adultery, even as Gomer's relationship with Hosea deteriorated through physical adultery. Both types of adultery lead to alienation, disappointment, estrangement, and hurt.

God knows everything. He is omniscient. God also sees everything. He is present everywhere (omnipresent). We dare not believe that we can go through life with no accountability. Israel persisted in her sinfulness and had contempt for divine justice. Several kings were murdered in coups. God's gracious dealings with Israel exposed the "sins of Ephraim . . . and the crimes of Samaria" (Hosea 7:1, NIV). Israel seemed to be useless to God.

Like Israel, we may be full of sin and even seem useless, yet we can have a relationship with God that makes us worthwhile in this world. God is holy and detests sin, but God is also love; therefore, He seeks the best for the sinner. When Jesus Christ died on the cross, justice met grace and mercy. They are gifts from God, and we could never merit them on our own. There is nothing the world can offer that is more worthwhile than a life lived for God and with God. We must turn and commit ourselves to living a life committed to God. God calls us to love and obey Him.

3. God's Disobedient People: God's Invitation (12:8–9)

Hosea teaches a lesson to Israel that is based on the story of Jacob, who wrestled with God. Jacob recognized his spiritual dependence on God. Hosea wanted Israel to recognize that she needed to return to God. The Children of Israel needed to reestablish a relationship with God based on justice and trust in Him completely. Likewise, we must submit to God in all areas of life.

Israel thought they were self-sufficient and ignored their history. They failed to realize that God had always provided for them. Israel continued to reject the messages from the prophets. God would send Israel into exile, away from their land and homes. God compared the exile to the Feast of Tabernacles, which commemorated His protection of the Israelites as they wandered through the wilderness for 40 years. Israel was condemned because she was materialistic and dishonest in her transactions. This condemnation would come in the form of bondage.

As believers, we expose ourselves to the judgment of God when we are disobedient to Him. God does not want to destroy or condemn us; He loves us, but He also desires that we as His children are loyal and just. We should never be arrogant about our accomplishments. God provides all opportunities, resources, and blessings.

Search the Scriptures

1. Why was Israel suffering (Hosea 4:1)?
2. How many of the Ten Commandments had Israel disobeyed (v. 2)?
3. What had Israel "considered not in their hearts" (7:2)?

4. What was God's promise to the Children of Israel (12:9)?

Discuss the Meaning

1. As believers, we must constantly seek to serve God and turn from sin. There is a constant battle between our flesh, or sinful nature, and our spiritual nature. When we sin, why doesn't God immediately confront us in our sin? Discuss the opportunities that God gives us to repent.

2. Ask the students to recognize that leadership is an important responsibility. Remind the students that God blamed Israel's leadership for not teaching the people the knowledge of Himself. Discuss why God blamed the leadership. Ask the students who serve in leadership positions if they realize the significance and the responsibility that accompany their position.

3. God compassionately loves all of humanity. When we sin and sever our relationship with God, He desires that we repent, or turn wholeheartedly from our sin to Him. Ask the students to personally consider their emotions when they sin.

Lesson in Our Society

In today's lesson, the prophet Hosea personally experiences the relationship that God had with Israel. As Christians, we must turn from the temptations of the world and turn to God. God desires a loving, faithful relationship with each one of us. Although all blessings come from God, we cannot hold them in higher esteem than we do God. When we sin, we must repent, make a definite change in our behavior, and return to a faithful relationship with God.

Although we sin, God loves us and desires to have an intimate relationship with us. When we sin, we create a barrier to our relationship with God. Our commitment to God has been affected because we have been disloyal to Him. When we live in total disregard for God and become self-sufficient, we no longer focus on Him. The safety and security of a relationship with God is gone. We must repent and ask Him for forgiveness. We must never let personal gain, material possessions, or achievement make us forget God.

As believers, we must not compromise with the standards of society. We are accountable to God. The world may be selfish, but we stand on the foundation of our Heavenly Father, who is able to sustain us. We base our standards on the Word of God, our "instruction book" for life.

Make It Happen

Reach out to someone who has been victimized. Tell him or her about the love of God and the strength that God gives. Encourage youth to seek a standard that transcends the idols of name brands, materialism, and wealth. Each of us as believers can make a difference when we pray to God for direction and take action. God does not want us to sit on our hands. We must set our standards according to God's Word. Seek God's guidance in starting a discussion of trends and standards of the world. Give God's response to the many things that keep us from being faithful to Him.

Follow the Spirit

What God wants me to do:

_____

_____

Remember Your Thoughts

Special insights I have learned:

_____

_____

More Light on the Text

Hosea 4:1–4; 7:1–2; 12:8–9

1 Hear the word of the LORD, ye children of Israel: for the LORD has a controversy with the inhabitants of the land, because there is no truth, nor mercy, nor knowledge of God in the land.

This chapter opens with a "call to attention" from the prophet. It has to do with God's lawsuit against His people Israel, because of their failure to keep the terms of their covenant with Him. The word "controversy" (Heb. *rib*, **reeb,** meaning "dispute, quarrel, case at law, or charge") in this context implies a vio-

lation or abuse of the terms of the covenant, which was founded on the principles of an intimate relationship like a marriage covenant. Given this unhappy situation, the Lord summoned His people to understand the reason why He was so concerned for them. They had created for themselves a bad situation by committing evil deeds. God brought a case against His own people. Truth, mercy, and knowledge were qualities that should have been the fruit of covenant faithfulness. Israel should have exhibited these qualities as manifestations of God's *grace,* but she took them for *granted.* The lack of these qualities resulted in untrustworthiness and infidelity. However, God called this lack to the Israelites' attention because these attitudes and actions were inconsistent with His nature and character.

God loves the sinner but hates sin. The obvious lesson to be learned from this fact is that no matter how far or deep one thinks he or she has gone into sin, it is important to realize that God does not readily give up on His children. His grace and love reach out to even the vilest sinner who has lived in the prison of evil or disobedience all of his or her life (John 3:16; Ephesians 2:8–10). The depth, length, width, and height of one's sin cannot surpass the capacity of God's saving grace. However, it is important to understand that this theological truth does not give sinners the freedom to callously continue in sin. God's love and mercy call us to repent in order to receive forgiveness from Him, but He will take us to task when we take His graciousness for granted (Hebrews 10:26–30; 6:3–6).

2 By swearing, and lying, and killing, and stealing, and committing adultery, they break out, and blood toucheth blood.

Some people wrongly think that just a "little sin" is not too serious an offense against God or a fellow human. Sin is always sin, and God will punish it if there is no repentance. However, there is enough evidence in both the Scriptures and human history to teach us valuable lessons. The "little" sinful habits and attitudes that people take for granted can become "big" having serious and damaging results for individuals and society (James 1:13–15).

The Hebrew word translated "break out," *parats* (**paw-rats**), means "to break through, burst out (from the womb or an enclosure), or breach." It suggests an outbreak of sin on an epidemic scale. Violent and bloody crimes were all too prevalent among God's people. When the people failed to repent of their "first sins" and turn to God for forgiveness and restoration, it led to breaking the covenant. The Bible teaches that by our arrogance and hardness of heart, we fail to submit to the convictions or dealings of God's Spirit. As a result, we slide down into the "deep waters" of sin. The fact is that we as believers may still fall into sin by yielding to temptation (1 John 1:8–10; 1 Corinthians 10:12–13). However, we should promptly seek God's grace, mercy, and forgiveness through confession and repentance. Failure to repent incurs God's judgment, since we are all accountable for our own words and actions. We need to rely on God's Holy Spirit as children of God's divine covenant of grace to help us live in ways that please Him.

3 Therefore shall the land mourn, and every one that dwelleth therein shall languish, with the beasts of the field, and with the fowls of heaven; yea, the fishes of the sea also shall be taken away.

The consequence of Israel's sin was that God judged her. Both individuals' lives and environmental

"Hear the word of the LORD, ye children of Israel: for the LORD has a controversy with the inhabitants of the land, because there is no truth, nor mercy, nor knowledge of God in the land" (Hosea 4:1).

conditions were negatively affected. The Hebrew word translated "mourn," 'abal (**aw-BAL**), means "to mourn or lament." The Hebrew word translated "languish," amal (**aw-MAL**), means "to be weak, droop, or be exhausted." These words express both the spiritual and physical consequences of God's judgment upon Israel because of her failure to repent of her sin. The effect of sin on people who are arrogantly living in ways contrary to God's perfect will can be devastating in many areas of their lives. When the first humans committed sin in the Garden of Eden, it affected them personally and environmentally (Genesis 3:15–24). The sins of individuals, families, and nations can have multiple direct or indirect effects on the social, spiritual, material, and economic situations of people. From the text, it is evident that God had a case against Israel because they had committed evil and abomination without repentance. God's judgment on them affected everything, including plants and animals.

According to the biblical worldview, everything we treasure has Almighty God as its source. Sin can deceive God's people into thinking that everything they possess or aspire to have in their lives can be acquired or achieved irrespective of their lifestyles. If we understand the principles of God's Word and the dealings of His Spirit, we should always keep in mind that God is the ultimate source, not only of what we have, but of who we are. Our vocation and identity are found in God. We should never allow anything or anybody to stand between us and our covenant relationship with God. God has the power and ability to take away everything we have acquired in this life if we do not continue walking with Him in holiness and integrity.

4 Yet let no man strive, nor reprove another: for thy people are as they that strive with the priest.

Israel's decision to prostitute themselves by following the evil leadership of King Jeroboam and paying tribute at the sanctuary in Bethel in the northern kingdom was greatly abhorred by God. This sanctuary symbolized the "heart and mind" of the nation's apostasy. Their state of apostasy represented an abuse of the grace God had lavished on them as His unique covenant people. It was the task of Israel's leaders to lead God's people in a way that prepared them to worship and serve God according to His perfect will. Whenever they failed in this task, the result was spiritual and social strife in the entire society. The nature and character of God does not permit consistent sin to continue forever. He judges ALL who walk in disobedience and ALL who mislead others.

7:1 When I would have healed Israel, then the iniquity of Ephraim was discovered, and the wickedness of Samaria: for they commit falsehood; and the thief cometh in, and the troop of robbers spoileth without.

Because God is holy and righteous, He not only rewards obedience, but punishes evil. Yet He will have mercy on whom He will have mercy and compassion on whom He will have compassion (Exodus 33:19). God would have healed Israel and restored her to Himself. But the sins of the northern kingdom (represented by Ephraim) were exposed. These crimes were most blatant in Samaria, the capital city. God declared judgment on the people of the northern kingdom for their attitude and behavior. The temptation was to assume that because God was not acting promptly against their wrongdoings, He approved of or did not really care about their sins.

2 And they consider not in their hearts that I remember all their wickedness: now their own doings have beset them about; they are before my face.

God's patience should not be mistaken as weakness on His part. God is omniscient; He knows all things. He is also omnipotent, or all-powerful. He rightly claims in this verse that He "remembers all their wickedness" in the land. God's judgment can be instant, progressive, or come in the future. In any case, God WILL judge sin. The nature and scope of sin is such that its perpetrators cannot escape God's justice (see Romans 1:18). However, when we confess our sins and repent, God promises to forgive and restore us. True repentance is not mere mental assent, but a sincere change of heart and spirit (1 John 1:8–9). It is important to remember that "it is with your heart that you believe and are justified" (Romans 10:10, NIV). Let us not be like those who "consider not in their hearts," but let us always search our hearts to make sure we are true to our covenant relationship with God. Let us, therefore, not be beset by sins and wrongdoings as were Ephraim and Samaria.

12:8 And Ephraim said, Yet I am become rich, I have found me out substance: in all my labours they shall find none iniquity in me that were sin.

Ephraim boasted in her prosperity in the midst of living in sin. The phrase "become rich" in the orthodox Hebraic sense speaks of advancement, growth, or maturity into a better, higher-quality life. However, the inhabitants of the northern kingdom were attempting to justify their evil deeds by their prosperity. They foolishly and arrogantly began to sing of and celebrate their so-called achievements, which had resulted from evil and injustice. Arrogant attitudes and oppression of the poor characterized Israel's society, yet they expected God to preserve this unjust status quo.

Similar situations exist today. Many who claim to be Christians exhibit behavior similar to that of the northern kingdom of Israel. We are called to test all things and to hold fast to what is good (1 Thessalonians 5:15). The experience of the northern kingdom teaches us that whatever we desire to have must be acquired ethically and with integrity. We should choose the right *means* to achieve our *end.*

9 And I that am the LORD thy God from the land of Egypt will yet make thee to dwell in tabernacles, as in days of solemn feast.

The Israelites had an arrogant sense of self-sufficiency because they had forgotten that it was God who had showed them mercy, choosing them as His special people from among the nations. They had also forgotten that He had delivered them with His mighty hand when they were slaves in Egypt, had provided for them supernaturally in the wilderness to meet their needs, and had defended them against other nations that were stronger than themselves. They were boastful about their own abilities as they worshiped false gods. Now, God would take away their prosperity and make them live in tents again, just as they had done after the exodus from Egypt in the days of their "solemn feasts." In other words, they would go into captivity. Yet God would graciously provide for them as He had in the wilderness.

Among the solemn feasts was the Feast of Tabernacles—a joyful reminder of God's blessing and generosity. The Israelites were to remember that even when God chastised them, He also displayed His grace. Likewise, we should always rely on the Lord as our sufficiency, wherever we find ourselves in this pilgrimage of faith. Let us also remember that He is our God and we are His people. We must commit ourselves to obey and faithfully serve Him in all circumstances.

Daily Bible Readings

M: The Fourth Generation
2 Kings 15:8–12
T: Repentance Brings Blessing
Hosea 14
W: God's Love for Israel
Hosea 11:1–5
T: God Cares
Hosea 11:6–11
F: A Nation Sins
Hosea 4:1–5
S: Evil Deeds Remembered
Hosea 7:1–7
S: Return to Your God
Hosea 12:5–10

TEACHING TIPS

June 17
Bible Study Guide 3

1. Words You Should Know

A. Law/Teaching (Isaiah 1:10) *torah* (Heb.)—The authoritative revelation of God to His covenant people, including instruction, command, and promise.

B. Wash (v. 16) *rachats* (Heb.)—The act of ceremonial cleansing so that one can take part in worship.

C. Judgment/Justice (v. 17) *mishpat* (Heb.)—A final and decisive declaration (by God) or performance (by humans) of what is right.

2. Teacher Preparation

A. Read the Bible Background and the Focal Verses.

B. Read Genesis 19 for background on Sodom and Gomorrah; also read Deuteronomy 27–29 for the backdrop against which Isaiah speaks of the covenant judgment threatening Israel.

C. Complete lesson 3 in the *Precepts For Living®️ Personal Study Guide*.

3. Starting the Lesson

A. Begin the class with prayer, thanking God for His perfect holiness and beautiful character, which inspire and demand true worship.

B. Share honestly your struggle to worship God with all your life, perhaps mentioning one way you feel your worship of Him is compromised.

C. Ask a volunteer to read the Keep in Mind verse.

D. Discuss the following question: If God is beautiful beyond compare and worthy of worship, why do we not spend all our time in wholehearted devotion to Him?

4. Getting into the Lesson

A. Ask a volunteer to read the Focal Verses.

B. Ask the students to think of the worst name for God to call them, and write down their answers. Use these later to talk about how God addresses Judah as "Sodom and Gomorrah."

5. Relating the Lesson to Life

A. Invite the class to tell how worship empowers them in their daily lives.

B. Allow your students to answer the Discuss the Meaning questions as a group.

6. Arousing Action

A. Have the students brainstorm how they plan to carry out the Lesson in Our Society exercise.

B. Challenge the students to complete the Make It Happen assignment.

C. Close the class with prayer.

Worship Guide

For the Superintendent or Teacher
Theme: Isaiah Calls for True Worship
Theme Song: "Come, Thou Almighty King"
Scripture: Isaiah 1:10–11, 14–20
Song: "Blessed Be the Name"
Meditation: Lord, You are worthy to be praised and worshiped. You are God and I magnify Your holy name. Amen.

ISAIAH CALLS FOR TRUE WORSHIP

Bible Background • ISAIAH 1:10–20; 2 KINGS 15:32–35
Printed Text • ISAIAH 1:10–11, 14–20   Devotional Reading • ISAIAH 58:6–12

Lesson Aim

By the end of the lesson, we will:

REVIEW Isaiah's words calling for true worship;

FEEL the need to let our worship overflow into a desire to please God in our behavior; and

PRAY to have lives that reflect genuine worship of God.

Keep in Mind

"Learn to do well; seek judgment, relieve the oppressed, judge the fatherless, plead for the widow" (Isaiah 1:17).

Focal Verses

Isaiah 1:10 Hear the word of the LORD, ye rulers of Sodom; give ear unto the law of our God, ye people of Gomorrah.

11 To what purpose is the multitude of your sacrifices unto me? saith the LORD: I am full of the burnt offerings of rams, and the fat of fed beasts; and I delight not in the blood of bullocks, or of lambs, or of he-goats.

1:14 Your new moons and your appointed feasts my soul hateth: they are a trouble unto me; I am weary to bear them.

15 And when ye spread forth your hands, I will hide mine eyes from you: yea, when ye make many prayers, I will not hear: your hands are full of blood.

16 Wash you, make you clean; put away the evil of your doings from before mine eyes; cease to do evil;

17 Learn to do well; seek judgment, relieve the oppressed, judge the fatherless, plead for the widow.

18 Come now, and let us reason together, saith the LORD: though your sins be as scarlet, they shall be as white as snow; though they be red like crimson, they shall be as wool.

19 If ye be willing and obedient, ye shall eat the good of the land:

20 But if ye refuse and rebel, ye shall be devoured with the sword: for the mouth of the LORD hath spoken it.

In Focus

When Thad turned his car onto the street where he lived, he saw an ambulance in his driveway. Once inside his home, he was shocked to find paramedics performing CPR on his wife, Sheila. His heart was in his mouth as he prayed in the ambulance as it sped toward the hospital.

In the emergency room, the doctor gathered Thad and his family together and said, "Sheila suffered a fatal aneurysm; I'm sorry, but she's gone."

After six years of marriage, Sheila was gone. Thad went into a downward spiral that plunged him into weeks of despair, followed by months of depression. He tried praying more and going to more Bible studies, but he struggled with his relationship with God and he felt forsaken. A year after the tragedy, he met with his pastor. During the visit, Thad asked, "Why

is it I no longer find any joy in my life? Why is God punishing me?"

"During your prayer time, are you praising and thanking God for the good years that you and Sheila shared, or are you simply focusing on your loss?" asked the pastor.

"What do you mean?" Thad asked.

"Thad, I realize that it is easy to loose heart when faced with the loss of a loved one; but *true* worship is when you focus on God and not yourself. You must begin to worship God for who He is despite your circumstances. Begin to thank Him for the gift of life and stop praying prayers of despair."

At that moment, Thad realized that since his wife's death his prayers were focused on his pain and despair at the loss of his wife. He had never truly entered into worship genuinely thanking God just because He is God. He realized that true worship should have a positive effect on his life.

Isaiah's words call for true worship. We see in today's lesson that it is not what we do, but the attitude of our hearts toward God that determines our relationship with Him.

The People, Places, and Times

Sodom and Gomorrah. Sodom and Gomorrah were cities that were destroyed by God in Genesis 19 with burning sulfur from heaven. The cities were proverbial in Bible times and continue to be so in our day. Their names are used to speak of an utterly evil group of people. Although the name Sodom has become associated with sodomy, it is likely that this was only one of many crimes of which those in the ancient city were guilty (Ezekiel 16:49). The use of Sodom and Gomorrah (and the neighboring towns, Admah and Zeboim) as a warning to God's covenant people, shows that these towns' greatest sin was idolatry, as was Israel's. God warns that if His covenant is broken, the land of Israel—a beautiful land flowing with milk and honey—will become a land of "brimstone, and salt, and burning" (Deuteronomy 29:23). Yahweh even uses Sodom-like punishment to coax His people to repent: "I overthrew some of you as I overthrew Sodom and Gomorrah . . . yet you have not returned to me" (Amos 4:11, NIV). Indeed, Israel and Judah responded, not with repentance, but with brazen and defiant rebellion: "they declare their sin as Sodom, they hide it not" (Isaiah 3:9). Ultimately, God brought about what was promised in Deuteronomy 29. The result was awful indeed as Israel's punishment was even worse than that of Sodom and Gomorrah, for the people of Israel and Judah had to live in a foreign land and continue to experience the consequences of their rebellion (Lamentations 4:6). No wonder, then, that the apostle Peter declares that Sodom and Gomorrah have become to all people "an example unto those that after should live ungodly" (2 Peter 2:6).

New moons and appointed feasts. The new moon offering (Numbers 28:11–15) was a monthly burnt offering. On the seventh new moon of each year, the ceremony corresponded with the Feast of Trumpets. The use of the term here corresponds with other prophetic uses, describing God's weariness with ritual that was empty of devotion and was performed alongside idolatrous worship. The new moon became a treasured symbol of Jewish worship; Ezekiel's prophecy of Israel's restoration in a renewed temple (Ezekiel 40–48) includes several mentions of the new moon once again being celebrated. Accordingly, the apostle Paul, knowing that all these expectations had been fulfilled in Christ and through the worship of Him by the church, the new temple of God, admonished the Colossian Christians to "let no man judge you . . . in respect of the new moon" (Colossians 2:16). In other words, Christian practice no longer requires the observance of such festivals, which were but a shadow of things to come, the substance of which is Christ.

Background

To whom do the warnings and invitations of Isaiah 1 come? We are told right away (1:1) that this prophecy concerns "Judah and Jerusalem," the southern kingdom (and its capital city) of once-united Israel. God summons the people of Judah to appear before Him as before a judge in court (v. 2). He calls for heaven and Earth to be His witnesses as He declares that Judah has been unfaithful to His covenant with her. Isaiah paints a picture of the most unnatural thing possible: a nation meant for God's praise has forgotten Him, and His own children pretend that their Father does not exist. As a result, the whole nation is covered with wounds, which God allows in order to show them the inevitable result of their persistent rebellion against and neglect of their Creator and Redeemer. Nevertheless, Isaiah says, God is merciful; because of His loving promise, He has not allowed Judah to experience the irreversible judgment once visited upon Sodom and Gomorrah. As we are about to see in the text, such mercy goes well beyond what unfaithful Judah deserves.

At-A-Glance

1. The Condemnation of Judah's Unholy Worship
(Isaiah 1:10–11)
2. The Worship God Rejects and the Worship He Accepts
(1:14–17)
3. Worship: A Matter of Life and Death
(vv. 18–20)

In Depth

1. The Condemnation of Judah's Unholy Worship (Isaiah 1:10–11)

Isaiah introduces a great and unexpected irony as he transitions from verse 9 to verse 10. Although verse 9 clearly states that Judah is *not* like Sodom and Gomorrah (for it has not been judged as severely as those cities), verse 10 now seems to say the opposite: that Judah is Sodom and Gomorrah! By calling Judah names that its people would have associated with hatred toward Yahweh and the worst possible judgment that could befall a nation, the Lord (through Isaiah) seeks to awaken the people to the awful reality of their sin. Imagine your shock if God were to speak to your church and say, "Listen, all sinners—everyone. . . !" But there are hints that something is different here, something unlike the destruction of Sodom and Gomorrah. In the latter case, no advance warning was given (except to Abraham's family); destruction came suddenly and irrevocably. Here, God offers the people "the word of the LORD" and "the law of our God." When reading the terrible warnings of judgment that we find in the Old Testament, we must always remember that God's advance warning is a miracle of mercy. The presence of God's Word is always a blessing and a sign that God has not forgotten His covenant promises. And so we have an interesting and mixed picture: God looks at the deeds of His people and justly compares Judah to the worst of all kingdoms; yet he condescends to speak to them as their God, which is a mercy altogether undeserved.

Verse 11 lists three observations about Judah's worship through sacrifices. First, this worship *means* nothing; God asks "to what purpose" these sacrifices are being made (v. 11). Because the people are bringing their sacrifices without repentance or righteousness, the sacrifices are nothing more than the senseless slaughter of animals and the spilling of blood. Second, this worship *adds* nothing; Yahweh says that He has "had enough" of it (v. 11). Although the people of Judah might smugly bring offerings as if they were doing the Lord a favor, He is rich beyond compare and needs nothing from His people. Third, this worship *does* nothing; God says, "I do not

delight" in it (v. 11). Later, we will see what kind of worship pleases God, but it is clear that a hypocritical offering from the hands of Judah did not please Him.

Source
Motyer, J. Alec, *The Prophecy of Isaiah: An Introduction & Commentary*. Downers Grove, Ill.: InterVarsity Press, 1993, 46.

2. The Worship God Rejects and the Worship He Accepts (1:14–17)

God's rejection of Judah's worship could not be more absolute: Yahweh says through Isaiah, "my soul hates" it (v. 14). God chose Jacob and his descendants for covenant blessing while leaving Esau and his descendants outside of that circle of blessing, or "hating" Esau (Malachi 1:2–3). So the warning here in Isaiah could hardly be more severe: If Judah's sacrifices are detestable to God, the people are in grave danger of being "hated" (rejected) themselves. How could this be? God's covenant calls for mutual *con-secration*; that is, the parties are to set themselves apart in devotion to one other. (See Genesis 17 for a graphic picture of God's devotion in the Abrahamic covenant.) But Judah's consecration (here represented by hands lifted up in prayer) has become tainted with blood—not the blood of faithful sacrifices, but the blood of cruel oppression and guilt (v. 15). As a result, God threatens to reject Judah's prayers of intercession (when they "spread out their hands," v. 15). What a picture of rejection: Judah's prayers would return to them unheard! This image reverses the picture of Moses' raised hands as the key to victory and blessing for the people (Exodus 17:8–16). Every time Moses interceded for Israel, God responded, as He did to Israel's priests and other anointed leaders. But now, the Lord threatens to reverse the beautiful blessing of Numbers 6:25 ("the LORD make His face shine upon you"); God will hide His eyes when the people turn to Him for help! Such is the disastrous totality of Judah's idolatry, which mocks God and defiles their worship.

But just in time, the light of the Gospel breaks through into this grim picture. Isaiah's prophecy moves from prediction to command, from condemnation to opportunity (v. 16), and although the face of God appears stern as He calls for wholehearted repentance, His offer is overflowing with mercy. The beauty of this invitation can be seen in the opening words: "wash yourselves, make yourselves clean" (v. 16). The meaning of this command would have been abundantly clear to the people of Judah, for this is the language of ceremonial cleansing. In other words, this is the language of sacrifice—the language of worship. Through Judah's sacrifices, God gave them a way to be forgiven of their sins and to be considered clean (that is, blessed by God and a recipient of all His good promises) rather than unclean (rejected by Him and cast out from among His people). But there is a problem: If sacrifice was the way to become clean, and the people of Judah were already bringing sacrifices that did *not* make

"Learn to do well; seek judgment, relieve the oppressed, judge the fatherless, plead for the widow" (Isaiah 1:17).

them clean, how were they to become clean again? This verse tells us that Yahweh is not setting aside the sacrificial system and the forgiveness of sins through the shedding of blood, but rather showing forth their true meaning. Sacrifice has meaning only in the light of true repentance, as demonstrated by an authentic change of heart and the works of righteousness and justice that result. In other words, God is calling for true worship to replace false, hypocritical worship.

God calls the people of Judah to "cease" (abandon) their old actions, which have made them guilty of blood; "learn" (develop) new ways of thinking, which are really the old ways of honoring God; and "seek" (pursue) different priorities: justice and goodness instead of idolatry and violence. This repentance will produce concrete results: The oppressor will be rebuked (rather than encouraged) and the oppressed will find comfort and justice (rather than abandonment and anguish). We cannot think too highly of this offer of mercy. By commanding repentance, God offers His people a "clean slate" and a chance to turn to Him; in so doing, He does not "hide his eyes" (v. 15), but turns *toward* them.

3. Worship: A Matter of Life and Death (vv. 18–20)

Having called His people to account and admonishing them to change their ways, Yahweh now does what no ancient god or king or judge would have ever considered doing: He discusses the case with His people! "Come now, and let us reason together" (Isaiah 1:18). To His dire warning and sober command, God now adds a tender plea to His rebellious people, showing His ever-compassionate heart toward Judah. He offers them the kind of repentance that will remove the blood from their hands and remove the stain of guilt from their hearts forever (v. 18). The stain of blood would have been considered a stain that all the washing in the world could not get out; indeed, righteous acts in and of themselves could not erase Judah's guilt, no matter how many times they were performed. Instead, God offers the cleansing that comes only from Him, a cleansing that would come through the people's repentance. And so, repentance is an integral and necessary part of worship; worship is empty and misguided without it.

As the people repent, God offers them the greatest life they could imagine: "you shall eat the good of the land" (v. 19). Judah's land was her dearest possession, and prosperity in that land her greatest desire. This was life indeed, expressed in the most graphic terms she could have imagined. On the other hand, the warning in verse 20 speaks of death if rebellion continued; to be "devoured by the sword" represented not only physical death, but capture and deportation to a foreign land, the worst kind of death imaginable for God's people.

In this warning of death and this promise of life, God upholds His covenant in two ways. First, the promise of judgment is made in the light of sin. Second, God's loyalty to His covenant people prompts Him to delay judgment and offer mercy and life to a nation of corrupt and undeserving sinners. It is important to remember that Isaiah prophesied after the northern kingdom (Israel) had been overrun by Assyria and sent into exile; after seeing this, Judah would have no excuse for thinking that God would not hold them to the same standard as He had Israel. But Isaiah prophesied approximately 100 years prior to the destruction of Judah and Jerusalem, indicating that this impending judgment was not a foregone conclusion in the Lord's mind. The Lord gives Judah one last chance to repent and to find life before being exiled. In the book of Isaiah, we see the incomparable riches of God's patience and mercy.

What kind of worship pleases God? The word used in verse 11 to describe worship in which God has no pleasure is again used in Isaiah 53:10, where the prophet says that "it *pleased* the LORD to bruise" Christ. The miracle of the Gospel is that, whereas our sacrifices did not delight the heart of God (quite the opposite!), God took delight—mystery of mysteries!—in having His own Son to be the sacrifice that was perfect, holy, and pleasing to Him. It is through this sacrifice that believers are made clean. Through Jesus' work, sins that were scarlet are washed away so that Christians are as white (clean) as freshly fallen snow in the eyes of God. And only through an eternal connection by faith with Christ can true worship take place. As the believer accepts Christ's sacrifice, which pleased the Father in its perfection, he or she is enabled by the Spirit's power to live the life of Christ. Thanks be to God that He has made us able to worship Him with all our lives as we live by the power of Christ!

Search the Scriptures

1. How are Judah's sacrifices described in Isaiah 1:11?

2. How does God feel about the religious festivals that Judah is observing? What typical context of worship is noticeably absent in the heavenly city (v. 14)?

3. What are the concrete ways in which Judah is commanded to "cease to do evil" and "learn to do good" (v. 17)?

4. Under what two conditions will Judah be allowed to "eat the good of the land" (v. 19)? What two transgressions will lead to their being "devoured by the sword" (v. 20)?

Discuss the Meaning

1. Why do you think God rejected Judah's sacrifices, even though verse 11 shows that they were abundant and involved the very best animals?

2. Why must God respond so harshly when His people are disobedient?

3. Why do you think promises of judgment and mercy so often go together in the Scriptures?

Lesson in Our Society

We are very prone to limiting our worship of God to one day a week; after all, the Lord's Day is still the day when most congregations gather, often with much pomp and circumstance, dressed in finery that is reserved only for Sunday worship. The worship of God on the Lord's Day is an event—and it should be! The Lord's Day is still the day on which God has called His covenant people to worship; however, this worship is meant to empower wholehearted worship the rest of the week, not *replace* it. It is helpful for us to consider how our worship of God once a week can best produce worship in all of life, rather than making worshipers feel they have done their duty and do not need to seek holiness and consecration every day.

Make It Happen

The prophet Isaiah called the Israelites to true worship of a holy and worthy God. God calls us as well to confess and repent of our sins so that we can engage in true worship as well. Therefore, think about how your worship of God might be compromised by: un-Christlike behavior toward your brothers and sisters, by failure to seek the justice God requires in your relationships and in society, or by idolatry: loving other things in your life so much that they compromise your worship of the true God. Truly, we all compromise in these ways! Think of specific examples of which you can repent, and pray for the grace to worship God more purely in each of these areas of your life.

Follow the Spirit

What God wants me to do:

_____

_____

Remember Your Thoughts

Special insights I have learned:

_____

_____

More Light on the Text
Isaiah 1:10–11, 14–20

God was faithful in keeping His part of the covenant with Israel. However, Israel (God's children) failed to fulfill their responsibility in achieving holistic development in accordance with God's purpose. Rather, they sinned by alienating themselves from God and involving themselves in habitual transgression and the abuse of religious rites. They did not sustain the kind of "family ecology" needed for healthy development. The result was a breakdown of what could have been an excellent family relationship in which children honor and reverence their parents, and the parents reward the children in every way possible. True worship can be likened to this family relationship: God's children honor and reverence God, and He, in turn, blesses and rewards them according to His purpose.

10 Hear the word of the LORD, ye rulers of Sodom; Give ear unto the law of our God, ye people of Gomorrah.

The character and behavior of God's people were beginning to resemble those of the people of Sodom and Gomorrah. Therefore, God called on the people and their rulers to pay close attention. The impact of the type of leadership displayed and the direction taken by those in authority over others cannot be overemphasized. Throughout human history, individuals and groups have either suffered or benefited depending on the values and characteristics of their leaders. However, when those they lead also fail to make morally sound choices, the leadership cannot always be blamed. This is why God takes both the "rulers of Sodom" and the "people of Gomorrah" to task in this passage. God wanted them to repent of their evil ways and make responsible choices.

11 To what purpose is the multitude of your sacrifices unto me? saith the LORD: I am full of the burnt offerings of rams, and the fat of fed beasts; and I delight not in the blood of bullocks, or of lambs, or of he-goats.

God was not impressed by the Israelites' sacrifices. The people were doing everything they could to be "religiously correct," but they lacked the qualities that help create a healthy family and spiritual ecology. Their religious observances did not bring about growth and fulfillment according to God's purpose. The sacrifices and offerings were mere empty rituals and ceremonies (Hebrews 10:5–7). God's people were merely conforming to the outward manifestations of religious ordinances without experiencing real inner transformation. In so doing, they were deviating from God's original intentions for establishing these ordinances. God's people had not been faithful to their covenant relationship with God, but instead had developed other ungodly allegiances to pursue their own selfish agenda. The root cause of their failing was that they had allowed sin into their camp.

We need to repent of our sin if we want to walk with God in a manner that pleases Him. God delights in the broken and contrite hearts of His children. This kind of heart attitude leads to obedience and commitment, important virtues that are expected in a God-centered family if we desire to walk according to His purpose. Responsible earthly parents nurture their children to develop "nonnegotiable" knowledge and character. They expect their children to be responsible and obedient and to conduct themselves properly whatever the situation. Parents desire that their children give ear to specific instructions and live accordingly. Good parents are interested in the achievements of their children that are accomplished with integrity. Children may climb to the topmost level of the social and economic ladder in life but fail to reflect important family values. Parents are disappointed when such family deficiencies occur. Similarly, God was disappointed with Israel's failure to truly worship Him—to revere, honor, serve, and adore Him. The Israelites were multiplying their sacrifices to the Lord but were living outside His perfect will.

Christian service and worship are important elements of a sound family ecology, which is rooted in God's purpose. Healthy growth and maturation in the context of the family prepares children to faithfully serve their parents as well as the larger community. Sodom and Gomorrah, to which God likened Israel earlier in the chapter, lived in selfishness, disobedience, greed, and arrogance. God did not delight in their sacrifices as forms of worship because they were not walking in integrity but were being disobedient and irresponsible. True worship is a total commitment to honor, revere, serve, and adore Almighty God for who He truly is.

1:14 Your new moons and your appointed feasts my soul hateth: they are a trouble unto me; I am weary to bear them.

The religious observances that God had ordained in the Old Testament to symbolize the good things to come in the New Testament (Colossians 2:13–17; Hebrews 10:1–2) had become acts of abomination; they were disgusting in the sight of God. The people perverted and abused these observances to serve their own selfish ends. God hated such hypocritical and misleading behavior in His people. He told them that He was not interested in their false spirituality. True worship and service, according to the principles of the kingdom of God, are intricately interwoven with right behavior. Genuine worship of Almighty God should overflow into a desire and commitment to behave in a manner consistent with His will and purpose.

15 And when ye spread forth your hands, I will hide mine eyes from you; yea, when ye make many prayers, I will not hear: your hands are full of blood.

According to the Scriptures, prayer is communicating with God. It is a two-way conversation between God and His people, who are actively involved in the process. God expects His people to "ask, seek, and knock" through acts of prayer and fasting to bring blessings upon themselves and others (1 John 5:14–15; Luke 11:9–10). However, sin primarily hinders believers' prayers from being answered. The sins of disobedience, cheating, hypocrisy, and deception were part of the lives of the Israelites, yet they still went before the Lord to "worship" Him with sacrifices and offerings. God rejected these empty rituals, saying, "I will hide mine eyes from you; yea, when ye make many prayers, I will not hear." Prayer reminds us that we are going to a holy God.

The other thing we need to understand is that there are different types of prayers—for example, prayers of thanksgiving, intercession, dedication, and praise (1 Timothy 2:1–2; Luke 11:1–4). When a believer dedicates him or herself totally to God in prayer, it becomes a form of worship. We can receive grace and mercy when we open our hearts and minds to God in sincere prayer and prepare ourselves to be touched by His Spirit (Ephesians 4:15–16).

16 Wash you, make you clean; put away the evil of your doings from before mine eyes; cease to do evil.

God exhorts His people to repent and to abandon their evil ways in order to restore their covenant relationship with Him. The phrase "wash you" should not be taken literally, but symbolically. God's people are to put away the uncleanness in their lives by asking the Holy Spirit to work in them by God's mercy and grace. In the Old Testament, people were "washed" by the shed blood of sacrificed animals (see Hebrews 9). In the New Testament, however, the shed blood of our Lord Jesus Christ makes atonement for all our sins. When we confess our sins to God, He forgives us and restores us to fellowship (1 John 1:8–9). After we have received forgiveness, God expects us to continue growing spiritually according to His perfect will. Moral development is a process, not a one-time occurrence, and for the believer, such development requires total submission to the Holy Spirit, who brings about true transformation.

17 Learn to do well; seek judgment, relieve the oppressed, judge the fatherless, plead for the widow.

God expected Israel to always stay connected to Him and learn, which would lead to growth in all aspects of their lives. The learning process for the believer is not so much behavioral as it is transformative. True spiritual maturity in God's people comes through a learning process that is guided by the Holy Spirit. God instructed Israel to reflect on the way they had treated the oppressed, the fatherless, and widows. To "seek judgment" here means to do things based on the sound moral and spiritual principles that God had revealed to them. The believer cannot claim to love God if he or she hates a fellow believer. A learning process that has the power to transform the hearts and minds of people prepares them to open up to, deal with, and serve others in love, integrity, and truth. We are called to do so because all humans are created equal in God's sight. As true worshipers of the living God, believers seek to love and serve others with all their hearts whenever and wherever they can.

18 Come now, and let us reason together, saith the LORD: Though your sins are as scarlet, they shall be as white as snow; though they be red like crimson, they shall be as wool.

God gave His people, while they were yet living in sin, a gracious opportunity to return to Him. It was a solemn act by a good Father—God Himself—who submitted the principles of His fatherhood to a discussion with His people. He invited His children to "reason together" with Him. God created humankind in His image. As a result, humans are free moral agents with the capacity to make choices for themselves. In Hebrew the phrase "let us reason together" denotes a kind of contention, such as that which occurs in a court of justice. The implication is that, even though God presented Himself as a Father to His people, He wanted them to walk faithfully with Him according to the tenets of His established covenant. When we receive forgiveness from God by repenting and obeying His Word, we are completely cleansed of ALL our sins. The "snow" and "wool" analogies used in this text help us to understand that God, in His great love and mercy, will not hold our sins against us when we repent and return to Him.

19 If ye be willing and obedient, ye shall eat the good of the land:

God did not attempt to impose His plans on the people of Israel but expected them to exercise their own power of choice in a responsible manner. He wanted them to voluntarily submit their wills to Him as an act of worship. The believer, who "presents his body as a living sacrifice" (Romans 12:1–2) on God's altar through obedience, is performing an act of true spiritual worship. God laid before the people of Israel the consequences for obeying or disobeying Him. Obedience would lead to blessings and peace, whereas disobedience would bring curses and misfortunes. God offered the Israelites both the carrot and the stick, but they were responsible for making the right choices for their own growth and development according to His will.

20 But if ye refuse and rebel, ye shall be devoured with the sword: for the mouth of the LORD hath spoken it.

An arrogant and hardened heart fails to submit to God's authority. The punishment that befalls a person rebelling against God may be psychological, physical, emotional, or spiritual. We must learn that even though God is a good Father who loves His children, His nature and character do not permit Him to overlook sin. He is righteous and just in all He does, rewarding and punishing as required. The love that parents have for their children in a typical family dictates that they provide for, protect, and defend their children, but also discipline, punish, and correct them so that they will become responsible, productive adults.

Let us worship God in spirit and in truth as we seek to walk in His perfect will in reverence and honor, serving and adoring Him according to His divine standard set in His Word.

Daily Bible Readings

M: Praise for God's Goodness
Psalm 65:1–8
T: Doing Right in God's Sight
2 Kings 15:32–36
W: Here Am I; Send Me
Isaiah 6:1–8
T: The Fast That Pleases God
Isaiah 58:6–12
F: Comfort for God's People
Isaiah 40:1–5
S: Not Desiring Sacrifices
Isaiah 1:10–14
S: Learn to Do Good
Isaiah 1:15–20

TEACHING TIPS

June 24
Bible Study Guide 4

1. Words You Should Know

A. Buy (Isaiah 55:1) *shabar* (Heb.)—To procure for oneself, especially the things necessary for life.

B. Wicked (v. 7) *rasha* (Heb.)—A broad term that refers to various kinds of sin and also to guilt before the law.

C. Return (v. 11) *shuwb* (Heb.)—The act of changing direction and returning to an original source.

2. Teacher Preparation

A. Read the Bible Background section and the Focal Verses.

B. Read Isaiah 52:13–54:17 as an important lead-in to today's text; read also John 4 for a similar invitation offered by Jesus Himself.

C. Think about how your church and the broader culture tend to view repentance. Is it something people believe is no longer necessary? Prepare yourself to teach about repentance through the holistic treatment of Isaiah 55.

D. Complete lesson 4 in the *Precepts For Living®
Personal Study Guide.*

3. Starting the Lesson

A. Begin the class with prayer, thanking God for the wonderful promises He gives to those who seem least deserving of them.

B. To set the stage for God's invitation in Isaiah 55, ask class members to share about the most exciting invitation they have ever received.

C. Ask a volunteer to read the Keep in Mind verse.

D. Discuss the following question: "When you receive an exciting invitation, how do you usually respond to that invitation?"

4. Getting into the Lesson

A. Ask a volunteer to read the Focal Verses.

B. Ask the class about an offer or an invitation

they believed was "too good to be true." Probe further to see if there are similar feelings about the invitation given in this passage.

5. Relating the Lesson to Life

A. Have the class compile a list of reasons why people are slow to respond to God's invitation, even when it is free.

B. Develop a regular prayer plan concerning the obstacles mentioned in class. Pray daily that these obstacles will be overcome.

6. Arousing Action

A. Allow your students to answer the Discuss the Meaning questions as a group.

B. Ask the students to brainstorm how they plan to carry out the Lesson in Our Society exercise.

C. Challenge the students to complete the Make It Happen assignment.

D. Close the class with prayer.

Worship Guide

For the Superintendent or Teacher
Theme: Isaiah Invites Us to God's Feast
Theme Song: "My Faith Looks Up to Thee"
Scripture: John 7:37–39
Song: "Just As I Am"
**Meditation: Dear Lord, help me to know You
more intimately through spending time in
prayer and studying and meditating on Your
Holy Word. Amen.**

ISAIAH INVITES US TO GOD'S FEAST

Bible Background • ISAIAH 55:1–11
Printed Text • ISAIAH 55:1–3, 6–11   Devotional Reading • 2 CORINTHIANS 9:10–15

Lesson Aim

By the end of the lesson, we will:

KNOW that God alone provides spiritual satisfaction;

FEEL the desire to know Him more intimately; and

INVITE God into our lives in a fuller way.

Keep in Mind

"Seek ye the LORD while he may be found, call ye upon him while he is near" (Isaiah 55:6).

Focal Verses

Isaiah 55:1 Ho, every one that thirsteth, come ye to the waters, and he that hath no money; come ye, buy, and eat; yea, come, buy wine and milk without money and without price.

2 Wherefore do ye spend money for that which is not bread? and your labor for that which satisfieth not? hearken diligently unto me, and eat ye that which is good, and let your soul delight itself in fatness.

3 Incline your ear, and come unto me: hear, and your soul shall live; and I will make an everlasting covenant with you, even the sure mercies of David.

55:6 Seek ye the LORD while he may be found, call ye upon him while he is near:

7 Let the wicked forsake his way, and the unrighteous man his thoughts: and let him return unto the LORD, and he will have mercy upon him; and to our God, for he will abundantly pardon.

8 For my thoughts are not your thoughts, neither are your ways my ways, saith the LORD.

9 For as the heavens are higher than the earth, so are my ways higher than your ways, and my thoughts than your thoughts.

10 For as the rain cometh down, and the snow from heaven, and returneth not thither, but watereth the earth, and maketh it bring forth and bud, that it may give seed to the sower, and bread to the eater:

11 So shall my word be that goeth forth out of my mouth: it shall not return unto me void, but it shall accomplish that which I please, and it shall prosper in the thing whereto I sent it.

In Focus

After 35 years of marriage, I have discovered that duty is good, but satisfaction is better.

Let me give you an example: Suppose I present my wife with a dozen roses, and she glows and says, "Oh, honey, they're beautiful! Why did you?" and I reply, "It's my duty." That probably would not be what she wants to hear. Why? Because duty can only take you so far. A more appropriate response might be, "I couldn't help myself, darling. The happiness you give me just brimmed to overflowing—and I can't wait to gaze into your eyes on our dinner date tonight." OK, that might be a bit overboard, but you get the picture, right?

The amazing thing about the latter response is that it does two things: It expresses my happiness and it makes my wife feel honored. Many people believe that if they do something because it makes *them* happy, it doesn't honor the other person. But it can! Doing something for someone simply to make them happy is a great tribute, and if you take pleasure in someone, two things happen: You receive joy, and they receive the glory.

This also holds true in our relationship with God. Once we understand that the pursuit of our happiness and the quest for God's glory are not at odds, we will be able to delight ourselves in the Lord.

In today's passage, the Lord (through the prophet Isaiah) invites us to His feast. When we accept God's invitation, we discover that it is not a duty to serve God, but a delight that surpasses all understanding.

The People, Places, and Times

Heaven. The term "heaven" is used of the physical heaven, especially in the expression "heaven and earth" (Genesis 14:19; Matthew 5:18). It also refers to God's dwelling place, but God is not alone there. We read in Nehemiah 9:6 of the "the host of heaven" that worships Him, and in Mark 13:32 of "the angels in heaven." Believers also may look forward to "an inheritance . . . kept in heaven" for them (1 Peter 1:4).

Background

Isaiah had just completed two wondrous and significant discourses: the discourse on the Suffering Servant (Isaiah 52:13–53:12), and the discourse on the future glory of Zion. The first discourse reveals in vivid detail the means by which God's people may enter into His glory (through the perfect sacrifice of the perfect Servant). The second discourse reveals the nature of that glory, describing rewards like numberless descendants, limitless prosperity, boundless security, fearless belonging, and faultless righteousness. Having shown the way into God's glory and the staggering rewards found in the midst of that glory, Isaiah still needs to provide a specific invitation into glory, which is precisely the purpose of Isaiah 55. With universal intent and magnificent mercy, the God of Israel sends forth this invitation to the people of the earth.

At-A-Glance

1. The Invitation to Hopeless Sinners
(Isaiah 55:1–3)
2. The Call to Turn Around to the Lord Who Invites
(55:6–7)
3. The Guarantee of Acceptance
(vv. 8–11)

In Depth

1. The Invitation to Hopeless Sinners (Isaiah 55:1–3)

"Ho!" begins one of the most gracious and glorious invitations in all of Scripture, with a word used to command the attention of those who hear. The use of this word indicates that, whatever follows, God's people would do well to listen to it; and what follows is a picture of God's grace to the utterly helpless. The Lord, through Isaiah, gives a call to *come* in three parts. First, God calls His people to "the waters," to a life of joy and satisfaction in the Holy Spirit. Second, God tells the people to "buy and eat," showing that the feast prepared will meet their needs, but that there is indeed a cost for such a great feast. Third, the people are called to "buy wine and milk," although "without money and without price." If wine and milk symbolize celebration and abundance, and yet those who come lack all resources to purchase such things, how can this invitation be real? We find a hint in Isaiah 52:3: "Ye have sold yourselves for nought; and ye shall be redeemed without money." We begin to understand the meaning and the magnitude of the Gospel: A people sold into slavery by their own sinfulness will now be bought back, but not through their own effort. This invitation will make sense to us only as we see it in light of the Suffering Servant of Isaiah 53, who took up our infirmities and by whose stripes we are healed. God's people freely possess His riches, not because these riches are of little value, but because their great cost has been paid through the suffering of the Servant. Moreover, God may now freely say, "Come."

How do we know that this passage is addressed to sinners like us? How do we know it's not addressed only to the poor and needy by the world's standards? The invitees here have plenty of resources (v. 2); the problem is that they "spend their labor on that which satisfieth not." Lest we think that Israel and Judah (and, by extension, the church) are guiltless (without sin) and helpless (unable to solve their sin problems), God makes it clear that they have dug their own way into spiritual poverty. They have lusted after things that in the end have left them bankrupt. Therefore, in great mercy, God calls to them three times to listen that they might "eat . . . that which is good" and "delight . . . in fatness." This is no mere

"Seek ye the LORD while he may be found, call ye upon him while he is near" (Isaiah 55:6).

vitamin pill or basic sustenance; it is "wine and milk," the richest of foods, a fare fit for kings. It is received by faith, for God says, "Hearken diligently unto me."

The true hearing of faith responds, repents, turns, and comes to the Lord who invites (v. 3). And in hearing and coming, the guest at the great banquet finds *life*—the life of the soul (v. 3). This does not mean life given only to the human spirit, but to the whole person, touching the deepest places of need and desire. This is what God's people receive through the simple act of hearing by faith! For the Servant has made the way open and procured the banquet on their behalf. What a glorious invitation to hopeless sinners!

2. The Call to Turn Around to the Lord Who Invites (55:6–7)

Isaiah now describes more fully what it means to respond to God's awesome invitation. He commands God's people to "seek" the Lord—not, of course, like someone looking for something that is lost, but rather like someone coming to something or Someone he knows is there. There is urgency in the command: The Lord may be sought only "while he may be found" (v. 6). In retrospect, these words have a chilling effect, because we know that Judah, in fact, failed to seek Yahweh in this way, and as a result suffered the fate of her sister Israel being forcibly ripped from her homeland and carried into captivity. But lest we modern-day Christians complacently feel that this warning doesn't apply to us, let us remember the New Testament's warning that we, like the first-century Christians, also live in the "last days" (Hebrews 1:2), during which Christ could return at any moment. The urgency of seeking the Lord has not faded with the coming of Jesus; it has only become more urgent, since His coming again will be final and repentance will no longer be an option.

Fortunately for Judah, God is now "near" (v. 6), a word used to describe the kinsman-redeemer (Leviticus 25:25), the close relative who had the responsibility of rescuing the one who is poor and helpless (as Boaz rescued Ruth in the book of Ruth). The good news is that, although Israel had willfully wandered far from Yahweh, He is as near to them as one of their own family and is seeking to rescue them. They will experience that rescue if their "seeking" and "calling" (v. 6) represent repentance (v. 7). In the wake of this repentance, God comes to them with mercy and forgiveness. The result is that fellowship with God is restored and His original intention accomplished.

3. The Guarantee of Acceptance (vv. 8–11)

It is understandable that a certain amount of disbelief would come in response to such a sublime invitation. How can God's people know that when they come, they will find the feast actually laid out for them? How can they know they will be accepted despite their foolishness and betrayal? On the other hand, if the invitation is free, why must God's people abandon their wickedness in order to be granted entry? All of these questions are answered in verses 8–11.

God makes clear that there is an unbridgeable gulf between Himself and His creation, just as there is between heaven and Earth (vv. 8–9). During his call to the prophetic ministry (chapter 6), Isaiah discovered the chasm between a holy God and sinful humankind. Here, he speaks once again of this chasm, but in a different way. The prophet now begins to talk about repentance in terms of both its necessity and its guarantee. Repentance is necessary because "my [God's] thoughts are not your thoughts, neither are your ways my ways." In other words, because God's thoughts and ways are high and holy beyond our imagining, His people must abandon their lowly, foolish, sinful thoughts and look to Him. Nevertheless, even as repentance is *necessary* for God's people, it is also *provided* by God (vv. 10–11).

God's Word is like the rain that comes down from heaven: "it is given freely and absolutely from above, it brings life in an effective way, and it totally provides for human need." But what kind of "word" are these verses talking about? Although it would not be wrong for us to apply this characterization to the whole Bible (for certainly the Bible does all the things just mentioned), the context shows us that the word spoken of here is the word of the invitation—the call to repentance. God's call to repentance is what theologians call *efficacious* or *effectual*—through the power of the Spirit, it actually does the work of getting a response! Unlike human beings, who cannot simply call things into existence, the God of the Bible speaks, and things come into being (cf. Genesis 1). In these verses, Isaiah reveals that when God speaks, those who are truly His are drawn to Him, for He speaks with great power. Therefore, His very word accomplishes "that which [He] please[s]" (v. 11). In other words, the repentance of His people "shall prosper in the thing whereto [God] sent it." Consequently, repentance brings about true spiritual prosperity; that is, the blessings of life and of God Himself all flow from the repentance that God grants to His people.

The idea of God giving repentance as a gift is also found in the New Testament. God works by His Spirit to give repentance to those He calls, so that they may inherit salvation (Acts 5:31; 11:18). We can see from these passages that repentance is closely connected with faith. When by faith we believe the promises of God in Jesus Christ, we repent and turn from the idolatry of the old self to worship the true God. Such is the glorious new covenant era that Christians enjoy; because of Christ's ascension to the right hand of the Father and His pouring out of the Holy Spirit, the invitation given to Judah in Isaiah 55 is guaranteed to us!

Source

Motyer, J. Alec. *The Prophecy of Isaiah: An Introduction & Commentary*. Downers Grove, Ill.: InterVarsity Press, 1993, 457.

Search the Scriptures

1. To what kind of people is the invitation in Isaiah 55:1 addressed?

2. In what does God call the soul to delight itself (v. 2)?

3. What are the wicked and the unrighteous called to forsake (v. 6)?

4. What is the result of the rain and snow coming down from heaven (v. 10)?

Discuss the Meaning

1. How is God's invitation in verses 1–3 different from an invitation given by a rich person to people who will repay him later?

2. Why is it vital that people seek the Lord without delay?

3. What is the significance of God's "word" in the process of invitation, repentance, and salvation as described in this passage (v. 11)?

Lesson in Our Society

"If you believe God enough, He will give you prosperity and health in this world." Many preachers and churches fall prey to this kind of thinking, which ties the promises of God to a worldly mind-set and leaves believers feeling entitled to God's blessings as something they deserve from Him. Usually lost in this way of thinking is the idea of *repentance,* which is the basic theme of today's passage. While the so-called "health and wealth" gospel might seem more inviting at first glance, it is counterfeit, since it tends not to acknowledge the biblical call to repentance—the call to turn away from our rebellion and acknowledge that we deserve nothing from the Lord. Perhaps this kind of thinking has crept into your church or into your own mind. Reflect on this passage from Isaiah 55 and consider what kind of damage this worldview could do to your spiritual life and to that of your church.

Make It Happen

Sometimes a preacher's or a Bible study's applications of Scripture can seem repetitive because so many passages in the Bible call people to repen-

tance. But each passage brings out a unique dimension that can help us understand repentance more fully. Today's passage shows us how free the invitation of God is, how superabundant the feast is to which He has called us, and how fully yet freely He provides us with the repentance He requires. We often think of repentance as totally our own work, but this passage teaches otherwise. If repentance is truly a free gift of God, we should seek it earnestly, rather than try to work up feelings of regret and holiness on our own. Use this lesson as an opportunity to begin praying regularly for the gift of repentance for yourself and for others.

Follow the Spirit

What God wants me to do:

_____

_____

Remember Your Thoughts

Special insights I have learned:

_____

_____

More Light on the Text
Isaiah 55:1–3, 6–11

The prophet Isaiah, son of Amoz, wrote the book of Isaiah to call the nation of Judah (the southern kingdom) back to God and to tell them of God's wonderful salvation through His Son Jesus, the coming Messiah. Bible scholars believe that chapters 40–66 of this great book may have been written near the end of Isaiah's life. The prophet wanted to comfort Judah during her captivity and after her release, bringing the nation consolation and hope through God's promise of future blessings through Jesus Christ. Therefore, his message is one of comfort, forgiveness, and hope.

The book of Isaiah has 66 chapters, just as there are 66 books of the Bible. Thirty-nine of these chapters pronounce judgment for the sins Israel had committed against the living God. They had disobeyed His commands and edicts, choosing instead to worship idols; because of their disobedience, they suffered the consequences and punishment of enslavement to a foreign ruler. However, the last 27 chapters of Isaiah offer comfort, forgiveness, and hope to a people who had suffered greatly and were ready to return to their God, who had rescued them time and time again, only to have them fall back into disobedience.

1 Ho, every one that thirsteth, come ye to the waters, and he that hath no money; come ye, buy, and eat; yea, come, buy wine and milk without money and without price.

The Hebrew word for "Ho" is *howy* (**HOH-ee**) and means "ah," "alas," "ha," "ho," "O," or "woe." The Hebrew word translated "come" is *yalak* (**yaw-LAK**) and means "to go, walk, come, depart, proceed, or move." Therefore, this passage is an invitation to take part in the Lord's salvation. The passage is calling everyone who is spiritually thirsty to God's well of living waters, which symbolize the eternal life that God offers through His Son. Therefore, if we drink from God's well—if we accept Jesus Christ as our Lord and Saviour—we will no longer be spiritually thirsty, since through Him we have eternal life.

We feed our physical body with food that costs money, and are filled for only a short time. However, the nourishment that God is offering will feed our souls for a lifetime and beyond.

2 Wherefore do ye spend money for that which is not bread? and your labor for that which satisfieth not? Hearken diligently unto me, and eat ye that which is good, and let your soul delight itself in fatness.

God lets us know that those who seek to satisfy their soul's hunger and thirst may be spending money on things that cannot satisfy these longings. The bread that the soul desires comes only from God Himself; only He can satisfy. The Hebrew word for "bread" is *lechem* (**LEKH-em**) and means "provision" (food in general). The bread that the soul longs for is a personal relationship with the living God. Without that personal relationship, the soul will forever be hungry and thirsty. Education, houses, land, money, prestige, or any other thing that we idolize will not

satisfy the inner longing of our souls. Things can never take the place of the God who holds the keys to death and hell. On the "Day of the Lord," we will have to answer to Him what we have done with Jesus. Did we accept His gift of salvation?

3 Incline your ear, and come unto me: hear, and your soul shall live;

God tells the Israelites (and us) to come to Him and listen to what He has to say. The Hebrew word translated "incline" is *natah* (**naw-TAW**) and means "to stretch out, extend, spread out, pitch, turn, pervert, bend, or bow." God's message is of grave importance because it involves the life of our soul. What we do with this message will determine where we will spend eternity—with God in heaven, or apart from God in hell. While we still have the breath of life, we must choose Jesus as our Lord and Saviour. When Jesus comes the second time, it will be too late to choose. He will come then as a righteous Judge; the season of forgiveness will be over.

55:6 Seek ye the LORD while he may be found, call ye upon him while he is near.

In Hebrew, the word for "seek" is *darash* (**daw-RASH**) and means "to investigate, enquire, practice, study, follow, or seek with application." Isaiah tells us that God wants us to intensively crave or desire Him. Enquire after Him right now, while He can still be found; don't hesitate, or it may be too late. He wants us to call upon Him right now, while He is near to us. He warns us not to wait until our sins have pushed us far away from Him, but to diligently seek God's forgiveness and mercy now.

7 Let the wicked forsake his way, and the unrighteous man his thoughts: and let him return unto the LORD, and he will have mercy upon him; and to our God, for he will abundantly pardon.

God desires that the wicked turn from their wicked ways. The word for "wicked" in Hebrew is *rasha* (**raw-SHAW**) and means "guilty one, one guilty of crime, one who is hostile (toward God), or one who is guilty of sin (against God or man)." God desires that the unrighteous man turn from his unrighteous thoughts. The word translated "unrighteous" is *aven* (**aw-VEN**) and means "wicked(ness), mischief, evil, unjust, vain, or trouble." God, then, wants to control even our thoughts. He wants to control our heart—the spirit that is within us—by empowering us with His own Holy Spirit.

The word translated "abundantly" (Heb. *rabah,* **raw-BAW**) means "to become many; to multiply; to be or grow great." God desires that we accept His gift of forgiveness through Jesus Christ so that we might be saved. This is God's invitation to abundant life.

8 For my thoughts are not your thoughts, neither are your ways my ways, saith the LORD. 9 For as the heavens are higher than the earth, so are my ways higher than your ways, and my thoughts than your thoughts.

Isaiah let the people of Israel know that they were foolish to even think or act as though they knew what God was thinking or planning. God's knowledge and wisdom are far above those of any human. After all, a human is God's creation. In view of this fact, we should never attempt to make God's will conform to ours, but rather seek God and His will.

10 For as the rain cometh down and the snow from heaven, and returneth not thither, but watereth the earth, and maketh it bring forth and bud, that it may give seed to the sower, and bread to the eater: 11 So shall my word be that goeth forth out of my mouth: it shall not return unto me void, but it shall accomplish that which I please, and it shall prosper in the thing whereto I sent it.

God shows Isaiah that He is indeed Almighty God, and that what He says will certainly come to pass. His Word will not return to Him void. "Void" in Hebrew is *reyqam* (**ray-KAWM**) and means "without effect." Thus, as believers we can count on God's Word. What He says is true because He is a God who cannot lie. His salvation is sure and secure for those who accept Jesus Christ as their Lord and Saviour.

Daily Bible Readings

M: Parable of the Great Banquet
Luke 14:15–24
T: God's Banquet
Isaiah 25:6–10
W: The Year of the Lord
Isaiah 61:1–6
T: Delight in the Lord
Isaiah 61:7–11
F: Blessed to Bless
2 Corinthians 9:10–15
S: God Invites Us
Isaiah 55:1–5
S: Seek the Lord
Isaiah 55:6–11

TEACHING TIPS

July 1
Bible Study Guide 5

1. Words You Should Know

A. Judgment (Micah 3:1) *mishpat* (Heb.)—A verdict, sentence, or formal decree.

B. Transgression (6:7) *pesha* (Heb.)—Moral or religious revolt.

2. Teacher Preparation

A. Begin preparing for this lesson by studying the, Bible Background, Devotional Reading, and the Daily Bible Readings listed at the end of the lesson. As you study, keep in mind the Lesson Aim.

B. Read the Focal Verses, consulting different Bible translations for clarity.

C. Complete lesson 5 in the *Precepts For Living® Personal Study Guide.*

3. Starting the Lesson

A. Before the students arrive, write the title of today's lesson, the At-A-Glance outline, and the Words You Should Know on the board.

B. After your students are settled, take prayer requests and pray, including the Lesson Aim in your request.

C. Ask the students to give their own definitions for the vocabulary words found in the Words You Should Know section. Then give biblical definitions and discuss.

D. Read and discuss the In Focus section.

4. Getting into the Lesson

A. Ask for volunteers to read the Background section and The People, Places, and Times. Discuss the material during or after each reading, tying it in with the theme.

B. Have volunteers read the Focal Verses, breaking the readings up according to the At-A-Glance

outline. Discuss the verses and relate them to today's Lesson Aim. After each section, review the appropriate Search the Scriptures questions.

5. Relating the Lesson to Life

Read and discuss Lesson in Our Society. Focus the students' attention on what God requires of His children in serving Him and each other.

6. Arousing Action

A. Direct the students to the Make It Happen questions. Explain that every day we struggle with distinguishing between right and wrong in complex ethical situations. We are overwhelmed by the magnitude of violence, injustice, and hatred in the world. But as Christians, we have the power to show God's mercy and do the right thing.

B. Encourage the students to read the Daily Bible Readings in preparation for next week's class.

C. Close the class with prayer.

Worship Guide

**For the Superintendent or Teacher
Theme: Micah Announces God's Requirements
Theme Song: "I Surrender All"
Scripture: Hebrews 12:6–12
Song: "Is Your All on the Altar?"
Meditation: Dear Father, guide us each and every day so that our actions reflect Your will. Help us to realize that right living and right worship require that we advocate justice and mercy for all humanity. Amen.**

MICAH ANNOUNCES GOD'S REQUIREMENTS

Bible Background • MICAH 2:1–4; 3:1–5, 8–12; 6:6–8
Printed Text • MICAH 3:1–4; 6:6–8   Devotional Reading • HEBREWS 12:6–12

Lesson Aim

By the end of the lesson, we will:

KNOW God's three requirements for a righteous life;

DESIRE to practice justice in our treatment of others; and

WORK toward justice for all people.

Keep in Mind

"He hath showed thee, O man, what is good; and what doth the LORD require of thee, but to do justly, and to love mercy, and to walk humbly with thy God?" (Micah 6:8).

Focal Verses

Micah 3:1 And I said, Hear, I pray you, O heads of Jacob, and ye princes of the house of Israel; Is it not for you to know judgment?

2 Who hate the good, and love the evil; who pluck off their skin from off them, and their flesh from off their bones;

3 Who also eat the flesh of my people, and flay their skin from off them; and they break their bones, and chop them in pieces, as for the pot, and as flesh within the caldron.

4 Then shall they cry unto the LORD, but he will not hear them: he will even hide his face from them at that time, as they have behaved themselves ill in their doings.

6:6 Wherewith shall I come before the LORD, and bow myself before the high God? shall I come before him with burnt offerings, with calves of a year old?

7 Will the LORD be pleased with thousands of rams, or with ten thousands of rivers of oil? shall I give my firstborn for my transgression, the fruit of my body for the sin of my soul?

8 He hath shewed thee, O man, what is good; and what doth the LORD require of thee, but to do justly, and to love mercy, and to walk humbly with thy God?

In Focus

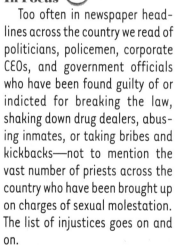

Too often in newspaper headlines across the country we read of politicians, policemen, corporate CEOs, and government officials who have been found guilty of or indicted for breaking the law, shaking down drug dealers, abusing inmates, or taking bribes and kickbacks—not to mention the vast number of priests across the country who have been brought up on charges of sexual molestation. The list of injustices goes on and on.

In most societies, leaders are held to a higher standard than those whom they serve. They are expected to obey not only the laws of God, but the laws of the land as well. They are expected to have compassion and respect for the people they serve. However, time and time again, greed and corruption have caused leaders to fall into a cesspool of crime and broken vows.

This is especially devastating when God's ministers and teachers succumb to Satan's temptations. It is most heartbreaking when these leaders do not serve the people out of a love for them and God, but for material gain.

Today's lesson tells us that God is not pleased when leaders refuse to lead by His standards or when His people do not stand on His Word.

The People, Places, and Times

Micah. Micah—whose name means "who is like the Lord?"—lived between 750 and 686 B.C. He was from the town of Moreshath Gath in southern Judah and delivered his prophetic message during the ministries of Isaiah and Hosea. Because of rampant injustice and apostasy throughout the divided kingdom, God had Micah predict the fall of Samaria, the capital of Israel, and foretell Judah's coming destruction. Although Micah's message concludes with God's promise to restore His people, his message of judgment highlights the fact that God requires justice as part of righteous living.

Background

Micah lived and ministered in the eighth century B.C., during the time of the divided kingdom. Samaria was the capital of Israel, the northern kingdom, and Jerusalem was the capital of Judah, the southern kingdom. Like Amos, Micah was from a small village in Judah. God would use this outsider, who was unfamiliar with political events in Jerusalem and Samaria, to deliver a message to all Judah and Israel.

Jerusalem was the center of religious practice for Jews throughout both kingdoms; hence, Micah's announcements of God's requirements for true worship were in stark contrast to the covenant rituals. God used Micah to inform the people that He considered true worship to consist of justice, mercy, and humility, not in empty ritual involving innumerable burnt offerings.

During Micah's ministry, injustice flourished in the land as wealthy landowners oppressed the poor and disregarded the Mosaic Law. This rampant injustice called for someone to protect the downtrodden and to preserve inherited property. Even though they adhered to the rituals of sacrifice and temple worship, the people with influence angered God because, using bribes and ruthless political maneuvering, they circumvented the laws that had been put in place to ensure justice.

Through Micah, God delivers the message that corrupt societies will be punished. However, God's grace is boundless, and He provides ample warning through His prophets. He delights in restoring His creatures despite their committing acts that do not merit such grace.

At-A-Glance

1. Micah Condemns Rulers' Actions (Micah 3:1–4)
2. God's Requirements Are Announced (6:6–8)

In Depth

1. Micah Condemns Rulers' Actions (Micah 3:1–4)

Micah vividly depicts the physical devouring of God's people and describes God's abhorrence of the ruthless acts that the rich and powerful were committing against the poor. At this time, there was an abundance of income flowing into Israel and Judah from the leasing of land to other nations. In addition to the apostasy of Israel and Judah, Micah also reports a covetous scheme that was being carried out by the rich and powerful.

The news about the powerful God of the Hebrews had spread throughout the ancient Near East. Other pagan nations concluded that the land of Israel and Judah had special power. The worshipers of false gods were paying top dollar to Jewish landowners to lease space atop hills and ridges throughout both kingdoms. As the wealth from these false worshipers poured in, the rich got greedier and sought to gobble up the land belonging to the poor. This was especially vile because God's law specifically forbade all idolatry, sought to preserve inherited land, and provided for the elimination of outstanding debts every seven years.

All such commands were ignored as the rich became intoxicated by greed. The prophets and schools of prophets in Israel and Judah should have been preaching against such widespread wickedness, but they were being silenced by bribes and favors. Micah condemned them as false prophets who preached for profit, leading the people further astray.

2. God's Requirements Are Announced (6:6–8)

Micah poses a question about what God values most in our worship of Him. Should we come before His throne with an abundance of sacrifices as required in ritual temple worship? Or does true worship begin with how we treat others in our day-to-day lives? According to Micah, true worship begins with acting justly, being merciful, and walking humbly with God (6:8).

God is more concerned that His people extend justice to others than that they place numerous sacrifices on the altar. God knows that as people stand up for the oppressed in the face of opposition, their actions will be like a sacrifice to Him. Sacrifices made according to God's principles serve to glorify His name. God expects us to imitate Him by being merciful. The taking of land from those who already had but little was the exact opposite of mercy.

Judah's rulers and Israel's arrogance and total disregard for God's law stand in stark contrast to the Lord's call to walk humbly before Him (v. 8). Being humble before God means that we know we were created to serve Him by also serving those around us.

We can be encouraged by the fact that God has provided the means for us to live out each requirement through our Saviour Jesus Christ. Without Him, we can fall into cycles of ritualistic church worship and end up dealing unjustly with others. We cannot expect that God will fail to judge individuals, communities, and nations who permit injustice to rule their land.

Search the Scriptures

1. Are leaders expected to lead justly (Micah 3:1)?

2. Does God answer the prayers of those who willfully do evil (v. 4)?

3. What type of offerings does God prefer (6:6–8)?

4. What are God's three requirements of His people (v. 8)?

Discuss the Meaning

1. Why are those entrusted with the responsibility of leadership in the church, in politics, or in the business world required to deal justly with people?

2. Why or why not is it that those in the midst of willful wrongdoing can or cannot expect to have their prayers answered or to sense God's presence?

3. Why is it that treating others with respect, showing mercy to humanity, and living humbly before God are included in righteous living?

"He hath showed thee, O man, what is good; and what doth the LORD require of thee, but to do justly, and to love mercy, and to walk humbly with thy God?" (Micah 6:8).

Lesson in Our Society

Most people want to do what is right—but how do we know what the right thing is? We should not assume that because we show up in church each week and tithe regularly, we are good Christians. God is not interested in ritualistic routines that show the world that we are believers. He requires us to show mercy as He does, treat others fairly, and live humbly.

Greed and fraud had become widespread among God's covenant people in Micah's day. Many of the elite, then as now, used money to secure acquittals, access the best health care, and influence public policy to increasingly marginalize the poor and the most vulnerable. Micah's call for the people of God to pursue justice in an affluent society is as pertinent today as it was in biblical times.

Make It Happen

God requires that our worship in our day-to-day lives be as authentic as the time spent inside the four walls of the church. Examine your life to see if you treat everyone justly, starting with your immediate family. Consider how you present yourself to others. Are you humble, or do you wear your faith on your sleeve for all to see? Is there mercy in your heart for those who are less fortunate, or do you jump on the bandwagon and assume that they must pull themselves up by their bootstraps?

After your self-checkup, ask God for forgiveness and for the power to show His mercy. Ask Him to make justice and fairness priorities in your life, as opposed to just getting to church on time. We must not forsake our call to collectively worship and honor God. Yet from Micah's message, we must understand that doing the right thing on a daily basis is God's priority for our lives. When we work for justice on the job, at home, and in our communities, our collective Sunday worship is holistic and authentic.

Follow the Spirit

What God wants me to do:

_____

_____

Remember Your Thoughts

Special insights I have learned:

_____

_____

More Light on the Text
Micah 3:1–4; 6:6–8

1 And I said, Hear, I pray you, O heads of Jacob, and ye princes of the house of Israel; Is it not for you to know judgment?

Micah lets his hearers know that they do not have the option of not listening to what he is about to say; they are commanded to listen. The word translated "hear" is the Hebrew imperative *shama* (**shaw-MAH**) and refers to a command. By God's authority, Micah is not asking his hearers if they would please listen; he is *commanding* them to listen.

There are seven main verbal patterns used in biblical Hebrew. Each pattern or stem gives a distinct nuance to any given verb. Thus, *shama,* in this context, represents the outcome of the implied action. By using this verbal form for the word *shama,* Micah can say, "Listen, and do not ignore what I am saying."

The combination of self-centeredness and political agendas was wreaking havoc on God's people, as the next few verses indicate. Micah dared the leadership to consider holding themselves responsible for the current state of affairs. The distractions of the Assyrian threat or the northern kingdom were not to blame.

Micah again uses a verbal form for the word "know." It is as if God, through Micah, was saying to the leaders of Judah, "You could have been different from the Assyrians. You did not have to treat your people the way the kings of the north treated their citizens. Nevertheless, you chose to treat *my* people in the same way your enemies treat you. You leaders of Judah chose to be unjust. You knew what you were doing and that your only intention was to seek your own good rather than the good of my people." To better understand Micah's condemnation of the leaders, we need to briefly examine what biblical justice is.

There are four words in the Hebrew language used to refer to "judgment" or "justice." The word that Micah, by the Spirit of the Lord, chooses to use in this context is *mishpat* (**mish-PAWT**). Like other Hebrew terms for justice, *mishpat* does not reflect modern-day distinctions between various types of justice such as judicial or civic justice. Justice in Middle Eastern cultures was to take into account the person, the society, and religious laws. If there is a distinction between *mishpat* and other Hebrew words for justice, it is that *mishpat* emphasizes justice as emanating from the very character of God. The problem the leaders had in practicing biblical justice was that they did not understand God or His ways.

The first step in administering biblical justice is to understand the goodness of God. When we dismiss God's desire to see good triumph among His people, any act of justice becomes nothing more than an expression of hate and evil intentions.

2 Who hate the good, and love the evil; who pluck off their skin from off them, and their flesh from off their bones;

With what indictment does Micah charge the leaders! They hate good and love evil. The Hebrew word for "hate" is *sane* (**saw-NAY**) and is the same word used in Genesis 37:4 to describe how Joseph's brothers felt about him. The Genesis passage says that Joseph's brothers were so jealous of their father's love for him that they hated him and found it impossible to show even the slightest degree of compassion toward him. Conceivably, then, justice denied to God's people is motivated by the desire to pervert the character of God. Goodness denied can only lead to evil promoted.

In this context, the leaders' hatred is directed outward toward humanity because they are caught up in selfishness. *Towb* is the Hebrew word translated "good." It means excellent; right (ethical); moral; and can refer to anything that has practical, spiritual, social, economic, or domestic benefit. To hate the good that God extends to His people is essentially to hate God: "Anyone who claims to be in the light but hates his brother is still in the darkness" (1 John 2:9, NIV.)

Ahab (**aw-HAB**) is the Hebrew word used here for "love," a love that is expressed in a close relation-ship. The Hebrew word used for "evil" is *ra* (**rah**). We usually think of the term "evil" as referring to something bad. However, loving evil is more than loving that which is bad; it means to be so consumed with hatred that it is impossible to be motivated by or do anything that might reflect the character of God. When leaders hate good by depriving God's people of justice, they become ambassadors for evil.

3 Who also eat the flesh of my people, and flay their skin from off them; and they break their bones, and chop them in pieces, as for the pot, and as flesh within the caldron.

Prayer and justice vanish when we don't listen to God (v. 3). We open ourselves up to doing the most unthinkable things to others, believing that we are justified in doing so.

Moses prophesied that such inhumane acts would result from breaking God's covenant (see Leviticus 26:29). Consumed with their own survival, the leaders of Judah began to act just like the ungodly in the northern kingdom and the invading Assyrians. When church leaders become more concerned with their own well-being than with trusting in the living God, God's people become mere pawns used to fulfill lustful and sinful personal and corporate desires.

The leaders of Micah's day had begun to administer justice as if the laws existed only for their own benefit. Justice that does not emanate from the character of God results in idolatry and the dehumanization of God's people (or of any person for that matter). God's people were being treated as if they were not even worthy of having the God-given right to sustain themselves.

The leaders blocked any attempts by the people to meet their daily needs (cf. Micah 2:2, 8). Because the leaders lusted for what others had worked for, they deprived others of their God-given rights. They oppressed men and their households, thereby denying the men their God-given right to try to provide an inheritance for their families. There is no question that these leaders had reached the epitome of selfishness. If others are not the object of our love, they will become the object of our scorn.

433

4 Then shall they cry unto the LORD, but he will not hear them: he will even hide his face from them at that time, as they have behaved themselves ill in their doings.

Micah begins the verse by stating, "then shall they cry," a phrase translated from the Hebrew word *za`aq* (**zah'-AK**), which means "a shriek or an outcry." In short, he tells the leaders that one day, they, too, are going to cry out for God's help. They would soon suffer the consequences of their own sins as God's principle of reaping what one sows would be in effect. The justice they had denied others would be in direct proportion to the justice they sought from the Lord. Upon closer examination of verse 4, we see that *as they* is the key phrase. The justice they had denied others would be the balance used to measure the justice they would receive.

If we want God to hear us when we cry to Him, we must be willing to hear and compassionately respond to the cries of others. Surely we do not want God to hide His face from us in our time of need. Thus, it is imperative for us to heed the cries of those around us.

The indictment in chapter 3 is truly horrific. It was not just the political leaders who were corrupt; it was the religious leaders as well. Everyone was motivated by the desire to build his or her own personal kingdom. So, what are the first steps in changing the way things are or have been to the way God wants them to be? Micah 6:6–8 gives us God's plan for how to get back up once we have fallen down. We can turn things around. We can repent and take a stand.

6:6 Wherewith shall I come before the LORD, and bow myself before the high God? shall I come before him with burnt offerings, with calves of a year old? 7 Will the LORD be pleased with thousands of rams, or with ten thousands of rivers of oil? shall I give my firstborn for my transgression, the fruit of my body for the sin of my soul?

Notice the question, "Shall I come before the Lord?" This would have been the natural response of anyone seeking to repent. These were the things that were required of every God-fearing Israelite—worship God, present Him with burnt offerings and thank offerings, and consecrate your firstborn for the Lord's service. These things were commendable, but according to Micah, they were not enough.

It may have been that these leaders and prophets had not engaged in personal worship and sacrifice for quite some time, and that they needed to get back into the house of the Lord. It was foolish, however, to think that they could get right with God without any attempt to correct the wrongs that they had done. Repentance and religious ritual without compassion for and restoration of the offended show lack of faith (see James 2:14–17).

If you want to get right with God, simply reciting creeds will not do it. Daily devotions are nice, but they don't cut the mustard. You can even call the assembly together and have a grand old worship service, singing every theologically profound hymn you know, and you still will not satisfy the Lord. "No," says God. "To get right with me, you are going to have to go back to the very people you abused and mistreated and fix things."

8 He hath shewed thee, O man, what is good; and what doth the LORD require of thee, but to do justly, and to love mercy, and to walk humbly with thy God?

What a powerful word Micah uses to begin verse 8! The word *nagad* (**naw-GAD**), translated as "showed," literally means "to flow" and figuratively implies telling or reporting with a purpose. The leaders were without excuse. They knew what to do. It may be that God does not tell us everything, but some things He has made very clear. To get right with Him, you are going to have to go back to the very people you abused and mistreated and address the problem.

Like the people of Micah's time, we, too, have choices. We can continue to ignore God and pay the price, or we can repent and do that which is good. However, our faith will be tested. Not only has God shown the *leaders* what to do, but He declares that this is what we must do—obey His commands.

Darash (**daw-RASH**) is the Hebrew word translated as "require" and means "to seek." God expects leaders to seek out His will as they interact with others. Grace not only saves us from sin; it also gives us the ability to do good to others. We cannot treat others badly and still maintain that our intimate relationship with God has not been negatively impacted.

"Do justly, love mercy, and walk humbly." This is another eye-opening set of verbs Micah uses: do, love, and walk humbly. *Asah* (**aw-SAW**), translated "do," means more than just doing something; the emphasis is on making something happen. Wow! God is not asking whether we want to be just; He is telling us to make godly justice a part of our modus operandi. However, the desire to be just as God is just can be sustained only by a love for mercy (see the earlier discussion of the word "love" in 3:2). Just as a love for evil inhibits our ability to respond to others in a godly manner, so a love for mercy keeps us looking for ways to express God's love and grace to others.

One of the most theologically significant words in the Old Testament is *checed* (**KHEH-sed**), which is translated as "mercy," "lovingkindness," or "goodness." The word is often used with the Hebrew term *towb,* or "good" (see comment on verse 2). Some scholars attempt to confine *checed* (mercy) to the covenantal relationship between God and His people. However, the abundant references to *checed* in the text indicate a broader application. Mercy is an attribute of a holy and loving God. The significance of the word in this passage is that God requires His people to demonstrate mercy as we are daily being made into His image.

Have you ever had to go back and say, "I was wrong"? If you have, you know how difficult confession can be. Nevertheless, confession that is not combined with corrective action is nothing more than worldly sorrow. Micah was essentially asking these leaders to put into practice what they should have been doing all along. Micah admonishes the leaders to confess their sin and to restore what had been gained in an unjust manner. God is commanding the leaders not just to *say* the right thing, but to *do* the right thing. This step requires supernatural power that only God can give. Therefore, Micah concludes these verses with a final challenge. "Walk humbly with God."

Tsana (**tsaw-NAH**) is the Hebrew word for "humble." It means to act in a way that demonstrates respect for the desires of someone else. In this context, to walk humbly with God means to behave in such a way that God Himself could say, "What you just did is exactly what I would have done in the same situation." That's why we have to act humbly. Walking humbly with God is what empowers leaders to show justice, love, and mercy. The implication is that if we cannot demonstrate these qualities, it is because we are not walking humbly with God. Moreover, when we are not walking humbly with God, we don't care what God thinks; thus, we don't care what action He might take. Equally important is the observation that when we are not walking humbly with God, it means we have forgotten how merciful He has been toward us.

Micah's indictment still applies to Christians today. At one time or another, we have all used others as little more than tools to reach the next level of success. Fortunately, we can "turn the tide" by learning to walk humbly before God. What is God putting on your heart to do right now that might take you out of your "comfort zone"? Is there someone you know who needs a manifestation of His love and mercy?

Daily Bible Readings

M: Fear the Lord
Deuteronomy 10:12–22
T: The Disciplined Life
Hebrews 12:6–12
W: Human Plans and God's
Micah 2:1–5
T: Sins Denounced
Micah 3:1–7
F: Micah Speaks Out
Micah 3:8–12
S: Water Flows Upstream
Micah 4:1–5
S: What Does God Require?
Micah 6:3–8

TEACHING TIPS

July 8
Bible Study Guide 6

1. Words You Should Know

A. Filthy (Zephaniah 3:1) *mara* (Heb.)—Rebellious.

B. Polluted (v. 1) *gaal* (Heb.)—Soiled or desecrated.

C. Oppressing (v. 1) *yanah* (Heb.)—Raging or violent; suppressing; maltreating.

D. Light (v. 4) *pachaz* (Heb.)—Literally, to bubble up or froth; hence, without substance; insignificant.

2. Teacher Preparation

A. Prayerfully read the entire Bible Study Guide, including the Bible text, the Bible Background Scripture, and the Devotional Reading for today's lesson.

B. Collect current news items that demonstrate depravity in the government, the judicial system, and the church.

C. Complete lesson 6 in the *Precepts For Living® Personal Study Guide*.

3. Starting the Lesson

A. Assign a student to lead the class in prayer, focusing on the Lesson Aim.

B. Ask a student to read the In Focus section.

C. With reference to some of the newspaper examples, ask the class what motivates this type of behavior and why it appears that there is no shame.

4. Getting into the Lesson

A. Allow each student to read some portion of The People, Places, and Times; Background; Keep in Mind; and the At-A-Glance outline.

B. Allow the students to read the Focal Verses based on the At-A-Glance outline. Be prepared to discuss them and to instruct the class using In Depth and More Light on the Text.

C. Use Words You Should Know to add intensity to the lesson discussion.

D. Ask if anyone can show ways in which God is making His impending judgment known to society.

E. Ask the students to respond to the Search the Scriptures questions.

5. Relating the Lesson to Life

A. Ask the students to respond to the Discuss the Meaning questions.

B. Have someone read Lesson in Our Society. Allow the students to pause for a moment and internalize the questions raised at the end of that section.

6. Arousing Action

A. Allow the students to read Make It Happen and to make a commitment to obey God's law—in other words, to be doers of the word and not hearers only.

B. Encourage the students to be prepared for next week's lesson by reading the Daily Bible Readings.

C. Close the class in prayer.

Worship Guide

For the Superintendent or Teacher
Theme: Zephaniah Announces God's Justice
Theme Song: "Balm in Gilead"
Scripture: Psalm 33:1–11
Song: "Praise Him, Praise Him"
Meditation: Heavenly Father, Creator of all things, shall not the Judge of all the earth do right? We pray for mercy because we deserve nothing from You. As we humble ourselves, give us more grace. Help us to comprehend our need for You, Lord. We thank You. We praise You. We glorify Your name. Amen.

ZEPHANIAH ANNOUNCES GOD'S JUSTICE

Bible Background • ZEPHANIAH 3:1–13; 2 CHRONICLES 34:1–3
Printed Text • ZEPHANIAH 3:1–5, 8–9   Devotional Reading • PSALM 27:7–14

Lesson Aim

By the end of the lesson, we will:
UNDERSTAND those things that will bring God's judgment upon us;
DEVELOP hearts that are not arrogant, treacherous, or profane; and
PRACTICE obedience to God's law.

Keep in Mind

"Therefore wait ye upon me, saith the LORD, until the day that I rise up to the prey: for my determination is to gather the nations, that I may assemble the kingdoms, to pour upon them mine indignation, even all my fierce anger: for all the earth shall be devoured with the fire of my jealousy" (Zephaniah 3:8).

Focal Verses

Zephaniah 3:1 Woe to her that is filthy and polluted, to the oppressing city!

2 She obeyed not the voice; she received not correction; she trusted not in the LORD; she drew not near to her God.

3 Her princes within her are roaring lions; her judges are evening wolves; they gnaw not the bones till the morrow.

4 Her prophets are light and treacherous persons: her priests have polluted the sanctuary, they have done violence to the law.

5 The just LORD is in the midst thereof; he will not do iniquity: every morning doth he bring his judgment to light, he faileth not; but the unjust knoweth no shame.

3:8 Therefore wait ye upon me, saith the LORD, until the day that I rise up to the prey: for my determination is to gather the nations, that I may assemble the kingdoms, to pour upon them mine indignation, even all my fierce anger: for all the earth shall be devoured with the fire of my jealousy.

9 For then will I turn to the people a pure language, that they may all call upon the name of the LORD, to serve him with one consent.

In Focus

Imagine for a moment that you have thrown open the patio doors of your oceanfront home after a powerful storm. A fresh breeze is stirring. In the distance, you hear the sound of children playing and yelling in delight.

Suddenly, you feel a powerful rushing wind, and screams of desperation fill the air. You realize that the morning peace was really the calm in the eye of a hurricane. You watch the backside of the storm lifting rooftops, bringing down chimneys, and crushing cars under the weight of 100-year-old tree branches. You gather your family and huddle away from the windows as you turn to God in desperate, heart-wrenching prayer.

In 2005, Hurricane Katrina brought that kind of swift destruction to New Orleans, killing over 1,000 people. However, that number didn't compare to the 10,000 lives taken by Hurricane Mitch in Honduras in 1998, a number that in turn was small compared to the 52,000 lives taken by the tsunami that struck Indonesia in 2004. Even that number pales in comparison to the 131,000 persons killed in a single day in 1991 by a cyclone in Bangladesh!

Most of these people were occupied with the routine of starting their day; the end of life probably seemed distant and unimportant. The ultimate question in the face of such raw, unstoppable power is: What is your relationship with God?

As we examine Zephaniah's message, we must ask ourselves: Are we living each day as though it were our last?

The People, Places, and Times

Zephaniah. The name Zephaniah means "the Lord hides" or "he whom the Lord hides." The first verse of the book that bears his name says that Zephaniah was the son of Cushi and the great-great-grandson of King Hezekiah. Thus, he was a prophet of royal blood. Zephaniah lived in Judah. The length of his ministry is not known. The word of the Lord came to him in the days of Josiah, king of Judah, placing Zephaniah's ministry between 640 and 609 B.C. and making him a contemporary of the prophets Jeremiah, Habakkuk, and Nahum. The central theme of the book of Zephaniah is "the day of the Lord."

Background

The nation of Judah was one of two kingdoms into which the unified kingdom of Israel under King Rehoboam (son of King Solomon) had split. Judah was the southern kingdom and was inhabited by the tribes of Judah and Benjamin. The ten tribes of the northern kingdom of Israel had already been judged by God for their evil practices. The Assyrians had come, devoured the land, taken Israel captive, and deported the people around 722 B.C. The kingdom of Judah seemed oblivious to these events and made the same mistakes. Their degeneration was accelerated by King Manasseh, the grandfather of King Josiah (2 Kings 21:1–26).

King Manasseh did evil in the sight of the Lord by adopting the same practices as the heathen nations the Lord had driven out from the Promised Land. Manasseh reinstituted idol worship in Judah after the death of his father, good King Hezekiah. Manasseh worshiped and served the gods of astrology, practiced soothsaying, used witchcraft, consulted spiritists and mediums, and established pagan places of worship. He went so far as to place an idol in God's temple and offer human sacrifices. Jerusalem was filled from one end to the other with the innocent blood that Manasseh had shed. The king seduced the nation of Judah to do more evil than all the pagan nations that surrounded them.

Judah failed to observe the commandments that the Lord had given them and broke their covenant with the Lord. They did much evil and provoked the Lord to anger. The Lord said that He would bring a great calamity on Jerusalem and Judah because of the great evil they were doing. This calamity would come at the hands of the Babylonians (Chaldeans) in a series of three attacks in 605 B.C., 597 B.C., and 586 B.C. Each time, captives would be taken back to Babylon. King Josiah was a "breath of fresh air" in the midst of the stench that permeated the nation. His father, Amon, who followed Manasseh, was assassinated after reigning for only two years, and Josiah became king when he was 8 years old.

Josiah reigned for 31 years and did what was right in the sight of the Lord. At the age of 16, he began to seek the Lord. Four years later, he had systematically torn down and removed all the idolatrous images and altars. In the 18th year of his reign, while the temple of God was being restored, the Book of the Law was found. When King Josiah heard the words of the Law, he humbled himself, tore his clothes, and wept before the Lord. He gathered the people of Jerusalem and read the Law to them, reestablishing proper worship practices in Jerusalem.

God honored King Josiah for his humility, obedience, and faithfulness. However, the nation as a whole was doomed; they could not stem the tide of corruption that had been set in motion by King Manasseh. They had passed the point of no return, and after the death of King Josiah they had gone back to their evil ways. The prophet Zephaniah spoke to this situation. We are not certain whether he spoke prior to or during the revival instituted by King Josiah, but he spoke to a deeply rooted condition of apostasy, one whose roots needed to be removed.

At-A-Glance

1. The Spiritual Condition of Jerusalem
(Zephaniah 3:1–2)
2. The Spiritual Condition of Jerusalem's
Leaders (vv. 3–5)
3. God's Justice Is Determined
(3:8–9)

In Depth

1. The Spiritual Condition of Jerusalem (Zephaniah 3:1–2)

"Woe" is a strong word of correction from the

Lord. The word refers to an outward expression of pain and grief. God is saying to the city of Jerusalem, to the nation that she represents, and to all the inhabitants of the land, "Great pain and grief be to you!" The people deserved punishment because they were filthy, they were polluted, and they were oppressing those who were powerless to resist.

Here was a highly favored nation of whom much was expected. God had formed them and had given them a place to call home. He had protected them from their enemies. God entrusted the oracles of the one true God to them. All they had to do to be successful was to be faithful to the God who loved them.

The people of Judah were filthy in the sense of being rebellious, abandoning the instruction of the Lord. When they knew to do right, they chose instead to do the things that provided instant gratification. The people were polluted in that they continued in sin while at the same time observing religious rituals, combining the pagan practices of other nations with the worship of God. But the Lord loathed this syncretistic "worship."

To make matters worse, the strong oppressed the weak, the poor, the orphans, and the widows. The strong had no regard for the rights of the poor. What could the poor do? They had no financial resources to pay for a defense, had no political connections, and posed no threat of retaliation. Because they were too insignificant, those in positions of power did not care about them. Those in power rushed to confiscate, by force, whatever property or valuables were left unprotected by a dead father or husband.

The people of Judah refused to keep the terms of the covenant. They cast aside or misapplied God's Word. God sent His prophets to warn them, but they ignored the warnings. Instead, they continued to pilfer from the poor and the oppressed. They built up their armies and fortified their cities, pursuing alliances with wicked nations rather than seeking security in God's lordship. Yet they expected God to reward them for continuing to observe their empty religious rituals.

2. The Spiritual Condition of Jerusalem's Leaders (vv. 3–5)

Zephaniah exposes the behavior of four groups of national leaders: the princes, the judges, the prophets, and the priests. The description of the princes is reminiscent of the way the apostle Peter describes the activity of the Devil, who goes about as a roaring lion seeking whom he may devour (1 Peter 5:8). A roaring lion is a lion preparing to attack. Likewise, these people in government were looking for every opportunity for personal gain at the expense of others. The judges were characterized as being insatiably greedy, leaving nothing until morning. They took bribes under cover of darkness and completed their business by morning. There was no justice in the land; God looked for justice but could not find any (Jeremiah 5:1). The poor, the orphans, and the widows were easy prey.

The "official" prophets committed adultery, declared false messages, encouraged evildoers, and became a stumbling block to any who might consider turning from wickedness (Jeremiah 23:14, 32). God had not sent these "prophets." They proclaimed peace and prosperity, if the price was right. The priests polluted the temple with idols and sacrifices to false gods. They distorted the intent of the law and replaced the teaching of God with their own traditions. Thus, they failed in their duty as advocates of repentance, justice, and righteousness.

However, godly prophets such as Zephaniah, Jeremiah, Nahum, and Habakkuk still proclaimed God's truth. The godly king, Josiah, rose above the corruption of society. When he heard the words of the Law, he was receptive and humbled himself. He then implemented substantial reform throughout Judah.

3. God's Justice Is Determined (3:8–9)

The godly in the nation of Judah were encouraged to look to the Lord and trust Him. The poor, the orphans, and the widows could rest assured that God would end the injustices being heaped upon them. In one great act of judgment, God would pour out His wrath and indignation on all evildoers in Judah. There seems to be a transition here from the impending destruction of Jerusalem to that yet future great day of judgment when God will gather all nations for the final judgment. Yet a godly remnant will emerge who will worship the Lord together with pure hearts because God Himself will purify them. They will call on the name of the Lord and serve Him in unity.

Search the Scriptures

1. How is the "city" described in the first verse of the lesson (Zephaniah 3:1)?

2. Whom did the city of Jerusalem refuse to trust (v. 2)?

3. What were the princes of the city like (v. 3)?

4. How are the judges of the city described (v. 3)?

5. What was the condition of the church leaders (v. 4)?

Discuss the Meaning

1. What is the affect on society when governmental and judicial leaders behave like those described by Zephaniah?

2. Why do you think people in the church continue to follow leaders who do violence to God's law?

3. What makes you obey or disobey God's law?

Lesson in Our Society

The pollution that the prophet Zephaniah identified in the nation of Judah in the 7th century B.C. is just as common in the 21st century. In recent years, adultery and fornication were reported in the highest office of the land: the presidency. Judges are promoting their own personal political agendas instead of rendering decisions based on the law of the land. Some people who claim to be representatives of God and spiritual advisors are committing the same acts as those they are supposed to be counseling. At least one church is still wrestling with a pedophile scandal in the priesthood. Those who do these things do violence to God's law. Many innocent people feel victimized and abandoned. However, God is not silent. Society may try to silence His messengers, but God still speaks to those in high places who abuse their position, as well as to the innocent. He is speaking to you; are you able to hear and obey? Will you trust God to correct the injustices of society and create righteousness in the hearts of humankind?

Make It Happen

God says to wait on Him to cleanse the world, but He requires us to clean ourselves now. We cannot be a friend of the world system and still be friends of God (1 John 2:15). Submit yourself to God and resist the activities of a fallen world. Draw nigh to God and He will draw nigh to you (James 4:7–8).

Follow the Spirit

What God wants me to do:

_____

_____

Remember Your Thoughts

Special insights I have learned:

_____

_____

More Light on the Text
Zephaniah 3:1–5, 8–9

In our last lesson, we saw that the leaders and the people had had many opportunities to repent. The "God of the second chance" had withheld His judgment for quite some time. Zephaniah is preaching about 100 years after Micah.

It is probable that Zephaniah ministered during the reign of Josiah (640–609 B.C.). Josiah was a good and godly king of Judah (2 Kings 22–23:30). Unfortunately, after 55 years of decadence under the wicked King Manasseh (697–642 B.C.), the die had been cast: "Nevertheless, the LORD did not turn away from the heat of his fierce anger, which burned against Judah because of all that Manasseh had done to provoke him to anger. So the LORD said, 'I will remove Judah also from my presence as I removed Israel, and I will reject Jerusalem, the city I chose, and this temple, about which I said, There shall my Name be'" (2 Kings 23:26–27, NIV). Zephaniah was God's prophet for the hour, sent to proclaim that the time for repentance was running out.

In the first two chapters of the book of Zephaniah, the prophet lumps Judah in with the other nations who deserve judgment. The book begins with the condemnation of Judah and describes how God will pour out His wrath on the people. Judgment does indeed begin with the household of God (1 Peter 4:17). It is time to stop blaming TV or other media, the government, the public schools, or the neighbors for our lack of commitment and repentance. These things may play a part in our choices, but ultimately responsibility for our actions rest within ourselves. From God's perspective, our lack of commitment to Him cannot be blamed on our circumstances. Our attitude and behavior, while walking through our circumstances, are our own responsibility. The real problem is often within us, not merely outside of us (Matthew 15:18–19). Zephaniah says that the corruption of God's people is what has defiled the nation and the city.

God's people had continued to ignore His call to repent. Because they had propped up merciless leaders and ungodly prophets, they would incur God's wrath. Reflection on the words of Micah spoken 100 years earlier lets us understand that these people had turned up their noses at God, and now God was about to "lower the boom."

As we know from TV crime shows, gathering evidence has taken on a new dimension. The tiniest amount of DNA or some other substance can be traced to an individual and provide the basis for a conviction. On the other hand, it takes only a shrewd lawyer to raise a question about how the evidence was gathered to get an acquittal. God had been "collecting evidence" for hundreds of years. He does not make a case against us; He allows us to make a case against ourselves. In today's lesson, the evidence was in, and the Lord God was about to proclaim judgment.

1 Woe to her that is filthy and polluted, to the oppressing city!

The first word in verse 1 is *Howy* (**HOH-ee**), translated "Woe," and is often used to express dissatisfaction. In this case, however, God was expressing more than just dissatisfaction; He describes the city as being *filthy, polluted, and the embodiment of oppression.*

The word translated "filthy" is *mara* (**maw-RAW**). This word can also be translated "lifted up," and its root form may be used of God. Likewise, the word translated "polluted," *ga'al* (**GAW-al**), has a form that can be translated as "redeem." Zephaniah is using wordplay to describe the situation. Ironically, although the city had become a place of oppression,

characterized by anything and everything that opposed God, the second half of the verse suggests that the people were usurping God's authority and misusing it at best. Instead of living as redeemed, covenant people, they were acting just the opposite.

2 She obeyed not the voice; she received not correction; she trusted not in the LORD; she drew not near to her God. Her princes within her are roaring lions; her judges are evening wolves; they gnaw not the bones till the morrow.

Just as in Micah's day 100 years earlier, the leaders hated good and loved evil. Now, however, it seems that these attitudes and behaviors have spread to the whole society. Large numbers of the people were completely disregarding the things of the Lord. Using a series of negatives, Zephaniah brings a threefold indictment against the people: they did not listen, they did not receive correction, and they did not trust the Lord.

The first part of verse 2 could be translated literally as "not hearing the voice," "not receiving" the correction of the Lord," "not trusting the Lord," and "not drawing near to the Lord." The phrase "received [not] correction" is a translation of the Hebrew words *laqach* (**law-KAKH**), meaning "received," and *muwcar* (**moo-SAWR**), meaning "correction." In the Old Testament, the word *muwcar* usually refers to discipline that is initiated by God. Thus, rather than accept God's corrective words of discipline, the people dismissed the Lord's purposes as unimportant and trivial.

The result is evident: When we refuse to accept God's discipline, we are distancing ourselves from God. *Qarab* (**kaw- RAB'**) is the Hebrew word for "draw near." In the qal form (refer to the previous lesson), *qarab* means to draw near to a point of reference. God was no longer the peoples' "reference point." The perfect-tense verbs (hearing, teaching, trusting, and drawing), each prefixed by the negative "not," speak of completed action. For Judah, God was no longer on the throne, and their past and present actions verified Zephaniah's indictment.

3 Her princes within her are roaring lions; her judges are evening wolves; they gnaw not the bones till the morrow.

The princes and judges are governmental and judicial officials, respectively, all of whom were acting like animals of prey. Those who should have been protecting the people had become like "animals" (Micah 3:3). Never satisfied with what they could deprive others of, they stripped the people of everything. The prophet compares them to wolves gnawing on their prey until all is devoured, leaving nothing but bones.

4 Her prophets are light and treacherous persons: her priests have polluted the sanctuary, they have done violence to the law.

The prophets spoken of in verse 4 trusted in themselves more than they trusted in God. In Hebrew, the first phrase is literally, "prophets *light* men." Whether these were prophets of God who had turned away from Him or prophets whom God had not called in the first place, the result was the same: "ministry" guided by the dictates of men. Apostasy had infiltrated every aspect of society. The rulers had given themselves over to evil, the prophets concocted sermons to support evil, and those who worked in the house of the Lord benefited from the evil.

The word translated "polluted" in verse 4 is different from that used in verse 1. This word, *chalal* (**khaw-LAL**), in the Piel form means "to treat with contempt" (specifically, those things that belong to God). Jesus said, "Many will say to me on that day, 'Lord, Lord, did we not prophesy in your name, and in your name drive out demons and perform many miracles?' Then I will tell them plainly, 'I never knew you. Away from me, you evildoers!'" (Matthew 7:22–23, NIV).

Even worse, the leaders of the city were trying to cover up their actions by distorting God's word. The leaders were doing violence (*chamac*, **khaw-MAS**) to the word of God. The word *chamac* means "to strip off," or tear something from that with which it is intimately connected. These rulers completely "stripped" the law of its intimate connection with the character of God.

5 The just LORD is in the midst thereof; he will not do iniquity: every morning doth he bring his judgment to light, he faileth not; but the unjust knoweth no shame.

The opening phrase of verse 5 literally reads, "Yahweh the righteous (just)." Again, noting the exact Hebrew phrase is helpful in understanding what Zephaniah is trying to communicate: "Yahweh the righteous in the midst (of a society of unrighteousness and injustice) is not doing unrighteousness or injustice." Instead, "morning-by-morning judgment (justice) gives light." The implication is that, when God is near, His light can direct us into paths of justice.

The phrase "he faileth not" is reminiscent of Isaiah 55:11, which says, "So shall My word be that goes forth from My mouth; It shall not return to Me void, But it shall accomplish what I please, And it shall prosper in the thing for which I sent it" (NKJV). Of course, the reverse is also true: If God is *not* near, the darkness increases.

The unjust do not understand that what they are doing is shameful. The nation of Judah had sunk so low and had become so "comfortable" with injustice that they no longer understood or cared how their actions were viewed by God. The priests, along with the rest of the leaders, had literally turned God's house, God's kingdom, into personal platforms to exalt themselves. As Jesus would later say, they had turned God's house into a den of thieves (Mark 11:17).

God had provided clear and undeniable evidence that safety and security could be found only in Him. He had even gone so far as to show Judah that relying on other nations would only lead to captivity. Yet, even though the nation had been reduced to subjects of Assyria, they refused to acknowledge their idolatry and wickedness, pretending that all was well.

3:8 Therefore wait ye upon me, saith the LORD, until the day that I rise up to the prey: for my determination is to gather the nations, that I may assemble the kingdoms, to pour upon them mine indignation, even all my fierce anger: for all the earth shall be devoured with the fire of my jealousy. 9 For then

will I turn to the people a pure language, that they may all call upon the name of the LORD, to serve him with one consent.

In verse 8, the word "wait" literally means "to wait for an unexpected event." The faithful could look for an unexpected deliverance, the unfaithful, for an unexpected judgment. There is encouragement for the faithful and a warning for the unfaithful.

God Himself will "raise up" (establish) the prey. The time will come, says the Lord, when the prey—all those who are opposed to God—will think the battle is over, not knowing that the battle—indeed, the entire war—is about to come to an end.

The Lord will gather the nations, all who have opposed him, and pour out His indignation. The Hebrew word for "gather" is *acaph* (**aw-SAF'**) and refers to the assembly of like kinds. The Hebrew word translated "kingdom" is *mamlakah* (**mam-law-kaw'**) and is often used to refer to earthly kingdoms. In the Old Testament, it is used to refer specifically to non-Israelite kingdoms. Just as the saints are marked as God's possession, so any who oppose the Lord are His enemies. We are either for God or against Him; there is no middle ground.

Also, during this time God will make "pure" (Heb. *barar,* **baw-rar'** meaning purge or cleanse) His people in order to unify everyone with one language so that we can all worship Him together in spirit and in truth.

Daily Bible Readings

M: Prayer for Help
Psalm 27:7–14
T: The Day of the Lord
Isaiah 2:12–22
W: God's Eternal Counsel
Psalm 33:1–11
T: Young Josiah's Reforms
2 Chronicles 34:1–7
F: Woe to Wrongdoers
Zephaniah 3:1–7
S: Deliverance Will Come
Zephaniah 3:8–13
S: The Call to Rejoice
Zephaniah 3:14–20

TEACHING TIPS
July 15
Bible Study Guide 7

1. Words You Should Know

A. Parable (Habakkuk 2:6) *mashal* (Heb.)—A portrayed object lesson.

B. Proverb (v. 6) *chiydah* (Heb.)—A puzzle; an enigmatic saying, question, or story whose meaning must be determined by the audience.

C. Spoil (v. 8) *shalal* (Heb.)—To drop or strip; to plunder.

D. Knowledge (v. 14) *yada* (Heb.)—A knowing gained by seeing.

2. Teacher Preparation

A. Prayerfully read the Bible Background and Devotional Reading.

B. Complete lesson 7 in the *Precepts For Living® Personal Study Guide.*

C. Be prepared to discuss Make It Happen.

D. Be prepared to discuss how people's actions can try the patience of Christians and make God seem indifferent. Consider familiarizing yourself with the reparations debate in America or other examples of ways in which people try to resolve injustices.

3. Starting the Lesson

A. Assign a student to lead the class in prayer, focusing on the Lesson Aim.

B. Ask a student to read the In Focus story.

C. Ask the students for examples of actions done by people that cause them to wonder if God is indifferent.

4. Getting into the Lesson

A. Allow each student to read some portion of The People, Places, and Times; Background; Keep in Mind; and the At-A-Glance outline.

B. Ask volunteers to read Focal Verses.

C. Use Words You Should Know to add intensity to the lesson discussion.

D. Since God promises to make everything right one day, ask the students why they should be concerned about conditions affecting believers today.

E. Ask the students to respond to the Search the Scriptures questions.

5. Relating the Lesson to Life

A. Ask the students to respond to the Discuss the Meaning questions.

B. Have someone read Lesson in Our Society. Ask the students if they feel justice was served.

6. Arousing Action

A. Allow the students to read Make It Happen and encourage them to not be indifferent to the ills of society and the church.

B. Ask the students to take a few minutes to respond to Follow the Spirit and Remember Your Thoughts.

C. Encourage the students to be prepared for next week's lesson.

HABAKKUK ANNOUNCES THE DOOM OF THE UNRIGHTEOUS

Bible Background • HABAKKUK 2:1–20; 2 KINGS 23:35–37
Printed Text • HABAKKUK 2:6–14   Devotional Reading • PSALM 37:27–34

Lesson Aim

By the end of the lesson, we will:

UNDERSTAND the reasons we can trust God in the midst of great suffering;

TRUST in the Lord for His final triumph; and

PERSEVERE in following the Lord.

Keep in Mind

"For the earth shall be filled with the knowledge of the glory of the LORD, as the waters cover the sea" (Habakkuk 2:14).

Focal Verses

Habakkuk 2:6 Shall not all these take up a parable against him, and a taunting proverb against him, and say, Woe to him that increaseth that which is not his! how long? and to him that ladeth himself with thick clay!

7 Shall they not rise up suddenly that shall bite thee, and awake that shall vex thee, and thou shalt be for booties unto them?

8 Because thou hast spoiled many nations, all the remnant of the people shall spoil thee; because of men's blood, and for the violence of the land, of the city, and of all that dwell therein.

9 Woe to him that coveteth an evil covetousness to his house, that he may set his nest on high, that he may be delivered from the power of evil!

10 Thou hast consulted shame to thy house by cutting off many people, and hast sinned against thy soul.

11 For the stone shall cry out of the wall, and the beam out of the timber shall answer it.

12 Woe to him that buildeth a town with blood, and stablisheth a city by iniquity!

13 Behold, is it not of the LORD of hosts that the people shall labor in the very fire, and the people shall weary themselves for very vanity?

14 For the earth shall be filled with the knowledge of the glory of the LORD, as the waters cover the sea.

In Focus

One of my all-time favorite movies is the 1994 drama, *The Shawshank Redemption.* Andy Dufresne (Tim Robbins), the main character, has been in prison for 19 years. Accused of murdering his wife, Andy (we discover) is innocent, convicted by circumstantial evidence. His fellow inmates and even the warden, who symbolizes justice and punishment, gradually learn of his innocence. The warden does not want Andy released because he has enlisted Andy's talent as an accountant to help him steal money from the prison appropriations to line his own pockets.

Meanwhile, Andy finds a way to use his relationship with the warden to create the prison's first library in the midst of evil forces conspiring to kill him.

In one scene, we find Andy musing over his situation with Red (Morgan Freeman), an older inmate who has become Andy's best friend. Andy asks Red whether he thinks that he (Red) will ever get out. Red says, "Sure. When I got a long white beard and about three marbles left rolling around upstairs. " Andy responds by saying, "I guess it comes down to a simple choice, really. Get busy living or get busy dying."

In the end, Andy escapes to Mexico. We learn that he has secretly been planning the escape for years. He writes to Red, now newly paroled, and ends his letter with the following observation: "Remember, Red, hope is a good thing, maybe the best of things, and no good thing ever dies."

This is the message of hope from our Lord: No matter what the hardship, no good thing ever dies.

Habakkuk questioned God as to why evil prevails. In today's lesson, we are reminded that we may experience suffering, but in the end, God will reward our right living.

The People, Places, and Times

Habakkuk. Information about Habakkuk is very limited. There are two references to him in the book of the Bible that bears his name. He was a prophet of God who probably lived during some portion of the reigns of Josiah, Jehoiakim, and other kings that followed. This dating is derived from a reference in Habakkuk 1:6 to the impending arrival of the Chaldeans in 605 B.C. It is possible that Habakkuk witnessed the decline and fall of the Assyrian Empire and knew about the fall of the Assyrian capital of Nineveh in 612 B.C. The sinful conditions in Judah he wrote about are also consistent with this time in history, which would make him a contemporary of the prophets Jeremiah, Zephaniah, and Nahum. The central theme of the book of Habakkuk is faith in the midst of problems and is beautifully expressed in 2:4, which says, "the just shall live by his faith." The name Habakkuk may mean "one who embraces," a fitting name for a man who struggled through the conflicts of life while continuing to "embrace" God.

Background

Habakkuk's complaints may reflect a time shortly after the death of King Josiah in 609 B.C. The death of King Josiah was a tragic event that occurred during a military campaign against Egypt in the valley of Megiddo, northwest of Judah in the upper part of Samaria (2 Chronicles 35:22–27). Godly prophets such as Jeremiah greatly mourned the death of King Josiah, who had faithfully served the Lord and had removed all the idolatrous images and altars from the kingdom of Judah. The kings who followed abandoned the spiritual reforms instituted by King Josiah and led Judah back into idolatry.

There was no justice in the land. Violence and wickedness continued apace. There was trouble everywhere. Contention and strife were out of control. Added to these tragic conditions were the con-

quering campaigns of the Babylonian (Chaldean) army led by Nebuchadnezzar, son of the Babylonian ruler. Nebuchadnezzar sliced through the surrounding territories of Assyria and Egypt. Egypt was defeated at the Hittite city of Carchemish, located far north of Judah and Samaria and west of Haran on the Euphrates River. The Assyrian Empire, which had destroyed the northern kingdom of Israel, was in turn overrun by the Babylonians. It is evident that God was punishing the wicked nations who were the enemies of Judah. However, Nebuchadnezzar continued on to Jerusalem in 605 B.C., removed King Jehoiakim, and carried away the best and the brightest of the royal family, along with many of the vessels in the temple (Daniel 1:1–7). The Babylonians would later return in 597 B.C. during the reign of Jehoiachin and again in 586 B.C. during the reign of Zedekiah to complete their conquest of Judah.

The silence of God in human affairs has always been perplexing. Habakkuk struggled with this "silence," calling on God for answers to questions like, "Where is the intervention of the righteous and just covenant Lord? He seems to be indifferent to all the wickedness occurring in the land. Should God not remove the affliction of the godly and punish the wicked? Is He not obligated to uphold His own law?" But God answered Habakkuk as He had answered Job in his time of deep turmoil and confusion. Habakkuk's prophecy differs from most prophetic messages, which typically represent a word from God to the people. Habakkuk's message is a record of his own experience with God and conversations with God. He is a prophet with a deeply rooted faith. From him comes the righteous cry for the Lord to rescue the godly and for godliness to prevail in the land.

The people of God can live by faith, knowing that whatever concerns them concerns God even more deeply.

At-A-Glance

1. Those Who Plunder Will Be Eliminated (Habakkuk 2:6–8)
2. Those Who Covet Will Be Incriminated (vv. 9–11)
3. Those Who Murder Will Be Incinerated (vv. 12–13)
4. Those Who Remain and Glorify God Will Be Exonerated (v. 14)

In Depth

1. Those Who Plunder Will Be Eliminated (Habakkuk 2:6–8)

Habakkuk's prophecy is described as a "burden" (1:1) because it tells of God's imminent judgment upon Judah and her enemies. It is a serious proclamation of God's wrath against sin. God sees the horribly sinful condition of His people and the even worse condition of their enemies. He will use the Babylonians to punish the wicked in Judah (1:6). The Babylonians are described as terrible and dreadful, who will take what does not belong to them. They move with speed and power and worship their own strength. The Babylonian insatiable desire for conquest is described as intoxicating. These vicious conquerors would ravage the sinful nation of Judah. This revelation caused another dilemma for Habakkuk: How could a holy God allow a nation that was more wicked than Judah to punish her when there were still some righteous people in her midst?

Abraham asked a similar question when God told him that He was going to destroy Sodom and Gomorrah: "Would God destroy the righteous along with the wicked?" (Genesis 18:24). Habakkuk is determined to wait for an answer from God. At some point, God responds with this command: "Write the vision, and make it plain upon tables, that he may run that readeth it" (Habakkuk 2:1–2). In other words, Habakkuk was told to write the message on tablets of stone in big, easy-to-read letters, so that many people could read the message and relay it to others. Hence, Habakkuk is not the sole reciter of the message.

Deliverance would not come immediately, but it would surely come. People were impatient with God, but there was no real delay with Him. He works according to His own plan and timetable. However, the godly, who were encompassed by wickedness, had to continue living day by day, trusting in God's timetable for restoration.

The vision that God gives Habakkuk contains five "woes" directed at the unrighteous nations. These woes are the taunts of the oppressed mocking their tormentors. It is as though someone who had previously been picked on now had his big brother by his side and was confidently saying, "You are going to get what you rightfully deserve." The oppressed are justified in reciting these threats because these are the words that God has given them to speak. The condemnation comes as a parable or riddle to those to whom the message is directed—obscure sayings that the listeners must decipher. Those who are not interested in making an effort to fully understand the consequences of their actions continue to heap more guilt upon themselves.

The first woe is directed at people who seek to take what is not theirs. They are now debtors to those whom they have plundered. How long did they think they could escape their just reward? "Him that ladeth himself with thick clay" means that those who take from others are, in reality, debtors to their victims. They have loaded themselves up with pledges, and now they have a debt that must be paid to their victims for their actions. In fact, the aggressor must pay back *more* than what he has taken (like interest on the principal). The avengers will come suddenly when they are called to act and will forcefully seize what is due them. The ravagers will now become the victims, spoils for those whom they have plundered.

The reason for the vengeance is further elaborated: The aggressors spoiled many nations. These were not actions taken in self-defense against an imminent threat. The oppressors plundered other nations just for the thrill of doing so, driven by arrogance and the desire to display their military might. As a result of their actions, much blood was shed, and many people lost their lives. The victims were not only professional soldiers, but all kinds of people: young and old, rich and poor, guilty and innocent. Families, communities, cities, cultures, and places of worship were destroyed. But the remnant (those who escaped destruction) and those who were yet to come would "turn the tables" by pillaging their oppressors.

2. Those Who Covet Will Be Incriminated (vv. 9–11)

The second woe is directed at those who are driven by a lust for invulnerability based on unjust gain. These aggressors put themselves in a secure place ("set [their] nest on high") to avoid the suffering that they inflict on others. As a result, they think they are impregnable and can do evil with impunity.

In reality, and unbeknownst to them, they bring the retribution of God upon themselves because they have sinned against their own souls. Their evil schemes will not go unpunished. The premeditated nature of their malevolence proves their utter depravity. They do not realize that the evil they have done to others has been done to themselves as well.

So apparent is their guilt that even the stone in the wall and the beam of finished lumber in buildings erected with materials and wealth taken from others will be a witness against them. God will respond to the "cries" of these inanimate objects.

3. Those Who Murder Will Be Incinerated (vv. 12–13)

The third woe is directed at those who murder and steal for personal gain. Babylon used the wealth gained from bloody wars to build palaces and cities. They took all the gold, silver, and precious metal and various other objects from the temples, government buildings, and homes of others and used this loot for their own edifices. They used their victims as slave labor to build their own homes, temples, and palaces.

But God is still in control. All of the oppressors' efforts will come to naught and they will face judgment by fire.

4. Those Who Remain and Glorify God Will Be Exonerated (v. 14)

The knowledge of the Lord will fill the earth when King Jesus establishes His earthly kingdom (Isaiah 11:9). Some see in Habakkuk 2:14 a fuller description of this Messianic kingdom. Not only will the earth be filled with the knowledge of the Lord, as prophesied in Isaiah 11:9; but it will also be filled with the knowledge of the *glory* of the Lord, even as the waters cover the sea. Now we know the Lord and His glory only in part (1 Corinthians 13:9); the fullness of His glory will be known when that which is perfect has come (1 Corinthians 13:10). Before all people can display God's glory (Numbers 14:21), all wicked people and nations must be judged and punished.

Search the Scriptures

1. How many times is the word "woe" used in Habakkuk 2:6–14?

2. What will the victims take up against the plunderers (v. 6)?

3. What shall the remnant of the people do (v. 8)?

4. The second woe is directed at those who do what (v. 9)?

5. The third woe is directed at those who do what (v. 12)?

Discuss the Meaning

1. Provide an example of plunder that has occurred in modern times.

2. When will the knowledge of the glory of the Lord fill the earth?

3. Why do you think the idea of reparations for slavery is controversial?

4. How was Habakkuk encouraged by the "woes"?

Lesson in Our Society

It was not until 2005—41 years after the fact—that a person was found guilty of manslaughter in the deaths of three civil rights workers in 1964. This person was finally held accountable for his actions. The families of the victims had longed for this day when justice would be served. The guilty person had probably thought that the crime could be committed with impunity and felt increasingly safe as the years passed. Such is the case with most perpetrators: When people are allowed to get away with wickedness, they are more inclined to increase their wickedness. However, they are failing to acknowledge the Lord of hosts, who will judge everyone for his or her deeds.

Make It Happen

The people of God should never be satisfied that sinful behavior seems to go unpunished. Uncontrolled wickedness affects our lives, our families, our nation, and our churches. We should support those who are committed to righteous judgments consistent with the moral law of God. We must pray for those in positions of authority. We must pray that the knowledge of the Lord will prevail in a fallen society as we wait on God, confident that He will one day cleanse the earth and establish righteousness.

Follow the Spirit

What God wants me to do:

_____
_____

Remember Your Thoughts

Special insights I have learned:

_____
_____

More Light on the Text
Habakkuk 2:6–14

The Hebrew word *Habakkuk* (**Hab-ak-KUK**) means "embrace." Habakkuk was a preexilic prophet (i.e., he lived prior to the Babylonian captivity), writing the book that bears his name before the Babylonian captivity in the seventh century B.C. His book is the eighth of the twelve books of the minor prophets. As a Levite, Habakkuk was set apart to serve in the sanctuary, as a musician in the temple.

Every prophet of God communicates God's word to his own generation and beyond. Habakkuk was assigned to prophesy concerning the kingdom of Judah. Chapter 1 begins with Habakkuk's ongoing cry to God, who has not yet answered him. Habakkuk

wanted to know how long God would continue to allow the righteous to suffer and the ungodly to prosper. The moral and spiritual condition of Judah was getting worse and worse (2 Kings 21–22), and Habakkuk could not understand why God was allowing this to continue. It was extremely hard for Habakkuk to continue to look on sin, and he wanted to know how a holy God could tolerate it. God answered Habakkuk by telling him that He was going to do a work that Habakkuk would not believe. He was going to raise up that bitter, hasty, terrible, dreadful nation of the Chaldeans (Babylon) to punish His people.

Habakkuk had such a good relationship with God (calling Him "LORD, my God, mine Holy One") that he could ask God about anything that was troubling him. So Habakkuk asked God another question: Why, Habakkuk wondered, would God use a wicked nation to punish Judah? After all, even the worst things that Judah had done were not as bad as the deeds of the wicked Chaldeans. Habakkuk had learned patience from his previous experience. This time, he would wait and watch expectantly for God's answer. The Lord answered him in a vision.

6 Shall not all these take up a parable against him, and a taunting proverb against him, and say, Woe to him that increaseth that which is not his! how long? and to him that ladeth himself with thick clay!

The Hebrew word for "parable" is *mashal* (**maw-SHAWL**), meaning "similitude" or "proverb." The Hebrew word for "taunting" is *meliytsah* (**mel-ee-TSAW**) and refers to a mocking poem or a satirical song.

One usually hears taunting songs or mocking from the wicked about the righteous, as when Job was mocked by his enemies, who made up a song to tease him about his afflictions (Job 30:9), or when Christians are teased, made fun of, picked on, or bullied. But when the righteous finally see God punish the unrighteous, they will boldly mock the wicked with their taunting songs. In the text that follows, God uses this sarcastic song or poem that the captives will sing to explain how He will punish the wicked

Chaldeans. The song has several woes and addresses the Chaldeans as individuals. The first woe is directed at those who increase their wealth with things that don't belong to them.

7 Shall they not rise up suddenly that shall bite thee, and awake that shall vex thee, and thou shalt be for booties unto them?

The Hebrew word for "booties," *meshiccah* (**mesh-is-SAW**), means "spoil." When a city was captured, everything belonging to the people of that city became the property of the conquerors. How the spoil was to be divided among the Israelites was called the "law of booty." The distribution of spoil became a joyous occasion (Isaiah 9:3). Now the tables were turned; instead of the righteous becoming spoil for the wicked, the wicked would become spoil for the righteous. The righteous would suddenly despoil the wicked, as if awakening them out of a deep sleep, to "vex" (Heb. *zuwa*, **ZOO-ah**) them, or make them tremble and shake.

8 Because thou hast spoiled many nations, all the remnant of the people shall spoil thee; because of men's blood, and for the violence of the land, of the city, and of all that dwell therein.

The oppressor will become spoil because of the many nations that he has despoiled, and the "remnant" (Heb. *yether*, **YEH-ther**)—those who are left in the land—will despoil him. What the Chaldeans have done to others will be done to them. They will become spoil because of the human blood that was shed and the violence inflicted on Judah.

9 Woe to him that coveteth an evil covetousness to his house, that he may set his nest on high, that he may be delivered from the power of evil!

Verse 9 contains the second woe of the taunting song. This woe refers to the household of "him that coveteth" (Heb. *batsa*, **baw-TSAH**), a word that means "to gain by unrighteous violence." Not only did the evildoer increase his wealth by violent means, but his gain represents an evil "covetousness" (Heb. *betsa*, **BEH-tsah**), a dishonest gain. Everything that

he gained was illegally obtained through unnecessary violence, just so that he could build a high place in order to be delivered from those who would harm him. Evil people know what evil people do and how they think, so they must constantly protect themselves from other evil people and from those whom they have victimized.

10 Thou hast consulted shame to thy house by cutting off many people, and hast sinned against thy soul.

The act of cutting off many people has brought "shame" (Heb. *bosheth*, **BO-sheth**), or a shameful thing, to the evildoer's house; he has sinned against himself.

11 For the stone shall cry out of the wall, and the beam out of the timber shall answer it.

Even the stones in the wall and the beams or splinters of wood used to build the house of the wicked will cry out, testifying to the evil that has been done. The familiar saying "if only these walls could talk" certainly applies here.

12 Woe to him that buildeth a town with blood, and stablisheth a city by iniquity!

Here we have the third woe of the taunting song. The Hebrew word for "stablisheth" is *kuwn* (**koon**), which means "to prepare." Verse 8 spoke of violence and the shedding of innocent blood. The city of the oppressors had been built with human blood; it had been prepared with iniquity.

13 Behold, is it not of the LORD of hosts that the people shall labor in the very fire and the people shall weary themselves for very vanity?

By referring to God as the LORD of "hosts" (Heb. *tsaba'*, **tsaw-BAW'**), Habakkuk introduces the imagery of warfare. God is the LORD of His host, the army of Israel. He fights their battles (Exodus 15:3) and controls their military operations. The taunting song turns into the question, Is it not of the LORD of warfare that the people should "labor" (Heb. *yaga*, **yaw-GAH**), becoming fatigued in the consuming fire, and "weary" (Heb. *yaaph,* **yaw-AF**) themselves for "vanity" (Heb. *riyq,* **reek**) (ie, in vain)? Babylon was the land of the Chaldeans, and this verse is describing how the LORD will destroy them with fire. Any attempt to stop the destruction will be in vain. The Chaldeans will wear themselves out for nothing. Jeremiah 51:58 helps clarify this verse. History records that Babylon fell in 539 B.C. to Cyrus, king of Persia, and was never rebuilt.

14 For the earth shall be filled with the knowledge of the glory of the LORD, as the waters cover the sea.

Verse 14 is a promise from God that one day the earth will be filled with knowing His glory, just as the waters cover the sea (cf. Isaiah 11:9). Isaiah 11 speaks about a " rod out of the stem of Jesse" (v. 1), who will judge and rule the earth wearing righteousness as his belt and faithfulness as the sash around his waist (v. 5). Verses 6–9 give a clear description of "the earth [being] filled with the knowledge of the glory of the LORD."

The animals will be gentle with each other and with mankind. The wolf and the lamb will dwell together, the leopard will lie down with the young goat, the calf, the young lion, and the yearling—with a little child leading them. The cow and the bear will feed together, and they and their young ones will lie down together. Animals of different species that normally fought and preyed on each other will live together in peace during this time. Every creature is earnestly awaiting that time (Romans 8:19). The nursing child will be able to play in the hole of the cobra, and the weaned child can put his hand on the viper's nest.

This promise of God is contained in the Davidic Covenant. God promised the Israelites that through the line of Jesse's son, David, He would send a King to rule the earth forever. That King came 42 generations later (Matthew 1:1–17) through the lineage of David, starting with Abraham, and His name was Jesus, the Christ. He was not only the Son of David, but also the Son of God (Luke 1:35).

God knew that it would be many decades before His promises would be fulfilled. This was why He comforted Habakkuk before He gave him the vision, telling him that the vision was for an appointed time and that he should wait for it because it would surely happen (2:3). Even though things looked as though they were not going to change, God told Habakkuk to keep waiting because he would see the fulfillment of God's promise in the end. Meanwhile, God encouraged him with the knowledge that "the just shall live by his faith" (v. 4), a recurring theme throughout the Bible (see Romans 1:17; Galatians 3:11; Hebrews 10:38).

Daily Bible Readings

M: The Lord Loves Justice
Psalm 37:27–34
T: Judah Becomes Egypt's Vassal
2 Kings 23:31–37
W: Habakkuk's Complaint
Habakkuk 1:12–17
T: The Lord Answers
Habakkuk 2:1–5
F: Woes Reported
Habakkuk 2:6–14
S: The Lord Will Act
Habakkuk 2:15–20
S: The Lord Is Our Strength
Habakkuk 3:13–19

TEACHING TIPS

July 22
Bible Study Guide 8

1. Words You Should Know

A. Works (Jeremiah 7:13) *maaseh* (Heb.)—An action, whether good or bad.

B. Evil (2 Kings 23:37) *ra* (Heb.)—Bad or adversity, affliction, calamity, wicked, worse, wretched, wrong.

2. Teacher Preparation

A. Pray for your students.

B. Read the Focal Verses in another translation.

C. Complete lesson 8 in the *Precepts For Living® Personal Study Guide*.

3. Starting the Lesson

A. Open the class in prayer.

B. Display the Lesson Aim and write the At-A-Glance outline on a chalkboard or poster board.

4. Getting into the Lesson

A. Have two students read the In Focus section.

B. After the students have heard the story, ask them why they think it is important to obey God.

C. Ask for volunteers to read the Focal Verses based on the At-A-Glance outline.

5. Relating the Lesson to Life

A. Give the students an opportunity to answer the Search the Scriptures questions.

B. Engage in conversation with your students as you answer the questions found in the Discuss the Meaning and Lesson in Our Society sections.

6. Arousing Action

A. Instruct the class to identify areas of disobedience in their lives and to write them down on a sheet of paper. Then have the class fold the paper in half, repent, and pray—asking God for forgiveness. Help them to understand that true repentance is not just confessing sin and apologizing for wrongdoing, but it is completely changing one's behavior.

B. Now, have the students bring you their folded sheets of paper as a symbolic gesture of entrusting God with their sins.

C. Rip the sheets of paper into little pieces and throw the pieces away as a symbolic gesture that God remembers their sins no more and casts their sins into the *sea of forgetfulness*.

JEREMIAH ANNOUNCES THE CONSEQUENCES OF DISOBEDIENCE

Bible Background • JEREMIAH 7:11–15; 2 KINGS 23:36–37

Printed Text • JEREMIAH 7:11–15; 2 KINGS 23:36–37   Devotional Reading • 2 CHRONICLES 7:11–16

Lesson Aim

By the end of the lesson, we will:

KNOW that there are consequences for trusting in a religious institution instead of trusting in God and obeying Him;

DESIRE to love and obey the Lord; and

PRAY that God will help us to be genuine in our heart attitudes as well as our deeds.

Keep in Mind

"And now, because ye have done all these works, saith the LORD, and I spake unto you, rising up early and speaking, but ye heard not; and I called you, but ye answered not. ... I will cast you out of my sight, as I have cast out all your brethren, even the whole seed of Ephraim" (Jeremiah 7:13, 15).

Focal Verses

Jeremiah 7:11 Is this house, which is called by my name, become a den of robbers in your eyes? Behold, even I have seen it, saith the LORD.

12 But go ye now unto my place which was in Shiloh, where I set my name at the first, and see what I did to it for the wickedness of my people Israel.

13 And now, because ye have done all these works, saith the LORD, and I spake unto you, rising up early and speaking, but ye heard not; and I called you, but ye answered not;

14 Therefore will I do unto this house, which is called by my name, wherein ye trust, and unto the place which I gave to you and to your fathers, as I have done to Shiloh.

15 And I will cast you out of my sight, as I have cast out all your brethren, even the whole seed of Ephraim.

2 Kings 23:36 Jehoiakim was twenty and five years old when he began to reign; and he reigned eleven years in Jerusalem. And his mother's name was Zebudah, the daughter of Pedaiah of Rumah.

37 And he did that which was evil in the sight of the LORD, according to all that his fathers had done.

In Focus

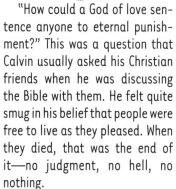

"How could a God of love sentence anyone to eternal punishment?" This was a question that Calvin usually asked his Christian friends when he was discussing the Bible with them. He felt quite smug in his belief that people were free to live as they pleased. When they died, that was the end of it—no judgment, no hell, no nothing.

But Carl had managed to shake Calvin's self-assurance. He had patiently explained to Calvin that God's love was only one aspect of His character. "God is also holy," Carl told Calvin, "which means that He hates sin. And He is just,

which means that He punishes those who practice sin." Carl made it clear to Calvin that it is because of God's love that He has revealed to us His revulsion for sin, the necessity for judgment, and the means of salvation. Carl explained that eternal punishment is not the result of breaking certain laws. Rather, it is based on our response to what has been revealed to us.

Finally, Carl told Calvin that God's judgments were not confined to some future time, but are already at work in our experience. "God reveals Himself to us," Carl said, "and we make decisions based on that revelation." Our decisions, Carl explained as he read John 3:19 to Calvin, demonstrate whether we love darkness or light.

Carl then asked Calvin, "Are you ready to make a decision based on the new information you've received? Not making a decision is the same as choosing darkness over light."

Calvin considered what he had heard. Carl had convinced him that God's judgment was true and His punishment real. He looked Carl in the eye and opened his mouth to speak.

The message of today's lesson from the book of Jeremiah is that if you trust God, He will keep you from "missing the mark" and suffering the consequences of sin.

The People, Places, and Times

Jeremiah. Jeremiah began his prophetic ministry during the reign of King Josiah (640–609 B.C.), the most righteous king of the nation of Judah (2 Kings 23:35). The 12-tribe nation of Israel had split into two kingdoms—Israel (Ephraim) to the north and Judah to the south—following the death of Solomon in 930 B.C. The larger northern kingdom had been conquered by the Assyrians of Mesopotamia in the late eighth century B.C. Several thousand of its citizens migrated south into Jerusalem at that time. Their long-held feelings of distrust toward the house of David probably made them reluctant residents of the southern capital. This reluctance would have been dissipated by the miraculous deliverance of Jerusalem from the hands of the same Assyrians in 701 B.C., during the reign of faithful King Hezekiah.

Shiloh. Shiloh, whose name means "place of rest," was a city of Ephraim. Judges 21:19 describes Shiloh as being "on the north side of Bethel, on the east side of the highway that goes up from Bethel to Shechem, and on the south of Lebonah." The city was one of the earliest and most sacred of the Hebrew sanctuaries. The Ark of the Covenant, which had been kept at Gilgal during the conquest (Joshua 17:1), was removed after the conquest of Canaan and kept at Shiloh from the last days of Joshua to the time of Samuel (Joshua 18:10; Judges 18:31; 1 Samuel 4:3). It was here that Joshua divided the land west of the Jordan among the tribes that had not yet received their allotted portion (Joshua 8:10; 19:51). In this distribution, or perhaps an earlier one, Shiloh fell within the limits of Ephraim (Joshua 16:5). The ungodly conduct of the sons of Eli caused the loss of the Ark of the Covenant. It was carried into battle against the Philistines and captured when the army of Israel was defeated. As a result, Shiloh was destroyed (Jeremiah 26:6, 9) and sank into insignificance. It stands in Jewish history as a striking example of divine indignation.

King Jehoiakim. King Jehoiakim reigned during the time of Jeremiah's greatest trials and opposition. Politically, the king and prophet were diametrically opposed: The king favored Egypt, whereas Jeremiah favored submission to Babylon. Spiritually, the two were even farther apart. Jehoiakim has been characterized as the worst and most ungodly of all the Judahite kings, a bloodthirsty tyrant and a habitual enemy of the truth. He cared nothing for the worship of the God of Israel, exacted exorbitant taxes, made use of forced labor, and had no regard for God's word or His prophet. The battle of Carchemish took place during Jehoiakim's 11-year reign. It was an event of permanent significance, for it marked the transfer of power over the Middle East from Egypt to Babylon. This defeat was the final blow to Egypt's aspirations and guaranteed the Chaldeans' supremacy in the West. It was the turning point of the period and also had important consequences for Israel's future.

The Babylonians made Jehoiakim their vassal and exiled a number of Jewish nobles (2 Kings 24:1), Daniel being among them (Daniel 1:1). Some scholars consider this first taking of Jerusalem by Nebuchadnezzar the beginning of the 70 years of Judah's exile in Babylon (2 Kings 25:11); with it, the dissolution of the Davidic kingdom had begun. In Jehoiakim's time, Jeremiah was persecuted, plotted against, maligned, and imprisoned. The king destroyed his written prophecies, but the prophet did not swerve from his divine mission. Jehoiakim died a violent death in Jerusalem in 598–597 B.C. in the 11th year of his rule, just as Jeremiah had predicted (Jeremiah 22:18–19). The book of 2 Chronicles records Jehoiakim's deportation to Babylon under Nebuchadnezzar (36:6–7; see also Daniel 1:1).

Background

Jeremiah's Temple Sermon—Jeremiah 7:11–15 is known as Jeremiah's "temple sermon." It shows the prophet in profound conflict with the dominant temple's faulty theology that lulled the people into a false sense of security because it did not address their disobedience to God's commands. In fact, the Israelites felt that God would not let any harm come to the temple nor the people who lived near it. They based their beliefs on what they deemed were unconditional promises of God made to their ancestors that assured them that Jerusalem would be continually blessed, intact, and protected. These distorted views were rooted in the temple and could be traced back to the royal claims of David and Solomon. Thus, the Israelites felt that God's judgment, in response to Israel's actions, was "limited" by God's promises to them. These beliefs were substantiated by the words spoken by Isaiah a century earlier (Isaiah 37:33–35) and were regularly celebrated in the book of Psalms (Psalm 132:6–10). Thus, obedience was not a crucial dimension of faith. Jeremiah deems these claims as "organized hypocrisy" and insists that the Israelites' living in obedience is a fundamental part of how God would deal with Jerusalem (Jeremiah 7). The state viewed his position as treason because it destroys the ideological foundation of the establishment.

At-A-Glance

1. God Sees (Jeremiah 7:11)
2. The Example of Shiloh (v. 12)
3. What Happened to Shiloh Can Happen to Jerusalem (vv. 13–15)
4. Jehoiakim Begins His Reign and Does Evil in the Sight of the Lord (2 Kings 23:36–37)

In Depth

1. God Sees (Jeremiah 7:11)

The temple, the house of God, was being treated like robbers treated their hideouts (v. 11). The leaders regarded the temple as a refuge where like thieves, they would hide until they went on their next rampage. In Jeremiah's day, limestone caves in Palestine were used as robbers' dens; thus, Jeremiah's hearers would have understood his metaphor. Jeremiah was opposing the corruption of the best and the holiest, saying that the Lord saw the situation and would deal with it accordingly (cf. Isaiah 56:7; see also Matthew 21:13; Mark 11:17; Luke 19:46).

2. The Example of Shiloh (v. 12)

The people were reminded of Shiloh, the city of Ephraim located on the main highway between Jerusalem and Shechem. During the era of the judges, Shiloh was the abode of the Ark of the Covenant. But it was at Shiloh that Israel lapsed into idolatry (1 Samuel 4:1–11), causing them to lose the battle of Ebenezer to the Philistines, who captured the ark. Shiloh was to the judges what Jerusalem was to the kings. Jeremiah was a descendant of Eli's family; consequently, the tragedy had personal implications for him. Jerusalem was not the first resting place for the ark; it had previously rested in Shiloh under the care of Eli and his sons. This was where God had first made a dwelling place for His Name (Jeremiah 7:12). The irreverent attitude of Jeremiah's own ancestors had led to the humiliating defeat of Israel's armies and the capture of the ark (1 Samuel 2–4). The destruction of Shiloh toppled the lie of the state's official position that Yahweh "was unalterably committed to an earthly temple and its preservation regardless of the moral state of the people."

3. What Happened to Shiloh Can Happen to Jerusalem (vv. 13–15)

Because the same irreverence characterized the people of Jerusalem, they did not listen when the Lord spoke through His prophets. Because they did not answer when God called to them, they were in danger of experiencing what had happened to Jeremiah's people more than four centuries earlier. Jeremiah makes it plain that the people were trusting in the temple of God (the sanctuary) rather than the

God of the temple. The outcome for Judah would be exile, as it had been for Ephraim (Israel), the northern kingdom, in 722–721 B.C.

4. Jehoiakim Begins His Reign and Does Evil in the Sight of the Lord (2 Kings 23:36–37)

King Jehoiakim was 25 years old, only slightly older than his predecessor Jehoahaz, when he was installed by Pharaoh Necho of Egypt. His mother came from Rumah in the former territory of Israel. Jehoiakim reigned for 11 years and apparently died of natural causes, after which he was buried in Jerusalem, although this is not explicitly recorded.

Sources

Gaebelein, Frank E., ed. *Expositor's Bible Commentary.* Grand Rapids, Mich.: Zondervan, 1989–1998.

Fritz, Volkmar. *1 & 2 Kings: A Continental Commentary.* Translated by Anselm Hagedorn. Minneapolis, Minn.: Augsburg Fortress Publishers, 2003, 414.

Search the Scriptures

1. What did God see (Jeremiah 7:11)?
2. How did God express Himself (v. 13)?
3. How did the people respond to God (v. 13)?
4. What verse reveals what the people were trusting in?
5. What would God do as a result (see question 4), and why?

Discuss the Meaning

1. What institution today is equivalent to what the people in today's lesson were trusting?
2. What consequences do you think people would face today if they committed the same sin?
3. How can we be genuine in our heart attitude as well as in our deeds?

Lesson in Our Society

We live in a society in which claiming to be a Christian is a cultural norm. The Christian religion is sometimes used by people without Christ's spirit to oppress, control, and exploit others. Be sure to develop a personal relationship with God that is cultivated through worship, the study of His word, and obedience to the Holy Spirit. Church attendance

should not be perceived as a way of affirming our relationship with God, validating our faith, or securing our salvation. Treat God as a visible and tangible person with whom you spend time walking and talking because you want a closer personal relationship with Him.

Make It Happen

The people of Judah were promised an earthly inheritance for changing their ways and living upright lives. New Testament believers are promised certain earthly blessings (Matthew 6:33; Mark 10:17), and a heavenly inheritance (1 Peter 1:4) for changing our ways and submitting to Christ as Lord. Is your life in total harmony with God's will? There is something in all of us that God wants to change. Over the next week, prayerfully identify those areas and seek to amend your behavior as needed.

Follow the Spirit

What God wants me to do:

_____

_____

Remember Your Thoughts

Special insights I have learned:

_____

_____

More Light on the Text
Jeremiah 7:11–15; 2 Kings 23:36–37

Jeremiah, the author of the book that bears his name, was another preexilic prophet (i.e., he lived prior to the Babylonian captivity) and was a contemporary of Habakkuk. Jeremiah had a twofold ministry: As a prophet, he represented God before the people; as a priest, he represented the people before God. Because God is holy and cannot approach sinful man, He appointed prophets to speak for Him. God's holiness also prevented sinful man from approaching Him, so God appointed priests to approach Him on behalf of the people. Jeremiah was known as the "weeping prophet"; no matter how much his own people persecuted him for telling the truth, he still had compassion for them.

God gave Jeremiah a message to give to Judah at the temple gates (Jeremiah 7). The people of Judah were coming to the temple to worship God. God told Jeremiah to tell the people to amend their ways so they could continue to dwell in the Promised Land that He had given their fathers. Many things they were doing made God angry (vv. 4–10). What especially fueled God's anger, however, was that they felt they could do anything they wanted as long as they came to worship Him in the temple. Nothing evil could happen to them, they thought, because God was among them (Micah 3:11). They lived ungodly lives and worshiped other gods, but they thought that going to the temple would excuse their sinful deeds (v. 10).

11 Is this house, which is called by my name, become a den of robbers in your eyes? Behold, even I have seen it, saith the LORD.

The house God is speaking of here is the temple, and He calls it the Lord's house (v. 2)—not Judah's house, the prophets' house, the priests' house, the congregation's house, or even Jeremiah's house, but the Lord's house. This house is called by His name. He tells Jeremiah to ask the people, who are going in and out of the temple gates, if the house that has His name on it has become a "den of robbers" in their eyes. He adds that even He has seen it to be so.

Not only was Judah ungodly outside the temple, but they had became ungodly in the house of the Lord, which kindled God's anger even more. Verse 11 is also quoted several times in the New Testament (Matthew 21:13; Mark 11:17; Luke 19:46). In Jesus' day, people were buying and selling in the temple. There were those who brought their tables to exchange currency and sell doves. Selling animals to be used for sacrifices was permitted, and people often had to exchange currency to make their purchases. But what made God angry was that the temple had been turned into a business. The money-

"And now, because ye have done all these works, saith the LORD....I will cast you out of my sight, as I have cast out all your brethren, even the whole seed of Ephraim" (from Jeremiah 7:13, 15).

changers and merchants were cheating people, making exorbitant profits, and causing His house to become nothing but a "den" (Heb. *mearah*, **meh-aw-RAW**, meaning "cave" or "hole") of robbers.

12 But go ye now unto my place which was in Shiloh, where I set my name at the first, and see what I did to it for the wickedness of my people Israel.

Shiloh was the city where the early sanctuary (tabernacle) was located, the place where the Lord first "set" His name and dwelt among His people. The Hebrew word for "set" is *shakan* (**shaw-KAN**), meaning "to make to settle down" or "tabernacle." Israel became so wicked that God allowed the Philistines to carry the Ark of the Covenant away from Shiloh. The Philistines were probably also responsible for the destruction of Shiloh (1 Samuel 4). God tells the Israelites to go to the former site of Shiloh and see what He had done to the tabernacle. God wanted them to understand that He had removed His divine presence from among His people in the past and was capable of doing it again.

13 And now, because ye have done all these works, saith the LORD, and I spoke unto you, rising up early and speaking, but ye heard not; and I called you, but ye answered not;

The Lord reminds the people that He had been speaking to them about their iniquity, but they had refused to hear and answer Him. This was not the first time He had told them about their wickedness. Neither did He let their behavior get out of hand before saying something about it. He spoke to them "rising up early." The Hebrew word for this phrase is *shakam* (**shaw-KAM**), meaning "in the morning" or "early." In other words, God had spoken to them when they had first acted wickedly. God did so "because he had compassion on his people, and on his dwelling place" (2 Chronicles 36:15). The Lord was giving a reason for the decision He was about to make.

14 Therefore will I do unto this house, which is called by my name, wherein ye trust, and unto the place which I gave to you and to your fathers, as I have done to Shiloh.

The Lord now accuses Judah of the same wickedness of which Israel had been guilty and promises to do the same thing to them as He had done to Israel. Because they had not heeded His warning, they would have to suffer the consequences. The Hebrew word for "trust" is *batach* (**baw-TAKH**), meaning "to lean on" or "to be confident in." The people had assumed that God would keep them safe and protect them, secure in the belief that He was with them.

However, they presumed upon God's protection. God was going to remove their "security blanket" because they could not count on His protection and be disobedient at the same time. Disobedience removes God's protection.

Long ago in Judah's history, Eli the high priest had had two sons who had taken the Ark of the Covenant from Shiloh to their camp to help them in battle against the Philistines (1 Samuel 4). The Philistines had won the battle, killed Eli's two sons, and taken the Ark of God. When Eli, who was 98 years old, heard about the ark being taken, he fell backward off his seat, broke his neck, and died. And when his pregnant daughter-in-law heard what had happened, she went into labor and died in childbirth. Her son was named Ichabod, which means "the glory is departed from Israel"(1 Samuel 4:21). Just hearing that the divine presence had left Israel was devastating and led to their deaths.

15 And I will cast you out of my sight, as I have cast out all your brethren, even the whole seed of Ephraim.

The Lord continues to add more punishment, telling the people that He is going to put them in a place where He cannot "see" them, just as He had done to the seed of Ephraim. Here, the LORD reminds Judah of the punishments He has inflicted in the past so that they will know exactly what their punishment will be like in the future. The word "brethren" refers to the northern kingdom of Israel, later called Ephraim.

Jacob, whose name God changed to "Israel," had 12 sons corresponding to the 12 tribes of the kingdom of Israel. When King Solomon reigned over Israel, he made God angry by worshiping other gods. When

Solomon's son Rehoboam succeeded Solomon on the throne, he made a bad situation worse by being arrogant and abusing his powers. Thus, God, in His anger, took 10 tribes away from Rehoboam and gave them to Jeroboam (1 Kings 11:9–13; 12). Israel was divided into two kingdoms, each with its own king. Ten tribes became the northern kingdom of Israel, also called Ephraim; the remaining two tribes, Judah and Benjamin, became the southern kingdom of Judah.

The throne of David was located in Judah. Through David's lineage, 42 generations later, would come the Messiah who would inherit David's throne (Matthew 1). This was God's covenant promise to David. According to this promise, David's throne would be established forever (2 Samuel 7:12–17; Psalm 89)—and the promise was unbreakable. Because God's promise to David's seed was unconditional, Judah assumed that what had happened to Israel would never happen to them. After all, the promised seed would come through Judah. Thus, they felt that they could do anything they wanted. They forgot the part of the promise that said they would still be chastised if they became disobedient (v. 14). In a similar way, salvation is a free gift (Romans 6:23), is unconditional, and can never be taken away; but disobedience brings chastisement.

2 Kings 23:36 Jehoiakim was twenty and five years old when he began to reign; and he reigned eleven years in Jerusalem. And his mother's name was Zebudah, the daughter of Pedaiah of Rumah.

Jehoiakim, whose name means "Jehovah raises up," was the 18th king of Judah, one of the last 3 kings of the southern kingdom. He reigned in Jerusalem for 11 years. His original name was Eliakim, the son of King Josiah and Josiah's wife, Zebudah. Eliakim's younger brother, Jehoahaz, was anointed king after his father's death, but reigned for only three months. He was bound and taken from Jerusalem to Riblah by Pharaoh Necho of Egypt, who then installed Eliakim as king and changed Eliakim's name to Jehoiakim (2 Kings 23:29–33).

37 And he did that which was evil in the sight of the LORD, according to all that his fathers had done.

Just like his ancestors, the 25-year-old King Jehoiakim did evil in God's sight. He did not follow in the footsteps of his father, King Josiah, who "did that which was right in the sight of the Lord, according to all that David his father did" (2 Kings 18:3). Instead of emulating his father, Jehoiakim followed in the evil ways of his grandfather, King Manasseh (2 Kings 21:1–18) and his great-grandfather, King Amon (2 Kings 21:19–26), joining those of his ancestors who refused to obey God.

Daily Bible Readings

M: Pay Greater Attention
Hebrews 2:1–4

T: Forgiveness Is Possible
2 Chronicles 7:11–16

W: Choices and Consequences
1 Kings 9:1–9

T: Disaster Is Coming
Jeremiah 19:1–6

F: Downfall Threatened
Jeremiah 26:1–6

S: Amend Your Ways
Jeremiah 7:1–7

S: Judgment of the Wicked
Jeremiah 7:8–15

TEACHING TIPS

July 29
Bible Study Guide 9

1. Words You Should Know

A. Peace (Jeremiah 29:11) *shalowm* (Heb.)—Being well, happy, friendly; also, welfare, health, prosperity, peace.

B. Captivity (v. 14) *shebiyth* (Heb.)—To be taken prisoner, removed from one's homeland to a foreign place and forced to live there.

2. Teacher Preparation

A. Begin preparing for the lesson by praying that God will reveal His will through the lesson about His people trusting Him.

B. Read the Scripture text from your own Bible.

C. Read Bible Study Guide 9.

D. Become familiar with Background; The People, Places, and Times; and In Depth.

3. Starting the Lesson

A. Open with prayer.

B. Display the Lesson Aim and the At-A-Glance outline on a chalkboard or poster board.

C. Briefly review the topic from lesson 8 and have the students share their thoughts.

4. Getting into the Lesson

A. Have five students read the In Focus section of the study guide.

B. After hearing the story, ask the students to express their thoughts.

C. Ask the students why they think it is important to trust God.

D. Have the students read the Focal Verses.

5. Relating the Lesson to Life

A. Ask the students to explain how the In Focus section and the Focal Verses section relate.

B. Ask the students to explain how trusting in God's promises can help us to have a positive outlook on life.

6. Arousing Action

A. Ask the class to identify three ways in which they have demonstrated that they trust God. One answer should be "through obeying God," but not merely obeying God when it is convenient or comfortable. Make sure that the students understand that trusting in God is demonstrated when we obey Him even when it is not convenient, comfortable, or "common sense" to do so.

B. Have the class create a prayer journal by writing down a list of prayer requests for the week that they expect God to answer.

C. Next, the students should ask God for forgiveness and pray for repentance, with the understanding that true repentance is not just confessing sin and apologizing, but having a complete change of mind and behavior.

Worship Guide

For the Superintendent or Teacher
Theme: Jeremiah Invites Jews in Babylon to Trust God
Theme Song: "Trust and Obey"
Scripture: Jeremiah 29:1–14
Song: "I Will Trust in the Lord"
Meditation: Dear Lord, help us always to obey and trust You. Thank You that You are a God who can be trusted. Amen.

JEREMIAH INVITES JEWS IN BABYLON TO TRUST GOD

Bible Background • JEREMIAH 29:1–14
Printed Text • JEREMIAH 29:1–14   Devotional Reading • PSALM 145:13–21

Lesson Aim

By the end of the lesson, we will:

KNOW the precious promises God makes to us for when we are in dire circumstances;

FEEL confident in the Lord in our present circumstances; and

PRAY that God will increase our trust in Him.

Keep in Mind

"For I know the thoughts that I think toward you, saith the LORD, thoughts of peace, and not of evil, to give you an expected end" (Jeremiah 29:11).

Focal Verses

Jeremiah 29:1 Now these are the words of the letter that Jeremiah the prophet sent from Jerusalem unto the residue of the elders which were carried away captives, and to the priests, and to the prophets, and to all the people whom Nebuchadnezzar had carried away captive from Jerusalem to Babylon;

2 (After that Jeconiah the king, and the queen, and the eunuchs, the princes of Judah and Jerusalem, and the carpenters, and the smiths, were departed from Jerusalem;)

3 By the hand of Elasah the son of Shaphan, and Gemariah the son of Hilkiah, (whom Zedekiah king of Judah sent unto Babylon to Nebuchadnezzar king of Babylon) saying,

4 Thus saith the LORD of hosts, the God of Israel, unto all that are carried away captives, whom I have caused to be carried away from Jerusalem unto Babylon;

5 Build ye houses, and dwell in them; and plant gardens, and eat the fruit of them;

6 Take ye wives, and beget sons and daughters; and take wives for your sons, and give your daughters to husbands, that they may bear sons and daughters; that ye may be increased there, and not diminished.

7 And seek the peace of the city whither I have caused you to be carried away captives, and pray unto the LORD for it: for in the peace thereof shall ye have peace.

8 For thus saith the LORD of hosts, the God of Israel; Let not your prophets and your diviners, that be in the midst of you, deceive you, neither hearken to your dreams which ye cause to be dreamed.

9 For they prophesy falsely unto you in my name: I have not sent them, saith the LORD.

10 For thus saith the LORD, That after seventy years be accomplished at Babylon I will visit you, and perform my good word toward you, in causing you to return to this place.

11 For I know the thoughts that I think toward you, saith the LORD, thoughts of peace, and not of evil, to give you an expected end.

12 Then shall ye call upon me, and ye shall go and pray unto me, and I will hearken unto you.

13 And ye shall seek me, and find me, when ye shall search for me with all your heart.

14 And I will be found of you, saith the LORD: and I will turn away your captivity, and I will gather you from all the nations, and from all the places whither I have driven you, saith the LORD; and I will bring you again into the place whence I caused you to be carried away captive.

In Focus

As Christians who believe in a loving Creator, we often have a problem interpreting pain. In a dark, secret moment, most of us might confess that pain was God's one mistake. As I prepared to write this article, I felt the same way. After briefly reviewing the medical studies showing the value of the millions of warning sensors of the pain network, I still had bad feelings. I reasoned that if pain was so beautiful, there should be statues erected in its honor or great hymns extolling its glory, like those that we create to recognize love.

The dictionary definition of pain repulsed me even more: *1: punishment; 2: usually localized physical suffering associated with bodily disorder (as a disease or an injury)*. Yuck! I resolved to write a nice, neat story of how God took some person's pain away instead of focusing on why pain was necessary.

While sitting in a golf cart one Saturday morning, I experienced excruciating pain that paralyzed my back and raced like fire through my left leg. It was a pinched sciatic nerve. Lying in bed for several days, unable to walk unassisted around my bedroom, I began to appreciate how the pain network bears the mark of God's creative genius.

When we feel the pain of loneliness, emptiness, meaninglessness, or suffering, we realize that something is terribly wrong with our world today. The pain in our lives demands the attention that God requires for our physical, as well as spiritual, healing.

My first weekend back on the golf course I stood erect on the first tee, thinking that maybe there should be a monument to pain. But after further reflection, I recognized that God had taken care of that—when Jesus took the pain of the world to the Cross.

While studying today's lesson, we should keep in mind Jeremiah's instruction to the Jews and trust God even during times of painful adversity.

The People, Places, and Times

Babylon. Located on the Euphrates River, Babylon was the capital of ancient Babylonia in Mesopotamia. The city was established as the capital in 1750 B.C. and rebuilt in regal splendor by Nebuchadnezzar II after its destruction by the Assyrians in 689 B.C. Babylon was the site of the famous Hanging Gardens, one of the Seven Wonders of the Ancient World.

"Babylon" is the Greek form of the word "Babel" (Semitic form, "Babilu"), meaning "the gate of God." In the Assyrian tablets, Babylon is the city of the dispersion of the tribes. The monumental list of the kings of Babylon reaches back to 2300 B.C. and includes Khammurabi, or Amraphel, the contemporary of Abraham. Babylon stood about 200 miles above the junction of the Tigris and Euphrates Rivers, the latter flowing through the middle of the city and dividing it into two almost equal parts. The Elamites invaded Chaldea (i.e., lower Mesopotamia, or Shinar, and Upper Mesopotamia, or Accad, now combined) and held it in subjection.

Some time later, Khammurabi delivered Babylon from its foreign oppressors and founded the new empire of Chaldea, making Babylon the capital city of the united kingdom. This city gradually grew in extent and grandeur, but after a time it became subject to Assyria. With the fall of Nineveh in 606 B.C., Babylon threw off Assyrian rule and became the capital of the growing Babylonian empire. Under Nebuchadnezzar, it became one of the most splendid cities of the ancient world. After passing through various vicissitudes, the city was occupied by Cyrus, king of Elam (Persia) in 539 B.C., who issued a decree permitting the Jews to return to their own land (Ezra 1).

Babylon then ceased to be the capital of an empire. It was again and again visited by hostile armies till its inhabitants were all driven from their homes. The city became completely desolate, its site being entirely forgotten. On the west bank of the Euphrates, about 50 miles south of modern Baghdad, there is a vast series of artificial mounds that represent the ruins of this once famous proud city.

These ruins are principally those of three ancient structures: (1) The great mound called Babil by the Arabs was probably the noted Temple of Belus, which was a pyramid about 480 feet high. (2) The Kasr (palace), or great palace of Nebuchadnezzar, is almost a square, each side of which is about 700 feet long. The little town of Hillah, near the site of ancient Babylon, is built almost entirely of bricks taken from this single mound. (3) A lofty mound, on the summit of which stands a modern tomb called Amran ibn-Ali, is probably the most ancient portion of the remains of the city and represents the ruins of the famous

Hanging Gardens or perhaps of some royal palace. The utter desolation of the city once called "the glory of kingdoms" (Isaiah 13:19) was foretold by the prophets (Isaiah 13:4–22; Jeremiah 25:12; 50:2, 3; Daniel 2:31–38).

Background

This unit deals with God's divine promises of restoration. The prophetic message is delivered by mail. King Zedekiah was sending couriers to Nebuchadnezzar in Babylon, and Jeremiah has them take a letter to the exiles living there (Jeremiah 29:1–3). The letter consists of five parts, each beginning with "Thus saith the LORD" (vv. 4, 8, 10, 17, 21). Jeremiah begins with a call for the people to "make themselves at home" in Babylon (29:4–7), a message that ran contrary to the message being spoken by other prophets (vv. 8–9). Jeremiah's message is that the future offers prosperity for those in Babylon (vv. 10–14) but death and destruction for those remaining in Jerusalem, in spite of what others might be saying (vv. 20–23).

At-A-Glance

1. Letter Carried to the Exiles (Jeremiah 29:1–3)
2. Make Yourselves at Home in Babylon and Pray for the City (vv. 4–7)
3. Do Not Believe the Dreams of the Prophets (vv. 8–9)
4. The Future Offers Prosperity for Those in Babylon (vv. 10–14)

In Depth

1. Letter Carried to the Exiles (Jeremiah 29:1–3)

The exact date for the sending of this letter is uncertain, but the reference to the exile of Jehoiachin and others (v. 2) suggests a time soon after that event (i.e., 597–596 B.C.). The letter is addressed to the nonroyal leaders among the exiles: the surviving elders ("the residue of the elders"), the priests, the prophets, and all the other people. The

two individuals who carry the letter (Elasah son of Shaphan and Gemariah son of Hilkiah) come from families who played important roles in Josiah's reform efforts (cf. 2 Kings 22:4–13; 23:4). These families appear to have been more sympathetic to Jeremiah's message than were others in the palace (cf. Jeremiah 36:10–16).

2. Make Yourselves at Home in Babylon and Pray for the City (vv. 4–7)

Jeremiah advises the exiles to move on with their lives, even though it was troubled times. They are to build houses, rather than live in tents; they are to plant gardens, rather than "eat what grows by itself" (Isaiah 37:30); they are to arrange marriages for their children, which points to long-term financial commitments. Most surprising, they are to seek the peace and prosperity of the city of their captivity (cf. Psalm 137). Even though this has an attractive component ("if the city prospers, you too will prosper"), it runs contrary to their natural inclination.

This passage reflects a situation that would also characterize Jewish and Christian life in the centuries that follow. These exiles found themselves to be in the minority in their society. They had little influence over the moral and ethical tone of the culture in which they lived and struggled with much in the culture. Their general economic welfare was tied to that of the society in which they lived. For this reason alone, the Lord tells them to pray for Babylon.

3. Do Not Believe the Dreams of the Prophets (vv. 8–9)

The immediate concern of this letter is that there are other prophets living among the Babylonian exiles who are promoting the position held by prophets like Hananiah in Jerusalem. Jeremiah does not give the exact message they are proclaiming, but it is fairly easy to deduce what their message is from what he writes here. Jeremiah repeatedly accuses them of prophesying lies (vv. 9, 21, 23). Such "lies" in Jerusalem were most often words of hope and appeasement, when the Lord's true message was one of devastation and punishment ("the sword, famine, and plague," vv. 17–18). Almost certainly, these false prophets were assuring the exiles that they would soon return to their homeland. Jeremiah had the unpleasant task of pointing out that these prophets were purveyors of false hope.

4. The Future Offers Prosperity for Those in Babylon (vv. 10–14)

Jeremiah now softens the blow of his harsh reply to this false assurance with his own true message of reassurance. He deemphasizes the fact that the return from exile is 70 years away (v. 10) in order to get to the words of comfort and encouragement. He opens and closes the balance of this section with the assurance that the Lord intends to bring back those who have been exiled (vv. 11, 14). He speaks of the Lord's gracious promise—a promise of prosperity, hope, and a future. Although the exiles are to settle down for awhile in Babylon, their "future" is not in Babylon, but back in Jerusalem; Babylon is merely a temporary "way station." The Lord's promise to their ancestors about a land still stands, but its realization is postponed for the present generation.

The Lord makes it clear, however, that, although He promises them prosperity and a future, He also expects their reverence and devotion. Through Jeremiah, the Lord indicates His expectations in a series of five verbs: "call," "come," "pray," "seek," and "find" (vv. 12–13). There is an implicit promise here of the restoration of the temple. There is also an expectation of something that had been missing from their worship. God says to the exiles, "You will search for me with all your heart." This is what had been missing from their worship in the days of Josiah,

"For I know the thoughts that I think toward you, saith the LORD, thoughts of peace, and not of evil, to give you an expected end" (Jeremiah 29:11).

but what had always been required of them. Such expectations would never change.

Search the Scriptures

1. What did God want the exiles to do while in Babylon (Jeremiah 29:5–6)?

2. What did God promise to do after they had spent 70 years in Babylon (v. 10)?

3. What were God's thoughts of His people in captivity (v. 11)?

4. How does God expect His people to respond to His thoughts (v. 13)?

5. What did God promise to do after being "found" (v. 14)?

Discuss the Meaning

1. God made promises to Israel through Jeremiah's letter at a time when they had been taken captive. Why do you think God made promises to them when things were bad as opposed to when things were good?

2. Which action best expresses true faith: hoping for and expecting the promises of God to come to pass when things are good, or when things are bad? Explain.

3. God gave Israel instructions in verses 5–7. What do these instructions say about the kind of attitude that He wants people to have in undesirable circumstances?

4. God foretold the future actions of Israel and how He would respond at that time in verses 12–14. What does this passage say about the role we play in changing undesirable circumstances in our lives?

Lesson in Our Society

Today's lesson emphasizes how God is faithful to send good news in bad times and to fulfill His promises when we respond in obedience and truly seek Him with all of our hearts. God desires for us to maintain a positive outlook on life that is inspired by His promises as we trust in His holy Word. He desires that we live life to the fullest and carry on with a disposition as though we were experiencing the reality of His heavenly kingdom on Earth. As we walk in love and

experience God's peace, our faith should be expressed in our countenance, in our praise and worship, and in our serving and giving to others.

Make It Happen

Write out three Scripture verses that contain a promise of God to His people. This week, meditate on these promises by reading and reciting the verses every day. Memorize these verses and be prepared to recite, reflect on, and share your experience with the class next week.

Follow the Spirit

What God wants me to do:

_____

_____

Remember Your Thoughts

Special insights I have learned:

_____

_____

More Light on the Text

Jeremiah 29:1–14

1 Now these are the words of the letter that Jeremiah the prophet sent from Jerusalem unto the residue of the elders which were carried away captives, and to the priests, and to the prophets, and to all the people whom Nebuchadnezzar had carried away captive from Jerusalem to Babylon; 2 (After that Jeconiah the king, and the queen, and the eunuchs, the princes of Judah and Jerusalem, and the carpenters, and the smiths, were departed from Jerusalem;) 3 By the hand of Elasah the son of Shaphan, and Gemariah the son of Hilkiah, (whom Zedekiah king of Judah sent unto Babylon to Nebuchadnezzar king of Babylon) saying, 4 Thus saith the Lord of hosts, the God of Israel, unto all that are carried away captives, whom I have caused to be carried away from Jerusalem unto Babylon;

The Hebrew word for "captives" is *gowlah* (**go-LAW**), meaning "exiles," or those who have not been allowed to return to their homeland. Although Jeremiah is in Jerusalem, he has a message of encouragement from the Lord for the leaders and others who had been deported from Jerusalem to Babylon in 597 B.C. and who were still alive after the recent unrest. Elasah and Gemariah, the royal messengers of King Zedekiah, appear to have been sympathetic toward Jeremiah's preaching or, at the very least, to have shown friendship and respect for him. They are willing to deliver Jeremiah's message, since they are on their way to Nebuchadnezzar in Babylon.

It is interesting to note that the Israelites, who were carried away into captivity, were craftsmen. Just as in the captivity of our forefathers in the days of slavery there were craftsmen (i.e., wrought iron workers, carpenters), so, too, the exiled Israelites were captured for their skills to serve the interests of Babylon. This is where the similarity ends, however. We must keep in mind that the Israelites' captivity was a result of their disobedience to God.

5 Build ye houses, and dwell in them; and plant gardens, and eat the fruit of them; 6 Take ye wives, and beget sons and daughters; and take wives for your sons, and give your daughters to husbands, that they may bear sons and daughters; that ye may be increased there, and not diminished.

Although God allowed the Israelites to be carried away into captivity, He did not forget them. God does not want the Israelites to die out or become a small population. In Hebrew, the word for "diminished" is ma`at (**maw-AT**), meaning "to be or become small" or "to be few." God's plan is for the Israelites to become many, to grow great, to increase greatly (Heb. rabah, **raw-BAW**). They are to make themselves content and be at home in Babylon. Paul demonstrates this mind-set in his letter to the Philippians: "I have learned to be content (satisfied to the point where I am not disturbed or disquieted) in whatever state I am" (Philippians 4:11, Amplified Bible). No matter what our circumstances, we can still live our lives with equanimity (calmness, self-control). We must constantly be mindful that God is always with us, no matter what our circumstances. We are reminded to "be content with what [we] have, because God has said, 'Never will I leave you; never will I forsake you'" (Hebrews 13:5, NIV).

7 And seek the peace of the city whither I have caused you to be carried away captives, and pray unto the LORD for it: for in the peace thereof shall ye have peace.

It would have been understandable for the exiles to hate their captors and strive to escape and return to Jerusalem. However, the Lord commands them to go against this all-too-human inclination and pray for peace (not escape), for themselves as well as for their captors. To further emphasize the importance of this instruction, God proclaims that when their captors have peace, they shall have peace as well, implying that if their captors do not have peace, neither will they.

The Hebrew word for "seek" is the verb darash (**daw-RASH**), meaning "to be sought or sought out; to be required." The exiles are to actively seek peace, or shalowm (**shaw-LOME**), meaning "completeness in number, safety, soundness in body, quiet, tranquility, contentment, friendship, peace from war." When the Lord speaks of seeking peace, He is speaking of more than just peace of mind for oneself. Therefore, when we talk of peace, we must consider other persons and all that such peace entails.

8 For thus saith the LORD of hosts, the God of Israel; Let not your prophets and your diviners, that be in the midst of you, deceive you, neither hearken to your dreams which ye cause to be dreamed. 9 For they prophesy falsely unto you in my name: I have not sent them, saith the LORD.

In referring to Himself as the Lord of hosts, God reminds the Israelites that He is Lord of all creation. The Hebrew word for "hosts" is tsaba' (**tsaw-BAW**), meaning "that which goes forth, army, host of organized army, host of angels."

True prophets were mouthpieces of the one true God. Therefore, when a prophet spoke, the people were to listen and obey. Consequently, God had to warn them of false prophets who were merely telling them what they wanted to hear. He even warned them not to pay attention to their own dreams (Heb. chalowm, **khal-OME**), which in Hebrew culture were often viewed as having prophetic meaning. Because these dreams were often merely the result of their own human desires, the exiles were to trust in the words of God alone.

The false prophets were among the exiles from Jerusalem and very much a part of the community. The Hebrew word for "midst" is *qereb* (**KEH-reb**), meaning "among," "inner part" (in the physical sense), "in the middle," or "among a number of persons." God lets the Israelites know that He has not sent these false prophets.

There are many times in our lives when we want to find an easy way out of unpleasant circumstances and anxiously await a "word from the Lord." In our anxiety, we look for a "word" in every conversation, especially if the other party claims to be a Christian. We must remember the words of an old Negro spiritual that says, "Everybody talkin' 'bout heaven ain't goin' there."

10 For thus saith the LORD, That after seventy years be accomplished at Babylon I will visit you, and perform my good word toward you, in causing you to return to this place.

Although the Israelites' hopes of escaping from Babylon were eliminated, God began to reveal His plan for them. He told the Israelites that their exile would not come to an end immediately. After 70 years (70 years being symbolic of the time of judgment of God's people), their exile would "be accomplished," or come to an end. The Hebrew word for "accomplished" is *male'* (**maw-LAY**), meaning "to be full, to be ended, to consecrate, to fill the hand." God's blessings would begin in the very place of their exile.

The Hebrew word for "visit" is *paqad* (**paw-KAD**), meaning "to attend to, muster, number, reckon, or pay attention to." The Hebrew word for "perform" is *quwm* (**koom**), meaning "to be established, to be confirmed, to be fulfilled, to make binding, or to carry out." The Hebrew word for "return" is *shuwb* (**shoob**), meaning "to turn back or to be returned, to be stored, or to be brought back."

11 For I know the thoughts that I think toward you, saith the Lord, thoughts of peace, and not of evil, to give you an expected end.

God reveals His thoughts (Heb. *machashabah*, **makh-ash-aw-BAW**, meaning "device, plan, purpose, or invention") toward the Israelites. He lets them know that they can expect peace and not misfortune. He even promises them a prosperous future.

The Hebrew word for "expected" is *tiqvah* (**tik-VAW**), meaning "hope, expectation, ground of hope, things hoped for, or outcome." The Hebrew word for "end" is *'achariyth* (**akh-ar-EETH**), meaning "latter time, prophetic for future time, or posterity."

Jeremiah 29:11 is a verse that we can live by. Knowing that God has already planned our lives should cause us to live with peace of mind concerning our future no matter how things appear to the natural eye. "You will keep him in perfect peace, whose mind is stayed on You, because he trusts in You" (Isaiah 26:3, NKJV).

12 Then shall ye call upon me, and ye shall go and pray unto me, and I will hearken unto you.

The Lord lets the Israelites know that at the end of the 70 years of exile, they will call on Him. The Hebrew word for "call upon" is *qara'* (**kaw-RAW**), meaning "to call, utter a loud sound, cry for help, or invite." The Israelites must "go and pray," which involves more than just sitting in a chair or standing in one place; God is calling for action on the part of the Israelites. In Hebrew, the word for "go" is *halak* (**haw-LAK**), meaning "to go, walk about, come, depart, proceed, move, or go away." If the Israelites pray as they have been instructed, God promises to "hearken" (Heb. *shama`*, **shaw-MAH**), meaning "to hear, listen to, or grant a request."

13 And ye shall seek me, and find me, when ye shall search for me with all your heart.

This verse is in the form of a covenant as God confirms His words in verse 12. The Hebrew words here are as follows: "seek" or *baqash* (**baw-KASH**), meaning "to seek, secure, desire, ask, or request"; "find" or *matsa'* (**maw-TSAW**), meaning "to find what is lost or attain to"; "search" or *darash* (**daw-RASH**), meaning "to resort to, seek with care, enquire, require, or allow oneself to be enquired of or consulted only of God"; and "heart" or *lebab* (**lay-BAWB**), meaning "inner man, mind, will, heart, soul, or understanding."

We have the Lord's promise that when we sincerely seek Him, He will answer us. God's answers are always far beyond our imaginations. In Psalm 50:15, God says, "Call upon me in the day of trouble; I will deliver thee, and thou shalt glorify me." Jeremiah 33:3 states; "Call to Me, and I will answer you, and show you great and mighty things, which you do not know." This same verse in the *New Living Translation* reads, "Ask Me and I will tell you some remarkable secrets about what is going to happen here."

A modern translation of this verse is found in the *New Living Translation*: "I will be found of you, says the Lord. I will end your captivity and restore your fortunes. I will gather you out of the nations where I sent you and bring you home again to your own land."

We learn from this account that, although we may suffer misfortune over the years, God can restore us to the place of honor we once held, and He has promised that He has plans to prosper us when our suffering is over. In the *Amplified Bible*, Jeremiah 29:11 reads, "For I know the thoughts and plans that I have for you, says the Lord, thoughts and plans for welfare and peace and not for evil, to give you hope in your final outcome." Let us hold fast to His promises.

14 And I will be found of you, saith the LORD: and I will turn away your captivity, and I will gather you from all the nations, and from all the places whither I have driven you, saith the LORD; and I will bring you again into the place whence I caused you to be carried away captive.

Again, the Lord promises to deliver the Israelites from captivity. The Hebrew word for "turn" is *shuwb* (**shoob**), meaning "to return or turn back." God promises to gather (Heb. *qabats*, **kaw-BATS**) the Israelites together in one place from the many nations (Heb. *gowy*, **GO-ee**, usually referring to non-Hebrew people) to which He had scattered or driven them. The Hebrew word for "places" is *maqowm* (**maw-KOME**), meaning "city, land, standing place, region, place of human abode, or region." The Hebrew word for "driven" is *nadach* (**naw-DAKH**), meaning "to impel, thrust, drive away; to be chased or banished."

Daily Bible Readings

M: The Goodness of the Lord
Psalm 145:13–21
T: God Restores
Jeremiah 30:18–22
W: Loved with an Everlasting Love
Jeremiah 31:1–9
T: Shepherd of the Flock
Jeremiah 31:10–14
F: They Shall Be My People
Jeremiah 31:33–37
S: Jeremiah Writes to the Exiles
Jeremiah 29:1–9
S: God's Good Plans
Jeremiah 29:10–14

TEACHING TIPS

August 5
Bible Study Guide 10

1. Words You Should Know
A. Wait (Lamentations 3:25–26) *qavah* (Heb.)—Look for, hope, expect.

B. Hope (vv. 25–26) *yachiyl* (Heb.)—Expecting, hoping, waiting.

C. Redeemed (v. 58) *ga'al* (Heb.)—To redeem; to act as a kinsman redeemer, avenge, revenge, ransom.

2. Teacher Preparation
A. Begin by praying and asking God to show you areas of your life in which you need to grow as you study today's lesson.

B. Read the Scripture for the lesson from several different Bible translations.

C. Make a list of all the words that you associate with "hope." Define hope in your own words.

D. Complete lesson 10 in the *Precepts For Living® Personal Study Guide* to gain further insight into today's lesson.

3. Starting the Lesson
A. Read the In Focus story. Ask your students, "What were you thinking as I read the story?" Discuss their answers.

B. Write the At-A-Glance outline on the board, along with the matching Scripture references.

4. Getting into the Lesson
A. Ask the students what words come to mind when they think of hope. Write these words on the board.

B. Present the information from Background and The People, Places, and Times.

C. As you deal with each point in the At-A-Glance outline, have a student read the Scripture relating to that portion of the lesson.

5. Relating the Lesson to Life
A. Lead your students in answering the Discuss the Meaning questions.

B. Ask your students if they have any other insights into today's lesson that they would like to share.

6. Arousing Action
A. Read Lesson in Our Society.

B. Ask the students to write out reasons why they can hope.

C. Have each student pray with a partner about areas in their lives in which they need to improve as they go through their troubles. Spend some time praising God for His care.

Worship Guide

For the Teacher or Superintendent
Theme: Lamentations Urges Hope in God
Theme Song: "Great Is Thy Faithfulness"
Scripture: Lamentations 3:25–33
Song: "God Never Fails"
Meditation: Dear Lord, thank You for hearing my desperate cry. You are a good God—always faithful, strong, and working on my behalf. In You, I have hope. Help me to rest in Your care. Amen.

LAMENTATIONS URGES HOPE IN GOD

Bible Background • 2 KINGS 25:1-2, 5-7; LAMENTATIONS 3:25–33, 55–58
Printed Text • LAMENTATIONS 3:25–33, 55–58   Devotional Reading • PSALM 23

Lesson Aim

By the end of the lesson, we will:

UNDERSTAND some reasons for maintaining hope in God;

FEEL God's compassion even when we are suffering; and

CONTINUE waiting on the Lord in the midst of our struggles.

Keep in Mind

"It is good that a man should both hope and quietly wait for the salvation of the LORD" (Lamentations 3:26).

Focal Verses

Lamentations 3:25 The LORD is good unto them that wait for him, to the soul that seeketh him.

26 It is good that a man should both hope and quietly wait for the salvation of the LORD.

27 It is good for a man that he bear the yoke in his youth.

28 He sitteth alone and keepeth silence, because he hath borne it upon him.

29 He putteth his mouth in the dust; if so be there may be hope.

30 He giveth his cheek to him that smiteth him: he is filled full with reproach.

31 For the Lord will not cast off for ever:

32 But though he cause grief, yet will he have compassion according to the multitude of his mercies.

33 For he doth not afflict willingly nor grieve the children of men.

3:55 I called upon thy name, O LORD, out of the low dungeon.

56 Thou hast heard my voice: hide not thine ear at my breathing, at my cry.

57 Thou drewest near in the day that I called upon thee: thou saidst, Fear not.

58 O Lord, thou hast pleaded the causes of my soul; thou hast redeemed my life.

In Focus

Dexter knew that this was the end. He gazed as if hypnotized at the machines recording his mother's last struggle with life. *She had such high hopes for me,* Dexter thought.

A few months ago he had been on top of the world, a young African American in good health with a rewarding career. The main supporter of his success was his mother.

Most often, Dexter and his mother were in a battle about conversion: He believed in self-empowerment, and she put all her faith in God. Her favorite phrase was: "I'm just going to leave it in the hands of the Lord."

"Mom," he would say, "the Lord gave you a brain, two arms and two legs, and everything else you need to make things happen, not to sit around waiting for divine intervention." His mother would smile and say, "Dexter, my greatest hope is that one day you will understand the power of prayer."

A month after being named vice president of his company, Dexter relocated his mother from the South to New York City so she could live near him. Finally he could take care of the person who had dedicated her entire life to him. He vowed to remove her financial worries and replace them with hope for the future.

Several weeks after the move, without warning, Dexter's mom was diagnosed with cancer. Radiation treatments, sickness, and vomiting soon followed, but still his mother remained steadfast in her faith. As a matter of fact, to Dexter's amazement, the events of the past several weeks seemed to have made her faith stronger.

Now, as Dexter leaned over his mother's hospital bed, he softly whispered prayers into her ear—prayers that she had taught him as a child. He whispered his acceptance of Christ. He prayed that he would see his mother in heaven. Moments before the machine beeped a flat line, he was certain that he heard his mother say, "That's all I have ever hoped for."

Lamentations is also called "the book of tears" because the prophet Jeremiah cries out to God from the depths of despair. But we see that God answers those who hope in Him.

The People, Places, and Times

Jeremiah. God told Jeremiah, "Before you were born I set you apart; I appointed you as a prophet to the nations" (Jeremiah 1:4, NIV). Jeremiah began his prophetic ministry in 626 B.C., as he stood at the threshold of manhood—when he was 13 years old. Thus, God called him to be God's mouthpiece, His spokesman to the world. God called him to lay aside his natural sensitivity and low self-esteem, and with the sword of God's words, "root out . . . throw down, build and plant." Jeremiah had lived through the reign of godly King Josiah and had witnessed Israel's return to idolatry after Josiah's death. Tirelessly he had warned the people of the coming destruction, but his warning had gone unheeded. He grieved over Jerusalem's hopeless attachment to idols. He saw Jerusalem partly destroyed in 606 B.C. by Nebuchadnezzar, further devastated in 597 B.C., and finally burned and made desolate in 586 B.C. He watched as the people of Israel were taken into exile. Jeremiah was chosen to provide God's last warning to the Holy City before its destruction.

Background

Lamentations consists of passionate expressions of grief composed by the prophet Jeremiah during the exile. He expresses his sorrow over Jerusalem, the city he had done his best to save, and the horror of being torn from the Jewish homeland and taken away to Babylon. The book of Lamentations must have been written after the death of King Josiah and between the burning of Jerusalem and the departure of the remnant to Egypt (Jeremiah 39:2; 41:1, 18; 43:7).

However, Jeremiah's sorrow was not without a mixture of faith. He believed that *beauty would come from the ashes of the city.* He had hope that the city would rise again from its ruins. In fact, Jerusalem did rise again and will give its name to the capital of a world of eternal glory (Hebrews 12:22; Revelation 21:2).

At-A-Glance

1. God Is Trustworthy and Good
(Lamentations 3:25–26)
2. God Uses Hardships for Our Good
(vv. 27–30)
3. God Allows Hardships for a Season
(vv. 31–33)
4. God Hears the Prayers of His People
(3:55–58)

In Depth

1. God Is Trustworthy and Good (Lamentations 3:25–26)

Verses 25–27 all begin with the Hebrew word for "good," communicating to us the fundamental idea that Yahweh is good to all. All of His creatures taste of His goodness, but He is especially good to those who silently (i.e., without complaining) and patiently wait for Him and seek Him, resting in His will.

Sometimes trouble can seem to last a long time, and we wonder whether we will ever see God's deliverance. These times provide an opportunity for us to learn to wait patiently by faith in confident expectation and to seek God prayerfully. He will be gracious to those who patiently wait on and seek Him. To such people, He will show His wonderful loving-kindness.

Hope is fundamental to faith. A person without hope cannot believe. If there is no expectation, there can be no confidence. In the Old Testament, hope is expressed by numerous words meaning "safety, security, and trust" (Psalm 16:9; 22:9). Another Hebrew word translated "refuge" or "trust" (Psalm 71:5) denotes a sense of firm and certain expectation. The word is also used in the sense of "refuge" or "shelter" (Jeremiah 17:7, 17; Joel 3:16). In another context, this word denotes something waited for (Ezra 10:2). Zechariah 9:12 refers to "prisoners of hope."

In the New Testament, hope relates to the expectation of good. The original term expressed a joyful and contented expectation of eternal salvation

"It is good that a man should both hope and quietly wait for the salvation of the LORD" (Lamentations 3:26).

(Acts 23:6; 26:7; Romans 5:4–8; 1 Corinthians 13:13). Because God has provided salvation through Christ, and because He is the believer's source of expectation, He is called the "God of hope" (Romans 15:13). The source of hope is the death, burial, and resurrection of Christ (1 Peter 1:3). "Christ in you" is the "hope of glory" (Colossians 1:27). In the New Testament, hope has to do with the coming of the Lord (Titus 2:13), the "blessed hope." As Christians, we can rejoice! We have much in which we can hope!

2. God Uses Hardships for Our Good (vv. 27–30)

Many of the young men in Israel had been carried away into captivity in Babylon. Jeremiah encouraged them to bear their yoke patiently and make the best of their situation, allowing God to do His work in their lives.

Certainly, it is good to develop good habits and to learn restraint while one is still young so that one can become a vessel to be used in advancing God's kingdom. Of course, discipline is always a part of early training! It would be wonderful if we, as adults, eventually no longer experienced hardships or needed discipline, but we always seem to have an area in which we still need to grow. Remember, *God is more concerned with our character than with our comfort.* Hardships can yield the fruit of righteousness if we allow that to happen.

God wants to make His people more like Himself. He desires that we become all we can be. To accomplish His will in our lives, He often uses hardships. Nevertheless, hardships can be used for our good only if we allow God to discipline us when we need it and learn what He wants to teach us. Allowing God to work in us, during times of trouble, requires several things: (1) an attitude of humility and submission (v. 27), (2) quiet reflection on what God wants (v. 28), (3) the practice of self-control in the face of trouble (v. 30), and (4) confident patience in God's desire and ability to bring about loving lessons in our lives (v. 26).

Jeremiah challenged the Israelites to not be vindictive toward their captors, but to have a forgiving spirit and "turn the other cheek" (Matthew 5:39) because vengeance belongs to God (Romans 12:19). Jesus was the perfect example of forgiveness, responding with kindness to those who abused Him (Isaiah 50:6; Matthew 27:27–31; Luke 22:64; John 18:22; 19:3).

3. God Allows Hardships for a Season (vv. 31–33)

In the Mosaic Covenant, if the people looked to God for salvation and demonstrated their faith by obeying His commandments, they would receive His promised blessings. If the people did not keep these terms, the covenant curses would be visited upon them. Unfortunately, the Israelites broke the terms of the covenant. They were not faithful to follow God's commandments and observe the Passover. They made and worshiped idols, involving themselves in despicable acts that were a common part of the idolatrous worship of those around them. Only for short periods of time—during the reigns of aggressively godly kings—did they turn their attention to worshiping the God of their fathers, the one true God. It seems doubtful, however, that they truly repented during those times, because as soon as a wicked king was on the throne, the people turned again to idolatry. True repentance requires a change of heart that also changes one's behavior.

Because of the Israelites' disobedience, God withdrew His hedge of protection from around them. They became vulnerable to attacks from the surrounding nations. They were taken from the land that they loved into Babylonian captivity. Yet God had not forgotten them. His deliverance was coming!

Even though God had temporarily withdrawn His protection from them, the Israelites still had their inheritance. God would still be true to the promises He had made to them in His covenant. Jeremiah encouraged the Israelites by telling them that God would graciously comfort them when their season of trouble was over (vv. 31, 32). They were to be penitent and patient because God is gracious and merciful.

As believers, we can take comfort in the fact that when we are cast down, we are not cast off. A father's correction of his son is not the same as his disinheriting him. Likewise, God does not take pleasure in our affliction, but uses it for our good. He uses the rod to save us. God is gracious because of His great mercy, not because of our merit.

As believers, we should not think that all difficulties come as a result of our disobedience. Sometimes things just happen. We are sinners, living in a sinful world, surrounded by ungodly people. When difficulties come, we can rest in Christ and take comfort in knowing that God has a purpose, even in difficult times.

4. God Hears the Prayers of His People (3:55–58)

Throughout this chapter, we read of the prophet Jeremiah's struggles between sight and faith, fear and hope. Ultimately it is faith that conquers and has the last word. Jeremiah comforts himself by meditating on his own experience of God's goodness in difficult times. During the lowest times of Jeremiah's life, God was there. When he had cried out in despair, God had answered. When despair began to overtake him, there was hope. God had not closed His ear to Jeremiah's prayer—nor will He close His ear to our prayers.

Jeremiah knew what it was like to be weak and left to die. At one point in his ministry, he had been thrown into an empty cistern and left in the mud to die (Jeremiah 38:6–13). But he had been rescued by Almighty God through the heroic actions of Ebed-Melech, a godly Cushite (African) official in the royal palace (Jeremiah 38:6–14). Jeremiah used this experience as an illustration of the nation of Israel sinking into sin. The prophet encouraged the people to turn to God so He could rescue them.

Jeremiah cried out to the Israelites on the authority of God, "Fear not! God will plead your cause and redeem you." These same words ring out to believers today: "Fear not! God is with you."

Sources

Moule, C. F. D. *The Meaning of Hope: A Biblical Exposition with Concordance.* Minneapolis, Minn.: Augsburg Fortress Publishers, 1963.

Zimmerli, Walther. *Man and His Hope in the Old Testament.* Atlanta: John Knox Press, 1976.

Search the Scriptures

1. What did Jeremiah say was good (Lamentations 3:25–27)?

2. Why can believers have hope when they face trouble (vv. 25–33, 55–58)?

3. What is the correct way for human beings to bear hardship (vv. 28–30)?

4. How does God view the affliction He allows (vv. 32–33)?

5. Why was Jeremiah able to speak about hope in the midst of trouble (vv. 55–58)?

6. Why does God say to us, "Fear not" (v. 57)?

Discuss the Meaning

1. What about today's lesson gives you hope?

2. When you have gone through hard times, have you followed the guidance given in Lamentations 3:25–33; 55–58? Why or why not?

3. Think about times when God has delivered you. Why should you "fear not"?

Lesson in Our Society

Both believers and unbelievers of all ages face trouble. At the very least, youth are troubled by physical "growing pains," peer pressure, and moral dilemmas. However, as we grow to adulthood, our problems become more complex due to increased responsibilities. Adults are concerned about financial problems, job problems, marital problems, and problems with their children. Personal expectations of how life was supposed to turn out are often not fulfilled, and we realize that sometimes bad things *do* happen to good people.

Even when we are suffering, we have reason to hope because God has promised to be good to those who hope in Him. He wants us to persevere in waiting on Him because maintaining hope in difficult times will strengthen us spiritually.

Make It Happen

Along life's way, we may experience injustices, trials, and catastrophes that we cannot logically comprehend. As time goes on, however, God will begin to unfold the reasons these things occurred in our lives. Can you think of anything that God allowed to happen that initially caused you to doubt Him? How long did it take you to realize that God was still in control? Share your experience with another believer to help strengthen that person in his or her walk with God.

Follow the Spirit

What God wants me to do:

_____

_____

Remember Your Thoughts

Special insights I have learned:

_____

_____

More Light on the Text
Lamentations 3:25–33; 55–58

In Lamentations 3, in the midst of his lament over the destruction of Jerusalem and the captivity of the Israelites, the prophet Jeremiah demonstrates strong faith in God, holding steadfastly to the promises and goodness of God.

25 The Lord is good unto them that wait for him, to the soul that seeketh him.

As in the previous lesson, Jeremiah speaks on behalf of the Lord (Heb. *Yehovah,* **yeh-ho-Vaw'**, meaning "existing One," the proper name of the one true God). Jeremiah lets us know that God is good (Heb. *towb,* **tove,** meaning "pleasant" or "agreeable") to those who silently inquire after Him or seek Him carefully (Heb. *darash,* **daw-RASH**) and look eagerly for Him. This "good" spoken of by the prophet does not mean that things always conform to our expectations. Rather, it is an expression of God's purpose and will. In essence, Jeremiah affirms the truth often spoken by our forefathers: "God has been better to us than we have been to ourselves." The all-surpassing goodness of God is showered on those who yield to and seek God's will and perfect timing.

26 It is good that a man should both hope and quietly wait for the salvation of the Lord.

Many times we complain and see only the negative side of events that occur in our lives. However, we are encouraged to always have hope. This is not an empty hope, nor is it mere wishful thinking. The hope God commends to us will never disappoint us (Romans 5:5). Therefore, this hope can bear the full weight of our faith. It can empower us to quietly learn *not* to worry. This is the discipline of true faith.

On the other hand, when people lose hope, they have lost the very desire to live. They see no way out of a dire situation, thinking that they have innumerable questions that have no answers. Unless they base their faith on the hope that God gives, they will never know the assurance of His continual presence. They may even conclude that the only way out is death. We must understand that God will never abandon us. He will make a way for us in the midst of the turmoil of this world. The Hebrew word for "salvation" is *teshuw`ah* (**tesh-oo-AW**), meaning "deliverance," usually deliverance by God through human agency.

27 It is good for a man that he bear the yoke in his youth. 28 He sitteth alone and keepeth silence, because he hath borne it upon him.

A yoke is a curved piece of wood fitted on the necks of oxen for the purpose of binding them together so they can pull a plough or do some other work. It is easier for a young ox to bear (Heb. *nasa',* **naw-SAW,** meaning "to carry or support") a load than for one who is old and tired.

For us as human beings, it is easier to carry heavy weights when our bodies are young and vibrant. As we grow older, the weight that we are able to carry becomes lighter and lighter. There are times when we wonder whether we have gotten weaker or the task has gotten heavier. So it is with life. It was much easier for us to bounce back from the stresses we encountered when we were younger. As we age, those same stresses become more difficult to deal with; they seem to linger a little longer, especially if we feel we have no one to share our burdens with.

The yoke God lays on us is one of service. It will transform our lives from the ordinary to the extraordinary. Whether we gain the favor or disfavor of others will not matter as long as we are in God's will.

Let us remember that God has a plan for our lives. Verse 27 in the *Amplified Bible* reads, "Let him sit alone uncomplaining and keeping silent [in hope], because [God] has laid [the yoke] upon him [for his benefit]." This truth is confirmed in Romans 8:28 (NLT): "And we know that God causes everything to work together for the good of those who love God and are called according to his purpose."

29 He putteth his mouth in the dust; if so be there may be hope. 30 He giveth his cheek to him that smiteth him: he is filled full with reproach.

Here we find a description of one who is so submitted to God that he is willing to endure humiliation. The "yoke" mentioned in verse 27 was a symbol of servitude; yet there is hope, in spite of being filled with "reproach" (Heb. *cherpah,* **kher-PAW**), or shame and disgrace at not being able to solve one's own problems. However, God has promised us, just as He promised His children in Isaiah 49:23, that "they shall not be ashamed that wait for me."

31 For the Lord will not cast off forever: 32 But though he cause grief, yet will he have compassion according to the multitude of his mercies. 33 For he doth not afflict willingly nor grieve the children of men.

Jeremiah realizes that although the Lord may bring sorrow and grief (Heb. *yagah,* **yaw-GAW**) into our lives, it will not last forever. He will not continue to reject someone because of his or her wrongdoing. The Hebrew word for "compassion" is *racham* (**raw-KHAM**), meaning "to love, love deeply, have mercy, be compassionate, have tender affection, or have compassion." The Hebrew word for "multitude" is *rob* (**robe**), meaning "abundance" or "greatness." The Hebrew word for "mercies" is *checed* (**KHEH-sed**), meaning "goodness, kindness, or faithfulness." The Hebrew word translated "children" is *ben* (**bane**), meaning "son, grandson, child, or member of a group of people (nation)." We can rest assured that it is not God's will for us to receive punishment from Him. Yet because He loves us, He will chastise us: "For the Lord disciplines those he loves, and he punishes those he accepts as his children" (Hebrews 12:6, NLT).

3:55 I called upon thy name, O Lord, out of the low dungeon. 56 Thou hast heard my voice: hide not thine ear at my breathing, at my cry.

Verse 55 is a description of the deepest depression possible. For the prophet Jeremiah to describe himself as being in a low dungeon is to see himself in the bottom or lower parts ("low" being the equivalent of the Hebrew word *tachtiy* [**takh-TEE**]) of a cistern or "dungeon" (Heb. *bowr,* **bore**), meaning "pit, well, or cistern," crying (Heb. *shav`ah,* **shav-AW**) to the Lord for help. The Hebrew word for "breathing" is *revachah* (**rev-aw-KHAW**), meaning "respite" or "relief." We can call on the name of the Lord wherever we are, and He will hear our cry.

57 Thou drewest near in the day that I called upon thee: thou saidst, Fear not.

As Jeremiah continues his conversation with the Lord, he acknowledges the Lord's response to his lament. We are not to be afraid, since God hears our voice wherever we may be in our journey through life. He is with us every step of the way, even when our enemies may strike at us from all directions. Therefore we must trust in the purpose of God for our lives and not worry about the opposing forces that may come against us.

58 O Lord, thou hast pleaded the causes of my soul; thou hast redeemed my life.

As an attorney would "plead" (Heb. *riyb,* **reeb,** meaning "to strive or contend; to conduct a case or legal suit") a case for his or her client, so the Lord takes up the case of His servants. The successful attorney will save the life of the client. Jeremiah acknowledges that our all-powerful God has "redeemed" (Heb. *ga'al,* **gaw-AL**) his very life. Our God is an awesome God. He has not left us without a Comforter, in the person of His Holy Spirit. As Christ has died to redeem us from sin, so the Holy Spirit is ever with us to redeem us daily. We need not worry about our unfortunate circumstances; we simply need to learn to wait patiently on the Lord (Psalm 27:14). Remember the words of King Darius to Daniel as Daniel was being cast into the den of lions: "Your God, whom you serve continually, He will deliver you" (Daniel 6:16, NKJV).

Daily Bible Readings

M: Promise of Deliverance
Isaiah 30:15–19
T: Jerusalem Destroyed
2 Kings 25:1–2, 5–7
W: God Is Our Hope
Psalm 33:12–22
T: My Soul Waits
Psalm 130
F: God Is Faithful
Lamentations 3:19–24
S: Wait for the Lord
Lamentations 3:25–33
S: God Hears My Plea
Lamentations 3:55–59

TEACHING TIPS

August 12
Bible Study Guide 11

1. Words You Should Know

A. Live (Ezekiel 18:22) *chayah* (Heb.)—To revive, keep, give (promise) life, nourish, preserve (alive), quicken.

B. Repent (v. 30) *shuwb* (Heb.)—To return or go back; bring back.

2. Teacher Preparation

A. Begin by praying and asking God to burn the message of this lesson into your heart and to help you communicate it to your class in a powerful way.

B. Read the Bible Background Scripture for the lesson, meditate on it, and make notes as the Lord illuminates.

C. Read the In Depth and More Light on the Text sections, highlighting information that you want to emphasize. In addition, complete lesson 11 in the *Precepts For Living® Personal Study Guide*.

D. Make a list of all the words you associate with "die" and "live."

3. Starting the Lesson

A. Write the three-point At-A-Glance outline on the board, along with the Scripture references.

B. Read the In Focus story. Ask your students, "What were you thinking as I read the story?" Discuss their answers.

4. Getting into the Lesson

A. Ask the students to list the words that come to mind when they think of "die" and "live." Write these words on the board.

B. Present the information from Background and The People, Places, and Times.

C. As you deal with each point in the outline, have a student read the Scripture relating to that portion of the lesson.

5. Relating the Lesson to Life

A. Lead your students in answering the Discuss the Meaning questions.

B. Ask your students if they have any other insights into today's lesson that they would like to share.

6. Arousing Action

A. Read the Lesson in Our Society section.

B. Ask the students to write out their reasons for hope.

C. Have each student pray with a partner about areas in their lives in which they need to improve as they go through their troubles. Spend some time praising God for His care.

Worship Guide

For the Teacher or Superintendent
Theme: Ezekiel Preaches about Individual Responsibility
Theme Song: "Sanctuary"
Scripture: Psalm 24:3–4
Song: "Lord, I Want to Be a Christian"
Meditation: "Wash me throughly from mine iniquity, and cleanse me from my sin. For I acknowledge my transgressions: and my sin is ever before me. Create in me a clean heart, O God; and renew a right spirit within me. Cast me not away from thy presence; and take not thy holy spirit from me. Restore unto me the joy of thy salvation; and uphold me with thy free spirit. Then will I teach transgressors thy ways; and sinners shall be converted unto thee" (Psalm 51:2, 3, 10–13). Amen.

EZEKIEL PREACHES ABOUT INDIVIDUAL RESPONSIBILITY

Bible Background • EZEKIEL 18

Printed Text • EZEKIEL 18:4, 20–23, 30–32   Devotional Reading • PSALM 18:20–24

Lesson Aim

By the end of the lesson, we will:

UNDERSTAND how God views responsibility for sin;

FEEL responsible for our own actions, but not guilty if we have done our best and still our children do not follow the Lord; and

CONSIDER the consequences of our actions when we are tempted to sin.

Keep in Mind

"For I have no pleasure in the death of him that dieth, saith the Lord GOD: wherefore turn yourselves, and live ye" (Ezekiel 18:32).

Focal Verses

Ezekiel 18:4 Behold, all souls are mine; as the soul of the father, so also the soul of the son is mine: the soul that sinneth, it shall die.

18:20 The soul that sinneth, it shall die. The son shall not bear the iniquity of the father, neither shall the father bear the iniquity of the son: the righteousness of the righteous shall be upon him, and the wickedness of the wicked shall be upon him.

21 But if the wicked will turn from all his sins that he hath committed, and keep all my statutes, and do that which is lawful and right, he shall surely live, he shall not die.

22 All his transgressions that he hath committed, they shall not be mentioned unto him: in his righteousness that he hath done he shall live.

23 Have I any pleasure at all that the wicked should die? saith the Lord GOD: and not that he should return from his ways, and live?

8:30 Therefore I will judge you, O house of Israel, every one according to his ways, saith the Lord GOD. Repent, and turn yourselves from all your transgressions; so iniquity shall not be your ruin.

31 Cast away from you all your transgressions, whereby ye have transgressed; and make you a new heart and a new spirit: for why will ye die, O house of Israel?

32 For I have no pleasure in the death of him that dieth, saith the Lord GOD: wherefore turn yourselves, and live ye.

In Focus

Gladys works for the city's consumer affairs department. Her work includes arbitrating lawsuits and personal cases between the public and the city. She is a conscientious worker who does what she can to help the "little person" get a fair shake from the city. So when she came home from work one day to find a large group of people at her doorstep, she was quite surprised.

She assumed that the group was there to discuss a case against the city—until she got to the door. "Gladys!" the group's spokesman called out as the group surrounded her. "Your son, Alex, is in deep trouble." As the group talked, she discovered that her 18-year-old son had been involved in an automobile accident.

He and another young man had been drag racing through the community. When he turned a corner to head for the home stretch, a woman with a baby stepped out in front of his car. To avoid hitting her, Alex jumped the curb and plowed into a number of parked cars. One of the cars he hit rammed into another car that was going in the opposite direction, pinning the driver of that car in the wreckage.

Gladys was devastated. Not only was her son hurt and another driver injured, but her car was damaged beyond repair. And because she had given Alex permission to drive the car, she would be held liable for his actions.

Should the mother be held responsible for the actions of her teenage son? Should she be held liable for the damages? These are questions that some people have probably asked themselves when they were in a similar situation—questions that will probably never be completely answered by any court of law. Sooner or later, each of us will be held accountable for our own actions, regardless of our age.

In today's lesson, the elders of Israel maintain that the people are suffering because of the sins of their parents. In other words, they themselves had not sinned, but they had been taken into captivity because of their parents' actions. They come to Ezekiel to get God's assessment of their situation.

The People, Places, and Times

Ezekiel. Ezekiel, a prophet from a priestly family, was carried off as a captive to Babylon in 597 B.C. when he was 25 years old. His call to the prophetic ministry came when he was 30 years old. Ezekiel prophesied to the captives who lived by the River Chebar at Tel Abib.

Ezekiel was a priest, the son of Buzi (Ezekiel 1:3). He was married to a woman whom he dearly loved (24:16). Her death was one of the saddest events of his life. She died on the very day the armies of Babylon laid siege to the Holy City of Jerusalem (Ezekiel 24:1–2). Believers have been called upon to suffer many tragedies down through the ages, but when we look at the suffering of Ezekiel, we learn more about God's suffering on behalf of His people.

Background

In the book that bears his name, Ezekiel shows us just how ugly and serious our sin is. God, against whom our sin is directed, is grieved and hurt. This is why God dealt so dramatically with the human condition by sending His Son Jesus to die in our place and set us free from sin's bondage.

The book of Ezekiel was written during the early years of the Babylonian captivity of God's covenant people Israel. Captives were taken from Jerusalem in three stages in 605 B.C., 597 B.C., and 587 B.C. Ezekiel must have been taken captive in 597 B.C. In 596 B.C., Nebuchadnezzar destroyed Jerusalem and sent most of the remaining inhabitants into exile.

Ezekiel wrote his early prophecies as a captive in Babylon who expected Jerusalem to be destroyed. Ezekiel 24 describes the beginning of the final siege of the city. The Lord had the prophet write down this important date as a memorial of the dreaded event (24:2). God indicated that it represented a clear judgment against Judah. God commanded Ezekiel not to mourn her death, as a symbol of His wrath upon the idolatrous nation (vv. 15–24).

Part of Ezekiel was written during the long siege of Jerusalem. Ezekiel and the other captives living in Babylon must have heard of the suffering of their fellow Israelites back home. Eventually, they heard that their beloved Jerusalem had fallen.

A key teaching throughout the book of Ezekiel is individual responsibility—as we stand before a Holy God, each of us is responsible for his or her own sin. During Ezekiel's time, the Jewish people emphasized their group identity as God's covenant people and tended to de-emphasize their responsibility as individuals to follow God and His will. Some believed that children were held accountable for the sins of their ancestors. But Ezekiel declared, "The soul that sinneth, it shall die. The son shall not bear the iniquity of the father, neither shall the father bear the iniquity of the son: the righteousness of the righteous shall be upon him, and the wickedness of the wicked shall be upon him" (18:20).

At-A-Glance

1. God Holds Us Responsible for Our Own Sins (Ezekiel 18:4, 20)
2. God Forgives Those Who Turn from Their Sins (vv. 21–23)
3. God Encourages Sinners to Repent (18:30–32)

"For I have no pleasure in the death of him that dieth, saith the Lord GOD: wherefore turn yourselves, and live ye" (Ezekiel 18:32).

In Depth

1. God Holds Us Responsible for Our Own Sins (Ezekiel 18:4, 20)

Chapter 18 clearly dispels the false notion that innocent children are held responsible for the sins of their fathers. Each of us must bear the guilt and punishment of his or her own sins (vv. 1–4). No one will die for sins that someone else has committed; and no one will be saved by another person's righteousness.

The Old Testament provides us with striking examples of kings who did not follow the wicked example of their fathers. Both Hezekiah and Josiah were such God-fearing kings who did not waver in seeking Him. They dedicated themselves to a life of reform and were noted as leaders who strove diligently by example and action to bring the Israelites back to God.

2. God Forgives Those Who Turn from Their Sins (vv. 21–23)

"I'm forgiven . . . set free!" cries the repentant sinner who has trusted in Christ alone for salvation. The dark cloud of bondage has lifted. A life has been transformed by the power of the living God. Such forgiveness and freedom are available to anyone who will turn from his or her sin to God. Oh, the joy of knowing and serving Him!

True repentance involves a change of mind (Genesis 6:6–7); a turning away from sin, disobedience, or rebellion; and a turning back to God (Ezekiel 18:21; Matthew 9:13; Luke 5:32). There is a sense of deep remorse or regret for past conduct (Matthew 27:3), a "godly sorrow" for sin that includes the act of "turning around" and going in the opposite direction. This is not the same as a "temporary regret" for sin that leads to only momentary change. True repentance results in a fundamental change in a person's relationship to God.

King David is a classic case of Old Testament repentance. David repented (Psalm 51) after the prophet Nathan exposed David's adultery with

Bathsheba and his murder of her husband Uriah (2 Samuel 12). David turned from his sin and was forgiven, even though there were painful personal consequences of his sin: The first child he bore with Bathsheba died (2 Samuel 12:18); it opened the door to murder being a constant threat in his family (13:26–30; 18:14, 15; 1 Kings 2:23–25); and David suffered the embarrassment of his wives being given to another in public view (2 Samuel 16:20–23).

Jesus' message related not only to "repentance," or turning away from sin, but also to "faith," or turning toward God by accepting the Lord Jesus Christ. Repentance and faith are two sides of the same coin. Both are necessary for entrance into the kingdom (Matthew 18:3). Jesus' message of repentance had a negative side for those who resisted: "Unless you repent," said Jesus, "you will all likewise perish" (Luke 13:3, 5). Repentance is a turning from an evil lifestyle and dead works (Ezekiel 18:21; Acts 8:22; Hebrews 6:1) toward Almighty God and His glory (Acts 20:21; Revelation 16:9), everlasting life (Acts 11:18), and a knowledge of His truth (2 Timothy 2:25).

God is fair in His dealings with people. Those who turn from their sin and walk in righteousness will find mercy. Repentant sinners are dealt with according to their repentance and faith, not according to their former sins. Sins are completely forgiven by God in His mercy, never to be mentioned again (Ezekiel 18:22).

God takes no pleasure in the death of the wicked (v. 23). Instead, God is better pleased when His mercy is glorified in the sinner's salvation than when His justice is glorified in their damnation. He sent His Son to die so that all might be saved. His name is love, and His nature is mercy. God does not abandon the sinner (1 Timothy 2:4; 2 Peter 3:9); He works and waits with His hands outstretched!

3. God Encourages Sinners to Repent (18:30–32)

God grieved over the house of Israel and, through prophets like Ezekiel (v. 31), admonished them to turn from their sins, just as He admonishes parents and children today. Because of sin, every person is disposed to reject the truth, but by grace we can accept it. The same is true about choosing between right and wrong. Parents can train a child to follow God, but that child will have to make his or her own choice. Thankfully, if we repent and turn toward God, asking Him to change our hearts, He will do it. When we earnestly call on God through Christ to save us, He will save us and help us to walk in His will and His way.

We cannot make a new heart and spirit for ourselves by our own power; God alone can give them (Ezekiel 11:19). Still, a person must come to God to receive them. When we turn to God, both heart and spirit are renewed by His Holy Spirit.

"Turn yourselves from all your transgressions; so iniquity shall not be your ruin," God warns (18:30). "For why will ye die?" (v. 31). Why go to hell when citizenship in the kingdom of God is available to you? Why should you be slaves of Satan when you may be free in Christ? Do not allow stubbornness or listlessness about salvation to prevent you. Are the lusts of this sinful world worth dying for?

God describes death as eternal separation from Himself and from the glory of His power (Ezekiel 18:31, 32)! Why die and forfeit all the purposes for which you were made (do not fulfill all that God has called you to be)? Today, the only barrier to salvation is that mentioned by the Lord Jesus: "You refuse to come to me to have life" (John 5:40, NIV).

Today, as in Ezekiel's day, it is common for people to try to blame their sin on others rather than take responsibility for their own actions. Then, when they suffer the consequences of their sin, they consider themselves merely unfortunate instead of guilty. If a child willfully follows the sinful tradition of his parents, it is only just that he shares in the parents' punishment. God made it clear in the Old Testament that "the fathers shall not be put to death for the children, neither shall the children be put to death for the fathers: every man shall be put to death for his own sin" (Deuteronomy 24:16). God reinforces this concept in the book of Ezekiel. Anyone who does not repent will perish, and their blood will be upon their own heads.

Whereas the sinner's inheritance is death, God

offers the repentant sinner life (Ezekiel 18:32). "I am come that they might have life, and that they might have it more abundantly" (John 10:10). Choose life today!

Search the Scriptures

1. Who belongs to God (Ezekiel 18:4)?

2. What do Ezekiel 18:20, 30 say will happen to sinners?

3. What does God say about sin as it relates to a father and son (v. 20)?

4. According to verse 21, what must a wicked person do to live?

5. What happens to a sinner who repents (vv. 21–22)?

6. How does God feel about sin (vv. 23, 32)?

Discuss the Meaning

1. What does God mean when He says, "All souls are mine" (Ezekiel 18:4)?

2. What type of death do you think God is talking about in verse 20?

3. What does "the righteousness of the righteous shall be upon him, and the wickedness of the wicked shall be upon him" mean (v. 20)?

4. In what ways is iniquity a person's ruin (v. 30)?

5. How can a person come to possess "a new heart and a new spirit" (v. 31)?

Lesson in Our Society

It's always easier to blame someone else for our problems than it is to take responsibility for what we have done to cause them. It can be hard to get children to take responsibility for their actions. Unfortunately, as adults, we, too, can have a hard time taking responsibility for our mistakes and sins. After all, we want to look good in the eyes of our spouse, boss, pastor, and coworkers; and admitting wrongdoing is often humiliating. Still, that is what God wants us to do. He sees all and knows all. When we stand before Him, we won't be able to blame our sin on anyone but ourselves. We won't be able to blame our sin on our parents, and our children won't be able to blame their sin on us. We will be held accountable for what we have done. Aren't we glad

that God can wash us as white as snow? Through Jesus, we can be set free of the sin that binds us—if we are willing to admit our sin, ask forgiveness, and follow Him. Praise God for His provision of grace!

Make It Happen

Are you able to take responsibility for the pain you cause others? When you make a mistake at home or at work, are you able to apologize? When you sin, do you take responsibility and repent of your sin before God? Are there areas in your life in which you need deliverance from sin? Allow the Holy Spirit to reveal areas in your life that need to change. "If we confess our sins, he is faithful and just to forgive us our sins, and to cleanse us from all unrighteousness. If we say that we have not sinned, we make him a liar, and his word is not in us" (1 John 1:9–10).

Follow the Spirit

What God wants me to do:

_____

_____

Remember Your Thoughts

Special insights I have learned:

_____

_____

More Light on the Text

Ezekiel 18:4, 20–23, 30–32

4 Behold, all souls are mine; as the soul of the father, so also the soul of the son is mine: the soul that sinneth, it shall die.

All people (parents, children, and grandchildren) belong to the Lord. The very "breath" we breathe, our "inner being," our "souls" (Heb. *nephesh,* **NEH-fesh**) belong to Him.

The Lord makes a distinction between those who follow His commandments and those who "go wrong." The *New Living Translation* says, "And this is my rule: The person who sins will be the one who dies." The Hebrew word for "die" is *muwth* (**mooth**), meaning "to die as a penalty, be put to death, perish as a nation, or die prematurely (by neglecting wise moral conduct)."

18:20 The soul that sinneth, it shall die. The son shall not bear the iniquity of the father, neither shall the father bear the iniquity of the son: the righteousness of the righteous shall be upon him, and the wickedness of the wicked shall be upon him.

The Lord is unyielding concerning sin and death. This verse is a repetition and expansion of verse 19, letting us know that we will not have to die for the sins that our parents or children commit. The Hebrew word for "bear" is *nasa'* (**naw-SAW**), meaning "to lift, lift up to carry, support, sustain, endure, or take." The only one who takes away our sins and the sins of our "kinfolk" is Jesus Christ. He endured suffering and death on the Cross in order to take away our sins.

The Lord also lets us know that we have a choice to make. We can be either wicked or righteous, and we will suffer (or rejoice over) the consequences of our actions. In allowing us this choice, the Lord shows forth both His mercy and His power.

21 But if the wicked will turn from all his sins that he hath committed, and keep all my statutes, and do that which is lawful and right, he shall surely live, he shall not die.

In this verse, the Lord gives hope to the sinner. This is good news for all of humankind, since "all have sinned, and come short of the glory of God" (Romans 3:23). When we obey the Word of God and repent of our sins, we can expect to live (Heb. *chayah*, **khaw-YAW**, meaning "to have life, remain alive, sustain life, live prosperously, live for ever, or be restored to life or health").

Many times, we as human beings will make promises with every intention of keeping them. However, sometimes our weaknesses overcome our intentions and we are unable to keep the promise we have made. But our Lord is always faithful to His promises: "God is not a man, that he should lie, nor a son of man, that he should change his mind. Does he speak and then not act? Does he promise and not fulfill?" (Deuteronomy 23:19, NIV).

In emphasizing the death of sinners, the Lord conveys His anger. We seldom study the wrath and indignation of the Lord. In today's lesson, we read about a God who is truly capable of stern correction that corresponds to a parent's response to the disobedience of a child.

22 All his transgressions that he hath committed, they shall not be mentioned unto him: in his righteousness that he hath done he shall live.

When we repent of our sins, the Lord promises that He will not even mention them again. The Hebrew word for "mentioned" is *zakar* (**zaw-KAR**), meaning "to be brought to remembrance, be remembered, be thought of, or be brought to mind." By repenting, we can avoid death and can look forward to receiving the Lord's promise of life and the blessings that go with it.

23 Have I any pleasure at all that the wicked should die? saith the Lord GOD: and not that he should return from his ways, and live?

The *New Living Translation* reads, "'Do you think,'" asks the Sovereign Lord, 'that I like to see wicked people die? Of course not! I only want them to turn from their wicked ways and live.'" In this verse, the Lord allows us to see His compassion for humankind. He desires that we all repent, "return from" (Heb. *shuwb*, **shoob**, meaning "to return unto or go back") our sin, and "live" (*chayah*, **khaw-YAW**).

18:30 Therefore I will judge you, O house of Israel, every one according to his ways, saith the Lord GOD. Repent, and turn yourselves from all your transgressions; so iniquity shall not be your ruin.

Through Ezekiel, the Lord seems to be pleading with His people to repent and save their lives. If they continue in their sin and rebellion, the Lord promises to "judge" (Heb. *shaphat*, **shaw-FAT**, meaning "to judge or punish") each of them individually. The Hebrew word for "iniquity" is `avon (**aw-VONE**), meaning "perversity, depravity, iniquity, guilt, or punishment of iniquity." The Hebrew word for "ruin" is *mikshowl* (**mik-SHOLE**), meaning "stumbling, a means or occasion of stumbling, or stumbling block."

31 Cast away from you all your transgressions, whereby ye have transgressed; and make you a new

heart and a new spirit: for why will ye die, O house of Israel?

The Israelites are told not only to repent, but to do so sincerely. The Hebrew word for "cast away" is *sha-lak* (**shaw-lak**), meaning "to throw, hurl, or fling." God's gracious invitation to Israel is poignant: "Why die when you can live?" The New Testament continues with this theme. We do not have to stay in our sins and die. "[T]hose who become Christians become new persons. They are not the same anymore; their old life is gone and a new life has begun!" (2 Corinthians 5:17, NLT). Ephesians 4:23 encourages us to "be constantly renewed in the spirit of your mind [having a fresh mental and spiritual attitude]" (*Amplified Bible*). We cannot help but ask the question, "Why would anyone want to die and not live?"

32 For I have no pleasure in the death of him that dieth, saith the Lord GOD: wherefore turn yourselves, and live ye.

The Lord continues to earnestly appeal to the Israelites (and to us today) to repent of our sins and live. The *Amplified Bible* renders this verse, "For I have no pleasure in the death of him who dies, says the Lord God. Therefore turn (be converted) and live!"

This passage teaches us that, although we may not be held responsible for the sins of our parents or children, we are indeed accountable for the sins that we ourselves commit. We are also made aware of the fact that our decision has consequences, whether it is to turn from the Lord or to turn toward Him and follow His commandments. Our compassionate God calls us to repentance, faith, and obedience. The consequences of our actions continue far beyond the moment of disobedience, and the blessings of obedience far outweigh what little pleasure we receive from our sin.

Each of us has the promise of Romans 8:1–2: "Therefore there is now no condemnation for those who are in Christ Jesus. For the law of the Spirit of life in Christ Jesus has set you free from the law of sin and of death."

Daily Bible Readings

M: One God and One Mediator
1 Timothy 2:1–6
T: God Rewards the Righteous
Psalm 18:20–24
W: God Judges Each One's Ways
Ezekiel 33:12–20
T: Those Who Sin Will Die
Ezekiel 18:1–4
F: The Righteous Will Live
Ezekiel 18:5–9
S: Those Who Repent Will Live
Ezekiel 18:19–23
S: God Judges Each of Us
Ezekiel 18:25–32

TEACHING TIPS

August 19
Bible Study Guide 12

1. Words You Should Know

A. Prophet (Zechariah 1:4) *navi* (Heb.)—Foreteller; God's spokesman; a divinely called minister who announces the will of God to His people.

B. Word (7:8) *babar* (Heb.)—A message from God.

2. Teacher Preparation

A. Pray and invite the Holy Spirit to guide you in teaching today's lesson.

B. Study the Bible Background, Printed Text, and Devotional Reading to enhance your comprehension of today's lesson.

C. Read through the lesson and prepare answers to the Search the Scriptures and Discuss the Meaning questions so that you will be able to facilitate discussion.

D. Study More Light on the Text in preparation for today's lesson.

E. Finally, complete lesson 12 in the *Precepts For Living® Personal Study Guide.*

3. Starting the Lesson

A. Lead the class in prayer, focusing on the Lesson Aim.

B. Instruct the class to silently read the In Focus section. Then discuss how the story relates to today's Lesson Aim.

C. Ask for volunteers to read The People, Places, and Times and the Background section. Discuss.

4. Getting into the Lesson

A. Review the Lesson Aim and highlight what the lesson should accomplish.

B. Have volunteers read the Focal Verses aloud based on the At-A-Glance outline.

C. Engage your students in discussion, reviewing the Discuss the Meaning questions to bolster their understanding of what it means to be repentant.

5. Relating the Lesson to Life

A. Share how the Focal Verses and the In Focus story relate to the Lesson Aim and the Lesson in Our Society section.

B. Using the In Focus story, the Lesson Aim, and the Lesson in Our Society section as focal points, allow the students to share some of their own experiences.

6. Arousing Action

A. Have the students read the Make It Happen exercise and challenge them to commit to completing it in the upcoming week.

B. Explain that praying, studying, and meditating on God's Word will help them cultivate an intimate personal relationship with God.

C. End the class with prayer and encourage the students to share their faith with others.

Worship Guide

For the Superintendent or Teacher
Theme: Zechariah Calls for a Return to God
Theme Song: "Trust and Obey"
Scripture: Zechariah 1:1–6; 7:8–14
Song: "I Have Decided to Follow Jesus"
Meditation: Father, I thank You for showing me the way and for helping me to "turn around" and give my life to You. Amen.

ZECHARIAH CALLS FOR A RETURN TO GOD

Bible Background • ZECHARIAH 1:1–6; 7:8–14; 8:16–17, 20–21, 23
Printed Text • ZECHARIAH 1:1–6; 7:8–14   Devotional Reading • ISAIAH 12

Lesson Aim

By the end of the lesson, we will:

KNOW that God is calling us to repent of our sins and will forgive us when we come to Him;

FEEL sorry for any wrong things that we have done; and

PRAY for forgiveness of our sins.

Keep in Mind

"Therefore say thou unto them, Thus saith the LORD of hosts; Turn ye unto me, saith the LORD of hosts, and I will turn unto you, saith the LORD of hosts" (Zechariah 1:3).

Focal Verses

Zechariah 1:1 In the eighth month, in the second year of Darius, came the word of the Lord unto Zechariah, the son of Berechiah, the son of Iddo the prophet, saying,

2 The Lord hath been sore displeased with your fathers.

3 Therefore say thou unto them, Thus saith the LORD of hosts; Turn ye unto me, saith the LORD of hosts, and I will turn unto you, saith the LORD of hosts.

4 Be ye not as your fathers, unto whom the former prophets have cried, saying, Thus saith the LORD of hosts; Turn ye now from your evil ways, and from your evil doings; but they did not hear, nor hearken unto me, saith the Lord.

5 Your fathers, where are they? and the prophets, do they live for ever?

6 But my words and my statutes, which I commanded my servants the prophets, did they not take hold of your fathers? and they returned and said, Like as the LORD of hosts thought to do unto us, according to our ways, and according to our doings, so hath he dealt with me.

7:8 And the word of the Lord came unto Zechariah, saying,

9 Thus speaketh the LORD of hosts, saying, Execute true judgment, and shew mercy and compassions every man to his brother:

10 And oppress not the widow, nor the fatherless, the stranger, nor the poor; and let none of you imagine evil against his brother in your heart.

11 But they refused to hearken, and pulled away the shoulder and stopped their ears, that they should not hear.

12 Yea, they made their hearts as an adamant stone, lest they should hear the law, and the words which the LORD of hosts hath sent in his spirit by the former prophets: therefore came a great wrath from the LORD of hosts:

13 Therefore it is come to pass, that as he cried, and they would not hear; so they cried, and I would not hear, saith the LORD of hosts.

14 But I scattered them with a whirlwind among all the nations whom they knew not. Thus the land was desolate after them, that no man passed through nor returned: for they laid the pleasant land desolate.

In Focus

Greg did not know what real freedom and hope were until he repented of his sins and accepted Jesus Christ as his Lord and Saviour. His eyes filled with tears as he shared his testimony in Bible study one evening:

"I know what God can do," he proclaimed. "I lived the life of a gangbanger and drug dealer. I was shot at, wounded, and now have to walk with a cane. After my mother's violent death when I was 13, I gave up on life and lived as a rebellious teenager. It finally caused me to spend 24 years in prison. One day, through a church's prison ministry, I heard the Word of God. They wrote me letters for more than 15 years, encouraging me and sharing their faith. Finally, I accepted Jesus Christ as my own Lord and Saviour, and He turned my life around. I regret all the terrible things that I did! I am truly sorry for my sins! I believe that God has forgiven me.

Now, I have earned my bachelor's degree and I am working on getting my master's in social work. I want to help others who have lost their way, as I was helped. I want to share with some lost boy, girl, man, or woman what God has given me."

In today's lesson, Zechariah teaches that we are called to repent and show compassion, justice, and mercy toward one another.

The People, Places, and Times

Zechariah. Zechariah, the 11th minor prophet, was born to a priest. His place of birth is thought to be Babylon. His prophetic ministry took place during a period of political strife and turmoil. The people had strayed from God (again). Through the divine intervention of God, Zechariah was called to minister and prophesy to the troubled people in a troubled time. He penned the first chapter of the book that bears his name in 524 B.C. About five years later (519 B.C.), he wrote the seventh chapter. The biblical events described in this lesson occurred during the restoration period. That is why Zechariah was known as a "restoration prophet." Zechariah is second only to Isaiah in the number of prophecies given about Jesus.

Chapters 1–8 of Zechariah speak of eight visions that the Lord gave the prophet to help the people overcome their problems in rebuilding the temple and their disobedience in worship. Here, we read Zechariah's prophecy about the second coming of the Lord and how He will rule over all nations and judge them. Zechariah was a priest who preached hope to the people. He called for righteousness, repentance, and spirituality in worship, home life, and politics.

Background

The prophet Zechariah was born in Babylon during the Exile. Zechariah was a young man when he returned to Jerusalem after King Cyrus of Persia defeated the Babylonians in 539 B.C. and decreed that the Israelites could return to their homeland in 538 B.C. As with all of His prophets, God called Zechariah for a specific purpose. He wanted

Zechariah to proclaim His word to the small remnant of Jews who had returned to Judah from exile to rebuild the temple and their nation. He also wanted to help them by pointing out and explaining the consequences of their sin and calling the Israelites to repentance and obedience. Here, Zechariah shares the first of eight visions that God gave Him through the night.

The people were aware that the temple they were building would not be as magnificent as the one that had been destroyed; still, they had begun to feel overwhelmed. They were ready to give up—to quit. Therefore, God called Zechariah to: (1) inspire the people and encourage them to finish rebuilding the temple, (2) restore their recognition of God in government, (3) restore their faith and hope during this period of despair, (4) bring them back to an orderly life and true worship of God, and (5) encourage them to repent of their sinful worship of false gods (idols).

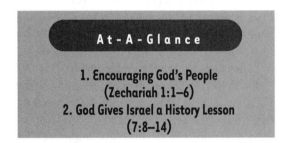

At-A-Glance

1. Encouraging God's People
   (Zechariah 1:1–6)
2. God Gives Israel a History Lesson
   (7:8–14)

In Depth

1. Encouraging God's People (Zechariah 1:1–6)

Ten years had passed since the exiles returned from captivity to rebuild the temple, and the work was still not completed. Like many of us who experience prolonged discouragement due to overwhelming trials and tribulations, the people were discouraged and began to ignore their service to God. They had lost their zeal for worship and were just "going through the motions." In fact, they had even begun fasting without being truly repentant for their sins. Zechariah let the Israelites know that halfhearted service was unacceptable to God.

Zechariah reminded the people that their forefathers had fallen prey to false leaders who had exploited them. God was angry with the Israelites' ancestors because they had ignored His prophets in the past. This disobedience was evidenced by worshiping idols and not acknowledging God as the one true God in their lives. As a result, they broke their covenant relationship with God time and time again, causing their intimate relationship with Him to suffer. They paid the consequences for their sins, finding themselves in bondage to the Babylonians for approximately 70 years. They were prisoners during the reigns of King Nebuchadnezzar, Belshazzar, Darius, and Cyrus. Now it was time for the next generation to pick up the reins and carry out God's mandates. It was time for the people to get right with God, renew their relationship with God, brush off their discouragement, pull themselves together, and obey God's command.

Through Zechariah, God promised the people that they did not have to fear any enemies while building the temple because He would protect the workmen and empower them to get the job done. At the same time, God expected them to fulfill their part of the bargain as well.

2. God Gives Israel a History Lesson (7:8–14)

The history lesson continues as Zechariah reminds the Israelites of how their ancestors had not listened to God's messengers. They had stubbornly turned away and would not listen to God's prophets. They were a hardheaded, stiff-necked people, and they suffered for their rebellion by being forced into slavery. God had not listened to their forefathers because of their disobedience and lack of repentance; likewise, He would not listen to them if they fell into the same rebellious behavior.

When we do not obey God's Word, we can expect God to respond to us in the very same way. When we sin or are disobedient, we open the door for Satan to build strongholds in our lives that imprison us. God expects His children to be genuinely sorry for their transgressions. True repentance, then, is completely turning away from sin. After repenting, if we ask God for forgiveness, He will restore our relationship with Him.

God wanted the Israelites to know that disobedience and sin have dire consequences. He warned the

Israelites that they did not want to experience His wrath again. God wanted them to come to Him with a sincere desire to know and love Him. He is a jealous God and wants believers' complete devotion, not their halfhearted service. We, too, must follow the instructions He has given us in His holy Word and remain pure until His Second Coming. If there is sin in our lives, we must repent and turn to Him for forgiveness.

Search the Scriptures

1. "The Lord has been sore _____ with your fathers" (Zechariah 1:2).

2. What did God want the Israelites to do (v. 3)?

3. Name two things that the Lord had wanted the Israelites' forefathers to do (Zechariah 7:9).

4. How did God want the Israelites and their forefathers to treat widows, the fatherless, strangers, and the poor (v. 10)?

Discuss the Meaning

1. Discuss what your church or denomination says about salvation and what it means to return to God.

2. What sacraments does your church regularly engage in that provide an opportunity for personal reflection, repentance, and renewal?

Lesson in Our Society

There is an old adage that says, "What goes around, comes around." This is another way of saying, "History repeats itself." The Old Testament cites numerous instances of the Israelites' disobedience, which resulted in punishments from God; subsequently, there was repentance by the Israelites, followed by the Lord's forgiveness. The New Testament follows the same pattern. There are many instances in which the Lord forgives sinners. Even on the Cross, Jesus asked His Father to forgive His murderers. Jesus wants His followers to be merciful and compassionate, just as He is.

We encounter similar disobedience in our present-day society. Every day, we meet people who harden their hearts when it comes to hearing the word of God. However, Zechariah says that when we return to the Lord, the wholeness and happiness we have in

Him leads to a right relationship with and true worship of Him. We must be patient and walk with the Lord. As we do so, He will keep us and encourage us in times of rejection and discord.

Make It Happen

We must think positively and focus on godly things so that we can live joyously. In this way, we will be encouraged to take positive actions. The Holy Spirit fills us with a joy that the world does not give and, therefore, that it cannot take away. We must bathe in that joy, especially in times of turmoil, for it is in these times that the Lord provides protection for us. When we are empowered by the Holy Spirit, we are to witness and to win souls for Christ. This is the mission of the church until the Lord comes again. Let Zechariah serve as a model for us, thereby encouraging us to continue ministering to others, helping, and encouraging them to turn to God.

Follow the Spirit

What God wants me to do:

_____

_____

Remember Your Thoughts

Special insights I have learned:

_____

_____

More Light on the Text
Zechariah 1:1–6; 7:8–14

1 In the eighth month, in the second year of Darius, came the word of the LORD unto Zechariah, the son of Berechiah, the son of Iddo the prophet, saying,

The Hebrew phrase *dabar* (**daw-baw'**), here translated "came the word," is a common way of referring to Jehovah's communication through His prophets by means of His Spirit (see also, for example, Hosea 1:1; Joel 1:1; Micah 1:1). This phrase, along with the phrase "word of the LORD" (Heb. *dabar Yevovah,* **daw-BAW Yeh-ho VAW**), leaves no room to doubt that the process often called "inspiration" is in view here. Drawing on the language of 2 Timothy 3:16, "All Scripture is given by inspiration" (literally, "God-breathed" or "breathed out by God"), Christians use the word "inspiration" to describe the process by which God speaks authoritatively and without error through the Scriptures. Zechariah gives us hints as to what this process looks like. First, the prophet's solemn declaration that it was Jehovah's own word that had come directly to him removes the possibility that inspiration can mean simply a heightened ability to perform or create (as in "The Knicks sure played inspired basketball tonight").

On the other hand, the Bible reader should avoid the other extreme of believing that God somehow dictated His words directly to a prophet in a way that ignored the prophet's personality or background altogether. Even a shallow reading of Zechariah—or of any other prophetic book, for that matter—will show that the prophet's personal characteristics are reflected in his prophecy. There is surely some mystery here, but the prophets spoke as they were "moved along by the Holy Ghost" (2 Peter 1:21), with this process of "moving" neither wiping out the personality of the prophet nor allowing the prophet's sinfulness and weakness to override the perfect transmission of God's holy Word.

The reign of Darius, king of Media and Persia, brought about an era of relative peace in the volatile region of the ancient Near East. The powerful Babylonian empire was in shambles, and, as the man in Zechariah's vision proclaims, "We have walked to and fro through the earth, and, behold, all the earth sitteth still, and is at rest" (1:11). God's providence had ushered in a time in which the tattered ruins of Jerusalem and the scattered remnant of the Jews might be rebuilt and restored.

2 The LORD hath been sore displeased with your fathers.

The phrase "sore displeased" is *qatsaph* (**kaw-tsaf'**) in Hebrew and means "to be angry, to be wroth, to be full of wrath." Therefore, the sentence literally reads, "The LORD hath been angry with a great anger." The old-fashioned language of the King James Version puts it nicely: The Lord is "sore displeased."

"Turn ye unto me, saith the LORD of hosts, and I will turn unto you..." (from Zechariah 1:3).

This ominous opening statement accomplishes several things. First, it provides an important backdrop for Zechariah's prophecy—specifically, the ongoing disobedience of God's people. The prophets are executors of God's covenant, and as such they often recall the curses in Deuteronomy, where God promised discipline if His people would not show covenant faithfulness. Without giving much detail, Zechariah establishes the fact that the Israelites as a nation have been wayward, and the Lord owes them nothing. Second, this opening statement introduces the concept of God's justice and wrath in response to sin. The fact that God had judged Israel before meant that He could do so again. Early on, then, the Israelites receive a warning. Third, the most important function of this opening statement is to set up a contrast with what follows. The merciful invitation that God extends to Israel (vv. 3–6) is all the more glorious in light of verse 2. Even though God owes these people nothing, He is offering them everything, if only they will turn to Him.

3 Therefore say thou unto them, Thus saith the LORD of hosts; Turn ye unto me, saith the LORD of hosts, and I will turn unto you, saith the LORD of hosts.

Three times in this verse, Jehovah presents himself in military terms. The "hosts" are angelic armies; therefore, the name "LORD of hosts" presents Israel's God as a conquering warrior, full of power. No wonder some translations render the phrase "Lord Almighty." Three times His voice thunders as He speaks to and through Jeremiah. The great and terrible King issues a command, but that command is full of grace and compassion! The King's simple command is to turn (Heb. *shuwb*, **shoob**), carrying the idea of turning back or returning. Notice the nature of the command: Jehovah does not say "come," but "turn (around)," meaning that the one invited is not facing Him but has his back turned toward Him! Although the Lord's terrible judgment, which had been carried out by the Babylonians as they swept through Jerusalem less than a decade earlier, is still fresh in the Israelites' minds, the unfinished temple in Jerusalem stands as a grim reminder that not much has changed among this people. Yet the Lord makes it known that "mercy rejoiceth against judgment" (James 2:13).

4 Be ye not as your fathers, unto whom the former prophets have cried, saying, Thus saith the LORD of hosts; Turn ye now from your evil ways, and from your evil doings: but they did not hear, nor hearken unto me, saith the LORD.

The Lord's words to Zechariah now demonstrate, by negative example, what it looks like to turn to the Lord. The prophetic call here brings to mind another common device used by Israel's prophets: rehearsing the history of the people. The reminder here is succinct: Zechariah refers to the prophets as a whole, probably referring to all those who prophesied during the reigns of Israel's and Judah's kings. The warning again mentions the "fathers," no doubt indicating those whose sins and idolatry had brought about the Babylonian Exile. Israel's faithlessness is rehearsed in the New Testament as well (Acts 7:51–53); however, the greater truth of the Gospel is also presented. The inheritance that Israel lost is now available, in a spiritual sense, to both Jews and Gentiles. In Jesus, all believers possess by faith the inheritance that was originally promised to Israel (Hebrews 3–4).

5 Your fathers, where are they? and the prophets, do they live for ever?

Often Israel's prophets—including Jesus, its ultimate and final Prophet—ask questions that are intended to be sarcastic and rhetorical (that is, with an obvious answer). The questions in verse 5 again speak of two groups of people: fathers and prophets (v. 4). The point is not that the people's ancestors were no longer alive on the earth—the fact that no one lives forever would have come as no surprise to

God's people—but that all memory of the fathers and prophets had been wiped out. All the visible reminders of Israel's enduring existence under God's gracious promise—Jerusalem, the temple, the king, the priest, etc.—had been wiped away in Judah's exile to Babylon. The prophets are presented as a separate category because as long as there was a prophet in Israel, the opportunity for repentance remained. In the midst of this painful reminder, God's grace endures in an ironic way, for who is it that reminds the people that the prophets in the kingdoms of Israel of Judah are no more? None other than a prophet—Zechariah himself. And so the offer of repentance in verse 3 rests on solid ground, for a prophet remains to extend the offer to God's people. One day, even that offer will be rescinded, as foretold earlier by the prophet Amos: "Behold, the days come, saith the Lord GOD, that I will send a **famine** in the land, not a **famine** of bread, nor a thirst for water, but of hearing the words of the LORD" (Amos 8:11). As we see in Malachi 1:1–7, Israel failed to fully heed Zechariah's warning, and so not until the coming of that great Prophet promised by Moses (Deuteronomy 18:15) would God speak in a way that restores His people to Him forever.

6 But my words and my statutes, which I commanded my servants the prophets, did they not take hold of your fathers? and they returned and said, Like as the LORD of hosts thought to do unto us, according to our ways, and according to our doings, so hath he dealt with us.

The little word "but" is the smallest Hebrew word in Scripture (only one narrow letter in Hebrew), yet it often turns out to be one of the most important words in a sentence. Here, it sets up an important and powerful contrast: Even though God's unfaithful people (and even the faithful messengers sent to them) have been blown away and have withered like the flowers of the field, one thing still remains: the enduring word of the Lord (Isaiah 40:6–8). The victory of the conquering Warrior, the Lord of hosts, is evident in the prevailing power and truth of His promises, decrees, and warnings. Zechariah presents these holy words as "take hold" (Heb. *nasag*, **naw-sag'**) meaning to reach, overtake, take hold upon. Thus, God's Word did not take hold upon the people's rebellious fathers. Although many of Israel's leaders and prophets insisted for a long time that God's holy city and nation could not possibly fall (see Jeremiah 26:9), they soon saw the light. The Judge, who had spoken from His holy law court, is now vindicated by the evidence: Jerusalem and the temple are no more. And so, as the people were commanded to *turn* in verse 3, Zechariah now uses the same word in reference to their fathers (Heb. *shuwb*, **shoob**). Here, however, the word does not mean that the fathers repented and received mercy, but that they *returned* (one might say "came around") to the right opinion. They had to admit that the Lord had indeed spoken rightly through his prophets! So Jehovah's word was vindicated.

The serious warning and the wondrous grace in the Lord's word to and through Zechariah are completely fulfilled. Jehovah's reminder that His past warnings were no idle threat leaves no doubt that His people face further calamity if they do not repent of their sinful idolatry and turn to their covenant King. But the very existence of such a warning—and of such an offer of grace and blessing through the presence of the living God—demonstrates the depth of God's mercy. Although spurned more times than anyone could possibly count, the great Lover of Israel will return to His bride once again as they return to Him.

7:8 And the word of the LORD came unto Zechariah, saying,

What connects this passage to the passage in chapter 1 is the mention of the preexilic prophets who spoke to Israel before their deportation to Babylon. The people of Bethel (a very important and symbolic town, for its name means "house of God") had sought out the priest and prophets to see if they should fast during a certain month, as was their custom. Jehovah takes this opportunity to recall to the people's minds the former prophets and their message. Zechariah realizes that Bethel's religious practice is similar to that of Israel and Judah before the Exile, who were practicing religious rituals but did not have any true heart involvement or genuine repentance behind it. Zechariah likely knew of the people of Bethel and suspected that their religious practice reflected this same kind of empty formalism. In light of this suspicion, he reminds the people that the prophets had, for years, warned the people about practicing ritual without true worship. Again, the word of God is "breathed out" (see comment on verse 1) through the prophet.

9 Thus speaketh the LORD of hosts, saying, Execute true judgment, and shew mercy and compassions every man to his brother:

At this point in the book of Zechariah, the building of the temple is well underway, so that in one sense, God's people are showing responsiveness and obedience to His command. However, it is clear from Jehovah's word through Zechariah that true covenant faithfulness is absent, as evidenced by the failure of the people to demonstrate justice and kindness "horizontally" in community. God's voice thunders with another verb-noun combination: *Shaphat* (**shaw-fat'**) and *mishpat* (**mish-PAWT**) are linked together in a phrase that might be literally translated as "judge a judgment." This word combination has a variety of meanings that, taken together, speak not only of "judgment" but of "judgment according to truth." Although the people have apparently shown some discernment and wisdom, the forceful repetition of this word group indicates that they have not extended true justice and mercy to their neighbor, even though the Lord has shown remarkable mercy to them. As a result, Jehovah demands conduct that simply reflects the way He has treated His people. "Mercy" and "compassions" do not refer to some heroic act or unreasonable demand, but rather to the natural and proper outgrowth of the mercy the people had received from the Lord's hand.

10 And oppress not the widow, nor the fatherless, the stranger, nor the poor; and let none of you imagine evil against his brother in your heart.

Zechariah's call for justice rather than oppression

repeats the calls of the prophets before the Exile, as well as God's command to show mercy to the helpless (Jeremiah 5:26; 6:13; Hosea 4:1–3; Deuteronomy 14:29; 16:11; 24:19–21). Although the verb *ashaq* (**aw-SHAK**) can often mean "defraud," "oppress" is a better translation here because, in this context, the word emphasizes the position of power in which the Israelites find themselves, relative to the helpless in their midst. Once again, these commands are full of sad irony: Although the Jews found themselves utterly helpless in Babylon and Persia, God showed them mercy and made a way for them to return to Jerusalem and build the temple. Yet, shockingly, the Jews have turned and looked on the powerless in their midst with contempt, perhaps even taking advantage of their lowly position.

The New Testament contains similar themes. The parable of the unmerciful servant (Matthew 18:21–35) graphically portrays the crimes the Israelites are guilty of here, and James 1:27 again speaks of widows and orphans in describing what "true religion" looks like. The covenant context provides the background in both cases: God's covenant people are supposed to mirror the covenant faithfulness He has shown them. In light of the Gospel revealed through Christ, the perfect Covenant Keeper, we understand that our failings are covered in the blood of the new covenant, shed by the Lamb. Because of Christ's sacrifice, we should strive to demonstrate His faithfulness to us in our dealings with each other!

11 But they refused to hearken, and pulled away the shoulder, and stopped their ears, that they should not hear.

The word "hearken" in the King James Version, although not commonly used today, brings out the sense of the Hebrew word *qashab* (**kaw-shab'**), which means more than just listening. It does not merely indicate that the Israelites had failed to hear the prophets' warnings; it means that they had heard these warnings all too well, but had stubbornly refused to repent and obey. Nevertheless, the focus on hearing is obvious; the phrase "pulled away the shoulder" might be expressed in more modern terms as "turned their backs" (implying a breaking of rela-

tionship and disobedience, but also making it harder to hear). The phrase translated "they stopped their ears" literally means that they made their ears heavy, suggesting that their ears were made of stone, or else that the act of listening was burdensome to them. The final clause shows the *purpose* of these actions on their part: They did not *want* to hear the warnings of the prophets, and although they no doubt heard the warnings, they made every effort to pretend that they hadn't. Zechariah's warning gains added force in that his hearers could hardly claim not to have heard *him!* The actions of their ancestors and the resulting destruction and despair would have made God's warning utterly impossible to ignore.

12 Yea, they made their hearts as an adamant stone, lest they should hear the law, and the words which the LORD of hosts hath sent in his spirit by the former prophets: therefore came a great wrath from the LORD of hosts.

The description of the covenant people's faithlessness continues, with a natural transition from the ears to the heart (which in the Bible always represents the center of both the understanding and the affections). There is no doubt as to who is the guilty party in this covenant violation; God is not even said to "harden their hearts," as He did with Pharaoh. On the contrary, the prophets before the Exile portray a God longing for His people to return to Him, pining for His adulterous bride (see Hosea, for example). The intentional hardening described here was heartbreaking, coming from a people who had seen the disastrous consequences of disobedience.

Zechariah mentions the Spirit as the agent of his inspiration. This reference brings out the seriousness of not heeding the prophets' commands and warnings—to do so was to deny the very Spirit of God. The New Testament shows us that denying the Spirit is blasphemy (Mark 3:22–30). Ananias and Sapphira paid with their lives for what is called "lying to the Holy Spirit" in Acts 5. It is no wonder that the military phrase "LORD of hosts" reappears, with God pictured as going to war against His own people! Their treason has brought about the King's inevitable response, despite centuries of patience.

13 Therefore it is come to pass, that as he cried, and they would not hear; so they cried, and I would not hear, saith the LORD of hosts:

The verbs in this passage suggest repeated, customary actions; the Lord's call to His people was, of course, repeated many times over, as was their unbelieving response. God in His mercy patiently offered restoration far beyond what His people deserved. Eventually, however, He executed His justice in a perfectly proportional way. Because He had called to them and they had not listened, he would not hear their cries. Yet, God provided safety and security (albeit in Babylon) for those who truly repented. Many of these same people returned to Jerusalem and were addressed by Zechariah. For them, the importance of hearing the Lord's call was abundantly clear.

14 But I scattered them with a whirlwind among all the nations whom they knew not. Thus the land was desolate after them, that no man passed through nor returned: for they laid the pleasant land desolate.

The term translated "scattered . . . with a whirlwind" occurs only three times in the Old Testament (see Isaiah 54:1; Habakkuk 3:4), and in each case it refers to a violent storm. This is not a literal storm, however, but the worst kind of curse imaginable: exile from the land of Canaan, where the people had rest, and forcible removal from that land into the terrible strangeness of foreign lands, with strange customs and foreign gods. It is no accident that the curses of Deuteronomy 28 focus primarily on assault and capture by a foreign people; this was the worst kind of judgment imaginable for a people whose very lifeblood, blessedness, and *shalom* depended on the land that had been promised to their great forefather Abraham hundreds of years earlier. And so the worst kind of upheaval took place: Whereas back in the glory days of Israel—the reigns of David and Solomon—the whole world traveled through the blessed land, now it had become desolate, without the hum of merchants traveling through it. Given that this land at the eastern end of the Mediterranean was a key crossroads, its desolation would have been a terribly striking reminder of God's rejection of His people.

As Zechariah now stands among the people to whom God has shown great mercy and to whom He has restored their land, his warnings and promises focus on making sure that the people retain the blessedness promised to them. Such warnings and promises are wonderfully relevant to people who are richly blessed in Christ. Believers must both hear and obey God's commands.

Daily Bible Readings

M: How to Return to God
James 4:6–10
T: God's Everlasting Love
Psalm 103:8–18
W: God Is My Salvation
Isaiah 12
T: Return to God
Zechariah 1:1–6
F: The People Refuse God
Zechariah 7:8–14
S: Divine Deliverance for God's People
Zechariah 8:1–8
S: Seek the Lord
Zechariah 8:14–17, 20–23

TEACHING TIPS

August 26
Bible Study Guide 13

1. Words You Should Know

A. Covenant (Malachi 3:1) *bariyth* (Heb.)—An agreement; a mutual commitment.

B. Refiner (3:3) *tsaraph* (Heb.)—One who purified metals; used figuratively to refer to God's purifying of His people.

2. Teacher Preparation

A. Prepare for today's lesson by reading the Daily Bible Readings throughout the week.

B. Read and study the Focal Verses in at least two different modern Bible translations.

C. Complete lesson 13 in the *Precepts For Living®* *Personal Study Guide.*

D. Read the Lesson Aim, focusing your attention on achieving the learning objectives for today's lesson.

3. Starting the Lesson

A. Open the class with prayer, using the Lesson Aim as a guide.

B. Read and discuss the In Focus section.

4. Getting into the Lesson

A. Discuss The People, Places, and Times and the Background section.

B. Have some students read the Focal Verses and the In Depth section according to the At-A-Glance outline.

5. Relating the Lesson to Life

Engage the students in a discussion to elicit their response to the question posed in the Lesson in Our Society section.

6. Arousing Action

A. The Make It Happen section challenges the students to make critical observations concerning the world and their own lives in the context of righteousness. Engage the students in a discussion about how to live responsibly within the community of faith.

B. Close the class with prayer.

Worship Guide

For the Superintendent or Teacher
Theme: Malachi Describes God's Just Judgment
Theme Song: "What a Friend We Have in Jesus"
Scripture: 1 Peter 3:12
Song: "Oh How I Love Jesus"
Meditation: We exalt You, O Lord. We pray that Your kingdom may come on Earth. Teach us to live uprightly before You. Amen.

MALACHI DESCRIBES GOD'S JUST JUDGMENT

Bible Background ● MALACHI 2:17–4:3
Printed Text ● MALACHI 2:17–3:5; 4:1   Devotional Reading ● PSALM 34:11–22

Lesson Aim

By the end of the lesson, we will:

KNOW that the Lord is coming again and will judge both our treatment of others and our heart attitude toward Him;

WORSHIP the Lord genuinely; and

PRACTICE justice and compassion toward others.

Keep in Mind

"Behold, I will send my messenger, and he shall prepare the way before me: and the Lord whom ye seek shall suddenly come to his temple, even the messenger of the covenant, whom ye delight in: he shall come, saith the Lord of hosts. But who may abide the day of his coming? and who shall stand when he appeareth? for he is like a refiner's fire, and like fullers' sope" (Malachi 3:1–2).

Focal Verses

Malachi 2:17 Ye have wearied the Lord with your words. Yet ye say, Wherein have we wearied him? When ye say, Every one that doeth evil is good in the sight of the Lord, and he delighteth in them; or, Where is the God of judgment?

3:1 Behold, I will send my messenger, and he shall prepare the way before me: and the Lord whom ye seek, shall suddenly come to his temple, even the messenger of the covenant, whom ye delight in: he shall come, saith the Lord of hosts.

2 But who may abide the day of his coming? and who shall stand when he appeareth? for he is like a refiner's fire, and like fullers' sope:

3 And he shall sit as a refiner and purifier of silver: and he shall purify the sons of Levi, and purge them as gold and silver, that they may offer unto the Lord an offering in righteousness.

4 Then shall the offering of Judah and Jerusalem be pleasant unto the Lord, as in the days of old, and as in former years.

5 And I will come near to you to judgment; and I will be a swift witness against the sorcerers, and against the adulterers, and against false swearers, and against those that oppress the hireling in his wages, the widow, and the fatherless, and that turn aside the stranger from his right, and fear not me, saith the Lord of hosts.

4:1 For, behold, the day cometh, that shall burn as an oven; and all the proud, yea, and all that do wickedly, shall be stubble: and the day that cometh shall burn them up, saith the Lord of hosts, that it shall leave them neither root nor branch.

In Focus

It was the last Sunday Pastor Long would address his congregation. Sitting behind his desk, he reflected on the first time he addressed his congregation. He remembered how humble he felt after a two-year search that the congregation chose him as their leader.

That was 40 years ago. Pastor Long remembered how he prayed that his new church would be a community of faith that would avoid lives of sinfulness and injustice. He prayed he would learn the personal stories of his congregants so he would feel the heartbeat of the congregation and that the congregation would show compassion toward one another. He prayed that his church would strengthen and challenge each other. He prayed for a community of faith that would bear each other's burdens and help the oppressed, the fatherless, and the poor, and he also prayed that his leadership would bring others to Christ.

On this last Sunday, Pastor Long walked out in front of the congregation feeling confident that God had answered all his prayers—God had done all he asked.

In today's lesson, Malachi tells us that the Lord is coming again and will judge both our treatment of others and our attitude toward Him. And in that day God will bless true worshipers as well.

The People, Places, and Times

Malachi. Although knowledge is scant regarding the birthplace and family of Malachi, records are available in some detail regarding his prophetic ministry. Malachi was yet another prophet whom God called to admonish the Jews in Jerusalem. He confronted and rebuked the Israelites as he told them about the coming Day of the Lord. Like Haggai and Zechariah before him, Malachi was a postexilic prophet to Judah. Whereas Haggai and Zechariah rebuked the people for their failure to rebuild the temple, Malachi confronted them for their neglect of and their false worship in the temple. When Malachi penned these last words of the Old Testament, the people had been released from captivity in Babylon and had returned to Judah. The temple had been rebuilt, and the priests had reinstated the custom of offering sacrifices to the Lord for the people. However, they were making wrong sacrifices, disobeying the laws of God, and mistreating the poor and downtrodden. The Lord, in His forgiving Spirit, continued to love the priests and the people. Despite the changes that they went through, despite their unfaithfulness and disloyalty, and despite their disobedience, the Lord remained the same. He is consistent, for He declares, "I change not."

The Lord was not pleased with the sinful lifestyles of the priests and the people, and He called Malachi to take a message to them. Malachi challenged the people to be faithful to the covenant the Lord had made with Israel. He admonished them to truly honor the Lord by offering the right kinds of sacrifices and by giving 10 percent of their income to Him. In return, the Lord would bless them for their repentance and obedience.

Background

God called Malachi to warn the Jews of their sin and to restore their relationship with God. He wrote the book that bears his name between 435 and 450 B.C. The city of Jerusalem and the temple had been rebuilt for nearly a century. Malachi was the last of the so-called minor prophets of the Old Testament. In this era, the people had a broken relationship with God. He brought a charge against false priests who were misleading the people. These priests were guilty of not teaching and leading the people in obeying God's commands. Therefore, they provoked God's anger as their forefathers did.

Malachi's twofold message from God was: (1) a rebuke to the sinful remnant of Israelites, and (2) prophecies of future purging (purification) and blessing from the Lord.

Throughout the first, second, and third chapters of Malachi, the prophet warns the people about: (1) neglect in the worship of God, (2) social wrongs and disorder in the home, and (3) robbery in the service of the temple by failing to tithe.

Although God proclaims His love for the people, Malachi, who was an advocate of obedience, was also confrontational in his approach, warning the priests and the people to turn from their wicked, sinful ways. Nevertheless, the Lord, who abhors sin, still loves the sinner. Therefore, Malachi announced that if the people would repent and obey the Lord, He would forgive them, cleanse them spiritually, and bless them. In essence, this book emphasizes God's love for the priests and the people, and His disappointment because of their sins.

At-A-Glance

1. Ceremonial Prayers and Broken Promises
(Malachi 2:17)
2. The Promised Messenger
(3:1–5)
3. The Day of Judgment Is Coming
(4:1)

Finally, at His coming, the Lord will refine and purify all believers, exposing and condemning sinners and unbelievers. We do not know the day or the hour that the Lord is going to return, but we can rest assured that He is coming back.

In Depth

1. Ceremonial Prayers and Broken Promises (Malachi 2:17)

The Lord loved Israel. Malachi expresses the Lord's love for His people in the opening words of his book. However, because of Israel's willful disobedience and refusal to honor the laws and the covenant, the Lord had grown weary of their repetitious, ceremonial prayers and sinful lifestyles. The Lord was weary of the way the priests and people were twisting His truth. Their prayers were vain and meaningless because of their refusal to honor the Lord with their hearts and their disobedience by offering the wrong sacrifices. Malachi challenged them to turn back to the Lord right away—not when they wanted to, not when it was convenient for them, but right away! Not only were they to return to the Lord, but Malachi told them that they would have to honor God first and foremost in their worship and praise.

2. The Promised Messenger (3:1–5)

The Lord promises to send a messenger to prepare the way for His coming. The prophet Malachi describes an individual (usually thought to be John the Baptist) who will bring the message of the coming Messiah (v. 1). At this point, Malachi paints a portrait of the second coming of Christ.

Verse 2 is a reference to the Second Advent, when Jesus will come as judge, and opens with two questions: "Who shall abide the day of His coming?" and "Who shall stand when He appeareth?" Notice the imagery of a smelter, a purifier, refiner's fire, and fullers' sope. When the Day of the Lord comes (i.e., Judgment Day), God will be like a "furnace," a refiner's fire (a refiner purified metals with intense fire), and all who are unworthy will be consumed. The term "fullers' sope" refers to a strong soap made with lye that was used for washing clothes.

The priests are required to bring an offering of righteousness. First, however, the priest must be prepared for service by the performance of a purification rite. The priests (the sons of Levi) would be the first in line for the "refiner," who would *purge* them. To purge means to purify and cleanse from guilt. After their purging, the priests would bring a true and righteous offering that would be pleasing to the Lord.

Malachi reminds the Israelites that they are to be good stewards. Because the Lord has blessed them and given them authority over others, they are also warned to be honest, to not cheat or abuse their subordinates and employees. The prophet reminds them that God is coming back to judge the wicked (i.e., all those who practice witchcraft, adultery, and lying). He will judge those who oppress, cheat, or steal the property of foreigners or refuse to respect the warning of the Lord.

3. The Day of Judgment Is Coming (4:1)

Malachi is giving written notice that the Lord will surely return. The Lord says, "Like a fiery furnace, He will come and judge" (CEV). The prophet says that the "flame will burn, and not a branch nor a root will be left." In other words, all that is not of the Lord will be consumed.

Search the Scriptures

1. "Ye have _____ the Lord with your _____" (Malachi 2:17).

2. "And He shall sit as a _____ and _____ of silver" (3:3).

3. "Then shall the offering of Judah and Jerusalem be _____ unto the Lord" (3:4).

4. "And I will come near to you to _____" (3:5).

5. "For behold, the day _____, that shall burn as an _____" (4:1).

Discuss the Meaning

1. Why do you think the Lord spoke of a day of change—"reckoning" or "judgment"?

2. Did the people realize that their repentance and faithfulness would be *eternally* rewarded? If so, why were they disobedient?

3. How has the knowledge that God will come to

judge and reign changed our larger community and the world?

Lesson in Our Society

Today's lesson describes a population of Jews who had strayed from the way of the Lord. As a result of their disobedience, they suffered dire consequences. Their punishments could have been avoided had they worshiped the Lord in Spirit and in truth. In the same way, we sometimes suffer the consequences of disobedience. For example, we may be guilty of putting other gods before the Lord. He has said that we must have no other gods before Him. We must learn to all of appreciate our blessings from God without idolizing those blessings.

In the light of His coming again, the Lord expects us not to live lives of sinfulness and injustice. We must remember that material things are temporal, whereas our love for and obedience to God are eternal. What habits would we need to change to measure up to God's expectations?

Make It Happen

There is an old hymn whose lyrics are, "Get right with God, and do it now/Get right with God, and He will show you how/Down at the Cross, where He shed His blood/Get right with God. Get right, get right with God." Not only in Malachi's era, but even today, God is calling all of His people to "get right"—to turn to Him, love Him, and obey Him.

Malachi obeyed the call of the Lord. He was bold in proclaiming the word of the Lord. The people knew where and for whom he stood. He admonished the people to obey the Lord. Using Malachi as your Christian model, share your testimony and witness in the same manner this week with your families, friends, neighbors, or coworkers in an effort to advance God's kingdom, by sharing the Gospel message.

Follow the Spirit

What God wants me to do:

_____

_____

Remember Your Thoughts

Special insights I have learned:

_____

_____

More Light on the Text

Malachi 2:17–3:5; 4:1

17 Ye have wearied the LORD with your words. Yet ye say, Wherein have we wearied him? When ye say, Every one that doeth evil is good in the sight of the LORD, and he delighteth in them; or, Where is the God of judgment?

This verse begins the fourth of four back-and-forth arguments Yahweh has with his people (through the mouth of the prophet Malachi). To understand how the people's words have "wearied the Lord," we must understand the historical background of Malachi's ministry as a prophet. Malachi likely wrote between 475 and 450 B.C., after the people of Judah had been granted safe return to Jerusalem by Darius, king of Media and Persia, and not long after the temple had been rebuilt under the prophetic ministry of Zechariah and Haggai. Despite 500 years of persistent idolatry and neglect of God's demands for true worship, righteousness, and justice, the Lord had promised a glorious future for Zion (a hopeful, prophetic name for Jerusalem). Countless times in the words of Isaiah and other prophets, both before and after the exile, Israel's God spoke tenderly about His remnant, which He would restore to the former glory of Israel. The people no doubt anticipated this restoration as they began returning to Jerusalem after three generations of exile (see Psalm 126).

Despite this great expectation, at least a generation had passed since the rebuilding of God's temple, and the glorious vision of the prophets did not seem to be coming about. The walls of Jerusalem remained in shambles, the Jews faced danger from many pagan peoples around them—in short, it seemed like the people whom God had *not* chosen were faring a lot better than the holy remnant of Israel, to whom such wonderful promises had been made.

With this grim picture before their eyes, the Jews in Jerusalem speak with bitter irony: "Every one that doeth evil is good in the sight of the LORD, and he delighteth in them," they say. We must keep in mind the intense sarcasm of this statement; these people very likely did not *really* believe that God rewards the unrighteous at the expense of those who do His will. After all, those who dwelled in Jerusalem at this point in Israel's history represented the faithful remnant whom God had favored most abundantly. First of all, the remnant were mostly, if not entirely, made up of the people of Judah, and although the tribe of Judah was ultimately judged for its unfaithfulness, it endured for more than 100 years after the fall of the northern kingdom of Israel because at times it demonstrated repentance and faithfulness, which delayed its oncoming calamity.

Second, as Jeremiah makes clear (Jeremiah 29), those inhabitants of Jerusalem who allowed themselves to be taken to Babylon were *more* obedient to God than were those who stubbornly remained in Jerusalem or attempted to escape to Egypt, thereby disobeying God and coming under His judgment (Jeremiah 42). Finally, after Babylon was conquered by Persia, those who "pulled up stakes" and took advantage of Darius's decree allowing them to return to Jerusalem showed the greatest faith in God's prophetic word that Jerusalem would be restored to her former glory. Surely these people knew all too well the justice and mercy of God!

In light of this background, we can understand the cry of verse 17 as the complaint of a suffering people resigning themselves to what was apparently their unfortunate lot in life. Although at some level they knew and believed God's promises, they were on the verge of giving up because these promises had seemingly not been fulfilled in a reasonable amount of time. Like any people oppressed for many years, they struggled with the idea that perhaps God was not going to show up after all. Putting it more directly, they cried out, "Where is the God of judgment?" (v. 17).

As reasonable as this complaint might seem, the righteous Judge sees such complaints as utterly wearisome, and this passage explains why. Verse 17 serves as an introduction to the rest of the passage, where specific sins of Judah are listed (see 3:5); it

also builds on the complaints that the Lord has brought against the Jews thus far in the book of Malachi. The people were offering polluted and insincere offerings (1:6–14), their priests were lazy and unfaithful in teaching and leading the people (2:1–9), and the Israelites had practiced divorce and had intermarried with the foreign pagans around them (2:10–16), a practice that in Israel's history always led to the idolatrous worship of other gods and the worship of Yahweh by inappropriate means (in other words, the breaking of the first two of the Ten Commandments).

Thus, it is readily apparent that these people were far from guiltless! We can now see why the complaint of verse 17 is without basis and is wearisome to the Jews' covenant God. Their complaint demonstrated their impatience and lack of faith, not to mention their failure to recognize that their lack of blessing was due to all the crimes they had committed against the Lord.

3:1 Behold, I will send my messenger, and he shall prepare the way before me: and the LORD, whom ye seek, shall suddenly come to his temple, even the messenger of the covenant, whom ye delight in: behold, he shall come, saith the LORD of hosts.

In response to the people's plaintive cry ("Where is the God of justice?"), the Lord gives a swift and unmistakable response: the long-awaited Messiah, the Anointed One, will come suddenly. The Hebrew word *hen* (**hane**), usually translated "behold," speaks of calling attention to a very important announcement. The announced event will not necessarily happen right away, but it will surely happen, and paying attention is of the greatest importance. After this attention-grabbing lead-in, four things are announced.

First, God will send a messenger. The messenger described here bears a striking resemblance to the messenger described in Exodus 23:20 (NKJV), where the Lord says, "Behold, I send an Angel before you to keep you in the way and to bring you into the place which I have prepared." In that verse, Yahweh promises to send an angel (the Hebrew words for "angel" and "messenger" are the same) to guide His chosen people through the desert and into the Promised Land. Similarly, the messenger here in Malachi will guide the people to the Messiah, who is the perfect fulfillment of everything represented by the Promised Land. The Hebrew word *panah* (**paw-NAW**), here translated "prepare," involves preparation by removing all obstacles. Thus, like the messenger in Isaiah 40:3–5, this messenger is pictured as taking away all obstacles to the coming of the Messiah—chiefly, no doubt, unbelief and disobedience. When we consider the identity of the Messiah in the New Testament, who can doubt that Malachi is speaking here of John the Baptist? Although other prophets might conceivably be seen as messengers who prepare the way for Jesus' coming, John the Baptist is the immediate and, therefore, the most important forerunner of the Messiah.

Second, the Lord will appear suddenly in his temple. This promise would have caught the Jews' attention, for their history showed them that the temple is the place where God always reveals Himself most fully and gloriously to His people. Yet the promise that the Lord would appear "suddenly" gives us a hint that when the Lord appears, people may not be prepared for His coming and may ultimately reject Him. Indeed, when Jesus came mysteriously not only *to* the temple (for He preached in the Jewish synagogues) but *as* the temple (John 2:18–22), many stumbled over this message, even though Malachi had spoken of it in advance.

Third, the Lord will come as the messenger of the covenant. It is important not to confuse the "messenger" here with the one spoken of in the first part of the verse; as the text that follows makes clear, Malachi is talking about the Messiah Himself (not His forerunner). The Jews would have known what it meant for this individual to be a "messenger of the covenant"; their minds would have returned to Deuteronomy, where God established His covenant with His people, pledging His own faithfulness and promising blessings for obedience and curses for disobedience. What was unknown to Malachi and the Jews, however, is that Jesus would come not only to enforce God's covenant, but also to embody that covenant and to seal it with His blood for His people. This reality is hinted at in the promise of a new covenant in Jeremiah 31:31–34.

Fourth, the messenger of the covenant will be the one the people are hoping for. Here we see the irony of this promise. The Jews have been complaining that the God of justice has not shown up to fulfill His promises; God's response is that the Messiah will surely come and do just that, but as verse 2 makes clear, the people to whom He comes may be getting more than they bargained for in longing for His coming. Jesus was the fulfillment of the Lord's people's hopes; He represented the apex of God's appearances to His people (often called theophanies). When Simeon, upon seeing the Baby Jesus, says, "This child is destined to cause the falling and rising of many in Israel" (Luke 2:34, NIV), it becomes clear that not everyone in Israel will find the news of the coming of the Lord's messenger joyful.

The announcer of these future events is the "Lord of hosts," a military reference to God in all His might. (See last week's commentary on Zechariah 1:1–6 and 7:8–14, especially 1:3.)

2 But who may abide the day of his coming? and who shall stand when he appeareth? for he is like a refiner's fire, and like fullers' sope:

Malachi now talks of the great Messenger's coming in terms of the all-important word "day"; here, "day of his coming" refers to the Day of the Lord (Heb. *ywom Yehovah*, **yome Yeh-ho-VAW**). This "day," like many repeated themes in the Bible, can refer to more than one event, which events may occur simultaneously or at different times. In the writings of the preexilic prophets, the phrase often refers to the time when God would do the unthinkable and judge His people for their covenant breaking. This "day" came about in 722 B.C. for the northern kingdom and in 586 B.C. for the southern kingdom. Here, "day" refers to another judgment: the Messiah's judgment. Malachi pictures His judgment as all-consuming ("who can stand?") and uses two familiar terms to describe it: fire and soap (or, better, lye used for washing). Both of these agents are pictured in the Bible as "burning" agents that are hot to the touch, but most importantly as agents of separation. The idea of "refining fire" occurs in both the Old and New Testaments (see 1 Peter 1:7), describing the process by which God removes the holy from the unholy, the clean from the unclean. Likewise, just as launderers' lye was used to cleanse clothing and separate it from dirt, the Messiah comes to reward the righteous and punish the unrighteous.

However, there is a twofold twist to this verse. The first twist is that the "day" of God's coming was a day that Israel looked forward to as a time when God would redeem them and judge their enemies. Yet, as God makes clear in the text that follows, Judah itself was to be judged on this Day. This was a surprising and divine reversal, but not altogether unprecedented; after all, God's people had been taken by surprise before when longing for the Day of the Lord (Amos 5:18–20). The second twist is the way in which the Messiah actually fulfills this promise of judgment.

Even when the messenger—John the Baptist—comes, he speaks of the Messiah's impending judgment, warning that His "fan is in his hand, and he will throughly purge his floor, and gather his wheat into the garner; but he will burn up the chaff with unquenchable fire" (Matthew 3:12). And yet the mystery of Christ's kingdom, and of the Gospel, is that His coming as Saviour and His coming as Judge are separated by a period in which grace is extended through the Gospel. Thus, the promise of Malachi and of John the Baptist still awaits fulfillment. Christ came the first time to meekly lay down His life for the salvation of all who believe; only at His Second Coming will the terror of His judgment finally be made known.

3 And he shall sit as a refiner and purifier of silver: and he shall purify the sons of Levi, and purge them as gold and silver, that they may offer unto the LORD an offering in righteousness.

"He will sit" suggests judgment or rule or both, sitting being the posture of judging (Exodus 18:13; Ruth 4:1–2; Daniel 7:9–10) and ruling (1 Samuel 1:9;

Psalm 29:10; 132:12; Jeremiah 17:25) in most ancient literature. The thought is continued as the ruling and judging Messiah separates the pure from the impure. Now, however, the focus is not simply on Israel as a whole but on a specific group of Israelites: the Levites. The inclusion of the Levites adds something to the metaphor of *separating*, since it was the Levites, as priests to God, who were already "set apart" from the rest of Israel. Unfortunately, as is clear from chapters 1 and 2 of Malachi, the priests had failed to conduct themselves according to their calling to holiness; ironically, without being truly and spiritually separate from the people, they were of no use to the people at all. Malachi says that at His coming, the Messiah will restore the priests so that their offerings are once again holy and true. This does not necessarily mean that the Levitical sacrificial system will be reinstituted, but that God's people will worship Him truly, as is His due.

4 Then shall the offering of Judah and Jerusalem be pleasant unto the LORD, as in the days of old, and as in former years.

According to the Holy Spirit speaking through Malachi, the Messiah's restoration includes both Judah and Jerusalem—in other words, all the people (both in the capital city and throughout the nation). Malachi envisions a time when sacrifices will be offered that please God, that are according to His will—much like "in the days of old, and as in former years." But one might rightly ask, "When were these 'days' and 'years'? When were the Israelites ever perfectly faithful in their priestly work?" The closest period is likely the time of Moses, who was a faithful mediator and priest for the people, but it is more helpful to recognize that the terms used here, especially the word *yowm* (**yome**), refers to day, time, year.

Malachi is not looking back to the "good old days" so much as he is looking ahead to a time when all that God intended for Israel will come about. At that time, sacrifices will be "pleasant unto the LORD," not because they are offered in a mechanically correct way, but—as we know from the New

Testament—because they are offered through Christ. Only the Lamb of God's perfect sacrifice brings about God's intention for His people; only by faith in His work do their sacrifices become acceptable to Him.

5 And I will come near to you to judgment; and I will be a swift witness against the sorcerers, and against the adulterers, and against false swearers, and against those that oppress the hireling in his wages, the widow, and the fatherless, and that turn aside the stranger from his right, and fear not me, saith the LORD of hosts.

Now Yahweh's response to His people's complaint is brought full circle: precisely the kind of people the Jews had in mind when they spoke of "every one that doeth evil" (2:17) are described here. Malachi lists seven kinds of sins (seven being a common number used in biblical lists to imply completeness, to signify that everything had been covered). All of these sins are violations of God's holy covenant because they are all condemned in Deuteronomy, where God's covenant with Israel is most fully laid down.

Sorcery was so odious in the mind of God that He prescribed the death penalty as punishment (Exodus 22:18). This sin was a clear violation of the Lord's command to worship Him only and to listen only to His Spirit, and was condemned in the Book of the Covenant (Deuteronomy 18:12, 19–22). Adultery was a crime both men and women could commit and was addressed directly in the seventh commandment; this also was a capital offense, similar to rape (Deuteronomy 22:22–27). Swearing falsely violated the third commandment, which suggested not only perjury but invoking Yahweh's name wrongly in any way (Deuteronomy 6:13). Cheating hired workers was a violation of God's perfect justice, whereby everyone was to receive what he was due, whether reward or punishment.

These workers were not slaves but those who worked for pay of their own accord (Deuteronomy 15:12–18). Oppressing widows and orphans was a grave offense, and the "oppressed" probably include people other than those without husbands or parents, since the phrase "widows and orphans" was usually used to describe all who were needy. The Lord is always depicted as being especially concerned for the needy (Deuteronomy 10:18). Likewise, "turning aside the stranger" was a crime that showed a sinfully short memory, since the Israelites themselves had been strangers and aliens in Egypt (Deuteronomy 10:19). Finally, failure to fear Yahweh was, in a sense, at the heart of all sins, a violation of the first commandment and of Deuteronomy 6:5, which Jesus later showed to be the greatest commandment (Matthew 22:37).

The fact that all these sins were present in the days of Malachi shows the depths to which the Jews had sunk. Now the whole story has been told; although the complaint in Malachi 2:17 might seem justified, we now see that God's people were suffering as a result of their *own* sin, and that they themselves were the ones who were doing evil. Consequently, they deserved the judgment of God, which the Messiah would ultimately bring.

One final point concerning these verses is important. The picture of the Messiah is not simply that of a messenger of Yahweh, but as Yahweh Himself! For who but Yahweh appears in the temple and makes a covenant with His people (3:1)? Who sits in rule and judgment over His people except Yahweh (vv. 2–3)? Who receives offerings from His people except Yahweh (vv. 3–4)? And finally, if the Messiah is not divine, why would the Lord switch from third person to first person (v. 5), referring to the messenger who was coming to judge as "I"? We can hardly be faithful to this passage without recognizing that, here and elsewhere, the Trinity is very much present in the Old Testament. Jesus comes as the LORD, Yahweh, the one and only God, as His own message and self-awareness show. It is Christ's divinity that, above all else, shows the truth, the certainty, and the finality of the judgment of which Malachi speaks.

4:1 For, behold, the day cometh, that shall burn as an oven; and all the proud, yea, and all that do wickedly, shall be stubble: and the day that cometh shall burn them up, saith the LORD of hosts, that it shall leave them neither root nor branch.

This final pronouncement repeats many of the

themes seen in 2:17–3:5. The idea of one great and cataclysmic "day" is repeated. The separation of pure from impure in the fire (here, "oven") is promised; the day is said to "burn up" evildoers. Yahweh appears once again as "LORD of hosts," waging war against the ungodly. This verse enhances the picture of judgment by including "the proud" (arrogant) among those who will be judged; surely this is a painful condemnation of the Jews themselves, who once again in the time of Malachi have grown complacent, believing that because they live in Jerusalem and worship at the temple they cannot be touched.

On the contrary, says the Lord, that great "tree" that was once in holy covenant with God will be pulled up once and for all; neither branch nor root will be left. As we see in the New Covenant, this does not mean that God forgets Israel, but that He *redefines* it. It is *God's church* that becomes the "Israel of God" (Galatians 6:14), and the "tree" of God's people includes both Jews and Gentiles, all who are of the faith of Abraham (Romans 9–11). God's faithfulness cannot be annulled by His people's unfaithfulness, but in the wonderful and holy mystery of His Providence, Israel's unfaithfulness becomes grace for the entire world. Thanks be to God for His indescribable gift!

Daily Bible Readings

M: God's Concern for the People
Psalm 34:11–22
T: Our Works Are Tested
1 Corinthians 3:10–15
W: God Judges Our Hearts
1 Corinthians 4:1–5
T: God Will Judge
Malachi 2:17–3:7
F: Will Anyone Rob God?
Malachi 3:8–12
S: Choosing between Good and Evil
Malachi 3:13–18
S: The Day of the Lord
Malachi 4:1–6